ANNUAL REVIEW OF IRISH LAW 1991

Annual Review of Irish Law 1991

Raymond Byrne
B.C.L., LL.M., Barrister-at-Law
Lecturer in Law, Dublin City University

William Binchy
B.A., B.C.L., LL.M., Barrister-at-Law
Regius Professor of Laws, Trinity College Dublin
Formerly, Research Counsellor, The Law Reform Commission

THE ROUND HALL PRESS
DUBLIN

The typesetting for this book was produced by
Gilbert Gough Typesetting, Dublin for
THE ROUND HALL PRESS
Kill Lane, Blackrock, Co. Dublin.

A catalogue record for this book
is available from the British Library.

ISBN 0-947686-78-9

ISSN 0791-1084

Printed by
Betaprint, Dublin

Contents

Preface

In this fifth volume in the Annual Review series, our purpose continues to be to provide a review of legal developments, judicial and statutory, that occurred in 1991. In terms of case law, this includes those judgments which were delivered in 1991, regardless of whether they have been (or will be) reported and which were circulated up to the date of the preface.

Once again, it is a pleasure to thank those who made the task of completing this volume less onerous. Mr Justice Brian Walsh (who, as we have mentioned in previous volumes, was the originator of the concept of an Annual Review of Irish Law) continues to be most supportive and we remain very grateful for this. Once again, we are in the debt of a number of people for providing access to library facilities. In particular, Ms Peggy McQuinn, of the Office of the Supreme Court, Ms Margaret Byrne and Ms Mary Gaynor, of the Library of the Incorporated Law Society of Ireland, and Mr Jonathan Armstrong and Ms Thérèse Broy, of the King's Inns Library, were very helpful with a number of queries. As on many previous occasions, Ms Jennifer Aston, Librarian in the Law Library, Four Courts, was also especially helpful in facilitating access to statutory material which otherwise proved elusive. We are also very grateful to Ms Lorna Moorhead who provided invaluable help at a late stage with a number of difficulties in the text.

William Binchy would also like to thank his many colleagues at Trinity College Law School for their help in relation to several of the matters discussed in this Review. Particular thanks are due to Hilary Delany, who read the Equitable Remedies chapter and made a number of very useful suggestions for improvement, and to Eoin O'Dell, whose comments relating to the decisions on Contract Law were most incisive. As with the 1990 Review, we are also very grateful to the Incorporated Law Society of Ireland, as Trustees of the Arthur Cox Foundation, for their generous financial research assistance in connection with the preparation of this volume.

Finally, we are ever grateful to The Round Hall Press, and in particular Michael Adams, Gilbert Gough and Martin Healy, whose professionalism ensures the continued production of this series.

Raymond Byrne and William Binchy,
Dublin

February 1993.

Table of Cases

A400025539

Other Tables

TABLE OF STATUTORY INSTRUMENTS

TABLE OF EUROPEAN COMMUNITY LAWS

TABLE OF COUNCIL OF EUROPE LAWS

ANNUAL REVIEW OF IRISH LAW 1991

Administrative Law

A most welcome publication during the year was Hogan and Morgan, *Administrative Law in Ireland*, 2nd ed. (Sweet & Maxwell, 1991). The first edition of this work was invaluable, a point which can be attested to not simply by reference to academic reviews but also to the empirical fact that extensive use was made of it by learned practitioners at the Irish Bar when engaged in research for forensic battle. The years since the first edition have seen an explosion of case law in the area, as can be seen from the length of the Administrative Law chapters in the five volumes of the *Annual Review* series. This has led to a significant increase in the size of Gerard Hogan and David Morgan's text over the first edition, and it is difficult to imagine that any less than 773 pages could have accommodated the breadth of material covered. The discussion and analysis ranges from the classical areas of judicial review of administrative action (including fair procedures and *ultra vires*) to the equally important matters of central institutions of control. Thus, for students of public law as well as of public administration, the second edition of this leading text will again be an essential reference tool.

GOVERNMENT FUNCTIONS

Appropriation   The Appropriation Act 1991 provided as follows. For the year ended 31 December 1991, the amount for supply grants was £7,199,991,000 and for appropriations-in-aid was £917,581,000. The 1991 Act also amends the Provisional Collection of Taxes Act 1927, allowing the Dáil 84 sitting days after budget day to complete the second stage of the Finance Bill. The limit of 30 sitting days in the 1927 Act was regarded as too short in view of the fact that the Dáil now sits on Friday.

European Bank for Reconstruction and Development   The European Bank for Reconstruction and Development Act 1991 incorporates into Irish law the Agreement establishing the Bank, which was brought into being in 1990 in the wake of the collapse of the Communist regimes of Eastern Europe. The Bank has two main purposes: to encourage the transition of the Eastern European states to market-based economic systems and to support democratic multi-party political structures. The Agreement establishing the Bank is included as a Schedule to the 1991 Act. The Act also authorises the financial contribution which the State must make as a member of the Bank. The sum represents about 0.3% of the total amount being subscribed. The European Bank for Reconstruction and Development (Designation and Immunities) Order 1991 (SI No. 65), made under the Diplomatic Relations and Immunities Act 1967, provides that the Bank will have diplomatic immunity.

Semi-State and State sponsored bodies

1 B & I Line   The B & I Line Act 1991 facilitated the complete privatisation of B & I Line plc through its sale to the Irish Continental Group plc. The sale followed a number of injections of State funds into B & I through legislation: see the 1988 Review, 4, and 1990 Review, 4. The sale of B & I, and the 1991 Act, contain a number of provisions which protect the interests of existing employees of B & I. For a more detailed comment, see the *Annotation in Irish Current Law Statutes Annotated.* The Act came into effect on 31 January 1992: B & I Line Act 1991 (s. 7) (Commencement) Order 1992 (SI No. 25 of 1992) and B & I Line Act 1991 (s. 8) (Commencement) Order 1992 (SI No. 26 of 1992).

2 Bord Trachtála: Irish Trade Board   The Trade and Marketing Promotion Act 1991 provided for the amalgamation of An Coras Trachtála (CTT) and the Irish Goods Council into a new body: Bord Trachtála, the Irish Trade Board. CTT had been responsible for assisting Irish companies with export marketing, while the Irish Goods Council had been involved in domestic marketing for Irish companies. The 1991 Act is aimed at ensuring that Irish companies will have continued support, from a single dedicated agency, in the context of the EC Single Market. The main provisions of the Act came into effect on 1 September 1991: see s. 2.

3 Foir Teoranta   The Foir Teoranta (Dissolution) Act 1990 (Commencement) Order 1991 (SI No. 55) brought the 1990 Act into force on 2 April 1991. The Act provided for the dissolution of the State rescue company, Foir Teo. Its assests and liabilities were transferred to the Industrial Credit Corporation plc.

4 IDA   The Industrial Development (Amendment) Act 1991 permits the Industrial Development Authority (IDA) to invest in companies through share purchases in sums of up to £1.5 million without government consent. Amounts in excess of this, of course, would require such consent. This power must be seen against the background of the provision for the dissolution of the National Development Corporation Limited (NADCORP) by the 1991 Act and the transfer of its assets to the IDA. The 1991 Act also provided for increases in the amount of government grants to the IDA (up from £700 million to £1,200 million) and to SFADCo (the Shannon Free Airport Development Co Ltd) (up from £130 million to £150 million). The Act had not been brought into force by Commencement Order at the time of writing.

5 Irish Sugar: Greencore The partial privatisation, and public flotation, of the Irish Sugar Co. plc (Siúicre Éireann cpt) was provided for in the Sugar Act 1991. The Act provided for the establishment of Greencore plc, the holding company for the shares in Irish Sugar, under which it now trades after the flotation which took place in 1991.

A significant provision is s. 2(9) of the Act which required the State to retain an unspecified 'special share' in Greencore after flotation. It had originally been intended to include a provision under which the State's share could be disposed of at some future date. By virtue of s. 2(9), amending legislation would be required to dispose of this 'special share' or Golden Share as is has become known. The then Minister for Agriculture and Food indicated that the special share would represent 45% of total shares in Greencore. In addition to the Government share, about 15% was also allocated to employees of the Sugar companies and to farmers who had been involved in beet processing: Irish Sugar (Prescribed Conditions) (Disposal of Shares) Regulations 1991 (SI No. 102).

The Sugar Act 1991 (Commencement) Order 1991 (SI No. 51) brought the Act, apart from s. 7, into effect on 19 March 1991. S. 7 of the Act, which provided for the repeal of the Sugar Manufacture Acts 1933 to 1982, came into effect on 9 April 1991: Sugar Act 1991 (Commencement) (No.2) Order 1991 (SI No. 76).

6 Marine Institute The Marine Institute Act 1991 provides for the establishment of the Marine Institute, whose primary function will be to undertake, co-ordinate, promote and assist in marine research and development. The stated intention in s. 4 of the Act is that the activities of the Institute will assist in promoting economic development and create employment as well as protect the marine environment. At the time of writing, the Institute had not yet been established by Order, as required by s. 2 of the Act.

7 NADCORP The Industrial Development (Amendment) Act 1991 provided for the dissolution of the National Development Corporation Limited (NADCORP) and the transfer of its assets to the Industrial Development Authority: see also above.

State in litigation The status of the Office of Public Works as occupier of national monuments to which the public has access was considered by the Supreme Court in *Clancy v Commissioners of Public Works* [1991] ILRM 567 discussed in the Torts chapter, 396-8, below).

JUDICIAL REVIEW

Deference to decision-making body   The reluctance of the courts to interfere with the decision-making power of a body whose decision is being
reviewed was expressly adverted to by the Supreme Court in *O'Keeffe v An
Bord Pleanála* [1992] ILRM 237 (see 16-18, below).

Fair Procedures/Natural Justice

1 Applicability: religious congregation   In *O'Dea v Ó Briain and Ors*
[1992] ILRM 364, Murphy J doubted whether judicial review could lie to
challenge the validity of a decision reached by a religious superior. It should
be noted immediately that Murphy J did not reach a concluded decision on
this point as the case involved an application for interlocutory relief. It was
later settled: see Barry (1992) 10 ILT 222. The case arose in the following
way.

The plaintiff, a nun who was a member of the Congregation of St Louis,
was also a teacher in a St Louis school. The board of management of the
school communicated in writing their dissatisfaction with the plaintiff's sick
leave absence and other aspects of her performance to the plaintiff's religious
superior. The board stated that they could take action against the plaintiff but
requested the superior to transfer the plaintiff to another school in exercise
of the religious superior's powers. (It may be noted that, because the
judgment delivered by Murphy J was *ex tempore*, the full text of the
communications from the board of management to the superior are not
recorded in the law report, which was based on a stenographer's note of
Murphy J's judgment: nonetheless, the account given here is the gist of the
communication involved.)

The plaintiff's superior held two meetings with the plaintiff concerning
the board of management's dissatisfaction. Subsequent to this meeting the
plaintiff was informed that she was to be transferred to a school in Monaghan.
The plaintiff claimed a mandatory injunction preventing the transfer from
proceeding pending full consultation with her on the issue of her transfer.
The plaintiff stated on affidavit that while the dissatisfaction with her was
discussed in her meeting with her religious superior, no mention was made
of the plaintiff's relocation to another school. Her superior stated that such
discussion had taken place. On the plaintiff's application for an interlocutory
mandatory injunction, Murphy J refused the relief sought.

Since the hearing was for interlocutory relief, Murphy J drew attention to
the fact that it was not necessary for him to decide whether the plaintiff could
succeed in her claim. However, he was of the (tentative) view that the plaintiff
faced great difficulty in sustaining her action, and he referred to three points
in this connection. First, he considered that the issue of fact as to whether her

transfer was discussed was likely to be resolved in favour of the plaintiff's religious superior. Second, he also felt that it was unlikely that mandatory relief would be granted to restrain an action which could be remedied merely by holding an interview.

The third point was whether the rules of fair procedures applied to the instant case at all. Murphy J accepted that while any action by the board of management would, as the board itself had acknowledged, require compliance with the rules of natural and constitutional justice, he felt that different considerations applied to a teacher who was also a nun. He stated:

> I know of no reason to accept or assume that the rules of constitutional justice or fair play which have evolved so clearly over so many years would apply to a decision made by a religious superior in relation to a member of his or her community.

Murphy J noted that the decisions of a religious superior were not necessarily made to ascertain truth but might also be made to inculcate humility or to advance the interests of the religious order, whereas a lay tribunal was required to ascertain truth and vindicate rights. Without expressing a final view on the matter, he felt that the power of a religious superior appeared to be absolute or virtually absolute, and that the vow of obedience seemed to be a converse of that power.

Although this was an interlocutory application, Murphy J's judgment reflected a strong leaning against fair procedures applying to decisions of religious superiors. There is some argument to be made for the case that fair procedures should not apply to the 'pure' religious discipline cases. However, as Murphy J acknowledged, the plaintiff's position involved a dual role, that of teacher and nun. In the instant case, it was surely her status as teacher, and thus employee, which was to the fore. In such a case, therefore, fair procedures ought apply even if it would not apply to the 'pure' religious discipline cases. This 'dual function' analysis has been used, for example, in the school discipline cases such as *The State (Smullen) v Duffy* [1980] ILRM 46. Moreover, there is clear Irish authority for the proposition that even 'pure' religious disciplinary decisions are sucbject to fair procedures. This arises from the well-known decision of the Supreme Court, *McGrath and Ó Ruairc v Trustees of Maynooth College* [1979] ILRM 166. In that case, the plaintiffs were priests and lecturers in Maynooth College who had been dismissed from their posts for failure to wear clerical dress and, in the case of one plaintiff, for writing articles which challenged the teaching of the Roman Catholic Church on certain issues. It was clear that the case involved 'pure' religious discipline matters, yet neither in the High Court or the Supreme Court was it argued that the rules of fair procedures did not apply. While this approach might, ultimately, be open to challenge on the ground that the point was not fully argued in the Maynooth case, it must in the meantime stand as clear authority in favour of the rules of fair procedures applying in such situations. In that light, the views of Murphy J in the *O'Dea* case must be open to doubt.

To revert to his judgment in the case, Murphy J finally considered the decision of the Supreme Court in *Campus Oil Ltd v Minister for Industry and Energy (No. 2)* [1983] IR 88 on the granting of interlocutory relief. He held that it it was not appropriate to grant interlocutory mandatory relief as there was no guarantee that this would give the plaintiff the remedy she sought, namely review of her transfer by another body. He considered that the court was not capable of ruling on her competence as a teacher and that this would in any event be intruding on the rights of others to take the action open to them. Of course, Murphy J's description of the court's function in such cases was correct in the sense that it would not be an appeal court. Nonetheless, the fact that he had already ruled that fair procedures did not apply deprived the plaintiff of her real remedy: a declaration that she was entitled to a fair hearing. The authorities we have referred to would appear to support her claim. As has been made clear on numerous occasions in the past, a finding that a decision was not in accordance with fair procedures may merely amount to a postponement of an adverse decision. Thus, with due respect to Murphy J, many cases on fair procedures amount to applications for 'an interview'. In the instant case, Murphy J appeared to consider this as a small matter, but it was the essence of the case, as with many others like it. The rules of fair procedures are not a guarantee of success for one side or the other in an interview or a hearing, but they are at the heart of administrative law.

2 *Audi alteram partem: delay*   A number of issues arose in the decision of Blayney J in *Gallagher v Revenue Commissioners* [1991] ILRM 632, many relating to the question of delay in proceeding with an adjudicatory hearing.

The circumstances giving rise to the case were, briefly, as follows. The plaintiff, a customs and excise officer, was interviewed in July 1985 about the seizure of certain vehicles for non-payment of relevant duties. The plaintiff was moved to other duties at that time. The officer investigating the seizures completed a written report in December 1985. Nothing further occurred until March 1987 when the seizures were further investigated and, in connection with this investigation, the plaintiff was interviewed in relation to 41 files in June and October 1987. During these interviews, it was put to the plaintiff that he had, *inter alia*, understated the value of vehicles seized and had fictionalised certain reports. By letter dated 25 January 1988, the plaintiff was informed that he was suspended from duty as it appeared he was guilty of grave irregularity and misconduct. His solicitors immediately wrote inquiring about the nature of the matters for which he was suspended, and were informed that details would be given at the end of March 1988. No details were furnished, and the solicitors wrote again in October 1988 seeking details. Details were furnished in January 1989, involving 18 separate transactions. The plaintiff issued proceedings contending, *inter alia*, that the suspension was invalid, that he was entitled to transcripts of the interviews conducted in June and October 1987 and to be legally represented at the oral hearing of the charges. Blayney J granted the plaintiff certain relief, though he rejected some of the claims put forward.

The plaintiff claimed that the initial suspension in January 1988 was invalid *ab initio*. Blayney J rejected this claim. Acknowledging that the plaintiff had not been informed in January 1988 of the reason for the suspension, this was not of itself sufficient because, he held, the plaintiff must have been well aware of the basis for the suspension, a point confirmed in the judge's view by the solicitor's delay between March and October 1988 in seeking particulars of the reasons for the suspension. However, on a connected issue the plaintiff was more successful. Applying the Supreme Court decision in *Flynn v An Post* [1987] IR 68 (see the 1987 Review, 228-9), Blayney J held that the suspension after May 1988 was invalid, because the plaintiff had been given a commitment in March 1988 that the reasons for the suspension would have been forwarded to him and May was set as the reasonable time within which reasons should have been furnished.

A second delay point raised by the plaintiff also received a mixed response from Blayney J. The plaintiff argued that further disciplinary proceedings should be prohibited in view of the delay in proceeding against the plaintiff in the instant case. The plaintiff relied on the case law emanating from the Supreme Court decision in *The State (O'Connell) v Fawsitt* [1986] IR 362 in this context (see the 1987 Review, 120-3 and 1988 Review, 147-51). He also cited the earlier decision of D'Arcy J in *The State (Cuddy) v Mangan* [1988] ILRM 720 (1988 Review, 151). Blayney J considered that these cases, which concerned delay in criminal trials, were not relevant to the instant case. He stated:

> In the instant case, the plaintiff has not been charged with a criminal offence. He is charged with grave misconduct and grave irregularity in the performance of his duties as a civil servant. What is at issue are matters appertaining to the law of master and servant, not matters appertaining to the criminal law.

While, of course, the plaintiff did not face the immediate threat of criminal proceedings it seems somewhat glib to describe the situation as relating to 'the law of master and servant'. Indeed, Blayney J himself appeared to acknowledge the inadequacy of the description in connection with another issue raised by the plaintiff, whether he was entitled to legal representation at the disciplinary hearings. Adopting the principles set out by Barron J in *Flanagan v University College Dublin* [1989] ILRM 449 (1988 Review, 14-5), Blayney J concluded that legal representation should be granted. On this aspect of the case, Blayney J stated:

> The consequences for the plaintiff if the charges against him are established could be extremely serious. He would be liable to be dismissed. So there is no doubt as to the gravity of the matter. Apart from this, the charges against him are extremely numerous. . . . And some of the charges, though not directly charging fraud, could clearly serve as a basis for such a charge. Finally, some of the reports discovered show that the question of having some of the charges investigated by the police was considered.

This passage reflects the true gravity of the plaintiff's position, and is in contrast with the passage previously quoted. The analogy with the *O'Connell* and *Cuddy* cases would appear to be apt in the particular circumstances of the plaintiff's case. If that analogy is not apt, then disciplinary proceedings would not appear to be subject to normal rules of prompt procedures which are at the heart of natural justice and that hoary principle 'Justice delayed, justice denied.'

3 Audi alteram partem: legal representation In *Gallagher v Revenue Commissioners* [1991] ILRM 632, above, Blayney J ordered that legal representation be granted to a person appearing before a decision-making body. See generally, Delany (1992) 14 DULJ 88.

4 Audi alteram partem: notice In *Haussman v Minister for the Marine* [1991] ILRM 382 (discussed in the Transport chapter, 461-2, below), Blayney J considered the extent to which the Minister was required to provide documentation to an interested party in a statutory merchant shipping inquiry.

5 Audi alteram partem: oral hearing In *O'Flynn and O'Regan v Mid-Western Health Board* [1991] 2 IR 223, the Supreme Court rejected the claim that an oral hearing was always required in order to comply with the requirements of fair procedures: see the discussion of the case in the Health Services Chapter, 260-1, below. A similar view emerged in the Court's decision in *Nolan v Minister for the Environment* [1991] ILRM 705 (discussed in the Local Government chapter, 319-20, below).

Costello J had also been of the same view in *Horan v An Post*, High Court, 18 January 1991. In the *Horan* case, the plaintiff challenged his dismissal from An Post. The Board of An Post had decided that the plaintiff's sick leave absence was unsatisfactory. The plaintiff had forwarded to the Board certain medical evidence to support his absence from work. This evidence had been considered by An Post's Chief Medical Officer, who reported to the Board that the plaintiff's evidence did not support the length of sick leave which the plaintiff had actually taken. It was on this basis that the Board decided to dismiss the plaintiff. As indicated, Costello J held that an oral hearing was not required, and it was sufficient that the Board had considered the written reports before it. Nor did he consider that the plaintiff was entitled to have seen a copy of the Chief Medical Officer's report in advance of the Board's decision to dismiss. Costello J thus concluded that there had been no breach of fair procedures requirements.

6 *Audi alteram partem: Tribunal of Inquiry* In *Boyhan and Ors v Tribunal of Inquiry Into the Beef Industry* [1992] ILRM 545, Denham J considered the nature of limited representation before a Tribunal of Inquiry having the powers granted by the Tribunals of Inquiry (Evidence) Acts 1921 and 1979.

The plaintiffs were all members of the United Farmers' Association (UFA). A Tribunal of Inquiry into the Beef Industry had been established on foot of an order of the Minister for Agriculture of 31 May 1991 after resolutions had been passed by the Houses of Oireachtas that such Tribunal be established. The effect of the resolutions was that the Tribunal was vested with the statutory powers conferred by the Tribunals of Inquiry (Evidence) Acts 1921 and 1979. The UFA submitted to the Tribunal that it use the evidence of some of its members in the Inquiry. The Tribunal indicated it would do so. The UFA applied for full legal representation before the Tribunal but this was rejected. The plaintiffs then sought a declaration that they were entitled to full legal representation. On applying for interlocutory relief Denham J dismissed the application.

She held that the Attorney General was the appropriate person to represent the public interest and the UFA had no interest over and above that of any member of the public. She was also prepared to hold that counsel for the Tribunal also represented the public interest. Applying dicta in *In re Haughey* [1971] IR 217, she held that since no allegations had been made against the UFA or its members, it was in the position of witness before the Tribunal; and since the Tribunal was required to comply with fair procedures, as it had indicated it would, the limited representation granted the plaintiffs by the Tribunal was sufficient to protect their interests and good name.

Turning to the 1921 Act, she held that the plaintiffs were not 'interested' persons within the meaning of s. 2 of the 1921 Act, and the Tribunal had acted within its jurisdiction in refusing the plaintiffs full legal representation. On this aspect of the case, she followed the approach taken in *K Security Ltd v Ireland* (High Court, 15 July 1977) and she also quoted with approval

certain passages from Appendix 4 of the *Report of the Tribunal of Inquiry
Into Whiddy Island Disaster* (Prl. 8911, 1980), which was conducted by
Costello J. Indeed, it is of interest to note that the approach taken by Costello
J in the Whiddy Inquiry has been adopted as a model since then in all
subsequent Tribunals.

Anticipating the view which was to be taken later by the Supreme Court
in *Goodman International v Mr Justice Hamilton* [1992] ILRM 145 (see the
Constitutional Law chapter, 109-11, below), Denham J rejected the plaintiffs' claim that the Tribunal constituted a court of law. She concluded that
the plaintiffs had misunderstood the purpose of the Tribunal, which was in-
quisitorial in nature, and was not adversarial in nature, nor a court of law,
civil or criminal. In the circumstances, she held that the plaintiffs' rights were
adequately protected by the observance of fair procedures and they had not
made out a ground for the exceptional relief of a mandatory injunction against
the Tribunal.

7 Bias   Murtagh v Board of Management of St Emer's National School
[1991] ILRM 549; [1991] 1 IR 482 involved a judicial review of school
disciplinary proceedings.

The applicants were the parents of a pupil in sixth class at St Emer's
National School, Longford. In the course of a class he wrote the words
'Noleen Bitch Rooney' on a sheet of paper. Mrs Rooney was a teacher in
another class. He was asked to apologise to Mrs Rooney but refused to do
so. The next day he left a note on Mrs Rooney's desk, the contents of which
indicated that she was interfering with the running of fifth and sixth classes
and which also stated that if she wanted to be headmistress she should apply
elsewhere. The Principal continued to require an apology and he subsequently wrote to the applicants seeking a meeting. This took place but the
applicants objected to the Principal dealing with the matter. The matter was
put before a meeting of the Board of Management who agreed to suspend
the pupil for three days. The applicants objected to the procedure and it was
agreed that they should attend a further meeting of the Board, pending which
the suspension was lifted. At the subsequent meeting of the Board with the
applicants present, the suspension was reimposed. In the High Court, Barron
J declined to grant a judicial review of the suspension (see the 1989 Review,
5-7), and this decision was unanimously upheld on the applicants' appeal to
the Supreme Court (Hederman, McCarthy and O'Flaherty JJ). On the substantive issue, the judges had relatively little to say, McCarthy J stating that
the evidence indicated that there had been no bias on the part of the Principal
or the Board of Management in the manner in which they dealt with the
suspension in the instant case, and that the trial judge had been correct in
dismissing the applicants' case.

The absence of any further analysis of the substantive issue in the *Murtagh* case may have been influenced by the judges' views of the 'merits' of the applicants' case and the apparent patience with which the school authorities dealt with the entire issue. The strongest comments came from O'Flaherty J, who described the instant proceedings as:

> a ridiculous waste of public time and should never have been initiated; having been inititated they should not have been entertained but should have been dismissed as quite inappropriate for judicial review.

The other two members of the Court did not comment as directly on this aspect of the case. Instead, Hederman J stated flatly that judicial review did not lie in respect of the suspension of a pupil from a national school since it did not amount to an adjudication on or determination of rights, or the imposition of any liability. More circumspectly, McCarthy J added to his view on the bias issue that the decision of the Court should not be taken to indicate that O.84 of the Rules of the Superior Courts 1986 applies to decisions of Boards of Management in circumstances such as arose in the instant case.

Both the procedural and substantive aspects of the decision merited more detailed discussion in the Supreme Court.

On the substantive side, none of the judges referred to the case law on bias in general or to the application of this rule to the nuances of the relationships created in the school context. At the least, one would have expected reference to the important decision of the present Chief Justice when President of the High Court in *The State (Smullen) v Duffy* [1980] ILRM 46 or to the decision of Barron J in *Flanagan v University College Dublin* [1989] ILRM 449 (1988 Review, 14-15). True, neither of these cases involved a primary level school, but the analysis in *Smullen* seems particularly apt. In that case, Finlay P had noted the duality of function which a school principal must balance, that of paternally maintaining general discipline (in connection with which the courts would be quite deferential) and also of making decisions which have a real impact on individuals (in respect of which the courts might intervene). This analysis owes something to the decision of Pennyquick VC in *Glynn v Keele University* [1971] 2 All ER 79 and can be seen reflected in, for example, the 1985 *Report of the Committee on Discipline in Schools* (Pl. 3437). That Report discussed, *inter alia*, a model procedure for dealing with discipline in the school in the wake of the 'abolition' of corporal punishment in 1982. That Report clearly expected that fair procedures must be applied. It is unfortunate that in *Murtagh*, some of the judges took a one-dimensional view of disciplinary powers in the school context. In effect, *Murtagh* failed to analyse to any extent the issues raised, perhaps, as noted already, because of an undue focus on the 'merits' of the case. In any future cases, reference might also usefully be made to the 'due process' case law arising from the United States Supreme Court decisions in *Goss v Lopez*, 419 US 565 (1975) and *Wood v Strickland*, 420 US 308 (1975). In this context see, for example, the articles in (1975) 4 *Journal of Law and Education* 565-623.

On the procedural issue raised in *Murtagh*, it is unfortunate that, for the second time in a year (see *O'Neill v Iarnród Éireann* [1991] ILRM 129, discussed in the 1990 Review, 12-14), the Supreme Court has been unable to state categorically the limits (if any) of the judicial review procedure. It may be that the limits are difficult to draw, but this does not excuse the current confusion. In the absence of any definitive ruling, applications under O.84 of the Rules are likely to continue in a wide variety of cases, due largely to the convenience of the procedure envisaged in O.84. The trenchant view of Hederman J in *Murtagh* is unlikely to hold sway, since it could be argued that the suspension of a pupil affects constitutional rights to education, and thus O.84 would be appropriate regardless of the contractual nature of the school-pupil relationship. For the foreseeable future, applications for judicial review in such situations are likely to be heard on a *de bene esse* basis, as indeed occurred in the *Murtagh* case itself.

8 *European Community comparison* In *Emerald Meats Ltd v Minister for Agriculture*, High Court, 9 July 1991, Costello J drew a comparison between what he described as the fair procedures requirements of 'Irish administrative law' and European Community law requirements to allow affected persons have their views be known before an adjudication is made: see the European Communities law chapter, 199-200, below.

9 *Reasons to be given* The move towards requiring decision-making bodies to furnish the reasons for their decisions (see the 1988 Review, 17-18 and the 1990 Review, 9-10) appeared to have been limited by the Supreme Court's decision in *O'Keeffe v An Bord Pleanála* [1992] ILRM 237: see 16-18, below. Nonetheless, the courts continue to consider the adequacy of reasons given by decision making bodies, so it remains a live issue in judicial review proceedings.

The adequacy question arose in *International Fishing Vessels Ltd v Minister for the Marine (No. 2)* [1991] 2 IR 93, a sequel to a previous decision on the same topic. The applicant company had been refused sea-fishery licences by the respondent Minister in respect of two fishing vessels. No reasons were given by the Minister in refusing the licence. The company sought judicial review challenging the validity of the refusal. In a preliminary application in the proceedings, the High Court ordered the Minister to furnish the applicant with the reasons for the refusal of the licences: *International*

Fishing Vessels Ltd v Minister for the Marine [1989] IR 149 (discussed in the 1988 Review, 18). In giving reasons pursuant to this order, the Minister referred to certain matters which had been communicated to the applicant prior to the refusal of the licence, but certain matters were also mentioned which had not been so communicated.

In the High Court, Gannon J held that the Minister's refusal of a licence was not invalidated by the failure to communicate some of the reasons to the applicant. This view was upheld on appeal by the applicant to the Supreme Court (Hederman, McCarthy and O'Flaherty JJ). Delivering the leading judgment, McCarthy J noted that in the instant case the reasons actually communicated to the applicant by the Minister prior to his decision to refuse the licence were valid grounds on which to base a refusal. Thus, while the other grounds referred to in the reasons given after the preliminary application also constituted grounds for refusal of a licence, the fact that they were not communicated to the applicant prior to the refusal did not invalidate that refusal. McCarthy J also added (though this should probably not be treated as anything greater than an aside) that the applicant was deserving of little sympathy from the Court in view of its failure to honour previous undertakings given to the Minister in respect of landings of fish and the employment of Irish citizens as crew. Concurring, O'Flaherty J noted that to grant the applicant relief would involve a moot since the company no longer sought a licence in respect of the vessels concerned in the original application. This comment reflects the long running nature of the proceedings in the case.

For a similar trend emerging in England, see the decision of the Court of Appeal in *R. v Civil Service Appeal Board, ex p Cunningham* [1991] 4 All ER 310.

Practice and Procedure

1 Additional grounds In *Molloy v Governor of Limerick Prison*, Irish Times LR, 2 December 1991, the Supreme Court held that, in an application under O.84 of the Rules of the Superior Courts 1986, a statement of claim may be amended at any time. The Court thus overruled the decision of Blayney J in *Ahern v Minister for Industry and Commerce (No. 2)* [1990] 1 IR 55 (1990, Review, 20).

2 Delay The question of delay was addressed by the Supreme Court in *O'Flynn and O'Regan v Mid-Western Health Board* [1991] 2 IR 223 (discussed in the Health Services Chapter, 260-1, below).

3 Locus standi The standing question was addressed, albeit in the context of declaratory proceedings, in *Chambers v An Bord Pleanála* [1992] ILRM 296; [1992] 1 IR 134 (see the Local Government chapter, 317-8, below).

4 Notice parties The Supreme Court in *O'Keeffe v An Bord Pleanála*

[1992] ILRM 237 (see below) issued what amounted to a Practice Direction on aspects of appeals in planning cases. Delivering the Court's leading judgment, the Chief Justice made two important points at the end of that judgment. First, an applicant for judicial review must seek to join, and the court should normally join, any party who is likely to be affected by the avoidance of the decision impugned. The second point, concerning an oral hearing, is discussed below.

5 *Oral hearing*   The second point made by the Chief Justice in *O'Keeffe*, above, was that where judicial review is by way of a plenary summons, the action should be presented by way of oral evidence, unless the court by express order directs a hearing on affidavit or accepts from the parties an expressly agreed statement of facts.

6 *Public law/private law*   The bounds of the O.84 procedure were adverted to, though not dealt with in a definitive manner, in *Murtagh v Board of Management of St Emer's National School* [1991] ILRM 549; [1991] 1 IR 482 (12-14, above).

7 *Time limits*   In *Tennyson v Dun Laoghaire Corporation* [1991] 2 IR 527 the applicants had applied for judicial review of a planning permission just one day before the expiry of the two month time limit in s. 82(3A) of the Local Government (Planning and Development) Act 1963, as inserted by s. 42 of the Local Government (Planning and Development) Act 1976. The application was adjourned by the judge dealing with the matter for over three weeks to seek clarification of certain matters. It was only at the adjourned hearing that leave to seek judicial review was granted. Barr J held that this adjournment had not brought the applicants outside the two month time limit, since it had not been established that the material considered at the adjourned hearing was fundamental to the success of the original application. See also the Local Government chapter, 321-2, below.

Proportionality   The developing area of challenging a decision for lack of proportion between the decision and the statutory jurisdiction on which it is based was raised in *Hand v Dublin Corporation* [1991] ILRM 556; [1991] 1 IR 409 (discussed in the Constitutional Law chapter, 104-5, below). See also the discussion of reasonableness in this Chapter, below.

Reasonableness   The question of reasonableness arose in two Supreme Court decisions in 1991. In the first, *O'Keeffe v An Bord Pleanála* (the 'Radio Tara' case) [1992] ILRM 237, the Supreme Court applied the test of reasonableness it had propounded in *The State (Keegan) v Stardust Victims Compensation Tribunal* [1987] ILRM 202; [1986] IR 642. In the second case, *Rooney v Minister for Agriculture and Food and Ors* [1991] 2 IR 539 the

Court was required to consider the reasonableness of a non-statutory grant scheme concerning agricultural animals.

O' Keeffe v An Bord Pleanála [1992] ILRM 237 was discussed in the 1990 Review, 16-19. However, it may be useful to reiterate here the Court's overall approach to this area as reflected in the judgment of the Chief Justice.

To reiterate the circumstances briefly, the applicant sought judicial review of the decision of the respondent Planning Board to grant planning permission to a company, Radio Tara Ltd, for the erection of a long wave radio transmitting station, including a 300 metre mast, in County Meath. The application for planning permission to Meath County Council had been rejected by the elected members pursuant to a motion under s. 4 of the City and County Management (Amendment) Act 1955 directing the County Manager to refuse planning permission. The County Manager declined to follow the direction, and he granted planning permission subject to certain conditions. The applicant appealed to the respondent Board, which upheld the planning permission, subject to certain conditions.

The judicial review focused on the decision-making procedures adopted by the Board and its, apparent, disregard for the views of experts. The Board had appointed an Inspector and an expert from Eolas, the Science and Technology Agency, to prepare a Report on the effect of the transmission station. The Eolas Report indicated that there would be 'widespread and sustained' electro-magnetic interference within a 7 km radius of the mast; electric fencing would require temporary earthing when not in use; telephones would be subject to consistent nuisance or impairment of enjoyment; radios and hearing aids would be difficult to operate free of interference and burglar alarms would be affected. The Inspector's report indicated the possible effect of the mast on the value of houses in the area surrounding the mast. S. 26(5) of the Local Government (Planning and Development) Act 1963 requires the Board, on appeal from a decision of the planning authority, to determine the matter as if made to it in the first place; and the Board is thus required in its decision to consider the proper planning of the area in question. The Board's formal decision was notified by means of a statement that the permission was granted as being consistent with the proper planning of the area. A Schedule of the conditions was attached to this statement.

In the High Court, Costello J had quashed the Board's decision, but this was unanimously overturned on appeal to the Supreme Court (Finlay CJ, Griffin, Hederman, McCarthy and Lynch JJ). Delivering the leading judgment of the Court, the Chief Justice adopted a quite conservative approach to the courts' role on judicial review. He referred to a number of authorities which had warned on the dangers of the judges themselves usurping another body's decision-making power, and reiterated the views of Lord Brightman in *Chief Constable of North Wales Police v Evans* [1982] 1

WLR 1155 on that topic (noting that Griffin J had quoted the same passage
in the *Keegan* case). He also noted that the courts cannot interfere merely
because they might have reached a different decision or because the case
against the decision made by the decision-making body under review was
much stronger than the case for it.

The Chief Justice felt that these considerations were particularly important in the planning context. He continued:

> Under the provisions of the Planning Acts the legislature has un-
> equivocally and firmly placed questions of planning, questions of the
> balance between development and the environment and the proper
> convenience and amenities of an area within the jurisdiction of the
> planning authorities and the Board which are expected to have special
> skill, competence and experience in planning questions. The Court is
> not vested with that jurisdiction, nor is it expected to, nor can it exercise
> discretion with regard to planning matters.
>
> I am satisfied that in order for an applicant for judicial review to
> satisfy a court that the decision-making authority had acted irrationally
> ... so that the court can intervene and quash its decision, it is necessary
> that the applicant should establish to the satisfaction of the court that
> the decision-making authority had before it no relevant material which
> would support its decision.

The Court held that, in the instant case, the applicant had not discharged
the onus placed on him in this regard. But even aside from the issue of onus
of proof, the Supreme Court held that the Board had been entitled to reach
the conclusion it did on a perusal of the entire of the Reports before it,
notwithstanding the strength and clarity of the actual recommendations
against granting permission made in them.

On the issue of the Board giving reasons for its decisions, the Supreme
Court looked at a combination of the decision itself and the conditions
attached to the decision; and having regard to the clarity of the conditions in
the instant case, the Board had complied with its obligation to give reasons
under reg. 48 of the Local Government (Planning and Development)
Regulations 1977.

For further comment on the effect of the *O'Keeffe* case on previous case
law in the area, see the 1990 Review, 19-20.

The second Supreme Court decision on reasonableness in 1991 was
Rooney v Minister for Agriculture and Food and Ors [1991] 2 IR 539. The
circumstances giving rise to the case were as follows.

In 1984, 20 of the plaintiff farmer's cattle were slaughtered as 'reactor'
cattle, that is, they were deemed to be infected with bovine TB in accordance

with the procedures provided for under the Bovine Tuberculosis (Attestation of the State and General Provisions) Order 1978. Under a non-statutory scheme operated by the defendant Minister, the plaintiff was paid certain sums in relation to each head of cattle so slaughtered. The plaintiff instituted proceedings claiming, *inter alia*, that the sums so paid were inadequate and thus in breach of Articles 40.3 and 43 of the Constitution, and that he should have been paid full compensation under the terms of the Diseases of Animals Act 1966. Ss.17 and 22 of the 1966 Act provide that the defendant Minister may institute a scheme of compensation by which the appropriate levels of compensation for slaughtered animals could, in the event of disagreement between the owner and the Minister, be referred to arbitration. No such statutory scheme had been instituted. In the High Court, the plaintiff's claim was dismissed by Lavan J, and this conclusion was unanimously upheld by the Supreme Court (McCarthy, O'Flaherty and Egan JJ).

Applying the approach taken in *Pine Valley Developments Ltd v Minister for the Environment* [1987] ILRM 747; [1987] IR 23 (see the 1987 Review, 24), McCarthy J (delivering the leading judgment) held that since the non-statutory scheme constituted a reasonable scheme for providing a measure of assistance to owners of diseased cattle the Court had no power to review the course of action adopted by the Minister in the instant case. Indeed, even if the scheme had not been reasonable, McCarthy J suggested that the Court might have no function to enjoin the Minister to introduce a statutory scheme under s. 20 of the 1966 Act, referring with apparent approval to the Court's decision in *The State (Sheehan) v Government of Ireland* [1987] IR 550 (see the 1987 Review, 16-21).

The Court was careful to note that the non-statutory scheme was in the nature of a grant scheme, whereas a scheme under the 1966 Act would be avowedly compensatory in its purpose. Despite this, the Court did offer the view that the Minister was providing a reasonable measure of compensation in the non-statutory scheme. Having made that observation, the Court seemed of the view that this appeared to comply with any constitutional requirements in this regard. This was, of course, on the assumption that any general constitutional right to compensation existed, which the Court did not concede. On the issue of compensation for interference with property rights under the Constitution, see generally Kelly, *The Irish Constitution*, 2nd ed., pp. 658-60.

For two other cases on reasonableness, see 316 and 380, below.

Agriculture

ANIMAL DISEASE ERADICATION

Brucellosis The Brucellosis in Cattle (General Provisions) Order 1991 (SI No. 114) replaces the 1980 Order of the same title (as amended). The 1991 Order includes comprehensive powers of the Minister for Agriculture to deal with reactor cattle.

Newcastle Disease The Diseases of Animals (Poultry Feed) Order 1991 (SI No. 364) outlines procedures for preventing Newcastle disease.

Schemes *Rooney v Minister for Agriculture and Food* [1991] 2 IR 539 concerned procedural aspects of the operation of one of the non-statutory schemes relating to animal disease: see the discussion in the Administrative Law chapter, 18-19, above.

ANIMAL REMEDIES

The Animal Remedies (Prohibition of Certain Sales) Regulations 1991 (SI No. 244) amounted to a further attempt to restrict the sale of items which might be used to artificially stimulate growth in farm animals. See also the Regulations referred to in the European Communities chapter in this context, 201-4, below.

DESTRUCTIVE PESTS AND INSECTS

The Destructive Pests and Insects (Amendment) Act 1991 provided for increased criminal penalties in connection with the Principal Act in this area, the Destructive Pests and Insects (Consolidation) Act 1958. For a discussion of the history of the legislation, see Humphreys' Annotation, *Irish Current Law Statutes Annotated*.

EUROPEAN COMMUNITIES

Meat imports *Emerald Meats Ltd v Minister for Agriculture*, High Court, 9 July 1991 (discussed in the European Communities chapter, 199-200, below) concerend the operation of EC provisions on importation of meat from non-EC States.

Regulations   A number of important EC-based statutory regulations concerning Agriculture are referred to in the European Communities chapter, 201-4, below.

HORSES

The Transit of Animals Order 1991 (SI No. 338) provide for fees in respect of horses being transported to Northern Ireland.

Commercial Law

ARBITRATION

Stay of proceedings: consumer In *McCarthy v Joe Walsh Tours Ltd* [1991] ILRM 813, Carroll J declined to stay proceedings under s. 5 of the Arbitration Act 1980 in relation to a package tour holiday dispute. The decision places a severe question mark over the continued enforceability of arbitration clauses in such cases.

The plaintiffs had booked a holiday through the defendant company, in relation to which they alleged breach of contract. The booking form, which the first plaintiff signed, contained a box beside the place for the signature in which the customer acknowledged that all terms included in the booking form had been brought to the customer's attention and that these had been accepted. The plaintiff stated that he was unaware that there was an arbitration clause in the standard booking conditions and that this had not been brought to his attention at the time of making the contract. Carroll J, applying common law principles, held that it would have been unreasonable for the plaintiff to assume that the contract was purely oral and that he was adding nothing by signing the booking form. She therefore concluded that the arbitration clause formed part of the contract between the parties.

However, this was not the end of the matter. Carroll J then considered the effect of ss. 39 and 40 of the Sale of Goods and Supply of Services Act 1980 on the contract. S. 39 of the 1980 Act provides that, subject to s. 40, in every contract for the supply of services it is an implied term that, *inter alia*, the service will be supplied with due skill, care and diligence. S. 40 provides that the s. 39 implied terms may be varied by agreement. In the case of the recipient of the service being a consumer, however, such variation must be fair and reasonable and have been specifically brought to the recipient's attention. A variation under s. 40 includes any term by which an implied term is restricted in some way.

Carroll J pointed out that, under the arbitration scheme operated by the defendant company, there was a ceiling of £5,000 for any single claim. She held that this clearly constituted an attempt to limit the terms implied under s. 39 of the 1980 Act. Since the arbitration clause was not specifically drawn to the plaintiff's attention, she held that the variation which it effected was not operable under s. 40 of the 1980 Act. She considered that, to be effective, the defendant was required to draw specific attention to the monetary limits and other limiting provisions (which purported to exclude liability for personal injuries) in the arbitration scheme.

These comments by Carroll J will have important implications for the effectiveness of arbitration clauses in all consumer services contracts, including those of airlines. Whether other considerations will apply in those cases, such as whether Air Transport Acts (implementing, for example, the Warsaw Conventions) which limit liability will take priority over the 1980 Act, remain to be considered.

Stay of proceedings: dispute In *Williams v Artane Service Station Ltd* [1991] ILRM 893, Lardner J applied the mandatory provisions of s. 5 of the Arbitration Act 1980 by granting the defendants a stay on the proceedings instituted by the plaintiff. The plaintiff claimed that the defendants had been in breach of contract in the manner in which they terminated the contract between them. The contract provided for a mandatory reference to arbitration in the event of a dispute between the parties, except for one particular situation. The plaintiff claimed that the instant case fell within that exception, but the notice of termination from the defendants purported to end the contract on a ground in relation to which arbitration was required. Lardner J held that, since there was a 'dispute' on this point, he was required to stay the proceedings under s. 5 of the 1980 Act. For previous cases under s. 5 of the 1980 Act, see the 1988 Review, 50-1, the 1989 Review, 20-1 and the 1990 Review, 28.

COMPETITION

The Competition Act 1991 represents a revolutionary change in domestic law on restrictive practices. It seeks to apply to the Irish market the EC competition rules contained in Articles 85 and 86 of the Treaty of Rome. S. 4 of the 1991 Act prohibits and declares void, subject to certain important exceptions, any agreements, decisions and concerted practices between 'undertakings' which have the effect of preventing, restricting or distorting trade in any part of the State—the text of this ban is borrowed directly from Article 85 of the Treaty of Rome. Similarly, s. 5 of the 1991 Act prohibits the abuse of a dominant position in the State, or a substantial part of the State—this section is based on Article 86. S. 6 of the Act introduces a novel cause of action—the right of any party aggrieved by any breach of ss. 4 and 5 to seek damages arising from such breach, including exemplary damages, in either the Circuit Court or the High Court.

The 1991 Act also establishes the Competition Authority which replaces the Fair Trade Commission. The Competition Authority continues to have powers to investigate restrictive abuses, but it also takes on another novel power, again by way of analogy with EC competition law. Rather like the European Commission, the Competition Authority has the power to determine whether agreements or practices comply with, or are in breach of, the 1991 Act. The Authority may issue, on application, a licence, which amounts to an exemption from the terms of the 1991 Act. In addition, the Authority has power to issue, again on application, a certificate, which amounts to a decision that the agreement or practice does not breach the 1991 Act.

Finally, relatively minor changes to the Mergers, Take-Overs and Monopolies (Control) Act 1978 are also effected by ss. 15 to 19 of the 1991 Act.

The Act came into effect on 1 October 1991: Competition Act 1991 (Commencement) Order 1991 (SI No. 249). Applications for licences or certificates are subject to a fee of £100: Competition (Notification Fee) Regulations 1991 (SI No. 250).

We do not intend in the present context to discuss in detail the existing case law on Articles 85 and 86 of the Treaty of Rome, nor on how precisely those Articles will be used in the context of the operation of the 1991 Act. There are very helpful discussions of this in Brown et al, *Competition Law and Regulation in Ireland* (Competition Press, 1991), Schuster (ed.), *The New Competition Legislation* (Irish Centre for European Law, 1991) and in Cregan's Annotation, *Irish Current Law Statutes Annotated*. Since these were written, the Supreme Court, in *Deane v Voluntary Health Insurance Board*, Supreme Court, 29 July 1992 has ruled on the question of what constitutes an 'undertaking' for the purposes of the 1991 Act. This important decision will be analysed in the 1992 Review.

For the present, however, we will comment briefly on some of the broad issues raised by the existence of the 1991 Act.

First, the effect of the 1991 Act on previous legislation. The wide-ranging and non-prescriptive sections of the 1991 Act are markedly different from any Irish legislative predecessors. Thus, for example, the Restrictive Practices Acts 1972 and 1987 provided for legislative bans of restrictive practices by Ministerial Order. However, such bans were made only after exhaustive investigation by the Fair Trade Commission followed—perhaps—by legislative action in a very narrow area of economic activity. The clear difference in the 1991 Act is that its provisions are, in effect, self-executing and declaratory. Ss. 4 and 5 of the Act obviate the need for investigations and Ministerial Orders. Indeed, the existing Restrictive Practices (Groceries) Order 1987 (which *inter alia* bans below-cost selling of certain groceries) fits uneasily into the free market thrust of the 1991 Act. To provide for a relatively easy transition, it was decided that the 1987 Order should not be repealed pending a review of its operation. Otherwise, however, the Restrictive Practices Acts 1972 and 1987 have been repealed and replaced by the 1991 Act.

A second problematic issue with the 1991 Act is the difficulty in predicting the likely effect of its exceptionally broad, and therefore bare, provisions. The 1991 Act is deceptively significant because its terms involve a move away from the detailed and prescriptive provisions of previous legislation to the non-prescriptive text based on Article 85 and 86. Because of this, there were concerns that the Act would, for example, prohibit all restrictive agreements. However, it may be said with some confidence that the 1991 Act does not ban all covenants in restraint of trade, nor does it prohibit all exclusive dealing agreements, nor does it prohibit all non-competition clauses. This can be said because the Competition Authority had, by early 1992, already granted certificates in respect of certain restrictive agreements, so the 1991 Act cannot be seen as banning all such arrangements. What the 1991 Act clearly does, however, is to cast a substantial doubt over the continued validity of such arrangements where a significant macro-distortion of trade in the State is brought about by their operation. Thus, for example, while the common law rules on restraint of trade continue to be important in their own terms, the 1991 Act adds a new dimension to litigation on restraint of trade: regardless of whether a restraint is reasonable as between two parties or reasonable in the public interest, the 1991 Act requires that such restraints do not involve a distortion of trade at the macro level.

That is certainly a new element in such cases, though it by no means presages a glut of decisions invalidating such arrangements. The experience with Articles 85 and 86 of the Treaty of Rome will, no doubt, prove instructive in this context: after all, the European Commission has accepted that certain 'distorting' arrangements must be allowed in order to protect, for example, intellectual property rights such as copyright and trade marks. The protections afforded by the Copyright Act 1963 or the Trade Marks Act 1964 could hardly be set at nought by the 1991 Act: it would be a gross distortion of the 1991 Act itself to describe these legislative provisions as condoning unacceptable restrictions on competition. The passage of the Patents Act 1992 by the Oireachtas (which increased the initial length of a patent from 16 to 21 years) also places the Competition Act in some context. The message of the 1991 Act is that some, but not all, trade distortions are invalid.

A third issue relates to enforcement of the terms of the 1991 Act. The Competition Authority clearly has a significant role in approving or disapproving of agreements and practices notified to it. Of course, the notification provisions are dependent on the willingness of private parties allowing the glare of an investigation by the Authority come to bear on their arrangements. Clearly, some are willing to do this, but this aspect of the 1991 Act is very much based on self-regulation. The Authority has been given no general prosecutorial role in relation to the 1991 Act, despite calls for such a role to be given it. Instead, s. 6 if the Act leaves positive enforcement to civil action in the Circuit Court and High Court by private parties aggrieved by the breach of ss. 4 and 5. Ultimately, of course, it will be the courts who decide whether the terms of the Act have been breached, and such decisions will be arrived at despite any decision which may have been made by the Competition Authority. No doubt, regardless of litigation, the 1991 Act has had the effect of requiring many organisations to seek opinions from counsel as to whether they are in breach of the 1991 Act. The test of any such opinions will come either in the form of decisions by the Competition Authority, where it is notified, and later by decisions of the courts.

EXCHANGE CONTROL

Gulf crisis   The Exchange Control Regulations 1991 (SI No. 48) required Central Bank approval for dealings with Iraq, in the light of the Gulf War. The 1990 Regulations (1990 Review, 31), which were revoked by the 1991 Regulations, had also required Central Bank approval for dealings with Kuwait.

FINANCIAL SERVICES

Banker and customer   In *Trustee Savings Bank Dublin v Maughan*, High Court, 8 October 1991 Costello J applied the rule that the courts lean against compound interest.

The defendant entered into an agreement with the plaintiff bank in 1983, in which the bank furnished the defendant with a current account overdraft facility of £5,000. On 11 August 1983, the defendant signed an application form which stated that 'charges may be made on this account, at a scale that the bank may from time to time decide.' On 23 August, the bank sent the defendant a letter stating that the overdraft was 'on the usual terms and conditions including interest repayable on demand.' On that date, the defendant had already drawn a cheque of over £4,000 on the account. In September 1983, the defendant obtained a further loan of £2,000 from the bank. On the defendant's default on the loans, the bank instituted proceedings claiming it was entitled, under the terms of the agreement, to compound interest annually and also to charge a default rate of interest of 6% over its normal rates for overdrawn current accounts. On the bank's calculations, the amount due in July 1991 in respect of the £7,000 loans amounted to £32,906.01. Costello J held that the bank was entitled to just over £21,000.

He concluded that the bank was not entitled, under the 11 August application form, to compound interest or to charge a default rate of interest, since the proposal referred to 'charges' and not to interest, and the bank was thus entitled to simple interest only. Nor did he think that the letter of 23

August could be effective to impose any new terms on the agreement reached on 11 August, since the contract had largely been performed on that date.

On the crucial question of compounding interest, he referred with approval to a passage in *Paget's Law of Banking*, 10th ed., p. 247, where the general presumption against compound interest is outlined. On this basis, he concluded that the loan of £2,000 was subject to the letter of 23 August, but that there was nothing in that letter which would allow the bank to compound interest annually or to a default rate of interest. Accordingly, he held that the bank was entitled to a sum of £21,313.14 only.

HIRE-PURCHASE

A.I.F. Ltd v Hunt and Hunt, High Court, 21 January 1991 was an important decision on the circumstances in which a Court may dispense with the letter of the requirements of a note or memorandum contained in s. 3 of the Hire-Purchase Act 1946.

The plaintiff company was the finance company in relation to a hire-purchase contract entered into by the defendants as co-hirers. The note or memorandum required by the 1946 Act overstated the hire-purchase price. This inaccuracy was known to the defendants and the dealer involved, but not the plaintiff company. The plaintiff had required the second defendant to enter into the transaction as co-hirer with the first defendant, his son. The second defendant directed his bank to repay the installments by monthly order. When 17 of the 36 installments had been repaid, the second defendant countermanded the order. The plaintiff instituted Circuit Court proceedings seeking enforcement of the agreement. The claim was dismissed as against the first defendant but was successful against the second defendant. The second defendant appealed against the Circuit Court decision; the plaintiff did not appeal the dismiss against the first defendant. Barron J dismissed the second defendant's appeal.

The judge held that, although the inaccuracy in the statement of the hire-purchase price meant that the requirements of s. 3 of the 1946 Act had not been complied with, it was just and equitable, within the meaning of s. 3 itself, that the Court dispense with such requirements having regard to the knowledge of the defendants and the lack of awareness of the inaccuracy on the part of the plaintiff. This decision is important as indicating that there are some unusual circumstances in which non-compliance with s. 3 will not invalidate a hire-purchase agreement. However, the case law in this area indicates that compliance will, in general, be required and finance houses in particular ought not rely on the special circumstances of the instant case as indicating a change in the judicial attitude to s. 3. For very strong comments on the importance of s. 3, see the judgments of Murnaghan J in *BW Credit*

Co. Ltd v Henebry (1962) 97 ILTR 123 and *UDT (Commercial) Ltd v Nestor* [1962] IR 140.

On a procedural point in *Hunt*, the second defendant had argued that the plaintiff was estopped by the dismiss of its claim against the first defendant in the Circuit Court from arguing that the first defendant had not signed the hire-purchase agreement. However, Barron J held that once the second defendant had appealed by way of re-hearing to the High Court, all issues debated in the Circuit Court were open again. Thus, he concluded, even if the Circuit Court had found that the first defendant had not signed the hire-purchase agreement, the plaintiff was not estopped from arguing the point. In any event, Barron J considered that such finding had not in fact been made since if it had been the plaintiff's claim against the second defendant could not have been successful.

INDUSTRIAL AND PROVIDENT SOCIETIES

The decision of Costello J in *Kerry Co-Op Creameries Ltd and Ors v An Bord Bainne Co-Op Ltd* [1990] ILRM 664 was discussed in the 1990 Review, 34-7. As indicated there, in 1991 the Supreme Court, on appeal, upheld all the domestic law conclusions reached by the trial judge but referred certain EC law matters to the Court of Justice: [1991] ILRM 851. It is appropriate to refer in more detail here to the reasoning of the Supreme Court on the domestic law issues raised. The case arose in the following way.

Bord Bainne (the Board), an industrial and provident society within the meaning of the Industrial and Provident Societies Act 1893, was formed in 1972 to market Irish dairy produce abroad. The Board membership consisted exclusively of dairy co-operatives. The members of the Board agreed that no dividends would be paid on the members' shares, but that instead profits would be distributed to those members who traded with it. Rules were adopted by the Board in 1975 which had the effect of guaranteeing members a fixed price regardless of the market price at the time, provided that the produce was sold to the Board. Membership could be terminated if a member failed to sell produce to the Board, but in fact no membership had ever been terminated. In 1981, the Board agreed a waiver to the 1975 Rules, without explicitly amending them, by which members were given a freer choice as to whether to sell produce to the Board or to export produce directly.

The plaintiffs, the first named also being an industrial and provident society and a member of the defendant Board, had traded exclusively with the Board up to 1987 when they decided to export some produce directly. In 1987 also the Board decided formally to alter its 1975 Rules. The plaintiffs, as members of the Board, sought unsuccessfully to oppose the changes in the Rules. The effect of the changes was that members who traded exclusively through the Board would be treated more favourably than those who exported some produce directly. The changes also involved changes in the composition of the Board itself as well as the issue of bonus shares. The plaintiffs challenged the validity of the rule changes on the grounds, *inter alia*, that the changes constituted an expropriation of property and a breach of property rights; that the rules constituted an unreasonable restraint of trade; that they were *ultra vires* the Industrial and Provident Societies Act 1893; and were in breach of Articles 85 and 86 of the Treaty of Rome.

In the High Court, Costello J rejected the claims: [1990] ILRM 664, and as already indicated, on appeal by the plaintiffs the Supreme Court (Finlay CJ, McCarthy and O'Flaherty JJ) upheld the conclusions of Costello J on the domestic law issues: [1991] ILRM 851.

The Court held that the wide power given to the Board to allot shares was such that it was circumscribed only by requirements as to good faith (which had not been questioned in the instant case). The power must also be exercised fairly as between different shareholders, but the Court held that this did not require identical treatment for all shareholders. The judges also agreed with Costello J that the plaintiffs had not acquired any proprietorial rights over the Board's 'net value' at the time of becoming a shareholder, so that the dilution involved in the 1988 Rules was not inconsistent with the Board's general power. On this point, the Supreme Court approved dicta in *Mutual Life Insurance Co. of New York v Rank Organisation Ltd* [1985] BCLC 11.

Turning to the *ultra vires* argument, the Court applied the principles in *Hole v Garnsey* [1930] AC 472. It concluded that the 1988 Rules were not *ultra vires* the Board, since they did not alter fundamentally the co-operative nature of the Board and it retained its same essential features. The Court expressly acknowledged that it was not prepared to concede the restriction on the Board's power to alter its Rules for which the plaintiffs contended. Clearly, the 1988 Rules amounted to quite substantial alterations to how the Board did business, but the Supreme Court, like Costello J, was prepared to concede what might be described as a wide margin of discretion in this context. Such deference is consistent with basic laissez faire principles of commercial law. This emerged later in the judgments when the Court held that although at first sight it appeared unfair for the 1988 Rules to have applied to the previous year's trading without advance notice, it was justifiable on the basis that otherwise members might have temporarily increased their trade with the Board in order to gain an artificial advantage in the change.

The next issue debated was restraint of trade. On this point, a question arose as to whether the doctrine applied at all in the absence of an express covenant in restraint of trade. All three Supreme Court judges seemed prepared to accept that, assuming the doctrine did apply in the instant case, the restriction imposed by the 1988 Rules amounted to a reasonable restraint as between the members of the Board and also by reference to the public interest. However, it was notable that on the actual point as to whether the doctrine applied, a distinct difference of opinion emerged.

Finlay CJ stated simply it was not necessary in the instant case to decide whether the doctrine of restraint of trade applied in the absence of an express covenant in restraint. McCarthy J stated that the doctrine was applicable even in the absence of an express covenant in restraint of trade; and he added that the provisions of Article 45 of the Constitution were relevant to the question of public policy reasonableness. However, O'Flaherty J considered that an express covenant in restraint of trade must exist for the doctrine to operate. Both McCarthy and O'Flaherty JJ referred to the discussion on this question in the Privy Council decision *Stenhouse Australia Ltd v Philips* [1974] AC 391. It remains for another case how this divergence of view will be resolved.

Finally, on the EC law issues raised, the Court held that Costello J had been correct in deciding that the Court had no jurisdiction to deal with the issue concerning Article 85 of the Treaty of Rome since the plaintiffs had not referred the 1988 Rules to the European Commission to determine their compatibility with the Council Regulation 26/62/EEC. Since this was a matter concerning the lack of jurisdiction of the Court rather than an issue of interpretation of the Treaty of Rome, the question of a reference to the Court of Justice did not arise. However, since Costello J's conclusions on Article 86 of the Treaty involved an interpretation of Community law, and since the Supreme Court was a court of final appeal and the judge's interpretation did not involve (in the eyes of the Supreme Court judges) a self-evident interpretation of Article 86, and since the determination of certain issues was necessary in order for the Court to give a decision in the case, the Court concluded that a reference under Article 177 to the Court of Justice was required. The issues relevant to the reference were outlined in the judgment of the Supreme Court of 14 May 1991: [1991] ILRM at 879.

INSURANCE

Disclosure of information   *Latham v Hibernian Insurance Co. Ltd and Peter J. Sheridan & Co. Ltd*, High Court, 22 March and 4 December 1991 was another case on non-disclosure in the insurance context.

The plaintiff was the owner of a shop premises. In August 1983 he entered into a policy of insurance with the defendant company to cover the building, stock, fixtures and fittings and loss of profits for one year. The second defendant acted as insurance broker for the plaintiff. The policy was renewed in August 1984. In November 1983, the plaintiff was arrested and charged with receiving stolen goods. He later pleaded guilty to the charge and was sentenced to a term of imprisonment. A fire occurred in the shop premises in May 1985 causing substantial damage to the building and its contents. When the plaintiff made a claim under his policy, the defendant company repudiated liability on the ground that the plaintiff's arrest and conviction had not been disclosed to it in 1983 or on the renewal of the policy. The plaintiff instituted proceedings against the two defendants, claiming that the insurance company was not entitled to repudiate and, in the alternative, that the second defendant had been negligent. Blayney J dismissed the claim against the insurance company but found the broker negligent.

Applying the leading decision of the Supreme Court in *Chariot Inns Ltd v Assicurazioni Generali SPA* [1981] ILRM 173; [1981] IR 199, he held that the commission of the offence of receiving stolen property was a material fact which should have been disclosed on renewal, since it would have affected the mind of a prudent insurer.

He went on to hold that the insurance company had no knowledge of the plaintiff's arrest in November 1983. Even if he had accepted certain evidence for the plaintiff that a clerk in the company's office was aware of the arrest, Blayney J noted that the clerk had not become aware in the ordinary course of his employment, and so knowledge could not be imputed to the company. Thus, the company was entitled to repudiate liability. A passage in *MacGillivray and Parkington on Insurance Law*, 7th ed., para. 674 was approved in this context.

Next, Blayney J held that the evidence established that the principal of the defendant broker had become aware of the plaintiff's arrest in November 1983, and he was in breach of his duty to the plaintiff by not advising him to disclose this information to the insurance company.

It then remained to determine the damages. In his judgment of 4 December 1991, Blayney J held that the matter was to be approached on the basis of whether the plaintiff would have received insurance cover from another company if the plaintiff's arrest and conviction was revealed, the onus being on the plaintiff. Since evidence had been given for the plaintiff that such cover could have been obtained from an English company, albeit at a higher premium, and this had not been disputed by the second defendant, the plaintiff was entitled to damages under the same headings as those in the policy he had obtained from the first defendant. Blayney J concluded that the plaintiff was not entitled to any loss of profits beyond the one year in the policy since the plaintiff's inability to borrow to reinstate his premises was not a direct consequence of the second defendant's negligence, though if he had been able to borrow to reinstate he would have been entitled to claim from the defendant any interest on a loan. He distinguished the Supreme Court decision in *Murphy v McGrath* [1981] ILRM 364 in this context.

Finally, he held that the plaintiff was entitled to interest on his damages under s.22 of the Courts Act 1981 since he would have been compensated over five years ago were it not for the second defendant's negligence. See further 410-11, below.

In *Superwood Holdings plc v Sun Alliance Insurance*, High Court, August 1991, O'Hanlon J dismissed a claim on account of non-disclosure after a hearing lasting 115 days, the longest ever civil action in the State. The judgment in the case, reported to be over 400 pages, has not been circulated.

European Communities   The European Communities (Non-Life Insurance) (Amendment) Regulations 1991 (SI No. 5), which came into effect on 11 January 1991, gave effect to Council Directive 87/343/EEC. They require that a credit insurance business must establish an equalisation reserve as set out in the Directive. The European Communities (Non-Life Insurance) (Amendment) (No. 2) Regulations 1991 (SI No. 142) gave effect to the Second Non-Life Services Directive, 88/357/EEC. The European Communities (Non-Life Insurance) (Legal Expenses) Regulations 1991 (SI No. 197) provide that legal expenses insurance is permissible, subject to avoiding conflict of interest situations.

INTELLECTUAL PROPERTY

Copyright: extension   The Copyright (Extended Application) Order 1991 (SI No. 101) extended copyright protection to services licensed under the Broadcasting Act 1988.

Copyright: fees   The Copyright (Proceedings before the Controller) Rules 1964 (Amendment) Rules 1991 (SI No. 105) provide for increase fees.

Copyright services   *Phonographic Performance (Irl) Ltd v Somers* [1992] ILRM 657 involved an interesting point on s. 17 of the Copyright Act 1963, in connection with liability for VAT: see the Revenue chapter, 364-5, below.

Protection for semiconductors   The European Communities (Protection of Topographies of Semiconductor Products) (Amendment) Regulations 1991 (SI No. 318) implement Decisions 90/510/EEC and 90/511/EEC by extending the protection given under the 1988 Regulations of the same title (1988 Review, 210).

SALE OF GOODS

Irish Telephone Rentals Ltd v Irish Civil Service Building Society Ltd [1991] ILRM 880 involved an important point on the status of contract terms under the Sale of Goods Acts 1893 and 1980: see the Contract Law chapter, 117-9, below.

Company Law

Several books on company law were published in 1991. The Honourable Mr Justice Keane produced a second edition of his excellent work, *Company Law in the Republic of Ireland*. Lyndon McCann published, as a companion volume, *A Casebook on Company Law*. Gerard McCormack's *The New Companies Legislation* analyses the two 1990 Acts in very helpful detail.

EXAMINERSHIPS

Appointment of Examiner   In the 1990 Review, 42, we noted that s. 2 of the Companies (Amendment) Act 1990 gives the court a broad discretion in deciding whether to appoint an examiner, in contrast to the specificity of s. 8 of Britain's Insolvency Act 1986. In *In re Atlantic Magnetics Ltd*, Supreme Court, 5 December 1991, affirming (with minor variations) Lardner J, 15-25 November 1991, considerable light was thrown on how the court should exercise its functions in this context. For a helpful analysis, see McCormack (1992) 14 DULJ 101.

Lardner J had expressed the standard, to be applied in cases where the evidence does not lead to a clearcut conclusion, as follows:

> [D]oes the evidence lead to the conclusion that in all the circumstances it appears worthwhile to order an investigation by the examiner into the company's affairs and see can it survive, there being some reasonable prospect of survival?

The Supreme Court upheld the substance of this test, but there was some internal disagreement as to precisely how much of it should be saved.

Finlay CJ (Hederman, O'Flaherty and Egan JJ concurring) approached the matter by noting that the examination procedure was designed to operate within a short time framework; the basic purpose of the appointment of an examiner was 'to do precisely what the word involves, *examine* the situation, affairs and prospects of the company'. There could be no onus on the petitioner to establish as a matter of probability that the company was capable of surviving as a going concern. The phraseology of s. 2(2) provided a strongly persuasive obligation to appoint where the court considered that to do so was likely to facilitate a survival of the company. The Chief Justice saw no warrant for incorporating into the exercise of the power the need to establish at that stage to the court's satisfaction 'a real prospect of survival of the company'. He thus rejected, *sub silentio*, the approach favoured by Keane J, extrajudicially, in *Company Law in the Republic of Ireland* (2nd ed.), 455, Finlay CJ accepted that, for a court to consider that there was a likelihood that an order would facilitate the survival of the company, which has received support in a number of English decisions on s. 8 of the Insolvency Act 1986: see McCormack, *op. cit.*, at 102-3, it had to engage in some evaluation as to the chances of the company surviving:

> The real importance of such an evaluation at the state of the petition for the appointment of the examiner goes no further than that a court should be very slow indeed to make an order pursuant to either of the sub-sections of s. 2 where it considers that there is no identifiable possibility of the survival of a company.

The Chief Justice approved of Lardner J's formula subject to deleting the word 'reasonable' from the last sentence.

McCarthy J went further. Like Finlay CJ, he also rejected the 'real prospect' test, going so far as to cite Keane J's textbook without disclosing its authorship—a curious exercise in judicial etiquette. Rather than merely delete a word from the final sentence of Lardner J's test, McCarthy J preferred to delete a phrase: 'there being some reasonable prospect of survival'. Thus McCarthy J's approach is nuanced slightly more in favour of the making of an order appointing an examiner under s. 2.

A couple of other issues of some importance arose in the case. Lardner J had made an order authorising the examiner to borrow sums not exceeding £429,000 and to apply these sums to certain specified purposes for the continuance of the company; he declared that these sums should be treated as expenses properly incurred by the examiner pursuant to s. 29(1) and should be repaid in full out of the assets of the company in priority to any other claim, whether secured or unsecured, in accordance with the terms of s. 29(3). Lardner J made another order authorising two banks to have recourse to funds standing to the credit of the company in the company's accounts in those banks, so far as was necessary for the purpose of lending to the examiner pursuant to his order as to borrowing. Finally he ordered that one of the banks should pay out the moneys standing to the credit of the company to the examiner, pursuant to the earlier orders.

The Supreme Court held that the declaration was not inappropriate by virtue of the fact that one of the banks had a fixed charge over all the assets of the company. It was impossible, said the Chief Justice, to construe s. 11 as impliedly amending s. 29(3) by inserting into that subsection, after the word 'secured' and before the words 'or unsecured,' the phrase 'by any means other than a fixed charge'. Ss. 11 and 29 were *separate* sections; to insert the suggested clause would clearly be to legislate and 'could not come under any doctrine or principle of interpretation'. The phrase 'before any other claim, secured or unsecured' was unambiguous and had to be given its literal meaning.

Counsel on behalf of the examiner did not seek to defend Lardner J's final order, requiring one of the banks to pay out the moneys standing to the company's credit to the examiner. The Supreme Court set it aside.

The Supreme Court upheld the order authorising the banks to have recourse to the funds standing to the company's credit so as to provide a loan to the examiner. In the court's view, the order had been made under the authority of s. 9, which enables the court to order that the borrowing powers of the directors should be performed by the examiner and to include such conditions in that order and make such other orders as it sees fit. It was true that, under s. 11, which gives the examiner power to deal with charged property, the court's authority to the examiner to dispose of property subject to a fixed charge as if it were not the subject of the security is on condition that the net proceeds should be applied towards discharging the sum secured by the security with a provision for a shortfall. Had Lardner J made the order under s. 11, it could not have been sustained; but he had *not* done so and his order had not been an attempt to achieve what was provided for in s. 11 by a different manner. The order had not involved the *disposal* of any of the company's property; it was merely a method of enabling the bank in question to grant 'back-to-back' loans to the examiner. The provisions of s. 9(3) were wide, and quite clearly intended to give full effect to an order such as the one made in the case.

Finlay CJ noted that, if the company's future inability to meet its debts were to result in a liquidation or receivership, repayment of the moneys borrowed pursuant to the order would clearly rank in priority to any claim of any form of secured creditor. Interpreting s. 9 as the court had done seemed to him clearly to achieve the legislative purpose. Any other interpretation would leave a situation where effectively a secured creditor with a charge over the entire of the assets of a company which had become fixed could always prevent the provisions for the appointment of an examiner (and other consequential provisions of the Act) from being operative in respect of that company at all.

The question of justice as between secured and unsecured creditors is not easy to resolve. An editorial in the *Irish Law Times* (vol. 10 (ns) 149 (1992)) notes that:

[w]hilst the financial insitutions may not be the weakest sector in the Irish business community it seems unjustifiable to force such insti-

tutions to bale out the other creditors of the company, particularly where
the insolvency has not been caused by them, but has resulted from mis-
management or from some other factor outside their control.

The examiner's report   The examinership system faced its first major test
in *In re Goodman International and related Companies*, High Court, 28
January 1991. The economic stakes were being high but the legal issues
raised in this context were slight enough.

At the end of August the examiner had been appointed to Goodman
International and related companies. A month later his remit was extended
to a further thirty companies. In his report under s. 15 of the Act, the examiner
expressed the opinion that the whole of the undertaking, with the exception
of certain non-essential subsidiaries, was capable of survival as a going
concern. He considered that the acceptance and confirmation of proposals
for a compromise scheme would facilitate that survival and that an attempt
to continue the whole of the undertaking was likely to be more advantageous
for the members as a whole and the creditors as a whole than a winding up.
These proposals received the virtually unanimous support of the companies
and the requisite majority of banking creditors. The Examiner presented his
report to the court in December, under s. 18 of the Act.

Hamilton P approved of the report, accepting a number of modifications
that had been suggested by counsel for Goodman International and by
counsel for a number of creditors; the examiner acknowledged that these
were not contrary to the spirit and terms of his proposals. The President
considered that, in the light of s. 24(3), the court had absolute discretion in
this regard and that it was not necessary to convene a further meeting of the
members and creditors of the companies to consider and approve of the
proposals thus modified. He noted that this was a discretion that had to be
exercised judicially and that, if the suggested modifications were to alter
fundamentally the proposals that had already been considered by the
members and creditors, a court 'would be slow' to modify the scheme in a
fundamental manner without having the modifications considered by the
members and creditors.

Hamilton P rejected the argument made on behalf of one of the creditors
that there should be separate proposals in respect of each company rather
than proposals relating to a group of companies; the purposes of the Act
would be nullified if the Examiner were not entitled to take into account the
position with regard to each and every one of the related companies and to
formulate a scheme of arrangement that would deal with the overall picture.
The President rejected without elaboration this creditor's contention that one
of the provisions in the proposals was contrary to public policy.

Finally, Hamilton P rejected the argument by another creditor that the proposed scheme was unfairly prejudicial to it because it was the only bank whose exposure would be increased if the scheme were implemented. The proposed scheme was admittedly prejudicial, but it was not *unfairly* so. The modification proposed by the bank had not been accepted by the examiner because its acceptance would violate the principle underlying the scheme that all the banking creditors should be treated equally. Accordingly Hamilton P, satisfied that the undertaking of the companies would be capable of survival as a going concern, approved the approved scheme subject to the agreed modifications.

Relationship with reckless trading provisions Under s. 33 of the Companies (Amendment) Act 1990 officers of a company might incur civil liability in respect of the company where they were knowingly a party to the carrying on of the business of the company in a reckless manner. (This provision later became s. 138 of the Companies Act 1990: see the 1990 Review, 88-9).

In *In re Hefferon Kearns Ltd* [1992] ILRM 51, Murphy J was called on to determine the precise relationship between the examiner procedure and the reckless trading sanction. An examiner had already been appointed under the Act when creditors of the company applied under s. 33 to have some of the officers made personally liable for reckless trading. Murphy J first had to decide whether the section was retrospective in rendering persons liable for conduct occurring before the Act came into force. He held that it was not. On this aspect, see Hilary Delany (1992) 10 ILT (ns) 133 and Lyndon McCann (1992) 10 ILT (ns), at 61-2.

Murphy J then turned to consider whether a s. 33 application could be made in respect of conduct alleged to have occurred *after* the Act had come into force. A seeming stumbling block was s. 5(2) which provided in sub-paragraph (b) that:

> [w]here, under any enactment, rule of law or otherwise, any person other than the company is liable to pay all or any part of the debts of the company:
>
> > (i) no attachment, sequestration, distress or execution shall be put into force against the property or effects of such person in respect of the debts of the company, and
> > (ii) no proceedings of any sort may be commenced against such person in respect of the debts of the company.

Subs. (3) provided that:

> [s]ubject to subs. (2), no other proceedings in relation to the company

may be commenced except by leave of the court and subject to such terms as the court may impose and the court may on the application of the examiner enable such order as it thinks proper in relation to any existing proceedings including an order to stay such proceedings.

Murphy J was struck by the difficulty of reconciling the legislative policies of proceeding against officers of a company for reckless trading and at the same time establishing a moratorium whilst the examiner conducted an examination and designed proposals under which creditors would compromise existing claims so as to facilitate the survival of the business. Nonetheless, s. 33 was drafted in such a way as to indicate that proceedings could indeed be pursued during an examinership. The right to proceed against an officer of the company for reckless trading arose only where it appeared in the course of proceedings under this Act that he or she had been a party to such conduct. Moreover, the section expressly conferred on the examiner (in addition to any creditor or contributory of the company) the right to apply for declaratory relief. Further, s. 16 confirmed that the Oireachtas had expressly directed its attention to the operation of s. 33 within the framework of a continuing protection since it provided that the examiner's report (under s. 15) should include 'his opinion as to whether the facts disclosed would warrant further enquiries under *ss. 33 and 34*' (emphasis added).

Murphy J was fully conscious of the anomalies that this interpretation generated. Proceedings under s. 33 would be likely to involve very considerable delays with detailed pleadings and the examination by experts of books and records prior to the hearing of the claim; these delays would be 'wholly out of tune' with the time limits envisaged by the Act. This might operate a considerable injustice to the creditors. Another difficulty was that execution could not be levied against an officer of the company as long as the protection continued and after the expiration of the protection the successful applicant under s. 33 would not derive any benefit from the court order if the scheme proposed by the examiner was sanctioned by the creditors and approved by the court. It seemed to Murphy J, therefore, that the reckless trading provisions in s. 33:

> would be unlikely to provide any significant benefit to a creditor save in the most exceptional circumstances and the more likely consequence of invoking that section would be to prejudice, if not defeat, the prospects of salvaging the business of the company. In fact it is difficult to envisage the effective operation of a clause such as s. 33 of the 1990 Act otherwise than in the context of an insolvent liquidation. It could be meaningless to look otherwise than to the primary debtor if it was in a position to pay its debts in full and certainly it would seem that the court would have great practical difficulty in exercising the discretion

conferred on it by s. 33 unless the assets and liabilities of the company in question had been finally established.

Nonetheless the existence of these anomalies 'would not justify the court in ignoring the express provision of s. 33. . . .'

Standing In *In re Jetmara Teoranta* [1992] 1 IR 147, Costello J was called on to determine the scope of the provisions in the Companies (Amendment) Act 1990 relating to standing. Under s. 24(2), only creditors whose claim or interest would be impaired if the Examiner's proposals were implemented can be heard when the court is considering the Examiner's report. Under s. 22(5), a creditor's claim is impaired if he receives less in payment of his claim than the full amount due in respect of the claim at the date of presentation of the petition for the appointment of the examiner.

In the instant case, the standing of the Bank of Nova Scotia, the only secured creditor, was challenged on the basis that its claim would not be impaired because it would be paid in full the amount due to it at the date of the petition. Costello J acknowledged that the Bank would indeed be paid in full, but he pointed to the fact that since this sum was to be paid by instalments it would be deprived of access to immediate repayment and would receive less in interest than the interest to which it was contractually entitled. This brought the bank within the scope of the statutory provisions, in his view.

As regards the report itself, Costello J approved of the proposals subject to certain modifications. Of most general interest is his insistence that the scheme of arrangement should be subject to an express provision that it was being confirmed without prejudice to any proceedings that the Bank might be advised to take against any of the directors of the company arising from allegations of wrongdoing in relation to the Company's contractual arrangements with the Bank and the security arising therefrom.

Requirement of Candour in Application for Appointment of Examiner *In re Selukwe Ltd*, High Court, 20 December 1991, is an interesting example of judicial discretion being used to accomplish the social policy of legislation. Costello J was faced with a situation where there had been a lack of candour on the part of directors applying for the appointment of an examiner. The company's debt to the revenue authorities had been greatly understated. Costello J emphasised that the utmost good faith was required in the making of *ex parte* applications of this type. (Costello J has reiterated this approach in *In re Wogan's (Drogheda) Ltd*, High Court, 7 May 1992).

In deciding whether to confirm the examiner's proposals, subject to important modifications, he was by 'no means certain' that the company was viable, but this consideration was outweighed by what he considered to be the main consideration in the case: the fact that thirty jobs were at stake. He did not think that the court should turn down the proposals if there was any prospect of saving them.

Two important modifications made by Costello J are worth noting. The first related to the examiner's proposal that the creditor bank be required to revoke the personal guarantees given by two of the directors. The reason advanced for this proposal was that the new investors did not wish the directors to face the problem of possibly having to face bankruptcy proceedings. Costello J deleted this requirement; he saw no justification for releasing these personal guarantees. The second modification was that the two directors should resign from the board, on account (*inter alia*) of the manner in which the directors had carried on the company's business and had acted in their dealings with the Revenue Commissioners.

Finally it may be noted that Costello J rejected the bank's argument that the examiner's proposals were invalid because they operated retrospectively to affect contracts entered into prior to the coming into operation of the Act.

WINDING UP

Set off S. 28(1) of the Companies Act 1963 provides that, where an insolvent company is being wound up by the court, the same rules are to prevail relating to the respective rights of secured and unsecured creditors and to debts provable as those applying under the law of bankruptcy. One of these rules is contained in s. 251 of the Irish Bankrupt and Insolvent Act 1857, which provides that, where there has been mutual credit given by the bankrupt and any other person or where there are mutual debts between the bankrupt and any other person, the court is to state the account between them and one debt or demand may be set out against another.

In *In re Baltimore Boatyard Co. Ltd* [1991] ILRM 817, an arbitration between Baltimore Boatyard Co. and Bord Iascaigh Mhara resulted in an award and costs being made in favour of the company. Bord Iascaigh Mhara claimed to be entitled to a set off against the balance of moneys due to them by the company in respect of property bought by the company from the Bord (the 'boatyard account') and in respect of a loan made by the Bord to the company for working capital (the 'loan account'). Blayney J held that the amount due for costs and the amounts due under the boatyard and loan accounts were 'clearly mutual debts' and that accordingly they might be set off as against each other. He rejected the argument that the matter was *res judicata* in that a court had earlier addressed the issue in the context of an application by the company under s. 41 of the Arbitration Act 1954 for leave to enforce the arbitration award in the same manner as a judgment to that effect. The two contexts were totally different. The set off claimed by the

Bord under s. 284 could not be affected in any way by the order made in the earlier proceedings which had nothing to do with the instant claim.

Fraudulent preferences   Under s. 286 of the Companies Act 1963, any payment or other act relating to property made or done by or against a company within six months before the commencement of its winding-up which would be deemed a fraudulent preference had it been made or done by or against an individual within six months before the presentation of a bankruptcy petition, is deemed a fraudulent preference of the creditors of a company. In *In re Citroen Sales (Ireland) Ltd*, Supreme Court, 1 May 1991, an accountant with full accounting function for four companies authorised a 'netting off' procedure whereby debts of one company were set off against debts of another. This procedure 'was carried out each year when the need arose to provide the material for the annual audit'. The companies were at the time in so parlous a state that, had the directors considered the question, they could not realistically have concluded that for the foreseeable future the companies would be able to discharge their liabilities as they fell due. The accountant was aware that the companies were in difficult trading and financial conditions but his knowledge of the situation was not as extensive as that of the directors. The manner in which he carried out his functions was that he brought what he thought necessary to the attention of the directors but otherwise worked or his own initiative.

The Supreme Court, overruling Lardner J, held that the 'net offs' were effective as payments and should not be disregarded by the liquidators. No suggestion of any impropriety, technical or otherwise, had been made against either the accountant or the directors. McCarthy J (Finlay CJ and Hederman J concurring), considered that, once it was established that what the accountant had done was an ordinary transaction in the course of business, carried out annually, a heavy burden lay on anyone seeking to set it aside. To do so, it would have to be shown that the accountant had lacked authority for his actions. Nothing in the evidence supported the view that the actual size of the transactions was relevant to the extent of his authority. Whereas a transaction of the kind engaged in by the accountant could not have been authorised by the directors if it had taken place a few weeks later, in view of the particularly vulnerable state of the companies then, it would be wrong to engage in hindsight to characterise as a fraudulent preference what had actually taken place.

Transfer of ownership of goods   In *In re J. & L.F. Goodbody (Exports) Ltd*, High Court, 22 March 1991, Murphy J was called on to unravel a system of internal business relationships between a parent (J. & L.F. Goodbody Ltd) and its subsidiary (J. & L.F. Goodbody (Exports) Ltd). A receiver had been appointed after Goodbody and Exports had been ordered by the court to be wound up. The subsidiary had been set up as a means of reducing the potential liability of the parent to Value Added Tax with respect to the purchase of expensive machinery which it was intended to buy during a modernisation proposal. Exports Ltd never owned or occupied any premises or employed any staff, nor did it have any significant permanent capital moneys or loan capital available to it from any financial institution. Such goods as it bought were funded by Goodbody Ltd.

There was evidence that both companies had intended that Exports Ltd should purchase raw materials and export them when processed. The financial records supported the inference that this intention had been to some extent implemented; there was, however, a hiatus in the evidence between the importation and the exportation. Clearly Exports Ltd could not have processed the goods since they had neither staff nor premises, but what was not known was whether the goods had been processed by Goodbody Ltd on their own account with perhaps the intention of reselling them to Exports Ltd or whether Goodbody Ltd had processed the materials on some form of commission basis.

The evidence indicated that Goodbody Ltd invoiced customers with the sale price of goods sold on the domestic market even though the raw materials had been purchased by Exports Ltd. This suggested to Murphy J that it had been intended that the ownership in some of the goods would pass to Goodbody. On the other hand, in relation to the goods that were exported, there was no evidence at all to suggest that it was intended that goods would be sold by Exports to Goodbody and then repurchased by Exports prior to resale.

Murphy J was called on to determine whether or not the moneys received by Goodbody on foot of invoices issued in respect of goods sold to non-resident customers and so issued in the name of Exports was the property of Exports. He admitted to the fact that there was no satisfactory solution to the question. It seemed to him that 'the better of two unsatisfactory solutions' was the inference that Exports, having become the owners of the raw materials, remained the owners of so much of them as were incorporated in finished products ultimately exported. Given the paucity of evidence, he thought it safer to base his conclusion on the known facts rather than to speculate or attempt to draw other inferences as to the transfer of ownership from Exports to Goodbody and perhaps back again.

Murphy J assumed that Exports incurred a liability to Goodbody 'on a *quantum meruit* basis if not otherwise' in respect of the work done by Goodbody on the goods provided by Exports. It might be the case that this liability had been discharged or reduced by a set-off of the cost price of the goods imported by Exports and ultimately resold by Goodbody for its own benefit on the domestic market. He admitted that these factors might require further argument and might involve 'troublesome computations'. They did not arise in the proceedings before the court at that time.

Floating charges   S. 288(1) of the Companies Act 1963 provides that, where a company is being wound up, a floating charge on the undertaking property of the company created within twelve months before the commencement of the winding up, unless it is proved that the company immediately after creation of the charge was solvent, is invalid, *except to the amount of any cash paid to the company at the time of, or subsequently to the creation of, and in consideration for, the charge*, together with interest on that amount at the rate of 5% per annum. In considering whether to apply this proviso, there is no single test to determine how long a time must elapse between the first payment and the execution of the charge.

In *In re Daniel Murphy* [1964] IR 1, at 6, Kenny J stated the rationale for allowing money paid before the execution of a charge to be regarded as being paid at the time of its creation:

> [I]t is desirable that lenders should be encouraged to advance money when a promise to create a charge has been given, for that is usually the time when the money is urgently needed.

In *Smurfit Paribas Bank Ltd v AAB Export Finance Ltd (No. 2)* [1991] 1 IR 19, Barron J said that, to treat payments made to the company before the execution of the charge as payments made at the time of the charge, the necessary elements are:

> an honest transaction, advances made before the execution of the charge; and reasonable expedition in and about the preparation and execution of the charge.

In the instant case the defendant bank had taken a floating charge over the assets of a company that became insolvent. The defendant bank had agreed with the plaintiff bank that this charge was to rank behind a similar charge to be taken by the plaintiff bank. Several months elapsed between the drafting and the execution of the plaintiff bank's charge. In Barron J's view this extended passage of time brought the plaintiff bank's charge outside the remit of the proviso to s. 288(1). The parties had envisaged that their agreement would be given effect by a deed of postponement. As matters transpired none was effected. Barron J did not regard this as a matter from which the plaintiff bank could derive any advantage:

> [Such a deed] would normally have included the term that the plaintiff would have had to bear the loss of failure to obtain a valid security.

Should it be presumed that any such deed would have included such a term and, if not, can the plaintiff now say that the court can enforce such a deed as if it existed without such a term[?]

This was not the case of an agreement to enter into an agreement, which would be no agreement at all. By advancing the money, the defendant executed the agreement on its part. The plaintiff remained entitled within a reasonable time to have a deed of postponement containing the usual terms of such a deed executed by the defendant. In Barron J's view, the time within which such a deed might have been submitted for execution by the defendant had long expired at the date of issue of the proceedings. Even if it had not, the defendant would have been entitled to insist on inclusion of a term whereby the plaintiff would have had to bear the loss of failing to obtain a valid charge. Accordingly, the plaintiff would not have been entitled to priority over the defendant.

Secured creditors In the 1989 Review, 58-60, we discussed Costello J's decision in *In Re McCairns (PMPA) plc (In Liquidation)* [1989] ILRM 501. The Supreme Court reversed: [1992] ILRM 19. Very briefly, the facts were as follows. The company had been wound up in 1987. One of its main assets was a site of which a bank was a secured creditor with three charges over it. The bank had consented to the sale of the site by the liquidator. After the sale had been completed, a number of disputes arose as to how much the bank could claim out of the proceeds and the basis on which their claim was sustainable.

The first issue concerned the bank's liability for court fees. Costello J rejected the bank's argument that the liquidator was precluded from claiming anything for the fees by virtue of an agreement he had made with the bank. The correspondence did not support this contention; but, more fundamentally, Costello J did not think that the liquidator, at all events without leave of the court, could agree to relieve the mortgagor of a tax liability and shift the burden onto unsecured creditors.

On this issue the Supreme Court held that Costello J had been in error. McCarthy J (for the Court) concluded that the correspondence supported a finding that the liquidator had agreed to deduct the court fees. If there was an error on the point, it was unilateral rather than mutual. Even assuming that the court's approval was necessary, it was for the liquidator to have sought it. Not having done so, he could not make a case based upon the absence of the approval.

The next issue concerned the basis on which the bank was entitled to claim interest after the date of the commencement of the winding up. Costello J had taken the view that s. 284(1) of the Companies Act 1963 should be construed as incorporating into the winding up of insolvent companies only those rules of bankruptcy that were consistent with the provisions of the 1963 Act. If the secured creditor were entitled to post-liquidation interest, this could significantly reduce the amount available for unsecured creditors. He could see no justification for construing the 1963 Act as modifying obligations so that no post-liquidation interest is payable if the debt is unsecured but as not modifying a similar obligation merely because it was a secured one. Such a distinction would breach the principle of equality and fairness. The 1963 Act, properly construed, modified companies' liability to pay post-liquidation interest whether the obligation was secured or not.

The Supreme Court reversed Costello J on this issue as well. McCarthy J conceded the attraction of the result of Costello J's analysis, but considered that it could not override the fact that a charge on registered land transferred as security for the debt the actual estate and interest of the registered owner with its attendant rights, subject to the equity of redemption. The registered owner of the charge had the power of sale:

> If the creditor, the legal owner of the property, chooses to bring it into bankruptcy or winding up, it may well be part of the assets; if he does not, it would appear more logical that the interest or estate of the liquidator in the property is limited to the equity of redemption, which, itself, may prove, as here, a valuable asset.

Having neither brought the property into the winding up nor sought to prove any claim in the winding up, the bank was entitled to be paid interest up to the date of redemption, in accordance with the terms of the charging documents. It followed that Costello J's decision in *In re Egan Electric Co. Ltd* [1987] IR 398 (noted in the 1988 Review, 68) could not be sustained. McCarthy J derived support from the fact that the Bankruptcy Law Committee Report, albeit without quoting authority, had stated the law in the terms that he had adopted. The most impressive authority for its accuracy was the composition of the Committee itself, whose chairman, Budd J, was the bankruptcy judge of the time and among whose members were some of the most experienced bankruptcy practitioners. If the Oireachtas had intended to exclude such a rule from the general application of the rules under the law of bankruptcy relating to the respective rights of secured and unsecured creditors, McCarthy J believed that it would have said so.

Guarantees In *In re PMPA Garage (Longmile) Ltd* [1992] ILRM 337, Murphy J had to determine whether a guarantee had been given *intra vires* the guarantor companies. The issue related to the PMPA saga. Guarantees had been executed in favour of the Private Motorists Provident Society Ltd

(PMPS) by a number of companies, including PMPA Car Leasing Ltd, PMPA Garage Division Ltd and a long list of subsidiary companies of the latter company, which included Longmile and Carrick. The guarantees had recited as follows:

> In consideration of your having at our request agreed to advance and advancing to us sums of money not exceeding at any time in the aggregate the sum of £3,000,000 . . . we jointly and severally guarantee to you the repayment of all such sums of money advanced by you to us as aforesaid.

These guarantees, made annually, were interpreted by Murphy J as being successive (the later *replacing* the earlier) rather than cumulative.

PMPS Car Leasing Longmile and Carrick were ordered to be wound up. In the course of the liquidations questions arose as to the legal efficacy of the guarantee.

Evidence was given that the guarantee had been the brainchild of the auditors of PMPS, as a way of solving the difficulty they would have in carrying out the audit and in certifying the accounts, since some of the debtor companies in the group were of doubtful solvency. The guarantee had been drafted by the in-house solicitor of PMPS and the company as a whole.

An important element in the case was the fact that PMPS and the other companies shared the same directors; this meant that these directors were required by law to view the matter of inter-company transactions from two different and perhaps opposing standpoints.

The managing director of the principal companies in the group gave evidence that those having control of the business interests of the companies constituting the group used to discuss the business problems on a day by day business and fitted their decisions into the complex corporate structure that existed. There had been considerable co-operation between the garage companies. One company with surplus funds might transfer them to another in need. There was the mutual transfer of potential customers. As to the guarantee, this had been given, on the advice of the auditors on the basis that it was 'one for all and all for each'. He emphasised that the companies had acted as a group and had to take the good with the bad, since 'it would look badly if one of the companies got into trouble'.

Murphy J accepted this evidence in full. What he had to say is of some general interest:

> In the nature of things companies associated with each other as parent and subsidiary or through common shareholders or who share common management and common titles or logos can not safely ignore the

problems of each other. Even the most independently minded director of any such related company seeking to advance the interests of a particular company would necessarily recognise that he should and perhaps must protect the interests of the group as a whole or else take steps to secure that the particular company disassociates itself from the group.

In the circumstances of the case, it seemed to Murphy J that, whilst the directors of the debtor companies might have accepted the need to give the guarantee without giving serious consideration to the benefits or burdens which could arise from them, their almost intuitive reaction to the request from the auditors for such a guarantee and its renewal each year was justifiable as a matter of law (although as a matter of commerce it had ultimately proved a disaster for the debtor companies).

Neither Longmile nor Carrick had executed the guarantee under seal; proof of consideration was thus vital. Murphy J was satisfied that this was supplied by the fact that it had been for the benefit of each company to ensure and promote the success of the other companies in the group; moreover, the individual companies also enjoyed at least the opportunity and perhaps the reality of advances from PMPS which could have been obtained only on the security of the fellow members of the group as a whole. A further benefit accruing to the individual guarantors was that subsequent guarantees discharged the earlier ones.

PMPS was registered under the Industrial and Provident Societies Act 1893, s. 40 of which states that:

> [t]he rules of a registered society may provide for advances of money to members on the security of real or personal property or in the case of a society registered to carry on banking business, in any manner customary in the conduct of such business.

Counsel for the debtor companies had argued that, in the absence of a comparable statutory provision, a society incorporated under the 1893 Act had no power to make advances to *non-members*, whether or not security was provided. This argument appeared to impress Murphy J, who noted that s. 39, authorising investment in a trustee savings bank or post office savings bank, 'would seem completely futile if a society could in fact advance all or any part of its monies to persons who are not members of the society . . .'.

Murphy J went on to observe that, even if the society could make advances to non-members, it was 'clear that this could be done in accordance with the existing regulations only on the basis of the society receiving "the security of property, real or personal" and manifestly no security of real property was ever obtained'. He rejected the suggestion that a promissory note, being a chose in possession, constituted 'personal security'. He preferred the argument that the Act envisaged a separate independent security to which the provident society might have recourse over and above any action it might have against a particular borrower either on the original debt or the bill of exchange promising the repayment of the debt. It followed that the advances made by PMPS to the companies in the PMPA group had been *ultra vires* the society.

In a supplementary decision ([1992] ILRM 349), Murphy J addressed the question whether the PMPA companies would be compelled to repay the moneys that had been thus advanced by PMPS. He considered several possible approaches. The first was that these companies should be entitled to retain the moneys for their own benefit. He noted that '[t]he monstrous injustice which would flow from the acceptance of such an audacious proposition would certainly render it unattractive to any court seeking to achieve justice in accordance with law'. Since Counsel for the PMPA companies had not attempted to make this argument, he did not pursue it any further. It seems clear that a simplistic conclusion that, because a contract is unenforceable as being *ultra vires*, there can be no remedy (though receiving some judicial support in *In re Cummins; Barton v Bank of Ireland* [1939] IR 60, at 70) has no place in the law to day.

Murphy J went on to consider whether an action *in rem* might be pursued. Counsel for the PMPA group of companies had conceded that this remedy was available to the PMPS and that it carried with it the right to follow the moneys provided by the donor in the hands of the donee into any other assets into which they could be traced. The House of Lords decision in *Sinclair v Brougham* [1914] AC 398 had given its benediction to such a claim but had been inspired to do so by its view that no claim *in personam* was warranted, since quasi-contractual remedies were based on an imputed promise and that the courts could not 'impute the fiction of such a promise where it would have been *ultra vires* to fill it'.

The 'imputed promise' rationale no longer commands support in Ireland or elsewhere. In the Supreme Court decision of *East Cork Foods Ltd v O'Dwyer Steel Ltd* [1978] IR 103, at 110, Henchy J said that claims for quasi-contract are usually dealt with in the books on contract:

> The plaintiff succeeds in this type of action because, it is said, the law imputes to the debtor a promise to pay the debt. The historical reason for this fiction was to enable the claim to be brought as a form of *indebitatus assumpsit*. It was a pleader's stratagem. In most cases, however, it is in the teeth of the facts to impute to the debtor a promise to pay. So long as the forms of action governed the course of litigation,

it was necessary for the courts to go along with this transparent fiction. Nowadays, however, when the forms of action have long since been buried, the concept of implied contract is an unreal and outdated rationale for the action for money had and received. Judges in modern times generally prefer to look at the reality of the situation rather than engage in the pretence that the defendant has promised to pay the debt.

Henchy J reiterated this view in *Murphy v AG* [1982]IR 241, at 316 where he noted that in *Moses v MacFerlan* (1760) 2 Burr 1005, at 1012, Lord Mansfield had put the claim on the footing of equity or unjust enrichment 'rather than under the fiction of an implied promise to repay . . .'.

This approach is replicated in Canada (*Deglman v Guaranty Trust Co. of Canada* [1954] 3 DLR 785, *Air Canada v British Columbia* (1989) 59 DLR (4th) 161), Australia (*Mason v New South Wales* (1959) 102 CLR 108, *Pavey and Matthews v Paul* (1987) 162 CLR 221), New Zealand (*AG (UK) v Wellington Newspapers* [1988] 1 NZLR 129) and (ultimately) England (*Lipkin Gorman v Karpnale* [1991] 2 AC 548, noted by Birks, [1991] LMCLQ 473 and McKendrick, (1992) 55 Modern L Rev 377). See further Eoin O'Dell's comprehensive analysis in (1992) 14 DULJ 123.

In *PMPA (No. 2)*, Murphy J, having quoted Henchy J's remarks in *East Cork Foods*, observed that:

> [t]he significance of this development is that by eliminating the need for an express or imputed promise to pay as an ingredient of the action for money had and received it overcomes the problem faced by the House of Lords in *Sinclair v Brougham*. If it is not necessary to infer some hypothetical or fictitious promise to pay then there is no impediment in availing of that remedy against a corporate body to recover monies received by it as a result of a transaction which was outside its corporate powers.

Murphy J was clearly correct in identifying the fact that, once the 'imputed promise' rationale was abandoned, the conclusion reached in *Sinclair v Brougham* was no longer inevitable. It is, however, quite another thing to suggest that there is *no* impediment against the court's availing itself of the restitutionary remedy with respect to *ultra vires* corporate transactions, if by this is meant that restitution should invariably be ordered. The task for the judiciary is to fashion restitutionary principles that do not subvert the *ultra vires* rule. It may well be that in many, or perhaps most, cases a restitutionary remedy will be appropriate, but there is nothing inevitable about this. While it is true that granting a restitutionary remedy is not the same as enforcing the *ultra vires* contract, it can amount to much the same thing in practice. If parties were to engage in *ultra vires* transactions in the firm, well-based, belief that the court will grant a restitutionary remedy of predictable para- maters, the policy underlying the invalidation of these transactions could be compromised, if not subverted.

The notion of *unjust* enrichment here needs analysis. It could perhaps be argued that the invalidity of the contract *per se* rendered the receipt of the moneys unjust; but can it be stated as an absolute rule that this is so? There must be many instances where money changes hands in the belief that there is a valid contractual relationship between the parties but in circumstances where the receipt of the money can be justified on independent moral or legal grounds. For example, if a deserting husband enters into a purported contract for the maintenance of his wife and children and the contract turns out for some reason to be invalid, one may doubt whether in many cases the recipients of the money would thereby have been unjustly enriched.

Murphy J went on to examine the proposition that the individual com- panies in the PMPA group were bound by their respective promises to repay the monies received by them and in respect of which they had furnished promissory notes and that all the companies that had joined in the guarantee were likewise committed by the express promise in it to repay the monies advanced. He considered that there was no inconsistency between the proper application by the *ultra vires* doctrine and the recovery by means of an action *in rem* or on a quasi-contractual basis of monies or goods in the hands of the party receiving them in consequence of the transaction. The problem was whether there was any *other* basis on which these moneys or goods could be recovered. It seems to him that the alternative basis was 'something akin to an estoppel'. He noted that there were differences of opinion as to whether the restriction imposed in the borrower was properly described as an estoppel but it seemed to him that the overwhelming body of judicial opinion was to the effect that the borrower was precluded from taking the point that the transaction was *ultra vires* where this would result in injustice. In most cases the injustice envisaged was that the competent party would retain for his own benefit the fruits of the *ultra vires* transaction; but the decision of the High Court of Australia in *In re K.L. Tractors Ltd* (1961) 106 CLR 318 showed that, when the competent party no longer had the property derived from the incompetent party, justice could be achieved only by allowing the invalid transaction to be implemented. In the instant case, none of the applicant companies had in their possession any moneys or assets derived from the PMPS nor were they themselves indebted to the society on foot of any promissory note. It had been conceded that the society had a right to recover all moneys in fact advanced to the individual companies in the group insofar as these moneys were now in their possession; to this extent the more obvious injustice was avoided. But Murphy J considered that this was 'a somewhat superficial view of the entire transaction'. It was clear that the accounts of the society would not have been certified at any time after 1977 unless either the auditors were satisfied as to the creditworthiness of the individual borrowers or else the successive guarantees were put into place. The society's continued existence turned on the existence of these guarantees. In these circumstances it seemed to Murphy J that it would be unconscionable to allow the borrowing companies or the guaranteeing companies to rely on any want of authority of the society to lend money in the manner it had done. He saw no difficulty in reconciling the propositions that a particular state of facts or law might exist but that a party might in particular circumstances be precluded from relying on them. In the circumstances, the society should be admitted as a creditor of each of the companies concerned on foot of the guarantee.

Murphy J's analysis is of considerable interest. While he used the term 'estoppel', it appears that he did not seek to bring the case within the scope of established principles of estoppel—promissory or otherwise—but was instead intending to prescribe the appropriate *in personam* legal response to the phenomenon of *ultra vires* contracts. What he sought to reject was the proposition that the law should seek merely to coerce the competent party to disgorge the benefit he retained. His approach can be interpreted as dispensing with the requirement of proof of enrichment of the party against whom the remedy is being sought. Quasi-contract thus has not been simply transformed into unjust enrichment but instead involves broader principles whereby injustice resulting from a legally ineffective contract requires judicial resolution. That resolution, as in the instant case, can take account of the circumstances in which the ineffective contract was purportedly made: PMPS was held entitled to assert the status of creditor (on an invalid contract) primarily on account of *the circumstances generating the ineffective contract* rather than because of *anything that the guarantor companies had done.* For further, wide-ranging analysis of the implications of the decision see O'Neill, *op. cit.*, at 126-40.

STOCK EXCHANGE

The European Communities (Stock Exchange) (Amendment) Regulations 1991 (SI No. 18) implement Directive 87/345/EEC, which amended Directive 80/390/EEC. The 1991 Regulations, which amend the 1984 Regulations of the same title, are to be construed as one with the Companies Acts 1963 to 1990.

Conflict of Laws

ADOPTION

Private international law rules for the recognition of foreign adoptions were slow to develop in Ireland or, indeed, in other common law jurisdictions, in the absence of direct legislative resolution. It seems that domicile was generally accepted as the relevant connecting factor but uncertainty prevailed as to whether the law of the domicile of the child or of the adoptive parents (or the laws of both) should control: see Binchy, *Irish Conflicts of Law* (1988), 372-6, *M.F. v An Bord Uchtála* [1991] ILRM 399, analysed in the 1990 Review, 126-9.

The Adoption Act 1991, introduced by Alan Shatter TD, sets out radically new rules. The Government, after initial hesitation, supported the measure, which underwent a number of changes in its progress through the Oireachtas, which involved a Special Committee in the Dáil.

Of course, the driving inspiration of the legislation was the phenomenon of a large number of adoptions by Irish couples (and single persons) of Romanian children. In 1990, about 150 adoptions of this type had taken place, and over 300 more occurred within the following six months.

The Act applies to 'foreign adoptions' of persons under the age of 21 (if the adoption was effected before the commencement of the legislation) or of 18 (if effected afterwards). The adoption must have been effected outside the State in accordance with the law of the place where it was effected and in relation to which the following five conditions, specified in s. 1, are satisfied:

(a) all consents required to be obtained or dispensed with under the foreign law were duly obtained or dispensed with;

(b) the adoption has essentially the same legal effect as respects the termination and creation of parental rights and duties with respect to the child in the place where it was effected as an Irish adoption order;

(c) the law of the place where the adoption was effected required an enquiry to be carried out, as far as was practicable, into the adopters, the child and the parents or guardians;

(d) due consideration was given to the interests and welfare of the child;

(e) the adopters did not receive or give any payment or other reward in consideration of the adoption (other than any payment 'reasonably and properly made in connection with the making of the arrangements for the adoption').

It may well be that varieties of partial adoption (*adoptio minus plena*) popular in several civil law and Asian countries will not fall within the definition of 'foreign adoption' under this legislation, since condition (b) requires that the foreign adoption should have 'essentially the same legal effect' as an Irish adoption order. The recognition of domicile-based adoptions relates to the time they were effected (since this ground was probably already part of our private international law); the recognition of adoptions under the other two headings is from the date of the commencement of the Act or the date they are effected, *whichever is the later*, since these grounds are new.

Broadly speaking, there are three categories eligible for recognition. The *first* involves recognition of foreign adoptions effected in, or recognised under the law of, a place in which either or both of the spouses was or were:

(a) domiciled;
(b) habitually resident;
(c) ordinarily resident for at least a year,

provided in any of these cases that this would not be contrary to public policy: ss. 2-6.

The *second* category relates to other foreign adoptions where the adopters were ordinarily resident in the State on the date when the adoption was effected and either (i) that date was *before 1 April 1991*, or (ii) the adoption was effected between 1 April 1991 and 1 July 1991, and the Minister for Justice had received a request in writing from the adopters before 1 April 1991 for an assurance in writing as to the admission to the State of a child the subject of a foreign adoption effected in their favour. These adoptions will be recognised if the Adoption Board declares in writing that it is satisfied that the adopters are persons in whose favour an adoption order may be made by virtue of s. 10 and the adoption would not be contrary to public policy. S. 10(1) requires that an adoption order be not made unless:

(a) the applicants are a married couple who are living together, or
(b) the applicant is the mother or father or a relative of the child, or
(c) the applicant is a widow or widower.

By way of qualification to these requirements, where the Adoption Board is satisfied that in the particular circumstances of the case it is desirable, an adoption order may be made in favour of an applicant who is neither the mother or father or a relative of the child nor is a widow or widower: s. 10(2).

In this context it is worth noting what the Minister for Health, Dr O'Hanlon, had to say in the Dáil on 8 May 1991:

The special procedures will apply to single people who have adopted a child through foreign adoptions, provided they meet the criteria in all other ways. Following the enactment of this legislation it will be a matter for the Adoption Board to decide on the special circumstances. As I see it, the special circumstances will be closely related to the bonding between the single person and the child, but it will be a matter for the Adoption Board to decide on individual cases': 408 Dáil Debates, col. 35.

S. 10 also provides (in subs. (3)) that, save where the applicants are a married couple living together, an adoption order is not to be made for the adoption of a child by more than one person.

A further limitation, provided by s. 10(4), is that the consent to an adoption by one spouse is required of the other spouse unless they are living apart by decree or a deed of separation or because the other spouse is guilty of actual or constructive desertion. Moreover, 21 is the minimum age for the applicant (or applicants, if they are a married couple save in the case where one of them is the parent or relative of the child, in which case it will suffice if *either* of them has reached 21): s. 10(5). A year's habitual residence leading up to the date of the making of the adoption order is also necessary: s. 10(6).

The third, and final, category of recognition relates to other foreign adoptions where the adopters were ordinarily resident in the State on the date when the adoption was effected and they did not get the benefit of the 1 April 1991 and 1 July 1991 deadlines. These adoptions have to pass s. 10 requirements, in fact and to the Adoption Board's satisfaction, as well as not being such that their recognition would not be contrary to public policy. But along with these hurdles, they also have to pass the requirement that the Adoption Board must declare in writing before the adoption is effected that, having had regard to a report by the local health board or a registered adoption society of an assessment carried out in relation to the adopters as respects the matters referred to in s. 13 of the Adoption Act 1952, the Board is satisfied in relation to the adopters as respects these matters. S. 13 requires that the applicant is of good moral character, has sufficient means to support the child and is a suitable person to have parental rights and duties in respect of the child. Thus, for the future at least, the controls on the recognition of foreign adoptions become more stringent than what is permitted up to April 1991.

CONTRACTS

The Contractual Obligations (Applicable Law) Act 1991 gives force of law to the EC Convention on the Law Applicable to Contractual Obligations (the Rome Convention) of 1980 and the 1984 Accession Convention of the

Hellenic Republic. For a stimulating, comprehensive analysis of the legislation see Gerard Hogan's *Annotation* [1991] ICLSA. The Irish Centre for Commercial Law Studies held a conference on the legislation on 8 December 1990. The papers from the conference may also usefully be consulted.

The purpose of the Rome Convention is to unify the choice-of-law rules as to contract within the European Community, not merely where the case relates to the Community, and regardless of whether the applicable law under the rules of Convention is that of a Member State. There was a clear need for a Convention to prevent forum shopping, which ironically became even more attractive on account of the Convention on Jurisdiction and Enforcement of Civil and Commercial Judgments, opening up new supplementary jurisdictional grounds in relation to contractual claims.

The Convention had originally been intended to cover the law applicable to both *contractual* and *non-contractual* obligations, but in 1978 the Brussels Working Group charged with the task decided that it would be better to press ahead with the first element alone, since there was a greater degree of uniformity among Member States on choice-of-law issues in torts.

The Convention has spawned a vast literature: see, e.g. Plender, *The European Contracts Convention* (1991), P. North ed., *Contracts Conflicts* (1982), Gill, 6 J of the Irish Society for European L 1 (1983), Lagarde, 22 Va J of International L 91 (1981), Delaume, *id*, 105 Juenger, *id*, 123, Weintraub, 17 Texas International LJ 155 (1982), Jaffey, 33 ICLQ 531 (1984), Williams 35 ICLQ 1 (1986), Binchy, *Irish Conflicts of Law* (1988) 552-66.

Scope of the Convention As has been mentioned, the scope of the Convention is very wide. The rules of the Convention, as a general principle, 'apply to contractual obligations in any situation involving a choice between the laws of different countries': Article 1(1). Moreover, any law specified by the Convention is to be applied, *whether or not it is the law of the Contracting State:* Article 2. In this respect the Rome Convention may be contrasted with the Brussels Convention, whose rules as to jurisdiction and the recognition of foreign judgments are essentially applicable only with regard to Community states.

The scope of the expression 'contractual obligations' needs some examination. Article 8(1) provides that the existence and validity of a contract are to be determined by the law which would govern it under the Convention if the contract or term were valid. Thus, if an Irish court has to deal with a promise supported neither by seal nor be consideration, it will refer to the applicable law the question whether a 'contractual obligation' is in existence, and be guided by its resolution. Cf. *In re Bonacina* [1912] Ch. 394.

The Convention does not give guidance on the question when, under

Article 1(1), a situation involves a choice between the laws of different
countries. It seems that, where the parties have made a choice that a foreign
law should govern, Article 1(1) comes into play. Where they have not,
'presumably the connection with one or more other countries must be
material and not merely fanciful': Williams, 35 Int & Comp LQ 1, at 7 (1986).

Exclusions   There are a number of significant exclusions from the scope of
the Convention, specified in Article 1(2) and (3). These nine exclusions are
as follows:

(a) *Questions involving the status or legal capacity of national persons,
without prejudice to Article 11*
Thus, questions relating to the validity of marriage, divorce, legitimacy and
custody of children fall outside the scope of the Convention, and will be
determined by the choice of law rules of the forum's private international
law system. Article 11 deals with the situation where persons who are in the
same country make a contract and one of them, a natural person, has capacity
under the law of that country but not under another law—for example, on
account of differing rules as to minority or mental capacity. We examine this
Article below.

(b) *Contractual obligations relating to:*

> wills and successions
> rights in property arising out of a matrimonial relationship
> rights and duties arising out of a family relationship, parentage,
> marriage or affinity, including maintenance obligations in respect of
> children who are not legitimate.

The intention here is to exclude from the scope of the Convention 'all
matters of family law': Giuliano-Lagarde Report, para 3. Family law and
commercial law principles do not easily mix, especially in an international
context. It was anticipated that most contracts relating to maintenance
obligations would fall within the scope of the Hague Convention on the Law
Applicable to Maintenance Obligations: Williams, *op. cit.*, at 8.

(c) *Obligations arising under bills of exchange, cheques and promissory
notes and other negotiable instruments to the extent that the obligations
under such negotiable instruments arise out of their negotiable character*
The Convention does not attempt to define what characterises a document
as a negotiable instrument: this is left to the *lex fori* (including its rules of
private international law). As may be seen, the exclusion from the scope of
the Convention only applies in relation to obligations arising out of the
negotiable character of the instrument. Thus, neither the contracts pursuant

to which the instruments are issued nor contracts for their purchase and sale are excluded.

The primary reason for excluding negotiable instruments is to avoid introducing unnecessary complexity into the Convention. The loss is not great for civil law jurisdictions, all of which are parties to the Geneva Conventions on Bills of Exchange (1930) and Cheques (1931): see E. Rabel, *The Conflict of Laws: A Comparative Study* (2nd ed., 1958), chs. 58-62. Neither Ireland nor Britain has adopted those Conventions, though the matter has been dealt with legislatively by the Bills of Exchange Act 1882, s 72: see Binchy, *op. cit.*, ch. 27.

(d) *Arbitration agreements and agreements on the choice of court*
These were excluded after much debate. The majority view was that they covered matters of procedure and judicial administration, which might have endangered ratification of the Convention. Moreover, questions as to the validity and form of jurisdiction agreements are already governed by Article 17 of the Convention on Jurisdiction and Enforcement of Judgments in Civil and Commercial Matters and the New York Convention on the Recognition and Enforcement of Arbitral Awards, 1958.

Of course the exclusion of arbitration agreements from the scope of the Convention does not mean that the *contracts containing arbitration clauses* are excluded: the *other* clauses in these contracts will be determined under the provisions of the Convention.

(e) *Questions governed by the law of companies and other bodies corporate or unincorporated and the general liability of officers and members as such for the obligations of the company or body*
The reason for this exclusion was that there was no point in trespassing on work already in progress on company law within the EC. All the complex acts relating to administration and registration, essential for the creation, internal organisation and winding-up of a company or firm, are excluded. But acts or preliminary contracts whose sole purpose is to create obligations between the promoters with a view to forming a company or firm fall within the scope of the Convention: Giuliano-Lagarde Report, para 6.

(f) *The question whether an agent is able to bind a principal, or an organ to bind a company or body, corporate or unincorporated, to a third party*
This exclusion affects only the relationships between the principal and third parties. It does not affect other aspects of agency, including principal-agent and agent-third party relationships. The reason given for the exclusion is that 'it is difficult to accept the principle of freedom of contract on this point': Giuliano-Lagarde Report, para 7.

(g) *The constitution of trusts and the relationship between settlor, trustees and beneficiaries*
Trusts, as understood in common law Member States, thus fall outside the scope of the Convention, being regarded as a feature of the law of property rather than contract. But similar institutions in the laws of civil law Member States will normally fall within the provisions of the Convention, where they are contractual in origin. Where, however, they exhibit the characteristics of a trust as understood in common law, they should be excluded from the Convention.

(h) *Evidence and procedure, without prejudice to Article 14*
The general principle is clear: evidence and procedure fall outside the scope of the Convention. These matters are governed by the *lex fori* under its private international law rules. We examine the important modification effected by Article 14 below.

(i) *Contracts of insurance which cover risks situated in the territories of the Member States*
This exclusion takes account of work being done in the EC in the field of insurance. It is worth noting what is *not* excluded. Article 1(4) explicitly provides that *re-insurance* contracts are within the scope of the Convention. These do not raise the same problem as insurance contracts where the protection of the insured person is of major significance. Moreover, contracts of insurance covering risks *outside the territories of the Member States* manifestly are within the scope of the Convention.

General rules under the Convention   The central provisions in the Convention for determining the applicable law are Articles 3(1) and 4(1). These contain principles which will be largely familiar to Irish and English conflicts lawyers, since they deal with the question of the governing, or proper, law of the contract, whether through the choice of the parties or otherwise. For an excellent analysis, see A.V. Gill, 'Identifying the Governing Laws of a Contract', paper delivered at the Irish Centre for Commercial Law Studies Conference, *International Contracts—The Rome Convention*, 8 December 1990. Let us first consider the position where the parties choose the governing law.

Applicable law based on parties' choice   Article 3(1) provides as follows:

> A contract shall be governed by the law chosen by the parties. The choice must be expressed or demonstrated with reasonable certainty by the terms of the contract or the circumstances of the case. By their choice the parties select the law applicable to the whole or a part only of a contract.

Article 3(1) 'simply reaffirms a rule currently embodied in the private international law of all the Member States of the Community and of most other countries': Giuliano-Lagarde Report, p. 15.

Article 3(1) gives the parties a very wide-ranging freedom in choosing the law to govern the contract. This has been welcomed by some commentators as being in harmony with the requirements of contemporary international contracts. On the other hand it has also being stigmatised as 'a surrender to the clever manipulation of connecting factors by interested contract draftsmen at the time of their negotiations': Delaume, *The European Convention on the Law Applicable to Contractual Obligations: Why a Convention?*, 22 Va J of Internat L 105, at 107 (1981).

It will be recalled that the Judicial Committee, in *Vita Food Products Inc v Unus Shipping Co.* [1939] AC 227, at 290, required that the parties' choice be *bona fide* and legal. In contrast, Irish decisions seemed to give the parties more or less untrammelled autonomy: *O'Callaghan v O'Sullivan* [1925] IR90, at 115 (Supreme Court, *per* Kennedy CJ), *Cripps Warburg Ltd v Cologne Investment Co. Ltd* [1980] IR 321, at 333, *Kutchera v Buckingham International Holdings Ltd* [1988] ILRM 501 [1988] IR 61, analysed in the 1988 Review 71-3.

In *O'Callaghan v O'Sullivan, supra*, at 115, Kennedy CJ observed that the parties were free to choose the Code Napoleon as the applicable law. Assuming that by this he intended to refer to the *former*, as opposed to contemporary, French codal provisions, the question arises as to whether such a choice would be permissible under Article 3. A related question concerns the choice by parties of *cannon law* as the applicable law; here the problem is one of geographical rather than temporal identification. In *O'Callaghan v O'Sullivan* at 109, Kennedy CJ expressed the robust opinion that canon law should be characterised as a foreign law because 'all law is foreign to these courts other than the laws which these courts have been set up under the Constitution of Saorstat Éireann to administer and enforce. ...'
Gerard Hogan, *op. cit.*, General Note to Article 3, has suggested that Kennedy CJ's observation as to the choice of the Code Napoleon would seem no longer to hold true because, under Article 15, the parties are restricted to choosing the 'law in force' in the country of the applicable law. This may well be the intended combined effect of Articles 3 and 15 and it would have some obvious good sense from a policy standpoint. Another view, of a somewhat technical nature, is perhaps worth considering. Article 3, para. 1 provides simply that a contract is to be governed 'by the law chosen by the parties'. It does not require that this law be the law of any particular country. Article 15 provides that the 'application of the law of any country specified by this Convention' means the application of the rules of law in force in that country other than its rules of private international law. The purpose of Article 15 is

clearly to exclude *renvoi* in respect of all cases where the Convention specifies the application of the law of any country. The Convention does this more than once: in Article 4, para 1, for example. Its failure to do this in Article 3 might be considered significant. It could perhaps be contended that it is implicit, but this may savour of boot-strapping. In view of the specific controls on party autonomy contained in Articles 3(3), 5, 6 and 7(2), the suggestion that Article 3(2), para 1 extends to the choice of a former law or a universal, non-municipal law, such as Canon Law, is perhaps worthy of some attention. The anomalies and the potential for abuse that such an extension would involve suggests that courts will be most reluctant to interpret the Article in this way.

Article 3(1) applies only where the choice of law is expressed or 'demonstrated with reasonable certainty' by the terms of the contract or the circumstances of the case. If neither of these requirements is fulfilled, Article 4 comes into place. This requirement of 'reasonable certainty' appears to be more stringent than the test adopted in many English cases, but has the advantage of 'preventing attempts to deduce an implied choice from minor indications, the presence of which cannot really be attributed to a real, but unexpressed, choice'. Williams, *op. cit.*, at 8. Moreover, it avoids 'creat[ing] a blur' between Articles 3 and 4. Lagarde, *The European Convention on the Law Applicable to Contractual Obligations: An Apologia*, 22 Va J of Internat L 91, at 97 (1981).

Article 3(2) permits the parties at any time to agree to subject the contract to a law other than that which previously governed it. Article 3(2) further provides that any variation by the parties of the law to be applied, made after the conclusion of the contract, 'shall not prejudice its formal validity under Article 9 or adversely affect the rights of third parties'. It seems clear that under Irish law previously, the Court would refuse to give effect to a purported change of the governing law where the purpose was to affect the rights of third parties adversely. Where this was the result, but was not the intention, the position was less certain, since the parties would have complied with the requirements of good faith in making their new selection.

Applicable law in the absence of choice   Among the Member States, the general approach to the problem of determining the governing law in the absence of express choice by the parties was for the courts to perform this task either on the basis of an inference as to what they 'really intended' or (increasingly) on a more frankly objective basis of selecting the law with the closest and most real connection with the transaction: Giuliano-Lagarde Report, pp. 19-20. An exception was Italy, whose legislation contained detailed specific rules to deal with different categories of contract.

Article 4 of the Convention deals with this question. Article 4(1) provides that, to the extent that the law applicable to the contract has not been chosen in accordance with Article 3, the contract is to be governed by the law of the contract with which it is most closely connected.

Thereafter, the Article becomes a good deal more complicated. Its structure is as follows. Paragraph 2 of the Article introduces a presumption that the contract is most closely connected with the country where the party to it, to effect the performance which is characteristic of the contract, resides or (if a business) has its central administration. Paragraphs 3 (dealing with contracts involving immovable property) and 4 (dealing with contracts for the carriage of goods) also minimise the scope of the presumption provided for in paragraph 2. But the presumption in paragraph 2 is subject to paragraph 5, which provides that paragraph 2 is not to apply if the characteristic performance cannot be determined and that the presumptions in paragraphs 2, 3 and 4 are to be disregarded if it appears from the circumstances as a whole that the contract is more closely connected with another country.

Let us look a little more closely at these provisions. Article 4(2) provides as follows:

> Subject to the provisions of paragraph 5 of this Article, it shall be presumed that the contract is more closely connected with the country where the party who is to effect the performance which is characteristic of the contract has, at the time of the conclusion of the contract, his habitual residence, or, in the case of a body corporate or incorporate, its central administration. However, if the contract is entered into in the course of that party's trade or profession, that country shall be the country in which the principal place of business is situated or, where under the terms of the contract the performance is to be effected through a place of business other than the principal place of business, the country in which that other place of business is situated.

This approach has some obvious advantages. But the important question concerns the notion of 'the performance which is characteristic of the contract'. What does it mean and how is it to be determined in specific cases?

Where a contract involves the payment of money, the idea is that this payment 'is not, of course, the characteristic performance of the contract. It is the performance for which the payment is done, i.e. depending on the type of contract, the delivery of goods, the granting of the right to make use of an item of property, the provision of a service, transport, insurance, banking operations, security, etc., which usually constitutes the centre of gravity and the socio-economic function of the contractual transaction': Giuliano-Lagarde Report, p. 20. See, however, D'Oliveira, 'Characteristic Obligation in the Draft EEC Obligation Convention', 25 Amer J of Compar L 303, at 328 (1977).

Of course, not all cases will be so easy: where *both* parties have to perform actions as well as pay money, or where the contract does not involve the payment of money at all, the court may have a difficult task in identifying either party as effecting '*the* performance which is characteristic of the contract'. (Emphasis added). The spectre of collateral contracts and *depeçage* must loom on the horizon.

Article 4(3) provides that, notwithstanding paragraph 2, to the extent that the subject matter of the contract is a right in immovable property or a right to use immovable property, it is to be presumed that the contract is most closely connected with the country where the immovable property is situated. This harmonises with our former rules on the question. It is easy to envisage a borderline case involving the sale to Irish residents of holiday villas abroad, where the parties have not specified an applicable law in accordance with Article 3(1). A difficult question may arise as to whether the case is governed by paragraphs 3 or 5 of Article 4.

Article 4(4) excludes contracts for the carriage of goods from the presumption, in paragraph 2. It goes on to provide that:

> [i]n such a contract if the country in which, at the time the contract is concluded, the carrier has his principal place of business is also the country in which the place of loading or the place of discharge or the principal place of business of the consignor is situated, it shall be presumed that the contract is most closely connected with that country.

For consideration of the International Carriage of Goods Act 1990, see the 1990 Review, 129-39.

Contracts for the carriage of passengers remain subject to the general presumption, when applicable, under Article 4(2).

The effect of Article 4(4) is that if, for example, an Irish airline transports goods between Ireland and France, there will be a presumption, in the absence of a choice of law by the parties, that the governing law is Irish. But if an Irish airline transports goods from Britain to France, no presumption would arise under either paragraph 2 or 4 of Article 4, and the court would have to resolve the question under the general provisions of paragraph 1: Giuliano-Lagarde Report, p. 22.

Consumer contracts   Article 5 contains some important modifications to the operation of the applicable law in relation to certain consumer contracts. This distinction between ordinary consumer contracts may be traced to Ehrenzwerg: see *Adhesion Contracts on the Conflict of Laws*, 53 Colum. L. Rev. 1072 (1953): Cf Juenger, *The European Convention on Law Applicable to Contractual Obligations: Some Critical Observations*, 22 Va. J. of

Internat. L. 123, at 135 (1981). See also Lando, *Consumer Contracts and Party Autonomy in the Conflict of Laws,* 42 Nordisk Tidsskrift for Internat. Ret. 208 (1972), Hartley, *Some Aspects of the Draft Convention from the Point of View of British Law,* in O. Lando, B. Hoffman & K. Siehr eds., *European Private International Law of Obligations,* 105 (1975). The Article applies to 'a contract the object of which is the supply of goods or services to a person (the consumer) for a purpose which can be regarded as being outside his trade or profession, or a contract for the provision of credit for that object' para 1. This definition is intentionally imprecise, to avoid conflict with the various definitions already given in the national legislation.

Para 2 of Article 5 provides that, notwithstanding Article 3, a choice of law made by the parties is not to have the result of depriving the consumer of the protection afforded to him by the mandatory rules of the law of the country in which he has his habitual residence if any one of three conditions is fulfilled.

The *first* of these conditions arises where, in the country of the consumer's habitual residence, the conclusion of the contract was preceded by a specific invitation addressed to him or by advertising, and he had taken in that country all the steps necessary on his part for the conclusion of the contract. Thus, if, for example, an English trader has engaged in door-to-door or mail-order selling in Ireland or has advertised in Irish newspapers or on Irish television, the mandatory rules of Irish law will apply where a consumer habitually resident here buys a product or services from the trader, regardless of any express choice of English, or other foreign, law. But if a person habitually resident here replies to an advertisement in a Canadian publication sold in Ireland, it appears that Article 5 would not apply "unless the advertisement appeared in special editions of the publication intended for European countries. In the latter case the seller will have made a special advertisement intended for the country of the purchaser': Giuliano-Lagarde Report, p24. This first condition has a parallel in the *torts* context: the Supreme Court of California in *Bernhard v Harrah's Club,* 16 Cal. 3d 313, 128 Cal. Reptr 215, 546 P 2d 719 (1976) accepted that out-of-state advertising may have important choice of law implications in tort proceedings.

The *second* condition enabling the mandatory rules of law of the country of the consumer's habitual residence to apply is fulfilled where the other party or his agent received the consumer's order in that country. There will, of course, be a considerable overlap between the first and second conditions, but it is quite possible to envisage cases where the order is received in the country of the consumer's habitual residence without having been preceded by any solicitation of advertising there.

The *third* condition is fulfilled where the contract is for the sale of goods and the consumer travelled from the country to his habitual residence to another country and there gave his order, provided that the consumer's journey was arranged by the seller for the purpose of inducing the consumer to buy. This could have special relevance in relation to cross-border shopping expeditions which have periodically been a feature of life in Ireland. It should be noted that Article 5 offers protection only where the consumer's journey was *arranged by the seller*, to induce him to buy. Thus, even in cases where a trader from north of the border advertises south of the border, and a consumer habitually resident south of the border is induced to make a purchase at the trader's premises, none of the three conditions of Article 5 will have been fulfilled.

Article 5(3) provides that, notwithstanding the provisions of Article 4, a contract to which Article 5 applies is, in the absence of choice in accordance with Article 3 to be governed by the law of the country in which the consumer has his habitual residence if it is entered into in the circumstances described in paragraph 2 of Article 5.

Paragraph 4 contains some important exclusions. It provides that Article 5 does not apply to:

(a) a contract of carriage; and
(b) a contract for the supply of services where the services are to be supplied to the consumer exclusively in a country other than in which he has his habitual residence.

Thus, for example, a person habitually resident in Ireland who has an uncomfortable stay at an hotel, on a weekend visit to London, may not invoke the mandatory rules of Irish contract law in his aid even where the hotel has advertised in the Irish papers. But paragraph 5 provides that Article 5 *will* apply to a contract which, for an inclusive price, provides for a combination of travel and accommodation. Thus, package tours are not excluded from the scope of Article 5, and will be subject to the mandatory rules of the law of the consumer's country of habitual residence, provided, of course, the conditions contained in the Article are fulfilled.

Individual employment contracts Article 6 contains important provisions for individual contracts of employment, designed to protect the employee. Where the parties have not chosen an applicable law in accordance with Article 3, Article 4 does not apply to individual employment contracts; instead, the contract of employment is governed:

(a) by the law of the country in which the employee habitually carries out his work in performance of the contract, even if he is temporarily employed in another country; or

(b) if the employee does not habitually carry out his work in any one country, by the law of the country in which the place of business through which he was engaged was situated.

If, however, it appears from the circumstances as a whole that the contract is more closely connected with another country, the contract will be governed by the law of that country: Article 6(2).

Where the parties to an employment contract have chosen a law in accordance with Article 3, that choice will be respected, but it is not to have the result of depriving the employee of the protection afforded to him by the mandatory rules of law which would be applicable under Article 6(2) in the absence of choice: Article 6(1). Thus, if the law applicable under Article 6(2) grants the employee protection greater than that resulting from the law chosen by the parties, the result is not to render the choice of law nugatory: 'on the contrary, in this case the law which was chosen continues in principle to be applicable. In so far as the provisions of the law applicable pursuant to paragraph 2 give employees better protection than the chosen law, for example by giving a longer period of notice, these provisions set the provisions of the chosen law aside and are applicable in their place': Giuliano-Lagarde Report, p. 25.

It appears that the mandatory rules from which the parties may not derogate extend beyond the provisions relating to the contract of employment itself to include 'provisions such as those concerning individual safety and hygiene which are regarded in certain Member States as being provisions of public law': *id*. It also appears that, although Article 6 does not affect an employee's trade union with regard to powers deriving from collecting agreements in its own country, it may have a beneficial effect on the employee's rights, since, if the law of the country designated by Article 6(2) makes a collective agreement binding on the employer, the employee may not be deprived of the protection which the agreement affords him by the choice of law of another State in the individual employment contract: *id*.

Mandatory rules The Convention contains three important modifications of the application of the proper law, to give effect to a state's mandatory rules. First, Article 3(3) provides that, where (a) the parties have chosen a foreign law, whether or not accompanied by the choice of a foreign tribunal, and (b) all the other elements relevant to the situation at the time of choice are connected with one country only, the fact that the parties have made this choice is not to prejudice the application of rules of the law of that country which cannot be derogated from by contract (which are referred to as 'mandatory rules'). Thus, if a contract is in all respects Irish save for the fact that the parties chose a foreign applicable law, then the parties will not be able to evade Irish mandatory rules. This will be so even if the matter is litigated in Britain or France, for example. It should be noted that, in contrast to Article 6(1), Article 3(3) does not necessarily apply where, in the absence of choice in accordance with Article 3, the proper law of the contract would have been (in our example) Irish, judged by the criteria specified in Article 4. It is essential that 'all the other elements [save that of choice] relevant to the situation at the time of the choice' be connected with Ireland only. Could this mean that such a contingent element as the place of contracting or the nationality, domicile or habitual residence of a party to the contract could ever (or always) be characterised as having sufficient relevance to knock out the application of Article 3(3)? The laconic analysis by Professors Giuliano and Lagarde provides no light on this question.

It may be argued that Article 3(3) is deficient in making the non-application of a state's mandatory rules depend on the connection with another state of as little as a single element that is relevant to the situation. That element need not be the dominant, or even relatively important, one. Of course, the task of characterising elements as 'relevant' gives courts a certain leeway; but why should they have to engage in *sub rosa* analysis rather than articulate openly the weighting process which that analysis may involve?

This brings us to another difficulty with Article 3(3). Does it refer to mandatory rules that relates exclusively to a state's domestic law? Is it restricted to mandatory rules that override the parties' selection of foreign proper law? Or, finally, does it apply to all mandatory rules of a state, whatever their international remit? The second interpretation would surely be the most satisfactory on principle but seems least easily reconcilable with the language of the convention as a whole. One had only to contrast the drafting of Article 7(1) which makes it clear that the mandatory rules there envisaged are ones that 'must be applied whatever the law applicable to the contract', and Article 7(2), which refers to rules that are 'mandatory irrespective of the law otherwise applicable to the contract'. Whether Article 3(3) should properly be interpreted according to the first or third options, the result is unfortunate, since in either of these cases the domestic mandatory rules of a state will require to be applied to a situation where the private international law of that state would not lead to the same conclusion. One does not have to be a Cavers or a Currie to lament his indefensible approach.

Article 7 contains the other two modifications in relation to mandatory rules; it provides as follows:

(1) When applying under this Convention the law of a country, effect may be given to the mandatory rules of the law of another country with which the situation has a close connection, if and in so far as, under the law of the latter country, those rules must be applied whatever the law

applicable to the contract. In considering whether to give effect to these mandatory rules, regard shall be had to their nature and purpose and to the consequences of their application or non-application.

(2) Nothing in this Convention shall restrict the application of the rules of the law of the forum in a situation where they are mandatory irrespective of the law otherwise applicable to the contract'.

Ireland has availed itself of its entitlement under Article 22 not to give paragraph 1 the force of law in the State. Article 7(1) was the most controversial provision of the Convention during the negotiations. Some of its more important features may be noted. First, the 'situation' must have 'a close connection' with the country whose mandatory rules of law are applied under paragraph 1. Just how close is 'close', for this purpose, is a matter for the courts to determine. It seems that the fact that the contract is to be performed in a country or that one party resides or has his main place of business there may be sufficient: Giuliano-Lagarde Report, p. 27.

Next it should be noted that paragraph 1 does not require the application of the mandatory rules once a close connection has been established. Instead it facilitates their application. In considering whether or not to give them effect, the court must have regard to their nature and purpose and to the consequences of their application or non-application. This involves to some degree the process of 'governmental interests' analysis, beloved of American scholars on conflicts of law, who, of course, tend to emphasise concern for the due effectuation of governmental interests underlying common law and statutory rules rather than an unthinking application of 'jurisdiction-selecting' rules. These concerns receive a partial refection in the *Restatement, Second:* cf. Lagarde, 22 Va J of Internat L, at 103, Delaume, *id.,* at 113-5, 119, Cavers, 'Re-Stating the Conflict of Laws: The Chapter on Contracts' in *20th Century Comparative and Conflicts Law,* 349 (1961).

In contrast to the *Restatement, Second's* provisions, which seek to provide guidelines for the solution of *all* conflicts situations involving contracts, Article 7(1) is 'only an exception to the operation of the traditional conflict rule': Lando, 30 Amer J of Comp L, at 33.

Article 7(1) has been subjected to strong criticism. This has concentrated on the uncertainty it introduces into international trade, in view of the fact that several countries may have 'a close connection' with the 'situation': see Mann, Contracts: Effect of Mandatory Rules, ch. 4 of K. Lipstein, ed., *Harmonisation of Private International Law by the EEC,* at 36 (1978). Moreover, the discretion given to the court and the uncertain scope of the examination of the 'nature and purpose' of rules and the consequences of their application, may lead to unpredictable results. Furthermore, since the provision regarding mandatory rules is not limited to those in existence at the time of the making of the contract, this makes the task of those drafting contracts a dangerous and frustrating one: see Gill, *op. cit.*, at 22-3.

Let us try to examine some of the specific questions raised by Article 7(1) in a little more detail. The first relates to the nature of a 'significant connection'. The original draft had required merely that the contract be 'also connected with a country other than the country whose law is applicable. ...' This was criticised by Collins (25 ICLQ, at 50-1) as being too wide-ranging and uncertain. Whether there is a significant change in the limitation that the connection be 'significant' and that this connection be with 'the situation' rather than 'the contract' may perhaps be doubted: cf. Diamond [1977] Current Legal Problems, at 174.

Professors Guiliano and Legarde (*op. cit.*, p. 27) explain that the Working Group

> decided that it is essential that there be a genuine connection with the other community, and that a merely vague connection is not adequate. For example, there would be a genuine connection when the contract is to be performed in that other country, or when one party is resident or has his main place of business in that other country. Among the suggested versions, the Group finally adopted the word 'close' which seemed the most suitable to define the situation which it wished to cover.

It may be wondered whether the residence of a party in a particular country is a sufficient reason, even *prima facie*, for opening up the possibility of the application to the contract of that country's mandatory rules. Of course it may be replied that Article 7(1) facilitates rather than requires the application of these rules and that, in considering whether to give effect to them, the court must have regard to their nature and purpose 'and to the consequences of their application or non-application'. Presumably this gives the court a discretion to engage in a type of 'comparative impairment' analysis but neither the Convention nor the Report gives any clear guidance on how this is to be done. As Professor Weintraub has observed of the elements specified in Article 7, '[t]hese are sound functional concepts, but they are the beginning, not the end point, of analysis': [1984] IV Hague receuil 239, at 285.

It is only fair to point out that some of the virulent British opposition to Article 7(1) sprang from concern about the uncertainties it involved, coupled with a potentially significant weakening of the dominance of party autonomy which might threaten the attractiveness of London as a centre of banking, commercial litigation and arbitration: Morse, *op. cit.*, at 146, fn 185. Nevertheless, the difficulties with Article 7(1) were sufficient in their own right to justify Ireland's making a reservation in its regard, even if the failure of some other states (notably France) to make such a reservation may lead to an

uneven application of the Convention. It is futile to blame either the reservers
the non-reservers for this outcome: that is the inevitable fate of a Convention
allowing for reservations. The real vice is the failure of those who drafted
the Convention to subject Article 7(1), or its original draft, to a sufficiently
detailed working-out of its probable implications in practice.

Let us now turn to consider Article 7(2). It springs from concern among
some of the delegations to safeguard the mandatory rules of the forum,
notably on cartels, competitions, restrictive practices, consumer protection
and rules concerning carriage: Giuliano-Legarde Report, p28. Whether the
forum is given too much latitude and whether this may encourage forum-
shopping are matters on which some fears have been expressed: cf. Williams,
op. cit., at 23-4, 31.

Perhaps the first comment that can be made about Article 7(2) is that we
are scarcely in a position to complain about it since we have a number of
statutory provisions drafted on just these lines. For example, a jilted fiance
or fiancee looking for his or her pound of flesh in an Irish court will get no
satisfaction here: s. 2(1) of the Family Law Act 1981 ensures this. Article
7(2) does no more than permit states to continue to draft laws of this type.

Morse, *op. cit.*, at 144, has expressed the following balanced views on
Article 7(2)'s treatment of these *lois d' application immediate*:

> The existence amongst the Member States of such inconsistent rules
> will, of course, not be conducive to the uniformity of result, irrespective
> of the forum seised of the dispute, at which the Convention is aimed.
> But, ultimately, a forum has to remain true to the dictates of its own law,
> a position which cannot as a matter of constitutional propriety be eroded
> by a choice of law convention even within the EEC. On the other hand,
> it is to be hoped that Member States will not seek to further the
> application of forum law by making rules internationally mandatory
> unless some serious forum interest or general interest is served by the
> process.

A troublesome question concerns the exact relationship between Articles
3(3) and 7(2). Let us take a case envisaged by Article 3(3), where the
mandatory rules of (let us say) Ireland apply to parties who have chosen the
law of France to apply to their contract, when all the other elements relevant
to the situation at the time of choice are connected with Ireland only. If a
dispute between them happens to be litigated in England, does this mean that
an English mandatory rule envisaged by Article 7(2) is to 'trump' the Irish
mandatory rules?

It seems that the answer has to be yes. In an elaborate and subtle textual
analysis, Patrick Ross Williams has come reluctantly to this conclusion,

finding that Article 16's *ordre public* clause is not capable of affording an effective barrier. The language of Article 7(2) is very strong and unqualified: *nothing* in the Convention is to restrict the application of these mandatory rules of the forum. In contrast, Article 3(3) concerns itself essentially with the resolution of a contest between the chosen law and the mandatory rules of the law of sole connection save for that choice. It confers no stronger claim for application of the latter law in any other battle against another adversary.

Perhaps the conclusion is not all that surprising. It seems clear that the forum's mandatory rules envisaged by Article 7(2) will universally defeat the mandatory rules of the otherwise applicable law. Why should the mandatory rules specifically identified by Article 3(3) have a claim to greater potency in relation to Article 7(2) merely by reason of the fact that they can knock down an applicable law where *all* the relevant elements save the choice lean towards the country with these mandatory rules?

Field of operation of the governing law Article 10(1) provides a non-exhaustive list of the matters falling within the scope of the law applicable to the contract. It provides as follows:

> The law applicable to a contract by virtue of Articles 3 to 6 and 12 of this Convention shall govern in particular;
>
> (a) interpretation;
> (b) performance;
> (c) within the limits of the powers conferred on the court by its procedural law, the consequences of breach, including the assessment of damages in so far as it is governed by rules of law;
> (d) the various ways of extinguishing obligations, and prescription and limitation of actions;
> (e) the consequences of nullity of the contract.

A few words about some of these elements may be called for. So far as interpretation is concerned, no difficulty arises for Irish law. In most cases, the proper law will determine questions of interpretation. Thus, in *St Pierre v South American Stores* [1937] 3 All ER 349, at 351 it was said that:

> [w]hen an action is brought in London on a contract which is a Chilean contract to be interpreted by Chilean law, the Chilean law in relation to matters which may be taken into account in interpreting the contract applies just as much as it would apply if it were to be interpreted in Chile.

In those rare cases where reference to another law may be necessary, the court may always resort to severance under either Article 3(1) or Article 4(1).

In this context it is worth noting Patrick Ross Williams's sensible argument (35 ICLQ, at 27, 58) that, in many cases where there is no express choice-of-law clause, the fact that an expression can be given a precise meaning only under a certain law may well lead to the conclusion that there is an implied choice of that law for the purposes of Article 3(1).

Article 10(2)provides that, in relation to the manner of performance and the steps to be taken in the event of defective performance, regard is to be had to the law of the country in which performance takes place. It does not attempt to define 'manner of performance', in view of the lack of a uniform meaning for this concept in the laws of the Member States: Giuliano-Legarde Report, p. 33. Thus, the question must be resolved by the *lex fori*, with all the consequential problems of inconsistency which this involves: Delaume, 22 Va J of Internal L, at 112. Among the matters that may fall within the scope of the concept are the rules governing public holidays, the manner in which goods are to be examined and the steps to be taken if they are refused: Giuliano-Legarde Report, p. 33. The reference to such precise and relatively unimportant matters in the report surely justifies Morse's surmise (*op. cit.*, at 153) that the envisaged control of the *lex solutionis* is 'confined' to minor matters. Nevertheless the wording of Article 10(1) contains no such express limits so the question is open.

It should be noted that Article 10(2) only requires the court to 'have regard' to the law of the place of performance. The court is free to apply this law to such extent, if at all, as it considers desirable in doing justice between the parties: Giuliano-Legarde Report, p. 33. This uncertainty is probably worth conceding in the broader interests of justice.

Article 10(1)(c) is in some respects novel, so far as Irish law is concerned, in that it refers questions relating to the assessment of damages to the applicable law. The traditional position in common law jurisdiction has been that the question of the measure, as opposed to the *remoteness*, of damages is matter for the forum: Binchy *op. cit.*, 642-6. It seems that under Article 10(1)(c) the *lex causae* is to control the measure as well as the remoteness of damages, subject only to the limits of the procedural machinery in the forum to apply the rules of the *lex causae*—scarcely a problem in the context of contractual claims. See Morse, *op. cit.,* at 154-5.

Paragraph (d), relating to limitation of actions, changes the present approach in most common law jurisdictions, which looks to the forum rather than the *lex causae*: Binchy *op. cit.*, 639-41. This traditional approach has few modern defenders and is already giving way to statutory reform in a number of countries. The Convention's solution has therefore been welcomed by many common law commentators.

Paragraph (e) provides that the applicable law is to govern the consequences of nullity of a contract. This proved too much for Britain, which made a reservation on the matter (permitted by Article 22(1)(b)) so as to preserve the application of the conflicts rules relating to quasi-contract. The policy in our 1990 legislation not to have recourse to their reservation is surely sensible, in view of the added clarity to our law which taking this course involves. It is nonetheless true that an argument can be made that the applicable law is not always the best one to decide this issue, especially where it is one that has no substantial connection with the situation: see Morse, *op cit*, at 135.

Capacity   We must now consider what the Convention has to say in relation to contractual capacity. The general rule, in Article 1(a), is to *exclude* from the scope of the Convention the legal capacity of natural persons and of bodies corporate or unincorporated. Thus, each Contracting State must continue to apply its own system of private international law to the question, subject to the single provision which we will address in a moment.

There is no clear modern Irish authority on the question of capacity. Historically the *lex domicilii* and the *lex loci contractus* were attractive to courts (cf. Binchy, *op. cit.*, 539-40) but today there is general support for determining capacity by the proper law objectively ascertained.

Article 11 contains the only rule in the Convention dealing positively with the question of capacity. It provides that, in a contract concluded between persons who are in the same country, a natural person who would have capacity under the law of that country may invoke his incapacity resulting from another law only if the other party to the contract was aware of this incapacity at the time of the conclusion or was not aware of it as a result of negligence.

This provision was designed to accommodate the anxiety of those whose private international law rules subjected the question of capacity to the law of nationality. Professors Giuliano and Lagarde note (p. 34) that:

> [a] rule of the same kind is also thought necessary in the countries which make capacity subject to the law of the country of domicile. The only countries which could dispense with it are those which subject capacity to the law of the place where the contract was entered into or the law governing the substance of the contract.

Let us take the case where a French student aged seventeen, working for the summer in Massachusetts, enters into a number of contracts there. If he breaches these contracts he will not be able to invoke his incapacity under French law as a defence unless he can discharge the burden of proving that the other parties to these contracts were, or ought to have been, aware of this incapacity when they concluded their contracts with him.

All of this is largely academic for our purpose. In a case such as the one mentioned, it seems clear that, under the rules of Irish private international law, our courts would not look to the *lex patriae* or *lex domicilii*, but would instead apply the proper law objectively ascertained, which in most if not all instances would be likely to be that of Massachusetts. The French youth's incapacity under the law of his nationality (and, let us also concede, domicile) will not avail him, even if he can show that the parties with whom he contracted were (or ought to have been) aware of that incapacity. The manner in which Article 11 is drafted does not silence the French youth's argument for immunity as conclusively as one might wish, but the commentary by Professors Giuliano and Lagarde, as well as considerations of common sense and justice, suggests strongly that it would fail.

Finally, it is worth recording Hartley's insights (4 Eur L Rev 36, at 39) regarding the function of rules as to incapacity in seeking to protect the young, the mentally disabled and the personally vulnerable from exploitation. These old-type rules:

> are generally regarded today as over-protective: the trend is towards increasing the capacity of the persons concerned. . . . In the case of the economically weak, on the other hand, the trend is in the opposite direction. The rights of workers and consumers are being strengthened as employers and manufacturers are subject to ever-increasing restrictions. This distinction is important in the field of conflict of laws: as between two potentially applicable rules of capacity, the more liberal is likely to be the more modern; in the cases of worker and consumer protection, on the other hand, the more protective is likely to be more modern. Consequently, one might expect choice of law rules to be more favourable towards provisions of the latter kind than to rule of capacity.

These trends are of some interest in the Convention's approach towards the questions of incapacity, and consumer and employment contracts.

Validity

1. Material validity Let us now turn to the question of material validity. First we must consider how the Irish courts, prior to implementation of the Convention, might best have determined the applicable law (or laws) to govern questions of offer and acceptance: see Gill, *op. cit.*, at 15-16, Jaffey, 4 ICLQ 603, at 604-13 (1975), Lewis, 10 ICLQ 908 (1961), Libling, 4 Modern L Rev 169 (1979). Under the Irish internal law, a contract normally is concluded when the acceptance of the offer is communicated to the offeror; but this rule is modified where the contemplated mode of acceptance is by post: in such a case the contract is completed when the letter accepting the offer is posted: *Wheeler & Co. Ltd v Jeffrey (John) & Co.* [1921] 1 IR 395

(CA, 1920), *Sanderson v Cunningham* [1919] IR 619 (CA), *Tedcastle McCormick Co. v Robertson* [1929] IR 597 (Supreme Court, 1927). Moreover, an offeror is not permitted to impose on the offeree the task of declining the offer under pain of being contractually bound: *Russell & Baird Ltd v Hoban* [1922] 2 IR 159 (CA, 1921). Finally, a distinction is drawn between an acceptance, a counter-offer and a mere request for further information; whether or not a contract exists depends on how the offeree's response is categorised. In several other countries, however, different rules as to offer and acceptance prevail. Thus, in some countries, an acceptance, though posted, is inefficacious until it reaches the offeror; or an offeror may require of an offeree that he either refuse the offer or be contractually bound: Wolff, *Private International Law* (2nd ed., 1950), 439. Finally, the principles as to what constitutues a counter-offer differ from country to country.

If, therefore, a contract exists from the standpoint of one country's law and does not exist according to another's on account of lack of acceptance, by what conflict rules should the efficacy of the contract be determined?

We may consider three possible approaches here. The first would refer to the *lex loci contractus*. This is satisfactory, so far as the question of communication of the acceptance is concerned, where the communications between the parties are instantaneous or 'virtually instantaneous' *(Mendelson – Zeller Co. Inc v T. & C. Providers Pty Ltd* [1981] 1 NSWLR 366, at 369) as, for example, where a person in Louth shouts his acceptance of an offer to the offeror who is standing just across the border in Armagh, or, more usually, where an offer is accepted by telephone or telex: *In re Modern Fashion Ltd*, 8 DLR (3d) 590 (1969), *Entores v Miles Far East Corporation* [1955] QB 37.

Where, however, communication of the acceptance is not so immediate, the *lex loci contractus* offers no clear guide, since the 'place of contracting' may itself vary according to which law's rules as to formation of a contract are chosen. Thus 'solv[ing] the problem by arbitrarily preferring one of the two relevant laws to the other is to beg the question'. Cheshire & North, *Private International Law* (10th ed.), 475. The temptation to apply the *lex fori* in such a case is no doubt a strong one, but this offers an unsatisfactory solution where the forum has only a fortuitous connection with the contract or the parties.

The third possible approach, advocated by many writers, with some judicial support, is to determine the question of offer and acceptance by reference to 'the putative proper law', that is, the law which 'would be the proper law of the contract if the contract was validly concluded': Dicey & Morris, *Conflict of Laws* (10th ed.), Rule 146.

Some difficulties with this approach have been identified: cf. Jaffey, 4 ICLQ, at 604-13. There may be disagreement between the parties as to which law should govern; in that event the selection of one of two (or more) competing laws on the basis that it is the 'putative proper law' has a potential for hardship and injustice. It is one thing to apply the proper law test to parties who, at the least, regarded themselves as being involved in a contractual relationship with each other. It is another thing to impose on persons who are only negotiating to enter into a contract the rules of offer and acceptance of the law of a country to which (so far as they are concerned) they have not yet bound themselves. Secondly, there is no reason to adopt a presumption that a valid contract has been concluded in a case where one person asserts and the other denies that this is the case.

Conversely, application of the 'putative proper law' test would defeat the contractual expectations of the parties in some cases, as, for example, where the parties both considered that there was, or would be, contractual efficacy because they were seeking to comply with the law of their country of residence or business, but the rules of the putative proper law specified otherwise. Thus, for example, if an Irish author and an Irish publisher were, in Ireland, to negotiate an agreement to publish a book in Ireland, but the law of Ruritania was specified as the proper law in the draft contract, and if the author posted a letter of acceptance of the contract in Ireland, and died the next day, it would surely defeat the expectations of the parties to hold that no contract had come into existence because in Ruritania postal acceptance must be received by the offeree before it is efficacious: cf. Jaffey, *op. cit.* at 609-10.

A contract may be void for lack of consent attributable to factors other than relating to offer and acceptance such as mistake, misrepresentation, duress or undue influence, for example. Although lack of consent affects the validity of contracts in every legal system, the extent to which it does, and the effect of its doing so, can vary widely from one law to another. By which law should this question be determined?

There was very little judicial authority in Ireland, or indeed in other common law jurisdictions, prior to implementation of the Convention. In the English case of *McKender v Feldia A.G.* [1967] QB 590, the Court of Appeal groped towards a distinction, which has some intuitive attraction, between cases where there simply was no meeting of minds and cases where minds did go some way towards meeting but the consent was what might be designated substandard. In the case of the first category the *lex fori* would apply since what had taken place did not constitute a contract at all according to that law. But in the second category, the proper law should determine whether the contract should stand or fall.

There are two principal difficulties with this approach. First, the distinction is difficult to apply in practice since there is a fairly wide band of cases where the lack of true consent could credibly be attributed to either of the two categories. Secondly, and more importantly from the standpoint of conflicts of law, legal systems contain widely differing rules in relation to consent. In Irish law, for example, the first category (of a complete absence of a meeting of minds) is clearly reflected in the doctrines of common mistake and *non est factum*, and to a lesser extent in other doctrines, such as duress and certain instances of unilateral mistake. But neither common mistake nor *non est factum* is restricted to this precise category. So far as the second category is concerned, several doctrines exist under Irish law: these include fraud, misrepresentation, non-disclosure, certain other instances of unilateral mistake and undue influence. Again, these doctrines, though substantially embracing the notion of substandard consent envisaged by the second category, are not specifically limited to this concept. The same can be said of other legal systems.

What *McKender v Feldia A.G.* attempted to do was to isolate certain specific doctrines of English domestic law of contract and categorise them for the purposes of conflicts of law. Thus Lord Denning MR and Diplock LJ accepted that *non est factum* was probably a matter for English law to determine since this raised the question whether there was any real *consensus ad idem*. In contrast, innocent misrepresentation or non-disclosure in insurance cases did not result in the absence of any consent; in these cases the affected party 'did in fact consent but would not have done so if he had known then what he knows now': [1967] QB at 604 (*per* Diplock LJ). Accordingly, the Court of Appeal held, the proper law rather than the *lex fori* should determine the outcome of the case, which was concerned with alleged non-disclosure in relation to an insurance contract.

Some troubling questions remained. Into which category did fraud fall? In *McKender v Feldia*, Diplock LJ (at 604) and Russell LJ (at 605) left this issue expressly unresolved. Libbing has suggested (4 Modern L Rev, at 178) that, since the victim of fraud may affirm the contract and be satisfied with damages in tort 'the doctrine of fraud does not affect consensus' and thus should be a matter for the proper law rather than the *lex fori*. The position was less clear in relation to duress, where there was a degree of fluidity of judicial thought on the question whether duress deprives a party of the *animus contrahendi* or merely renders his or her consent revocable.

Finally when dealing with the matter of material validity, we should mention briefly the subject of consideration. Under Irish law , a contract not under seal requires consideration. In many civil law jurisdictions there is no necessity for consideration, the concept of *cause* playing an important role. What was the position, before the Convention was implemented, regarding a contract without consideration? It appears that where the contract was connected exclusively with a foreign law which did not require consideration, it should be treated as valid here: *Re Bonacina* [1912] 2 Ch 394. Where the connection was less than exclusive the position was less certain, but the putative proper law had scholarly support.

Article 8(1) of the Convention provides that the existence and validity of a contract, or of any term of a contract, is to be determined by the law which would govern it under the Convention if the contract or term were valid. Article 8 (2) modifies this general principle by providing that a party may rely on the law of the country in which he has his habitual residence to establish that he did not consent if it appears from the circumstances that it would not be reasonable to determine the effect of his conduct in accordance with the law applicable in Article 8(1).

The approach adopted here is designed, among other things, to solve the problem of the implications of silence by one party as to the formation of the contract. The solution is a broad discretionary one which is a good way of ensuring justice in these cases. The reference to 'the circumstances' enables the Court to have regard, not merely to the particular alleged contract from which one party wishes to abstract himself, but also to the previous dealings between the parties. Thus, if an Irish company, traded for many years with a foreign company, the proper law being that of a country where silence constitutes acceptance, it would be quite unjust for the Irish company to invoke the Irish rule to the contrary. Having regard to the circumstances and exercising its discretion under Article 8(2), the Court would be able to hold that Article 8(1) continued to apply.

It may be noted that the application of Article 8(2) can result in a decision releasing a party who would otherwise have been bound under Article 8(1), 'but it can never produce the opposite effect of holding that a contract exists which is non-existent by its proper law': Giuliano-Lagarde Report, p. 8.

Article 8(2) is capable of dealing with cases other than merely those of offer and acceptance. Thus, the courts may have to consider, for example, whether it would be appropriate to relieve a party from liability under a contract where, according to the law of his habitual residence, but not the applicable law, he failed to consent on account of undue influence or unilateral mistake. The notion of *reasonableness* as the criterion for determining whether or not to apply the law of habitual residence in such a case is a good deal less helpful that in an offer-and-acceptance case. We can all understand the unreasonableness of a silent acceptor's invoking the law of his habitual residence in order to escape a liability where the other party, perhaps on the basis of previous dealings, reasonably relied on his adhering to the requirements as to acceptance in the putative proper law. But once we venture outside offer and acceptance, the concept of reasonableness has to carry a huge responsibility in determining what essentially may be a clash of values as to the appropriate degree of paternalism which a state's law should extend to vulnerable persons.

2. Formal validity   Prior to the 1991 Act, there was no clear modern Irish judicial authority on the private international law aspects of the formal validity of contracts. All that we had were a few decisions in the nineteenth century, when the *lex loci contractus* was in vogue, dealing, not so much with commercial contracts as with contracts in the family law area, such as marriage and family property. The bold adherence in these decisions to the place of contracting as providing the exclusive test of formal validity should not therefore be regarded as offering any real barrier to contemporary thinking on the matter, which in both the common law and the civil law systems tends to favour strongly the minimising of formal requirements as barriers to upholding contracts: see Wolff, *op. cit.*, 466. Thus the general position prior to the legislation was that a contract that complied with the formal requirement of either the *lex loci contractus* or of the proper law would be treated as formally valid: *Sharn Importing Ltd v Babchuk*, 1 DLR (3rd) 349 (BC, 1971), *In re Dunn: ex parte Andrew*, 3 ALR 466, at 471 (Fed Ct of Austr, 1981).

It is worth noting that, in some cases, a country's law may require parties to a contract to comply with rigorous formalities, the purpose being to alert an economically weak or dependent party and to discourage others from exploiting him or her. If the forum has such a law the court may well choose to apply the *lex fori* regardless of the proper law, in order to protect the weaker party. To do so would give effect to a basic policy of that state's law. A Canadian scholar has suggested that compliance with the *lex loci contractus* should not suffice where:

> (i) the place of contracting is fortuitous, bearing no real relation to the transaction and the parties;
> (ii) the formal requirements of the system of law with which the transaction has its most real and substantial connection have been disregarded;
> (iii) these latter requirements are designed for the protection of the parties; and
> (iv) the involve the implementation 'a strong social policy': J.G. Castel, *Canadian Conflict of Laws*, vol., 546 (1975).

Finally, we must recall an important qualification to the principles regarding formal validity. The Statute of Frauds (IR) 1695 provides that no action is to be brought to enforce certain specified agreements and undertakings unless they are in writing. This requirement was treated as a matter of procedure, to which the *lex fori* rather than the *lex* cause applied. Thus if a contract of guarantee, for example, was not in writing by fulfilling the formal requirements of the proper law it would not be enforceable here because it fails to comply with the Statute of Frauds: cf. *Leroux v Brown*, (1852) 1 CB 801, 138 ER 1119.

The Convention adopts quite a flexible approach to the question of formal validity, giving good effect to the *favor negotii* principle. Where a contract is concluded between persons who are in the same country, it will be formally valid if it satisfies the formal requirements of either the law which governs it under the Convention or the law of the country where it is concluded: Article 9(1). Where the parties are in different countries, the contract will be formally valid if it satisfies the formal requirements of either the law which governs it under the Convention or the law of one of those countries: Article 9(2).

In either case, where a contract is concluded by an agent, the country in which the agent acts is the relevant country: Article 9(3).

Article 9 also deals with an 'act intended to have legal effect relating to an existing or contemplated contract'. This type of act might be a notice of termination or remission of a debt or a declaration of rescission or repudiation, for example: Giuliano – Lagarde Report, p. 9. Such an act will be formally valid if it satisfies the formal requirements of either the law which under the Convention governs or would govern the contract or the law of the country where the act was done: Article 9(4).

Paragraphs 1 and 4 of Article 9 do not apply to consumer contracts, the formal validity of which is governed by the law of the country in which the consumer has his habitual residence: Article 9(5). In view of the social importance of many formal requirements for consumer contracts where the whole purpose of the formal requirements is to protect the consumer, and put him on notice of the implication of the transaction which he is contemplating, there is much to be said in favour of letting the law of his habitual residence have exclusive control. So far as immovable properties are concerned, a contract (the subject matter of which is a right in immovable property) is subject to the mandatory requirements of the form of the law of the country where imposed irrespective of the country where the contract is concluded and irrespective of the law governing the contract: Article 9(6).

Article 3(3) should not be overlooked. It empowers the parties at any time to change the applicable law; but it goes on to provide that this is not to prejudice the formal validity of the contract under Article 9 or adversely affect the rights of third parties. It may be, of course, that a contract, having been formally valid under the originally applicable laws is invalid under the newly chosen law; this cannot affect the rights of third parties. But what of the reverse case, where the contract was formally invalid under the originally applicable law and is valid under the newly chosen law? If, for example, a third party had a good defence by reason of such invalidity to an action for inducing a breach of the contract, is there any prospect that he will retrospectively lose that defence? Patrick Ross Williams (*op. cit.*, at 1) thinks not and we are inclined to agree, but the reference in article 3(3) to the 'rights' of third parties is unfortunate. Should the courts really have to engage in hand-to-hand Hohfeldian combat to establish that the word 'rights' really means 'legal position'?

3. Evidential and procedural aspects   The general principle is clear: evidence and procedure fall outside the scope of the Convention. These matters are governed by the *lex fori* under our conflicts rules: cf. Binchy, *op. cit.*, ch. 34.

Article 14 modifies the full force of this exclusion in two respects. It provides as follows:

> (1) The law governing the contract under this Convention applies to the extent that it contains, in the law of contract, rules which raise presumptions of law or determine the burden of proof.
> (2) A contract or an act intended to have legal effect may be proved by any mode of proof recognised by the law of the forum or by any of the laws referred to in article 9 under which that contract or act is formally valid, provided that such mode of proof can be administered by the forum.

Article 14(1) raises difficult questions of characterisation. The essential issue concerns the relationship between the law of evidence and the law of contract. Article 14(1) is premised on acceptance of the proposition that it is possible to speak with propriety of rules "*in the law of contract*" which raise presumptions of law or determine the burden of proof. There is perhaps little difficulty in accepting that irrebuttable presumptions are in truth rules of substantive rather than adjectival law and to that extent are capable of forming part of the law of contract. Thus, for example, if the applicable law contains a rule, expressed as an irrebuttable presumption, that a letter duly posted arrived at its intended destination, this should properly be treated as what it is, in reality if not in conceptual dress, a rule of substance rather than evidence, which forms part of the law of contract'.

When we move away from irrebuttable presumptions to consider rebuttable presumptions and the interrelated question of the burden of proof, the distinction between substantive and adjectival law becomes far more difficult to draw. The truth of the matter is that in these areas the rules are part of both the law of evidence and the law of contract. Evidence law has no existence in isolation: it can exist only in relation to specific applications, in relation to contract, tort, family law and so on. It is true that some rules of evidence have a seemingly generic aura. The burden of proof is one such rule, but beneath its seemingly simple formulae lurk a teeming mass of policy choices. Thus, any characterisation of these rules as belonging to 'the law of contract' will inevitably give the false impression that there is a coherent conceptual basis for the distinction.

INTERNATIONAL CHILD ABDUCTION

International child abduction is a problem that has grown in the past thirty years or so. The reasons are easy to discern: a growing incidence of divorce in Europe and America, the reduction in the price of airfares and, paradoxically, the greater willingness on the part of the courts to investigate the welfare of the children involved as the paramount factor in determining questions of custody and access. In the context of the removal of a child from one country to another, the delay which such investigation can involve works in favour of the abducting party. If he or she can spin things out long enough—and this may be for as short a period as a few months—the psychological and psychiatric evidence may well convince the judge that, whatever demerits attach to the abducting parent, the welfare of the child, and the need to avoid long term or short term trauma require that the child stay with the abducting parent.

The prospects of a successful international abduction are enhanced where the abducting parent brings the child 'home' from a foreign land where the parent and the child had been living as a family with the other parent. International experience suggests that courts in such cases tend to be more forgiving than perhaps they should. They find it relatively easy to be convinced that the welfare of the child will be best served in the home country (with whose culture the court is of course totally familiar) rather than the foreign country with whose culture the court may have only a limited acquaintance.

Against the background of these difficulties two Conventions were formulated over a decade ago: the Hague Convention on the Civil Aspects of International Child Abduction (1980) and the Council of Europe (Luxembourg) Convention on Recognition and Enforcement of Decisions concerning Custody of Children and on Restoration of Custody of Children (1980). These Conventions contain important administrative and judicial measures designed to secure the return of children who are removed to any Contracting State in defiance of a court order made in another Contracting State or against the wishes of a parent with custody rights. See the Department of Justice's *Explanatory Memorandum to the Child Abduction and Enforcement of Custody Orders Bill 1990*, as passed by Both Houses of the Oireachtas and enacted, Marta 1991, para 2 (hereinafter cited as '*Explanatory Memorandum*').

The Child Abduction and Enforcement of Custody Orders Act 1991 gives the force of law in the State to both Conventions. This is in accordance with the proposals of the Law Reform Commission in their *Report on the Hague Convention (LRC 12-1985)* that Ireland should ratify the Hague Convention, without prejudice to our becoming a party also to the Luxembourg Convention. For a detailed, helpful analysis of the Act see Timothy Bird's *Annotation* [1991] ICLSA. This Act came into force on 1 October 1991: SI No. 235 of 1991.

The Conventions share many common features. The most important is the goal of ensuring that an abducted child should be returned to the state from which he or she was abducted as quickly as possible. Both Conventions envisage that a Central Authority in each State should have specifically assigned functions to assist in the practical operation of the Convention, depending on whether the child has been abducted to or from the State in question. Neither Convention applies to children who have reached the age of sixteen. The Luxembourg Convention (Article 1(a)) does not apply to a child *under* sixteen who has the right to decide his own place of residence under the law of his habitual residence, the law of his nationality or the internal law of the State addressed.

There are some distinctions between the Conventions, so it is useful to consider aspects of them separately.

The Hague Convention   The Hague Convention (in contrast to the Luxembourg Convention, as we shall see) applies in cases of wrongful international abduction, *whether or not* the parent from whom the child was abducted was exercising rights *pursuant to a court order*. Article 3 provides that the removal of a child is to be considered wrongful where:

> (a) it is in breach of rights of custody attributed to a person, an institution or any other body, either jointly or alone, under the law of the State in which the child was habitually resident immediately before the removal . . . ; and
> (b) at the time of the removal . . . those rights were actually exercised, either jointly or alone, or would have been so exercised but for the removal. . . .

Article 3 goes on to provide that the rights of custody mentioned in sub-paragraph (a) 'may arise in particular by operation of law or by reason of a judicial or administrative decision, or by reason of an agreement having legal effect under the law of that State'.

Chapter III of the Convention deals specifically with the return of children wrongfully removed or retained in breach of custody rights. It prescribes detailed administrative rules involving the active assistance of the relevant

Central Authority. Article 12 is a core provision. It provides that where a child has been wrongfully removed or retained and less than a year has elapsed at the time proceedings are begun in the Contracting State where the child is, the judicial or administrative authority must order the return of the child *forthwith*. In cases where a year or more has passed, the obligation to return remains, qualified only by an exception arising where it is demonstrated that the child is now settled in its new environment.

Article 13 relieves the judicial or administrative authority of the obligation to order the return of the child in cases where the proper custodian was not actually exercising the custody rights at the time of the removal or retention or had consented to the removal or retention or later acquiesced in it. Nor need the return be ordered if there is 'grave risk that this would expose the child to an intolerable situation'. In either case the onus of proof rests on the party opposing the return. See *In re Y.A.A. an Infant; M.A. v P.R. (otherwise known as P.A.)*, High Court, 23 July 1992; cf. *W. v W.*, High Court, 9 February 1992. Finally Article 13 permits (but again does not require) the authority to refuse to order the return of the child if the child objects and has attained an age and degree of maturity at which it is appropriate to take account of its view.

Article 20 has an important potential in the Irish context. It provides that the return of the child under the provisions of Article 12 may be refused if this would not be permitted by the fundamental principles of the requested State relating to the protection of human rights and fundamental freedoms. Clearly there is a potential for the application here of Article 41 of the Constitution. An important, interrelated question concerns the international remit of Article 41. So far our courts have managed to deal with cases in which this issue was raised by specific resolutions which do not in any final sense attempt to answer the fundamental question at stake: see the 1989 Review, 257-64 and Binchy, 'Constitution Remedies and the Law of Torts', in J. O'Reilly, ed., *Human Rights and Constitutional Law*, at 218-222 (1992).

The Luxembourg Convention In contrast to the Hague Convention, the Luxembourg Convention is restricted to cases where the applicant spouse has obtained in one Contracting State a *decision* relating to the custody of a child and wishes to have it recognised or enforced in another Contracting State. This is spelt out in Article 4. Again the central authorities play a vital role in assisting this process.

Article 7 makes decisions relating to custody in one Contracting State recognisable and (where enforceable in the State of origin) enforceable also in every other Contracting State. In the case of an improper removal, the central authority of the State to which the child is removed must cause steps to be taken 'forthwith' to restore the custody of the child where:

(a) at the time of the institution of the proceedings in the State where the decision was given or at the time of the improper removal, if earlier, the child and his parents had as their sole nationality the nationality of that State and the child had his habitual residence in the territory of that State, *and*

(b) a request for restoration was made to a central authority within *six months from the date of the improper removal.*

By virtue of Ireland's exercising its power of reservation under Article 17, restoration of custody may be refused in any of the following cases:

(a) if the effects of the decision in the State of origin are manifestly incompatible with the fundamental principles of the law relating to the family and children in the State addressed;

(b) if as a result of a change in the circumstances (other than merely a change in the residence of the child after an improper removal) the effects of the original decision are manifestly no longer in accordance with the welfare of the child;

(c) if the child at the time of the institution of the proceedings in the State of origin was either:

(i) a national of the State addressed or habitually resident there, no such connection existing with the State of origin, or

(ii) a national both of the State of origin and of the State addressed and habitually resident in the State addressed;

(d) if the decision is incompatible with one given in the State addressed or enforceable there after being given in a third state in proceedings begun before the submission of the request for recognition or enforcement, and if the refusal is in accordance with the welfare of the child.

See further the *Explanatory Memorandum*, paras 52ff.

Paragraph (a) is not dissimilar to Article 20 of the Hague Convention, but the manner in which it is drafted suggests that it would be more difficult for parents with less than coercive connections with Ireland to succeed in invoking the protection of paragraph (a) than it would for them to call Article 20 in aid.

Article 9 deals with cases of improper removal falling outside Article 8—in other words where there are somewhat less close links between the parties and the State of origin. Again the request must come within six months from the date of removal. Article 9 requires the recognition and enforcement of the original order save in *seven* cases. Four of them (by virtue of our reservation under Article 17) are identical with the four attaching to Article

8. The other cases are (in summary):

(a) the absence of due service on the defendant of the document instituting the proceedings in sufficient time to enable him to arrange his defence, the decision being given in the absence of the defendant or his legal representative;

(b) again where the decision was given in the absence of the defendant or his legal representative, the fact that the competence of the authority giving the decision was not founded on the *habitual residence* of any of the parties, and

(c) and the fact that the decision is incompatible with one relating to custody which became enforceable in the State addressed before the removal of the child (unless the child has had his habitual residence in the requesting State for a year before the removal).

Finally Article 10 deals with cases falling outside the scope of Article 8 and 9—in other words, cases where a request is not made within six months of the removal. It provides that recognition and enforcement may be refused not only on the three grounds provided for in Article 9 but also on any of the four extra grounds which (by virtue of our reservation under Article 17) apply to cases falling under Articles 8 and 9.

The 1991 Act, in giving effect in Irish law to both Conventions, provides that the High Court is to have jurisdiction to determine applications under them. It is 'the judicial or administrative authority' to which the Hague Convention refers. The Minister for Justice is to be the Central Authority for the purposes of that Convention unless and until he appoints another body to discharge these functions: s. 8. The Central Authority is obliged to ensure that, where a child has been abducted *into* the State, steps are taken to trace the child, to seek its return or secure access to it and to arrange if necessary for court proceedings to achieve this. Where a child has been abducted *from* the State, the Central Authority must assist the wronged party is seeking the return of the child and liaise with other Central Authorities as to welfare reports, for example, regarding the child: see Articles 6 and 7 of the Hague Convention and Articles 2 to 6 of the Luxembourg Convention. In practice, incoming applications will be referred by the Central Authority to the Legal Aid Board for relevant proceedings to be taken in the High Court. Applicants under both Conventions are entitled to legal aid: see the useful discussion by Timothy Bird, *op. cit.*, General Note to s. 8.

The High Court is given power to order a person to disclose a child's whereabouts: s. 36. This power is designed to overrule any right not to incriminate oneself: subs. (1). The Act also gives Gardaí an emergency power to detain a child whom they reasonably suspect is about to be wrongfully removed from the State: s. 37. This provision was inspired by the Law Reform Commission, which made a recommendation on these lines in its Report on the subject.

Proceedings under the Act are to be as informal as is practicable and consistent with the administration of justice; wigs and gowns are not to be worn: s. 39, modelled on s. 33(3) and (4) of the Judicial Separation and Family Law Reform Act 1989.

JURISDICTION

Contract Not surprisingly, contractual disputes have dominated juris-dictional issues under the Act. Several decisions in this area were handed down in 1991.

In *Olympia Productions Ltd v Mackintosh et al.* [1992] ILRM 204, the plaintiff, owner of the Olympia Theatre in Dublin, claimed that it had a right to perform the musical play *Les Misérables*, on the basis of a contract whereby the defendants, who owned the performing rights, had agreed to grant it the sole and exclusive right to perform the play in Ireland. The defendants sought to have service of the summons set aside, arguing that they were domiciled in 'the United Kingdom' and that the Irish courts had no other basis for jurisdiction under the Convention.

Article 5 provides that:

> [a] person domiciled in a contracting State may, in another contracting State, be sued:
>
> (1) in matters relating to a contract, in the court for the place of performance of the obligation in question. . . .

Two issues thus arose: *what* was the 'obligation in question', and *where* was the place of performance of that obligation? As to the first, Costello J cited the judgment of the Court of Justice in *De Bloos v Bouyer* (Case 24/76) [1976] ECR 1497, to the effect that the word 'obligation' refers to *the contractual obligation forming the basis of the legal proceedings.* Applying this principle to the facts of the case, it seemed to him that the obligation forming the basis of the plaintiff's claim was an obligation to grant the sole and exclusive right to perform the play in Ireland. This obligation would be performed by the execution of a valid legal document by which performing rights were granted. The execution of such a document 'would take place in England and not in this country. . . .' Accordingly, Article 5(1) was of no avail to the plaintiff.

The plaintiff had sought to rely on *Ivenel v Schwab* (Case 133/81) [1982] ECR 1891, where the Court of Justice had held that, in a contract containing a number of different obligations, regard should be had to *the obligation that characterises the contract*. The plaintiff had contended that the draft licence that had been submitted by the defendants envisaged their participation in the production of the work, and that the obligation characterising the contract was the performance of the play in Dublin. Costello J rejected this argument for failing to recognise the distinction between the performance by the grantor of his obligation to grant a right and the exercise of the right by the grantee once that obligation had been fulfilled. Here the contractual obligation on which the plaintiff's claim was based was the promise to grant an intellectual property right, and that obligation was to be performed in England. Once that obligation was fulfilled by the grant of performing rights, those rights would of course be exercised in Ireland; but the fact did not confer jurisdiction on the Irish courts.

In *Unidare plc and Unidare Cable Ltd v James Scott Ltd* [1991] 2 IR 88 the plaintiffs sued for monies due under a contract with a Scottish company whereby the plaintiffs had supplied conductors for electric current. The defendant company sought unsuccessfully to have service of notice of the summons set aside, on the basis of either Article 17 or Article 5 of the Convention.

The facts were simple enough. The plaintiffs had made an offer to the defendant company for the supply of cable. The defendant had replied by telex accepting the offer and noting that its formal order would follow shortly. Three days later the formal order was communicated to the plaintiffs, containing a provision for inclusion of standard terms and conditions which were printed on the reverse side and which included a clause providing that the parties agreed that the governing law was to be English law and that the English courts should have jurisdiction.

The Supreme Court, affirming MacKenzie J, declined to set aside service of notice of the summons. Finlay CJ (Hederman and McCarthy JJ concurring) dealt first with the argument that Article 17 applied. This gives exclusive jurisdiction to the courts of a particular Contracting State if the parties (one of whom must be domiciled in a Contracting State) have chosen these courts to exercise jurisdiction to settle any disputes arising in connection with their legal relationship: see Binchy, *op. cit.*, 190-1. The Chief Justice was satisfied that the terms of the contract had been completely agreed between the parties by the telex issued by the defendant; the fact that it contained a request to the plaintiff to proceed with the manufacturing process in advance of the receipt of any formal order made it clear that complete agreement had been reached. In these circumstances the Chief Justice was quite satisfied that the clause providing for choice of jurisdiction did not form part of the contract arrived at between the parties. He noted that there was no written acceptance of this formal order in the documents that passed between the parties.

This conclusion may perhaps be questioned. The proper issue was not simply *when* the contract was concluded but whether the parties had ever expressly or impliedly agreed upon a choice of exclusive jurisdiction. There is no reason in principle why, having initially come to a contractual agreement with no choice of exclusive jurisdiction, the parties might not subsequently have come to an agreement as to an exclusive choice of jurisdiction. The evidence indicated that the plaintiffs had not repudiated the second communication from the defendant company. Why therefore should its additional provision, relating to choice of jurisdiction, not be deserving of legal recognition?

The defendant's second argument was that the place of performance, in accordance with Article 5 of the Convention, was outside the jurisdiction of the Irish Courts. This also was unsuccessful. The Chief Justice noted that the particular obligation that was the subject matter of the proceedings was payment for the goods manufactured and supplied. Payment 'fell to be performed where the creditor was, namely, in Ireland.'

In *Campbell International Trading House Ltd v Van Aart* [1992] ILRM 26, the question of jurisdiction arose in respect of the plaintiffs' proceedings against the defendant, a German national domiciled in Germany, arising from a contract whereby the parties entered into a joint venture for the marketing of Irish products within the German market-place. The defendant entered an appearance requiring delivery of a statement of claim. He raised particulars to the statement of claim, to which the plaintiff replied.

The defendant sought to have the proceedings struck out, arguing that the court had no jurisdiction to entertain the case by reason of Article 2 of the Judgments Convention, which provides that persons domiciled in a Contracting State are to be sued in the courts of that State. Morris J noted that Article 5, s. 2 qualified Article 2, by permitting a party to be sued, in matters relating to a contract, in the courts for the place of performance of the obligation in question. If this obligation was at least in part to be performed in Ireland, then the plaintiff would be entitled to sue here. A prior question, however, arose in relation to Article 18, which provides as follows:

> Apart from jurisdiction derived from other provisions of this Convention, a court of a Contracting State before whom a defendant enters an appearance shall have jurisdiction. This rule shall not apply where appearance was entered solely to contest the jurisdiction, or where another court has exclusive jurisdiction by virtue of Article 16.

Morris J noted that no machinery existed under Order 12 of the Rules of the Superior Courts for the entry of an appearance solely to contest the jurisdiction. The practice of the Central Office to accept appearances marked

'Without Prejudice' or 'Under Protest' was not recognised under these Rules. The Rules of the Superior Courts (No. 1) 1989 (SI No. 14 of 1989) recognised the existence of the procedure for entering appearances solely to contest the jurisdiction, but nowhere in the Rules of 1989 was provision made for any such limited appearances. A defendant was thus left with no option but to enter an appearance that was sanctioned by Order 12 of the Rules.

Morris J considered that the leading case of *Elefanten Shuh v Jacqmain* [1981] ECR 1671 was authority for the proposition that if the court ascertained that, from the time of the defendant's first defence, it was intended to contest the jurisdiction of the court, the defendant would have complied with the requirements of the second paragraph of Article 18. Morris J noted that the procedural steps in the various jurisdictions vary widely but in his view *Elefanten Shuh* was authority for the proposition that, providing the defendant wished to raise the issue of jurisdiction, he might do so *at any time prior to delivering his defence within the jurisdiction.*

In the instant case, no defence had been delivered. Morris J was of opinion that the delivery of a notice for particulars and the receipt of a reply did not constitute 'a defence addressed to the Court'. On the contrary, he could 'well understand circumstances in which by reason of the short form of pleadings it becomes necessary for a defendant to deliver a notice for particulars and receive replies before he can know whether he wishes to raise a jurisdiction point'.

Morris J went on to address the question whether jurisdiction was conferred on the court by Article 5.1, in that Ireland was 'the place of performance of the obligation in question' under the contract. He referred to *de Bloos v Bouyer* [1976] ECR 1497, where the Court of Justice had concluded that the obligation to be taken into account was that corresponding to the contractual right on which the plaintiff's action was based; in a case where the plaintiff asserted the right to be paid damages or sought dissolution of a contract on the grounds of the wrongful conduct of the other party, that obligation 'was still that which arose under the contract and the non-performance of which was relied upon to support such claims'.

In the instant case, the joint venture envisaged the sale and supply of Irish products into the German marketplace. In Morris J's opinion it was clear that the 'place of performance of the obligation in question', insofar as the defendant was concerned, was Germany. Accordingly he held that the proceedings should be struck out under Order 19, rule 28 of the Rules of the Superior Courts 1986. The Supreme Court in an *ex tempore* judgment, reversed Morris J's decision: [1992] ILRM 663. We will discuss the Supreme Court judgment in the 1992 Review.

Necessary and proper parties to an action In *O'Toole and GPA Group* *plc v Ireland* [1992] ILRM 18, Costello J had to consider the meaning of Order 11, rule 1(h) of the *Rules of the Superior Courts 1986*, which provides that service out of the jurisdiction of an originating summons (or notice of that summons) may be permitted by the court whenever any person out of the jurisdiction is a necessary or proper party to an action properly brought against some other person duly served within the jurisdiction. See Binchy, *op. cit.*, 157-9.

Hence the plaintiffs' plenary summons generated two completely separate matters of controversy. It was only with regard to one of these matters that the fourth named defendant, The European Organisation for the Safety of Air Navigation (Eurocontrol), objected to being joined. This involved a claim by the plaintiffs that certain provisions of the Air Navigation and Transport Act 1988 were unconstitutional.

Costello J held that Eurocontrol should not be joined in respect of this claim. Manifestly it was not a *necessary* party; nor was it a *proper* party, since it was not involved in the dispute as to the constitutionality of the statutory provisions. The fact that it might in a very indirect way have some interest in the outcome of the proceedings did not suffice to make it a proper party.

Civil and commercial matters   In *O'Toole and GPA Group plc v Ireland*, above, Costello J discussed briefly, but did not seek to determine, the question whether the proceedings involved a *civil and commercial matter* within the meaning of Article 1 of the Brussels Convention. The plaintiffs contended that they did not. Whilst not expressing a final view, Costello J went so far as to acknowledge that it would appear that there was 'considerable force' in the plaintiffs' contention. He noted that he had been referred to a decision of the Court of Justice in relation to the meaning of the term.

SOVEREIGN IMMUNITY

In *Government of Canada v Employment Appeals Tribunal* [1992] ILRM 325, the Supreme Court, reversing MacKenzie J ([1991] ELR 57), held that the proper scope of the doctrine of state immunity was that which had been set out by Lord Wilberforce in the House of Lords decision of *I Congresso* [1983] 1AC 244, at 267, to the effect that,

> in considering, under the 'restrictive' theory, whether state immunity should be granted or not, the court must consider the whole context in which the claim against the state is made, with a view to deciding whether the relevant act(s) upon which the claim is based should, in that

context, be considered as fairly within an area of activity, trading or commercial, or otherwise of a private law character, in which the state has chosen to engage, or whether the relevant act(s) should be considered as having been done outside that area, and within the sphere of governmental or sovereign activity.

In the instant case, a chauffeur of the Canadian embassy, who was not a member of the Canadian foreign service and who enjoyed no diplomatic privileges, had bought unfair dismissal proceedings before the Employment Appeals Tribunal. The Government of Canada contended that the Tribunal had no jurisdiction to entertain the claim on the ground of state immunity, which had not been waived by the state. The tribunal had rejected this submission, held that it had jurisdiction and awarded the chauffeur a sum in compensation. Mackenzie J declined to make an order quashing these fundings but the Supreme Court allowed the appeal.

After a detailed review of the development of the law on the subject, O'Flaherty J came to four conclusions. *First*, he doubted whether the doctrine of absolute sovereign immunity had ever been conclusively established in Ireland. It had not received Hanna J's support in *Zarine v Owners of SS 'Ramava'* [1942] IR 148, thought in the subsequent Supreme Court decision of *Saorstát and Continental Streamship Co. v de las Morenas* [1945] IR 291, O'Bryne J appeared to give support, *obiter* to Lord Atkin's articulation of absolute immunity in *The Christina* [1938] AC 485, at 490. *Secondly*, assuming that the absolute immunity doctrine *had* been part of our law, it had by now expired. *Thirdly*, and relatedly, the doctrine had flourished at a time when a sovereign state was concerned only with the conduct of its armed forces, foreign affairs and the operation of its currency. Today, with so many states engaged in the business of trade, direct or indirect, the rule of absolute immunity was not appropriate to such conditions. *Finally*, if the activity in question truly touched the actual business or policy of the foreign government, then immunity should still be accorded to that activity.

Applying these conclusions to the facts of the case, it was clear that the embassy's employment of a chauffeur was not a commercial contact in the ordinary sense of the word; it was a contract of service. It thus differed from a contract of repair of the heating system in an embassy, which had been characterised as a commercial contact in *Empire of Iran* (1963) 45 ILR 57. O'Flaherty J thought that:

once one approached the embassy gates one must do so on an amber light. *Prima facie* anything to do with the embassy is within the public domain of the government in question It may be that this presumption can be rebutted as happened in the *Empire of Iran* case. I believe that

the element of trust and confidentiality that is reposed in the driver of
an embassy car creates a bond with his employers that has the effect of
involving him in the employing government's public business organisation and interests.

Accordingly O'Flaherty J held that the doctrine of restrictive state
immunity applied in the case.

Hederman J was a good deal less disposed to adopt a narrow interpretation
of the immunity doctrine. He was satisfied that the chauffeur's service related
to the exercise of the ambassador's diplomatic functions. This fell within the
area of sovereign immunity envisaged and adopted by the Constitution. For
the purpose of the case it was unnecessary to express any view on the extent
to which the doctrine of sovereign immunity might have been modified or
limited in respect of commercial activities conducted or undertaken by a
foreign sovereign.

McCarthy J accepted O'Flaherty J's conclusion that the general principles
of international law had so developed as to depart radically from the absolute
State immunity doctrine to a much more restrictive view of sovereign
immunity. He rightly identified the possibility that Lord Wilberforce's
alternatives might not express the total range of possibilities:

> Is there some other category, neither commercial nor governmental, in
> which the embassy may be engaged?

In a detailed analysis of the Supreme Court's decision (14 DULJ 160
(1992)), Liz Heffernan suggests that the issue of state immunity is too
complex to be regulated by judicial pronouncement alone and that Ireland
should contemplate accession to the European Convention on State
Immunity and its Additional Protocol, as well as the Brussels Convention on
Immunity of State-owned Vessels of 1926 and its Protocol of 1934.

SUCCESSION CONVENTION

The Law Reform Commission's Report on the Hague Convention (1989) on
the Law of Succession to Estates of Deceased Persons (LRC36 – 1991) is
worthy of attention as the Hague Convention of 1989 seeks to reach a *via
media* between the traditional common law approach, involving scission as
between movable and immovable property and the unitary approach
favoured in civil law jurisdictions. Whether the compromise is, on balance,
acceptable is a matter on which Irish scholars and practitioners have yet to
make their contribution.

Under present law, as a general principle, the *lex situs* governs succession to immovables and the *lex domicilii* at the time of death determines succession to movables: see Binchy, *op. cit.*, ch. 23. These rules are subject to some fairly important qualifications, especially in relation to testate succession and powers of appointment.

It is a long-established rule that succession to movable property in the case of intestacy is determined by the *lex domicilii* of the testator at the time of death: *In bonis G.M. Deceased; F.M. v T.A.M.*, 106 ILTR 82, at 86.

It is also well established that, where a person with an interest in immovables dies intestate, the *lex situs* determines the question of descent or distribution. This is so, regardless of the domicile of the intestate person: *In bonis Gentili*, IR 9 Eq 541 (1875), *De Fogassieras v Duport*, 11 LR Ir 123 (1881) *In re Rea Deceased; Rea v Rea* [1902] 1 IR 451.

The general rule in Ireland (*In re Adams, Deceased. Bank of Ireland Trustee Co. v Adams* [1967] IR 424), and other common law jurisdictions is that the *lex domicilii* of the testator at the time of his death exclusively determines testamentary succession to his movable property, and that the *lex situs* governs testamentary succession to his immovable property. The fact that Irish assets must be administered in accordance with Irish law does not detract from this principle, since the duty of the Irish executor will be to distribute the movable property to the persons entitled under the *lex domicilii*.

The question of requisite formalities was the subject of a Hague Convention in 1961: *The Hague Convention on the Conflicts of laws relating to the Form of Testamentary Dispositions*. The philosophy of the Convention is very much in favour of upholding the formal validity of testamentary dispositions whenever it is reasonably possible to do so.

Giving effect to this Convention, Part VIII of the Succession Act 1965 provides (in s. 102(1)) that a testamentary disposition is valid as regards form if its form complies with the internal law of any of a number of possible countries, that is, the internal law:

(a) of the place where the testator made the testamentary disposition;
(b) of a nationality possessed by the testator either at the time when he made the disposition or at the time of his death;
(c) of a place in which the testator had his domicile either at the time when he made the disposition or at the time of his death;
(d) of the place in which the testator had his habitual residence either at the time when he made the disposition or at the time of his death; or
(e) so far as immovables are concerned, of the place where they are situated.

As regards matters of essential validity, legislative provisions in many countries, including Ireland, confer specific entitlements on intestacy as well as restricting the freedom of a testator to dispose of the whole of his estate as he wishes. Normally the members of his family will have the right to some specific or discretionary share in his estate. There is a wide divergence in the types of legislation in different countries.

The problem with Irish law is that there has been a dearth of cases in which the courts could have been given the opportunity to develop a sophisticated analysis of the policy considerations. What we have is a single case, with some shafts of understanding of the issues but essentially a blinkered perception of the full picture.

In *In re bonis G.M. deceased; F.M. v T.A.M*, 106 ILTR 82 (1970), a testator, domiciled in Ireland, left, among other property, a farm in England. An adopted child of the testator took proceedings under s. 117 of the *Succession Act 1965*, claiming that the testator had not provided for him as a prudent and just parent should.

Kenny J said:

> The duty is not to make adequate provision but to make proper provision in accordance with the testator's means and, in deciding whether this has been done, the court may have regard to immovable property outside the Republic of Ireland owned by the testator. The court, therefore, when deciding whether the moral duty has been fulfilled, must take all the testator's property (including immovable property outside the Republic of Ireland) into account, but if it decides that the duty has not been discharged, the provision for this child is to be made out of the estate excluding that immovable property.

After a review of the evidence, Kenny J came to the conclusion that a prudent and just parent would have given one half of the estate, excluding the immovable property in England, to the adopted son.

The implications of this case are interesting. Kenny J took into account the immovable property in determining how much the testator should have given his adopted son. Kenny J came to this conclusion without regard to the content of the legislation in England or to the conflict rules of that country. If the Irish court chooses to be blind to those considerations in other cases there is a danger that the claimant may receive undue compensation. The foreign court may award, or have already awarded, compensation in blithe disregard of the international remit of s. 117.

It seems that Kenny J's reference in the *G.M.* case to the *lex domicilii*, so far as movables are concerned, suggests that he might not have countenanced a claim brought against a testator not domiciled within the State and having no immovable property here: Cf. *In re Found, Found v Seemens* [1924]

SASR 237 (Supreme Court, Murray CJ, 1924), *In re Butchart (Deceased): Butchart v Butchart* [1932] NZLR 125 (CA, 1931) and *In re Paulin* [1950] VR 462 (Sholl J). If the testator had immovable property here but was not domiciled within the jurisdiction, it seems clear that the Irish court could make an order under s. 117, so far as the immovable property is concerned, and, on Kenny J's approach, in doing so, it would have regard to the value of the movable property elsewhere. What is not so clear is whether the Irish court could in this case go further and attempt to determine the statutory entitlements, akin to s. 117, of claimants under the *lex domicilii* so far as the movables are concerned. The inhibition which affected Kenny J against trespassing on the jurisdiction of the *lex situs*, so far as immovables are concerned, would not arise in this case. Moreover, the general rule that the essential validity of a will of movables is determined by the *lex domicilii* would appear to permit our courts to attempt to determine statutory claims arising under that law.

If this approach is favoured, the risk of overcompensation by the laws of two separate countries would obviously be reduced. But it may be considered too much to ask of an Irish court to attempt to exercise discretion in the same manner as required of courts in the country of the domicile by the *lex domicilii*: Cf. *In re Paulin* [1950] VLR 462, at 467 (Sholl J).

It may be argued that questions relating to moral duties to family members raise value judgments best resolved in the context of the culture in which they arise. This last observation brings to the surface yet again the inadequacy of a blind adherence to the *lex situs* in relation to immovables; for why should the contingent location of immovable property in a particular country result in the application of the mores of *that* country on an issue which is not its primary concern? If a German domiciled and resident in the Federal Republic of Germany buys a site in County Cork for a holiday home, Irish law should have little interest in imposing on him the mores of our Succession Act 1965, so far as the compulsory entitlements of his wife and children are concerned. The doctrine of total *renvoi* could mitigate the dangers of a 'culture clash' here. Cf. Scoles & Rheinstein, *Conflict Avoidance in Succession Planning*, 21 L & Contemp. Prob. 499, at 510-511 (1956). Under this doctrine the Irish court would apply whatever law the German courts would apply if they were dealing with the case.

It would be unfortunate if the traditional deference afforded to the *lex situs* were allowed to get in the way of basic justice to surviving family members. In the *G.M.* case, no difficulty arose, since the assets within the reach of the Irish court were capable of satisfying the claim of the testator's adopted child. But it is possible to think of cases where all the testator's roots and life experiences were in Ireland but the large part of his property at the time of his death consisted of an immovable, perhaps recently purchased in a foreign country whose domestic law had no equivalent of s. 117, and whose conflicts rules did not refer the question back to Irish law. In cases such as this, the risk of injustice would be high.

When we come to consider the 'legal right' of the surviving spouse, more difficulties arise. If Ireland is the country of the testator's domicile, and the portion of the estate consisting of immovable property is situated abroad, it would appear from the *G.M.* case that the 'legal right' would be measured against the *whole* of the estate, but that only that amount of the estate comprising movables would be available to satisfy this claim. The surviving spouse, regardless of whether the 'legal right' claim had been fully satisfied against the movable property, would appear free to proceed independently under the *lex situs* of the immovable property for such further claim as that law might support. It is hoped that the foreign court would have regard to the claim already made before the Irish court, but with the present lack of international harmony on this general question, there is no guarantee that this will be so.

The *Hague Convention on the Law of Succession to Estates of Deceased Persons* (1989), as we have mentioned, attempts an interesting compromise between the laws of common law and civil law countries. The Convention dispenses with differing rules of movable and immovable property. Instead succession is to be governed by the law of the State in which the deceased at the time of his death was habitually resident, if he was then a national of that State. If the deceased was *resident* in a State for at least five years preceding his death, and died *habitually resident* there, the law of that State will govern his succession save in exceptional circumstances, where he was at the time of his death 'manifestly more closely connected' Article 3(2) with the State of his nationality, in which case the law of that State of nationality applies. In other cases succession is governed by the law of the State of nationality of the deceased at the time of his death, unless at that time he was more closely connected with another State, in which case the law of that other State applies.

Article 5 of the Convention allows for designation by a testator of the governing law, where the designation is of the State of nationality or habitual residence of the testator at the time of designation or of death.

The Law Reform Commission, in their Report on the Convention, recommend that Ireland should incorporate the Convention into our law. The Commission consider that the principal advantage of the Convention is that it removes the problem of the *de facto* dominance of the courts of the *situs*. Moreover, the concept of domicile, so far as it affects the fate of movable property, has the disadvantages of complexity and potential arbitrariness, especially where the deceased was a minor or mentally disabled.

The Commission note that the choice of law rules set out in Article 3 are very much designed to facilitate the testator or testatrix by providing greater certainty, as well as unity, in the rules applicable to the essential validity of the will which he or she makes; these rules are thus centred on the movements and contacts of the testator or testatrix rather than his or her family. As against this, the Commission doubt that the Convention would have the effect of encouraging attempts to disinherit the surviving spouse. S. 29 of the Judicial Separation and Family Law Reform Act 1989 contains provisions, similar to those contained in s. 121 of the Succession Act 1965, enabling the court to set aside 'reviewable dispositions', *inter vivos*, intended to defeat the claim of the applicant: see the 1989 Review, 239, and the 1990 Review 309-11. The Commission consider that this is the most usual context in which the neglect of family responsibilities will be addressed.

The Commission recommend that Ireland should avail itself of the option, under Article 24, paragraph 1d, not to recognise a designation under Article 5 if:

(i) Irish law would otherwise have been the applicable law;

(ii) application of the designated law would totally or very substantially deprive the spouse or child of the deceased of an inheritance or family provision to which they would have been entitled under Irish mandatory rules; and

(iii) the spouse or child is habitually resident in or a national of Ireland.

The Commission express the view that a designation of the type envisaged here 'appears fundamentally out of harmony with our Constitution'. Accordingly, the entitlement to make a reservation is opportune and makes the Convention far more attractive to Irish legislators.

Constitutional Law

ACCESS TO COURTS

Court fees In *MacGairbhith v Attorney General* [1991] 2 IR 412, the constitutionality of court fees was raised, though not resolved. The plaintiff instituted proceedings claiming that his right of access to the courts had been infringed by the requirement that stamp duty be paid on legal documents. He also claimed that access was restricted by the failure of the State to make available a law library for lay litigants. O'Hanlon J dismissed his claim.

He stated that to resolve what he described as the 'difficult' question raised by the applicant would require detailed evidence on the intervention by the State in the work of the law courts for the purpose of raising revenue. O'Hanlon J suggested that it would be difficult to establish that all such interventions involved a breach of constitutional rights without regard to the question of whether hardship had resulted, and in the absence of actual evidence, he concluded that it was not appropriate to determine the issue. In addition, he also noted that, since it was apparent that the plaintiff had exercised his right of access to the courts on a number of occasions and there was no evidence that he had actually been prevented from exercising his right, the question of his *locus standi* to raise the issue was in doubt, and this was another reason why he considered that the resolution of the matter should be left to another time.

As to the question of a law library, O'Hanlon J noted that it was a traditional feature of court proceedings that lay litigants were afforded every opportunity by judges and court staff to exercice their right of access to the courts. This was achieved through helping such litigants understand the formal pleading requirements as well as being as helpful as possible where such litigants were presenting a case in court. However, he did not consider that the further provision by the State of a law library to lay litigants was an unenumerated right under Article 40.3 of the Constitution.

While the plaintiff's claims were thus dismissed by O'Hanlon J, he also made a number of comments on the issues raised which indicate a somewhat hostile view of the generality of court fees. He stated that court fees had risen to a level which would have appeared unthinkable some years ago, and he noted that VAT on legal fees had also been introduced. He commented:

I have no doubt that the frightening cost of litigation, made up in part by these heavy charges levied by the State, are a major deterrent to people who wish to have access to the courts established under the Constitution and may in many cases actually prevent parties from availing of rights nominally guaranteed to them under the Constitution.

As already indicated, he did not consider that the instant case was apt to consider the actual effect of these fees. However, O'Hanlon J went out of his way to refer to the decision of the United States Supreme Court in *Boddie v Connecticut*, 401 US 371 (1971), in which he noted that the Court had decreed that an apparently neutral law fixing general court fees could be deemed unconstitutional if it blocked access to people of little means. O'Hanlon J pointed out that the Court in that case stated that its decision did not involve a total ban on court fees, but only those which were not proportional to a legitimate State interest.

This reference to the *Boddie* case may prove important in future litigation. It is unfortunate, however, that O'Hanlon J was apparently not referred to the decision in *Cosgrove v Legal Aid Board* [1991] 2 IR 43 (see the 1990 Review, 144-7), in which Gannon J had taken a less expansive view of the question of impediments to access to the court. Whether the decision in *MacGairbhith* will ultimately result in a change in the arrangements for court fees, the decision adds further weight to previous extra-judicial comments expressing doubt on their constitutionality: see the 1990 Review, 441-2.

Discovery as action In *Megaleasing UK Ltd v Barrett* [1992] 1 IR 219, the Supreme Court adverted to the question whether discovery could constitute a substantive action: see the Practice and Procedure chapter, 335-6, below.

Locus standi *Chambers v An Bord Pleanála* [1992] ILRM 296; [1992] 1 IR 219 raised the issue of *locus standi* as an aspect of the right of access to the courts: see the Local Government chapter, 317-8, below.

Oaths In *Mapp v Gilhooley* [1991] ILRM 695; [1991] 2 IR 253, the Supreme Court held that the requirement that evidence be given on oath by an 8 year old child in a civil action was not an impermissible restriction on the right of access to the courts: see the discussion in the Practice and Procedure chapter, 348-9, below.

ADMINISTRATION OF JUSTICE

Definition of administration of justice The term was considered in *Goodman International v Mr Justice Hamilton* [1992] ILRM 145 (see 109-11, below) and in *Keady v Garda Commissioner* [1992] ILRM 312 (see 256-7, below, in the Garda Síochána chapter).

Independence of judiciary   Article 35.2 was considered in relation to a temporary Judge of the District Court in *Magee v Culligan* [1992] ILRM 186; [1992] 1 IR 223: see 155-8, below, in the Criminal Law chapter.

AVOIDANCE OF CONSTITUTIONAL ISSUE

The normal rule of avoiding a constitutional issue where possible was applied by the Supreme Court in *Director of Public Prosecutions v McCreesh*, Supreme Court, 7 March 1991: see 131-2, below, in the Criminal Law chapter.

CITIZENSHIP

Aliens   In *Ji Yao Lau v Minister for Justice* [1993] ILRM 64, the applicant sought an inquiry into his detention in Mountjoy Prison on foot of an order made by an Immigration Officer of the Department of Justice under the Aliens Order 1946, as amended by the Aliens Order 1975.

The respondent, a national of the People's Republic of China, had applied for refugee status. His detention under the 1946 Order, as amended, was ordered pending determination of his application. A number of issues were addressed to Hamilton P as to whether it was lawful for detention for any period pending such decision to be made. However, the President was not required to reach that issue. He held that, on the true interpretation of Article 7 of the 1946 Order, as amended, the maximum time permissible for detention was two months. Since this time had elapsed in the applicant's case, he ordered his immediate release.

DAMAGES

Conway v Irish National Teachers Organisation [1991] ILRM 497; [1991] 2 IR 305 (discussed in the Torts chapter, 448-53, below) concerned the level of damages to be awarded where a constitutional right was breached.

FAIR PROCEDURES

Much of the case law on fair procedures in 1991 is discussed in the Administrative Law chapter, 6-15, above. The issue is also discussed in

Cowzer v Kirby, High Court, 11 February 1991, in the Criminal Law chapter, 145-7, below.

LIBERTY

Prisoner's rights In *Murray and Anor v Ireland* [1991] ILRM 465 the Supreme Court examined the impact which loss of personal liberty has on a convicted prisoner's other constitutional rights. The analysis by the Court was disappointing.

The plaintiffs, wife and husband, were prisoners serving sentences of life imprisonment for murder: see *The People v Murray* [1977] IR 360. They had no children, but wished to be provided with facilities to procreate while serving their sentences. Such facilities were refused by the prison authorities, and the plaintiffs instituted proceedings claiming that the absence of such facilities amounted to a denial of their rights as a married couple to beget children. The plaintiffs were allowed to visit each other regularly but the prison authorities required that, for security reasons, these took place in the sight and hearing of prison officers. In evidence in the High Court hearing in 1985, it was stated that by the time of their possible date for release the first plaintiff (at that time 36 years of age) would be unlikely, by reason of her age, to be able to conceive a child. Costello J dismissed the plaintiffs' claim in a judgment which analysed the issues raised with his customary skill: [1985] ILRM 542; [1985] IR 532.

The plaintiffs appealed against this decision to the Supreme Court, but the appeal did not come on for hearing until January 1991. This delay (which was not explained in the judgments delivered in the Supreme Court) had had two effects, one straightforward the other quite unusual. The first was that the first plaintiff was, by the time of the Supreme Court hearing, over 40 years of age, and the plaintiffs proposed to adduce new evidence as to her medical fitness to bear children. The second effect was that, during Christmas 1990, the plaintiffs had for the first time since their initial imprisonment both been granted two and a half days temporary release (parole) from prison (an event which was, in fact, reported in the media at the time, in itself an unusual event).

The plaintiffs wished to introduce their parole to counter the security argument made by the State in the case. However, the Supreme Court (Finlay CJ, Hamilton P, McCarthy, O'Flaherty and Keane JJ) unanimously decided that neither of these events should be taken into account on the hearing of the appeal. The Court held that since no application to adduce additional evidence had been made between the time of the High Court judgment in 1985 and the hearing of the appeal in January 1991, it would not be consistent with fair procedures for the Court to admit further evidence, whether relating to the ability of the first plaintiff to bear children or to their temporary release in December 1990. Accordingly, the appeal was based on the evidence adduced in the High Court in 1985.

While the Supreme Court's recent approach to fresh evidence (1989 Review, 341) has indicated a reluctance to allow such evidence to be introduced, the judges have always indicated that a discretionary approach should be taken in this connection. Given the central importance of the security argument in the instant case, to ignore the fact of the plaintiffs' parole appears contradictory. The authorities had argued that to allow intimate contact between the plaintiffs would not be consistent with security considerations, yet by their actions the authorities had allowed the plaintiffs temporary release for over two days. It is difficult to think of a more convincing trump argument for the plaintiffs, and yet the Supreme Court concluded that they should be blind to the existence of the release.

A more striking 'absence' from the Supreme Court judgments is any sustained analysis of the jurisprudence on prisoner's rights. The judgments are strong on conclusory views but weak on analysis.

The first point raised was whether there was any significance in the fact that the plaintiffs were both prisoners. The Supreme Court was of the view that the arguments put forward by the plaintiffs applied equally where one spouse only was imprisoned. Nor did the Court consider that a distinction could be drawn between a couple with children who wished to beget more, on the one hand, and a couple who have no children, on the other. No supporting arguments were put forward to bolster these conclusions, but they appear rather strange at first sight. Assuming that the first plaintiff had not been a convicted prisoner, surely there would be a quite different case to be argued on behalf of a person who has committed no crime and where any child born to her would be born and brought up outside the prison environment. Even if security considerations could overcome the argument for allowing sexual relations with the convicted husband, surely the starting point for any constitutional argument would be wholly different from that in the instant case. On the question of a difference between a childless couple and a couple who wish to have their first child, it is perhaps more difficult to raise a constitutional objection to the Court's 'no difference' approach, but at the very least the margin of discretion which might arise for consideration would be different had the Court been minded to allow discretion into the balance.

In the end, however, the Court was not prepared to accept that there was any room for discretion in the instant case. It adopted a traditional 'hands off' approach to the whole question of the plaintiffs' (and it seems all other prisoners') constitutional rights while in prison. The Chief Justice in his leading judgment stated that an inevitable practical and legal consequence of imprisonment as a convicted person was that a great many constitutional rights arising from the married status are, for the period of imprisonment, suspended or placed in abeyance. He considered that Costello J had been correct to conclude that the right to beget children was a right which was, in general, put in abeyance for the period of imprisonment. On the question of the judgment to be exercised by the prison authorities, Finlay CJ held that the general regulation of prison conditions was a matter for the executive, subject to supervision by the courts for constitutional validity and to ensure that the executive did not operate its power in a capricious, arbitrary or unjust way.

In language reminiscent of the approach taken in many other areas of public law in recent years (see the 1990 Review, 19-20) he stated that the courts would not intervene merely because they would have reached a different conclusion on the appropriateness of particular restrictions. Having regard to the evidence as to the difficulties associated with giving the plaintiffs, and others in a like situation, the facilities for procreation claimed, the Chief Justice concluded that the trial judge had applied the correct approach in dismissing the plaintiffs' claim.

The extent of the deference to the executive in the instant case was best illustrated by the fact that the Chief Justice stated that the courts would not intervene in relation to whether the executive ought to exercise its power to grant temporary release to prisoners in the position of the plaintiffs in the instant case. Given that the authorities had by the time the judgments were delivered (February 1991) already exercised their discretionary powers to *grant* temporary release, this comment by Finlay CJ appears to put the notion of 'blind justice' in a strange light.

It is a great pity that the conclusion reached by the Supreme Court should have been arrived at without any analysis of the difficult issues posed. This is in stark contrast with the sophisticated analysis of Costello J in the High Court where, of course, the trial judge reached the same conclusion. The stark deference to executive discretion and the unwillingness to consider the new evidence in the case hardly does justice to the arguments undoubtedly addressed to the Court. One might have expected that, since the Court was addressing the effect of imprisonment on the convicted person's rights, it would first of all have analysed the text of Article 40.4 of the Constitution. This could have led on to a discussion, which Costello J engaged in in his High Court judgment, as between the *power* of the authorities to imprison and the remaining *rights* which a prisoner retained. There is no discussion in the Supreme Court of the difference between 'power' and 'right' in this context. This is so despite the fact that the distinction is fundamental to an analysis of the relationship between the citizen and the State, in other words, an issue which is fundamental to the Constitution itself. At first sight, perhaps, the instant case would not appear to be fertile ground for such discussion, but Costello J certainly found it so.

This criticism of the Supreme Court decision is not simply about the length of the judgments or of the level of sophistication, however. The approach taken by the Supreme Court (and ultimately of course by Costello J also) is just one approach to such prison cases, and it is particularly disappointing that the Supreme Court did not even sketch out the alternative analysis which places a stronger emphasis on rights. Thus, for example, the judgment of Barrington J in *The State (Richardson) v Governor of Mountjoy Prison* [1980] ILRM 34 was not even referred to, let alone analysed. In that case, the emphasis on rights had led the judge to conclude that the courts should intervene in the prison regime where the rights of bodily integrity and of privacy were being interfered with. Of course, the subsequent retreat from *Richardson* by the Chief Justice (then President of the High Court) in *Cahill v Governor of Curragh Military Detention Barracks* [1980] ILRM 191 might explain why in *Murray* there was a distinct absence of any rights analysis, but this hardly excuses the failure of the Supreme Court to engage the question at all.

While the message of the *Murray* case is very clear, namely that the Irish courts are unlikely to look favourably on prisoners' rights cases, the reasoning on which this is based can only be found (if at all) in the judgment of Costello J.

LIVELIHOOD

The right to earn a livelihood was considered by the High Court in *Browne v Attorney General* [1991] 2 IR 58: see 359-60, below, in the Revenue Law chapter. The right was also considered in two Supreme Court decisions, which are discussed here.

Casual trading   In *Hand and Ors v Dublin Corporation* [1991] ILRM 556; [1991] 1 IR 409, the Supreme Court rejected a constitutional challenge to certain aspects of the Casual Trading Act 1980.

The plaintiffs were traders in Dublin who had been in dispute for some years with Dublin Corporation as to the operation of the 1980 Act. In the course of the dispute the plaintiffs had been convicted of offences under the Act on two or more occasions. The plaintiffs had, however, reached the position that Dublin Corporation was prepared to provide them with permits to trade under the 1980 Act. However, to be entitled to receive such permits, the plaintiffs required a licence from the Minister for the Environment and the Minister had refused such licence in accordance with the mandatory terms of s. 4(6) of the 1980 Act. S. 4(6) prohibits the granting of a licence to a person who has been convicted of two or more offences if the latest conviction occurred less than five years before and where 'two, at least, of the convicitons occurred after the expiration of the last period (if any) of disqualification by virtue of this subsection. . . .' The plaintiffs argued in the High Court that s. 4(6) was inoperable as it was impossible to construe the intention of the Oireachtas. Alternatively, it was argued that the 1980 Act was invalid as being in breach of their right to earn a livelihood since the penalty of loss of licence was disproportionate to the seriousness of the offences involved.

In the High Court, Barron J dismissed the plaintiffs' claims: [1989] IR 26 (see the 1988 Review, 281-3). The plaintiffs unsuccessfully appealed on the constitutional issue to the Supreme Court (Finlay CJ, Griffin, Hederman, McCarthy and O'Flaherty JJ).

The case centred on the status of the right to earn a livelihood. The Court accepted the views of Costello J in *Attorney General v Paperlink Ltd* [1984] ILRM 373 that the right to earn a livelihood under Article 40.3 was not an unqualified right and that it could be subjected to legitimate legal constraints. Applying this to the instant case, the Court considered that the 1980 Act struck a balance between the legitimate rights and interests of those who might be affected by it. It held that it was open to the Oireachtas to provide for strict control and regulation of casual trading having regard to the exigencies of the common good. Reflecting a deference which has become a staple of recent decisions (see *Murray v Ireland* [1991] ILRM 465, above) the Court concluded that since these were matters which were peculiarly within the competence of the Oireachtas, the courts would not interfere with the decision made by the Oireachtas unless injustice was thereby done to traders.

Turning finally to whether injustice had in fact been done, the Court held that since s. 4 of the 1980 Act made perfectly clear the circumstances in which a licence may be lost, the Act provided for what amounted to a statutory disqualification for obtaining a licence for the period fixed by s. 4(6), and this did not constitute an unjust or unreasonable attack on the plaintiffs' rights. The Court referred in this context to *Conroy v Attorney General* [1965] IR 411, the decision upholding the validity of driver disqualification under the Road Traffic Act 1961.

Finally, the Court refused to accept that the principle of proportionality was relevant to the claim put forward by the plaintiffs. This point is of some relevance in the context of the second case on the right to a livelihood considered by the Court in 1991, *Cox v Ireland*, Supreme Court, 11 July 1991, to which we now turn. We will return to discuss the *Hand* case after discussing *Cox*.

Special Criminal Court convictions *Cox v Ireland*, Supreme Court, 11 July 1991, was a successful challenge to the constitutional validity of s. 34 of the Offences against the State Act 1939. As we mentioned in the 1990 Review, 173, doubts had been expressed judicially and extra-judicially about the validity of s. 34: see Walsh J in *The People v Quilligan* [1987] ILRM 606; [1986] IR 495 and Hogan and Walker, *Political Violence and the Law in Ireland* (1989), 265-6.

The plaintiff, a qualified vocational teacher, had pleaded guilty in the Special Criminal Court to certain firearms offences and was sentenced to two years' imprisonment. While serving his term of imprisonment, his teaching position was filled on a temporary basis. On his release he was informed that, by virtue of s. 34 of the 1939 Act, his teaching position had been forfeited and that he was disqualified from holding the position for a period of seven years. The plaintiff instituted proceedings claiming that s. 34 of the 1939 Act was in breach of the Constitution. In the High Court Barr J granted the declaration sought, and this decision was upheld by the Supreme Court (Finlay CJ, Hederman, McCarthy, O'Flaherty and Egan JJ).

Like Barr J, the Supreme Court analysed the case primarily in the context of Article 40.3. The Court acknowledged that s. 34 of the 1939 Act constituted an attack and major inroad on the unenumerated right of the person involved to earn a living as well as certain property rights of that person protected by the Constitution, such as the right to a pension or the right to the advantages of a subsisting contract of employment.

The central issue, however, was whether such inroad and attack constituted an 'unjust attack' on such rights within the meaning of Article 40.3. On this, the Court noted that the State was entitled, for the protection of public peace and order and to maintain its own stability, to provide by law for far-reaching penalties to deter major crimes threatening the State, and to ensure that persons who commit such crimes are not involved in carrying out the functions of State. However, it held that any such laws must also protect the constitutional rights of the citizen. It was on this aspect that s. 34 failed to meet constitutional requirements.

S. 34 of the 1939 Act was mandatory in terms and forfeiture followed a conviction in the Special Criminal Court without any reference to whether the scheduled offence in question involved an attack on the maintenance of public peace and order, such as conviction in the Special Criminal Court for possession of a sporting gun without a licence. Thus, as had already been noted by Hogan and Walker, supra, since the ultimate factor triggering s. 34 was the venue of the trial, the section failed 'as far as practicable' to protect the constitutional rights of the citizen within Article 40.3. The Supreme Court thus held in *Cox* that s. 34 was impermissibly wide and indiscriminate and not warranted by the objectives it was sought to secure; and it concluded that the power of the government under s. 34 to remit in whole or part the effects of a forfeiture did not save s. 34 from its constitutional invalidity.

The description of s. 34 as impermissibly wide and indiscriminate and not warranted by the objectives it sought to secure would appear to indicate that some principle of proportionality was being applied by the Supreme Court. It is unfortunate that only a few months previously in *Hand v Dublin Corporation*, supra, the Court had rejected the proportionality principle in the context of another case based on the right to earn a livelihood. It is appalling to think that, if the proportionality argument had been presented as one relating to the impermissible breadth of s. 3 of the Casual Trading Act 1980 (which was at issue in *Hand*), it might have been more favourably viewed by the Court. In *Hand* the Court would certainly appear to have been keen to steer away from the concept of proportionality, perhaps because (though this is somewhat speculative) proportionality was seen as a concept more appropriate to general judicial review and not constitutional judicial review.

The reality, of course, is that the proportionality principle is surely no more than the application of one aspect of the liberal rule of law, namely that laws be clear in scope and be no wider than necessary. It would also appear to be similar to the general constitutional test put forward in *East Donegal Co-Op Ltd v Attorney General* [1970] IR 317, a test which has stood the test of time. Indeed many constitutional cases can be reduced to the question whether a particular legislative provision can be justified as being proportional to its purpose when viewed in the light of a constitutional interest. This is inevitable in a constitutional text where few provisions are stated in absolute terms. No doubt, proportionality or its associates will not be relevant in all constitutional cases. But the differing approaches in *Hand* and *Cox* suggest that the use of one word rather than another, similar, word may cost a litigant a full analysis of their constitutional argument. It may thus be time for the courts to attempt an overhaul of some of the most common tests for constitutional validity so that an argument may not be lost in a superfluity of terms.

For further comment on the case, including a consideration of the quality of the judgments delivered in the Supreme Court, see Humphreys (1991) 13 DULJ 118.

LOCUS STANDI

Chambers v An Bord Pleanála [1992] ILRM 296; [1992] 1 IR 134 raised the issue of *locus standi* as an aspect of the right of access to the courts: see the Local Government chapter, 317-8, below.

PRESIDENT

Presidential establishment   The Presidential Establishment (Amendment) Act 1991 arises out of the election of President Mary Robinson in December 1990. During the election campaign, it was accepted that the non-salary emoluments and expenses of the Presidential Establishment, which had not been raised since 1973, were too low. The 1991 Act provides for an increase in such emoluments and expenses to £100,000 per annum, effective from the President's election. S. 2 of the Act also provides that this sum may be increased (not decreased) by Order of the government. Thus, no amending legislation will be required in future.

The second element of the 1991 Act was to make provision for the payment of a pension to the widow 'or widower' of a President. The Presidential Establishment Act 1938 had provided for a pension to a widow only. The pension lapses on the re-marriage of the widow or widower.

In his Annotation to the 1991 Act, *Irish Current Law Statutes Annotated*, Gerard Hogan queries the constitutional validity of raising the President's emoluments and expenses by Order and also the lapsing of the pension on remarriage.

Presidential speeches   The issue of the extent of the government's power to limit the contents of the President's speeches was discussed by Duffy, *Irish Times*, 22 June 1991.

PROPERTY

The issue of compensation for interference with property rights was adverted to in *Rooney v Minister for Agriculture and Food* [1991] 2 IR 539: see 18-19, above, in the Administrative Law chapter.

RETROSPECTIVE CRIMINAL LAWS

The provisions of Article 15.5 which prohibit legislation creating retrospective criminal acts was considered in *Magee v Culligan* [1992] ILRM 186; [1992] 1 IR 223: see the Criminal Law chapter, 155-8, below.

SEPARATION OF POWERS

Criminal trial   The 1991 decision of the Supreme Court in *The People v Gallagher* [1991] ILRM 339, *sub nom Application of Gallagher* [1991] 1 IR 31, concerning the respective roles of the judicial and executive branches in 'guilty but insane' cases, is discussed in the 1990 Review, 164-6.

Tribunal of inquiry *Goodman International and Goodman v Mr Justice Hamilton and Ors* [1992] ILRM 145 involved an unsuccessful challenge to the constitutional validity of a Tribunal of Inquiry invested with the powers of the Tribunals of Inquiry (Evidence) Acts 1921 and 1979.

The first respondent, who was also President of the High Court, had been appointed the sole member of a Tribunal of Inquiry into the Beef Industry. The appointment was on foot of an order of the Minister for Agriculture of 31 May 1991 establishing the Tribunal of Inquiry after resolutions had been passed by the Houses of Oireachtas that such Tribunal be established. The effect of the resolutions was that the Tribunal was vested with the statutory powers conferred by the Tribunals of Inquiry (Evidence) Acts 1921 and 1979. The Tribunal was empowered to investigate certain allegations made in the Oireachtas and on an ITV 'World in Action' documentary concerning alleged fraud and malpractice in the beef industry in Ireland. These allegations involved references to the activities of the first applicant, Goodman International (a company), and the second applicant, Mr Goodman who was the chief executive of Goodman International.

The Tribunal of Inquiry prepared a document headed 'Statement of Allegations' which was read out at the first sitting of the Tribunal, and which received widespread publicity in the media. The applicants objected to the form the Inquiry was taking and they then brought a constitutional action claiming that the Tribunal could not validly inquire into allegations which were the subject matter of current civil proceedings, or of criminal proceedings which had either been heard or which might be heard in the future. The applicants also claimed relief in relation to the rules of evidence to be employed by the Tribunal. Costello J dismissed the claim and, in an expedited appeal, the Supreme Court (Finlay CJ, Hederman, McCarthy, O'Flaherty and Egan JJ) unanimously affirmed this decision.

In his judgment, Costello J first deal with the question of the presumption of constitutionality. He held that, in carrying out its functions as defined in the order establishing it, and having regard to the resolutions of the Oireachtas, the Tribunal was entitled to assume that the Oireachtas had acted constitutionally. This view was upheld by the Supreme Court on appeal which adopted *mutatis mutandis* the approach taken by the Court in *East Donegal Co-Op Ltd v Attorney General* [1970] IR 317. The Court held that since the presumption derived from the respect of one branch of government for another, it was appropriate that it apply to the resolution made by both Houses of the Oireachtas in the instant case.

Turning to the substantive issues raised, both Costello J and the Supreme Court rejected the argument that the Tribunal would be engaged in the administration of justice, which is of course reserved exclusively for the courts by Article 34.1. Costello J quoted the tests as to what constitutes the administration of justice set out in *McDonald v Bord na gCon* [1965] IR 217 and *Kennedy v Hearne* [1988] ILRM 531; [1988] IR 481 (see the 1988 Review, 355-6). Applying these, he held that although the Tribunal would express an opinion on the matters referred to it, such opinion was of no legal effect, and the Tribunal would determine no legal rights and impose no legal obligations, its conclusions being for the guidance of the legislature and the executive. Thus, he concluded that the Tribunal could not be regarded as being concerned in the administration of justice within the meaning of Article 34.1, and its establishment did not breach the principle of separation of powers. A similar view was taken by the Supreme Court, where it was noted that while the Tribunal was engaged in a controversy as to the existence of legal rights or the violation of the law, it would not make legally binding determinations but would report its findings of fact to the legislature *in vacuo*. Like Costello J, the Supreme Court approved dicta of the High Court of Australia to this effect in *Victoria v Australia Building Contractors and Building Labourers Federation* (1981-82) 152 CLR 26.

In addition, the Supreme Court held that the added powers conferred on the Tribunal by s. 6 of the Tribunals of Inquiry (Evidence) (Amendment) Act 1979 allowed it to operate more effectively, but did not, in the view of the Supreme Court, go over the line into the administration of justice. The Supreme Court also held that the proceedings of the Tribunal had none of the ingredients of a criminal trial within the meaning of Article 38 of the Constitution, applying the approach taken in *Deaton v Attorney General* [1963] IR 170 and *The State (Murray) v McRann* [1979] IR 133 in this context.

Costello J went on to deal with the impact of the Tribunal on civil and criminal proceedings. He stated that the establishment of a Tribunal of Inquiry did not in any way inhibit the judicial power from dealing with any civil dispute which may be pending, so that no interference with the judicial domain was involved and the same considerations applied to matters which might in the future become the subject of civil proceedings. He acknowledged that the Tribunal might in practice affect the due course of a criminal trial which might later arise from the matters under its consideration, but he concluded that this could be overcome by the observance of fair procedures. Thus, the Tribunal was not prohibited from inquiring into matters which might in the future be the subject matter of criminal proceedings; nor was the Tribunal precluded from inquiring into the circumstances surrounding past criminal prosecutions, provided it did not purport to re-open such prosecutions. In the Supreme Court, the approach taken was that any potential impact on civil or criminal trials would not affect the validity of the resolutions establishing the Tribunal, and that any actual effects would be dealt with if and when they arose by way of judicial review proceedings for prohibition if that was the appropriate remedy.

The plaintiffs also argued that since the Tribunal was established to inquire into a matter of public interest it was inappropriate to investigate what might, essentially, be disputes between private parties. Costello J held that where, as in the instant case, there was no challenge to the opinion expressed in the resolutions of the Houses of the Oireachtas that it was in the public interest to inquire into the allegations concerned here, the Tribunal was not precluded from inquiring into disputes between private parties. He referred to the decision of the United States Supreme Court in *Watkins v United States*, 354 US 178 (1956) in this context. This issue would not seem to have been relitigated in the Supreme Court.

Finally, on the procedures to be observed by the Tribunal, Costello J and the Supreme Court rejected the suggestion that the Tribunal was required to observe the rules of evidence. However, it was accepted that the Tribunal must act judicially and thus was required to observe the requirements of fair procedures, something which the Tribunal had already indicated. On this, Costello J considered that since it must observe fair procedures it would be required to hear parties affected by the admission of hearsay, as it had also indicated it would do in the instant case. Nor did he consider that the Tribunal was required to hear evidence in advance of testimony being given at a public hearing of the Tribunal, although the Tribunal indicated that in most instances it would attempt to obtain statements in advance from witnesses.

SUPREME COURT JURISDICTION

The limits on the Supreme Court's appellate jurisdiction under Article 34.4.3 were discussed in *Minister for Justice (Clarke) v Wang Zhu Jie* [1991] ILRM 823: see the Practice and Procedure chapter, 350-1, below.

TRIAL OF OFFENCES

Role of District Court The question whether the District Court should address constitutional issues was discussed by Denham J in *Coughlan v Patwell* [1992] ILRM 808: see the Criminal Law chapter, 147, below.

Summary trial The constitutional aspect of summary trial was addressed in *Cowzer v Kirby*, High Court, 11 February 1991: see the Criminal Law chapter, 145-7, below.

Contract Law

OFFER AND ACCEPTANCE

In *Boyle v Lee* [1992] ILRM 65, which we consider below, 124-7, in relation to the Statute of Frauds, the Supreme Court divided on the question whether the parties had entered into a complete and binding oral agreement for the sale of a house. The parties had failed to come to any agreement as to the amount of the deposit to be paid by the purchaser, the time at which it was to be paid or the terms under which it was to be held. No closing date had been prescribed; nor had the nature and terms of the tenancies in flats contained in the premises been precisely identified. The majority, reversing Barrington J, held that no agreement had been made. In the view of Finlay CJ (Hederman J concurring) the amount of a deposit to be made, even if the purchaser was willing to make a deposit of the appropriate or usual amount, was 'too important a part of a contract for the sale of land in the large sum of £90,000 to be omitted from a concluded and complete oral agreement unless the parties in such an agreement had agreed that no deposit would be paid.' Here, although the parties had agreed that there had to be a deposit, they had not agreed on its amount and thus no concluded agreement had been arrived at.

O'Flaherty J, concurring, stressed the failure of the parties to identify the nature and terms of the tenancies; it was easy for the plaintiff to say at trial that he had been prepared to take the property subject to the tenancies, whatever their nature, but one of his answers suggested that he might have had to engage in litigation because of what he felt was a misrepresentation in relation ot the length of a particular tenancy. Moreover, no closing date had been agreed.

Egan J, dissenting, saw no problem with the tenancies: as was 'abundantly clear on the evidence' that the plaintiff had agreed to accept them as they stood. As to the closing date, it had long been established that, where no time for performance was agreed, the law implied an undertaking by each party to perform his part of the contract within a reasonable time. The parties had agreed that the closing date was to be 'as speedily as the legal formalities have been completed'. These words should be interpreted as importing the reasonableness test rather than being so uncertain in their meaning as to negative the existence of an oral agreement. Nor did the absence of specific agreement in relation to the payment or amount of the deposit have this effect.

While it was *usual* to have a deposit in the case of sales of land, it was *not essential in law* to do so. The trial judge's finding that the plaintiff was at all times prepared to pay even a substantial deposit, had it been accepted from him, made it unrealistic for the Court to hold that the failure to pinpoint a specific sum rendered the agreement incomplete.

BREACH OF CONTRACT

In *Varios Fabriken BV v Horgan (t/a Irish Welding Co.)*, High Court, 19 April 1991, an Irish sole agent of a Dutch company, who was appointed in 1972, found in 1981 that the company's products were coming into the country other than through the company. In spite of complaints, the position did not improve; the only change was that the products started coming in to rival distributors in unmarked boxes. There was a price war, which affected the sole agent's turnover. Matters continued for a further five years, at which time the sole agent failed to pay for products sent to him by the company. The company sued for their price; the sole agent counter-claimed for breach of contract.

The quality of the pleadings and the presentation of the case did not impress Barron J. He came to the conclusion that the company had knowingly permitted the practice whereby its products reached other Irish distributors. This was a breach of contract. The sole agent had acquiesced in the breach since he had taken no steps to terminate the agency. He was not, however, *obliged* to treat the company's actions as a repudiation of the contract; to have done so would only have increased his loss.

Barron J adjourned the case to give the sole agent the opportunity to call further evidence on the issue of damages, provided satisfactory particulars were furnished to the company in advance.

CONTRACTUAL TERMS

Implied terms *Sun Fat Chan v Osseous Ltd*, Supreme Court, 30 July 1991 involves a less than impressive disposition of the interrelationship between implied contractual terms and the estoppel doctrine. The plaintiff had agreed to buy a site from the defendant and had paid a deposit. The contract provided that the plaintiff should apply for planning permission to build a house on the site and should pursue the application with all due diligence. If permission was not obtained within six months, either party might rescind the contract, with a refund of the deposit to the plaintiff.

As matters transpired, planning permission was *not* obtained within the six month period. McCarthy J's judgment notes that '[n]either party took any positive action in respect of the contract; the vendor encouraged the purchaser to proceed with an application which succeeded' but which was overturned on appeal. Subsequently the defendant on one week's notice purported to rescind the contract.

The plaintiff's claim for a declaration that the contract was valid and subsisting was dismissed by Blayney J on the application of the defendant, on the basis that the claim could not succeed. The Supreme Court affirmed. On appeal, the plaintiff argued that 'a form of estoppel' arose on the basis that, after the six month period had long passed, far from rescinding the contract, the defendant had encouraged the plaintiff's efforts to obtain planning permission. In view of the fact that the plaintiff had, albeit temporarily, been successful in this regard, he should be given another chance to pursue the application by renewing it in a form that would be acceptable not merely to the planning authority but also to the Appeal Board.

McCarthy J observed that the plaintiff's claim 'to be given time, so to speak' was 'based on an argument of implied terms of the contract'. As he understood the law to imply a term in a written contract, in its simple form, it required the conclusion that, if the parties had thought of it, they would have incorporated such a term:

> Here it requires the concession that if the parties [at the time of the making of the contract] had considered that approximately eighteen months after the date of the signing of the contract planning permission would have been refused, they, and, in particular, the vendor, would have agreed that a further unspecified time would have been made available to the purchaser to secure final planning approval; all in the light of the contract which provided that the deposit would be returnable if planning approval were not obtained. In my view such a proposition is unacceptable.

With respect, the analysis and outcome can be criticised. McCarthy J was doubtless correct in his argument that the *Moorcock* principle gave little support to the plaintiff's case. But it would be quite misconceived to conflate an estoppel-based argument with the implied term doctrine. In the large majority of cases where an estoppel-based argument applies, the circumstances would either be directly antithetical or entirely irrelevant to a case based on an implied term.

It is clear that the plaintiff's case was thin enough. But plenty of these cases have been found on close examination to have sufficient merit to succeed. Rather than become fixated with the implied term doctrine, the Supreme Court should have addressed in detail the plaintiff's possibility of success under the estoppel principle. The fact that McCarthy J did not even attempt to identify the category of estoppel on which the claim was based suggests that the plaintiff may have concentrated his guns in the contractual field. It is unfortunate that we have no judicial consideration of the extent to which conduct by one party antithetical to the terms of a contract can operate to modify or restrict the operation of contradictory contractual terms. It would have availed the defendant nothing in *High Trees* to have invoked either the express or implied terms of the contract.

Reference to the equitable estoppel doctrine raises the interesting question in relation to *Sun Fat Chan v Osseous Ltd* as to which party was the 'real' defendant. If we accept that the doctrine is a shield and not a sword and may be invoked only by *defendants*, does this mean that the plaintiff in the instant case was automatically debarred from invoking *High Trees*? Arguably not. The plaintiff was (on appeal) looking for a *declaration* as his rights. Whilst a declaration can have a remedial dimension, it should surely be categorised jurisprudentially in neutral terms: a declaration may be invoked by a prospective defendant in hypothetically or actually forthcoming judicial proceedings just as much as by a prospective plaintiff. In the instant case the party seeking the declaration was the one *against whom* putative legal rights had been asserted. If not a victim, he was on the receiving end of ostensibly legally-sanctioned conduct. It was an accident of time and legal strategy that he sought a declaration after rather than before the defendant invoked its entitlement to rescind.

Morris J's decision in *Aga Khan v Firestone* [1992] ILRM 31, though largely involving the resolution of issues of fact, contains some interesting points of law. The plaintiff sought specific performance of an alleged contract for the purchase of the defendants' stud farm, bloodstock and shares in a bloodstock sales company for over fourteen million dollars. The defendants denied that the parties had made a completed contract and argued that, even if they had, there was no sufficient note or memorandum to satisfy the Statute of Frauds (Ir.) Act 1695. The essence of the defendants' case was that the negotiations had taken place on the basis that a third party, Mr Akazawa, had a first refusal. In separate proceedings, Mr Akazawa sought specific performance of a contract to purchase the stud farm in the exercise of his right to first refusal.

After a detailed review of the evidence, Morris J concluded that there was a completed verbal contract between the defendants and the Aga Khan. As to the Statute of Frauds, he expressed complete agreement with Keane J's approach in *Mulhall v Haren* [1981] IR364 which, in his view, had 'at least the tacit approval' of the Supreme Court, as a result of comments made in *McCarthy v O'Neill* [1981] ILRM 443. (This subject is analysed in more detail below, 124-7).

Morris J was satisfied that the language of the letter alleged to constitute the note or memorandum recognised the existence of the prior verbal contract and thus satisfied the Statute. Expressions such as 'confirm', 'terms' and 'the transaction' supported that conclusion; their impact outweighed that of other terms suggestive of a more tentative meeting of minds.

Morris J also rejected the argument by the defendants that the document was defective because it did not contain all the essential terms, such as provisions dealing with the need to obtain permission under the Mergers, Takeovers and Monopolies (Control) Act 1978 and the consent under s. 45 of the Land Act 1965. He accepted the evidence of an experienced conveyancing solicitor that the fundamental terms of the contract existed; he also accepted the solicitor's opinion that Land Act consent and ministerial permission would be forthcoming. No doubt such evidence was helpful so far as it threw light on conveyancing *practice;* it should not be overlooked, nevertheless, that the question whether a particular document contains all the essential provisions of the contract is one in the legal order which only the court can determine.

Morris J rejected the defendants' argument that the contract contained an *implied* term that the transaction would be carried through by means of formal contract to be executed by the parties. He noted that Bowen LJ in the *Moorcock* (1889) 14 PD 64 had expressed the principle of implied terms as having 'the object of giving the transaction such efficacy as both parties must have intended that at all events it should have'. In the present case, to imply the term suggested by the defendants would 'destroy the contract and, far from giving efficacy to it, would in effect prevent its operation'. Morris J was satisfied that the *Moorcock* principle applied only where through mischance the implied term had been omitted and was necessary in order to give the contract efficacy and to prevent its failure. It could not in his view be logical to ask the court to imply into a contract a term so as to give it business efficacy when it would have the contrary effect.

One may express a doubt as to whether there is any clear legal principle preventing a court, in appropriate circumstances, from holding that there was an implied term where the effect of doing so is to render the contract unenforceable in the circumstances of the case. The *Moorcock* principle strives to give business efficacy to agreements, it is true; but this is not its sole function. As PS Atiyah points out (*An Introduction to the Law of Contract* (4th ed., 1989), p. 225), '. . . the principle is that the court can only read a term into the contract if it is essential to give 'business efficacy' to the agreement, *or if the matter is so obvious that it goes without saying'* (emphasis added). This latter function has been recognised in several cases, most notably in *Shirlaw v Southern Foundries (1926) Ltd* [1939] 2 KB 206.

Morris J also rejected the defendants' argument that the note or memorandum reflected two separate contracts, one for the lands and bloodstock, the other for the defendants' shares in the bloodstock company; the defendants had contended that the document was defective in failing to allocate the part of the total consideration attributable to each contract. Morris J considered that the defendants had been divesting themselves of their assets in Ireland as they had lost interest in their Irish enterprise. The shares were no more than one element in the sale. The need for a separate valuation for the shares was attributable to the fact that there was a separate closing date for their disposition. This did not take away from the fact that the parties had made an 'overall contract' governing the sale of the land, bloodstock and shares.

Turning to Mr Akazaw's claim for specific performance of an earlier contract between him and the defendants, Morris J, after a detailed review of the evidence, came to the conclusion that the document of first refusal on which he sought to rely was unsupported by any consideration and was a voluntary document given in the course of cementing business relationships. So far as this matter impinged on the Aga Khan's claim, Morris J held that, even if the right of refusal had contractual status, if would not have constituted an interest in land such as would affect the defendant's capacity to enter into a contract for the sale of the stud farm to a third party. English authority supported that holding: *Manchester Ship Canal Co. v Manchester Racecourse Co.*, [1901] 2 Ch 37, *Murray v Two Strokes Ltd* [1973] 3 All ER 357.

Contracts for the supply of services   In *Irish Telephone Rentals Ltd v Irish Civil Service Building Society Ltd* [1991] ILRM 880, Costello J addressed important issues relating to the terms of a contract. The plaintiff company had entered into contracts for the hire of telephone installations and an internal paying system with the defendant. In 1988 the defendant terminated these contracts, claiming that the defects in both systems justified it in doing so. The plaintiff sued for damages.

As regards the telephone installations, the relevant contract provided that the rent was to be paid 'for the hire of the installation and for maintenance of same in good working order'. The evidence established to Costello J's satisfaction that the plaintiff was in breach of this express term. Incoming callers had experienced very long delays in having their calls answered; calls transferred internally were subject to being cut off and reverting to the switch; there was not a sufficient number of 'hold-buttons' on the operators' consoles.

These difficulties also amounted, in Costello J's view, to a breach of s. 39 of the Sale of Goods and Supply of Services Act 1980. That section provides that, where goods are supplied under a contract for the supply of a service, there is an implied term that they will be of merchantable quality.

Goods are of merchantable quality if they are fit for the purpose for which
goods of that kind are commonly bought and as durable as it is reasonable
to expect. Durability was not in issue in the instant case; but the goods which
the plaintiff supplied were not fit for the purpose of providing a reasonably
efficient telephone system.

Costello J applied the test for entitlement to repudiate which Diplock LJ
had set out in *Hong Kong Fir Shipping Co. Ltd v Kawasaki Kisen Kaisha
Ltd* [1962] 1 QB 26, at 65-66:

> The test whether an event has this effect or not has been stated in a
> number of metaphors all of which I think amount to the same thing:
> does the occurrence of the event deprive the party who has further
> undertakings still to perform of substantially the whole benefit which it
> was the intention of the parties as expressed in the contract that he should
> obtain as the consideration for performing those undertakings?

In Costello J's view, there could be only one answer to this question. The
'event' that had occurred was the development of a situation in which the
installation hired by the defendant had significantly failed to fulfil its
purpose. This had deprived the defendant of the whole of the benefit which
it had been intended the defendant would obtain from the hiring agreement.

Costello J then turned to the internal paging system. He considered that
the difficulties the defendant had experienced with it could have been
resolved if the plaintiff had been given the opportunity to do so. Even if a
breach of contract had been established it was not one that would have
entitled the defendant to repudiate the contract.

The contract included a clause that, if the hirer repudiated the contract and
the company accepted this repudiation so as to terminate the contract, the
company might remove its installation and the hirer would be obliged to pay
to the company all payments then accrued plus a sum equal to the present
value on a 5% basis of the remaining rentals that would have been payable
under the contract less an allowance of 25% to cover the estimated cost of
maintenance and value of recovered material. The clause went on to provide
that these sums were payable as liquidated damages on an agreed estimate
of the loss that the plaintiff company would suffer.

Costello J held that this clause amounted to a penalty rather than a genuine
pre-estimate of damages. He accepted the test prescribed by Lord Dunedin
in *Dunlop Pneumatic Tyre Co. Ltd v New Garage and Motor Co. Ltd* [1915]
AC 70, at 87:

> It will be held to be a penalty if the sum stipulated for is extravagant in
> comparison with the greatest loss that could conceivably be proved to
> have followed from the breach.

Costello J had a number of reasons for reaching his conclusion. The evidence had established that the 5% figure had excluded the wages of the maintenance staff. The clause made no allowance for other deductions, such as finance charges, administrative costs and engineering costs. Part of the 25% deduction was based on an estimate of the value of the materials obtained at the date of premature termination. This was based on the assumption that this value would be 20% of the discounted gross rents. This, in Costello J's view, was an entirely arbitrary figure and could not be regarded as a genuine pre-estimate of the value of the recovered installations. The effect of operating the formula prescribed by the clause would be to yield a sum equal to 71.25% of the gross rent, less 5% for accelerated payment. This was 'quite an enormous net profit'. The defendant had discharged the onus of showing that the clause was a penalty. The plaintiff's damages were thus awarded on the basis of the court's estimate of lost profits, appropriately discounted for accelerated payment.

Terms relating to interest on bank loans *Trustee Savings Bank Dublin v Maughan*, High Court, 8 October 1991 is an important case on the question of how interest may be charged on bank loans. The defendant obtained an overdraft facility on a current account with the plaintiff bank for £5,000 in August 1983. This was extended by £2,000 the following month. The loan was unpaid and the bank sought over £32,000 in its regard by claiming compound interest annually plus a default rate of interest of 6% over its normal rates for overdrawn current accounts.

The defendant, when applying for the £5,000 facility, had signed an application form which stated:

I hereby apply to open a current account in the Trustee Savings Bank Dublin subject to the rules and regulations of the bank. I declare that the account will not be operated either wholly or partly as a business account. I understand that charges may be made on this account, at a scale that the bank may from time to time decide.

The application was duly accepted by the bank and, in Costello J's view, a contractual relationship was thereby established. The defendant was immediately given a cheque book. Some days later, after the defendant had drawn a cheque on the account which used up most of the facility but before that cheque had been debited to his account, the bank wrote to him a letter stating that a facility had been sanctioned subject to conditions in the following terms:

£5,000 in the way of overdraft on the usual terms and conditions including interest prepayable on demand. The current rate of interest is 19%, and the facility extends until the 17 August 1984, at which time it will be reviewed.

Costello J did not think that this letter was effective to impose any new terms into the original loan agreement, which had by then been largely performed. It was thus necessary to examine the terms of the original agreement. That said nothing about the payment or rate of interest. Its reference to 'charges' were to bank charges rather than to the interest that might be payable on outstanding loans. Whereas a customer borrowing from a bank would know that he would have to pay interest on an outstanding balance and a term should be implied that this would be at the bank's prevailing rate on overdrafts on current account, there was no justification for implying a term into the original contract entitling the Bank to capitalise any outstanding interest, either annually or at any other interval of time. Nor should a term be implied that it could charge a higher rate of interest to be determined by it at its discretion in the event of default in repayment of the sums due on the current account. As far as the original loan was concerned, therefore, the bank was entitled to charge only simple interest on any outstanding balance at its current rates.

When the defendant applied for a further facility of £2,000 some weeks after he had received this letter, he must be taken to have agreed to be bound by its terms. In Costello J's view this meant that two-sevenths of the sum advanced by the bank were subject to the contractual terms contained in the letter.

In Costello J's view, nothing in the terms of the letter entitled the bank to charge compound interest or interest at a specially high default rate. The test to be applied was *what a customer receiving the letter would reasonably understand it to mean*. The letter referred to the loan's being 'on the usual terms and conditions'. In view of the fact that a review of the facility was to take place in a year's time, which might or might not mean that the loan would then be called in, the letter could not be construed as meaning that the customer was agreeing that the onerous terms regarding interest would be included should the facility be extended.

Even if it was the bank's practice to compound interest annually this did not in Costello J's view entitle it to do so under the particular contract. Parties might expressly agree that compound interest should be paid on an outstanding loan or such an agreement could be implied or payable by virtue of a custom of the trade. Here no trade custom was relied on, nor had it been suggested that an agreement to pay compound interest could be implied. Costello J noted that, in banking, the law leans against compound interest and that a clear manifestation to charge such interest is required by the law of mortgages. He referred to the recent English Court of Appeal decision in *National Bank of Greece SA v Pinios Shipping Co. No. 1: The Maira* [1989] 1 All ER 213 which had held that a mortgage under which the mortgagor had consented to pay the mortgage bank all moneys due 'so that interest shall be computed according to agreement or failing agreement at the usual mode of the bank' did not entitle the bank to change compound interest, in spite of evidence that this was the bank's practice.

Costello J applied the same rule to unsecured bank loans. The term relating to compound interest would have to be brought to the customer's attention and accepted either expressly or impliedly by him.

The reason why the claim to interest at a default rate must also fail was that a term entitling a bank to charge a higher rate of interest in the event of a default might be void as being a penalty. It could be justified if it was a genuine pre-estimate to the bank's loss in the event of default. The agreement to pay a default rate of interest:

> must therefore be an express one, and an attempt to incorporate such a term by reference to 'usual terms and conditions' which are not brought to the customer's attention cannot be successful because no genuine mutually agreed pre-estimate would have been made.

MISTAKE

In *O'Neill v Ryan (No. 2)* [1991] ILRM 672; [1992] 1 IR 166, Costello J addressed important questions relating to the operation of the doctrine of mistake in the law of contract. The plaintiff, a former shareholder and employee of Ryanair Ltd, had taken legal proceedings against a number of defendants in respect of alleged wrongs, including wrongful dismisssal, misrepresentation and conspiracy, as well as proceedings under s. 205 of the Companies Act 1963. The defendants' solicitors wrote a letter to the plaintiff offering to purchase his shares in the company in terms which the plaintiff understood to mean that acceptance on his part would involve his foregoing his proceedings under s. 205 but not the other proceedings. The defendants' solicitors' intention in making the offer was otherwise: that the price of acceptance was the termination of all proceedings save those for wrongful dismissal. The plaintiff sought specific performance of the offer in the terms that he had understood and accepted it.

Costello J held in favour of the plaintiff. He reviewed the jurisprudence on the doctrine of shared common mistake, noting that cases in the previous forty years had shown that the circumstances in which it would nullify a contract were 'extremely limited'. He quoted with approval in this context

Denning LJ's well known observation in *Solle v Butcher* [1950] 1 KB 671, at 691.

Costello J then addressed the category of mistake that arises where each party is mistaken as to the other's intention, although neither appreciates that he is misunderstood by the other. He applied the objective test of intention whereby '[t]he language used by one party, whatever his real intention may be, is to be construed in the sense in which it would be reasonably understood by the other, or at least in the sense in which a reasonable person would construe it': *Chitty on Contracts*, vol. 1, para 351 (1989 ed.). the defendants solicitors' offer, in his view, should be reasonably understood as one to settle the s. 205 proceeding only.

Costello J saw three reasons why the court should adopt this rule. Echoing the Supreme Court in *Mespil Ltd v Capaldi* [1986] ILRM 373, at 376, he referred to the undesirable uncertainty into which business relations would be thrown if a party could renounce his agreement on subjective considerations. Moreover, to permit such a defence 'would be to open the door to perjury and to destroy the security of contracts' (*Fry on Specific Performance*, 5th ed., p. 765). Finally, it seemed to Costello J that an *estoppel* arose, precluding an offeror from adducing evidence of intention:

> if an offeror intends his offer in one sense but fails to convey that sense in the words he uses (as objectively determined) and the offeree accepts it in the sense in which the words could reasonably be construed it seems to me that the offeror is estopped from relying on his own error if detriment would thereby be suffered by the offeree.

It should be noted that the latter ground differs radically from the first two in that it would apply only in cases where detriment would otherwise be suffered by the offeree. This contingent element would not exist in some cases.

As regards the question of *construing* the letter of offer, Costello J endorsed the principles set out in *Prenn v Simmonds* [1971] 3 All ER 237, which O'Hanlon J had applied in *British Leyland Exports v Britain Manufacturing Ltd* [1981] IR 335, at 346. Costello J considered that, while *Prenn* afforded justification for hearing extrinsic evidence of the general circumstances in which the offer of settlement had been made and accepted, it was not authority for the propositon that the parties could advance evidence as to *their intention in entering the agreement*. The Supreme Court decision in *Mespil* did not challenge this approach. *Mespil* was an example of a case where, looking at the words used by the parties, the court could come to the conclusion that, objectively speaking, they suffered from such ambiguently that it was impossible to conclude that the parties had reached an agreement.

This was not the position that pertained in the instant case since the words used by the defendnts' solicitors 'could only be construed as an offer to settle the s. 205 proceedings only'.

In deciding whether or not to make an order for specific performance, Costello J applied what was in essence a 'balance of hardship' test. The defendants' solicitors had intended that their offer was to settle the two sets of proceedings rather than merely the s. 205 proceedings, and so the defendants would suffer a hardship by a decision holding them bound to a different contract. But an award of damages based on the difference between the actual value of the shares and the price offered would leave the plaintiff holding shares in a company engaged in a business in a highly volatile industry whose value would be liable to fluctuate and in a company from whose employment he had been dismissed and over which he had no control. Moreover, the plaintiff had in no way contributed to the situation that arose. The balance of justice accordingly lay in favour of an order for specific performance.

In an ex tempore judgment, the Supreme Court affirmed Costello J's decision: [1992] 1 IR at 193-6.

RESTRAINT OF TRADE

In the chapter on Commercial Law, above, 28-30, we discuss the decision of *Kerry Co-Operative Creameries Ltd v an Bord Bainne Co-Operative Ltd* [1991] ILRM 851. The issue of restraint of trade was there considered, resulting in a direct split between O'Flaherty J and McCarthy J with the Chief Justice staying neutral. O'Flaherty J referred to the distinction to be drawn between contracts of services and contracts for the sale of a business: a restraint might be imposed more readily and more widely on the vendor of a business in the interests of the purchaser than on an employee in the interests of an employer:

> [I]t is thought that, in general, businessmen are best able to look after their own interests and that the public interest is best guarded by reliance on legislation. However, it appears to me that the protection that the law affords to employees continues with the same force as before. This is a distinction which I think it is important to preserve and to emphasise.

Counsel for Bord Bainne argued that the restraint of trade doctrine was premised on the existence of a covenant in restraint of trade. O'Flaherty J agreed, at all events where a restraint as between businesses was alleged. In so far as the English decisions of *Wyatt v Kreglinger* [1933] 1 KB 793 and *Bull v Pitney Bowes* [1966] 3 All ER 384 created an anomaly, this could be explained by saying that 'the courts must continue to pay particular attention to the need to safeguard and protect the rights of employees despite the fact that many of their rights are now, of course, guarded by legislation, too'. The instant case involved a dispute between competing giants of the market-place. If either of them wished to invoke the restraint of trade doctrine, it had the obligation to point to a clear covenant so restraining trade and to its breach.

As regards the instant case O'Flaherty J was of opinion that, except in the sense that whenever one takes any course in the business world it will operate as a restraint either on one's own activities or some form of clog on one's competitors, there was no question of restraint of trade. Even if there was a restraint of trade, it was reasonable as between the parties and in the public interest.

McCarthy J disagreed with O'Flaherty J's view that a restraint of trade must be an express covenant or condition in a contract. The impact of the new rules on the trading of the members *was* a restraint of trade but a reasonable one in the circumstances. Finlay CJ was also of the view that the restraint, if it was such, was reasonable. As to the need for an actual covenant or condition in a contract, he preferred to reserve his decision on this issue, having regard to its general importance, until it arose in a case as a question necessary for the determination of the claim.

THE STATUTE OF FRAUDS

Perhaps the most troublesome aspect of the law of contract in the Irish courts in recent years has been the formal requirements of the Statute of Frauds (Ir) Act 1695. In substantial part the difficulties reflect rapidly changing social and economic factors—the growth of house purchase, the relative ease in financing the transaction and the sudden rises and falls in the market. Apart from these phenomena, the more legal debate, without beginning or end, between certainty and individual equity, rolls on.

It will be recalled that in *Kelly v Parkhall School Ltd* [1979] IR 340 and *Casey v Irish Intercontinental Bank Ltd* [1979] IR 364, the Supreme Court held that, where parties had reached an oral agreement, a memorandum recording that agreement, but with the addition of the phrase 'subject to contract', was sufficient to pass the requirements of the Statute of Frauds. In *Mulhall v Haren* [1981] IR 364, Keane J, acting within the hierarchical constraints of precedent, characterised *Kelly* and *Casey* as exceptional cases and held that the use of that phrase was inconsistent with the existence of a concluded agreement, save in the most exceptional cases. In the Supreme Court decision of *McCarthy v O'Neill* [1981] ILRM 443, Henchy J (for the Court) referred to Keane J's careful examination of the law in *Mulhall*; he pointed out that 'unfortunately' *Mulhall* had not been opened to the court; and he went on to distinguish the facts in *McCarthy* from the 'special circumstances' discussed in *Kelly*. In *Silver Wraith Ltd v Siuicre Éireann*, High Court, 8 June 1989 (noted in the 1989 Review, 131-3), Keane J, without any reference to the Supreme Court decision, reiterated the position he had adopted in *Mulhall*. In *Aga Khan v Firestone* [1992] ILRM 31, considered above, 115-6, Morris J, expressed complete agreement with Keane J's approach in *Mulhall*.

The Supreme Court returned to the subject in *Boyle v Lee* [1992] ILRM 65. The plaintiff had sought to purchase the defendants' premises as an investment property. He had carried out negotiations with the defendants' auctioneers and had settled on the price of £90,000. Several matters were, however, left up in the air. These included the position relating to planning permission, the precise nature of the tenancies by which the premises had been let, the closing date and, perhaps most significantly, the question of a deposit. We consider this aspect of the case in the section of this chapter dealing with terms of a contract. A member of the auctioneers' staff wrote to the plaintiff on behalf of the defendants. His letter confirmed that the auctioneers had received instructions to accept the offer of £90,000 'subject to contract'. It requested the plaintiff to prepare the contract, which should incorporate a number of specified 'agreed terms', including the proposed purchase price, which was expressed as '£90,000, subject to contract'. The member of the auctioneers' staff had gone on to write that, '[i]n the meantime, you will appreciate that this letter is for information purposes only, and does not, by itself, constitute part of a binding contract'.

Barrington J held in favour of the plaintiff's claim for specific performance on the basis that a binding agreement had been concluded before the letter was composed; the letter constituted an effective memorandum, the phrase 'subject to contract' being dismissed as *'nihil ad rem'*.

The Supreme Court unanimously reversed. The basis of the reversal was not, however, unanimous. Four judgments were delivered: by Finlay CJ (Hederman J concurring), McCarthy, O'Flaherty and Egan JJ.

The Chief Justice rested his judgment on the absence of a complete oral contract in view of the uncertainty as to the question of the deposit: we discuss this aspect of the decision in the section of this chapter entitled 'Offer and Acceptance'. He went on, however, to 'express a view' (surely *obiter*) on the meaning and effect of the Supreme Court's earlier decision on the Statute of Frauds.

Finlay CJ noted that s 2 required the memorandum to record the *agreement*, not merely its important or necessary *terms*. In some instances a total recital of all the necessary ingredients of the contract could, without any other expression indicating an acknowledgment of a binding or completed contract, necessarily imply the existence of such a contract. Where, however, a document containing a recital of certain terms purported to *deny* the existence of a completed or concluded contract, or made use of *expressions specially adapted to exclude* the existence of a completed contract, it did not seem to the Chief Justice that as a matter of first principle the terms of s. 2 could be complied with.

Finlay CJ conceded the attraction of the argument that a party to an orally concluded agreement which was complete and intended to be complete should not be permitted by the unilateral insertion of the phrase 'subject to contract' in the memorandum to escape from the enforcement of the contract. Nevertheless he considered that such an argument:

> necessarily involves the precise mischief which the Statute of Frauds ... was intended to avoid, and that is that it invites the court to amend by deletion, or by ignoring one of its terms, the note or memorandum relief upon by the plaintiff and signed by the defendant, such amendment or deletion depending on the finding by the court on oral evidence as to what was the agreement between the parties.
>
> Such a principle clearly puts the oral evidence as superseding the only written evidence that is available. In broad terms, it is the clearest possible purpose of the Statute of Frauds 1695 to put the written evidence as dominant and superseding any oral evidence.

The Chief Justice went on to identify *policy* considerations pointing in the same direction. Central among these was the goal of avoiding doubt and consequent litigation, concerning contracts for the sale of land. In modern times, 'probably the most important legal transaction' which a great number of people made in their lifetime was the purchase or sale of their home.

The requirement of certainty meant that the note or memorandum would satisfy the statute only when it directly or by very necessary implication recognised, not only the terms to be enforced, but also the existence of a concluded contract between the parties. This rule would not, in the view of the Chief Justice, allow for the 'exceptional cases' mentioned by Keane J in *Mulhall v Haren*. Nor should the Court follow its earlier decision in *Kelly v Parkhall School*, so far as it appeared to amend by deletion the note or memorandum in writing, signed on behalf of the vendor, by reference to the evidence of the oral agreements which had previously been arrived at between the parties. Similar considerations might apply to *Casey v Intercontinental Bank*, though a decision on the validity of the concept of oral waiver of a suspensory condition in the writings which were part of the formation of the contract was not required in the instant case.

McCarthy J, in his concurring judgment, agreed that neither *Kelly* nor *Casey* should be followed.

O'Flaherty J, concurring, was of the view that expressions such as 'subject to contract' amounted to *'prima facie* a strong declaration that a concluded agreement does not exist'. There would have to be cogent evidence of a contrary intention before such a phrase was to be put to one side. In this regard, *Kelly* and *Casey* should be considered to be exceptional cases and confined to their particular facts and to the era in which they were decided.

O'Flaherty J went on to advocate that the Statute of Frauds should be amended to provide that all contracts for the sale of land should be in writing:

> This is because life has not got any less complicated over the intervening centuries: nowadays . . . there are often planning aspects to a sale; there is finance to be arranged; there is the tax end of matters to be sorted out . . .; family law legislation may often have some relevance and, further, there is the fact that the boundaries of negligence in relation to people involved in the buying and selling of property have been widened over the last number of decades. In these circumstances, I would rather the occasional gazumper go unbound than that people should be involved in needless uncertainty leading often to long drawn out litigation'.

O'Flaherty J thought that such a law would accord with the view taken by the average person, not versed in the mysteries of conveyancing law.

Egan J held that there had not been sufficient compliance with the Statute of Frauds because of the failure of the auctioneer's letter expressly to exonerate the vendors from any liability to the purchasers if the Corporation should require that steps be taken to remedy a breach of planning permission in respect of the tenancies. He went on to express support *obiter*, for Henchy J's approval in *McCarthy v O'Neill* of Keane J's explanation of *Kelly* as being a decision based on exceptional factual circumstances.

Criminal Law

1991 saw the welcome publication of *Judgments of the Court of Criminal Appeal, 1984 to 1989*. This is the third volume in the series begun by former Registrar of the Court of Criminal Appeal, the late Gerard L. Frewen. Although this third volume has been edited by Eithne Casey, Barrister-at-Law, it was decided to retain the citation '3 Frewen' as a mark of respect for Gerard Frewen as well as to indicate continuity with the first two volumes. The three volumes represent a highly significant corpus of law, some of which had become lost to practitioners before the publication of the first volume.

All three volumes consist of the full text of hitherto unreported judgments of the Court together with the headnote of any reported cases. An additional feature of the third volume edited by Eithne Casey is the inclusion of *ex tempore* judgments of the Court. This was made possible by the initiative of Geraldine Manners, current Registrar of the Court, in ensuring the taping and subsequent transcription of *ex tempore* judgments of the Court. Since February 1992, *ex tempore* judgments of the Court from the year 1990 to date are also now circulated in the same manner as judgments of the other superior courts. As a result, practitioners will have available a hugely increased volume of material on Irish criminal law.

In the current Review we refer to the *ex tempore* judgments published in 3 Frewen (which cover the period June 1987 to December 1989) as well as those circulated in early 1992 (which cover the period January 1990 to December 1991). The effect of these cases can be seen in particular in the increased section dealing with sentencing principles, but many other issues were also addressed by the Court in these important *ex tempore* judgments.

ARREST

Criminal Justice Act: detention In *The People v Boylan* [1991] 1 IR 477 the Court of Criminal Appeal (McCarthy, Barr and Blayney JJ), in an *ex tempore* judgment, dealt with an important point in connection with a detention under s. 4 of the Criminal Justice Act 1984.

The applicant had been detained by gardaí when they stopped a lorry at Dublin port being driven by the applicant. The gardaí believed that the lorry contained controlled drugs, and a search of the lorry the next day revealed that it contained a large quantity of cannabis. A crucial event on the day of the initial detention of the applicant was that he was brought to a shed at the port where he was detained for two hours. He was then brought to a garda station where he was detained in purported compliance with s. 4 of the 1984 Act. In the course of this detention the applicant made a statement which, apparently, admitted a part in the importation of the cannabis.

The question arose as to whether the applicant's initial detention under s. 4 was valid. This centered around the validity of his being brought to a shed in Dublin port after the lorry had been seized initially. The prosecution argued that this was in accordance with s. 23 of the Misuse of Drugs Act 1977, as amended by s. 12 of the Misuse of Drugs Act 1984, which relates to the power of the gardaí to require a person found in control of a vehicle to accompany the gardaí during a search of the vehicle. The defence argued that, since there had been no real search of the lorry while the applicant was brought to the shed in Dublin port, s. 23 of the 1977 Act (as amended) was not relevant to the case. The Court of Criminal Appeal accepted this argument, noting that the search while the applicant was held in the shed had been 'minimal' and that he had, in any event, not been present when this initial search was being conducted.

In the circumstances, the Court concluded that the applicant had been arrested from the time he was taken to the shed at Dublin port. Since it was another two hours before he had been brought to a garda station, the Court held that this did not comply with s. 4 of the 1984 Act.

It is significant that s. 4 of the 1984 Act merely states that a person arrested may be brought to a garda station, and no specific time period is specified. Nonetheless, the Court in the instant case stated:

> The requirement of section 4 of the Criminal Justice Act 1984 is that after arrest a person would be brought to a garda station and there the member in charge . . . can make the appropriate detention order. This requires that [the applicant] be brought as soon as reasonably possible after arrest and if he were arrested [two hours earlier] then he was not brought to the garda station as soon as reasonably possible.

This important passage, albeit in an *ex tempore* judgment, indicates that the Court requires compliance with what amounts to fair procedures in the operation of s. 4 of the 1984 Act as well as strict compliance with its provisions.

Colourable device: Offences against the State   In *The People v Walsh* (1989) 3 Frewen 260, the applicant had been convicted on charges arising from the stabbing of two women. In the course of the stabbing, the women's clothing had been damaged. The applicant was arrested by the gardaí under s. 30 of the Offences against the State Act 1939 on the basis that the damage to the clothes constituted malicious damage, a scheduled offence under the Act. During the applicant's subsequent interrogation, he made an in- criminating statement or confession to the gardaí.

The Court of Criminal Appeal (Walsh, Barr and Johnson JJ), in an *ex tempore* judgment, held that the applicant's arrest under s.30 of the Offences against the State Act 1939 was invalid, and thus the confession was not admissible. Although the applicant had been arrested for malicious damage to clothing, his subsequent interrogation was directed entirely at the stabbing during which the victim's clothing had been damaged. The Court held that an arrest under s. 30 could only be valid if the scheduled offence under which the arrest took place was itself worthy of investigation. The Court thus distinguished the instant case from the circumstances in *The People v Quilligan* [1986] IR 495 and *The People v Howley* [1989] ILRM 629 (see the 1988 Review, 139-42). The Court accepted that the gardaí had mistakenly believed that, once the case fell within the letter of s. 30 of the 1939 Act, this was sufficient to justify any subsequent interrogation. However, this im- portant decision of the Court indicates that there are limits to the 'non terrorist' use of s. 30, first authorised by the *Quilligan* case, above.

Detention as arrest   The case law on whether a detention can amount to an arrest was added to by the *ex tempore* decision of the Court of Criminal Appeal in *The People v McGinley (D.)* (1987) 3 Frewen 233. In this case, the applicant had been stopped at a garda and army road checkpoint. He was held there in order, he was told, for his driving licence to be checked. In fact, it appeared that no check was made but he was detained for over an hour in the presence of a garda and member of the army. The applicant was subsequently arrested under s.30 of the Offences against the State Act 1939, during which it appeared that he made a confession concerning, *inter alia*, robbery and aggravated burglary. He was charged with these offences in the Circuit Criminal Court. The trial judge ruled that the applicant's detention for the hour before his s. 30 arrest did not amount to an arrest, and he concluded that the s. 30 arrest was not in any way tainted with illegality. The applicant was convicted on the charges.

The Court of Criminal Appeal (Hederman, Gannon and Barrington JJ) differed from the trial judge as to the effect of the one hour detention. The Court held that, in fact, this had amounted to an arrest, since it could not be interpreted as being connected with the operation of the powers contained in the Road Traffic Acts 1961 to 1978. However, the Court did not fully accept the defence contention that the detention had been a colourable device to facilitate the s. 30 arrest. Therefore the Court ordered a re-trial, though noting that the prosecution would be required to establish that there was no con-nection between the detention and the subsequent s. 30 arrest. The editorial note in 3 Frewen, at p.234, notes that a *nolle prosequi* was subsequently entered by the Director of Public Prosecutions.

Trespass In *Director of Public Prosecutions v McCreesh*, Supreme Court, 7 March 1991, the Court held that s.49 of the Road Traffic Act 1961 did not confer a power of arrest on the gardaí while trespassing. The case arose in the following way.

The defendant, while driving his car, came to the attention of a garda patrol. He was followed for some time and the patrol car flashed its lights with a view to requesting him to pull in to the side of the road. The defendant failed to do this. He was followed by the patrol car to the driveway of his house. He was approached by a garda from the patrol car as he was walking towards the door. The defendant told the garda that he was a trespasser and that he should leave. The garda then arrested the defendant in purported compliance with s. 49 of the 1961 Act. The defendant was brought to a garda station but he was unable to provide a urine sample as required under s. 13 of the Road Traffic (Amendment) Act 1978. He was charged with the offence of failure to provide a sample having been arrested under s. 49 of the 1961 Act, as amended by s. 12 of the 1978 Act.

The defendant argued in the Circuit Court that the arrest under s.49 was invalid on two alternative grounds: (a) the arrest was in breach of the defendant's right to inviolability of the dwelling under Article 40.5 of the Constitution and (b) the arrest was invalid on the ground that the garda was a trespasser and was not authorised by s. 49 to effect an arrest in such circumstances. On a case stated to the Supreme Court (Griffin, Hederman and McCarthy JJ), the Court decided to address the non-constitutional issue first, in accordance with practice.

On the question of the extent of the power granted by s. 49 of the 1961 Act, the Court followed the virtually identical decision of the House of Lords in *Morris v Beardmore* [1981] AC 446. The Court held that since s. 49 of the 1961 Act did not in express terms confer a power of arrest on the gardaí where they were trespassing, the Court would not assume that the Oireachtas had intended to permit a valid arrest where the gardaí were engaging in tortious acts. On the evidence in the instant case the gardaí were trespassing, the arrest was thus invalid and the charge against the defendant had to be dismissed. Noting the distinction between the instant case and the circum-stances in *Director of Public Prosecutions v Gaffney* [1987] IR 173; [1988] ILRM 39 (see the 1987 Review, 85-6), Griffin J stated that there would appear to be a need for legislative intervention, as occurred in England in the wake of the *Morris* decision, to avoid repetition of the result arrived at in the instant case. No such legislative intervention has been made at the time of writing.

It should be noted, however, that while legislation might legitimise an arrest involving tortious acts, the constitutional dimension of trespassing on a person's dwelling would have to be considered by those drafting any amending s. 49. Thus, while Article 40.5 of the Constitution does authorise certain invasions of the dwelling, there could be no carte blanche for legislative provisions: see the cases discussed in the 1988 Review, 191-4 and the 1990 Review, 202-5.

CONFISCATION OF THE PROCEEDS OF CRIME

Until relatively recently, most of those accused of crimes in the Irish courts were poor people with little or no assets. In the past few years, the pheno-menon of defendants with substantial assets has become apparent, especially in relation to drugs offences. The popular sentiment is that 'something should be done' to ensure that criminals are stripped of their ill-gotten gains. Confiscation of their property seems the obvious solution, but some important issues of justice must inevitably be confronted.

For example, should the mere fact that a person known or suspected to be engaged in a life of crime has the trappings of affluence be a justification for the State's relieving him of his assets? Should it be necessary to establish that the seized property was actually the proceeds of a specific crime? Should only certain criminal offences such as those relating to drugs, handling stolen goods and forgery, be the basis for seizure? And, more fundamentally, does confiscation serve a *punitive* function exclusively or at all? If it does, what are the constitutional implications?

The Law Reform Commission addresses questions such as these in its Report on the subject (LRC 35-1991). The model for reform that it favours is based on designating certain offences as offences warranting mandatory confiscation of assets on conviction. These 'scheduled' offences would include drug trafficking, handling stolen or smuggled goods, demanding money with menaces and fraud-related offences. With regard to scheduled offences, the Gardaí would be given wide ranging powers of search and seizure, based on a warrant granted by a District Judge, in conjunction with a restraint order against the suspected person. To obtain either a warrant or an order, there would have to be reasonable grounds for suspecting that a scheduled offence had been committed. Where it was proved that a person convicted of a scheduled offence owned property, or had done so within ten years before his conviction, it would be presumed that such property repre-sented the proceeds of a scheduled offence or offences. The convicted person would be able to rebut the presumption by proving on the balance of probabilities that the property did not represent such proceeds. Where he failed to do so, the court would be obliged to order the forfeiture to the State of that property to the extent that it exceeded in value the sum of £1,000. The range of confiscation envisaged by the Commission goes even wider. Where any property in the possession of *another* person was acquired from a person convicted of a scheduled offence within the period of ten years preceeding the conviction, the court would be obliged to order its forfeiture to the State unless that other person could prove as a matter of probability that he had acquired it *bona fide* for reasonable value.

The draconian nature of these proposals raises some interesting constitutional issues, addressed in the Report. Most obviously, it may be debated whether placing on the convicted person the onus of proving that his property was not the proceeds of a scheduled offence is consistent with the due process guarantee of Article 38.1. The mere fact that a person convicted of a scheduled offence has assets of more than £1,000 could not warrant the inevitable inference that these assets were the fruits of that offence. Of course in some cases, where the assets are extensive and the convicted person's means of generating them, apart from through criminal activity, are not apparent, the inference would indeed be justified, but to create a statutory presumption in *all* cases, albeit one capable of rebuttal, would seem close to offending against the test carefully prescribed by Costello J in *O'Leary v Attorney General* [1991] ILRM 454 (1990 Review, 178-82).

Barrington J's decision in *Clancy v Ireland* [1989] ILRM 670; [1988] IR 326 (1988 Review, 127-30) offers some support for the constitutional validity of the 'freezing and seizing' strategy, but the two contexts are far from identical. The legislation in *Clancy*—the Offences Against the State (Amendment) Act 1985—involved the protection of the security of the State; the process of freezing funds was conditional on Ministerial intervention, based on the Minister's opinion that the moneys, but for s. 22 of the Offences Against the State Act 1939, would be the property of an unlawful organisation. In the Commission's proposals, neither of these elements exists, nor is it necessary that a rational inference arise that the convicted person's assets derive from the commission of a scheduled offence.

As regards the proposal that all property received by others for less than a reasonable value from a person convicted of a scheduled offence should be obliged to be forfeited, again constitutional doubts arise. Even if the recipient was entirely in good faith—a charity, for example—this would not prevent the forfeiture. The proposal is drafted in such a way that forfeiture would be obligatory even where the property was not in fact the proceeds of crime. One may assume that this is simply a mistake and that what is envisaged is that the recipient of the property could resist its forfeiture on such a basis.

Precisely how in practice a recipient such as a charity could be in a position to discharge such an onus is not clear. The general strategy of the recommendations, both in regard to convicted persons and recipients for less than reasonable value, is to treat them as the modern equivalents of outlaws, whose property was subject to escheat. There is a danger that, in doing so, modern constitutional values of due process may be infringed.

Among other recommendations in the Report are the proposals that there should be an offence of assisting another to enjoy or dispose of the proceeds of scheduled offences, that the Revenue Commissioners be obliged to disclose tax information to the prosecution authorities on production of a court order, that informants be immune for liability for the disclosure of information to the Garda and that provision be made for the enforcement of search, restraint and confiscation orders of other countries, on the basis of international agreements, on the application by the relevant foreign authorities to the Irish courts.

CONTEMPT OF COURT

In *Orion Pictures Corp v Hickey*, High Court, 18 January 1991, Costello J sentenced the defendant to one month's imprisonment for his refusal to obey the terms of an order of the Court to which the defendant had in fact consented. The case arose out of breach of copyright proceedings taken by the plaintiff companies.

The Law Reform Commission published a Consultation Paper on Contempt of Court in July 1991. Its Report on the subject was promised for 1992.

CRIMINAL DAMAGE

The Criminal Damage Act 1991 gives effect to the substance of the recommendations of the Law Reform Commission in its *Report on Malicious Damage* (LRC 26 – 1988), analysed in the 1988 Review, 158-161. In place of the myriad offences prescribed by the Malicious Damage Act 1861, the 1991 legislation provides for *three* main offences of damage to property in general. These are, *first*, the simple offence of damaging another's property (s. 2(1)), *second*, the aggravated offence of damaging any property with intent to endanger the life of another or with recklessness in that regard (s. 2(2)), and, *third*, the offence of damaging property with intent to defraud (s. 2(3)). Where any of these offences is committed by damaging property by fire, it is to be charged as arson (s. 2(4)). (The common law offence of arson is abolished by s. 14(1)). The maximum sentence for arson under the first and third of these offences and for the second (regardless of an arson dimension) is life imprisonment and a fine. Otherwise the maximum is ten years' imprisonment and a fine of £10,000 (s. 2(5)).

The Act provides for two ancillary offences: threatening to cause damage to property (s. 3) and possessing anything with intent to cause damage to property (s. 4). The maximum sentence for these offences is again ten years' imprisonment and a £10,000 fine.

The question of *mens rea* for these five offences is dealt with by the requirement that the prosecution establish intention or recklessness on the part of the accused, while enabling the defendant to be acquitted if he or she has a 'lawful excuse'. The Law Reform Commission had recommended that recklessness be defined in terms based on a tentative draft of the American Law Institute's *Model Penal Code*. This proposal was in line with the Commission's general approach to recklessness evident in its Reports since the *Report on Receiving Stolen Property (LRC 23 – 1987)*. The Act departs from this recommendation. The Minister of State at the Department of Tourism, Transport and Communications, Mr. Lyons, explained to the Seanad that, '[p]ending the consideration of such a common approach, the Government did not implement the Commission's recommendation based on the U.S. model scheme': 130 Seanad Debates, vol. 1620 (12 December 1991). Instead, s. 2(6) provides that a person is reckless 'if he has foreseen that the particular kind of damage that in fact was done might be done and yet has gone on to take the risk of it.' Mr. Lyons suggested that s. 2(6) defined recklessness 'in the sense in which it has been developed by the courts in these cases': *id.*

This departure from the Law Reform Commission's recommendation, for no pressing reason, is unfortunate. There appears to be an ingrained resistance within the system to any approach that would lead Irish criminal law any appreciable distance from the British model.

The Act deals with interferences with computers in two ways. First, s. 1(1) provides that the term 'to damage, in relation to data, includes adding to, altering, corrupting, erasing or moving to another storage medium or to a different location in the storage medium in which they are kept (whether or not property other than data is damaged thereby).' Thus all the damage offences that have been mentioned can include interference of this type. Secondly, s. 5 deals with 'hacking' by making it an offence for a person without lawful excuse to operate a computer within the State with intent to access any data kept either within or outside the State or outside the State with intent to access any data kept within the State. The offence is con-summated regardless of whether the defendant succeeds in accessing any data, and regardless also whether the defendant intended to access any particular data.

S. 9 contains an important feature of the legislation. It gives power to the court on convicting a defendant of any of the three offences of damaging another's property prescribed by s. 2 to make a *compensation order*, requiring the defendant to pay to the injured party a sum, no greater than the injured party would have received in a civil action, but also having regard to the means of the defendant—a factor which has no place in the assessment of damages in civil proceedings, save in the exceptional case where exemplary damages are awarded. The court may order that this payment is to be made in instalments; it may vary the amounts subsequently in the light of the convicted person's changing circumstances. Of course damages in civil proceedings must take account of the compensation order: s. 11.

This admixture of criminal and civil law is a feature of contemporary legislation—witness the Criminal Justice Act 1992—and has received almost universal acclaim. The desideratum of paying greater attention to victims of crime—whom the criminal process largely ignores (and in the case of sexual offences historically treated very badly)—has encouraged commentators to give their blessing to any legislative change that improves their position. It would be wise, nonetheless, to be fully conscious of the wider implications of merging the criminal and civil law. The purposes of the criminal law in society are no doubt controversial but they clearly are of some considerable importance. They had better be; otherwise the policy of locking people up and depriving them of their property needs some explanation. The purposes of the civil law are very different but again they are of real social importance. There must surely be limits to the extent to which criminal law can be privatised into a machine for vengeance or retribution rather than serving the function of social concern which underlies the philosophy of the criminal law.

Finally, reference may be made to s. 14 of the Act, which introduces a number of minor and consequential changes in existing law. Subs. (3) is a transitional provision which maintains in operation, for the purposes of the Criminal Law (Jurisdiction) Act 1976, certain offences of malicious damage to property made punishable by the 1976 Act if committed in Northern Ireland. Subs. (4) makes provision for updating the 1976 Act to take account of the replacement of these offences by the arson offences prescribed by s. 2 of the 1991 Act: see Para. 16 of the Explanatory Memorandum to the Bill, published by the Department of Justice in October 1990. Subs. (4) was brought into operation by Ministerial order (SI No. 226 of 1992) on 10 August 1992, in conjunction with reciprocal provisions in Britain, whereupon subs. (3) ceased to have effect.

CRIMINAL LIBEL

In December 1991 the Law Reform Commission published its *Report on the*

Crime of Libel (LRC41 – 1991), containing its final recommendations on the subject. The previous July it had published a Consultation Paper, setting out its tentative proposals. The report deals with four matters: defamatory, seditious, blasphemous and obscene libel.

Seditious libel   Least contentious is the proposal that the common law offence of seditious libel be abolished without replacement. There have been no reported cases involving this offence since the foundation of the State and our criminal code is endorsed with an elaborate array of offences relating to State security, notably the Offences against the State Act 1939 and the Broadcasting Authority Act 1960 (as amended).

Obscene libel   With regard to obscene libel, the Commission proposes that the offence be abolished without replacement. It does so on the basis, first, that the offence is superfluous in view of the wide-ranging statutory controls, such on the Censorship of Publications Act 1929, the Indecent Advertisements Act 1889 and the Customs Consolidation Act 1876, and secondly, that the offence 'is well nigh obsolete' (*Consultation Paper*, para 257). Whether it is reasonable to infer that it is obsolete from the paucity of prosecutions would seem debatable: the stringency and greater breadth of the legislative provisions may have made them a more attractive option, without any implication that, in the event of their abolition, the vitality of the common law offence would not become apparent.

The Commission's analysis of this offence studiously avoids taking a position as to the merits of the various viewpoints regarding the legal control of pornography or other explicit depiction of sexual activity. It goes no further than to express the opinion that, of a number of possible rationales for the offence, perhaps the strongest argument for suppression of obscene matter is that '[t]he law on behalf of society wishes to prevent the corruption and depravity of minds in society because in the long term it may create an atmosphere in which harmful activity is encouraged, a harmful act in this context being an act which is a criminal offence'. (*Id.*, par 247). It characterises as being 'arguably open to objection' certain other possible rationales which would identify harmful acts with acts harmful from a moral viewpoint. The objection here is that the law should not be 'asked to accept a given morality on a specific issue, when in fact society reflects a number of different moralities and it is the freedom of each person to choose his or her own, within limits which are not transgressed in this context' (*Id.*).

The Commission is here again reflecting the philosophic approach of Mill and Hart, in this instance supplemented by the Williams Committee Report on Obscenity, published in England in 1979 (Cmnd 7772). A similar preference was apparent in earlier Reports of the Commission, notably those relating to child sexual abuse (LRC 32 – 1990) and sexual offences against the mentally handicapped (LRC 33 – 1990): see the 1990 Review, 246-58.

The Commission goes on to recommend that an examination should be undertaken of the legislation on obscene and indecent matter and the various schemes of censorship in order to determine whether they are consistent with the requirements of the Constitution as to freedom of speech and are appropiate in modern conditions. Those carrying out this examination should have the task of formulating, if necessary, changes to the existing law: *Report*, para 22.

It seems curious that law reform proposals on obscenity should be framed in such a way as to recommend (for the time being, at all events) the retention of the entire machinery of censorship and prior restraint while proposing the abolition of the substantive offence of publishing obscene material. A more attractive approach from the liberal standpoint would have been to remove or restrict the scope of censorship laws while retaining on updated offence of publishing obscene material. The effect of the Commission's recommendations if implemented, could well be to make it politically more difficult to re-establish a criminal offence if the censorship controls were later removed. The subject is one that is not best served by piecemeal, somewhat lop-sided, statutory reform.

Defamatory libel   The Commission makes detailed proposals in relation to the common law offence of defamatory libel. In contrast to the other three offences, the Commission considers that this offence should be retained. It does, however, recommend that its scope be substantially confined. The prosecution would be required to prove that the statement was false as well as defamatory and that the defendant knew it to be defamatory and either knew it to be false or was recklessly indifferent as to the question of truth or falsity.

The shift from the present law is striking, especially in relation to the question of the falsity and knowledge of the falsity of the statement (or reckless indifference in its regard). At present, truth does not always afford a defence. It is one thing to propose that a plaintiff in civil proceedings for defamation should have to prove the falsity of the statement, on the balance of probabilities; it is quite another that the prosecution should have to do so beyond reasonable doubt, coupled with a similar task in relation to the defendant's *mens rea*. The justification for the differing approaches is that criminal proceeding is here serving a quite separate function from civil libel. Society has no legitimate interest in punishing people for making true defamatory assertions or even false ones where the matter lacked the *mens rea* characteristic of most offences. Nonetheless, the realistic prospects of convicting anyone for the offence thus narrowed must be slight enough.

The Commission goes on to recommend that there should be no defences of justification, comment or qualified privilege in proceedings for criminal defamation but that the defence of absolute privilege should apply in respect of judicial proceedings and fair and accurate reports of them. The effect of this recommendation is that communications between the members of the executive could give rise to a criminal prosecution. One wonders how such a proposal coheres with the law as stated by the majority in *Attorney General v Mr Justice Hamilton*, Supreme Court, 21 August 1992.

The Commission proposes that there should be no special defence available to distributors and printers:

> It would in most cases be impossible to prove knowledge on their part and while proof of recklessness might not be so difficult, there seems no reason why the printer and distributor should not be liable in such a case. (*Report*, para 10)

Perhaps this analysis needs further development. It is surely the hall-mark of distributors (and to a lesser extent printers) not to concern themselves with the content of the publication. One should hesitate before turning into a criminal a newspaper boy who reads a seemingly defamatory headline in the paper he is selling, wonders whether it might be false, and continues with his job of selling newspapers.

The Commission proposes that the offence of defamatory libel should be triable on indictment or summarily at the option of the Director of Public Prosecutions, whose consent should be obtained for all prosecutions for this offence. It recommends the repeal of ss. 8-10 of the Defamation Act 1961, requiring leave of a High Court judge to be obtained for prosecution for defamation against newspapers and enabling the District Court to dismiss or dispose of such prosecution summarily. The maximum penalty on indictment would be five years' imprisonment and a fine of £10,000; on summary disposal, the maximum would be a year's imprisonment and a fine of £2,000.

One commentator, Michael McDowell SC, writing in the *Irish Times*, 23 August 1991, criticised aspects of these proposals when they had just appeared, in the Consultation Paper. He was particularly concerned with the recommendation that the Director of Public Prosecutions be given power to elect for summary trial. This would deprive the accused of the right to a jury trial as well as the valuable safeguard of the entitlement to be heard by a High Court judge before the prosecution was commenced. The Commission's rebuttal of Mr McDowell's criticism is narrowly focused, concentrating on small points relating to the wording of the critique rather than addressing the wider and important question of whether jury trial is appropriate for all prosecutions for defamatory libel. The jurisprudence on Article 38 of the

Constitution, itself far from a paragon of judicial coherence, cannot provide an answer to that question since all that it can concern itself with is whether or not an offence is a minor one, not the related but ultimately separate question of whether jury trial is appropriate for it in any or every case. The effect of *Conroy v Attorney General* [1965] IR 411 and *The State (Rollinson) v Kelly* [1984] ILRM 625; [1984] IR 248, is that the Oireachtas, aided by an election provision such as the Commission proposes, can ensure that an accused will be deprived of a jury trial. The maximum summary penalties recommended by the Commission are such as would seem to guarantee that no defendant could ever invoke Article 38 successfully in support of his or her being tried by a jury. Only if the Supreme Court were to hold that defamatory libel is such a serious offence as to warrant a jury trial in spite of a low maximum penalty for summary trial would the accused have any way of avoiding summary trial. The kind of offences that have been mentioned thus far as having such seriousness are of a clearly different order of gravity.

Blasphemous libel   Blasphemous libel presents distinctive difficulties for those who would wish to recommend a change in the law. This is because it has an express constitutional status. Article 40.6.1.i provides that the publication or utterance of blasphemous matter is an offence punishable in accordance with law. Clearly abolition of the offence—a course the Commission favours—is simply not possible, unless the constitutional provision is changed in a referendum. The Commission considers that a referendum having such a repeal as its sole object 'would rightly be seen as a time wasting and expensive exercise' (*Report*, para 18). It proposes that, in any more extensive revision that may be taken of provisions of the Constitution which are generally considered to be anachronistic or anomalous, the opportunity should be taken to delete the provision relating to blasphemy.

In the event of this recommendation's not being accepted, the Commission recommends the abolition of the common law offence of blasphemous libel and its replacement by a new offence entitled 'publication of blasphemous matter'. Blasphemous matter would be matter the sole effect of which is likely to cause outrage to a substantial number of the adherents of any religion—Christian or otherwise—by virtue of its insulting content concerning matters held sacred by that religion. The prosecution would have to show, first, that the defendant had known the matter was likely to outrage the adherents of any religion and, secondly, that its sole intent was to outrage the adherents of any religion.

One wonders whether even the most rabid of bigots would face the serious prospect of conviction under an offence thus confined, however intemperate his outpourings. The requirement that his *sole* intent be to outrage the adherents of any religion would exclude almost all of those who attack other people's religion. An odd cynical mocker of religion might have such a distilled intent but this type of person would be a *rara avis*.

The common law offence of blasphemy in its original manifestation is unquestionably inconsistent with contemporary attitudes to freedom of religion and the Commission in its Consultation Paper presents a useful analysis of the difficulty of capturing the modern *actus reus* of the offence. The movement of legal thought in Britain has been away from a definition based on religious heterodoxy to one centring on the *feelings* of believers. A similar movement of thought is apparent in relation to obscenity where value judgments regarding published material have been replaced by the goal of protecting people from being offended by the material. The law in both cases is thus able to adopt a comfortably neutral posture on the basis that it is better to treat these religious and moral issues as in essence raising no more thanb the question of psychological tranquility.

Doubtless, the norms of pluralism and freedom of thought and speech have encouraged this transformation. The decline in religious belief in Western Europe and the United States has also surely contributed to the trend. What is lacking in the British jurisprudence is any serious attempt to articulate acceptable principles for the legal protection of freedom of religion from undue restriction by blasphemous denigration. There would seem merit in proceeding on the basis that a religious perspective should be regarded as integral to the human personality. The notion of a religious perspective should not be narrowly construed as embracing merely deist conclusions; what is here envisaged is the natural reflection by human beings as to the ultimate questions of being, value human responsibility and destiny. Clearly there is no universal consensus as to how these questions should be answered but they are nonetheless issues of supreme importance. No doubt the answers at which people arrive vary in their intellectual power and moral attraction, but the future development of the law of blasphemy may be in the direction of affording respect to the process of addressing these issues because that process is inherently deserving of that respect, rather than merely catering for emotional sensitivities. For an interesting recent discussion, see Bohlander, 'Public Peace, Rational Discourse and the Law of Blasphemy' (1992) 21 Anglo-Amer L Rev 162.

DEFENCES

Insanity   The decision of the Supreme Court in *The People v Gallagher* [1991] ILRM 339, *sub nom. Application of Gallagher* [1991] 1 IR 31 was discussed in the 1990 Review, 164-6.

It may be noted that, in the wake of the *Gallagher* case, an Advisory

Committee was established to assist the Department of Justice in determining whether persons found 'guilty but insane' should be released. Arising from the recommendations of that Committee the Minister for Justice released the applicant who had been involved in *The People v Ellis* [1991] ILRM 225; [1990] 2 IR 291 (discussed in the 1990 Review, 160-2): see *Irish Times*, 22 November 1991.

Provocation   In *The People v Kehoe* [1992] ILRM 481, the Court of Criminal Appeal (O'Flaherty, Murphy and Blayney JJ), in an *ex tempore* judgment, dealt with certain aspects of the defence of provocation.

The applicant had been charged with murder. The applicant had had a relationship with a particular woman and they had had a child together. The applicant's best friend had then begun a relationship with this woman, and this enraged the applicant. The two men had, on one occasion, had a fight over this question and the applicant had also written to the woman that he had it in mind to kill the victim. On a particular evening, the applicant was invited back to the woman's apartment. Here the applicant looked into their child's bedroom, where he found the victim sleeping. The applicant gave evidence at his trial to the effect that, in a rage, he went out of the bedroom and obtained a knife with which he fatally stabbed the victim.

It was accepted that the only issue in the case was whether the applicant was guilty of murder or manslaughter. The Court of Criminal Appeal accepted that the trial judge had correctly directed the jury, in line with the decision in *The People v MacEoin* [1978] IR 27, that where the defence of provocation is raised the prosecution must establish beyond reasonable doubt that the accused was not provoked to such an extent that having regard to his temperament, character and circumstances he lost control of himself at the time of the wrongful act. The other matter for the jury would be to consider whether the force used was excessive in relation to the provocation.

The only other issue which was dealt with in detail by the Court was the relevance of the evidence of a psychiatrist at the applicant's trial. The psychiatrist had given evidence that in his opinion the applicant had been under huge emotional distress at the time of the stabbing, that he believed the applicant had no intention to kill and that the accused was telling the truth. In the course of his charge to the jury, the trial judge stated, inter alia, that the psychiatrist had based his opinion on hypotheses and not on the actual testimony of the applicant, and that the jury was ultimately required to make an assessment of the applicant's state of mind from their interpretation of the applicant's own testimony. The applicant, on appeal, submitted that the trial judge had erred in being so scathing in his comments.

Ultimately, the Court of Criminal Appeal concluded that the trial judge had not erred in this respect. The Court accepted that, in provocation cases, the accused is in the best position to give evidence as to his state of mind at the time of the wrongful act. It concluded that psychiatric evidence would only be relevant where the accused's sanity is being raised. The Court thus agreed with the view expressed by the Court of Appeal (Criminal Division) in *R. v Turner* [1975] QB 834 that psychiatric evidence is of little or no value in provocation cases. The Court recommended that, in future such cases, defence counsel should canvass in advance with the trial judge the introduction of such evidence and that its relevance should be assessed before the evidence is given. The effect of the *Kehoe* case is that such evidence is unlikely to be regarded as relevant in many provocation cases.

DELAY

Yet more decisions on the impact of delay in criminal procedures were made in the High Court in 1991. The general pattern emerging indicated a preparedness to accept that, in summary cases, a certain margin of appreciation be allowed to the prosecution.

The first case on this topic was *Director of Public Prosecutions v Corbett* [1992] ILRM 674; [1991] 2 IR 1. The defendant was charged, inter alia, with an offence under s. 49 of the Road Traffic Act 1961, the summons originally alleging the offence took place on 19 September 1989. The summons was applied for on 9 February 1990, and the hearing was set for 3 May 1990 in the District Court. At the hearing, the defence sought to have the case struck out for prejudice to the defendant arising from the delay involved. No evidence being led on this point, the District Court dismissed the application. The prosecution then applied, under r. 88 of the District Court Rules 1948, to change the date of the alleged offence on the summons from 19 September 1989 to 18 September 1989, and to change the number of the defendant's dwelling on the summons from '27' to '25'. The District Court refused to amend the summonses and dismissed the charges. On a case stated, Barr J remitted the case to the District Court.

On the delay issue, he held that, although there had been a delay in applying for the summonses, this was within the appropriate statutory limit and therefore *prima facie* the summons was good; and since there was no unreasonable delay between application and the trial, the District Court had correctly dismissed the defendant's application in the absence of evidence as to prejudice.

On the refusal to amend the summons, Barr J disagreed with the Judge of the District Court. Citing the decision in *The State (Duggan) v Evans* (1978) 112 ILTR 61, he noted that the District Court had a discretion under rr. 21 and 88 of the 1948 Rules as to whether to grant the application to amend the summons. He held that the District Court Judge should not have taken account of the delay factor since there was no indication that this would prejudice the defendant, and he should have confined himself to considering prejudice from the point of view of the defendant's alibi evidence which he had intended to introduce and also whether the prosecution had taken the relevant blood or urine sample on the date in the summons or on the date sought to be inserted. On this basis, he remitted the matter to the District Court.

The second case on delay was *Director of Public Prosecutions v Carlton*, High Court, 24 June 1991. Here the defendant had also been charged with an offence under s. 49 of the Road Traffic Act 1961, alleged to have taken place on 11 November 1989. The summons was due to be heard on 12 March 1990 but owing to an oversight the prosecuting garda had not been informed about this and the charges were struck out. The garda applied for a fresh summons and this was issued on 21 June 1990, returnable for 26 July 1990. On the latter date, the defendant sought to have the charges struck out on the basis that the 8 month delay was unfair, and this application was granted. On a case stated, Morris J remitted the case to the District Court.

Referring to the decision of D'Arcy J in *The State (Cuddy) v Mangan* [1988] ILRM 720 (see the 1988 Review, 151) and to *dicta* of Barr J in *Director of Public Prosecutions v Corbett*, above, Morris J helpfully noted in his judgment that the District Court could strike out charges on the alternative grounds that: (a) there had been excessive or unconscionable delay in bringing the case, where the onus is on the State to justify delay; or (b) the defendant would be prejudiced by a delay in bringing the case, where the onus is on the defendant to prove prejudice.

He went on to note that, in the absence of evidence of prejudice, the District Court Judge must have based his decision on the excessive nature of the delay; but, having regard to the six month time limit permitted in s. 1(7) of the Courts (No.3) Act 1986 for the making of a complaint, it was unreasonable for the District Court Judge to decide that an eight month delay was excessive. On the unreasonableness issue, Morris J referred with approval to the decision of the Supreme Court in *O'Keeffe v An Bord Pleanála* [1992] ILRM 237 (see the Administrative Law chapter, 16-18, above).

Morris J also noted that the District Court Judge might have been influenced by the fact that the previous summons had been struck out, but he considered that this was an irrelevant matter in the instant prosecution. As already indicated, the case was remitted to the District Court to enter continuances.

The third case which raised the delay issue was *Director of Public Prosecutions v McKillen* [1991] 2 IR 508. This case arose in the following way. On 3 August 1989, a summons alleging dangerous driving by the defendant on 13 March 1989 was applied for under s. 1 of the Courts (No.3) Act 1986. Due to difficulties in serving the defendant, a second summons was issued on 27 September 1989, returnable for 16 November 1989. In the District Court, the charge of dangerous driving was dismissed on the ground that the second summons was applied for outside the six month time limit specified in s.1 of the 1986 Act. On a case stated Lavan J remitted the case to the District Court.

He noted that proceedings pursuant to s. 10 of the Petty Sessions (Ireland) Act 1851 had permitted the re-issue of a summons and that the second summons would be deemed to have been grounded on the first complaint, citing *Ex p. Fielding* (1861) 25 JP 759 as authority. He then pointed to the provision in s. 1(7)(a) of the 1986 Act that its parallel procedure was subject to 'any necessary modifications' to the procedure under the 1851 Act. Lavan J concluded that this must be deemed to include the possibility of seeking a second summons in circumstances such as the present. Indeed, as he noted, this approach was anticipated in the leading decision of the Supreme Court in *Director of Public Prosecutions v Nolan* [1989] ILRM 39; [1990] 2 IR 526 applied (see the 1988 Review, 184-6). This decision of Lavan J is of some significance since it also overruled a decision of Judge Sheehy to the contrary in *Director of Public Prosecutions (Moran) v Ayton*, Circuit Court, 26 February 1990, which had been relied on by the defendant in the instant case.

Finally, it may also be noted that in *The People v Ryan* (1989) 3 Frewen 237, the Court of Criminal Appeal (Walsh, Barr and Blayney JJ), in an *ex tempore* judgment, held that a four year delay in bringing a charge of falsifying accounts, contrary to the Falsification of Accounts Act 1875, was acceptable having regard to the complexity of the case and that the applicant had not been prejudiced by the delay.

DISTRICT COURT

Advance notice of evidence   In the 1990 Review, 197, we discussed the decision of Gannon J in *Kelly v O'Sullivan*, High Court, 11 July 1990. In *Kelly*, it was held that there was no obligation on the prosecution in a summary trial to give notice of any evidence to the defence. In *Cowzer v Kirby and Director of Public Prosecutions*, High Court, 11 February 1991 Barr J reached the opposite conclusion.

The applicant had been charged with demanding money with menaces on a particular date, contrary to s. 29 of the Larceny Act 1916. The applicant was brought before the first respondent in the District Court and elected for summary trial, the first respondent indicating that he was prepared to accept jurisdiction. On the date set for trial, the applicant proposed to adduce alibi evidence to indicate that he could not have committed the offence on the date indicated in the charge. At the outset of the hearing, however, the prosecution applied to have the date in the charge amended and this was accepted by the first respondent and the trial was adjourned. The prosecution also indicated that the s. 29 charge was being abandoned and that a charge of demanding money with intent to steal, contrary to s. 30 of the 1916 Act, would be brought instead. The applicant's solicitor then sought from the second respondent a copy of the statement from the complainant on which the original charges had been brought, but this was refused. The applicant then sought an order of prohibition preventing his prosecution and trial on the existing or any substituted charges unless all witness statements were furnished to him before the trial. Barr J granted the prohibition order.

Barr J was of the view that the charges against the applicant were not in any way trivial in nature, since he ran the risk of a prison sentence of up to 12 months. Looking at the case from the constitutional perspective, he referred to the seminal decision in *The State (Healy) v Donoghue* [1976] IR 325. He was of the view that the constitutional guarantees of fair procedures and of a trial in due course of law required that the applicant be afforded every opportunity to defend himself. He also then referred to the decisions in *Clune v Director of Public Prosecutions* [1981] ILRM 17 and *Kelly v O'Sullivan*, High Court, 11 July 1990. He did not consider that these were authority for the view that in summary proceedings an accused is not in *any* circumstances entitled to receive, prior to his trial, copies of written statements made by prosecution witnesses. While one might disagree with this interpretation of the *Kelly* decision in particular, it is understandable that Barr J did not wish to refuse to follow the decision of Gannon J. However, the reality is that the two cases stand uneasily together.

Barr J went on to hold that there was no logic in the proposition that merely because the applicant elected for summary trial he should lose rights which he would have if he had elected for trial on indictment and would then have been served with a book of evidence under s. 6 of the Criminal Procedure Act 1967. While he accepted that the applicant was not entitled to receive a formal book of evidence, the constitutional principles of fair procedures required that he receive, at the least, copies of the statements of all witnesses whose evidence was crucial to the prosecution case against him, particularly having regard to the change in the dates and in the charges themselves which the Director of Public Prosecutions had indicated.

In conclusion, it must be said that the approach of Barr J in *Cowzer* appears more flexible than that adopted by Gannon J in *Kelly*. As we stated in the 1990 Review, 198, the virtual ban on advance information which Gannon J appeared to espouse was difficult to reconcile with other decisions of the courts on the guarantee of fair procedures. The decision of Barr J is more in line with analogous case law. Nonetheless, the position is now somewhat unsatisfactory, with two conflicting High Court decisions on this specific topic. It may that the Supreme Court will receive an opportunity to clarify the matter, but a more satisfactory arrangement would surely be for new District Court Rules to incorporate the flexible approach suggested by Barr J and which is in place in the United Kingdom in relation to summary trial in Magistrates' Courts.

Amendment of summons The discretion to amend a summons was discussed by Barr J in *Director of Public Prosecutions v Corbett* [1992] ILRM 674; [1991] 2 IR 1: see 143, above.

Constitutional issues The question whether the District Court was required to entertain constitutional arguments was addressed by Denham J in *Coughlan v Patwell* [1992] ILRM 808. The applicant had been charged with offences under the Road Traffic Acts 1961 to 1978. On his appearance before the respondent judge of the District Court, he argued that his rights under Article 40.5 of the Constitution had been breached in the process of obtaining his name and address when the summons against him had been sought. The respondent refused to hear the point being put forward by the applicant, taking the view that such a constitutional issue could only be raised in the High Court and that he had jurisdiction to hear the case once the defendant appeared in court to answer the summons.

On judicial review, Denham J quashed the respondent's decision. She accepted the general point that procedural irregularities in summonses were cured by an appearance in court, and referred with approval to the decision in *Director of Public Prosecutions v Clein* [1983] ILRM 76 (see the discussion in the 1988 Review, 187-8).

However, Denham J also noted that this principle was modified where constitutional points were at stake. Invoking, inter alia, dicta of Walsh J in *The People v Lynch* [1981] ILRM 389; [1982] IR 64 and *Ellis v O'Dea* [1990] ILRM 87; [1989] IR 530 (1989 Review, 160-1), she concluded that since the District Court was a court established under the Constitution, it had a residual power and duty to uphold the constitutional rights of the persons appearing before it. She opined that the respondent should have allowed the argument to be put forward, and then decided whether it would be appropriate to grant a case stated or to allow a judicial review to proceed. In the instant case, she concluded that the appropriate course was to quash the decision and remit the matter to the District Court under O.84, r.26(4) of the Rules of the Superior Courts 1986.

Committal warrants   The Courts (No. 2) Act 1991 is a short Act which rectified a perceived problem in the District Court Rules 1948 concerning committal warrants. The 1948 Rules provided that committal warrants may be made at any time after default of payment of a fine or when the Court is satisfied that a condition in a court order has not been satisfied. However, s. 23 of the Petty Sessions (Ireland) Act 1851 provides that a committal warrant must be made directly on the expiration of the time for payment of the fine or at the next sitting of the court. It was felt, therefore, that the 1948 Rules were *ultra vires* and that legislation should be enacted to avoid any possible challenge to court orders. The 1991 Act provides for a period of up to to six months for committal warrants to be made. Changes in the 1948 Rules will follow from this.

The Act does not contain any provisions concerning committal warrants made under the previous regime. This may be contrasted with the Courts (No.2) Act 1988, which gave rise to *Shelly v Mahon* [1990] 1 IR 36 (1989 Review, 94-5) and *Glavin v Governor of Training Unit Mountjoy Prison* [1991] ILRM 478 (1990 Review, 155-7). In light of these decisions, it seems doubtful that such warrants would survive judicial review proceedings. Note however the comments in the 1990 Review, 157, on 'mending' legislation.

Remand on station bail   In *Maguire and Ors v Shelly and Ors*, High Court, 20 December 1991, Barron J dealt with an issue arising out of the remand of the applicants on station bail.

Each applicant was arrested on 26 May 1991 on suspicion of larceny and then remanded in Mullingar Garda Station on station bail pursuant to s. 31 of the Criminal Procedure Act 1967, having entered into recognisances to appear in the District Court in Mullingar on 14 June 1991. In fact the next sitting of the District Court in that area was in Longford on 30 May 1991. On their appearance in Mullingar on 14 June 1991, the applicants submitted that they were not lawfully before the Court. This issue then came on for judicial review.

S. 31 of the 1967 Act, which deals with station bail, provides that when station bail is granted the person charged must enter into a recognisance to appear before the District Court 'at the appropriate time and place.' As Barron J noted, s. 31 of the 1967 Act is a re-enactment of s. 14 of the Criminal Justice Act 1951. He noted this for the purposes of referring to s. 15 of the 1951 Act, which deals with remands by the District Court. S. 15 of the 1951 Act (as substituted by s. 26 of the Criminal Justice Act 1984) provides that remands on bail must be to 'the next sitting of the Court.'

Barron J also referred to the decision of the Supreme Court in *The State (Lynch) v Ballagh* [1987] ILRM 65; [1986] IR 203 in which the Supreme Court had held that Rule 39(1) of the District Court Rules 1948 was *ultra vires* since it appeared to allow a long remand period to facilitate the availability of the arresting garda. Walsh J had also indicated in that case that 'at the appropriate time and place' in s. 31 of the 1967 Act could be equated to 'the next sitting of the court' contained in s. 15 of the 1951 Act. However, as Barron J pointed out in the instant case, Griffin J had stated in the *Lynch* case that the practice for over 100 years had been that station bail could be granted for a period longer than to the next sitting of the court, so that the two phrases should not be equated.

In the instant case, Barron J appeared to lean towards the view expresseed by Griffin J in *Lynch*. However, he was not required to reach a final conclusion on this point, since he considered that the issue did not affect the jurisdiction of the District Court to hear the cases against the applicants. The Court's jurisdiction depended on the complaint and not on the validity of the recognisances which had been entered into by the applicants. He thus declined to grant judicial review.

Second summons The possibility of seeking a second summons under the 'parallel procedure' introduced by the Courts (No. 3) Act 1986 was discussed by Lavan J in *Director of Public Prosecutions v McKillen* [1991] 2 IR 508: see 144-5, above.

Service of summons by post S. 22 of the Courts Act 1991 (see also the Practice and Procedure chapter, 346-8, below) is a general provision permitting the service of a summons by registered post. This provision came into effect on 15 October 1991: see s. 23(5) of the Act. Prior to s. 22 of the 1991 Act, s.12 of the Petty Sessions (Ireland) Act 1851 generally required personal service of a summons. It was estimated by the Minister for Justice, in the course of the debate on the 1991 Act, that s. 22 would free up to 130 gardaí engaged in summons service, particularly in road traffic offences. An instance of a provision permitting service of summonses by registered post is s. 3 of the Safety, Health and Welfare at Work Act 1989 (on the Act in general, see the 1989 Review, 379-93). S. 22 of the 1991 Act also applies to the 'parallel' procedure in the Courts (No.3) Act 1986.

EVIDENCE

Additional evidence In *The People v Ward*, Court of Criminal Appeal, 6 December 1990, the Court (O'Flaherty, Keane and Lavan JJ), in an *ex tempore* judgment, held that a trial judge has no discretion as such to refuse to accept into evidence additional evidence tendered by the prosecution under the Criminal Procedure Act 1967. The Court accepted that evidence could be excluded if its prejudice to the accused outweighed its probative value, but the instant case did not involve such an issue. The Court accepted that the only issue was whether an adjournment should have been granted to defence counsel to consider the effect of the additional evidence. Since such application had not been made by the experienced counsel appearing for the defendant, the Court of Criminal Appeal held that the trial judge had not erred in admitting the additional evidence.

Appeal: additional evidence   In *The People v Quirke*, Court of Criminal Appeal, 20 March 1991, the Court (O'Flaherty, Blayney and Johnson JJ), in an *ex tempore* judgment, ordered that new evidence be taken in the appeal under s. 33 of the Courts of Justice Act 1924, applying the test established in *Attorney General v McGann* [1927] IR 503. The evidence in question had been taken by the gardaí but not included in the book of evidence. Solicitor and counsel for the prosecution were unaware of the evidence at the date of the trial, which was for rape, and the defence was likewise unaware. The defence only became aware of the evidence after the trial, owing to the publicity attaching to it.

The Court also ordered the gardaí to conduct certain further inquiries into the events surrounding the offence. In the light of the new evidence and the inquiries, the Court quashed the applicant's conviction and ordered a retrial, without opposition from the Director of Public Prosecutions: *The People v Quirke (No.2)*, Court of Criminal Appeal, 16 May 1991.

In *The People v Walsh* (1989) 3 Frewen 248, the Court (Finlay CJ, MacKenzie and Lavan JJ) had declined to hear additional evidence concerning the opinion expressed by gardaí at the applicant's trial that he had been involved in the preparations for the armed robbery in respect of which he had been convicted. The Court also accepted that the trial judge was entitled to hear such opinion in determining the sentence to be imposed.

Common design   In *The People v Farrell (A.)*, Court of Criminal Appeal, 7 May 1990, the Court dealt with a case in which common design or acting in concert was inferred from circumstances. The defendant had been found, apparently asleep, in the back of a van containing stolen goods shortly after they had been stolen and been seen to be placed in the van. The defendant denied knowledge of the circumstances in which the stolen goods had been placed in the van, whose ownership was not established. The trial judge had charged the jury on the question of common design, in effect applying the principles set out by the Court of Criminal Appeal in *The People v Madden* [1977] IR 226. The Court of Criminal Appeal considered that, in these circumstances, there had been no error in the trial.

Confession: no corroboration required In *The People v Kavanagh* (1989) 3 Frewen 243, the Court of Criminal Appeal (Finlay CJ, Barron and Johnson JJ), in an *ex tempore* judgment, noted that the corroboration rule did not apply to confessions, but that statements made in garda custody were subject to the protections contained in the Judges' Rules. It is noteworthy that, in the context of whether the law should be reformed to require such corroboration, the Martin Committee on Criminal Procedure, which reported in March 1990, did not recommend any change in this respect. For discussion of the Martin Report see the 1990 Review, 240-2.

Confession: right to silence In 1991, the Director of Public Prosecutions continued to call for further restrictions on the right to silence at a conference on Criminal Law in the 1990s organised by the Incorporated Law Society: see *Irish Times*, 18 November 1991 and Editorial, *Irish Law Times*, December 1991.

Corroboration: sexual offence The decision of the Court of Criminal Appeal in *The People v Reid*, Court of Criminal Appeal, 20 February 1991 provided some useful *dicta* for practitioners on the effect of the Criminal Law (Rape) (Amendment) Act 1990 on the need for corroboration in sexual offences. It should be noted, however, that the trial in question took place before the 1990 Act came into force.

The applicant had been convicted of rape in the Circuit Criminal Court. In evidence he accepted that sexual intercourse had taken place with the complainant but averred that it had been consensual. His application for leave to appeal to the Court of Criminal Appeal related primarily to the trial judge's warning to the jury as to the dangers of convicting on the uncorroborated evidence of the complainant. The trial judge indicated that the jury was entitled to convict without corroborative evidence but that it was dangerous to do so. The trial judge later referred to medical evidence which indicated that there was no bruising on the complainant's body, but that the indications from her vagina were that sexual intercourse had recently taken place and that some force was used. The trial judge also referred to the evidence of the distressed condition of the complainant at the time. The trial judge did not deal specifically with the question as to what constituted corroborative evidence, having indicated to counsel that he would give the usual warning in relation to corroboration and would allow the jury to decide whether there was in fact corroboration. The Court of Criminal Appeal (O'Flaherty, Keane and Lavan JJ) dismissed the application for leave to appeal.

The Court referred to the existing case law on the subject, in particular the decisions in *The People v Williams* [1940] IR 195 and *The People v Egan (L.)* [1990] ILRM 780 (see the 1990 Review, 193-4). It noted that there was no requirement in law that the warning to be given in cases such as the present should be in any particular form. Having regard to the course which the trial judge had indicated to counsel he was going to take in his charge, it was understandable that he did not deal in any detail with the matters which the jury might have treated as being corroborative of the complainant's account.

Noting, however, that the Criminal Law (Rape) (Amendment) Act 1990 had come into force after the trial in the instant case, the Court of Criminal Appeal indicated that trial judges might feel that a warning may still be required; and in general, the Court considered that it might be of assistance for the trial judge to draw the jury's attention to those aspects of the evidence which are capable of corroborating the complainant's version.

In the instant case, the Court considered that there was ample evidence to corroborate the complainant's version, but if the jury mistakenly believed that there was no such corroboration then, in the light of the trial judge's warning, they could only have applied a standard which was unnecessarily favourable to the applicant. Thus, the application for leave to appeal was refused.

Finally, the Court rejected an application for leave to appeal to the Supreme Court pursuant to s. 29 of the Courts of Justice Act 1924. The *ex tempore* judgment on this point was circulated under the new arrangement by which Court of Criminal Appeal judgments are recorded. The Court considered that the question as to whether the charge to the jury in the instant case was adequate—despite the lack of an objection in the court of trial to the failure of the trial judge to identify those items of evidence which were capable of amounting to corroboration—did not appear to raise a point of law, and certainly did not raise a point of law of exceptional public importance which would merit a certificate of appeal to the Supreme Court pursuant to s. 29 of the 1924 Act.

Hearsay: effect   In *The People v O'Donoghue*, Court of Criminal Appeal, 29 July 1991, the Court (O'Flaherty, Barr and Morris JJ), in an *ex tempore* judgment, held that certain hearsay evidence which had been introduced in the applicant's trial did not affect the validity of his conviction.

The applicant had been charged with burglary, and he had served a notice of alibi in accordance with s. 20 of the Criminal Justice Act 1984 to the effect that he had been with his girlfriend at the time of the burglary. In the course of his cross-examination at his trial, he stood over his alibi, but accepted that his girlfriend would be unable to assist the jury in the matter as she could not remember the night in question. Prosecution counsel then put to him that his girlfriend had made statements to the gardaí which did not protect the applicant and did not refer to the night of the burglary at all. The applicant replied that he did not know about these statements. His girlfriend was not called to give evidence in the case.

The Court of Criminal Appeal held that, although the initial questioning on the applicant's alibi was permissible under s. 20 of the 1984 Act, the reference to the garda statements was improper since they constituted hearsay evidence in light of the fact that the applicant's girlfriend was not called. The Court, however, concluded that the refereence to these statements had not affected the outcome of the trial and since it had not been objected to at the time it would not allow the appeal on this ground. The Court did, however, refer with apparent approval to the decision of the Court of Appeal (Criminal Division) in *R. v Windass* (1989) 89 Cr App R 259, though noting that the circumstances in that case were quite different to those in the instant case.

Production of objects not required In *The People v Glass*, Court of Criminal Appeal, 19 March 1991, the Court (Finlay CJ, Johnson and Morris JJ), in an *ex tempore* judgment, affirmed the approach taken in *Hocking v Ahlquist Bros Ltd* [1944] KB 120 that the prosecution is not obliged to produce in court the physical evidence on which a criminal charge is founded.

In the instant case, the applicant had been charged with receiving stolen goods, and a number of witnesses testified that they had identified relevant component parts of motor cars as having been stolen from them when they were shown the parts in garda stations. The Court accepted that such evidence was admissible as identifying the objects in question, expressly applying the decision in the *Hocking* case. It may be noted that the *Hocking* case followed the view taken by the Court for Crown Cases Reserved in *R. v Francis* (1874) LR 2 CCR 128, which was a receiving case.

The Court in *Glass* noted that a judge would be obliged to comment to the jury on the non-production of the physical evidence, and the trial judge in the instant case had indeed warned the jury that the applicant should be acquitted if there was any doubt about the identifications given by the witnesses. Thus, it is clear that in many cases non-production will not be fatal to the prosecution and that the strict rigours of the best evidence rule will not, therefore, apply.

On another aspect of the case, see 170, below.

Visual identification: video evidence In *The People v Reid*, Court of Criminal Appeal, 29 February 1990, the Court (McCarthy, Egan and Blayney JJ), in an *ex tempore* judgment, noted that cases of visual identification were nowadays of a different character where video tape evidence was available to assist a jury in evaluating the testimony of a witness. While the Court emphasised the continued importance of the warning required by *The People v Casey (No.2)* [1963] IR 33, and quoted in full the warning given by the trial judge in the instant case, it is clear that juries are given more information by such videos in evaluating the credibility of eye witness evidence.

Visual identification: warning   In *The People v Connor*, Court of Criminal
Appeal, 5 December 1990, the Court (O'Flaherty, Keane and Lavan JJ), in
an *ex tempore* judgment, noted that a visual identification warning was
required, in accordance with *The People v Casey (No. 2)* [1963] IR 33, even
where the witness previously knew the accused. In the instant case, the trial
judge had in fact given such a warning.

In *The People v Craig*, Court of Criminal Appeal, 17 December 1990, the
Court (Finlay CJ, Egan and Johnson JJ), in an *ex tempore* judgment, approved
a warning on visual identification given by the trial judge in the instant case.
Of some significance in the instant case was that there was some 'bolstering'
evidence to support the visual identification evidence.

However, in *The People v McDermott* [1991] 1 IR 359, the same Court
(Finlay CJ, Egan and Johnson JJ), also in an *ex tempore* judgment delivered
in the same date as the *Craig* case, upheld an appeal against conviction in a
visual identification case. The Court held that although the trial judge had
given an impeccable general warning on the dangers of convicting on visual
identification, he had not brought home to the jury the particular circumstances of the instant case which made a conviction especially problematical.
The absence of an identification parade was a matter to which the Court drew
attention. Although the Court approved the decision of the Court in *The
People v O'Reilly* [1991] ILRM 10; [1990] 2 IR 415 (1990 Review, 207-8)
that formal identification parades are not in any sense mandatory, it concluded that a special warning should be given in such cases.

EXPLOSIVES

In *Hardy v Special Criminal Court* [1992] 1 IR 204, Carroll J held that the
designation of sodium chlorate as an explosive was not *ultra vires* the
Explosives Act 1875.

Sodium chlorate was designated an explosive for the purposes of the 1875
Act by the Explosives (Ammonium Nitratre and Sodium Chlorate) Order
1972. S. 3 of the 1875 Act defines 'explosive' as being certain named
substances. However, s. 104 of the 1875 Act also provides that an Order made
by the government under that section may declare that any substance is
explosive if it appears to the government that the substance is 'specially
dangerous to life or property by reason either of its explosive properties or
of any process in the manufacture thereof being liable to explosion.'

Carroll J said that the question of the true interpretation of s. 104 should
be approached by examining first whether sodium chlorate had explosive
properties and then considering whether it was specially dangerous to life or
property.

On the first question, the expert evidence indicated that sodium chlorate was a strong oxiding agent, that is, it would cause an explosive reaction when mixed with, and detonated with, certain other substances such as sugar or oil. Carroll J concluded that this action of transforming otherwise innocuous substances into explosive substances indicated that sodium chlorate could be deemed to have 'explosive properties' within the meaning of s. 104 of the 1875 Act. She rejected the submission that 'properties' should be interpreted as being confined to a characteristic of the substance itself to the exclusion of other substances. She took the word 'properties' to refer to attributes, inherenet qualities, characteristics or abilities.

On the second question, Carroll J concluded that, arising from the powerful explosive effect brought about by the mixture of sodium chlorate with other substances, it was specially dangerous to life or property within s.104 of the 1875 Act. She noted that it was being put into use in explosions by 'subversive organisations' at the time the 1972 Order had been made. She did not indicate whether this had been put in evidence in the case. On this basis, Carroll J concluded that the 1972 Order had not been *ultra vires* the 1875 Act.

EXTRADITION

The year saw three more high-profile extradition cases which ended up in the Supreme Court. Each of the cases involved, to a greater or lesser extent, an examination of the amendments made to s. 50 of the Extradition Act 1965 by the Extradition (European Convention on the Suppression of Terrorism) Act 1987. The three cases were *Magee v Culligan* [1992] ILRM 186; [1992] 1 IR 223, *Sloan v Culligan* [1992] ILRM 194; [1992] 1 IR 223 and *McKee v Culligan* [1992] 1 IR 223.

In the first case, *Magee v Culligan* [1992] ILRM 186; [1992] 1 IR 223 the applicant had been charged in the courts of Northern Ireland with murder and attempted murder of members of the British army. The deaths had involved the use of an M60 machine gun. The applicant escaped from custody in Crumlin Road Prison on 10 June 1981, two days before the conclusion of his trial for the offences referred to, and he was convicted in his absence. The applicant was arrested in the State in January 1982 and was charged with and convicted of offences arising from his escape from custody, pursuant to the provisions of the Criminal Law (Jurisdiction) Act 1976. He was sentenced to 10 years imprisonment on foot of these convictions. On 23 October 1989, a temporary Judge of the District Court ordered the applicant's delivery to Northern Ireland on foot of warrants seeking his extradition in respect of the 1981 murder and attempted murder convictions. The applicant sought judicial review of this decision. The applicant argued, *inter alia*, that the Extradition (European Convention on the Suppression of Terrorism) Act 1987 created retrospective criminal liability contrary to Article 15.5 of the Constitution by excluding offences involving the use of automatic firearms from the definition of political offences within s. 50 of the Extradition Act 1965. He also raised the issue of a temporary District Court Judge being involved in his extradition. Lynch J dismissed the application and, on appeal by the applicant on the constitutional issues, the Supreme Court (Finlay CJ, Hamilton P, Hederman, McCarthy and Egan JJ) dismissed his appeal.

In the High Court, Lynch J held that the 1987 Act was not inconsistent with Article 15.5 of the Constitution, since it did not create a retrospective criminal act but involved the exclusion of certain offences from being regarded as political offences and thus merely developed the law on political offences. In the Supreme Court, a similar view was taken, the Court holding that Article 15.5 of the Constitution did not contain any general prohibition against retrospective legislation, but only against legislation which declares acts retrospectively to be infringements of the law. On this basis, the Court dismissed the claim under Article 15.5.

The next point raised by the applicant was that the 1987 Act had deprived him of a right not to serve a sentence of imprisonment, by altering the rules on political offences. However, Lynch J considered that any such right was not one protected under Article 40.3 of the Constitution and so the removal of the protection of the political offence exception by the 1987 Act in respect of the offences for which the applicant had been convicted was not unconstitutional. Again, in the Supreme Court a similar view was taken. The Court held that the applicant did not have any vested right to be dealt with in accordance with any law which might have applied in 1982, and fair procedures required only that the application for his extradition would be dealt with in accordance with the law applicable at the time of the application, and thus the use of the 1987 Act in the instant case did not involve the State in infringing the applicant's rights under Article 40.3. It may be noted that a similar view had been taken by the Divisional High Court in *Finucane v McMahon* [1990] ILRM 505 (SC); [1990] 1 IR 165 (HC & SC) (discussed in the 1989 Review, 157-9, and 1990 Review, 212-16).

The next constitutional point raised by the applicant concerned the temporary Judge of the District Court who had ordered his extradition. Here, the Supreme Court was much stronger in its view than Lynch J had been. In the High Court, Lynch J had relied on to a large extent on the presumnption of constitutionality in rejecting the applicant's claim. He held that s. 51 of the Courts of Justice Act 1936, which provides for the appointment of temporary Judges of the District Court, and which was re-enacted to apply to the present District Court by s. 48(8) of the Courts (Supplemental Provisions) Act 1961, must be presumed constitutional. In the absence of any evidence in the instant case that the power to appoint had been used in an improper manner, he held that the applicant had not established that s. 51 was inconsistent with the Constitution. While the Supreme Court did not disagree with this analysis, it went somewhat further. The Court held that although the Judge of the District Court in the instant case was a temporary Judge within s. 51 of the 1936 Act, this did not in any way affect his independence of function under Article 35.2 of the Constitution since his warrant of appointment was held under the President and for the period of his appointment he was free in the exercise of his functions. The fact that as a temporary Judge his removal would not be subject to the same protections as for permanent members of the judiciary did not, in the Supreme Court's view, affect his independence and the 1936 Act was a permitted regulation of the business of the courts under Article 36.iii of the Constitution.

The remaining points raised by the applicant in the High Court were not renewed in the Supreme Court. Lynch J held that, having considered the evidence presented to the Court, the applicant had not established that he would be ill-treated if returned to Northern Ireland. On the question of the delay in seeking the applicant's extradition, he noted that this had arisen from the applicant's imprisonment in the State on foot of his 1982 conviction and thus no ground relating to delay had been made out. The applicant also argued that the extradition would be oppressive or unjust within the meaning of s. 50(2)(bbb) of the 1965 Act, as inserted by the 1987 Act. However, since the Northern authorities did not seek extradition in respect of the applicant's prison escape and they had given undertakings that the term served in this State would be taken into account, the application would not be refused under s. 50(2)(bbb).

Finally, Lynch J turned to the political offence question. Applying the test put forward by the Supreme Court in *Finucane v McMahon* [1990] ILRM 505; [1990] 1 IR 165 (1990 Review, 212-16), Lynch J held that the offences relating to possession of firearms could be regarded as political offences within the original provisions of s. 50 of the Extradition Act 1965, since although they were committed on behalf of the IRA they did not as such involve subversion of the Constitution. However, he noted that this con-clusion was subject to the effect on the 1965 Act of the provisions of the Extradition (European Convention on the Suppression of Terrorism) Act 1987. On this point, he held that since the firearms offences had resulted in the commission of murder, the application of the political offence exemption was precluded by s. 3(3)(a)(v) of the 1987 Act and the plaintiff's application for release under s. 50 of the 1965 Act was therefore dismissed. As already indicated, the applicant did not appeal this finding to the Supreme Court, and the effect was that he was therefore liable to extradition.

While the *Magee* decision appeared to indicate that the 1987 Act had effectively narrowed the political offence exception in the 1965 Act, the other two cases heard in 1991 indicated that further amendments were required if that objective was, in fact, to be achieved.

In *Sloan v Culligan* [1992] ILRM 194; [1992] 1 IR 223 the applicant had been charged in the courts of Northern Ireland with possession of automatic weapons with intent to endanger life and with false imprisonment. He escaped from custody in Crumlin Road Prison on 10 June 1981, two days before the conclusion of his trial for these offences, and he was convicted in his absence. The longest sentence he received on these charges was one of five years. He was arrested in this State in January 1982 and charged with and convicted of offences arising from his escape from custody, pursuant to the Criminal Law (Jurisdiction) Act 1976. In October 1989, the District Court ordered his extradition to Northern Ireland in relation to the 1981 convictions. The applicant sought his release pursuant to s. 50 of the Extradition Act 1965. In the course of the hearing, an undertaking was given that the applicant would only be required to serve the balance of his 1981 sentence and that the term served in respect of the convictions in this State would be taken into account. In the High Court, Lynch J dismissed the applicant's claims, though his judgment also exposed a gap in the Extradition (European Convention on the Suppression of Terrorism) Act 1987, the effect of which was that, by the time his appeal reached the Supreme Court, no extradition order was made.

The applicant had, like the applicant in *Magee*, above, argued that the 1987 Act was inconsistent with Article 15.5 of the Constitution. This point was rejected by Lynch J.

The substance of the *Sloan* case concerned, however, the political offence issue and the effect of the 1987 Act on the 1965 Act. Relying again on the decision in *Finucane v McMahon* [1990] ILRM 505; [1990] 1 IR 165, Lynch J noted that the aims and purposes of the IRA, in connection with which the offences in question had been committed, involved an attempt to overthrow the institutions established by the Constitution, but since the particular offences with which the applicant had been involved might not have had such a purpose he felt that they could be regarded as political within s. 50 of the 1965 Act. Again, as in the *Magee* case, this finding in the applicant's favour was subject to the effect of the 1987 Act.

This required a close analysis of s. 3(3)(a) of the 1987 Act, which states that the political exemption shall not apply to possession of firearms 'if such use endangers persons'. Lynch J held that since the circumstances of the applicant's possession of the automatic weapons involved in the offences alleged did not, at that time, involve a present danger to persons, the possession offence did not fall within the exclusion in s. 3(3)(a) of the 1987 Act, and he was thus entitled to rely on the political exemption in respect of that offence.

On the false imprisonment issue, Lynch J considered that the offence of false imprisonment with which the applicant was involved was a 'serious false imprisonment' within s. 3(3)(a) of the 1987 Act and thus the applicant was not entitled to rely on the political offence exemption in s. 50 of the 1965 Act in respect of that offence. It was on this basis alone that Lynch J ordered his extradition.

When the appeal in *Sloan* came on to the Supreme Court, only two issues issues were raised: whether the possession of firearms fell within the terms of s. 3(3)(a) of the 1987 Act and the effect of the undertaking given by the Northern authorities. In effect, the Supreme Court (Finlay CJ, Hamilton P, Hederman, McCarthy and Egan JJ) upheld the reasoning of Lynch J, but the passage of time had had a significant effect on the undertaking given by the Northern authorities.

On the interpretation of s. 3(3)(a) of the 1987 Act, the Supreme Court agreed that the exclusion in s. 3(3)(a) should be strictly construed. Since it referred to the use of firearms in the present tense the Court agreed with Lynch J that it should not be interpreted as applying to the case where firearms possession might in the future endanger persons. The Court made the usual comment in such cases that if this had been the intention of the Oireachtas, it could have used clear language to indicate that intention.

On the effect of the undertaking, the Court pointed out that since the Northern authorities had undertaken that the applicant would only serve the balance of his five year sentence (giving credit for the sentence served in this State) the effect at that stage (November 1991) was that the applicant would be released immediately on rendition to Northern Ireland. Since the courts would not act in vain, the applicant's release was ordered. It is of note that McCarthy J, in a concurring judgment, queried whether a requesting State should be encouraged to give undertakings that its laws would not be enforced in respect of a citizen of its own State, citing *dicta* in *Bourke v Attorney General* [1972] IR 36 on this point.

The third major extradition case of the year was *McKee v Culligan* [1992] 1 IR 223. The circumstances were quite close to those in *Sloan* and the outcome was, inevitably, to refuse to extradite him.

The applicant had been charged in the courts of Northern Ireland with possession of automatic weapons with intent to endanger life. He escaped from custody in Crumlin Road Prison on 10 June 1981, two days before the conclusion of his trial for these offences, and he was convicted in his absence. He was arrested in this State in December 1981 and charged with and convicted of offences arising from his escape from custody, pursuant to the Criminal Law (Jurisdiction) Act 1976. In October 1989, the District Court ordered his extradition to Northern Ireland in relation to the 1981 convictions. The applicant sought his release pursuant to s. 50 of the Extradition Act 1965.

Similar arguments were raised in connection with Article 15.5 of the Constitution, and were rejected as in *Magee* and *Sloan*, above.

On the political offence issue, it was held that since it had not been established that the particular offences with which the applicant had been involved were intended to overthrow the Constitution, they could be regarded as political within s. 50 of the 1965 Act, subject to the 1987 Act, again relying on the decision in *Finucane v McMahon* [1990] ILRM 505; [1990] 1 IR 165. Turning to the 1987 Act, again as the circumstances of the applicant's possession of the automatic weapons involved in the offences alleged did not, at that time, involve a present danger to persons, the possession offence did not fall within the exclusion in s. 3(3)(a) of the 1987 Act, and he was thus entitled to rely on the political exemption in respect of that offence, and was thus entitled to his release.

The effect of the *Sloan* and *McKee* decisions in particular were that calls were made for the amendment of the 1987 Act to deal wuth what were perceived as loopholes in the 1987 Act: *Irish Times*, 16 November 1991. While it appeared that there was general agreement that some amendments were required, no legislative proposal had been published at the time of writing.

FIREARMS

Offensive weapons   The Firearms and Offensive Weapons Act 1990 (Offensive Weapons) Order 1991 (SI No. 66) is discussed in the 1990 Review, 225. The full text of the Order is helpfully reproduced in the amended Annotation to the 1990 Act in *Irish Current Law Statutes Annotated*.

Revocation of licence   *Hourigan v Kelly and Ors*, High Court, 26 April 1991 concerned the application of fair procedures in the revocation of a firearms licence.

The applicant, a farmer, had held a shotgun licence under the Firearms Act 1925. In 1990, he was involved in an incident with a neighbour. No assault had taken place and no firearms had been involved, but the gardaí requested both parties to surrender their shotguns with a view to their licences being revoked and both parties complied with this request. The first respondent revoked the applicant's licence based in part on a report of the incident. He also had regard to a conviction of the applicant in 1984 for assault, in an incident in which it was alleged that the applicant had discharged his shotgun, but in relation to which no charge under the 1925 Act was brought. S. 5 of the 1925 Act provides that a licence may be revoked where a Superintendent is 'satisfied', *inter alia*, that the holder is a person who cannot, without danger to the public safety or to the peace, be permitted to possess firearms. The applicant challenged the revocation on the ground that he had had no opportunity to reply to or deal with the grounds of the decision.

Egan J granted judicial review and quashed the revocation order. He held that, although s. 5 of the 1925 Act did not provide for a hearing, any licence revocation must be conducted with fair procedures. He accepted that, in some circumstances, an instant revocation would be perfectly permissible, but stated that this was not such a case having regard to the fact that the shotgun was in garda custody. Thus, he concluded that the applicant was entitled to a hearing on the basis of the *audi alteram partem* principle.

INDEXATION OF FINES

The Law Reform Commission's *Report on the Indexation of Fines* (LRC 37-1991) is a most interesting contribution to jurisprudence on a subject whose title savours of the mundane. The problem about fines is obvious to anyone who has perused the criminal code: there is a patchwork of offences, often going back more than a century, with a register of fines reflecting the monetary values of a bygone age. Inflation over the past generation has made a mockery of any sense of proportionality. Offences of some significance can carry maximum fines of as low as £2.

Lethargy has characterised the response of the Oireachtas thus far. The problem could be radically improved by a single, comprehensive, piece of legislation, covering all criminal offences, backed by a suitable formula for increases in line with the decreasing value of money. The Commission recommend that this be done. The specific approach it favours involves the introduction of between three and five categories, extending retrospectively to embrace equivalent band of fine values for earlier periods. The categories and time periods would be fixed by reference to tables of relative money values based on the Consumer Price Index, drafted on the model of s. 3(1) of the Capital Gains Tax (Amendment) Act 1978 so as to avoid constitutional problems as to delegated legislation such as arose in *McDaid v Sheehy* [1991] ILRM 250; [1989] ILRM 342; [1991] 1 IR 1. See the 1989 Review, 111-14 and the 1990 Review, 464-5.

This general approach involves a *standard fine system*, in contrast to a *variable fine system*, which seeks to give effect to the principle of equality of impact of the criminal penalty on offenders of differing financial circumstances. A fine of £10 may cause significant hardship for a poor person while a fine of £1,000 may not be noticed by a rich offender. Of course there is some flexibility within a standard fine system for giving weight to the question of the convicted person's financial position, but clearly there are limits to the extent for which this can reduce disparity in impact, especially where the maximum fine is not very high.

Finland, well over half a century ago, and Sweden more recently, developed a 'day fine' mechanism which seeks to equalise the impact of fines. The *number* of day fines represents the measure of punishment, and the *amount* of each day fine is estimated in accordance with the financial situation of the accused. The day fine is calculated by multiplying these two numbers together. See paras 100-114 of the Report.

The Commission expresses considerable interest in the 'day fine' approach. Among its advantages, as well as achieving a modicum of equality of impact on those sentenced, is the fact that day fines do not require any adjustment for inflation. Moreover, they promote efficiency in fine collection, as defaults are substantially reduced. The Commission is nonetheless conscious of the objections to variable fine systems. Perhaps its greatest drawback is that it diminishes the economic disincentive to crime created by the penalties of the criminal law. The Commission acknowledges that much crime is opportunistic, thus excluding cerebral considerations as to the balance of advantage resulting from likelihood of apprehension and conviction and the quantum of sentence. Nonetheless, the Commission comments that 'the apparent undermining by day fines of the general deterrence which criminal sanctions are supposed to provide is disturbing' (para 131).

A further difficulty with the variable fine approach is that it cannot easily deal with cases where the offender has a low income or no income at all. As against this, the Commission points out that the standard fine approach leads to even greater problems, since it results in high imprisonment rates for non-payment. A more telling practical objection to the variable fine system is that it depends on a correct assessment of offender's means. The existing evidence suggests that this is a real problem.

A final objection to the variable fine approach arises in the constitutional context, regarding jury trial for non-minor offences. The Commission state (*id.*) that:

> A day fine scheme cannot easily be grafted onto our present system of jurisdictional allocation, with its rigid (though uncertain) monetary limitation on competence of the District Court. The same offence might be either minor or non- minor, depending on the means of the offender, which might make him liable to a fine either above or below the threshold. While a means-based variation in the level of penalty imposed has been submitted to be fully in accordance with the equality guarantee of Article 40.1 of the Constitution, it is inconceivable that the choice between jury and summary trial should be made available, or denied, depending on a person's means. As long as the courts adhere to their

present scheme for differentiating between minor and non-minor offences, it is likely that a day fine system would be very vulnerable to constitutional challenge.

The Commission is far from convinced that this challenge would succeed, but is sufficiently impressed by the difficulty to come to the conclusion, after consideration of all the arguments for and against a day fine system, that it should not recommend its introduction *at this stage*. The Commission remains confident of its potential merits, and suggests that the question be considered again, after a standard fine system has been introduced and in the light, in particular, of British experience (as to which see Morris & Gelsthorpe, 'Not Paying for Crime: Issues in Fine Enforcement', [1990] Crim L Rev 839, at 850).

JURY

Visit to locus in quo In *The People v Connor*, Court of Criminal Appeal, 5 December 1990 the Court (O'Flaherty, Keane and Lavan JJ), in an *ex tempore* judgment, noted that a trial judge had a discretion as to whether to allow a jury to visit the scene of a crime, in accordance with s. 22 of the Juries Act 1976.

LARCENY

In *The People v Gilligan (No. 2)* [1992] ILRM 769, the Court of Criminal Appeal considered the effect of a statutory provision which substituted a new section in existing law. In the instant case, the provision in question was s. 3 of the Larceny Act 1990, which provides that the Larceny Act 1916 be amended by the substitution for s. 33 of the 1916 Act of the section set out in s. 3 of the 1990 Act. The 1990 Act replaced the old offence of receiving stolen property with the new offence of handling.

The applicant in *Gilligan* had been charged with receiving stolen property, contrary to s. 33 of the 1916 Act, as originally enacted. The offence was alleged to have taken place in January 1988. The crucial point in the case was that the 1990 Act came into force in August 1990 and the applicant was put on trial in November 1990. It was argued that the applicant could not have been tried in November 1990 with the receiving offence since this had been abolished by the 1990 Act.

The case turned on s. 21(1)(e) of the Interpretation Act 1937. This provides that the 'repeal' of statutory provisions shall not affect pending civil or criminal proceedings. The applicant argued that s. 3 of the 1990 Act had not repealed s. 33 of the 1916 Act but had merely substituted a new section for the original s. 33. The Court of Criminal Appeal (O'Flaherty, Keane and Barron JJ) rejected this argument. The Court relied on passages from Bennion, *Statutory Interpretation* (ss. 170 and 178) in concluding that since the 1990 Act had altered the legal meaning of the 1916 Act this amounted to a repeal of s. 33 of the 1916 Act. Thus, s. 33 was regarded as still extant for the purposes of the charge against the defendant. The Court therefore dismissed the application on this ground. This view of s. 21 of the Interpretation Act 1937 is, no doubt, of great practical interest given the proliferation of the 'substitution' or 'scissors and paste' approach to statutory amendment which exists in the State. For another issue considered by the Court in the instant case, see 167-8, below, and for the Court's decision on the applicant's seeking bail, see *The People v Gilligan*, Court of Criminal Appeal, 10 December 1990, below, 166.

The Court also dismissed an appeal against sentence by the applicant in an *ex tempore* judgment: *The People v Gilligan (No. 3)* [1992] ILRM at 775. The trial court had imposed a sentence of 4 years, which the Court of Criminal Appeal described as at the low end of the scale for the robbery in question, which it stated had been well planned. The trial court had been told by a garda witness that, to his knowledge, the applicant had never worked legitimately. In fact, the applicant had been a seaman between 1966 and 1976. However, the Court of Criminal Appeal held that this point did not affect the validity of the sentence imposed and it affirmed the sentence. It may have been influenced in particular by the evidence that the applicant had been convicted on a number of previous occasions in respect of similar offences.

LEGAL AID

Attendance fees   The Criminal Justice (Legal Aid) (Amendment)(No. 2) Regulations 1991 (SI No. 70), which came into effect on 1 January 1991, amended the fees payable for a solicitor's attendance in the District Court as well as those for solicitor's and counsel's attendance in prison.

Mileage allowance   The Criminal Justice (Legal Aid) (Amendment) Regulations 1991 (SI No. 24), which came into effect on 1 January 1991, increased the motor mileage allowance for solicitors attending a client.

PROCEDURE

Accusatorial nature of trial   In *Director of Public Prosecutions v Holmes*, High Court, 19 December 1991, the accusatorial nature of criminal trials was adverted to: see 171-2, below.

Another aspect of the accusatorial nature arose in *The People v Boylan* [1991] 1 IR 477, discussed in another context above, 128-9. The Court, in an *ex tempore* judgment, stated that where there was a conflict between prosecution and defence witnesses it was not suffi- cient for the trial judge to leave the jury 'at large' to determine which witnesses it believed. Rather, the trial judge should direct the jury that, in deciding between the witnesses, it was required in a criminal trial to give any benefit of a doubt to the accused where such doubt arose.

Additional evidence In *The People v Ward*, Court of Criminal Appeal, 6 December 1990 the Court (O'Flaherty, Barr and Lavan JJ), in an *ex tempore* judgment, dealt with the admission of additional evidence: see 149-50, above.

Appeal: ground not argued in trial court In *The People v Walsh and Tynan*, Court of Criminal Appeal, 28 January 1991, the Court (McCarthy, Barr and Lardner JJ), in an *ex tempore* judgment noted that the Court was reluctant to hear an appeal against conviction on the basis of a ground on which experienced counsel in the trial court had not requisitioned the trial judge.

For an instance of the Court allowing such a point to be raised, however, see the decision in *The People v Martin*, Court of Criminal Appeal, 1 July 1991, below, 175.

Appeal: new evidence In *The People v O'Brien (K.)*, Court of Criminal Appeal, 29 January 1990, the Court (McCarthy, Egan and Blayney JJ), in an *ex tempore* decision allowed the applicant to adduce new evidence in his application for leave to appeal in circumstances where this evidence had not been disclosed prior to his trial. Although the Court doubted whether the evidence in question would have materially affected the trial, it considered that there would be an apparent injustice if he was not permitted to rely on the material in the appeal.

Appeal to Supreme Court In *The People v Reid*, Court of Criminal Appeal, 20 February 1991, the Court refused a certificate of leave to appeal to the Supreme Court under s. 24 of the Courts of Justice Act 1924: see 152, above.

Bail: appeal In *The People v Smith*, Court of Criminal Appeal, 2 April 1990, the Court (O'Flaherty, Barr and Lavan JJ), in an *ex tempore* judgment, admitted the appellant to bail, having granted him leave to appeal, in accordance with the principles laid down in *The People v Hayden* (1970) 1

Frewen 347. The Court was satisifed, without prejudicing the full appeal, that an arguable point had been made out. Judgment in the substantive appeal, in which the appellant was successful, was discussed in the 1990 Review, 229.

In *The People v Gaffey*, Court of Criminal Appeal, 10 December 1990, the Court (O'Flaherty, Lynch and Johnson JJ), in an *ex tempore* judgment which also applied the *Hayden* case, declined to admit the applicant to bail, concluding that the applicant had not been able to isolate an arguable point in advance of the full transcript of the trial being available. The Court noted, of course, that this was without prejudice to the applicant's full application for leave to appeal, and it is of some interest to note that the applicant was, ultimately, successful, though on a different point to that relied on in the application for bail: see *The People v Gaffey (No. 2)*, Court of Criminal Appeal, 10 May 1991: 183, below.

In *The People v Gilligan*, Court of Criminal Appeal, 10 December 1990, the Court (O'Flaherty, Lynch and Johnson JJ), in another *ex tempore* judgment which also applied the *Hayden* case, declined to admit the applicant to bail, again concluding, as in the *Gaffey* case of the same date, that the applicant had not put forward any arguable point. In this case, it may be noted that the substantive application for leave to appeal was not successful: see *The People v Gilligan (No. 2)* [1992] ILRM 769, above, 163-4.

In *The People v Barr*, Court of Criminal Appeal, 17 June 1991, the Court (O'Flaherty, Costello and Keane JJ), in another *ex tempore* judgment declined to admit the applicant to bail in a case where the grounds argued did not appear to touch on one of the offences for which the applicant had been convicted. As with the previous cases in this area, the Court pointed out, of course, that this was without prejudice to the applicant's full application for leave to appeal.

Book of evidence: discrepancies   In *The People v Marsh, Irish Times*, 28 February 1991, Barron J directed the acquittal of the accused on a murder charge after discrepancies emerged in the evidence given by a number of prosecution witnesses. The judge commented on the discrepancies between the evidence given in the book of evidence and that given in court. In a subsequent statement by the Director of Public Prosecutions, the Director stated that criticisms made by the trial judge as to the procedures adopted in the prosecution of the case were 'without foundation and . . . unjustified': see *Irish Times*, 2 March 1991.

Chambers hearing   In *The People v McGinley (J.)* (1989) 3 Frewen 251, the Court of Criminal Appeal (Hederman, Lynch and Blayney JJ), in an *ex tempore* judgment, held that it was not appropriate for the trial judge to consider a sentencing matter in his chambers with a probation officer where the defence did not have the opportunity to put its side. The Court stated that hearings must be in open court.

Confession: not challenged   In *The People v Kearney*, Court of Criminal Appeal, 20 March 1991, at the applicant's trial his confession had not been challenged as being involuntary. However, at the end of the case, counsel for the defence invited the jury to reject the confession on the ground that it had been obtained in oppressive circumstances. The trial judge, in his direction, informed the jury that the defence had not challenged the confession and that there had, therefore, been no *voir dire* procedure in the case ('trial within the trial'). On appeal, the Court of Criminal Appeal (O'Flaherty, Blayney and Johnson JJ), in an *ex tempore* judgment, held that the trial judge's comments were not wrong in law.

While the Court accepted that any reference to the *voir dire* would be unacceptable if a *voir dire* had actually taken place, there was no objection to the course adopted by the trial judge in the instant case.

Counsel's duty to court   The obligation of counsel for the prosecution and defence to give all assistance to the trial judge, including reference to relevant statutory provisions, was adverted to by the Court of Criminal Appeal in *The People v Dennigan* (1989) 3 Frewen 253.

'Direction' in Special Criminal Court   In *The People v Gilligan (No. 2)* [1992] ILRM 769, the Court dealt with the role of the Special Criminal Court at the end of the prosecution case when an application is made by the defence that the case be dismissed, in other words, what would amount in a jury trial to an application for a direction.

In the instant case, it was suggested that the Special Criminal Court had dismissed the defence application by, in effect, rejecting certain evidence tendered for the prosecution, which appeared to exonerate the defendant and preferring certain other prosecution evidence which appeared to point towards the defendant's guilt. It was argued that where there was a contradiciton in the prosecution's evidence, there should be an acquittal at the 'direction' stage. This interpretation of the trial court's function was rejected by the Court of Criminal Appeal (O'Flaherty, Keane and Barron JJ). The Court concluded that there was evidence on which a prosecution could succeed, and thus the trial court had been correct in allowing the case to proceed. In this context, the Court approved certain dicta of the Court of Appeal (Criminal Division) in *R. v Galbraith* [1981] 2 All ER 1060. Significantly, however, the Court accepted that the Special Criminal Court was required, as far as possible, to emulate the role of a trial judge in a jury trial at the 'direction' stage.

Other issues in the case are discussed above, 163-4.

Duplicity in charge   *Devereaux v Kotsonouris* [1992] ILRM 140 was a case involving, *inter alia*, claims that a summons was bad for duplicity. The case arose against the background of the Criminal Justice Act 1984.

S. 6(1) of the Criminal Justice Act 1984 empowers a member of An Garda Síochána to do a number of things in relation to a person detained under s. 4 of the 1984 Act. S. 6(1)(c) empowers a garda to photograph such person, and s. 6(1)(d) empowers a garda to fingerprint such person. S. 6(4) of the 1984 Act states that any person who obstructs or attempts to obstruct a garda exercising such powers shall be guilty of an offence. The applicant had been convicted before the respondent Judge of the District Court on a summons which alleged that he had unlawfully obstructed a member of An Garda Síochána by refusing to allow himself 'to be photographed or fingerprinted'. The particulars in the summons stated that such was 'contrary to s. 6(1)(c)(d) Criminal Justice Act 1984.' The order of the District Court recorded that this was treated as a single offence, and the applicant was sentenced to 8 months imprisonment. The applicant appealed the conviction to the Circuit Court and then applied for judicial review of the District Court decision. The Circuit Court appeal was adjourned generally pending the judicial review pro- ceedings. The argument centred largely around whether the summons was bad for duplicity.

Lavan J ultimately refused judicial review, but in analysing the issues arising in the case, he made a number of important and useful comments on the general principles in the area.

In relation to s. 6 of the 1984 Act, he accepted that there were no offences *created* by s. 6(1)(c) or (d) of the 1984 Act, but rather that s. 6(4) created a number of offences in respect of the powers *conferred* by s. 6(1) of the 1984 Act. Applying the general approach in *The State (McGroddy) v Carr* [1975] IR 275, he pointed out that to lay more than one charge of 'obstructing' or 'attempting to obstruct' would be bad for duplicity.

However, Lavan J went on to conclude that, since the applicant was charged under s. 6 of the 1984 Act, he was not prejudiced in the conviction entered against him and was thus not entitled to judicial review *ex debito justitiae*. He referred with approval to, but distinguished, the leading decision in *The State (Vozza) v Ó Floinn* [1957] IR 227 in this respect. And adopting another Supreme Court decision, *The State (Roche) v Delap* [1980] IR 170, he held that since the applciant had appealed the conviction to the Circuit Court it was not appropriate to grant judicial review.

Remitting the case, Lavan J commented that since the Circuit Court would be entitled to confirm, vary or reverse the decision of the District Court, the Circuit Court could deal with any problems of duplicity in the summons. He commented (though no doubt this was obiter) that the evidence on affidavit indicated that the applicant had been guilty of one of two offences provided for by s. 6(4) of the 1984 Act; but, perhaps with a view to the ultimate function of the Circuit Court on this point, he stated that this was assuming that such evidence was established to the satisfaction of the Judge of the Circuit Court.

Expert witnesses In *The People v Sloan (G.)*, Court of Criminal Appeal, 26 November 1990 the Court (Finlay CJ, Lardner and Blayney JJ), in an *ex tempore* judgment held that a trial court was entitled to prefer the evidence of one expert witness over another in relation to the correct interpretation of foreign law, in the instant case the law of Northern Ireland.

On the expression of opinion by a garda, see *The People v Walsh* (1989) 3 Frewen 248 (see 180, below).

Judicial review: quash or remit In two judgments delivered by Barron J on the same day, he quashed on *certiorari* two decisions of the District Court in criminal trials. In one case, *Sweeney v Brophy and DPP* [1992] ILRM 479, the case was not remitted to the District Court whereas, in the second, *Director of Public Prosecutions v Brennan* [1992] ILRM 532, he ordered remittal to allow the prosecution to proceed. The cases illustrate that, in some but not all circumstances, *certiorari* can amount to an acquittal.

In *Sweeney v Brophy and DPP* [1992] ILRM 479, the applicant had been convicted of assault before the respondent Judge of the District Court. The applicant sought certiorari to quash the verdict on the ground that a number of improprieties had occurred during the hearing of the case. The respondents did not oppose the application for certiorari but sought to have the matter remitted to the District Court. Barron J declined to remit the case.

He held that the improprieties which had occurred did not make the trial void *ab initio*, but rather the resulting conviction was voidable so that *certiorari* lay to quash it. He approved dicta in *R. (Drohan) v Waterford Justices* [1901] 2 IR 548 and in *R. (McGrath) v Clare Justices* [1905] 2 IR 510 in this context.

Since the applicant had been put in peril in a trial which had initially been valid, Barron J concluded that he was entitled to plead autrefois acquit and it was thus not appropriate to remit the case. In this respect, he distinguished *Singh v Ruane* [1989] IR 610 (see the 1989 Review, 181-2).

The second case on this topic, also a decision of Barron J, was *Director of Public Prosecutions v Brennan* [1992] ILRM 532. In this case, the respondent Judge of the District Court was the trial judge in a prosecution of two persons for malicious damage and burglary. The two defendants had been arrested under s. 30 of the Offences against the State Act 1939 on suspicion of malicious damage. The defendants made confessions of their involvement in the malicious damage, and at about 4.30 p.m. on the date in question they were visited by their solicitor. The gardaí wished at this stage to bring them before a court, but the respondent was unavailable at the time. The defendants were, accordingly, released from their s. 30 custody and immediately re-arrested at common law and were charged with malicious damage and burglary. They were detained overnight in garda custody and brought before a court the following morning. The defendants elected for summary trial and indicated that they would plead guilty. At the hearing of their case, their solicitor argued that their detention after 4.30 p.m. on the date in question was unlawful and that accordingly the charges should be dismissed. The respondent Judge acceded to this submission. On judicial review by the Director Barron J quashed the respondent's decision and remitted the case to the District Court.

He held that the respondent had acted improperly, and should have allowed the case to proceed and then dealt with any submissions as to unlawful custody in the course of the trial, and so his decision was quashed on this ground. However, unlike the *Sweeney* case, above, he concluded that the respondent's decision was a nullity, and since he never entered into an adjudication on the charges against the defendants it was appropriate to remit the case to the District Court to deal with the matter. In this context, Barron J applied the decision in *R. (McGrath) v Clare Justices* [1905] 2 IR 510.

Jury: majority verdicts   In *The People v Glass*, Court of Criminal Appeal, 19 March 1991 the Court (Finlay CJ, Johnson and Morris JJ), in an *ex tempore* judgment, affirmed the view that a trial judge is not obliged, at the beginning of their deliberations, to inform a jury of the majority verdict provisions in s. 25 of the Criminal Justice Act 1984. In this instance it was acceptable if the jury were informed after they had told the court that they were unable to agree a verdict on a unanimous basis. See also the decision in *The People v O'Callaghan*, Court of Criminal Appeal, 30 July 1990 (1990 Review, 210).

Jury: withdrawal by judge   In *The People v Farrell (A.)*, Court of Criminal Appeal, 7 May 1990 the Court (O'Flaherty, Keane and Lavan JJ), in an *ex tempore* judgment, applied the decision of the Supreme Court in *The People v O'Shea (No. 2)* [1983] ILRM 529 on the circumstances in which a trial judge should not withdraw a case from the jury. The same principles were applied by a differently constituted Court (Finlay CJ, Gannon and Blayney JJ) in its *ex tempore* decision in *The People v O'Shea (P.)*, Court of Criminal Appeal, 21 May 1990.

ROAD TRAFFIC

Arrest: opinion The adequacy of the opinion required to found an arrest under s. 49 of the Road Traffic Act 1961 was again discussed in *Director of Public Prosecutions v Brady* [1991] 1 IR 337.

The defendant had been charged with driving a vehicle when his blood-alcohol level was in excess of the limit prescribed by s. 49 of the 1961 Act, as inserted by s. 10 of the Road Traffic (Amendment) Act 1978. The defendant had been stopped at a garda checkpoint. The arresting garda had noticed that the defendant's eyes were bloodshot, that his speech was slurred and his appearance untidy. He asked the defendant to provide him with a breath test, informing him that refusal would be an offence. The breath test proved positive, the garda formed the opinion that the defendant was unfit to drive the vehicle and informed him that he was arresting him on suspicion of an offence under s. 49 of the 1961 Act. In the District Court, the charge was dismissed on the ground that there was no formal proof that the garda had formed the opinion that the defendant had consumed intoxicating liquor. On a case stated O'Hanlon J remitted the case to the District Court.

He accepted that a charge under s. 49 could be dismissed if the result of the breath test formed the sole basis for the garda's opinion that the person was unfit to drive the vehicle. However, in the instant case the garda had given evidence of an observational nature as to the defendant's condition, and the failure to give formal proof of his opinion that the defendant had consumed intoxicating liquor could not, in O'Hanlon J's view, invalidate all the subsequent steps taken by the garda. On this basis, O'Hanlon J distinguished the instant case from the circumstances in *Director of Public Prosecutions v Gilmore* [1981] ILRM 102.

He added the important rider that if the defendant had been charged with the offence of failure to provide a breath test under s. 12 of the 1978 Act, it would be a good defence if no evidence had been adduced to show that the garda had formed the necessary opinion that the defendant had consumed intoxicating liquor before requiring the defendant to undergo the breath test.

Arrest: trespass In *Director of Public Prosecutions v McCreesh*, Supreme Court, 7 March 1991 (see 131-2, above) the Supreme Court held that s. 49 of the Road Traffic Act 1961 did not confer a power of arrest on the gardaí while trespassing.

Course of evidence In *Director of Public Prosecutions v Holmes*, High Court, 19 December 1991 the central issue concerned the refusal of a District Court Judge to hear certain evidence.

The defendant had been charged, *inter alia*, with the offence of driving a mechanically propelled vehicle when it was in a condition that was dangerous, contrary to s. 53 of the Road Traffic Act 1961, as inserted by s. 10 of the Road Traffic (Amendment) Act 1978. Evidence was given that the gardaí were called to the scene of a crash involving a minibus driven by the defendant. A garda began giving evidence of his examination of the minbus after the accident. Objection was taken on the basis that the scene of the accident had not been fully preserved, that the chain of evidence had been broken and that the examination had taken place three hours after the accident. The prosecution stated that the evidence would relate solely to the pre-accident condition of the minibus. The District Court Judge declined to hear the evidence and dismissed the dangerous driving charge. On a case stated Lavan J remitted the case to the District Court.

Lavan J relied primarily on *dicta* of Walsh J in *The State (O'Connor) v Larkin* [1968] IR 255, in which the accusatorial nature of criminal proceedings was stressed. On that basis, he held that there was no sound basis in law for the trial court refusing to hear the evidence being tendered by the prosecution in relation to the pre-accident condition of the minibus, and he ordered that continuances be entered in the case.

Disqualification from driving   In *The People v O'Byrne* (1989) 3 Frewen 241, the Court of Criminal Appeal (Finlay CJ, Barron and Johnson JJ) lifted a 10 driving disqualification which had been imposed on the applicant after he had been found guilty of driving a car without the driver's consent. The Court noted that under s. 29 of the Road Traffic Act 1961, restoration of a licence was not to be considered solely by reference to the circumstances of the original offence but must be determined by taking account of the character of the applicant, his conduct since conviction, the nature of the offence and any other relevant matters.

Medical practitioner: proof of designation   In *Director of Public Prosecutions v O'Donoghue* [1991] 1 IR 448, O'Hanlon J dealt with the question whether a medical practitioner had been sufficiently identified as a designated practitioner.

The defendant was charged with failing to provide a blood or urine sample to a registered medical practitioner, contrary to s. 13 of the Road Traffic (Amendment) Act 1978. The defendant had been presented to a doctor in the garda station and told he was 'the designated medical practitioner.' In the District Court the doctor was asked: 'I think you are a registered medical practitioner?', to which he replied 'I am.' He was also asked in Court: 'Were you designated by the gardaí on the night in question?', to which he replied: 'I was.' The charge was dismissed on the ground that there was no sufficient evidence that the doctor was a registered medical practitioner at the time the defendant was requested to supply a blood or urine sample. On a case stated O'Hanlon J affirmed the dismissal.

He accepted that while doctor's testimony, that he was at the time of the request a registered medical practitioner, was *prima facie* evidence of that fact, this was a relaxation of the best evidence rule, and the prosecution could not ask for a further relaxation of the rule by reference to the maxim *omnia praesumuntur rite esse acta*. As the evidence in the instant case did not amount to an express confirmation of the necessary formal proof, he concluded that the charge had been correctly dismissed. O'Hanlon J cited with approval the decision of the Supreme Court in *Martin v Quinn* [1980] IR 244, where, of course, the circumstances were somewhat different.

While the decision in *O'Donoghue* might appear, at first sight, to be harsh on the prosecuting authorities, it indicates the continued insistence of the courts to regard road traffic offences as mainstream criminal offences, thus drawing the strict interpretation associated with such legislation.

SENTENCING

As mentioned at the beginning of this Chapter, the case law on sentencing policy in the Court of Criminal Appeal shows a remarkable increase in the current volume as a result of the initiative in the recording and subsequent circulation of *ex tempore* decisions of the Court. The very informative article in the *Irish Criminal Law Journal*, O'Malley, 'Principles of Sentencing' (1991) 1 ICLJ 138 predated the circulation of many of the decisions referred to in this Review. However, in addition to decisions of the Court of Criminal Appeal which had been circulated prior to 1992, the article also includes first instance sentencing decisions which would not otherwise have become known.

Age In *The People v Murray (J.)*, Court of Criminal Appeal, 26 November 1990 the Court (Finlay CJ, Lardner and Blayney JJ), in an *ex tempore* judgment, affirmed a conviction of 15 years imposed on a 55 year old man for wounding with intent to do grievous bodily harm contrary to s. 18 of the Offences Against the Person Act 1861.

It had been argued that the sentence was 'merciless' in that, allowing even for remission, the applicant would not be released until he was 66 or 67. However, the Court took account of the fact that the applicant had previously been convicted of manslaughter for which he received a lenient sentence and that there had been no question but that the applicant had criminal intent in attacking the woman who had been wounded in the instant case in what the Court described as a 'savage' attack which had 'destroyed' the woman's life.

Accordingly, although the Court noted that the sentence was at the upper range for this offence, it did not interfere with the sentence imposed.

However, in *The People v Kearney*, Court of Criminal Appeal, 20 March 1991, the Court (O'Flaherty, Blayney and Johnson JJ) reduced a sentence of 12 years to one of 8 years in respect of a serious sexual assault imposed on a 58 year old man: see 182-3, below.

At the other end of the age spectrum, the Court in *The People v Farrell (M.)*, Court of Criminal Appeal, 23 July 1990 (see 175-6, below) reduced the combined effect of consecutive sentences from 15 to 11 years in relation to a 23 year old person.

In *The People v Fitzgerald*, Court of Criminal Appeal, 22 July 1991 (see 182, below), the Court did not alter a 10 year sentence on a 21 year old, although it did indicate that the executive might consider exercising clemency during the course of the term of the person in question.

In *The People v McGrath*, Court of Criminal Appeal, 22 July 1991, the Court (O'Flaherty, Keane and Barron JJ) reduced a sentence on a person who was 18 years of age in an explosives case: see 177, below.

AIDS In *The People v Connington*, Court of Criminal Appeal, 17 December 1990 the Court (Finlay CJ, Egan and Johnson JJ), in an *ex tempore* judgment, rejected the submission that the fact that the applicant suffered from AIDS should be a ground for altering an otherwise appropriate sentence. The Court considered that any alteration would be a matter for the executive exercising its clemency power. In the instant case, the applicant had been sentenced to 8 years in respect of robberies.

Assault and robbery In *The People v Rolleston*, Court of Criminal Appeal, 11 February 1991 the Court (Finlay CJ, Johnson and Lavan JJ), in an *ex tempore* judgment, reduced a sentence of 7 years for assault and robbery to four years. Although the assault and robbery had been on a semi-crippled person, and was described by the Court as brutal, it considered that the reduction might facilitate the rehabilitative element. The Court took account of the applicant's history of alcoholism and that, as the offence had been committed while the applicant was on temporary release or parole (which the Court noted was in some ways an aggravating factor), the applicant would be losing any right to remission on the sentence he was already serving.

Attempted burglary In *The People v Kearney (T.)*, Court of Criminal Appeal, 29 July 1991 the Court (O'Flaherty, Barr and Morris JJ), in an *ex tempore* judgment, affirmed a 2 year sentence imposed in the Circuit Criminal Court for attempted burglary of a garage. The trial judge had adverted to evidence of an assault on a garda in the course of attempting to evade arrest, which was the subject of a separate charge in the District Court. The Court of Criminal Appeal stated that this evidence should not have been given, but that, having regard to the seriousness of the burglary charge and the large number of such offences in Dublin, the sentence was not inappropriate. However, it did comment that since the assault matter had been taken into account by the trial judge, the prosecution in the District Court should not proceed.

Bad reputation In *The People v Martin*, Court of Criminal Appeal, 1 July 1991 the Court adverted to the issue of bad reputation. The applicant had pleaded guilty to maliciously causing grevious bodily harm with intent to disfigure, contrary to s. 18 of the Offences against the Person Act 1861. In the Circuit Court, evidence was given by the arresting garda that certain people would not testify against the applicant because they were in fear of their lives, and he also stated the applicant was a violent person. The trial judge sentenced the applicant to seven years imprisonment, having regard to the evidence of the garda and the applicant's previous convictions.

Application for leave to appeal against sentence was dismissed by the Court of Criminal Appeal (McCarthy, Barr and Lavan JJ). The Court accepted that evidence of bad reputation should, as a general rule, be restricted and should not be allowed to found a view that the applicant had committed previous offences. However, the Court concluded from the transcript that since the trial judge had not actually drawn such conclusions in the instant case the application would be dismissed and the sentence allowed to stand. Despite this, the decision stands as a timely reminder about the correct practice in cases of this kind.

On a procedural point, it may be noted that the Court stated that, although the arguments made on appeal had not been advanced in the trial court, this did not preclude the applicant from raising them on appeal. The Court referred to the decision in *The State (O'Connor) v Ó Caomhanaigh* [1963] IR 112 in this context.

Chambers hearing inappropriate In *The People v McGinley (J.)* (1989) 3 Frewen 251, the Court of Criminal Appeal (Hederman, Lynch and Blayney JJ), in an *ex tempore* judgment held it was inappropriate for the trial judge to have had a discussion of the case in chambers with a probation officer. Accordingly, the Court reduced a sentence of five years detention to three years in respect of a number of offences including unauthorised taking of vehicles, burglary and receiving stolen goods.

Consecutive sentence In *The People v Farrell (M.)*, Court of Criminal Appeal, 23 July 1990 the Court (O'Flaherty, Egan and Barr JJ), in an *ex* *tempore* judgment, considered the application of s. 11 of the Criminal Justice Act 1984, which deals with consecutive sentences in respect of offences committed on bail.

The applicant had been convicted of a robbery on a 70 year old man in which the man had been stabbed. He was sentenced to seven and a half years imprisonment for this offence. While on bail in respect of this charge, the applicant had committed an aggravated burglary in which staff members of a boutique had been, in the words of the Court, terrorised by the applicant. For this offence, the applicant was sentenced to 8 years imprisonment to commence on the expiration of the sentence for the first offence, thus bringing the total to over 15 years.

The Court of Criminal Appeal accepted that both sentences had been correct in principle. However, it also accepted that their combined effect, or the totality, would be that the applicant would spend the rest of his young manhood in prison (he was 23 at the time of the appeal). Accordingly, the Court suspended the last 4 years of the second sentence to encourage the applicant in his efforts to reform and to deal with the drug addition to which the Court also referred, bringing the possible total back to just over 11 years. The Court thus applied a similar approach taken in *The People v Dennigan* (1989) 3 Frewen 253 and in *The People v Farrell* (1989) 3 Frewen 257. The Court also referred with approval to the *dicta* of the Court on s. 11 in *The People v Healy (N.)* [1990] 1 IR 388 (see the 1989 Review, 183-4), particularly in relation to the totality of sentence imposed.

A similar approach was taken by the Court (Finlay CJ, Lardner and Blayney JJ) in another *ex tempore* decision, *The People v Ward (S.)*, Court of Criminal Appeal, 26 November 1990. Although in the *Ward* case, the Court did not suspend any part of the sentences imposed, it reduced the totality to reflect its intention to encourage the applicant's rehabilitation.

Contempt of court   In *The People v Cochrane*, Court of Criminal Appeal, 28 January 1991, the Court (McCarthy, Barr and Lardner JJ) held, in an *ex tempore* judgment that a sentence of 6 months for contempt of court should be reduced to 3 months. The applicant, who was already serving a sentence of imprisonment for stealing cattle, refused to testify in the trial of a person described as an accomplice. The Court took account of the fact that the refusal to testify appeared to have been connected with the applicant's grievance at his prison conditions.

Defence allegations   In *The People v McNally*, Court of Criminal Appeal, 2 April 1990, the Court (O'Flaherty, Barr and Lavan JJ) held, in an *ex tempore* judgment, that a trial judge would err if he had taken account at the sentencing stage of defence counsel allegations against the gardaí in the course of the trial. Consequently, although it was not certain that the trial judge in the instant case had actually been influenced by the defence allegations, the Court reduced a sentence of eight years for unlawful possession of firearms to seven years. The Court emphasised the importance of counsel being free to put the prosecution on full proof of its case, and that such a course must not attract any additional penalty where a conviction results.

However, the Court also emphasised that, in relation to those involved in the preparation of weapons for armed robberies, particularly sawn-off shotguns, it would be failing in its duty if it did not support heavy sentences of imprisonment for persons involved in such offences.

Disability In *The People v McEvoy*, Court of Criminal Appeal, 16 December 1991, the Court (O'Flaherty, Keane and Barron JJ), in an *ex tempore* judgment, took into account that the applicant had, at a young age, lost the sight of one eye and had later suffered an industrial accident in which the sight of his other eye was damaged. The applicant had been sentenced to three years for assault occasioning actual bodily harm, and the Court reduced this to 2 years taking account of the applicant's disability as well as the fact that the victim of the applicant's assault in the instant case had been compensated out of the damages received by the applicant from his industrial accident claim.

Drugs: possession In *The People v Foley*, Court of Criminal Appeal, 25 November 1991 the Court (Hederman, Barr and Lavan JJ), in an *ex tempore* judgment altered a five year sentence for possession of drugs to one of seven years but suspending the last four years of the sentence, thus reducing the custodial element from five to three years. The Court took account of the applicant's changed circumstances since the imposition of sentence which the Court otherwise considered had been correct.

Escape from custody In *The People v Sloan (G.)*, Court of Criminal Appeal, 26 November 1990 the Court (Finlay CJ, Lardner and Blayney JJ), in an *ex tempore* judgment, affirmed a sentence of five years for unalwful escape from custody in a prosecution brought under the Criminal Law (Jurisdiction) Act 1976.

Explosives In *The People v McGrath*, Court of Criminal Appeal, 22 July 1991, the Court (O'Flaherty, Keane and Barron JJ), in an *ex tempore* judgment, reduced a sentence of five years to three years in a case involving unlawful possession of explosives contrary to s. 4 of the Explosive Substances Act 1883. The applicant was 18 years of age at the time of the offence, he had in effect pleaded guilty, had agreed to sever all connections with unlawful organisations and it was also accepted that he was not the ring-leader. He had been induced to commit the crime by a person in his 40s, who also received a five year sentence subsequently confirmed on appeal. The Court accepted that, while the five year sentence for the older co-accused was at the lower end of the scale, the sentence on the applicant should be reduced to three years.

The People v Carmody, Court of Criminal Appeal, 22 July 1991 (below, this page) also concerned possession of explosives.

Firearms offences   In *The People v McNally*, Court of Criminal Appeal, 2 April 1990, the Court (O'Flaherty, Barr and Lavan JJ) alluded to the seriousness of possession of sawn-off weapons in particular: see 176-7 above. Similar comments were made by the Court in *The People v Hardiman*, Court of Criminal Appeal, 18 February 1991 (see 182, below), in *The People v Fitzgerald*, Court of Criminal Appeal, 22 July 1991 (below, 182) and in *The People v Carmody and O'Dwyer*, Court of Criminal Appeal, 22 July 1991. In the *Carmody* case, the Court (O'Flaherty, Keane and Barron JJ), in an *ex tempore* judgment, confirmed sentences totalling 10 years for possession of firearms and explosives. See also *The People v Cahill and Ors*, Court of Criminal Appeal, 22 July 1991 (182, below) and *The People v Mahon*, Court of Criminal Appeal, 9 December 1991 (182, below).

In *The People v Sheridan*, Court of Criminal Appeal, 14 December 1990, the Court (Hederman, Barr and Lavan JJ) dealt with a case of possession of imitation firearms: 181, below.

Incest   *The People v P.F.*, Court of Criminal Appeal, 25 November 1991 was an incest case. In an *ex tempore* judgment, the Court (Hederman, Barr and Lavan JJ) suspended the balance of a five year sentence on the applicant, which the Court acknowledged had been a very lenient sentence in the first place. The major factor which influenced the Court was that it had available new evidence since the applicant's trial, in which he pleaded guilty. This evidence indicated that the applicant's daughter, the victim of the incest committed by him, had recovered well from the ordeal of the criminal acts committed and that if the applicant were returned to prison custody this would have an adverse effect on her. Bearing in mind this paramount factor, the Court suspended the balance of the sentence.

The Court also commented on the apparent delay by the health authorities in alerting the gardaí about the offence after the applicant had been referred for treatment. The Court also expressed the hope that future such cases would be dealt with under more modern legislation than the Children Act 1908 or the Punishment of Incest Act 1908. Since the Court's decision, some provisions of the Child Care Act 1991 have been brought into force, though others which will repeal provisions of the Children Act 1908 have yet to be brought into effect: see the Family Law chapter, 232, below. The Punishment of Incest Act 1908 remains in effect, of course.

Leniency or clemency In *The People v Church*, Court of Criminal Appeal, 17 December 1990, the Court (Finlay CJ, Egan and Johnson JJ), in an *ex tempore* judgment, noted that while it could deal with issues of leniency in sentence, it had no function to grant clemency, in the sense, as the Court described it, of giving the applicant gift. In the instant case, however, the Court reduced a 7 year sentence to one of 4 years in the case of the assault and robbery by the applicant, who was 20 years of age, and who had no previous record of serious offences. The Court considered that this reflected the correct rehabilitative element for the offence.

In *The People v Connington*, Court of Criminal Appeal, 17 December 1990 (see 174, above) and *The People v Fitzgerald*, Court of Criminal Appeal, 22 July 1991 (see 182, below), the Court indicated that the executive might exercise its clemency power in these cases in which the Court itself considered it could not alter the sentences imposed.

See also *The People v Walsh* (1989) 3 Frewen 248, 180, below.

Manslaughter In *The People v Johnston* (1989) 3 Frewen 276, the Court of Criminal Appeal (Finlay CJ, Carroll and Murphy JJ), in an *ex tempore* judgment, applied the decision in *The People v Conroy (No. 2)* [1989] ILRM 139; [1989] IR 160 (1988 Review, 181) in reducing a life sentence to 17 years in respect of a conviction for manslaughter.

Misleading information The effect of a trial court being misled into believing that a defendant had never worked legitimately was considered in *The People v Gilligan (No. 3)* [1992] ILRM 769: see 164, above.

More serious offence considered In *The People v Waters and Ors*, Court of Criminal Appeal, 21 May 1990 the applicants successfully appealed to the Court (Finlay CJ, Gannon and Blayney JJ) against severity of sentence in respect of unlawful possession of explosive substances. The applicants had each pleaded guilty to these offences. The Special Criminal Court had, however, in its judgment suggested that the explosives in question were bound for the IRA. The Court of Criminal Appeal, in an *ex tempore* judgment, considered that such reference was improper and that, although the injustice thereby arising might be more apparent than real, it was appropriate to reduce the sentence from 10 years to seven years, beginning from the date of their trial.

In a connected case, *The People v O'Reilly*, Court of Criminal Appeal, 21

May 1990 the applicant also successfully appealed to the same Court in respect of a sentence imposed for the same incident. Having regard to the more central role played by the applicant in the obtaining of the explosives involved in the case, however, the Court, also in an *ex tempore* judgment, substituted an eight year sentence from the date of its judgment.

Opinion of garda   In *The People v Walsh* (1989) 3 Frewen 248, the Court of Criminal Appeal (Finlay CJ, MacKenzie and Lavan JJ), in an *ex tempore* judgment, held that a trial judge was entitled to hear the expression of opinion of a garda as to the applicant's level of participation in the preparations for the armed robbery in respect of which he had been convicted. The Court also stated that evidence as to the applicant's model behaviour in prison since sentencing was not appropriate for consideration by the Court, but was a matter for the executive in the exercise of the clemency power. The Court affirmed a sentence of eight years.

'Professional' criminal   In *The People v O'Donoghue*, Court of Criminal Appeal, 29 July 1991, the Court (O'Flaherty, Barr and Morris JJ), in an *ex tempore* judgment, deprecated the description of the applicant as a 'professional' criminal. The Court stated that garda witnesses should confine themselves to a stark description of the record of a convicted person. In the circumstances, the Court reduced a 5 year sentence for burglary to 4 years in a case in which the Court would otherwise have not altered the sentence.

Rape   In *The People v Smith*, Court of Criminal Appeal, 17 December 1990, the Court (Finlay CJ, Egan and Johnson JJ), in an *ex tempore* judgment, affirmed a sentence of 8 years on the applicant, who had pleaded guilty to rape. The Court held that the guilty plea was not sufficient to allow the Court reduce the sentence imposed.

In *The People v Egan (L.) (No. 2)*, Court of Criminal Appeal, 4 February 1991, the Court (Hederman, O'Hanlon and Barr JJ), in an *ex tempore* judgment, affirmed a sentence of 10 years for rape. The appeal against conviction had previously been dismissed by the Court and the Supreme Court: see *The People v Egan (L.)* [1990] ILRM 780 (1990 Review, 193-4). On the question of sentence, the Court approved the principles established in *The People v Tiernan* [1989] ILRM 149; [1988] IR 250 (1988 Review, 181-4). It is significant that the Court also provided what appears to be a comprehensive list of appeals against sentence to the Court since the *Tiernan* case up to the instant case. This list will undoubtedly prove of great interest to practitioners. Among the cases referred to was *The People v Maguire* (1989) 3 Frewen 265, which had not been published at the time of the *Egan* case.

In *The People v Donohoe*, Court of Criminal Appeal, 20 March 1991, the

Court (O'Flaherty, Blayney and Johnson JJ), in an *ex tempore* judgment, reduced a sentence of 14 years to one of 12 years. In this instance the Court took account of the guilty plea by the applicant. The Court indicated that it might have reduced the sentence slightly further but did not do so in the light of a previous conviction for indecent assault which bore certain similarities to the circumstances of the instant rape. It is also noteworthy that the Court refused to take into account, one way or the other, the fact that the applicant had been beaten by relations of the rape victim, for which he required 200 stitches. While deploring the fact that these relations had taken the law into their own hands, the Court stated that such was irrelevent to the sentencing decision.

In *The People v Maher*, Court of Criminal Appeal, 14 May 1991, the Court (Egan, Costello and Lynch JJ), in an *ex tempore* judgment, reduced a sentence of 17 years to one of 12 years. The applicant had no previous convictions and had immediately confessed to the gardaí when found by them after the rape and subsequently pleaded guilty. The Court noted that, although the applicant had a history of mental illness, he had not previously been involved in any criminal activity.

See also *The People v Kearney*, Court of Criminal Appeal, 20 March 1991, a case involving a girl under 15 years of age, dealt with under s. 1 of the Criminal Law Amendment Act 1935 (182-3, below).

Refusal to name accomplice   In *The People v Maloney* (1989) 3 Frewen 267, the Court of Criminal Appeal (Finlay CJ, Costello and Blayney JJ), in an *ex tempore* judgment, held that the refusal of the applicant to name a 'fence' in a receiving case should not be a basis for imposing a higher sentence than would otherwise have been imposed.

Robbery and firearms   In *The People v Sheridan*, Court of Criminal Appeal, 14 December 1990, the Court (Hederman, Barr and Lavan JJ), in an *ex tempore* judgment, affirmed a sentence of 7 years on the driver of a 'getaway' car involved in a robbery who had also been in possession of an imitation firearm.

Although the applicant had no previous involvement in robberies, he had a number of convictions for unauthorised taking of vehicles. The Court alluded to the fact that a sentence of 7 years on a co-accused had been affirmed by the Court, but counsel for the applicant sought to distinguish the applicant's case on the basis that he had no previous convictions for robbery whereas the co-accused had two such previous convictions; in addition the applicant had pleaded guilty to the charge. This was not regarded by the Court as a basis for reducing the sentence, nor the fact that the applicant had been in possession of imitation firearms, which it stated could have a very traumatic effect on victims. The Court also stated, in conclusion, that it took 'a very severe view of the escalation of violence in society and particularly in [Dublin].'

In *The People v Hardiman*, Court of Criminal Appeal, 18 February 1991, the Court (Hederman, O'Hanlon and Lynch JJ), in an *ex tempore* judgment, affirmed a sentence of five years for robbery involving a sawn-off shotgun. Although the applicant had no previous convictions, and the trial judge had referred to him as 'an ardent rogue and an outlaw', the Court of Criminal Appeal considered that the sentence imposed was correct. The Court drew attention to the fact that s. 23 of the Larceny Act 1916, as inserted by s. 5 of the Criminal Law (Jurisdiction) Act 1976, had increased the maximum sentence for the offence charged to life imprisonment. In fact, the Court stated that, had it not been for the particular circumstances of the applciant to which counsel had drawn attention, it would have raised the sentence to 7 years.

In *The People v Fitzgerald*, Court of Criminal Appeal, 22 July 1991, the Court (O'Flaherty, Keane and Barron JJ), also in an *ex tempore* judgment, affirmed a sentence of 10 years in respect of a series of armed robberies, taking account that the applicant was 21 years old.

In *The People v Cahill and Ors*, Court of Criminal Appeal, 22 July 1991, the Court (O'Flaherty, Keane and Barron JJ), also in an *ex tempore* judgment, reduced sentences in a case of robbery and possession of firearms. This resulted in a sentence of 16 years imposed on the first applicant (who had previous convictions for similar offences) being reduced to 14 years. This reduction was only for the purpose of maintaining a differential between his sentence and those of his two co-accused, whose sentences of 12 years were reduced to 7 years to take account of their relatively unblemished previous records.

In *The People v Mahon*, Court of Criminal Appeal, 9 December 1991, the Court (O'Flaherty, Keane and Barron JJ), also in an *ex tempore* judgment, dealt with a fourth member of the group who had been involved in the same robbery as in the *Cahill* case, above. In order to preserve a proportion between the cases, the Court reduced a sentence of 7 years to 5 years in view of the fact that the applicant in the instant case had not played a substantial role in the offence.

Sexual assault on girl under 15   In *The People v Kearney*, Court of Criminal Appeal, 20 March 1991, the applicant had been convicted of defilement of a girl under 15 years of age, contrary to s. 1 of the Criminal Law Amendment Act 1935, and was sentenced to 12 years imprisonment. He was also convicted of indecent assault. On appeal, the Court of Criminal Appeal (O'Flaherty, Blayney and Johnson JJ), in an *ex tempore* judgment, reduced the sentence to 8 years. The Court took account of the applicant's age (58) as well as the unusual circumstances of his life. However, it is notable that the Court regarded the offence under s. 1 of the 1935 Act as equivalent to rape, and applied the general sentencing principles in the Supreme Court decision in *The People v Tiernan* [1989] ILRM 149; [1988] IR 250 (1988 Review, 181-4).

SEXUAL OFFENCES

Consent In *The People v Gaffey (No.2)*, Court of Criminal Appeal, 10 May 1991, the Court (Finlay CJ, Lynch and Morris JJ), in an *ex tempore* judgment, ordered a re-trial of the applicant, who had been convicted of rape.

The Court considered that, in the circumstances which arose, it was necessary for the trial judge to direct the jury that they must have regard to whether the applicant believed that the complainant had consented to sexual intercourse. The Court consdiered that the trial judge should have given a direction to the jury in the terms of s. 2 of the Criminal Law (Rape) Act 1981. The Court noted that a direction on this point would not be required in all cases but that it arose in the circumstances of the instant case.

YOUNG OFFENDERS

Absence of facility to detain In *The People v D.E.*, Court of Criminal Appeal, 11 February 1991, the Court (Finlay CJ, Johnson and Lavan JJ), in an *ex tempore* judgment, quashed a sentence of imprisonment imposed on the applicant, who had been convicted of a number of offences, many consisting of larceny from cars.

The applicant was 15 years of age, a 'young person' within s. 131 of the Children Act 1908. The trial judge had ordered that the applicant be detained in prison under s. 102 of the 1908 Act. This permits imprisonment of a 'young person' where found to be unruly or 'depraved.' In fact, as the Court of Criminal Appeal observed, the trial judge had made findings that the applicant had, to some extent, changed his ways prior to his trial and had taken a FAS training course without being regarded as disruptive. On this basis, the Court of Criminal Appeal held that no order could have been validly made under s. 102 of the 1908 Act and it quashed the order of the trial judge as being illegal.

This left the Court with a problem which counsel for the Director of Public Prosecutions accepted as fact: namely, that at the time of the appeal, there was no suitable detention facility available in the State for 'young persons' who were not unruly or depraved within the meaning of the 1908 Act. In those circumstances, the Court felt that it could not make any form of suspensory order but was confined to quashing the sentence and leaving no order in its place. As the Court noted, the executive's inaction provided the applicant with an unusual opportunity for reform.

For previous discussion of the absence of facilities in the State in this context, see the 1990 Review, 264. See also the helpful article in the *Irish Criminal Law Journal*, Ring, 'Custodial Treatment for Young Offenders' (1991) 1 ICLJ 59.

'Depraved and unruly': constitutional challenge   *G. and McD. v Governor of Mountjoy Prison* [1991] 1 IR 373 was an unsuccessful challenge to the constitutional validity of ss. 102 and 131 of the Children Act 1908.

The applicants were both 15 years of age, and were 'young persons' within s. 131 of the 1908 Act. They were both convicted of assault and other offences, and had been sentenced in the District Court (Children's Court) to terms of imprisonment ranging from three to 12 months imprisonment. The Judge of the District Court before whom they appeared certified that both applicants, both of whom had a number of previous convictions, should serve their sentences in a prison since they were, within the meaning of s. 102 of the 1908 Act, 'of so depraved a character' that they were not fit to be detained in an institution for young offenders. The applicants sought an enquiry pursuant to Article 40.4 of the Constitution, seeking various forms of relief, including a declaration that s. 102 of the 1908 Act was inconsistent with the Constitution, that the word 'depraved' lacked clarity and that there was no evidence on which the applicants should be detained in a prison, and that their conditions of confinement were in breach of the 1947 Prison Rules. The applicants did not seek release from custody but sought orders that some form of secure accommodation be provided. Blayney J dismissed the application for the main relief sought.

On the central issue as to whether it was permissible to imprison a young person, he held that the power to order detention of a 'young person' in prison under s. 102 of the 1908 Act was not inconsistent with the applicants' personal rights under Article 40.3 of the Constitution since, on the contrary, it defended their rights by prohibiting the detention in prison of the young person except in certain specified circumstances. He considered that the requirement that the young person be 'depraved' was perfectly fair as the other young persons in a place of detention must be protected against anyone who is so depraved as not to be fit to be detained there.

On the interpretation of 'depraved', he held that the absence of any definition of 'depraved' in the 1908 Act, or of any judicial decision on its interpretation, did not mean that the Court should refuse to construe it. Taking account of dictionary definitions, which defined depraved as 'immoral, vicious, unprincipled, wicked', Blayney J concluded that there was ample evidence on which the Judge of the District Court could conclude that the applicants were of so immoral and vicious a character that they were not fit to be detained in a place of detention provided under the 1908 Act.

Finally, on the claim that the Prison Rules were being violated, Blayney J accepted that, on the evidence, the applicants were not being detained in accordance with rr. 223 and 224 of the Rules for the Government of Prisons 1947 (requiring separate detention of young persons). However, citing the decision of Barrington J in *The State (Comerford) v Governor of Mountjoy Prison* [1981] ILRM 86 (which, he said, he had not been referred to in argument), he doubted whether in an Article 40.4 application such non-compliance entitled the applicants to any form of relief, since they did not seek release from custody. He therefore ordered that further argument on this point take place. At a resumed hearing, Blayney J was satisfied that adequate arrangements had in fact been made in the meantime to comply with the 1947 Rules: see [1991] 1 IR, at 378.

Defence Forces

MILITARY DISCIPLINE

Death penalty abolition   The Rules of Procedure (Defence Forces) 1991 (SI No. 27) amend the Rules of Procedure (Defence Forces) 1954 to 1987 to take account of the abolition of the death penalty by the Criminal Justice Act 1990. On the Act see the 1990 Review, 195.

Legal Aid   The Courts-Martial (Legal Aid) Regulations 1991 (SI No. 210) are self-explanatory.

REPRESENTATIVE ASSOCIATIONS

The Defence (Amendment) Act 1990 (Commencement) Order 1991 (SI No. 119) brought the 1990 Act, which concerns representative associations, into effect from 16 May 1991. On the Act see the 1990 Review, 266-7.

Education

EDUCATIONAL EXCHANGE

The Educational Exchange (Ireland and the United States of America) Act 1991 gives effect to the 1988 Agreement between Ireland and the United States of America in order to increase the number of academic and educational exchanges between the two countries. The 1991 Act provides that the Ireland—United States Commission for Educational Exchange will administer the exchanges. The Ireland—United States Commission for Educational Exchange (Establishment Day) Order 1991 (SI No. 354) provided that the Commission came into being on 3 February 1992.

The Commission replaces the Scholarship Exchange Board, which administered the Fulbright exchange programme under the Scholarship Exchange (Ireland and the United States of America) Act 1957. The 1957 Act is now, in effect, obsolete since the establishment of the Commission under the 1991 Act.

For a full commentary on the background to the 1991 Act, which arose from a commitment made by President Reagan on his 1984 visit to Ireland, see Barniville's Annotation, *Irish Current Law Statutes Annotated*.

RECOGNITION OF EC QUALIFICATIONS

General   The European Communities (General System for the Recognition of Higher Education Diplomas) Regulations 1991 (SI No. 1) give effect to Directive 89/48/EEC, and provide the general basis on which higher level diploma qualifications in EC states must be recognised in this State. They came into effect on 4 January 1991.

Pharmacy   The European Communities (Recognition of Qualifications in Pharmacy) Regulations 1991 (SI No. 330) give effect to Directive 90/658/EEC. They further update the European Communities (Recognition of Qualifications in Pharmacy) Regulations 1987 and also amend s. 22A of the Pharmacy Act (Irl) 1875 and s. 2 of the Pharmacy Act 1962 (as inserted by the 1987 Regulations).

Solicitors   The Solicitors Acts 1954 and 1960 (European Communities)

Regulations 1991 (SI No. 85) specify the basis on which lawyers qualify for recognition in accordance with the European Communities (General System for the Recognition of Higher Education Diplomas) Regulations 1991 (SI No. 1).

THOMOND COLLEGE/UNIVERSITY OF LIMERICK

The University of Limerick (Dissolution of Thomond College) Act 1991, as its name indicates, provides that Thomond College of Education be dissolved and that its staff and property be transferred to the University of Limerick. The Act came into effect on 8 July 1991: University of Limerick (Dissolution of Thomond College) Act 1991 (Commencement) Order 1991 (SI No. 181).

The passage of the Act was marked by concern that the ethos of Thomond might be lost in the new regime. To some extent this was provided for in s.10 of the 1991 Act which states that the University shall have due regard to the Irish language and culture in performing its functions, including those in connection with teacher training. The Act also provides for an increase in the membership of the University's ruling bodies, thus providing for a voice for the former staff members of Thomond.

Electricity and Energy

ELECTRICITY

The European Communities (Transit of Electricity) Regulations 1991 (SI No. 275) gave effect to Directive 90/547/EEC.

NATURAL GAS

Installation safety zone   The Continental Shelf (Protection of Installations) (Ballycotton Field) Order 1991 (SI No. 226) provides for a 500m safety zone around the Ballycotton Natural Gas Field. The effect is that shipping may not enter this area without the permission of the Minister for Energy. The Order was made under the Continental Shelf Act 1968. A similar Order had been made in respect of the Kinsale Gas Field, to which Ballycotton is connected: Continental Shelf (Protection of Installations) (Kinsale Head Gas Field) Order 1977 (SI No. 285 of 1977).

Transit   The European Communities (Transit of Natural Gas) Regulations 1991 (SI No. 343) gave effect to Directive 91/296/EEC.

PETROLEUM

Whitegate offtake   The Petroleum Oils (Regulation or Control of Acquisition, Supply, Distribution or Marketing) (Continuance) Order 1991 (SI No. 336) continued for a further year the regime outlined in the 1988 Order of the same title: see the 1988 Review, 198.

Equitable Remedies

INTERLOCUTORY INJUNCTIONS

Defamation proceedings In *Connolly v Radio Telefís Éireann* [1991] 2 IR 446, the plaintiff sought an interlocutory injunction in July 1991 to prevent RTE from using film taken at a garda checkpoint during its Christmas campaign against drunken driving. It had been broadcast a number of times in December 1990. The portion to which the plaintiff objected showed her car stopped and a garda talking to her as the driver although she could not be seen. This was intercut with another shot of a woman driver being breathalysed and a voice-over saying that this woman was just below the limit. Such a sequence had been broadcast twice. A variant, also broadcast twice, showed a driver handing out a breathalyser from the car followed by a shot of the plaintiff standing at the rear of the car talking to a garda. The plaintiff stated in her affidavit that she recalled having been stopped by a garda on the road in question and asked to show him the contents of the boot of her car; there had been no question of drink consumption at all throughout the conversation with the garda. There were only three models of the same colour as the particular brand of car that she was driving in the jurisdiction.

The gravamen of the plaintiff's case was that the film sequences, in conjunction with the commentary about drunken driving, defamed her. She had sought an undertaking from RTE that it would not use the film again; its reply was that, whilst it had no intention at present of using the film, it had the right to do so if it wanted to. The plaintiff was not identified on the film, her face did not appear and the registration number of her car did not appear. The film had been shot at night and was relatively indistinct. Nevertheless, as Carroll J noted, it was sufficiently clear for the plaintiff (who had not seen the original transaction) to have been told by others that they had identified her.

Carroll J refused to grant the interlocutory injunction. She saw no reason why she should not apply in conjunction the *Campus Oil* principles and the principle that in defamation cases injunctions are very rarely granted and never if the defendant claims justification as a defence:

> So that in considering the balance of convenience, the court must take into account the right to freedom of expression balanced against the plaintiff's right to a good name and reputation in the light of the law on injunctive relief in defamation cases.

Given that there was an issue to be tried and 'the fact that damages are not an adequate remedy for defamation', it came down to a consideration of the balance of convenience judged in the light of the case law. In Carroll J's view, that balance lay against granting an injunction. In spite of the plaintiff's fears, there was no immediate danger of the footage being used and RTE had promised to co-operate in bringing the matter to an early trial. It was preferable in the circumstances of the case that the alleged libel, which was contested, should be tried by a jury rather than that an injunction should issue.

Carroll J's approach is consistant with earlier precedents leaning against prior restraint in defamation cases. Perhaps the clearest, and most controversial, recent example is the Supreme Court decision in *[X] v RTE*, 27 March 1990, affirming High Court, Costello J, 27 March 1990, *Irish Times*, 28 March 1990, which we analysed criticially in the 1990 Review, 534-8. If an asserted risk of being killed is not sufficient to override the defendant's stance of a willingness to plead justification, then, *a fortiori*, the plaintiff in the instant case would seem to have had a forlorn hope of success at the interlocutory stage. Carroll J's reference 'to the right of freedom of expression' seems clearly to connote a right of constitutional dimensions. In the 1990 Review, 537, we examined the argument whether an unthinking application of a constitutional gloss of this type to the law of defamation is necessarily justifiable. We repeat here this concern. For further analysis of this general question, see O'Dell (1990) 12 DULJ (ns) 50 and (1991) 9 ILT (ns) 181.

Passing off In *Mantruck Services Ltd v Ballinlough Electrical Refrigeration Co. Ltd*, Supreme Court, 30 July 1991, the plaintiffs sought an interlocutory injunction restraining the defendant from dealing in transport refrigeration equipment under a particular brand name within the jurisdiction and from passing itself off as a dealer of products of this brand. The plaintiffs held some form of sole distributorship agreement within the State for this brand. Denham J granted the injunction. She concluded that, on the face of it, the sole distributorship agreement was valid, despite the provisions of Article 85(1) of the Treaty of Rome. She was of opinion that damages would not be an adequate remedy for the plaintiffs.

The Supreme Court allowed the appeal and restricted the injunction to restraining the defendant from holding itself out as an appointed distributor and from using the brand name or logo on its publicity material. McCarthy J (Finlay CJ and Hederman J concurring) set out succinctly the *Campus Oil* test for interlocutory injunctions: 'Has the plaintiff made out a fair case and where does the balance of convenience lie?' He then proceeded to adopt a somewhat unconventional mode of analysis. Under the heading of 'the balance of convenience' he addressed first that issue and secondly the issue of whether the plaintiff had made out a fair case.

As to the balance of convenience, he was satisfied that this lay against granting the injunction. The defendant's entire operation would be set at risk, 'not by competition, but by legal restraint'. It would, moreover, be very difficult to assess in money terms the damage to a growing business.

Turning to the question of a fair case, McCarthy J quoted the following passage from Bellamy & Child's *Common Market Law of Competition*, para 6-13 (3rd ed., 1987):

> It is a basic principle of community law that an exclusive distribution agreement falls within the prohibition of Article 85(1) where it impedes, in law or in fact, either re-export of the contract products by the distributor to other Member States or import of such products by third parties from other Member States. That is so whether the prevention of imports or exports results from export bans, discriminatory pricing policies or other measures.

McCarthy J noted that it might be the case that the plaintiffs could identify in law a construction whereby the prohibition of Article 85 did not apply. The argument on the interlocutory appeal had necessarily been limited. At first sight, however, it appeared to him that Article 85(1) was directly in point. In those circumstances, it seemed to him that the plaintiffs had fallen short of establishing a fair case on this aspect of their claim. McCarthy J differed from Denham J's view that, on the face of it, the agreement was valid.

Reconciliation of civil and religious norms   *O'Dea v Ó Briain* [1992] ILRM 364 raises important jurisprudential issues as to the relationship between legal and religious authority in the context of *civil* as opposed to criminal law. Much has been written about the proper relationship between the two in the area of criminal law. Little attention has so far been given to the more troublesome question of the extent to which a religious vow—in this case of obedience—should be integrated with civil law notions of the fair exercise of authority, the law of contract and the process of adjudication. See further Barry (1992) 10 ILT (ns) 222.

In the Administrative Law chapter above, 6-8 we analyse aspects of the decision. Here our attention is on the injunction issue. Very briefly, the case concerned a transfer of the plaintiff, a teaching nun, under the purported exercise of a power contained in an article of her congregation's constitution, and the withdrawal of her nomination to the school at which she had been teaching for over forty years. The plaintiff sought a mandatory injunction directing her superior to remove the transfer and the withdrawal of nomination.

Murphy J declined to grant an interlocutory injunction. He noted that it was not necessary for him to decide whether or not the plaintiff could sustain a case on either of the grounds she alleged; he was of the view that there would be 'great difficulty' in doing so. He nonetheless observed that this was 'not to dismiss entirely the possibility that that would happen. Not only the facts require further consideration but it is proper to say that matters of complicated law can only be adjudicated on finally at the full hearing'. It seemed to him that the matter should be dealt with 'like other interlocutory applications' by considering the balance of convenience and the nature of the damage which could be done or avoided by granting or withholding the relief sought.

This approach may appear to understate the strength of the hurdle laid down by the Supreme Court in *Campus Oil Ltd v Minister of Industry and Energy (No. 2)* [1983] IR 88 at 109. There O'Higgins CJ (Hederman J concurring) expressed the view that 'the test to be applied is whether a fair *bona fide* question has been raised by the person seeking relief'. Perhaps Murphy J's remarks can best be understood an being premised on the admitted compliance by the plaintiff with that test; but the only express language he used to describe the strength of the plaintiff's case appears to fall some distance short of the test prescribed in *Campus Oil*. The point is moot, because Murphy J decided against the plaintiff on the balance of convenience.

In coming to this conclusion, Murphy J noted that the plaintiff was residing alone in a private dwelling, with the use of a car. If she accepted the transfer, similar facilities would await her where the went. Her financial, physical 'and, presumably, religious' welfare would be comprehensively safeguarded. To that extent the plaintiff was not in peril as might be others who sought relief from the Court. Nonetheless, the plaintiff's concern was that her reputation had been challenged by what had happened and that she had not had the opportunity of vindicating it.

The defendants counterposed their concern about safeguarding the reputation of the school, the quality of its teaching and the interests of the children and their parents. The effect of granting a mandatory injunction would be to create a new state of affairs rather than merely preserve the *status quo*.

Murphy J acknowledged that under *Campus Oil (No. 2)*, it was possible in some circumstances to grant a mandatory injunction, but that this was rare. He would be 'extremely reluctant' to do so, in spite of his sympathy with the plaintff's concern to have her capacity as a teacher reviewed by an appropriate and competent body. His reluctance sprang from the fact that no order that he could make could guarantee that such a review would take place. The balance of convenience was against granting an injunction. If the plaintiff succeeded in her action at the plenary hearing, the court could neither be reluctant nor prescribed from granting a range of remedies, including a declaratory order, monetary compensation if the plaintiffs rights had been infringed and a mandatory order.

Murphy J's reluctance to grant a mandatory order at the interlocutory stage reflects the approach he adopted four years previously in *Bula Ltd v Tara Mines Ltd* [1988] ILRM 157, which we analysed in the 1987 Review, 167-9. It can be reconciled with Costello J's decision in *Capemel Ltd v Lister (No. 2)* [1989] IR 323 (analysed in the 1988 Review, 193-4) on the basis of the exceptional factual circumstances in *Capemel* which had no parallel in *O'Dea v Ó Briain.*

Torts affecting economic relations   A constant complaint by workers and trade unions has been that the law relating to interlocutory injunctions operates in practice in aid of employers since the balance of convenience will usually tilt in their favour. S. 19 of the Industrial Relations Act 1990 goes some way towards modifying the impact of this rule, albeit in a robust way which scarcely takes proper account of the interests of third parties: see our comments in the 1990 review, 353-4. *Westman Holdings Ltd v McCormack* [1991] ILRM 833; [1992] 1 IR 151 is of interest because it was decided at a time when s. 14 of the Act had not yet been implemented, though other provisions of the Act had come into force. Since the benefit of s. 19 was contingent on s. 14, it was not available to the defendants.

The case involved an application for an interlocutory injunction restraining picketing of the plaintiff company's licensed premises. Shortly beforehand the business had been sold to the plaintiff company by a company that terminated the employment of all its employees after giving each of them a sum of money in discharge of all claims due to them arising out of their employment. The picket was an official one, on behalf of these employees, who claimed that they were entitled to be employed by the plaintiff company by reason of the European Communities (Safeguarding of Employees' Rights on Transfer of Undertakings) Regulations 1980 (SI No 306 of 1980), which implemented the Council Directive No 77/187/EEC of 14 February 1977.

Two issues of law arose to be tried. The first was whether the defendants' picketing was protected by s. 11(1) of the 1990 Act on the basis that the plaintiff should be deemed their 'employer'. (In the 1990 Review, 347, we examine the scope of this term.) The plaintiff argued that it was not the defendants' employer since it had never employed them. The defendants replied that the term should be construed as including an *alleged* employer, since otherwise the subsection would lose its obvious purpose of protecting picketing in support of a dispute concerning non-employment. The second issue related to the transfer of the business. The defendants argued that the prohibition of termination by reason of the transfer rendered invalid any purported termination of the contract of employment between them and the transfer of the business to the plaintiff company, and that accordingly they were entitled to seek the enforcement of what was a novated contract of employment.

Finlay CJ (O'Flaherty and Egan JJ concurring) was satisfied that there was a fair question to be tried on both issues. Applying the *Campus Oil* test, he was satisfied that, once this threshold was crossed, the court should not express any view on the strength of the contending submissions but should proceed to address the balance of convenience and the question of irreparable damage. One may here interpose the observation that in trade disputes there is surely no less pressing a case for modifying the general rule than there is in passing off litigation whereby the absence of a significant conflict of *fact* between the parties should enable the court in interlocutory applications to address the legal issues as it would on plenary hearing. Cf. *Benckiser GmbH v Fibrisol Service Ltd*, High Court, 13 May 1988. There are of course some drawbacks to this approach; we noted some of them in the 1988 Review, 200. But the injustice to workers which the conventional test so often involves must be a reason for giving serious thought to a modification of this type.

In *Westman Holdings*, consideration of the balance of convenience led to a foreseeable outcome. If the injunction were granted and later overturned on plenary hearing, the greater part of the losses suffered by the defendants would be recoverable from the plaintiff company; if it were refused and the plaintiff subsequently succeeded on plenary hearing, the plaintiff would face the prospect of seeking enforcement against defendants at least some of whom would not be able to pay, with the trade union having a potential immunity from liability. The Court accordingly upheld the interlocutory injunction which Lardner J had granted.

MANDATORY INJUNCTIONS

In *Boyhan v The Tribunal of Inquiry* [1992] ILRM 545, Denham J declined to grant an interlocutory mandatory injunction in favour of the United Farmers' Association directing that they be granted full representation at the Beef Tribunal. Denham J noted that no allegations had been made against the plaintiffs at the Tribunal, which was not a court. There was no evidence that the plaintiffs would be prejudiced by the Tribunal, which had clearly stated that the rules of natural justice would apply to its deliberations. The Tribunal had manifestly been acting within its discretion and jurisdiction in making its decision to decline to authorise full representation for the plaintiffs.

Denham J observed that the mandatory injunction was 'a powerful instrument'. On the facts of the case, it would effectively mean an order of mandamus to the Tribunal. If the proceedings were an application for mandamus, they would not succeed.

Denham J stated:

> In seeking this exceptional form of relief, a mandatory injunction, it is up to the plaintiffs to establish a strong and clear case—so that the court can feel a degree of assurance that at a trial of the action a similar injunction would be granted.

The plaintiffs failed this test.

In the section on interlocutory injunctions, 192 above, we discuss Murphy J's decision in *O'Dea v Ó Briain* [1992] ILRM 364, which also involved an unsuccessful application for a mandatory interlocutory injunction.

SPECIFIC PERFORMANCE

In the Chapter on Contracts, we discuss the decisions of *Aga Khan v Firestone* [1992] ILRM 31, *Boyle v Lee* [1992] ILRM 65 and *O'Neill v Ryan* [1991] ILRM 672; [1992] 1 IR 166 which addressed questions relating to specific performance.

TRUSTS

Charitable trusts In *Eastern Health Board v Commissioners of Charitable Donations and Bequests for Ireland,* High Court, 17 December 1991, Denham J was called on to determine a dispute about the appointment of trustees of a charitable trust, relating to a library of 4500 books established for Dr Stevens's Hospital under the will of Dr Edward Worth in 1723. The bequest had required that the books be kept in some convenient room in the hospital, for the use of the physician, chaplin and surgeon. Three catalogues were to be made of them, one of which was to be kept in Trinity College, Dublin. For stimulating accounts of Dr Worth's library, see T.P. Kirkpatrick, vol. 1, no. 3, Bibliographical Society of Ireland (1919) and Muriel McCarthy, Irish Arts Review, no. 3 (1987), p. 29.

The terms of the trust were complied with for over two and half centuries. In 1988, Dr. Stevens's Hospital closed. The Governors of the hospital, who were the trustees of the Worth trust, sought the agreement of the Commissioners to their wish to have Trinity College act as trustee in their stead and asked them to prepare a *cy près* scheme which would take into account the long connection of Trinity with the hospital since its foundation, its possession of a large ancient library and its technical competence because of its skill in conservation. Since the hospital buildings had to be sold, and the Governors were concerned with the safekeeping of the books in the Worth Library, they sought and obtained authorisation from the Commissioners to have the books housed temporarily in Trinity.

S. 43 of the Charities Act 1961, as amended by the substitution set out in s. 14 of the Charities Act 1973, deals with the procedure for appointing new trustees. Subs. (4) provides that the Board shall:

> (a) not less than fourteen days before the date on which they propose to make an [appointment], give public notice of the proposed order, and
> (b) within ten days after the date of the making of the order give public notice of the making, and of the date of making, of the order in such manner as [it] considers most effectual for ensuring publicity for the proposal or order, as the case may be, and for bringing it to the attention of persons interested.

Subs. (5) entitles any person with an interest to appeal to the High Court against the making of the appointment. In February 1991 the Commissioners made an order appointing Trinity and the Director of the National Library to be trustees in place of the Governors of the hospital. This was challenged by the Eastern Health Board on procedural and substantive grounds.

As to procedure, the background to the 1991 order must be considered. In 1988 the Commissioners had issued notice of their intent to appoint Trinity to be trustee of the Worth trust. The notice had been displayed on the notice board of the Federated Dublin Voluntary Hospitals at St James's Hospital. The Eastern Health Board had written to the Commissioners, objecting to the proposed appointment. It stated that the hospital premises would be the headquarters of the Board and it wished to give full effect to the trust in its original room, which was being refurbished. Correspondence had followed, and no appointment was made at that time. From 9 October to 25 October 1990, a new notice was placed on the same notice board on a clearly visible part of the board. It was not seen by the person who, so far as may be gleaned from the judgment, would have been the employee of the Board most likely to have heeded such a notice.

Denham J rejected the Board's argument that there had been no public notice and that it should have been specifically informed of the revised proposal to appoint new trustees. The 1990 notice had been exactly the same type as the 1988 counterpart. No objection as to this form of notice had been made in 1988. The 1988 notice had come to the attention of the Board. It had been reasonable to assume that it would do so again. In the circumstances it had not been necessary for the Commissioners to write to the Board alerting them about the notice.

Two points of substance were also considered. The first was that the appointment of the new trustees was premature in that it prejudiced the position of the Eastern Health Board in the *cy près* application. Denham J rejected this argument. The relocation of the library at Trinity for safekeeping had been a correct decision as, at the time when the hospital building was being closed, no one could have foreseen that the Board would buy it and wish to run the Worth Library in the building as a heritage exhibition. It was not for the court to second guess the form of the *cy-près* scheme; it was manifestly obvious that both Trinity and the Eastern Health Board had an interest in the matter. The second point of substance related to the appropriateness of appointing Trinity and the Director of the National Library as trustees. Denham J acknowledged that the Board had an interest in the library but she noted that they were not experts in the conservation of old books nor were they running a hospital on the premises. The books were now in the care of Trinity and the Director and it was appropriate that they be appointed trustees.

Resulting trusts   *Greyside Ltd v McKenna*, High Court, 2 July 1991 is an example of how the legal principles relating to resulting trusts can take second place to evidential considerations. The defendant had been engaged in a series of transactions relating to property development, in association with two other persons, one of whom was managing director of the plaintiff company. The defendant bought a site which, the plaintiff company claimed, was subject to a resulting trust in its favour. Barron J engaged in a detailed review of the evidence. He was not satisfied that there was a resulting trust in favour of the plaintiff because he was satisfied that there had been some agreement the terms of which had not been disclosed. He could not speculate as to the nature of this agreement. It was for the plaintiff to establish its claim; this it had failed to do.

Trusts relating to family property   In the Family law chapter, below, 216-24, in the section dealing with family property, we analyse two important Supreme Court decisions relating to the traditional trusts approach towards family property. These are *L. v L.* [1992] ILRM 115 and *N. v N.* [1992] ILRM 127. Another significant decision, relating to retirement and death benefit schemes, is *In re Doyle deceased; Crowe Engineering Ltd v Lynch*, High Court, 24 July 1991. We examine this case in the Family Law Chapter 228-9.

European Communities

ABUSE OF DOMINANT POSITION

The issue of abuse of a dominant position was raised in *Kerry Co-Op Creameries Ltd v An Bord Bainne Co-Op Ltd* [1990] ILRM 664 (HC); [1991] ILRM 851 (see 28-30, above, in the Commercial Law chapter). It also arose in *Mantruck Services Ltd and Anor v Ballinlough Electrical Refrigeration Co. Ltd*, Supreme Court, 30 July 1991: see 191-2, above, in the Equitable Remedies chapter.

In *Commission v Radio Telefís Éireann and Ors*, the Court of Justice, in its decision of 12 July 1991, held that the prohibition on the publication by Magill TV Guide Ltd from publishing a full TV listing guides was in breach of Community law. For the domestic litigation in this case, in which the courts had granted injunctive relief to RTE and the other television stations involved in the case, see the 1989 Review, 200-1.

AGRICULTURAL IMPORTS

The lengthy judgment in *Emerald Meats Ltd v Minister for Agriculture and Ors*, High Court, 9 July 1991 concerned the correct allocation of a national quota for the importation of non-EC meat under Council Regulation 4024/89. Briefly, the plaintiff company had, over a number of years, purchased the importation quotas for non-EC meat of certain meat processors. These processors had been allocated their quotas by the Department of Agriculture and Food as the relevant national authority under previous Council Regulations. The Department was aware that these quotas had been sold to companies such as the plaintiff, who were known as meat brokers. Under Council Regulation 4024/89, the quotas for importation of non-EC meat were to be allocated only to those who had been 'importers' of such meat under the previous Council Regulations in this area. After representations to the Department of Agriculture by the meat processors, the Department determined that the meat processors were the 'importers' for the purposes of the Regulation, and forwarded their names only to the European Commission which was responsible for allocating the quotas under Regulation 4024/89.

The plaintiff company sought a mandatory injunction that it was the 'importer' for the purposes of the Regulation, since it had in reality purchased the quotas under the previous regime and the meat processors had not in fact imported the meat. Costello J held that the Department had misapplied the relevant provisions of Regulation 4024/89. A significant factor in the plaintiff's favour had been that, where meat had been imported under the previous regime, the Single Administrative Document (SAD) concerning the meat had, on most occasions, described the plaintiff as the importer. This was the basis on which the Department was required to determine the matter under Regulation 4024/89. Costello J held that once the plaintiff had put the meat into free circulation, the Department retained no role in adjudicating any dispute between the meat processors and the plaintiff as to who were correctly described as importers: Costello J concluded that the evdience simply pointed to the plaintiff.

In any event Costello J held that even if the Department did have an adjudicatory role in this area, it had failed to comply with Community law by not allowing the plaintiff to make its views known, citing *Transocean Marine Paint Assoc v Commission* [1974] ECR 1063 in this context. He noted that this requirement approximated to the requirements of fair procedures in Irish administrative law. He concluded that the Department was thus in breach of its duty under the Regulation to grant an import licence to the plaintiff.

For 1990, Costello J awarded the plaintiff £385,922 and a further sum of 662,926 Belgian francs, being the sums which, it was agreed, would have been realised by the plaintiff if it had received the licence.

COUNCIL MEETINGS

In *Duff and Ors v Minister for Agrculture and Food and Ors* [1992] 1 IR 198, Lardner J rejected a claim to privilege in respect of documents prepared for meetings of the Council of Agriculture Ministers: see the Practice and Procedure chapter, 336-7, below.

IMPORTATION BAN

In *United States Tobacco (Irl) Ltd v Ireland*, High Court, 19 February 1991, Article 36 of the Treaty of Rome was discussed: see the Safety and Health chapter, 376-7, below.

IRISH REGULATIONS

The following regulations and orders were made in 1991 pursuant to the provisions of s. 3 of the European Communities Act 1972 (or other statutory powers) involving implementation of Community law obligations.

European Communities (Additives in Feedingstuffs) (Amendment) Regulations 1991 (SI No. 124): further amended the 1989 Regulations.

European Communities (Additives in Feedingstuffs) (Amendment) (No. 2) Regulations 1991 (SI No. 345): further amended the 1989 Regulations and gave effect to Directives 91/248/EEC, 91/249/EEC, 91/336/EEC, 91/508/EEC and 91/620/EEC.

European Communities (Beef Carcase Classification) (Amendment) Regulations 1991 (SI No. 223).

European Communities (Beet Seed) (Amendment) Regulations 1991 (SI No. 108.

European Communities (Classificationn, Packaging and Labelling of Pesticides) (Amendment) Regulations 1991 (SI No. 88).

European Communities (Control of Oestrogenic, Androgenic, Gestragenic and Thyrostatic Substances) (Amendment) Regulations 1991 (SI No. 198): authorise stop and search powers for the Gardai in connection with the 1988 Regulations, which control the use of substances such as hormone growth promoters in animals.

European Communities (Cosmetic Products) (Amendment) Regulations 1991 (SI No. 352): amended the 1990 Regulations to give effect to Directive 91/184/EEC.

European Communities (Customs and Excise) Regulations 1991 (SI No. 57): see the Revenue chapter, 363, below.

European Communities (Customs and Excise) (Amendment) Regulations 1991 (SI No. 174): see the Revenue chapter, 363, below.

European Communities (Customs and Excise) (Amendment) (No. 2) Regulations 1991 (SI No. 368): see the Revenue chapter, 363, below.

European Communities (Egg Products) Regulations 1991 (SI No. 293: give effect to Directive 89/437/EEC on the marketing of egg products, and came into effect on 1 December 1991.

European Communities (Electrically, Hydraulically, or Oil-Electrically Operated Lifts) Regulations 1991 (SI No. 41): see the Safety and Health chapter, 369, below.

European Communities (Extraction of Solvents in Foodstuffs) Regulations 1991 (SI No. 334): see the Safety and Health chapter, 367, below.

European Communities (Feeding Stuffs) (Tolerances of Undesirable Substances and Products) (Amendment) Regulations 1991 (SI No. 241).

European Communities (Fruit Jams, Jellies and Marmalade and Chestnut Puree) (Amendment) Regulations 1991 (SI No. 319): implement Directive 88/593/EEC and amend the 1982 Regulations of the same title.

European Communities (General System for the Recognition of Higher Education Diplomas) Regulations 1991 (SI No. 1): see the Education chapter, 187, above.

European Communities (Good Laboratory Practice) Regulations 1991 (SI No. 4): see the Safety and Health chapter, 366, below.

European Communities (Health Act 1947, Amendment of Sections 54 and 61) Regulations 1991 (SI No. 333): see the Safety and Health chapter, 367, below.

European Communities (Indication of Prices of Foodstuffs and Non- Food Products) Regulations 1991 (SI No. 329): replace the European Communities (Indication of Prices of Foodstuffs) Regulations 1983.

European Communities (Labelling, Presentation and Advertising of Foodstuffs) (Amendment) Regulations 1991 (SI No. 228).

European Communities (Marketing of Feedingstuffs) (Amendment) Regulations 1991 (SI No. 11).

European Communities (Marketing of Fertilizers) Regulations 1991 (SI No. 284).

European Communities (Materials and Articles Intended to Come into Contact with Foodstuffs) Regulations 1991 (SI No. 307): see the Safety and Health chapter, 366, below.

European Communities (Merchandise Road Transport) Regulations 1991 (SI No. 60): see the Transport chapter, 465, below.

European Communities (Motor Vehicle Type Approval) Regulations 1991 (SI No. 186): see the Transport chapter, 463, below.

European Communities (Motor Vehicle Type Approval) (No. 2) Regulations 1991 (SI No. 367): see the Transport chapter, 463, below.

European Communities (Non-Life Insurance) (Amendment) Regulations 1991 (SI No. 5): see the Commercial Law chapter, 32, above.

European Communities (Non-Life Insurance) (Amendment) (No. 2) Regulations 1991 (SI No. 142): see the Commercial Law chapter, 32, above.

European Communities (Non-Life Insurance) (Legal Expenses) Regulations 1991 (SI No. 197): see the Commercial Law chapter, 32, above.

European Communities (Paints etc.) (Classificationn, Packaging and Labelling) (Amendment) Regulations 1991 (SI No. 152): see the Safety and Health chapter, 369, below.

European Communities (Protection of Topographies of Semiconductor Products) (Amendment) Regulations 1991 (SI No. 318): see the Commercial Law chapter, 32, above.

European Communities (Protein Feedingstuffs) (Amendment) Regulations 1991 (SI No. 195): further amend the 1986 Regulations.

European Communities (Recognition of Qualifications in Pharmacy) Regulations 1991 (SI No. 330): see the Education chapter, 187, above.

European Communities (Retirement of Farmers) Regulations 1991 (SI No. 227).

European Communities (Road Passenger Transport) Regulations 1991 (SI

No. 59): see the Transport chapter, 463, below.

European Communities (Road Traffic) (Vehicle Type Approval) Regulations 1991 (SI No. 34): see the Transport chapter, 463, below.

European Communities (Sampling and Analysis of Fertilizers) Regulations 1991 (SI No. 282).

European Communities (Scheduled Air Fares) Regulations 1991 (SI No. 54): see the Transport chapter, 461, below.

European Communities (Seed of Fodder Plants) (Amendment) Regulations 1991 (SI No. 110).

European Communities (Seed of Fodder Plants) (Amendment) (No. 2) Regulations 1991 (SI No. 179).

European Communities (Seed of Oil Plants and Fibre Plants) (Amendment) Regulations 1991 (SI No. 109).

European Communities (Self-Propelled Industrial Trucks) Regulations 1991 (SI No. 12): see the Safety and Health chapter, 369, below.

European Communities (Sharing of Passenger Capacity and Access to Scheduled Air Service Routes) Regulations 1991 (SI No. 54): see the Transport chapter, 461, below.

European Communities (Simple Pressure Vessels) Regulations 1991 (SI No. 115): see the Safety and Health chapter, 369, below.

European Communities (Statistical Confidentiality) Regulations 1991 (SI No. 111).

European Communities (Stock Exchange) (Amendment) Regulations 1991 (SI No. 18): see 51, above.

European Communities (Surveillance of Certain Textile Products Imports) Regulations 1991 (SI No. 29): revoke SI No. 35 of 1990 and give effect to Commission Decisions 87/433/EEC and No. C(90) 2767 (19 December 1990).

European Communities (Surveillance of Import of Certain Iron and Steel Products) Regulations 1991 (SI No. 106).

European Communities (Tar Yield of Cigarettes) Regulations 1991 (SI No. 327): see the Safety and Health chapter, 377, below.

European Communities (Television Broadcasting) Regulations 1991 (SI No. 251): see the Telecommunications chapter, 383, below.

European Communities (Trade with Iraq and Kuwait) Regulations 1991 (SI No. 52). gave effect to Council Regulation 542/91, in the wake of the Gulf War.

European Communities (Trade with Iraq and Kuwait) (No. 2) Regulations 1991 (SI No. 100): give effect to Council Regulation 811/91 by allowing additional medical supplies to be exported to Iraq.

European Communities (Transit of Electricity) Regulations 1991 (SI No. 275): see the Electricity and Energy chapter, 189, above.

European Communities (Transit of Natural Gas) Regulations 1991 (SI No. 343): see the Electricity and Energy chapter, 189, above.

European Communities (Use of Sewage Sludge in Agriculture) Regulations 1991 (SI No. 183).

European Communities (Vegetable Seeds) (Amendment) Regulations 1991 (SI No. 107).

European Communities (Vehicle Testing) Regulations 1991 (SI No. 356): see the Transport chapter, 464, below.

Health (Official Control of Food) Regulations 1991 (SI No. 332): see the Safety and Health chapter, 367, below.

Restriction of Imports from Iraq and Kuwait (Amendment) Order 1991 (SI No. 68): amended the 1990 Order (1990 Review, 286) by deleting Kuwait, to take account of the Gulf War.

Road Traffic (Construction, Equipment and Use of Vehicles) (Amendment) Regulations 1991 (SI No. 273): see the Transport chapter, 463, below.

Road Traffic (Construction, Equipment and Use of Vehicles) (Amendment) (No. 2) Regulations 1991 (SI No. 358): see the Transport chapter, 463, below.

Road Traffic (Construction, Equipment and Use of Vehicles) (Amendment) (No. 3) Regulations 1991 (SI No. 359): see the Transport chapter, 463, below.

Safety, Health and Welfare at Work Act 1989 (Control of Specific Substances and Activities) Regulations 1991 (SI No. 285): see the Safety and Health chapter, 370, below.

Solicitors Acts 1954 and 1960 (European Communities) Regulations 1991 (SI No. 85): see the Solicitors chapter, 381, below.

Solicitors Acts 1954 and 1960 (European Community Lawyers) (Fees) Regulations 1991 (SI No. 84): see the Solicitors chapter, 381, below.

In addition to the above Regulations, some EC Directives and EC- related law were implemented by primary legislation.

The Liability for Defective Products Act 1991 implemented the Products Liability Directive 85/374/EEC: see the Torts chapter, 420, below.

The Contractual Obligations (Applicable Law) Act 1991 implemented the 1980 Convention on the Law Applicable to Contractual Obligations: see the Conflict of Laws chapter, 54-81, above.

S. 36 of the Finance Act 1991 implemented Directive 90/435/EEC on the taxation of parent and subsidiary companies see the Revenue Law chapter, 357 below.

Finally, the Competition Act 1991 implemented a domestic regime of competition law by direct analogy with Articles 85 and 86 of the Treaty of Rome: see the Commercial Law chapter, 23-6, above.

NECESSITATED BY MEMBERSHIP

A very helpful discussion of the extent to which provisions of the Constitution may not be invoked to invalidate requirements 'necessitated' by membership of the Communities, pursuant to Article 29.4.3 of the Constitution, is found in Whelan, 'Article 29.4.3 and the meaning of "necessity"' (1992) 2 *Irish Student Law Review* 60. The case law on this area is discussed in the 1987 Review, 92-4, the 1989 Review, 99-100 and the 1990 Review, 283-4.

REFERENCE TO COURT OF JUSTICE

The circumstances in which the Supreme Court will refer a case to the Court of Justice under Article 177 of the Treaty of Rome were referred to in *Kerry Co-Op Creameries Ltd v An Bord Bainne Co-Op Ltd* [1990] ILRM 664 (HC); [1991] ILRM 851 (SC) (see 30, above, in the Commercial Law chapter).

ROAD TRANSPORT

The European Communities (Road Passenger Transport) Regulations 1977 (since replaced) were referred to in *D.P.P. (Jennings) v Go-Travel Ltd* [1991] ILRM 577: see 464-5, below, in the Transport chapter.

SERVICES

The 1991 decision of the Court of Justice in *Society for the Protection of Unborn Children (Irl) Ltd v Grogan* [1992] ILRM 461 will be considered in the 1992 Review along with the 1992 decisions of the High Court and Supreme Court in *Attorney General v X.* [1992] ILRM 401; [1992] 1 IR 1.

TRANSFER OF UNDERTAKINGS

The European Communities (Safeguarding of Employees' Rights on Transfer of Undertakings) Regulations 1980 were adverted to in *Westman Holdings Ltd v McCormack and Ors* [1991] ILRM 833; [1992] 1 IR 151: see 194, above, in the Equitable Remedies chapter.

TREATIES AS CONSTITUTIONS

The debate as to whether the Treaties establishing the Communities contain principles of 'European constitutional law' was raised in John Temple Lang's important article 'The Development of European Community Constitutional Law' (1991) 13 DULJ 36.

Family Law

NULLITY OF MARRIAGE

Mental incapacity   In the 1990 Review, 291-7, we analysed the important Supreme Court decision of *F. (otherwise H.C.) v C.* [1991] ILRM 65, which endorsed the developments that had taken place at High Court level since Barrington J's judgment in *R.S.J. v J.S.J.* [1982] ILRM 263. In *G.M. (otherwise G.) v T.G.* High Court, 22 November 1991, Lavan J applied the test set out by Costello J in *D. v C.* [1984] ILRM 173, at 188, which the Supreme Court had approved of specifically in their 1990 decision.

In *G.M.*, the petitioner sought a decree of nullity on the ground that, at the date of the ceremony, the respondent was, by reason of psychiatric illness, incapable of entering into and sustaining a normal functional martial relationship with her. The evidence indicated that the parties had become engaged in 1983 and had had a reasonably uneventful courtship until 1985. The respondent then underwent a tonsillectomy which resulted in his being out of work for six months. During that time he became severely depressed and received specialist psychiatric treatment. He experienced problems on his return to his employment and lost his job in 1986. The couple's plan to marry in August of 1986 was put back to June 1987, mainly on account of his condition. A week before the ceremony the respondent told the petitioner that he wished to call off the wedding but she prevailed on him to go through with it.

After the ceremony, the parties cohabited for only fifteen months. The expert psychiatric evidence was to the effect that the respondent suffered from a severe psychotic endogenous depression, and that he had been advised by two psychiatrists not to marry until he had fully recovered. The respondent had received no treatment on a continuing basis for some six to twelve months from April 1986, in spite of the advice of the psychiatrists.

Lavan J was satisfied that there was no collusion. He accepted the need for the petitioner to prove her case to a high standard of proof. He regard the Supreme Court decision in *F. (otherwise H.C.) v C.* as authority for this approach: on this issue, see our comments in the 1990 Review, 295-6. The question he addressed was whether the respondent, at the time of the ceremony, was 'a sick man and a man who was not in a position to make significant decision for himself, and in particular, not in a position to make a decision which would involve him in a life-long union as contemplated by the test as set out [in *D. v C.*]'. In answering this question he disregarded evidence led by both parties as to the relationship between them *after* the ceremony. This is an unusual strategy, since events after the ceremony can often throw light on a party's mental condition at the time of the ceremony, as *D. v C.* indicates. In the light of the evidence Lavan J concluded that the respondent's severe depression had affected his capacity to consent to enter into and sustain a lifelong union with the petitioner, that in this state he had clearly indicated his unwillingness to make a lifelong commitment to marriage, and that, suffering this condition, on account of 'the features of the serious mental illness', he had been unable to resist the petitioner's understandable pressure to proceed with the marriage. Accordingly Lavan J granted a decree of nullity.

A couple of points are worth noting about the case. The Master had ordered that two questions in particular be tried: *first*, whether the respondent was incapable of entering into and sustaining a normal marriage relationship with the petitioner by reason of *psychiatric illness and/or personality disorder*, and secondly, whether he was thus incapable by reason of *emotional immaturity*. Lavan J answered both questions in the affirmative. It is easy to see how the first was so answered; the second, on the evidence, seems more problematical.

It is also interesting to note that, while the grounds exclusively related to the incapacity described, the respondent's inability to resist the petitioner's pressure to marry was a factor in Lavan J's reaching that conclusion. There was no need to characterise this pressure as duress, which is of course a separate ground for nullity.

Duress In the 1990 Review, 297-301, we examined the most recent Supreme Court decision on duress, *D.B. (otherwise O.'R.) v O.'R.* [1991] ILRM 160; [1991] 1 IR 536, which reviewed the earlier jurisprudence on the subject. In *P.W. v A.O.C. (otherwise W.)* [1992] ILRM 536, Blayney J referred to *D.B.* and its predecessors in distilling the test for duress as being whether the effect of the duress was such that the party's consent to the marriage 'was an apparent consent only, that is to say, that it was not a fully free exercise of an independent will'. He noted that the nature of the duress seemed no longer to be an essential element. It was not necessary, as *Szechter v Szechter* [1971] P 286 had required, that the will of the party have been overborne 'by genuine and reasonably held fear caused by threat of immediate danger, for which the party himself is not responsible, to life, limb or liberty. . . .'

In the instant case, the parties had become engaged in 1956, when they were in their mid-twenties. The petitioner had not intended marrying for a couple of years. Shortly after their engagement, the respondent, a woman of domineering character, wrote to the petitioner threatening suicide unless he married her immediately. The petitioner, not wishing her to die, went through a ceremony of marriage with her.

Blayney J held that the petitioner had not acted freely in taking this course, and that there had not been a valid consent. Blayney J's consideration of the issue of delay is discussed below.

Delay as a bar   In *P.W. v A.O.C. (otherwise W.)* [1992] ILRM 536, which we have just analysed in relation to the ground of duress, Blayney J held that a petition for nullity brought over thirty years after the parties had gone through a ceremony of marriage, in 1956, should not be defeated by delay. He accepted the petitioner's explanation that he had told his legal advisers the full facts about his marriage as long ago as 1964 but that he had not been advised until 1987 that he had grounds for having his marriage annulled. Blayney J thought the explanation likely to be true because the petitioner, had he known earlier of his entitlement to do so, would have petitioned for a decree of nullity as this would have relieved him of the legal obligation to pay maintenance to the respondent, which he had been doing since 1966.

JUDICIAL SEPARATION

Grounds for a decree   *V.S. v R.S.*, High Court, 10 June 1991 is important in offering the first recorded judicial interpretation of the grounds for judicial separation under the 1989 legislation. The plaintiff's application for a decree under s. 2 of the Judicial Separation and Family Reform Act 1989 was based on three grounds. The first—adultery—Lynch J rejected on the evidence. The second, under paragraph (b) of s. 2(1), was that the respondent had behaved in such a way that the applicant could not reasonably be expected to live with him. This ground is the statutory successor to the old ground of cruelty under the divorce *a mensa et thoro* regime: see Duncan & Scully, *Marriage Breakdown in Ireland: Law and Practice* (1990), para 7.018. The essence of the applicant's case was that the respondent had assaulted her on occasions when he was drunk. Lynch J was satisfied on the probabilities that there had been rows from time to time during the history of the marriage (which had been celebrated in 1982) and that the respondent had 'physically abused' the applicant 'on a few occasions in the course of mutual quarrelling and that likewise, though to a lesser extent', the applicant had 'offered or attempted physical abuse' of the respondent. Lynch J refused to grant a decree on this ground as he was not satisfied that on the probabilities that the applicant had made out a case.

This holding merits comment. It may be recalled that the old ground of cruelty looked both backwards and forwards: backwards in that it required proof that the respondent had engaged in conduct (not *necessarily* subjectively morally blameworthy: *McA. v McA.* [1981] ILRM 361, *Gollins v Gollins* [1964] AC 644); forward in that the impugned conduct must have been such 'as to render the continued performance of the obligations of marriage impossible': *D. v D.*, High Court, 20 December 1966 (Butler J). In regard to physical violence it was sufficient to show that the respondent had engaged in conduct that gave rise to a reasonable apprehension of *future* physical abuse. Thus, a spouse who had thrown a knife, or fired a shot, at his or her partner could make nothing of the fact that it had missed its target. Ground (b) under 2(1) also looks backward and forward. Unless the respondent has 'behaved' in some *particular* way such that the applicant cannot reasonably be expected in the future to live with him or her, the ground is not made out. Manifestly acts of violence, even thwarted ones, are capable of constituting behaviour of the kind envisaged by ground (b). So why did the petitioner fail here? Presumably because Lynch J considered that the level of 'physical abuse' was within a range of tolerability. Stated so baldly, the proposition may prove controversial. Indeed, one suspects that courts would in future be somewhat shy about articulating with any specificity what precise acts one spouse may practice on the other without fear of having a decree made against him or her under ground (b). Language here seems a dangerous servant. Words describing physical contact are simply unable to capture fully its potential for aggression. A 'push' may seem innocuous enough, but people have been pushed to their death,not simply over cliffs, but also with the flick of a wrist onto a kitchen floor. A 'dig', in some social quarters, connotes attempted grievous bodily harm. Perhaps the courts could scarcely go no further than to deny the proposition that *every* act of physical contact to which a spouse does not consent automatically entitles that spouse to a decree under ground (b). This is scarcely very helpful but it may seem preferable to judicial comments that could lead to the conclusion that certain forms of *physical abuse* are within the matrimonial pale.

One possible interpretation of Lynch J's remarks, which must surely be rejected, is that the applicant's own 'offer' or 'attempt' at physical abuse should have the effect of disentitling her to a decree under ground (b). The relevant legal principles are, however, somewhat complex. Provocation for a husband's violence did not *per se* constitute a bar under the divorce *a mensa et thoro* regime: *Holden v Holden* (1810) 1 Hag Con 453, 161 ER 614. (Cf. Finlay P's address to the jury in *O'Reardon v O'Reardon* High Court, February 1975, as quoted by Shatter, *Family Law in the Republic of Ireland* (3rd ed., 1986), 221, fn 34.) So far as it induced a physical response limited to that of reasonable self-defence, however, it would have this legal effect: *Waring v Waring* (1813) 2 Hag Con 153.

Under the 1989 Act, what remains unanalysed in express terms by Lynch J is the extent to which the *reasonableness* requirement specified in ground (b) requires or authorises the court to take into account the character and conduct of the *applicant* in determining what that applicant should be required to put up with in a marriage. In England the courts have interpreted a ground for divorce expressed in the same language as our ground (b) as connoting a reference to such subjective dimensions. In *Ash v Ash* [1972] Fam 135, at 160, Bagnall J considered that the proper question for a judge to ask was whether '*this* petitioner with his or her faults and other attitudes, good and bad, and having regard to his or her behaviour during the marriage [can] reasonably be expected to live with *this* respondent'. Duncan & Scully, *op. cit.*, para 7.024, express uncertainty as to whether the same approach will be adopted here:

> On the one hand, it could be argued that to apply the standard of 'ordinary men and women' fails to take into account any special characteristics, whether in the constitutions and personalities of the parties, or the history of their relationship, which might make it reasonable not to expect the particular applicant to continue cohabitation. However, an entirely subjective approach cannot be adopted, because to do so would ignore the requirement of reasonableness in relation to what the applicant can be expected to tolerate. A middle path seems likely.

Perhaps assistance may usefully be sought here from the manner in which courts apply the test of reasonableness in negligence litigation. Much emphasis is there placed on the objective quality of this criterion and on the fact that, as Lord Macmillan observed in *Glasgow Corporation v Muir* [1943] AC 48, at 457, the test 'eliminates the personal equation'. Yet, when one looks closer, considerably more deference to individuating personal factors is apparent. Cf. Seavey, 'Negligence—Subjective or Objective?', 41 Harv L Rev 1 (1927). Indeed, negligence law may provide another useful analogy in the manner in which it enables the particular elements of a personal inter-relationship to fashion the contours of the duty of care: see *McComiskey v McDermott* [1974] IR 75, McMahon & Binchy, *op. cit.*, 100-1.

At all events, even if we concede that ground (b) requires the court to have regard to the particular qualities and circumstances of the applicant as well as those from the respondent, this falls well short of the proposition that some tacit rule of recrimination should be re-introduced whereby a violent applicant should be refused a decree of separation from an equally, or still more, violent partner. This is not permitted by s. 44 of the Act: see the 1988 Review, 242.

One puzzling aspect of Lynch J's disposition of the applicant's claim under ground (b) is his reference to the fact that the respondent had had a barring order made against him some years previously. Lynch J does not refer to the evidence on which the barring order was obtained, but if the Supreme Court's test in *O'B. v O'B.* [1984] ILRM 1 was faithfully applied, some serious misconduct on the part of the respondent might well have been in question. Some interesting issues could arise as to the extent to which the ordinary evidential rules of issue estoppel ought to be displaced by distinctive rules applying to interspousal litigation. Forty years ago the English courts constructed an elaborate scaffolding of law based on the policy of retaining a high degree of judicial control so as to preserve society's interest in protecting the institution of marriage. In the light of the radical social and legal shift in England from treating marriage as a matter of status to the contemporary emphasis on individual fulfilment, these cases have a very dated air. While the Irish position is far from identical, it is to be hoped that the Irish courts would not too readily adopt some of the elaborate distinctions favoured in these cases.

The third, and final ground for a decree of judicial separation on which the applicant relied was ground (f):

> that the marriage has broken down to the extent that the court is satisfied in all the circumstances that a normal marriage relationship has not existed between the spouses for a period of at least one year immediately preceding the date of the application.

On this ground she was successful. Lynch J was satisfied that, from about the beginning of 1988, the relationship between the parties had deteriorated significantly. Since then they had not had any sexual intercourse. The applicant had left the family home about half a dozen times. When living in the family home she and the respondent slept in different rooms. During one of the periods of separation, which had lasted nearly a year, the applicant had lived with one of their children, while the respondent had remained in the family home with the other child. Although the parties had been living under the same roof again for nearly a year, they had been doing so 'very abnormally'. The applicant rarely remained in the house alone with the respondent and the parties communicated with each other as little as possible. In holding that ground (f) applied, Lynch J was satisfied that a normal marriage relationship had not existed for the previous three and a half years.

It would have been interesting to know how the applicant would have fared had she sought to rely on ground (e), under which a decree may be granted on the basis that the parties have lived apart for the last three years. S. 2(3)(a) provides that spouses are to be treated as living apart from each other unless they are living with each other in the same household. There is no judicial authority thus far on the meaning of the expression 'living with each other'. In England it has been held that the absence of sexual intercourse does not, of itself, prevent a couple from being characterised as living with each other: see *Mouncer v Mouncer* [1972] 2 All ER 246, the facts of which were not dissimilar to those in *V.S. v R.S.*

Lynch J's judgment throws little light on the analytic basis for determining whether ground (f) had been made out. The language of the ground presents some difficulty. It is capable of dealing with clear cases of marital disharmony where communication between the spouses has virtually ended, but it is far more troublesome in other contexts.

Three possible interpretations may be hazarded of the concept of a 'normal marital relationship's not having existed for the previous year. The *first* is that what is envisaged is the absence of a marital relationship *that is statistically common*. The idea here is that *most* marriages involve the parties living together, in the company of their children, with at least some degree of positive communication between the spouses and between parents and children. Under the *second* interpretation, a 'normal marital relationship' connotes the particular relationship which, prior to its 'breakdown', the spouses had enjoyed. Normality would thus embrace *the state of the marital relationship before matters went wrong*. A possible attraction of this interpretation is that it saves the court the troublesome task of having to articulate the ingredients of a 'normal relationship' in objective terms. The obvious disadvantage is the consequential uncertainty and subjective nature of the ground. Such a test would make it very difficult for the respondent to defend himself or herself against the applicant's claim that the relationship had deteriorated significantly from what it 'normally' had been. The wear and tear of family life inevitably involves ups and downs in relationships. A selective, albeit *bona fide*, recollection of the low points could be very difficult to refute.

The *third* interpretation of a 'normal marital relationship' is that it connotes a relationship of a kind that is necessary for the normal incidents of married life to function adequately. On this approach, marriage, as a freely chosen, mutual commitment for the joint lives of the spouses, involves certain elements without which that commitment cannot normally be lived out effectively. Thus, for example, where one spouse refused to have any sexual relationship with the other or where the spouses did not otherwise communicate it could properly be said that a normal marital relationship had not existed.

This interpretation has the attraction of harmonising with the law of nullity of marriage, where the courts have articulated, as a ground of nullity, incapacity to form a normal relationship with the other party. See the 1988

Review, 230-2 and above 206-7.

Where does Lynch J's analysis fit into these competing interpretations? It would seem unwise to read too much into the brief treatment of the issue in his judgment, which amounts to no more than a statement of the relevant evidence and the holding that 'in all the circumstances' a normal marital relationship had not existed between the spouses for the previous three and a half years. Nevertheless, *each* of the three interpretations finds some implicit support. As to the first, the notion of statistical abnormality underlines Lynch J's statement that, although the family had lived under one roof since August 1990, they had done so 'very abnormally' so far as the spouses were concerned. As to the second, the notion of 'things having *gone wrong*' is inherent in Lynch J's reference to the fact that from the beginning of 1988 the relationship between the parties had 'deteriorated significantly'. The third interpretation is consistent with Lynch J's approach in that the essential matters he deemed relevant to mention are those impinging on precisely the elements of communication, physical and emotional, which the third interpretation highlights.

Maintenance and Property adjustment orders   In *J.C. v C.C.*, High Court, 15 November 1991, the spouses married in 1972 and had two children. Before the marriage, the defendant, the husband, had bought a suburban house in his own name for £10,000, subject to a mortgage, and this had become the family home. The husband was a pilot, the wife an air hostess. On her marriage, she had been obliged to resign. (This *ancien regime* incidentally, raised a general issue of some considerable legal contention: cf. *Aer Lingus Teoranta v Labour Court* [1990] ILRM 485 [1990] ELR 113, and the 1990 Review, 342-4). The wife subsequently qualified as a Montessori teacher; she was a part-time professional artist without formal qualifications. The couple had two children, born in 1974 and 1976.

The parties agreed to separate in 1982 but did not then do so. The husband obtained temporary leave of absence from his employers and took up service abroad for the following three years, during which time he made considerable savings out of high earnings. The parties separated in 1985. The husband bought a derelict old mill on ten acres for £190,000. With the services of an architect he spent £90,000 on building a house 'of exceptional interest and character', which incorporated the mill. This venture entailed the raising of a £22,000 mortgage. Barr J characterised it as financially unwise, with hindsight. It ate up all the husband's savings, and involved an £8,000 overdraft in addition to the mortgage.

This house, though not fully completed and suffering from some damp, was valued at £120,000. The former family home (still so designated under the Family Home Protection Act 1976) also had a value of £120,000. It was in need of substantial maintenance work costing around £10,000 including rewiring the electricity supply and remedying damp. Since 1982, the plaintiff had spent about £5,000 on the property, including the installation of gas-fired central heating and an alarm system.

On her resignation in 1972, the plaintiff had received a £1,450 gratuity. This remained her property. It had been lodged to a joint deposit, from which the defendant had drawn to finance his house-building project.

At the time of the proceedings the husband's earnings were over £60,000. Out of his net income of over £35,000, he was paying his wife nearly £15,000 per annum for her maintenance and that of the children. He also paid the mortgage and insurance on the former family home: these cost £1,321 *per annum*. The wife's net income from her work as an artist was about £2,500. Her net earnings from all sources were unlikely to exceed £12,800. The wife claimed that her husband should increase the maintenance by £3,125 per annum.

Barr J acknowledged that the wife's claim was 'modest and reasonable in all the circumstances'. He ordered an increase of only £2,000, however, because he considered that the wife would not have too much difficulty making up the difference by using her qualifications. Such employment seemed to him to be suited to her present circumstances; it would not interfere with her duties as a mother. Barr J apportioned the maintenance between the wife and the children. He did not make a secured maintenance order as there was no evidence to suggest that this was required.

Barr J went on to make a lump sum order of £5,000 to cover the present capital value of the money the wife had lodged in the joint deposit in 1972. He made a further lump sum order of £10,500 to cover maintenance and improvements which the wife had carried out on the family home after 1982, as well as further substantial expenditure that would need to be carried out on the home in the future.

Turning to property adjustment orders, Barr J held that the wife was entitled to a right of residence in the family home for her life and to 'a half interest in her husband's title to that property'. (Whether that interest involved a joint tenancy or a tenancy in common was not specified in the judgment). She had never had any connection with the home her husband built after the separation and 'therefore' was not entitled to any interest in it. One may perhaps question the suggestion that the conclusion followed *logically* from the premises (if the latter word is not confusing in the present context). The powers of the court in making property adjustment orders under s. 15 of the 1989 Act are in no sense as limited as they would be in proceedings under s. 12 of the Married Women's Status Act 1957. There is no need to establish any prior beneficial interest in the property on the part of the spouse in whose favour a property adjustment order is made: *cf. Hanlon v The Law Society* [1980] 1 All ER 763, at 770 (*per* Lord Denning MR).

It may be useful to consider some of the implications of a court's making a property adjustment order in respect of the former family home. An English commentator (Cretney, *Principles of Family Law* (4th ed., 1984), 775-6) has observed in relation to a provision similar to s. 15 of our 1989 Act, that orders for the transfer of property should not prejudice the interests of third parties who are not before the court:

> Thus, if the matrimonial home is subject to a mortgage, a transfer of it to the wife cannot affect [a mortgagor] husband's contractual liability to pay the mortgage instalments, nor the rights of the mortgagee to take action if the mortgage contracts are broken. In practice mortgage deeds usually contain provisions forbidding the mortgagor transferring the property without the mortgagee's consent: hence the mortgagee should have notice of the application and be given an opportunity to be heard.

Finally, it may be noted that the wife expressed concern that her husband might on his retirement opt for a tax-free sum of £100,000 and a reduced pension (of £30,000 per annum) rather than accept a pension of two-thirds his gross salary. Evidence was given that nearly all pilots favoured the former option. In view of the husband's undertaking to give his wife one month's notice if he took that option, Barr J thought there was no need to make any order in that regard.

Exclusion orders   In *K. v K.*, High Court, 25 October 1990, the plaintiff wife had obtained a decree for judicial separation from her husband in the Circuit Court on the basis of ground (f) of s. 2 of the Judicial Separation and Family Law Reform Act 1989. The Circuit Court did not make any ancillary order directing the husband to leave the family home or directing that the home be sold. The wife appealed on the ground (*inter alia*) that, by virtue of s. 19, the court must make an order under which the parties must live apart either by reason of an exclusion order under s. 16(a) or a barring order under s. 16(e) or by directing a sale of the home under s. 16(b).

Barron J interpreted s. 16 as giving the court a discretion whether or not to make any one or more of the orders set out in the section. S. 19 provides as follows:

> The court shall exercise its jurisdiction under s. 16(a) and (b) above as an additional jurisdiction to that which arises under the Family Law (Protection of Spouses and Children) Act 1981 and the Family Home Protection Act 1976 and shall in exercising such jurisdiction have regard to the welfare of the family as a whole and in particular shall take into consideration—

(a) that where a decree of judicial separation is granted it is not possible for the spouses to continue to reside together;

(b) that proper and secure accommodation should, where practicable, be provided for a dependant spouse and any dependant children of the family;

(c) the matters referred to in s. 20 of this Act.

Barron J was of the view that, having regard to the provisions of paragraph (a) of s. 19, the court 'must . . . ensure that the parties shall no longer reside together'. The court might accordingly make an order under s. 16(e). If it did not do so, it had to choose between s. 16(a) and s. 16(b).

In the circumstances of the case before him, Barron J did not consider that the facts warranted the making of a barring order. There were several reasons why the family home should not be sold: the youngest child of the family was going to school in the area and the wife had interests in the community; nor did the family finances require the home to be sold. In these circumstances he made an order under s. 16(a) excluding the husband from the home.

FAMILY PROPERTY

The Constitutional dimension In the 1988 Review, 213-21, we discussed in detail Barr J's judgment in *L. v L.* [1989] ILRM 528, which held that Article 41.2 of the Constitution generated a proprietary interest in the family home for wives who work within the home. The Supreme Court unanimously reversed Barr J: [1992] ILRM 115. For incisive comments, see, Sora Doherty (1992) 2 Ir. Students L. Rev. 5 and Hilary Delany (1992) 14 DULJ 153.

The plaintiff was the wife of a very rich man, whom she had married in 1968. She had not worked outside the home and had been 'a devoted full-time home-maker and mother from the beginning'. She obtained a decree of divorce *a mensa et thoro* on the grounds of her husband's adultery and cruelty. In concurrent proceedings, Barr J had held she was entitled to a half-interest in the family home.

Article 41.2 provides as follows:

1°. In particular, the State recognises that, by her life within the home, woman gives to the State a support without which the common good cannot be achieved.

2°. The State shall, therefore, endeavour to ensure that mothers shall not be obliged by economic necessity to engage in labour to the neglect of their duties in the home.

Finlay CJ accepted the plaintiff's contention that the obligation which subs. 2 imposed on the State was imposed on the *judiciary* as well as on the legislature and the executive. He was, however, satisfied that there was no warrant for interpreting the subsection as granting the courts jurisdiction to award any particular interest in the family home to a wife and mother 'where that would be unrelated to the question of her being obliged by economic necessity to engage in labour to the neglect of her duties'. If a court was assessing the alimony or maintenance payable by a husband to a wife and mother in proceedings for judicial separation or under the Family Law (Maintenance of Spouses and Children) Act 1976, it 'should . . . have regard to and exercise its duty under this subsection of the Constitution in a case where the husband was capable of making proper provision for his wife within the home by refusing to have any regard to a capacity of the wife to earn herself, if she was in addition to a wife a mother also, and if the obligation so to earn could lead to the neglect of her duties in the home. In other words, maintenance or alimony could and must be set by a court so as to avoid forcing by an economic necessity the wife and mother to labour out of the home to the neglect of her duties in it'.

In cases (such as the 1989 Act) where the Oireachtas had chosen to confer on the court power to declare a right in a spouse to a beneficial interest in the family home as part of a general judicial jurisdiction on the granting of a separation to make monetary provisions arising from it, then, the Chief Justice thought, the court might exercise that expressed statutory power in obedience to and furtherance of subs. 2.

Finlay CJ's analysis provokes reflection. As to the first part of it, no one would contest the proposition that subs. 2 does not give the judiciary jurisdiction to award a wife a share of the home where to do is *unrelated* to the question of her being obliged by economic necessity to work outside the home. But it does not in any sense follow from this undeniable fact that the court's jurisdiction under subs. 2 should be limited to orders for *maintenance or alimony*. Of course these orders have a clear relationship with the court's constitutional obligation under subs. 2, but neither logically nor in practice is the court's obligation *limited* to cases where it is making orders of this kind.

Take, for example, the case of a husband with plenty of assets but (perhaps on account of a recent accident) no earning power. Let us assume that the husband is not disposed to share any of his assets with his wife who, as a result, is forced to contemplate working outside the home in circumstances captured by subs. 2. Why should the court be obliged to exercise its constitutional function under subs. 2 only if the wife seeks a maintenance order under the 1976 Act or a maintenance or alimony order under the 1989 Act? The wife may not wish to obtain a judicial separation. The court's powers to award lump sum payments as part of the exercise of its maintenance jurisdiction are wider under the 1989 Act than under the 1976 Act. In a case such as the one outlined above, clearly lump sum payments would be preferable to orders for periodical payments without a lump sum element. One effect of limiting the power of the court to discharge its constitutional obligation under subs. 2 on the lines envisaged by the Chief Justice is that the wife would be pressurised into seeking a judicial separation as the price of obtaining access to the constitutional protection for her under subs. 2. One wonders why such constitutional protection which (on the Chief Justice's own analysis) imposes an obligation on the judiciary should be subject to such a self-imposed judicial restraint, contingent on the extraneous decision of the Oireachtas and so capable of creating unwarranted pressures on married women whose husbands, though perhaps very rich, are not earning salaries or other income which can be the basis of a maintenance order. In this context, it may be noted that the Supreme Court in *Sachs v Standard Chartered Bank (Ireland) Ltd* [1987] ILRM 297 held that an order for financial provision made in favour of the wife should be treated as involving the provision of maintenance: see further Binchy, *Irish Conflicts of Law* (1988), 291-2.

A further aspect of the passage quoted from Finlay CJ's judgment merits comment. The Chief Justice proposes that, when assessing maintenance or alimony in cases where the husband can make proper provision for his wife, the court must '*refus[e] to have any regard to a capacity of the wife to earn herself*', if she is a mother and if the obligation so to earn could lead to the neglect of her duties in the home. At first sight this might seem to be an uncontroversial conclusion, but on further reflection it touches on more contentious themes. It forces the court for the first time to identify what are the wife's duties in the home and what constitutes neglect of those duties. In the 1990s, this is a task that the judges might well wish to dodge. See our discussion of this issue in a somewhat different, but nonetheless related, context in the 1990 Review, 568-74.

The temptation not to answer these questions springs from the diversity of attitudes towards gender roles in contemporary Irish society. As we noted in the 1989 Review, 239, there was formerly a fairly general consensus that children were best reared in the home by their mothers. This consensus has been diluted in recent years: some argue that domestic duties are equivalent to servitude and reflect a patriarchal imposition on women; others contend that the distribution of childbearing functions should be a matter of the couple to decide for themselves; still others suggest that women who rear their children in the home do a much better job than any creche can do, in terms of constant loving attention. The Chief Justice's approach forces the court, when determining maintenance, to identify the 'duties in the home' which are distinctively those of mothers. Have fathers *any* duties in the home? If so, are they as extensive as those of mothers? And must *they* be recognised and respected by the courts even though receiving no express constitutional identification or protection akin to subs. 2?

The plaintiff in *L. v L.* had not contested on appeal Barr J's rejection of her claim to a share in the family home based on 'common law' (surely equitable?), non-constitutional, principles. Finlay CJ accepted the inconsistency in the existing law between the respective positions of wives working outside and within the home; nevertheless he agreed with Barr J that to extend these principles to benefit stay-at-home wives would 'not . . . develop any known principle of the common law' but rather would 'identify a brand new right', which would constitute judicial legislation and a usurpation by the courts of the function of the Oireachtas.

A question arises as to why s. 12 of the Married Women's Status Act 1957 should not be interpreted as a legislative conferment of jurisdiction on the courts to discharge their obligation under subs. 2 of Article 41.2 when determining spousal entitlements to property. The reply may be that, in contrast to the 1989 Act, s. 12 professes to confer on the court merely a declaratory, and not a rights-generating, function. Whatever the formal merits of this rebuttal, it would seem naive to believe that this is how s. 12 operates in practice.

Egan J's concurring judgment clearly endorses the Chief Justice's approach to the question of extending the equitable principles. His laconic disposition of the plaintiff's constitutional argument suggests a difference from Finlay CJ in failing to identify any obligation on the part of the *courts* under subs. 2 of Article 41.2, and in failing to identify the family home as a legitimate subject matter for effectuation of the obligation imposed on the State by that subsection. The Chief Justice, as we have seen, was willing to accept that, subject to legislative conferment of jurisdiction (as under the 1989 Act) the courts would have to take the subsection into account in determining property rights relating to the home.

O'Flaherty J's concurrence is slightly less laconic than Egan J's but nonetheless raises a number of questions. Having agreed that Barr J's approach should be rejected, but not having given any express endorsement of the Chief Justice's analysis, he went on to note that Article 41.2 referred to 'mothers' rather than 'wives and mothers'. This, in his mind, made clear that the section could not be called in aid to govern the division of property rights between spouses:

> What it does do is to require the State to endeavour to ensure that mothers with children to rear or to be cared for are given economic aid by the State. If a mother in dire economic straits were to invoke this section it would be no answer for the State to say that it did not have to

make any effort in her regard at all, though it would be open for it to say that it was doing its best having regard to the State's overall budgetary situation.

There is nothing logically compelling in the argument that, because the section refers to mothers, rather than wives and mothers, it *cannot* be called in aid to govern the division of property rights between spouses. It is perfectly possible to envisage an approach whereby the court would invoke the section in respect of the division of property rights between spouses and invoke the section identically or with modification in respect of property rights of unmarried, cohabiting couples. Cf. *McGill v L.S.* [1979] IR 283, *P. v C.*, High Court, 22 February 1980, Cooney, 'Wives, Mistresses and the Law', (1979) 14 Ir Jur 1, at 7ff.

O'Flaherty J was alone in unambiguously interpreting the section as extending to mothers who are not wives. McCarthy J reserved his position on the point in terms suggesting some sympathy towards it. Neither Finlay CJ nor Egan J addressed the issue squarely.

As a matter of textual analysis (as opposed to an argument based on justice), the tenor of Article 41.2 suggests that it envisaged mothers who were wives. The Article proceeds progressively and consequentially. Under Section 1.1° the State recognises the family (based on marriage) as the natural primary and fundamental unit group of society. Under Section 1.2° the State 'therefore' guarantees to protect the family. Section 2.1° deals with a specific aspect of what has gone before: *'[i]n particular'*, the State recognises that by her life within the home, woman gives the State a support without which the common good cannot be achieved. The 'woman' whose 'life within the home' is mentioned would seem to be a woman who is part of a family based on marriage: a wife (or widow). Section 2.2° provides that the State shall *'therefore'* endeavour to ensure that mothers are not to be obliged by economic necessity to engage in labour to the neglect of their duties *in the home*. These two italicised phrases appear to provide a clear consequential link with Section 2.1°. The idea that 'mothers' should be treated as embracing mothers of children outside families based on marriage, however desirable that extension, is not easy to harmonise with the language of the Section, and Article, as a whole. To modern minds, this seems highly regrettable; but since subs. 2 is so embarrassing for judges, the more likely development is for them to continue to interpret it narrowly rather than breathe vitality into it by extending its remit to single mothers.

The tenor of O'Flaherty J's analysis is to reject the Chief Justice's view that subs. 2 of the section imposes an obligation on the *courts* as well as the State. His remarks are unclear on the extent to which the courts can second-guess the assertion by the State that it is doing its best having regard to the

State's overall budgetary situation. It will be recalled that in *O'Reilly v Limerick Corporation* [1989] ILRM 181 (1988 Review, 114-5), noted by Whyte (1988) 10 DULJ 189 and Elder (1988) 6 ILT 171, Costello J, held that the division of the 'national cake' was a matter for political rather than judicial resolution. O'Flaherty J's reference to the State's 'overall budgetary situation' seems narrower in focus. Several years of economic stringency may have encouraged us to assume that the budgetary situation will remain troubling for the indefinite future, but the day may come when it can no longer be contended credibly that the State cannot afford the financial outlay necessary to give practical effect to Article 41.2.

McCarthy J's analysis also raises unanswered questions. Having noted that the plaintiff had no entitlement to a share under non-constitutional 'common law' principles, he went on to state that:

> [i]t would be making a quantum leap in constitutional law to hold that by her life within the home the mother acquires a beneficial interest in it. This would be in recognition of the support that the mother gives by her life within the home in carrying out her constitutional role as a mother. No complementary role is accorded a father, although such a role reversal is, nowadays, by no means uncommon. That does not, necessarily, dispose of the matter. It may be that in another instance circumstances may arise whereby, on the true interpretation of the relevant Article, it would prove necessary to accord to the mother some proprietary interest in the home. Such is not the case here. . . .

It is difficult to pin down the logical process here involved. As to the reference to 'making a quantum leap in constitutional law', one may contest the implicit suggestion that the springboard consists of the 'common law' rules of spousal property entitlements. Those rules represented the fruits of nineteenth century statutory reforms of the British parliament designed largely to deal with the property entitlements of the aristocracy and *haute bourgeoisie*. True, there had been some small amount of judicial modification of traditional principles, in both England and Ireland, in the previous twenty years or so, but what is striking about the Irish jurisprudence, from Kenny J's decision in *C. v C.* [1976] IR 254 to the Supreme Court judgment in *McC. v McC.* [1986] ILRM 1, is its dependence for all creative thought upon the members of the English Court of Appeal and of the House of Lords. That there should now be a 'quantum leap' between this body of law and the asserted constitutional entitlement in *L. v L.* is perhaps a comment, not on the radical nature of the claim, but on the persistently passive quality of judicial analysis of the subject and of its failure earlier to examine traditional principles of family property law in the light of constitutional norms. The complexity and lack of coherence of the jurisprudence on Articles 40.3 and 43 must have contributed to this situation.

McCarthy J appears to argue that a reason for the courts' not giving practical effect to Article 41.2 by way of recognising a beneficial interest for the stay-at-home mother is that '[n]o complementary role is accorded a father, although such a role reversal is, nowadays, by no means uncommon'. One would have wished this argument to have been further discussed. A seem- ingly obvious difficulty is that, in 1937 (and for decades afterwards), such a role reversal was quite uncommon. Is the suggestion that as role reversal increased in popularity, a wife's constitutional entitlement, *on that account*, was sacrificed? Can changing social practices thus extinguish constitutional rights? Or is the argument that the constitutional guarantee of sexual equality (to the extent that it exists) has the effect of neutralising an entitlement which a wife would otherwise have under Article 41.2?

Finally, one can only guess as to what circumstances McCarthy J had in mind as being possibly capable of generating 'some proprietary interest' for mothers in the family home. It may be that what was here envisaged was the case of a mother 'in dire economic straits'—an example mentioned, for a different purpose, by O'Flaherty J.

The traditional trust-focused approach   In the 1989 Review, 240-4, we analysed Barron J's judgment in *E.N. v R.N.* [1990] 1 IR 383. The plaintiff wife's claim to a share in the family home, based on the principles articulated by Barr J in *L. v L.* [1989] ILRM 528, did not convince Barron J for reasons not dissimilar to those favoured by the Supreme Court on appeal in *L. v L.* Having rejected the wife's claim on this constitutional ground, Barron J went on to address her claim based on the traditional trust-focused ground. He held that she was entitled to only a one-fifteenth share, applying with some regret what he perceived to be the established principles on the issue. In our discussion of the case in the 1989 Review, we set out the facts in detail. Here we need record merely that the essence of the wife's claim was that she had played a continuous active role in managing bedsitter apartments in the house, the rents from which went to servicing five mort- gages taken out on the premises over a period of time. Barron J held that this work should generate a proprietary interest only in so far as it contributed to the discharge of the original mortgage and to the servicing of a mortgage taken out several years later for the extension of the house.

The Supreme Court partially reversed Barron J and awarded the wife a half interest in the home: [1992] ILRM 127. Finlay CJ (with whom Hederman, McCarthy, O'Flaherty and Egan JJ concurred) had no problem with Barron J's rejection of the Article 41.2 claim. But, with regard to the trust claim, the Chief Justice considered that Barron J had been mistaken in his refusal to have regard to the *other* mortgages which had been raised and apparently repaid on the premises. The wife's activities in managing the bedsitters, followed by a period when she had worked as a nurse, had contributed to the discharge of all of these mortgages.

Finlay CJ was happy to rely on *dicta* from his earlier judgment in *W. v W.* [1981] ILRM 202, as President of the High Court. He had there said that in cases where a wife expends monies or carries out work in the improvement of a property that has been originally acquired by her husband, in whom legal ownership is solely vested, the wife will have no claim in respect of that contribution unless she establishes that, from the circumstances surrounding her conduct, she was led to believe, or it was specifically agreed, that she would be recompensed, in which case compensation should be 'in monies only and . . . not [by way of] a right to claim an equitable share in the estate of the property concerned.' He had also been of the view that the *redemption* of a mortgage on property consisted in essence of the acquisition by the mortgagor of an estate in that property and that there could be no distinction in principle between a contribution made to the acquisition of that interest and a contribution made to the acquisition of an interest in property by an original purchase. Since in *E.N. v R.N.* the plaintiff had contributed to the redemption of *all* mortgages, by conduct that was 'different from and not to be identified with the activities of a wife and mother in the home', her share in the property should be identified as being *one half*.

The Supreme Court was surely correct on the facts of the case to have found as it did. Nevertheless, its unwillingness to examine the possibility of extending of the law is a source of regret. The distinction between acquisition of property and the redemption of a mortgage, on the one hand, and the improvement of property, on the other, is one that needs reconsideration. Whilst it may have some attraction where the parties are not spouses and the property is not a family home, it is far less acceptable in cases (such as in *E.N. v R.N.*) where one spouse contributes to the improvement of the family home which is in the legal ownership of the other spouse. It is hard to see why there is not a presumption of agreement that the contribution should generate a proportionate proprietorial interest. All that Finlay P in *W. v W.* (or as Chief Justice in *E.N. v R.N.*) would allow is a *compensatory* claim which *cannot* constitute a right to claim an equitable share in the property; that claim is conditional on either a specific agreement or proof that the wife 'was led to believe' that she would be compensated for it. It seems that what is envisaged here is a situation where the husband, by assertion or conduct, caused the wife to act to her detriment. In the absence of such conduct, no claim to recompense apparently lies, even in the clearest of cases of implied agreement. This seems indefensible. Even if one concedes that the label of implied contract can at times disguise the reality of a restitutionary norm (cf.

East Cork Foods v O'Dwyer Steel [1978] IR 103, at 111 (*per* Henchy J)), it must be asked why restitution, in respect of the enhanced value of a family home, should *not* be computed by reference to a proprietary interest. If a wife contributes £25,000 to the improvement of a home worth £50,000 and as a result the value of the home increases by 50%, why should she be limited to a claim for £25,000 two years later if the home's value has by now appreciated to £150,000 on account of a rise in market values. To allow the husband to hold onto the increased value save for the £25,000 is to enrich him unjustly.

Registration of title   In *Friends Provident Life Office v Doherty* [1992] ILRM 372, Blayney J was called on to resolve an issue of wide-ranging dimensions in relation to family property: the interrelationship between s. 72(1)(j) of the Registration of Title Act 1964 and spousal property interests that may be declared under s. 12 of the Married Women's Status Act 1957. S. 72(1)(j) defines as a burden affecting land without registration:

> the rights of a living person in actual occupation of the land or in receipt of the rents or profits thereof, save where, upon enquiry made of such person, the rights are not disclosed.

In the present case Mr Doherty had bought a site on which a house was constructed, with Mrs Doherty paying for the cost of construction. He later borrowed money from the plaintiff, secured by a mortgage on the premises. In reply to requisitions on title he made a statutory declaration that none of the burdens set out in s. 72 affected the lands. Both Mr and Mrs Doherty made statutory declarations which stated (correctly) that the premises were in the sole name of Mr Doherty. Mrs Doherty fully consented to the mortgage which was a charge by her husband as sole registered owner of the property.

When the money owing on the mortgage was not paid, the plaintiff sought vacant possession of the premises. Mrs Doherty resisted this, and brought an application under s. 12 of the 1957 Act, claiming a declaration that she was entitled to an interest in excess of 50% in the family home. The Circuit Court Judge rejected her application. Blayney J dismissed the appeal.

Blayney J was satisfied that Mrs Doherty had indeed an interest in the premises at the time of the mortgage and that it was a burden taking effect without registration. It could not be said, on the evidence, that any enquiry had been made *of her* by the plaintiff as to whether she had any interest in the home. Nonetheless, she could not assert her interest against the plaintiff because of the principle of *estoppel by representation*. Mrs Doherty, by her statements in writing and her conduct at the time of the mortgage, had represented to the plaintiff that she had no interest in the family home and that her husband was solely entitled and thus in a position to mortgage the entire interest. The plaintiff had been under no duty to enquire from her whether she had any interest, since there was nothing to put the plaintiff on notice that she might have an interest.

The decision is of significance because it raises the question whether, in every case where one spouse whose name does not appear on the title consents to the sale or mortgage of a family home registered in the name of the other spouse, in such a way as to render the disposition valid under the Family Home Protection Act 1976, the process of giving that consent *necessarily* amounts to estoppel by representation. Surely the answer must be that there should be no such necessary connection. One has only to envisage situations where the unregistered spouse was somewhat mentally disabled or was virtually illiterate. In a stimulating analysis of *Doherty*, John Mee has argued that the onus should have been on the plaintiff to prove that Mrs Doherty had understood the nature of the transaction and had been aware of her rights: 'The Family Home Protection Act and Priorities in Land Law' (1992) ILT (ns) 213.

It should also be noted that there will be cases involving the sale of the family home where the unregistered spouse's consent is *not* required (or consequently, obtained) because (for example) he or she is in desertion, but nonetheless that spouse has a proprietal interest in the home by virtue of contributions that he or she has made to its acquisition.

Another issue concerns the relationship between s. 12 of the 1957 Act and s. 72 of the 1964 Act: in a case where the unregistered spouse had not initiated proceedings under s. 12 at the time the property was registered or subsequently disposed of, how can an adjudication under s. 12 at some *later* time have the effect of determining *retrospectively* the interest of the unregistered spouse at the time of registration or disposition? Such an adjudication speaks to the present time rather than the past. Moreover, it is based on broad equitable principles which do not easily lend themselves to chronological character- isation.

Sale in lieu of partition   In *First National Building Society v Ring*, High Court, 5 July 1991, Denham J addressed the important question of balancing the interests of non-owning spouses and judgment creditors. The facts were straightforward. The plaintiff society obtained judgment for over £150,000 against the first named defendant, a farmer, who was then in hospital and likely to stay there for some time. The plaintiff had registered a judgment mortgage against the farm. It now sought, *inter alia*, a declaration that it was entitled to a valid mortgage or charge over the first defendant's interest and an order that, in default of payment of the moneys due (reduced to £145,000 on account of part payment), payment should be enforced by sale in lieu of partition or by the appointment of a receiver, or both.

The farm was a family home jointly owned by the first named defendant and his wife, the second named defendant. The wife was in no way personally indebted to the plaintiff. The couple had three children, the youngest of whom was eleven, two of whom were receiving fulltime education.

Denham J's sympathetic observations in relation to the wife's position are worth recording. She noted that the wife had contributed a great deal to the purchase of the home:

> The premises are the family home and are central to the family life and its location is central to the family activities and education. If the family home were sold the disruption of family life would be enormous and very detrimental. She would be unable to purchase another dwelling-house with her share of the net proceeds of the sale of the home and her family would be homeless and destitute. She is an innocent party. No judgment has been obtained against her. She shares no guilt or blame for any actions of the first named defendant.

Denham J had no difficulty in making a well-charging order and a declaration as to the amount owing on foot of the judgment mortgage. She declined, however,to make an order for sale *in lieu* of partition under s. 4 of the Partition Act 1868. She noted that the section required the court to direct a sale, *'unless it sees good reason to the contrary'*. Here the court suffered from a lack of information as to the persons interested in the premises, their shares and proportions, or the current market price. She ordered an inquiry as to these questions and as to the possibility of the wife's making financial arrangements to purchase her husband's share at an agreed price.

Denham J's resolution of the case combines realism and humanity. The farm premises seemed to be worth between £40,000 and £80,000. When divided by two to take account of the wife's proprietary interest, this sum would not go very far in meeting the amount outstanding under the judgment mortgage. Denham J acknowledged that this fact, of itself, was not a valid reason for refusing an order for sale but it clearly seems to have been a *factor* in the exercise of her discretion against making the order *instanter*.

Denham J was conscious of the jurisprudence holding that the registration of a judgment mortgage is not a conveyance under the 1976 Act. She cited Carroll J's judgment in *Containercare (Ireland) Ltd v Wycherley*. (See also *Murray v Diamond*, [1982] ILRM 113, Shatter, *op. cit.*, 543-4, Duncan & Scully, *op. cit.*, paras. 11.16-11.17). Nevertheless Denham J considered that the fact that the premises was a family home was a fact which she could include as a relevant factor in exercising her discretion under s. 4 of the 1868 Act.

Prior to *First National Building Society v Ring*, it was clear that in *interspousal* litigation under s. 4, the court was entitled—indeed *obliged*—to take into account the existence and social policy of the 1976 Act. In *O'D. v*

O'D., High Court, 18 November 1983,Murphy was of the view that a court 'would be justified in concluding in the circumstances of our present times, under the Constitution and of the rights conferred by the Family Home Protection Act 1976, that the loss of the statutory veto represented good reason within the meaning of s. 4 of the Partition Act 1968'. Similarly, in *A.L. v J.L.*, High Court,7 February 1984, Finlay P held that an order for sale *in lieu* of partition could not be made unless the court was also satisfied that it should dispense with the consent of the non-agreeing spouse under s. 4 of the 1976 Act.

Denham J's problem was different in principle. The wife here had no protection under s. 3 of the 1976 Act since the order sought did not involve a conveyance by a spouse of any interest in the family home. She could not claim that any specific provision of the 1976 Act would be breached or frustrated by an order for sale under s. 4 of the 1868 Act. Her claim was in the broader domain of social policy. Yet how should that social policy be identified? Plainly it would be quite wrong to argue that the 1976 Act sought to protect wives against their husbands' creditors. Such a policy may have much to commend it and underlies the 'homestead' legislation in several states in the United States of America but, whatever its merits, was expressly disclaimed by Mr Cooney, the Minister for Justice, during the Oireachtas Debates on the Bill. The drafting of s. 3 in particular makes it plain that much effort was made to ensure that the legislation should not be judicially interpreted as venturing into this new area of social policy.

Having said this, it must also be stressed that the 1976 Act should not be interpreted as being devoid of social policy in regard to the relationship between wives and creditors. True, it prevents a non-owning wife from vetoing under s. 3 the sale of the family home pursuant to a judgment mortgage obtained by a creditor of her husband; but the intent of other provisions of the Act—notably ss. 5 to 8—is clearly to buttress as far as possible the interests of non-owning wives where this can be done without improperly trespassing on creditors' rights.

What Denham J rightly perceived is that the spirit of the 1976 Act is to encourage courts to be as flexible as possible in dealing with creditors' claims against the family home. They should investigate every reasonable option that may result in optimum protection for the wife and children. Rather than perceive these claims as *simply* involving creditors' rights, they should approach the matter on the basis that society has a legitimate interest in encouraging security of occupation of the family home.

One aspect of the case should be noted. The wife was not in fact a non-owning spouse. On the contrary she was joint owner of the home and had contributed substantially to its purchase. In *Nestor v Murphy* [1979] IR 326, the Supreme Court held that a conveyance of a family home jointly owned by the spouses fell outside the protection of s. 3(1) of the Act (on the basis that to bring such a transaction within its scope would be otiose and would encourage some spouses to repudiate contracts 'unfairly or dishonestly'). Nevertheless, in other respects the policy underlying the 1976 Act goes far enough to encompass the protection of the wife who is a joint owner as much as that of non-owning spouses.

Retirement and death benefit scheme In *In re Doyle Deceased; Crowe Engineering Ltd v Lynch* High Court, 24 July 1991, the question arose as to the interpretation of the rules of a company's retirement and death benefit scheme. The deceased, an employee of the company, had separated from his wife some years before his death. In 1985 the spouses had entered into a separation agreement which provided for the sale of the family home and an equal share of the proceeds. Both spouses renounced all rights accruing to them by the marriage under the Succession Act 1965 and 'any other legislation conferring rights, status and obligations on married persons'. The wife specifically undertook not to make any claim for maintenance against her husband.

For a period before his death in 1989, the deceased cohabited with a married woman whose husband was still living. She had been in employment at a wage of £75 per week until 1986 but had been obliged to stop working on account of ill-health. She was wholly dependent on the deceased, who paid her a personal weekly allowance. The deceased bought a house, which he put into the joint names of himself and the woman.

The scheme defined 'dependant' as meaning (i) the spouse of the deceased; (ii) any person who at his death or retirement was 'dependent on him for all or any of the ordinary necessities in life'; (iii) any other person whom the trustee might consider to have been dependant as described in (ii), or (iv) any other person whom the employee had required the trustee in writing to consider as a possible recipient of a benefit arising under the scheme on his death.

The trustee of the scheme sought answers to a number of questions of interpretation. The first presented no difficulty. All parties agreed that the benefits from the scheme did not form part of the deceased's estate. The purpose of such schemes, in the event of the death of an employee in service, said Carroll J, was 'to provide a sum of money not available to creditors of the deceased'. The next question concerned the nature of trustees' discretion as to payment to any one or more of the persons defined as 'dependant'. Carroll J held that the trustees had an absolute discretion. She rejected the argument that, because the superannuation money represented deferred earnings on emoluments of the deceased, it was his right to direct the trustees and the trustees' obligation in equity to follow:

All the court is concerned with are enforceable rights, whether expressed as legal or equitable rights. The deceased did not have an enforceable right to direct where the payment of the moneys should go. The discretion of the trustees is exactly that, a discretion.

Carroll J also addressed the question of whether the woman with whom the deceased had been living at his death was his 'dependant'. His wife argued that the woman was not, as she had a husband alive who would have been responsible for her necessaries. Carroll J disagreed: the definition in the scheme referred to a *factual situation* as well as a legal obligation. A person might be dependant on another for the ordinary necessaries of life without there being any legal obligation on that other to pay.

A final issue of general interest related to the separation deed. Carroll J held that the wife, in giving up her rights under the Succession Act and all other legislation conferring rights, status and obligations on a married person, had *not* ceded the right to be considered as a beneficiary under a superannuation scheme; this did not form part of the estate of the deceased and did not concern a right conferred by statute.

MAINTENANCE ENTITLEMENTS

In *P.J. v J.J.* [1992] ILRM 273, Barr J addressed an important issue of principle, concerning the relationship between contractual freedom and maintenance obligations. The issue has no easy answer. Barr J's solution is likely to inspire a useful discussion of the competing arguments.

The facts were relatively straightforward. The spouses had been married for thirty-nine years, with a grown up family all of whom had long since left home. The spouses had ceased to live with each other in 1978; at that time the husband went to live with another woman. Two years later, the spouses entered into a separation agreement, which was made a rule of court under s. 8 of the Family Law (Maintenance of Spouses and Children) Act 1976. It provided that the wife was to remain for her lifetime in the family home, bought by her husband some years previously and subject to a mortgage. The husband agreed to pay £527 per month to the wife, free of all deductions, the amount to be adjusted annually in accordance with the consumer price index, as well as the mortgage, the electricity and telephone accounts, the wife's VHI, household insurance, 'a sum' (unspecified in the judgment) for household maintenance and the provision of a car for the wife. There was no provision for the reduction of maintenance in the light of changed circumstances that might occur.

In late 1990, the husband, who was in poor health, sold his business, which had been in decline for some years, for £110,000. He subscribed £50,000 of this sum towards the purchase of a house for himself and the woman with whom he was living. The woman contributed a further £85,000 to the purchase price. He and the woman embarked on a plan to extend the house so that it would have eight bedrooms and would be suitable for use as a guest house from 1992 onwards. The husband was endeavouring to sell the house in which he and the woman had been living. Its market value was around £80,000. His intention was to run it as a guest house also if he could not sell it.

Until 1989, the husband had not only honoured all the financial terms of the separation agreement but had also made substantial additional payments for the benefit of his wife and children, including presents of £5,000 to each of the children when they married and also the costs of their weddings. Barr J was satisfied that arrears which had accrued subsequently 'arose out of the decline of the husband's business, leading to an inability on his part to meet his financial obligations to the wife as previously'. (When Barr J here spoke of the husband's 'inability' to meet his financial obligations, it seems clear that he was using this term broadly: a husband with business assets worth £110,000, and with a house worth £80,000 would seem able to pay the amount to which he had contractually bound himself, though the question whether it would be fair just or appropriate for him to do so is, of course, entirely separate.)

The wife sued for maintenance and other payments due under the separation agreement. Her claim was compromised in November 1990 on payment of £10,000 by the husband out of the £110,000 proceeds of sale of his business interest. The wife was sixty five years old. Like her husband, she had health problems. She was employed as a records clerk. The retirement age for her job was sixty five and no pension was payable; it appeared that her employers were not yet aware of her actual age. Her net earnings were £700 per month, 'including interest on £7,000, being the balance remaining out of the arrears of maintenance paid by the husband in 1990'. (A point that perhaps may be noted is that the interest derived from a sum offered in settlement to an applicant for arrears of maintenance should not be treated as income on her part when computing the defendant's *subsequent* maintenance obligations. It represents no more than the delayed benefit of what should have been received earlier).

The wife's overheads, (*excluding* social expenditure and the cost of holidays) came to £750 per month. Barr J was satisfied that this sum was 'fair and reasonable in all the circumstances'. It included ESB and telephone accounts which ought to be paid by the husband under the terms of the separation agreement. Barr J had no doubt that, when the wife's employment came to an end, as it surely would within the following three or four years at the latest, she would be in serious financial difficulties, having only the State contributory old age pension. Even at the time of the proceedings she was suffering financial hardship on account of her husband's failure to comply with the terms of the agreement. Arrears amounted to nearly £5,000.

The husband sought an order *varying downwards* the maintenance provisions of the separation agreement to take account of his financial circumstances. The wife resisted this application and claimed arrears of maintenance. The net point of law, as Barr J perceived the matter, was whether the maintenance provisions of a separation agreement that had been made a rule of court under s. 8 of the 1976 Act are reviewable under s. 6 of that Act, with the possibility of downward adjustment.

Barr J came to the conclusion, as Carroll J had done in *J.D. v B.D.* [1985] ILRM 688, that s. 6 is *not* available as a vehicle for the review of maintenance provisions in a separation agreement which itself contains no such machinery. The relevant sections were clear in their terms. A court was entitled to interpret legislation so as to resolve any ambiguity or obvious error in it but, where the statute was clear in its terms, the court had no power to extend its provisions to make good what was perceived to be a significant omission:

> If the court took that course it would entail going beyond statutory interpretation and into the realm of law-making, a function which under the Constitution is reserved to the Oireachtas. Occasionally circumstances arise where the court is powerless to avoid injustice and, sadly, this case is one of them.

Barr J considered himself 'obliged' to hold that the husband was not entitled to a review of the maintenance provisions of the separation provisions under s. 6. He noted that the alternative claims which the husband had made (not identified in the judgment) were 'patently devices in effect to secure indirectly the benefit of a review under s. 6', and accordingly he rejected them. Barr J held that the wife was entitled to the arrears of maintenance.

Barr J went on to indicate what his attitude *would* have been had he the power to review the maintenance provisions. This would have involved the reduction of the husband's maintenance liability to £300 per month, with all ancillary payments as provided in the agreement continuing to be paid. The matter would have been reviewed again in October 1992 or sooner if the wife lost her employment in the meantime.

CHILD CARE

The Child Care Act 1991 modernises the law in relation to the care of children. It is not a comprehensive measure in regard to child law: other aspects have already been addressed, by the Status of Children Act 1987 and the Adoption Act 1988, for example. The Act is the result of a slow process of law reform extending over a period of a quarter of a century. Noteworthy landmarks include the Kennedy Report on Reformatory and Industrial Schools Systems, in 1970, CARE's Memorandum on Deprived Children and Children's Services in Ireland, *Children Deprived*, published in the same year, the Task Force on Child Care Service's Interim Report of 1975 and its Final Report in 1980, the Report of the Working Party on Child Care Facilities for Working Parents in 1983 and the Report of the Review Committee on Adoption Services, in 1984.

The Act substantially amends the Children Act 1908. Its main provisions include the following:

(i) imposing a statutory duty on health boards to promote the welfare of children who are not receiving adequate care and protection;

(ii) strengthening the powers of health boards to provide child care, adoption and family support services;

(iii) improving emergency intervention procedures;

(iv) introducing new procedures for care or supervision by health boards where children have been assaulted, ill-treated, neglected or sexually abused or their health, development or welfare has been neglected;

(v) establishing provisions for the inspection and supervision of pre-school services;

(vi) revising the provisions in relation to the regulation and inspection of residential centres for children.

See the *Explanatory Memorandum to the Child Care Bill 1988, As Passed by both Houses of the Oireachtas and enacted as the Child Care Act 1991*. (An Roinn Sláinte, Iúil, 1991).

PART I: PRELIMINARY PROVISIONS

The Act comes into effect very gradually, by Ministerial Orders: s. 1(2). This delay was much criticised but was defended on the basis that the radical changes made by the Act required time for their full implementation. Part I and ss. 71 and 74 ('glue sniffing' offence) came into effect on 1 December 1991: SI No. 292 of 1991. Ss. 9, 10 and 66 came into operation on 1 June 1992: SI No. 123 of 1992. S. 79 and the Schedule came into operation on the same date, for the purpose of effecting the repeal of s. 65(2) of the Health

Act 1953. Ss. 3, 7 and 8 came into effect on 1 December 1992: SI No. 349 of 1992. S. 2 defines 'child' as a person under the age of 18 years other than one who is or has been married. Formerly 16 was the age at which the responsibility of health boards ceased. The definition of 'parents' includes adoptive parents, not only under our domestic law but also under those so recognised under our rules of private international law: see further 392 Dáil Debates, cols 1202-3 (1 November 1989). These rules were greatly extended by the Adoption Act 1991, see our analysis above 52-4.

PART II: PROMOTION OF WELFARE OF CHILDREN

Health board's functions S. 3(1) provides that it 'shall be a function' of every health board to promote the welfare of children in its area who are not receiving adequate care and protection. In the performance of this function, the health board, having regard to the rights and duties of parents, whether under the Constitution or otherwise, must have regard to the child's welfare as the first and paramount consideration; it must, moreover, in so far as is practicable, give due consideration, having regard to the child's age and understanding, to his or her wishes: subs. (2)(a) and (b). Further the health board must have regard to 'the principle that it is generally in the best interests of a child to be brought up in his own family': subs. (2)(c).

A few comments about s. 3 seem in order. The first concerns the nature of the function thus established. It is not described as a *duty* but there would seem scope for arguing that this is what is entailed. The concept of function is a generic one, capable of embracing duties and powers. It would be hard to characterise the function prescribed by s. 3 as simply a power. The whole tenor of the provision is to establish an agenda for health boards and to set out the detail of how they are to exercise the function. Nevertheless, the section nowhere prescribes a sanction for failure to exercise the function properly or at all. Doubtless public law remedies would be available, but could a child (or a parent or foster parent) base a claim for breach of statutory duty on s. 3? One suspects that the court would be reluctant so to hold. Of course the provision seeks to protect an identifiable group—children—but it also clearly has a broad social dimension. Cf. *Siney v Dublin Corporation* [1980] IR 400. Another possible avenue of recovery in tort is that of common law negligence. Here the court may take account of relevant legislative policy in determining whether or not to impose a duty of care: cf. *Ward v McMaster and Louth County Council* [1989] ILRM 400; [1988] IR 337, analysed in the 1988 Review, 407-10, 428-33, and *Sunderland v Louth County Council* [1990] ILRM 658, analysed in the 1990 Review, 545-9.

It will be recalled that, in *K.C. & A.C. v An Bord Uchtála* [1985] ILRM

302, the Supreme Court articulated the principles governing the relationship between Articles 41 and 42 and the 'welfare' test specified in s. 3 of the Guardianship of Infants Act 1964. Finlay CJ, delivering the judgment of the Court, accepted the contention that s. 3 'must be construed as involving a constitutional presumption that the welfare of the child, which is defined in s. 2 of the Act in terms identical to those contained in Article 42.1, is to be found within the family unless the court is satisfied on the evidence that there are compelling reasons why this cannot be advanced or unless the court is satisfied that the evidence establishes an exceptional case where the parents have failed to provide education for the child and continue to fail to provide education for the child for moral or physical reasons'.

The Supreme Court addressed the meaning of 'failure' of parental duty, in *In re the Adoption (No 2) Bill 1987* [1989] IR 656; [1989] ILRM 266, analysed in the 1988 Review, 246-52. Sub-clause (1)(A) of s. 3 required that, for at least twelve months previously, the parents, for physical or moral reasons, should have failed in their duty towards the child whose adoption was in prospect. The Court was of the view that the reference to physical or moral reasons did 'not mean that the failure must necessarily in every case be blameworthy, but it does mean that a failure due to externally originating circumstances such as poverty would not constitute a failure within the meaning of the sub-clause'. Presumably, the principles underlying this analysis should colour the courts' interpretation of subs. 2.

Voluntary care   S. 4(1) imposes a duty on a health board to take a child into its care where it appears that the child, resident or found in its area, requires care or protection that he is unlikely to receive unless he is taken into its care. This duty is qualified by s. 4(2) which prevents the health board from so acting against the wishes of a parent having custody of the child or person acting *in loco parentis*; moreover, the health board may not maintain the child in its care under s. 4 if that parent or person *in loco parentis* wishes to resume care of him.

The section is drafted in such a way that the veto of one parent where both have custody (or of one person *in loco parentis* where there is more that one such person) will prevent the health board from acting under it. In such circumstances the health board will be able to proceed only under Parts III, IV and VI of the Act. Clearly, the basis of intervention under these parts is more restrictive than the test prescribed by s. 4(1).

Where a health board has taken a child into its care under s. 4, it must maintain the child in its care so long as the child's welfare appears to require it (but not beyond adulthood): s. 4(3)(a). During this period the health board must have regard to the wishes of parents having custody or any person acting *in loco parentis* in the provision of that care.

S. 4(4) provides that (without prejudice to Parts III, IV and VI), where a health board takes a child into its care because it appears that he is lost or that a parent having custody of him is missing or that he has been deserted or abandoned, the board is to endeavour to re-unite the child with that parent 'where this appears to the board to be in his interests'. The question arises as to the relationship of this provision with ss. 4(2) and 4(3). If the health board takes a child into care because, for example, he is lost, the basis for doing so under s. 4(1) must be that the child requires protection that he is unlikely to receive unless he is taken into its care. That basis would normally (though perhaps not invariably) exist. What happens if the child's parents emerge and seek the return of their child? S. 4(2) would appear to require that the board should comply with their wishes (subject of course to taking proceedings under Part III, IV or VI). By virtue of s. 4(3), the board is under a duty to maintain the child in its care only so long as its welfare appears to *require it.*

Therefore the question may be posed in relation to s. 4(4). Does it entitle the board to *retain the child in its care* for any longer than it would a child who is not lost, deserted or abandoned or whose custodial parent is missing? The answer appears to be that it does not. All that it provides is that the board is to endeavour to re-unite the child with the absent parent where this appears to be in the child's best interests.

Homeless children S. 5 deals with the needs of homeless children. Where it appears to a health board that a child in its area is homeless, the board must enquire into the child's circumstances. If satisfied that there is no accommodation available to the child which he or she can reasonably occupy, the board must take reasonable steps to make suitable accommodation available, unless the child is received into care. The section does not define the concept of homelessness. It appears, however, that it does not connote the absence of *any* abode but rather the lack of accommodation available to the child which he or she can reasonably occupy. This notion 'is wide enough to include [the position of] children who have a family home but whose circumstances there are intolerable': 129 Seanad Debates, col. 495 (Mr Noel Treacy).

Originally this section required that the board should be satisfied, not merely that there is no accommodation available to the child which he or she can reasonably occupy, but also that the child is unable to provide or arrange accommodation for himself. This latter requirement was removed by amendment at Report Stage in the Seanad.

Provision of adoption service S. 6 requires each health board to provide or ensure the provision in its area of an adoption service. It empowers health boards to enter into arrangements for this purpose with registered adoption societies.

Child care advisory committees   S. 7 requires each health board to establish one or more child care advisory committees to advise it on the performance of its functions under the Act. The board must 'consider and have regard to' any advice so tendered to it. Thus proceedings for judicial review would be available if the board ignores this advice or treats it in bad faith. Where, however, the board considers the advice but concludes nonetheless that it would be better not to follow it, having given it *bona fide* attention, it will not be in breach of the section.

The child care advisory committees are to be composed of those with a special interest or expertise in matters affecting the welfare of children, including representatives of voluntary bodies providing child care and family support services. The Minister has a role here. He or she must give general directions in relation to child care advisory committees; these may include directions on matters relating to the membership, constitution or business of the committees. The directions must be followed: subs. (5).

The functions of the child care advisory committees are fourfold:

> (a) to have access to non-personal information in relation to child care and family support services in their area;
> (b) to consult with voluntary bodies providing child care and family support services in their area;
> (c) to report on child care and family support services in their area, either on their own initiative or when requested to do so by the health board; and
> (d) to review the needs of children in their area who are not receiving adequate care and protection: sub-s(7).

Annual review of services   S. 8 requires health boards to have an annual report prepared on the adequacy of child care and family support services available in their area. The Minister is to receive a copy, as well as such bodies as the board sees fit whose purpose includes the provision of child care and family support services.

Services by voluntary bodies   S. 9 enables health boards to make arrangements with voluntary bodies or other persons for the provision by them of child care and family support services which the boards are empowered to provide under the Act. This entitlement is restricted in a number of ways. First, a health board may not thus delegate its duty under s. 4 to receive children into care or its power to apply for an order under Part III, IV or VI of the Act. Secondly, with regard to areas where the power of delegation exists, the Minister may give general directions as to how it is to be exercised. S. 9 came into effect on 1 June 1992: SI No. 123 of 1992.

Assistance for voluntary bodies S. 10 enables health boards, subject to general directions given by the Minister, to assist financially voluntary bodies or other persons providing child care or family support services similar or ancillary to those which health boards may provide under the Act.

Research S. 11 enables the Minister to conduct, or assist in, research in relation to child care and family support services.

PART III: PROTECTION OF CHILDREN IN EMERGENCIES

Part III enables the Gardai and health boards to intervene quickly where there appears to be an immediate and serious risk to a child's health or welfare.

Garda powers S. 12 spells out the powers of the Gardai. Where a Garda has reasonable grounds for believing that there is an immediate and serious risk to the health or safety of a child and that it would not be sufficient for the protection of the child from that risk to await the application for an emergency care order by a health board under s. 13, he or she may remove the child to safety: subs. (1). No warrant is necessary; force may be used to gain entry to the place where the child is, if required. The Garda may be accompanied by 'such other person as may be necessary': *id*.

A child so removed must be delivered up as soon as possible to the custody of the health board for the area in which the child is for the time being: subs. (3). Unless the health board returns the child to the custodial parent (or parents) or person *in loco parentis*, it must make application for an emergency care order at the next sitting of the District Court held in the same district court district: subs. (4). If that next sitting is not due to be held within three days, the application must be made at a sitting of the District Court specially arranged under s. 13(4).

Emergency care orders S. 13 deals with emergency care orders. If a judge of the District Court is of opinion on the application of a health board that there is reasonable cause to believe that—

> (a) there is an immediate and serious risk to the health or welfare of a child which necessitates placing the child in the care of a health board, or
> (b) there is likely to be such a risk if the child is removed from the place where he is for the time being,

the judge may make an emergency care order: subs. (1). Its effect is to place the child under the care of the health board for the area in which the child is for the time being for eight days (or shorter): subs. (2). The order may be accompanied by a warrant to the Garda to enter premises, with powers of entry similar to those specified in s. 12.

Normally the judge for the district in which the child resides or is for the time being makes the order, but, if he or she is not immediately available, any other judge of the District Court may do so: subs. (4). *Ex parte* applications are permitted in emergencies: *id*. The urgency of the matter can also warrant the holding of the application and the making of the order elsewhere than at a public sitting of the District Court: *id*. An appeal does not stay the operation of the order: subs. (5).

The judge making an emergency care order has power to give such directions as he or she thinks proper with respect to withholding the address of the place where the child is being kept from its parents, access issues *and* the medical or psychiatric examination, treatment or assessment of the child: subs. (7).

Notification   The health board must notify the custodial parent (or parents), or person *in loco parentis*, of the delivery or placement of the child as soon as possible: s. 14.

Provision of accommodation   S. 15 requires health boards to provide or make arrangements with the registered proprietors of children's registered centres or other suitable persons for the provision of suitable accommodation for the purposes of Part III.

PART IV: CARE PROCEEDINGS

Part IV enables the court to make a *care order* when satisfied that a child has been or is being mistreated or neglected, and a *supervision order* when satisfied that there are reasonable grounds for believing that such circumstances exist.

Duty to institute proceedings   S. 16 imposes a duty on the health board to apply for a care order or supervision order where it appears that a child resident or found in its area requires care or protection which he or she is unlikely to receive unless a Court makes a care order or supervision order in respect of the child. This test does not require that the health board be of the view that any wrongdoing of any description has occurred. Indeed it would appear to impose on the health board a duty to apply for one of these two orders even where the parents are entirely blameless. The grounds on which the court may make either such order are not, *expressis verbis*, co-extensive with the criteria for obligatory application under s. 16. Indeed, the criteria specified in s. 16 are necessary to establish *in addition* to any one of three *other* grounds before a care order or supervision order may be made.

Interim care orders S. 17 deals with *interim care orders*. The District Judge may make such an order if satisfied that an application for a care order has been or is about to be made and that there is reasonable cause to believe that any of the three circumstances specified in s. 18(1) exists or has existed with respect to the child and that it is necessary for the protection of the child's health or welfare that he or she be placed or maintained in the care of the health board pending the determination of the application for the care order.

The effect of an interim care order is to require the child to stay in the care of the health board for up to eight days or longer if the custodial parent or person *in loco parentis* consents: subs. (2). An extension of this period may be granted if the judge is satisfied that grounds for the making of an interim care order continue to exist with respect to the child: *id.*

Care orders S. 18 deals with *care orders*. Subs. (1) sets out the grounds. Where, on the application of a health board with respect to a child resident or found in its area, the court is satisfied that—

(a) the child has been or is being assaulted, ill-treated, neglected or sexually abused, or
(b) the child's health, development or welfare has been or is being avoidably impaired or neglected, or
(c) the child's health, development or welfare is likely to be avoidably impaired or neglected,

and that the child requires care or protection which he is unlikely to receive unless the court makes an order under the section, the court may make a care order in respect of the child.

The care order commits the child to the care of the health board for so long as he or she remains a child or such shorter period on the court determines: subs. (2). In the latter case, there is a judicial power of extension where the court is satisfied that grounds for the making of a care order continue to exist: *id.*

Where a care order is in force, the health board has the like control over the child as if it were his parent; it must do what is reasonable in all the circumstances to safeguard or promote the child's health, development or welfare: subs. (3). In particular, the board has authority to:

(i) decide the type of care to be provided for the child under s. 36 (which deals with his or her accommodation and maintenance);
(ii) give consent to any necessary medical or psychiatric examination, treatment or assessment with respect to the child; and
(iii) give consent to the issue of a passport to the child or of the provision of passport facilities to him or her to enable the child to travel abroad for a limited period: *id.*

Any consent given by a health board in accordance with s. 18 is sufficient authority for the carrying out of a medical or psychiatric examination or assessment, the provision of medical or psychiatric treatment, the issue of a passport or the provision of passport facilities, as the case may be: subs. (4).

S. 18(5) provides that, where, on application for a care order, the court is satisfied that—

(a) it is not necessary or appropriate that a care order be made, and
(b) it is desirable that the child be visited periodically in his home by or on behalf of the health board,

the court may make a supervision order under s. 19. The precise relationship between ss. 18(5) and 19 is not entirely clear. The better view seems to be that a court may make a supervision order under s. 19, by virtue of s. 18(5), in circumstances where the desirability of the child's being visited periodically is unaccompanied by any reasonable grounds for believing that the child is being ill-treated or that the child's health, development or welfare has been, is being or is likely to be avoidably impaired or neglected. An alternative interpretation is that, whereas the health board's application for a *supervision* order can be dealt with under s. 19 only, s. 18(5) enables the court, in a case where the health board has applied for a *care* order, to make a supervision order, but only where satisfied that s. 19 grounds, *in addition to those specified in s. 18(5)*, exist.

Where a court makes a court order under s. 18, it may in addition make an order requiring the parents of the child (or either of them) to contribute to the health board a sum towards the cost of maintaining the child, which having regard to their means, the court thinks fit: s. 18(7). An order for maintenance thus made may be varied or discharged subsequently: subs(8).

Supervision orders   S. 19 deals with supervision orders. Where, on the application of a health board, with respect to a child residing in its area, the court is satisfied that there are reasonable grounds for believing that—

(a) the child has been or is being assaulted, ill-treated, neglected or sexually abused, or

(b) the child's health, development or welfare has been or is being avoidably impaired or neglected, or

(c) the child's development or welfare is likely to be avoidably impaired or neglected,

and it is desirable that the child be visited periodically by or on behalf of the health board, the court may make a supervision order in respect of the child: subs. 1.

The supervision order authorises the health board to have the child visited on such periodic occasions as the board may consider necessary, to satisfy itself as to the welfare of the child and to give his parents (or the person *in loco parentis*) any necessary advice as to the care of the child: subs. 2.

If the parent (or person *in loco parentis*) is dissatisfied with the manner in which the health board is exercising its authority to have the child visited, he or she may apply to the court for directions, with which the health board must comply: subs. 3.

Where a court makes a supervision order, it may, on the application of the health board, either when making this order or during its currency, give such directions as it sees fit as to the care of the child: subs. 4. These may include requiring the parents (or person *in loco parentis*) to cause the child to attend for medical or psychiatric examination, treatment or assessment at a hospital, clinic or other place specified by the court: *id*. Failure to comply with the terms of a supervision order is a summary offence with a maximum penalty of 6 months' imprisonment or a fine of £500 or both: subs. 5.

A supervision order remains in force for a maximum period of 12 months; the court may specify a shorter period: subs. 6. After its expiration, a new supervision order may be made on the application of the health board: subs. 7.

Adjournment of family proceedings to investigate child's circumstances
S. 20(1) provides that, where, in any proceedings under s. 7, 8 or 11 or Part III of the Guardianship of Infants Act 1964 or in any case to which s. 3(3), 11(b) or 16(g) of the Judicial Separation and Family Law Reform Act 1989 relates, or in any other proceedings for the delivery or return of a child, it appears to the court that it may be appropriate for a care order or a supervision order to be made, the court may, either on its own motion or on the application of any person, adjourn the proceedings and direct the health board for the area in which the child resides or is for the time being to undertake an investigation into the child's circumstances. During the period of adjournment, the court may give such directions as it sees fit as to the care and custody of the child; alternatively it may make a supervision order in respect of the child: subs. 2.

Where the health board is thus charged with the task of investigation, it must consider whether it should—

(a) apply for a care order or for a supervision order,
(b) provide services or assistance for the child or his or her family, or
(c) take any other action with respect to the child: subs. 3.

If the health board decides *not* to apply for a care order or a supervision order, it must inform the court of its reasons for so deciding and of any service or assistance it intends to provide, as well as of any other actions it has taken or proposes to take: subs. 4.

Stay of order on appeal   An appeal from an order under Part IV, stays the operation of that order only if the court that makes it or the court to which the appeal is brought so determines; the stay may be ordered on such terms as may be imposed by the court making the determination: s. 21.

Variation or discharge of orders   The court, either on its own motion or on the application of any person, may vary or discharge a care order or supervision order, or any condition or direction attaching it, or, in the case of a care order, discharge the care order and make a supervision order instead in respect of the child: s. 22.

Powers of court where orders are invalid   S. 23 specifies the powers of the court in cases where a care order proves to be invalid. If a court makes such a finding or declaration of invalidity in any proceedings for whatever reason, it may refuse to exercise any power to order the delivery or return of the child to a parent or any other person if of opinion that to do so would not be in the best interests of the child. In these circumstances, the court has power to make a new care order or remit the matter to the relevant District Court so that it can consider whether to make a new care order.

When the Bill was originally published, it was drafted in such a way that, if an order proved to be invalid (even for a technical reason), the court would have no option but to return the child to the environment from which he or she had emerged, however detrimental this might be to the child's welfare. After discussions with the Attorney General, this section emerged.

Senator Brendan Ryan expressed some concern at the breadth of the section so far as it enables a court to refuse to return the child to the parents where a care order *for whatever reason* proves to be invalid. He was worried that health boards might consider that, as long as they had a plausible case, 'the legal niceties need not trouble them too much because if somebody contested a case in a higher court the legal niceties would not be at issue. ...

There is a slightly Kafkaesque tone about this provision and one could imagine parents in the centre of it all feeling they had got somewhere and then discovering they were actually back where they started': 129 Seanad Debates, para 537.

PART V: JURISDICTION AND PROCEDURE

Part V sets out the jurisdiction, powers and procedures of courts in relation to child care proceedings.

Paramountcy of child's welfare   S. 24 provides that, in any proceedings before a court under the Act in relation to the care and protection of a child, the court, having regard to the rights and duties of parents, whether under the Constitution or otherwise, is to regard the welfare of the child as the first and paramount consideration and, in so far as is practicable, to give due consideration, having regard to his age and understanding, to the wishes of the child.

Joinder of the child   S. 25(1) enables the court in any proceedings under Part IV or VI to join the child as a party. For this power to arise, the child must not already be a party and the court must be satisfied, having regard to his or her age, understanding and wishes and the circumstances of the case, that it is necessary in the interests of the child and in the interests of justice to do so. As an alternative, the court in such circumstances may order that the child is to have such of the rights of a party as may be specified by the court in either the entirety of the proceedings or such issues in the proceedings as the Court may direct. The making of any such order does not require the intervention of a next friend in respect of the child.

Where a court makes an order joining the child as a party (or giving the child specified rights of a party) or where a child is a party to the proceedings otherwise than by reason of such an order, the court may, if it thinks fit, appoint a solicitor to represent the child in the proceedings and give directions as to the performance of his or her duties (which may include, if necessary, directions in relation to the instruction of counsel): subs. 2.

The fact that a child is party to the proceedings (whether as a result of subs. (1) or otherwise) does not limit the court's power under s. 30(2) to refuse to accede to a request of a child to be present during part or all of the proceedings. (Under s. 30(2), the Court must grant this request unless it appears to it that, having regard to the age of the child or the nature of the proceedings, it would not be in the child's interests to accede to the request).

Where a solicitor is appointed under s. 25(2), the costs and expenses

incurred on behalf of a child exercising any rights of a party in any proceedings under the Act are to be paid by the health board: subs. 4.

The court which has made an order under s. 25(2) may, on application to
it by a health board, order any other party to the proceedings to pay to the
board any costs or expenses payable by the board under subs. 4: subs. 5.

Appointment of guardian ad litem   S. 26 provides for the appointment of
a guardian *ad litem* for the child. If, in any proceedings under Part IV or VI,
the child to whom the proceedings relate is not a party, the court may make
such an appointment, if satisfied that it is necessary in the interests of the
child and of justice to do so: subs. 1.

Any costs incurred by a person thus acting as a guardian *ad litem* are to
be paid by the health board (subs. 2), subject to the court's ordering any other
party to the proceedings to pay to the board any costs or expenses payable
by it (subs. 3).

Where a child in respect of whom a guardian *ad litem* has been appointed
becomes a party to the proceedings in question, the order appointing the
guardian *ad litem* ceases to have effect: subs. 4.

Procurement of reports on children   S. 27(1) empowers the court, in any
proceedings under Part IV or VI, to procure a report from a nominated person
on any question affecting the child's welfare. In deciding whether or not to
do so, the court is to have regard to the wishes of the parties before the court
where these are ascertainable; the court is not, however, to be *bound* by these
wishes: subs. 2.

A copy of the report is to be made available to the counsel or solicitor of
each party in the proceedings or to the party himself or herself if he or she is
not legally represented. The report may be received in evidence in the
proceedings: subs. 3.

The court, if it thinks fit, or any party to the proceedings, may call the
person making the report as a witness: subs. 5. The fees and expenses of a
person preparing a report are to be paid by such party or parties to the
proceedings as the court orders: subs. 4. For an examination of what welfare
reports should contain, see Davies, 22 Family L 210 (1992).

Jurisdiction   S. 28 deals with jurisdiction. The District Court and the
Circuit Court on appeal have jurisdiction to hear and determine proceedings
under Part III, IV or VI.

Privacy of proceedings   Proceedings under Part III, IV or VI are heard
otherwise than in public: (s. 29(1)) and are to be as informal as is practicable
and consistent with the administration of justice: (s. 29(4)).

Power to proceed in child's absence S. 30(1) gives the court power to hear proceedings under Part III, IV or VI in the absence of the child for part or all of the hearing unless satisfied that the child's presence is necessary for the proper disposal of the case. Where the child requests to be present during the hearing or a particular part of the hearing, the court must grant that request unless it appears to the court that, having regard to the age of the child or the nature of the proceedings, it would not be in the child's interests to accede to the request: s. 30(2).

Restrictions on publication S. 31 introduces stringent restrictions on the publication of matter likely to lead members of the public to identify a child who is or has been the subject of proceedings under Part III, IV or VI. It prescribes a summary criminal offence with a maximum penalty of 12 months' imprisonment or £1,000 or both. This is without prejudice to the law as to contempt of court. Paragraph (c) of subs. 3, prior to Report Stage in the Seanad, imposed liability on 'any person' who transmits or provides the programme. Concern was expressed that this might catch a technician or other employee who physically transmitted material contravening the section. An amendment to 'any body corporate', at Report Stage, sought to place it 'beyond doubt that it will be the owners of the broadcasting station who will be responsible in the matter, together with any person having functions in relation to the programme corresponding to those of an editor of a newspaper': 129 Seanad Debates, col. 845.

Determination of child's age S. 32 provides that, in any application for an order under Part III, IV or VI, the court is to make due enquiry as to the age of the person to whom the application relates and the age presumed or declared by the court to be the age of that person is to be deemed to be the true age until the contrary is proved.

Rules of court S. 33 enables rules of court to be made to facilitate procedural aspects of proceedings under Part III, IV or VI of the Act.

Failure or refusal to deliver up a child S. 34 deals with the failure or refusal to deliver up a child. It provides that, without prejudice to the law as to contempt of court, where the District Court has made an order under Part III or IV directing that a child be placed or maintained in the care of a health board, any person having the actual custody of the child who, having been given or shown a copy of the order and having been required, by or on behalf of the health board, to give up the child to the board, fails or refuses to do so, is guilty of a summary offence with a maximum penalty of 6 months' imprisonment and a £500 fine.

Search warrants   S. 35 deals with search warrants. Where a judge of the District Court has made an order directing that a child be placed or maintained in the care of a health board, a judge of the District Court may for the purpose of executing that order issue a warrant authorising a member of the Garda Síochána, accompanied by such other members of the Garda Síochána or such other persons as may be necessary, to enter (if need be by force) any house or other place specified in the warrant where the child is or where there are reasonable grounds for believing that he or she is and to deliver the child into the custody of the health board.

PART VI: CHILDREN IN THE CARE OF THE HEALTH
BOARD

Part VI sets out the arrangements which health boards may make in looking after children in their care.

Accommodation and maintenance   S. 36 empowers a health board to place a child in foster care or in a children's residential centre or other institution (such as a special school). It may make other suitable arrangements for his care, including placing him with a relative. Moreover, where the child is eligible for adoption, the health board may place him with a view to his adoption.

Access   S. 37 deals with *access*. Where a child is in the care of a health board, the board must facilitate reasonable access to the child by his parents, any person acting *in loco parentis*, or any person who, in the opinion of the board, has a *bona fide* interest in the child: subs. 1. Access includes allowing the child to reside temporarily with such a person: *id*.

Anyone dissatisfied with arrangements for access made by a health board may apply to the court, and the court may make such order as it thinks proper regarding access: subs. 2. The court order may be varied or discharged subsequently: *id*. The court, on the application of a health board, and if it considers it necessary to do so to safeguard or promote the child's welfare, may make an order authorising the board to *refuse* to allow a named person access to a child in its care: subs. 3. This order may also be varied or discharged subsequently: *id*.

Residential care   S. 38(1) requires health boards to make arrangements with the registered proprietors of children's residential centres or with other suitable persons to ensure the provision of an adequate number of residential places for children in its care. Subs. 2 permits health boards, with Ministerial approval, to provide and maintain residential centres or other premises for the provision of residential care for children in care.

The Minister is required to make regulations with respect to the conduct of homes or other premises provided by health boards under s. 38: subs. 3. Subs (4) provides the detail for what these regulations may cover.

Regulations   Ss. 39 to 41 require the Minister to make regulations as to the placing of children in foster care, residential care and with relatives.

Review of cases of children in care   S. 42 requires the Minister to make regulations requiring the case of each child in the case of a health board to be reviewed in accordance with the provisions of the regulations.

Removal from placement   S. 43(1) empowers a health board, in accordance with Ministerial regulations, to remove a child in its care from the custody of any person with whom he or she has been placed by the board under s. 36. If the person refuses or neglects to comply with this request, the board may apply to the District Court, and the judge, if he or she considers that it is in the best interests of the child to do so, may make an order to deliver up the child to the custody of the board: s. 43(2). Failure to comply with this order is an offence, with a maximum penalty of six months' imprisonment or fine of £500 or both, without prejudice to the law as to contempt of court: s. 43(3).

Where a child is removed from the custody of a person in pursuance of s. 43, any contract between the board and that person in respect of the child terminates immediately upon the removal: s. 43(5). The section as originally drafted made it an offence for a foster parent wilfully to refuse or neglect to deliver up the child to a health board empowered under the section to remove the child from his or her custody. As a result of representations from the Irish Foster Care Association, the Minister for State introduced an amendment at Committee Stage in the Seanad restricting criminal liability to cases of refusal to obey a *court order* to return the child to the health board: 129 Seanad Debates, col. 634.

Children who become adopted   S. 44(1) deals with the adoption under Irish domestic legislation of children who were being maintained in foster care by a health board with the adopter or adopters immediately before the adoption. The health board may, subject to any general directions given by the Minister and subject to such conditions as the health board sees fit, contribute to the maintenance of the child as if he or she continued to be in foster care. Where a child becomes adopted under Irish domestic legislation, any care order in force in respect of the child ceases to have effect: s. 44(2).

Aftercare S. 45 provides for aftercare. Subs. 1 enables a health board to assist a child who leaves its care for so long as the board is satisfied as to his need for assistance, until he reaches the age of 21 or completes the course of education in which he is engaged. Subs. 2 sets out the ways in which the health board may provide this assistance:

(a) by causing him to be visited or assisted;
(b) by arranging for the completion of his education and by contributing towards his maintenance while he is completing this education;
(c) by placing him in a suitable trade, calling or business and paying the requisite fee;
(d) by arranging hostel or other forms of accommodation for him;
(e) by co-operating with housing authorities in planning accommodation for children leaving care on reaching the age of 18 years.

In providing assistance under s. 45, the health board is to comply with any general regulations given by the Minister: subs. 4.

Recovery of children removed from care S. 46 deals with the recovery of a child removed without lawful authority from care or prevented from returning to the custody of the health board at the end of any period of leave. The board may request the Garda Síochána to search for the child and deliver him up to the custody of the board and the Garda Síochána may take all reasonable measures to comply with this request: subs. 2. A judge of the District Court, if satisfied by information on oath that there are reasonable grounds for believing that a person specified in the information can produce the child named in the application, may make an order (which may be *ex parte* (subs. 7) directing that person to deliver up the child to the custody of the board: subs. 3. Failure or refusal by a person having actual custody of the child to comply is a summary offence with a maximum penalty of six months' imprisonment and a fine of £500, without prejudice to the law as to contempt of court: subs. 4.

Two matters may here be noted. First the offence is drafted in such a way as not to include any express defence such as lawful authority or reasonable excuse. The shadow of the robust policy underlying civil contempt seems to fall over this provision. Secondly, the offence applies where there were reasonable grounds for believing that the defendant could produce the child at the time the court made the order. It may be that, in spite of these reasonable grounds, the defendant could not in fact have produced the child at that time or later. It seems wrong that he or she should be guilty of an offence for failure to comply with an order which is impossible to obey in the circumstances.

Application for directions   S. 47 provides that, where a child is in the care of a health board, the District Court may, of its own motion or on the application of any person, give such directions and make such order on any question affecting the welfare of the child as it thinks proper. It may vary or discharge that direction or order subsequently.

S. 48 contains transitional provisions.

PART VII: SUPERVISION OF PRE-SCHOOL SERVICES

Part VII contains detailed provisions for the supervision of pre- school services. These services embrace pre-school, play group, day nursery, creche, day-care or other similar services which cater for pre-school children, including those grant-aided by health boards: s. 49. By way of clarification, s. 58 makes it plain that Part VII does not apply to the care of pre-school children undertaken by their relatives *or* by a person taking care of the pre-school children of one family (other than the care-taker's own such children) in the care-taker's home *or* by a person taking care of not more than three pre-school children of different families (other than the care-taker's own such children).

This section was inserted at Report Stage in the Seanad. Its purpose is to make it absolutely clear that the provisions of Part VII do not apply to the case of pre-school children undertaken by a relative or a neighbour of the parents. This is a matter which greatly, and understandably, had exercised Senators at Committee Stage: 129 Seanad Debates, cols. 679-681 (5 June 1991). Clearly, a cut-off point had to be selected in the case of persons who mind children of *different* families. The Minister for State, Mr Tracey, considered that *three* children was 'a reasonable threshold': 129 Seanad Debates, col. 854.

S. 50 requires the Minister to make regulation for securing the health, safety and welfare and promoting the development of pre-school children attending pre-school services.

S. 51 requires those carrying on a pre-school service to give notice to the relevant health board in the prescribed manner. An interesting debate took place at Committee Stage in the Seanad as to whether the requirements of notification should be elevated into that of registration. Senators O'Reilly and Norris argued that it should. The charge against this proposal was led by Senator Brendan Ryan, whose energetic contribution emphasised the huge administrative burden which pre-inspection would involve as well as the inhibitive effect which such elaborate machinery would have on the development of pre-school services. The professional bodies had submitted that registration, backed by pre-inspection, would be preferable: 129 Seanad Debates, cols. 666-7.

The absence of a registration requirement should not be viewed in isolation: ss. 50 and 52 provide for the making of, and compliance with, Ministerial regulations as to the health, safety and welfare of pre-school children; s. 53 provides for visitation; and s. 55 empowers the health boards to inspect premises where pre-school services are being carried out.

S. 52 imposes a statutory duty on persons carrying on pre-school services to take all reasonable measures to safeguard the health, safety and welfare of their charges and to comply with Ministerial regulations under Part VII. It would seem that breach of this duty could well generate civil liability as the beneficiaries of the prescribed duty seem clearly to constitute a well-defined class. Of course there is already a well-established common law duty resting on those having care of children to ensure that they are not unreasonably exposed to risk: see McMahon & Binchy's *Irish Law of Torts* (2nd ed., 1991), ch. 16. There also appears, moreover, to be an overlap with the Safety, Health and Welfare at Work Act 1989 (see the 1989 Review, 379-93).

The other provisions of Part VII are unexceptional: health boards must arrange for the inspection of pre-school services (s. 53); the inspectors thus appointed (s. 54) have wide-ranging powers of inspection (s. 55) backed by criminal sanction (s. 57)); health boards may, moreover, provide pre-school services and make available information on pre-school services (s. 56).

PART VIII: CHILDREN'S RESIDENTIAL CENTRES

Part VIII contains provisions for the regulation and inspection of residential homes for children. These are largely similar to those of Part VII, save that registration rather than notification is required.

S. 59 excludes from the definition of 'children's residential centre' five particular categories of institution. Paragraph (a) refers to institutions managed by or on behalf of a Minister of the Government or a health board. During the Committee Stage in the Seanad, the Minister for State explained that 'it would make no sense' to have such institutions subject to regulation and inspection by a health board, perhaps the same health board. He did 'not understand how one could register oneself, inspect oneself and verify and vouch for oneself. It would be illogical and impractical': 129 Seanad Debates col. 817. Paragraph (b) refers to hospitals and similar institutions. Paragraph (c) refers to centres for mentally and physically handicapped children. These were excluded, the Minister for State explained, because 'it would not make sense to have [them] subject to statutory registration while all other hospitals and centres dealing with handicapped adults are not subject to similar controls': *id*, col. 812. There were different views as to whether centres for the handicapped should be subject to this kind of control; it would not be realistic to attempt to resolve this contentious issue in the context of this legislation. Paragraph (d) refers to certain mental treatment institutions. Paragraph (e) refers to certain industrial and reformatory schools. These are already subject to statutory control under other legislation and it was not considered necessary to subject them to a second layer.

PART IX: ADMINISTRATION

This Part contains several technical provisions dealing with the administration of the legislation. S. 66, which deals with superannuation of staff of children's residential centres, came into effect on 1 June 1992: SI No. 123 of 1992. The details are dealt with in the Child Care Act 1991 (Children's Residential Centres) (Superannuation) Order 1992 (SI No. 124 of 1992) and in the Child Care Act 1991 (Children's Residential Centres) (Superannuation) (No. 2) Order 1992 (SI No. 125 of 1992). S. 68 gives the Minister power to make regulations. S. 69 gives the Minister power to give directions to health boards in relation to the performance of their functions under the Act and to cause any service provided or premises maintained by a health board under the Act to be inspected. S. 70 enables health boards to charge for certain services. S. 71 provides for prosecution of offences under the Act, prescribing that summary proceedings are to be brought by the health board for the area in which the offence is alleged to have been committed. S. 72 assigns certain functions under the legislation to chief executive officers of health boards: subs. 1. These may be delegated by them to other officers of the boards: subs. 3.

PART X: MISCELLEANEOUS AND SUPPLEMENTARY

Of the several miscellaneous and supplementary provisions, almost all are of a technical nature. S. 74, however, is of some considerable significance. It makes it an offence for a person to sell, offer or make available a substance to a person under eighteen years or someone acting on his behalf if he knows or has reasonable cause to believe that the substance is, or its fumes are, likely to be inhaled by the person under eighteen for the purpose of causing intoxication: subs. 1. Two defences are available: first that the provider was acting otherwise than in the course of or furtherance of a business (subs. 2) and second that the provider took reasonable care to assure himself that the recipient, or person to whom the substance was made available or the person on whose behalf he was acting, was under eighteen: subs. 3. These defences involve a legal rather than evidential burden of proof on the defendant.

Conviction involves a maximum fine of £1000 and imprisonment for twelve months (subs. 4), as well as forfeiture of anything shown to the satisfaction of the court 'to relate to' the offence (subs. 5), subject to the entitlement of any interested person to show cause why forfeiture should not be made (subs. 6). S. 74 came into effect on 1 December 1991: SI No. 292 of 1991.

Fisheries

ANGLING LICENCES

The Fisheries (Amendment) Act 1991 was the legislative attempt to bring to an end the rod licence dispute which arose from the Fisheries (Amendment) (No. 2) Act 1987: see the 1987 Review, 214 and xiii. See also *Kelly v O'Sullivan*, High Court, 11 July 1990, a case arising out of the dispute (discussed in the 1990 Review, 197-8).

The 1991 Act replaces the need for a licence and provides for the establishment of fisheries co-operative societies for the development and regulation of trout and coarse fishing. These are charitable societies, who will raise funds through the issuing of share certificates which will entitle the holders to manage the societies and elect members of the Regional Fisheries Boards. The 1991 Act also revises the various licence duties. Grants will be payable by the government to make good the shortfall in income arising form the replacement of the rod licence.

The Act came into effect on 30 November 1991: Fisheries (Amendment) Act 1991 (Commencement) Order 1991 (SI No. 301). Refunds on licences were provided for by the Salmon Licence Duty (Refund) Regulations 1991 (SI No. 346). Finally, the passage of the 1991 Act resulted in the postponement of elections to the Regional Fisheries Boards: Regional Fisheries Boards (Postponement of Elections) Order 1991 (SI No. 339).

FISHERY HARBOUR CENTRE

In *Island Ferries Teo v Minister for the Marine and Aran Ferries Teo*, High Court, 31 July 1991, Barron J considered the validity of a restriction on the size of passenger ferries using a fishery harbour centre under the Fishery Harbour Centres Act 1968.

The applicant company had, for many years, operated a passenger ferry service into Rossaveel harbour, Galway. The harbour was designated by Order as a fishery harbour centre under the Fishery Harbour Centres Act 1968. The second respondent also operated a passenger ferry service into Rossaveel. In 1988, the Minister had decided that no ferry in excess of 100 feet should be allowed operate into the harbour. Both the applicant and the second respondent had applied a number of times since then to operate a vessel in excess of 100 feet, but these had been turned down by the Minister. In December 1990, the second respondent again applied for permission to use a 108 foot vessel and this was rejected on 21 March 1991. The second respondent sought a meeting with Departmental officials on 22 March 1991, during which discussions took place with the Rossaveel harbour master by telephone. Having heard that additional berthing facilities would be in place when the 108 foot vessel would be operating, the second respondent was given permission to use the vessel.

The applicant had, prior to 21 March 1991, become aware that the second respondent was proposing to use a vessel in excess of 100 feet into Rossaveel, and had contacted the Department of the Marine on 21 March 1991 to confirm that the 100 foot limit still stood; this was confirmed to the applicant. The applicant was informed, after 22 March, that the second respondent's application had been granted after a full consideration of the application.

The applicant sought judicial review on the alternative grounds that the decision allowing a vessel of 108 feet in length amounted to a bye-law which could only be validly made in accordance with the procedures set out in s. 4 of the 1968 Act and that, even if it was not a bye-law, the decision made in the instant case did not comply with fair procedures. Barron J accepted both arguments but, for reasons to be explained later, made declaratory orders only.

Barron J referred with approval to Lord Russell CJ's definition of a bye-law in *Kruse v Johnson* [1898] 2 QB 91. It is to be regretted that Barron J was apparently not referred to the decision of the Supreme Court in *The State (Harrington) v Murphy* [1988] IR 290 (1988 Review, 301-2) in which the Court had also approved that definition. Be that as it may, Barron J concluded that the decision to allow vessels in excess of 100 feet into Rosaveel constitued a bye-law within s. 4 of the 1968 Act. Since the Minister in the instant case had argued that this did not constitute a bye-law, it is hardly surprising, therefore, that the s. 4 procedures had not been complied with. Indeed, it is a curious feature of the instant case that all parties accepted the validity of the previous 100 foot limit decided in 1988. Barron J arrived at a neat solution to the forensic dilemma posed by this circumstance. He granted the applicant a declaration that the 1988 decision as well as the decision in the instant case were invalid. He allowed the Minister an adjournment of 3 months to enable him decide whether to make an appropriate bye-law. He indicated, to some extent, his own tentative view on the matter when he adverted to concerns expressed by local fishing interests who had also objected to the decision to allow a 108 foot vessel into the harbour. Barron J noted that, under the 1968 Act, the Minister had clear responsibilities to those interests, notwithstanding the general powers of development given by the 1968 Act.

On the second ground raised in the case, Barron J also accepted that the Minister's decision was flawed for lacking fair procedures. Given the confirmation of the 100 foot limit to the applicant on 21 March, Barron J concluded that the decision to grant the second respondent's application on 22 March. He concluded:

> In my view administrative decisions come to in such an arbitary manner cannot be supported.

Garda Síochána

DISCIPLINE

The constitutional validity of the Garda disciplinary procedure was upheld by the Supreme Court in *Keady v Garda Commissioner* [1992] ILRM 312.

The plaintiff, then a member of An Garda Síochána, was charged with a number of offences relating to claims in respect of night duty while a member of the gardaí. Having opted for trial on indictment, a nolle prosequi was subsequently entered. Disciplinary proceedings under the Garda Síochána (Discipline) Regulations 1971 (since replaced by the Garda Síochána (Discipline) Regulations 1989) were then instituted against the plaintiff arising out of the same facts which had given rise to the criminal proceedings. The plaintiff was dismissed from the Garda Síochána arising from these proceedings. The plaintiff then challenged the constitutional validity of these proceedings, but in the High Court Costello J dismissed the claim, High Court, 1 December 1988. On appeal, the Supreme Court (Finlay CJ, Hederman, McCarthy, O'Flaherty and Egan JJ) unanimously upheld Costello J's view.

In the leading judgment of the Court, O'Flaherty J referred with approval to the decision of the Divisional High Court in *The State (Murray) v McRann* [1979] IR 133, a case on prison disciplinary procedures which was also approved by the Court in its decision earlier the same month (November 1991) in *Goodman International v Mr Justice Hamilton* [1992] ILRM 145: see 109-11, above, in the Constitutional law chapter. Following *Murray*, O'Flaherty J held that the requirement in Article 38 of the Constitution that all criminal matters must be tried in the courts did not preclude the investigation of parallel matters before administrative or domestic tribunals such as that constituted under the 1971 Regulations.

In a connected argument, the plaintiff had argued that the inquiry under the 1971 Regulations constituted an administration of justice within Article 34.1 of the Constitution. This required the examination of the case law on what constitutes the administration of justice, an issue which has been much discussed in recent years (see the 1987 Review, 82-3, the 1989 Review, 91-5 and the 1990 Review, 154), including the decision of the Court in the *Goodman* case, above. In *Keady*, the plaintiff relied on the decisions of the Court in *In re the Solicitors Act 1954* [1960] IR 239 and dicta in *K. v An Bord Altranais* [1990] 2 IR 396 (see the 1990 Review, 339-40). O'Flaherty J distinguished these cases on the basis that there was no determination as such arising from an inquiry under the 1971 Regulations; and although the plaintiff was deprived of a particular means of earning his livelihood, he was not deprived of any qualification in the process.

Again echoing the approach in *Goodman*, O'Flaherty J pointed out, however, that any inquiry proceedings must be conducted in a judicial manner in accordance with fair procedures.

The plaintiff's final argument was based on the terms of the 1971 Regulations. He argued that a specific reference in the Schedule to the 1971 Regulations to disciplinary charges arising from criminal conduct in respect of which there was a conviction in the courts precluded an investigation of conduct with criminal connotations under separate headings, as had occurred in the instant case. The Court rejected this argument, which was consistent with its approval of the *Murray* case.

It is of interest to note, however, that O'Flaherty J expressly pointed out that no argument had been addressed to the Court as as to a possible estoppel arising against the authorities on this aspect of the case. It would appear, therefore, that the Court did not have an opportunity to explore the impact of its decision a year before in *McGrath v Garda Commissioner* [1990] ILRM 817, in which estoppel had been successfully raised: see the 1990 Review, 330-1.

Health Services

CANCER

The National Cancer Registry Board (Establishment) Order 1991 (SI No. 19) provided for the establishment of the eponymous Board. The Order was made under the Health (Corporate Bodies) Act 1961.

ELIGIBILITY

S. 3 of the Health (Amendment) Act 1991 amended s. 46 of the Health Act 1970 to abolish the income limit for 'limited eligibility' for hospital services. The effect is that all persons, regardless of income, are entitled to avail of a free hospital bed (subject to out-patient and in-patient charges) and free hospital consultant services. S. 10 of the 1991 Act also revoked a number of Regulations to give effect to this. This significant change in the health service regime was made as part of the commitments contained in the Programme for Economic and Social Progress (PESP) which was agreed between the government and the social partners in February 1991.

S. 2 of the 1991 Act amended s. 45 of the 1970 Act by providing that eligibility for full health services is dependent on ordinary residence as well as the other factors provided for in s.45 of the 1970 Act. S. 4 of the 1991 Act (by inserting section 47A into the 1970 Act) empowers the Minister for Health to issue guidelines to health boards on what constitutes 'ordinary residence' for the purposes of the Act.

The 1991 Act also made a number of other changes to the provision of in-patient and out-patient services. S. 5 of the 1991 Act amended s. 52 of the 1970 Act by providing that a person who opts for private treatment thereby loses their right to full or limited eligibility to free services.

S. 6 of the 1991 Act amends s. 55 of the 1991 Act by ensuring that public in-patient facilities will be provided to non-residents, in particular EC nationals. S. 9 of the 1991 Act also deals with EC nationals. The Minister is also empowered under s. 55 of the 1970 Act to make Regulations filling in the detail. The Health Services (In-Patient) Regulations 1991 (SI No. 135) were made under this power. A similar Regulation-making power was conferred in respect of out-patient services by s. 7 of the 1991 Act (amending s. 56 of the 1970 Act). This resulted in the Minister making the Health Services (Out-Patient) Regulations 1991 (SI No. 136).

Finally, s. 8 of the 1991 Act removed the income ceiling in respect of health contributions (amending the Health Contributions Act 1979 to achieve this).

The 1991 Act came into effect on 1 June 1991: Health (Amendment) Act 1991 (Commencement) Order 1991 (SI No. 134).

FITNESS TO PRACTICE COMMITTEE

Phillips v Medical Council [1992] ILRM 469 arose out of complaints of professional misconduct alleged against the applicant, a consultant neuro-surgeon in Beaumont Hospital, Dublin. The complaints were made by letter from two other consultant neurosurgeons in the hospital. After the complaints had been made, the board of Beaumont Hospital requested, pursuant to s. 45 of the Medical Practitioners Act 1978, that the Fitness to Practice Committee of the Medical Council conduct an inquiry into the complaints.

In May 1990, the Fitness to Practice Committee decided that there was a *prima facie* case for holding an inquiry into the applicant's conduct. The Committee's registrar received legal advice that an independent report on the applicant's conduct be obtained. A preliminary report from the independent consultant who was asked to provide evidence for the Committee appeared to indicate a view favourable to the applicant. In addition, in separate High Court proceedings involving one of the other consultants who had brought one of the complaints against the applicant, the chairman of Beaumont Hospital stated on affidavit that the board had confidence in the applicant.

In these circumstances, the applicant sought judicial review of the May 1990 decision of the Fitness to Practice Committee that there was a *prima facie* case against him and also an order of mandamus seeking to end the inquiry. He also sought an order of certiorari quashing an order for production of documents directed to the hospital from the Fitness to Practice Committee in relation to 16 cases in which the applicant had been involved. Carroll J declined to grant most of the relief sought, except for the *certiorari* quashing the Committee's notice to produce documents directed to the hospital.

She held, firstly, that once the Committee had determined that there was a *prima facie* case it was obliged to carry through with the inquiry; this was the essential threshold which needed to be passed. She did not therefore accept that any of the material which had emerged since May 1990 could prevent the Committee from proceeding to hear and determine all the evidence in the case.

Nor did she consider that the principles of fair procedures required the Committee's registrar to evaluate the material which had emerged since May 1990 and to put it before the Committee for it to express a view on such material.

Carroll J declined to order mandamus to direct the Committee that it was prohibited from making a finding of unfitness to practice on the basis of the preliminary report prepared by the indpendent expert, since this was a matter for the Committee to determine and not for the Court.

Finally, Carroll J did determine one issue in the applicant's favour. The Fitness to Practice Committee had ordered the hospital to produce, under s. 45 of the 1978 Act, all documents in its possession relating to 16 cases in which the applicant had been involved. Such documents were to be produced to all the parties in the case. Carroll J held that this was *ultra vires* the Committee since the power given to the Committee under s. 45 was to order production of documents to the Committee, not in effect an order of discovery under which all parties would obtain sight of the documents in question. She did not consider that discovery was an inherent power of the Committee. She distinguished the instant case from *Nolan v Irish Land Commission* [1981] IR 23, where discovery was held to be an inherent part of the proceedings of the Land Commission. Carroll J held that since that decision was based on ensuring fair procedures, the instant case could be decided on the basis that discovery to all parties was not required provided that the other two consultants could, through other mechanisms, fully present their allegations of misconduct to the Committee.

HEALTH BOARD

Health Board Investigation *O'Flynn and O'Regan v Mid-Western Health Board* [1991] 2 IR 223 was an, ultimately, unsuccessful challenge to the procedures followed by a health board when investigating a complaint against medical practitioners under the general medical services scheme.

In 1981, the applicant doctors had entered into agreements to provide a general medical service to the respondent health board pursuant to s. 58 of the Health Act 1970. In June 1986, a complaint was received by the board that the applicants were in breach of their contracts in that they allegedly obtained fraudulent payments for pharmaceutical products alleged to have been prescribed for their patients. Between June and October 1986, the board investigated the complaint and then referred the matter to the Garda Síochána. In October 1987, the Gardaí informed the board that the Director of Public Prosecutions had decided that no prosecutions be brought. The board subsequently wrote to the applicants informing them that, under clause 24 of their agreement with the board, it was pursuing the complaint, and setting out in general terms the nature of the complaint. The applicants by letter denied the complaint and requested details of the allegations made against them. By subsequent letter from the board, they were informed that the chief executive officer had requested the Minister for Health to establish a Committee to inquire into the complaint pursuant to the Health Services Regulations 1972. The Minister subsequently established such a Committee.

The applicants sought judicial review of the appointment of the Committee on the ground, *inter alia*, that thay had not been given an opportunity to make representations to the chief executive officer of the board prior to his referral of the matter to the Minister as envisaged by para.24 of the applicants' agreement with the board. In the High Court, Barr J granted judicial review: [1989] IR 429 (see the 1989 Review, 375-6). However, on appeal by the board the Supreme Court (Finlay CJ, Griffin, Hederman, McCarthy and O'Flaherty JJ) allowed its appeal and dismissed the judicial review claim.

Two reasoned judgments were delivered, by Hederman and McCarthy JJ, and they were in agreement on the approach to be taken to the case. They accepted that the chief executive officer was required to act in accordance with fair procedures, but they held that he was not obliged to provide the applicants with an oral hearing in the performance of his functions. The same approach was taken by the Court later in the year in *Nolan v Minister for the Environment* [1991] ILRM 705; [1991] 2 IR 548 (see 319-20, below, in the Local Government chapter).

The Court in *O'Flynn* went on to held that since the chief executive officer acted primarily as a filter in respect of complaints against doctors, and did not have any adjudicatory role, he had not been in breach of any rules of fair procedures in requesting the Minister to establish a committee of inquiry pursuant to the 1972 Regulations where, as in the instant case, there was an irreconcilable conflict of fact between the person who had made the complaint and the applicants.

The Supreme Court would also have refused judicial review in the instant case in the absence of any reasonable explanation by the applicants as to why they sought relief outside the time limits specified in O.84, r.21 of the Rules of the Superior Courts 1986. On this aspect of the case, the judgments referred to the quite lenient approach taken in *The State (Furey) v Minister for Defence* [1988] ILRM 89, where delay had been excused. Clearly, even on the *Furey* test, there are circumstances in which that test's author, McCarthy J, would refuse judicial review for delay.

Finally, the Court dealt with the plaintiffs' argument that the board's investigation should not have been deferred pending the outcome of the criminal investigation of the complaint against the applicants. Referring to its decision in *Dillon v Dunnes Stores Ltd* [1966] IR 397 the Court held that, while such a deferral was not an immutable rule, the board had acted correctly in the instant case in deferring the appointment of a committee under the 1972 Regulations pending the conclusion of the criminal investigation against the applicants.

Health Board Resolution The question of fair procedures also arose in *Farrell v South Eastern Health Board* [1991] 2 IR 291. In this case, the applicant was a medical consultant and a member of the South Eastern Health Board. The question of where to locate the acute general hospital for South Tipperary had been the subject of intense debate on the board, with support divided between Cashel and Clonmel. The applicant was concerned that Clonmel hospital did not meet fire safety standards and expressed this view at meetings of the board. After initiating High Court proceedings in which Blayney J ordered permission to have a fire inspection of Clonmel hospital, the applicant inspected Clonmel hospital with fire safety experts, with a view to preparing a report on whether it met fire safety requirements. On the day after this inspection, the health board met to consider a medical consultants' report (from which the applicant had dissented) that all acute services be provided in Clonmel. At the meeting of the board, the applicant had a limited number of copies of one of the reports prepared by the fire safety experts on Clonmel hospital, and he was allowed two minutes to put his views to the meeting. After a vote, the medical consultants' report was adopted by the meeting.

The applicant sought judicial review of the decision of the board on the grounds that fair procedures had not been adopted and also that the medical consultants' report had been adopted without consideration of any report on the costs of implementing the report, contrary to standing orders. Barron J granted judicial review relying primarily on the first ground.

He noted that, since the board does not act judicially and makes no determination between members, the strict requirements of natural justice did not apply to its deliberations. Nonetheless, he also held that the principles of fair procedures did apply and that these required that all members be given a reasonable opportunity to express their views on matters under discussion. Having regard to the attempts to inhibit the applicant to obtain evidence to substantiate his views, and to the manner in which his views were stifled at the meeting of the board, Barron J concluded that the board had been in breach of fair procedures. He noted in particular in this context that the chief executive officer of the board had placed obstacles in the applicant's attempts to obtain information on fire safety in Clonmel. Barron J commented:

> Speaking for myself, I would have thought that a member of the Board was entitled to the information likely to be acted upon by the members of the Board. The chief executive officer clearly thought otherwise. His position is that of a servant of the Board not the other way around. He appears to have forgotten that.

As to whether there had been a breach of standing orders, Barron J did not express a concluded view, though he did refer to the fact that, although it had previously been resolved that costings for the consultants' report would be prepared by the chief executive officer, these were not before the meeting which considered the consultants' report. However, as indicated, Barron J relied primarily on the fair procedures point.

Finally, Barron J concluded that the applicant should be granted *certiorari* to quash the Board's decision. Although he accepted that the applicant appeared to be in a minority on the board, he noted that there had been a number of absentees from the board meeting which considered the consultants' proposal and that, of those present at the meeting, a number had abstained. In those circumstances the Court would not be acting in vain in quashing the decision since a full meeting hearing all the arguments might come to a different conclusion.

MENTAL TREATMENT

In *O'Reilly v Moroney and Mid-Western Health Board*, High Court, 7 June 1991, Murphy J declined to give leave to the plaintiff to institute proceedings under s. 260 of the Mental Treatment Act 1945. The plaintiff had been committed to a psychiatric hospital under the following circumstances.

Her husband and her father had gone to the husband's general practitioner, the first named defendant, who was not the plaintiff's general practitioner. There was some dispute as to whether the plaintiff's father had expressed concern to the doctor about the plaintiff's mental health—the doctor averred that he did, but the father denied this in evidence. The doctor heard from the plaintiff's husband that the plaintiff was in an agitated state and had threatened her life. The doctor was aware that there were marital difficulties between the plaintiff and the husband. He went with the plaintiff's husband to the family home where, he said, the plaintiff was violent towards the husband. He signed committal papers. The Gardai were called to the house, and the Garda who arrived observed that the plaintiff was quiet and appeared normal. She was brought to a psychiatric hospital under the control of the second named defendant, where she was examined by a doctor. This doctor phoned the general practitioner to check the basis on which he had signed the committal papers, and she also rang a consultant psychiatrist attached to the hospital. She admitted the plaintiff to the hospital where she was detained for three days.

Having preferred the first defendant's evidence to that of the plaintiff's father, Murphy J concluded that he had exercised reasonable care and that leave should not be granted under s. 260 of the 1945 Act in respect of his actions. He accepted the view of McCarthy J in *Murphy v Greene* [1991]

ILRM 404; [1990] 2 IR 566 (see the 1990 Review, 147-50) that the standard of care in a psychiatric committal may be less than that in 'ordinary medical practice', having regard to the immediate danger which a person may be in when a committal is made. Murphy J accepted in the instant case that, although the first defendant had not actually examined the plaintiff at close hand, his decision to commit the plaintiff was not lacking in reasonable care.

In relation to the examination and decision made in the psychiatric hospital, Murphy J was satisfied that the doctor in question had reached an independent decision to admit the plaintiff and that her two phone calls had not been the sole basis on which the admission was made. Accordingly, he held that leave should not be granted in this connection either.

Finally, of some interest is that, as Murphy J noted, he had had the benefit of hearing all the evidence in the case on oral testimony (the initial application having been on affidavit) over a period of three days. In effect, therefore, the application under s. 260 of the 1945 Act amounted to a full hearing of the actual action for negligence against the defendants. It is clear that nothing further could have been added. For this reason, Murphy J addressed an issue which had not arisen before in such cases. He accepted that if he considered the plaintiff's evidence alone she might have a *prima facie* case for leave to proceed within the test laid down by the Supreme Court in *Murphy v Greene*, above. However, having rejected the plaintiff's evidence in the light of the oral testimony of the defendants and the other witnesses in the case he concluded that it would have been futile to allow the plaintiff proceed any further when all the evidence had been heard in the instant hearing.

The decision of Murphy J in the instant case to hear all the evidence on oral testimony is to be welcomed. The case illustrates, however, the strange anomaly which s. 260 of the 1945 Act represents (see the 1990 Review, 148-50). In the instant case, Murphy J felt constrained to hear all the evidence as in a full civil action before determining the s. 260 issue, which in theory was designed to be a preliminary filter for claims. It would seem, therefore, that not only is s. 260 an anomaly but that, at least in cases where the judge must hear oral evidence, it also fails to serve the purpose for which it was avowedly inserted into the 1945 Act.

NURSING

1 Nursing homes In *O'Sullivan v Minister for Health* [1991] ILRM 744, the applicants owned and managed a nursing home, which had been approved by the Minister, under s. 54 of the Health Act 1970, as a place in which in-patient hospital treatment could be given. The nursing home was also subject to the provisions of the Health (Homes for Incapacitated Persons)

Act 1964. Under s. 2 of the 1964 Act, the Minister had made the Homes for Incapacitated Persons Regulations 1985, under which health boards were empowered to limit the number of persons accommodated in each nursing home. Under the 1985 Regulations, the Southern Health Board imposed a limitation of 40 on the number of in-patients in the applicants' nursing home.

The applicants then purchased a new premises in which they intended to have 90 in-patients. They applied to the Minister for approval for such premises under s. 54 of the Health Act 1970, though without indicating the number of persons they wished to accommodate in the premises. The Minister granted the approval, but subject to a limit of 40 on the number of persons to be accommodated in the premises.

The applicants sought judicial review of the Minister's decision, contending that it was *ultra vires* s. 54 of the 1970 Act for the Minister to impose a number limit, since this was a matter for the health board under the 1985 Regulations.

Barron J dismissed the application. He noted that the Minister was required under s. 54 of the 1970 Act to consider whether the institution for which approval is sought is a fit and proper place for eligible persons to receive in-patient services. In this context, he held that the Minister would therefore be required to examine the proposed number of patients in relation to the available space, staff and facilities. He did not consider that there was anything in s. 2 of the 1964 Act (under which the 1985 Regulations were made) which curtailed the Minister's function in this area, notwithstanding the health board's powers under the 1985 Regulations. Finally, Barron J stated that the onus was on the applicants to have put the Minister on notice that they were seeking approval for an institution for 90 patients.

It may be noted that the 1964 Act will be superceded by the Health (Nursing Homes) Act 1990 when that Act is brought into effect: see the 1990 Review, 340.

2 *Register* In *Fennessey and Anor v Minister for Health* [1991] 2 IR 361, the plaintiffs instituted proceedings claiming that An Bord Altranais (the Board) was not entitled, under the Nurses Act 1985, to alter the basis on which nurses were registered under the Nurses Act 1950. The plaintiffs also claimed that the Board was not entitled to charge a retention fee for registration in 1987 since it had not established a register under the 1985 Act until 1988. Blayney J rejected the claim in relation to registration, but granted the plaintiffs limited relief in relation to the retention fee.

The argument on registration centred on whether it was statutory or contractual in nature. Some correspondence produced in evidence from the Board to the applicants appeared to indicate a contractual basis. However, Blayney J concluded that the basis on which nurses had been registered pursuant to s. 42 of the 1950 Act was statutory in nature, not contractual, notwithstanding any communications to the plaintiffs which might have indicated the contrary. Since the right to registration was statutory in nature it could not be argued, he stated, that it was not capable of repeal or amendment by the 1985 Act. Blayney J therefore rejected the plaintiffs' claim that nurses registered under the 1950 Act had a right not to be removed from the register maintained under the 1985 Act. He approved a similar view expressed in *R. v United Kingdom Central Council for Nursing, Midwifery and Health Visiting, ex p. Bailey, The Independent*, 14 March 1989 (Queen's Bench Division, 13 March 1989).

When Blayney J came to deal with the retention fee issue, he noted that s. 27 of the 1985 Act required the Board to prepare, in accordance with rules made under s. 26 of the Act, a register 'as soon as may be' after its establishment under the Act. He held that this indicated a lapse of time for preparation of a register. Since the register adopted in 1988 under new rules (approved by the Minister) included new categories of nurses, it was not possible for the Board to argue that the old register could be capable of adaptation under the 1985 Act. Thus, he concluded that while the Board was entitled under s. 25 of the Act to charge retention fees in respect of the register, the Board had not been entitled to charge a fee in 1987 when it had not yet prepared a register under the 1985 Act. To that extent only, the plaintiffs succeeded. In the long term, of course, the decision indicates that retention fees levied since the 1988 Rules came into effect may be charged by the Board under the 1985 Act.

POISONS

Agricultural use   The Poisons (Prohibition of the Use of Certain Substances for Agricultural Purposes) Regulations, which came into effect on 1 January 1992, introduce bans on the use of certain substances as part of the attempt to reduce the risk to human health.

General   The Poisons (Amendment) Regulations 1991 (SI No. 353) amend the Principal Regulations of 1982 of the same title.

Labour Law

PENSIONS

In *In re Cavan Rubber Ltd* [1992] ELR 78, the Tribunal held that the definition of 'occupational pension scheme' in s. 1 of the Protection of Employees (Employers' Insolvency) Act 1984 included a claim submitted to the Department of Labour by the liquidator of a company for payment under the 1984 Act of a sum of money which comprised employers' and employees' unpaid pension contributions. The Trust Deed accompanying the claim had not been signed; the rules of the scheme had never been adopted and the Revenue Commissioners had not yet approved of it. The Tribunal considered that the absence of these elements did not prevent the scheme from falling within s. 1.

EMPLOYMENT EQUALITY

In *Moran v Revenue Commissioners* [1991] ELR 189, the Equality Officer addressed the relationship between the status of spouse and that of widow. The claimant had been required to resign from the Revenue Commissioners in 1969 on account of her marriage. At that time, of course, the marriage bar was in full sway. When she applied for re-entry in 1990, she was obliged to establish that she was not being supported by her husband. Had she been a woman of unmarried status or a widow she would have been eligible automatically for reinstatement. She contended that this amounted to less favourable treatment of her because of her marital status.

The respondent contended that the same onus was placed on all applicants for reinstatement, in that each had to establish that she was not being supported by a husband. The evidence obviously varied, depending on the basis of the application, but the onus was the same in each case.

The Equality Officer held in favour of the claimant. Widowhood was a marital status different from that of a woman who was married. If a widow was treated differently, because she was a widow, from the way a woman who was married was treated, the treatment had to be regarded as being 'because of her marital status'. It was true that in very many cases widows would qualify for reinstatement on grounds of hardship but there were other cases where their assets could far exceed those of the claimant but they would still qualify for reinstatement. This amounted to more favourable treatment for them.

The Equality Officer did not accept the merit of the respondent's argument that the claimant had not been treated less favourably than widows or unmarried women because each category was required to establish the common denominator of the absence of a husband's support. To afford more favourable treatment to persons on the basis of non-support by a husband constituted direct discrimination contrary to s. 2(6) of the Employment Equality Act 1977.

The Equality Officer went on to find that the Minister for Finance had contravened s. 9 of the Act by producing a circular which required the Revenue Commissioners to act in a way that the Equality Officer had found to be discriminatory.

MATERNITY LEAVE

In the 1988 Review 266-7, we discussed the High Court decision of *Ivory v Skyline Ltd* [1988] IR 399, where Egan J dealt with the requirement of written notification by an employee of intention to return to work after maternity leave. In *Scott v Yeates & Sons* [1992] ELR 83, the claimant had been pregnant on two previous occasions and, by agreement with the employer, taken maternity leave and returned to work in due course without complying with the Maternity Protection of Employees Acts 1981 and 1991. Her failure on the third occasion to give written notice of her intended return to work ruled out a claim under these Acts. But, said the Tribunal, the maternity leave on the third occcasion was not governed by these Acts at all: it was a *contractual* maternity leave, established by the two earlier precedents, enabling the claimant to return to employment. The decision throws no light on why the third leave, even if contractual, should have been on different terms from what had gone before.

PAYMENT OF WAGES

The Payment of Wages Act 1991 brings to a further stage the modernisation of the law relating to modes of payment of employees. The 1991 Act came into force on 1 January 1992: Payment of Wages Act 1991 (Commencement) Order 1991 (SI No. 350). The Truck Acts had the beneficial goal of preventing exploitation of employees by employers. With the development of a non-cash culture of cheques, credit cards and credit transfers the law's insistence that wages be in cash came to be in many respects a liability. The Payment of Wages Act 1979 permitted employers to pay wages by non-cash means, *if the employees agreed* to this. The 1991 Act goes substantially further. S. 1 requires employers to pay wages in a number of specified cash and non-cash modes (including credit transfers and postal orders). These modes include 'any other mode of payment . . . specified . . . by Regulations made by the Minister [for Labour] after consultation with the Minister for Finance': clause (h). This introduces the flexibility necessary to take account of future technological changes and the consequential development of novel modes of payment.

S. 3 repeals the Truck Acts. It preserves, however, the right of employees paid in cash before the 1991 Act commenced to continue to be paid in this way unless any of the non-cash modes specified in s. 2 is agreed upon by the employer and the employees (or their trade unions). A somewhat similar transitional rule applies to manual workers receiving wages by a method other than cash, under s. 3 of the Payment of Wages Act 1979. That section enabled the employees to revert to payment in cash at the end of the agreement with their employees to be paid by the other mode, or on four weeks' notice if there was no such termination point specified. The purpose of s. 2 is to preserve for these employees their entitlement to return to a cash regime for payment of their wages.

S. 4 of the Act requires employers to give their employees a written statement of gross wages and deductions. This should normally be done at the time of payment, in circumstances of confidentiality. S. 5 prohibits unauthorised deductions by employers from their employees' wages. S. 6 enables an aggrieved employee to complain to a Rights Commissioner. As to procedure, see SI No. 351 of 1991.

For consideration of the Act, see the very helpful analyses by Tony Kerr, *Annotation* [1991] ICLSA, Michael Forde, *Employment Law* (1992), 88-96 and Éilís Barry, 19 ILT (ns) 78 (1992).

REDUNDANCY

In *Fox v Des Kelly Carpets Ltd* [1992] ELR 182, the Tribunal left for another day the important question of whether or not conduct can be a factor in selecting an employee for redundancy. The claimant's employment had been terminated on the professed basis of restructuring within the company. The case made to the Tribunal, however, on behalf of the employer was that the decision to make the claimant redundant had been based on his behaviour and ability as observed by the employer during his term of employment, and that the claimant had misconducted himself by late attendance, non-attendance and by threatening customers. One customer gave evidence of an alleged incident involving the claimant. The employee's manager explained that, while this alleged incident was considered serious, he had not dismissed the claimant as he was always prepared to give him a chance. When, however, the redundancy situation arose, the incident was taken into account as part of the claimant's general conduct. The claimant denied in evidence that he had threatened the customer.

The Tribunal declined to determine whether conduct could be a factor in selection for redundancy because it considered that the issue did not arise in the case, on the basis of estoppel. This was because the employer had continued to employ the claimant after the alleged incident. Since a more junior person had been retained when the claimant was subsequently let go, the claim for unfair dismissal was upheld.

One may perhaps question the merits of this analysis. There are surely levels of misconduct on the part of an employee ranging from the trivial to the serious. If an employee is guilty of misconduct, not sufficient to warrant his or her dismissal, why should not that be taken into account by the employer when contemplating who should be let go in a redundancy context? To require employers to ignore all misconduct when making that decision would seem unwise. It would, moreover, encourage employers to take the harshest view of misconduct for fear of later being met with the bar of estoppel. Of course, the redundancy process should not be turned into an unofficial procedure for firing employees who misconduct themselves to a degree that would not warrant their dismissal; but the idea that this factor should be exorcised from the decision-making process in relation to redundancy seems on balance to be misconceived.

In *Ward v M.C.M. Builders Ltd* [1991] ELR 134, the Tribunal followed the approach followed in the High Court decision of *The Minister for Labour v O'Connor* (1985) 4 JISLL 72, to the effect that:

> compensation paid to the employee on dismissal for redundancy can be treated as payment by the employer of the statutory lump sum only when the employer proves to the satisfaction of the Tribunal (i) that the employee at the time of the payment knew the amount of the statutory lump sum to which he was entitled at the date of the dismissal and (ii) that the employee agreed to accept the sum paid in discharge of his claim for the statutory lump sum.

The Tribunal held on the evidence that the claimant was entitled to a redundancy payment.

TRADE UNIONS

In *National Union of Journalists and the Irish Print Union v Sisk* [1992] ILRM 96, Keane J and, on appeal, the Supreme Court confronted the ugly patchwork of statutory law which comprises the compendium of trade union legislation over the past two centuries. From 1800 to 1992, when Ireland was part of a political union with Britain, the model of legislation was to apply to both islands unless the particular Act contained a specific delimitation to the contrary. After Independence, the Adaptation of Enactments Act 1922 went some way towards integrating this volume of legislation into the new regime. The solutions it adopted were inevitably rough at the edges and failed to concentrate on the underlying socio-political context which spawned the particular pieces of legislation and on how that context had been modified, not only by the passage of time but also by the fact of independence.

In the instant case, the NUJ was a trade union registered under the relevant legislation in Britain. It had over two thousand members in Ireland and carried on negotiations on behalf of its members with employers in both Britain and Ireland. It had a negotiation licence here but was not registered as a trade union under the Trade Union Acts 1871 to 1982. The IPU was a trade union registered here under that corpus of legislation.

The two unions agreed that the IPU's engagements should be transferred to the NUJ. They sent the necessary documentation to the respondent, the Registrar of Friendly Societies, for his approval. Having taken counsel's advice, the Registrar declined to adhere to the application as he was satisfied that jurisdiction under the Trade Union Act 1975 was limited to trade unions registered in the State except in the case of a body of persons expressly provided for under s. 9, and that the NUJ could not be regarded as a trade union for the purposes of the 1975 Act.

Keane J dismissed an application by the unions for judicial review. He thought that nothing in the Acts would justify the court in imputing to the legislature at any stage an intention to bring within its scope bodies properly described as trade unions under the law of another country and having no connection of any sort with Ireland. For analysis of Keane J's decision, see Anthony Quinn, 'Vital Issues in Trade Union Law' (1991) 85 Incorp L Soc of Ireland Gazette 239.

The Supreme Court reversed Keane J. Finlay CJ (Hederman, O'Flaherty and Egan JJ concurring) did not consider that counsel for the unions in the High Court should have conceded that, if the unions came within the definition of 'trade unions' in ss. 2 to 4 of the 1975 Act, it followed inevitably that the provision of these sections would become applicable to any trade union in any part of the world, even though it had no connection with Ireland. It was quite clear that the terms of s. 2 referred to engagements here. This arose from the fact that the entire scheme of the relevant portion of the 1975 Act was to protect the rights of members against an unfair imposition of a transfer of engagements, and the members involved were clearly members within the State. Thus, for example, the provisions of s. 3(1)(e) requiring publication in at least one daily newspaper published in the State would be applicable only if the provisions dealt with by the section affected the rights of members of trade unions who were within the State. Furthermore, the Chief Justice was satisfied that the precondition contained in s. 2(4)(a) that the union should have undertaken to fulfil the engagements must, in the case of a transfer of engagements to a union not registered in the State, ordinarily involve a capacity to negotiate with employers within the State, 'in the case at least of a trade union consisting of a combination of workmen'.

Article 40.6.1° of the Constitution featured, by way of addendum, in the judgments of both High Court and Supreme Court. Keane J considered that paragraph (iii) of the subsection, guaranteeing 'the right of freedom of association', did not assist the unions' case. It was not in dispute that the right in question might be regulated and controlled by law and that was what the legislation under consideration sought to do. The constitutional guarantee of right to form associations and unions did not require him to read the legislation so as to extend the benefits of the Act to unions in other countries, except so far as the legislation itself actually provided.

This interpretation of the international remit of the Constitution has the attraction of simplicity in transmitting to the legislature, in the exercise of its undoubted regulatory function, the *exclusive* entitlement of breathing an extra-territorial dimension into Article 40.6.1°, paragraph (iii). Of the several constitutional rights, the right to form associations certainly involves considerable difficulty in developing a coherent convincing judicial analysis of its international remit. But the difficulty of this task is no reason to settle for the solution of letting the legislature determine the issue. It is quite clear that, in formulating legislation affecting trade unions which has an international dimension, the Oireachtas is likely to be seeking a solution to a problem with significant political dimensions. The last thing on its mind is the international remit of the constitutional right to form associations. More fundamentally it may be asked what is the basis for the holding that the Oireachtas is charged with such a significant constitutional function. Admittedly, the willingness by the judiciary on occasion to cede such a role to the Oireachtas is striking: see our comments in the 1988 Review, 442-3.

In the Supreme Court it appeared to Finlay CJ that the right of members of a trade union to vote in favour of a transfer of its engagements to another union, whether one registered in the State or not, was 'a necessary and valuable expansion of the general right to form trade unions and belong to them.' If ss. 2 to 4 of the 1975 Act were interpreted as preventing this, they would fail to be justified in the public interest. McCarthy J expressed the view that the constitutionally guaranteed right of free association 'should not be lightly hampered; if the enforcement of that right requires a more liberal construction of restrictive legislation, then so be it'.

While this may be true, the process by which the Supreme Court reached its conclusion seems to have concentrated on considerations in which Article 40.1.6° played only a secondary role.

TRANSFER OF UNDERTAKINGS

In *Yorke and Tuite v Teenoso Ltd (in receivership)* [1992] ELR 161, the Tribunal held that acceptance of a redundancy payment by the employer of a company when it was being purchased by another company did not prevent the continuity of the employment of that employee from being preserved having regard to Reg. 5 of the European Communities (Safeguarding of Employee's Rights on Transfer of Undertakings) Regulations 1980 (SI No. 306 of 1980).

UNFAIR DISMISSAL

Fairness The position of an employer responding to a suspicion that an employee is guilty of dishonesty is not an easy one. If the employer dismisses the employee, the employer must be able to establish that his belief in the employee's guilt was a reasonable one and furthermore that he has carried out a full and fair investigation in the course of which the requirements of natural justice have been satisfied: *Hennessy v Read and Write Shop Ltd* (UD 192/78).

In *Burke v Form Print Ltd* [1992] ELR 163, the employer's manager, while doing his best in a difficult situation, failed both of these requirements. Cheques had been stolen from the company and one of them had been cashed at the company's bank. The manager's claimed identification from the bank's video of the claimant as the person who cashed the cheque did not greatly impress the Tribunal as the manager had earlier claimed to identify the claimant at a point in the video which was not in fact the relevant time. The manager had conducted an investigation in which he had interviewed the claimant, who denied any involvement but made no reference to an alibi. The manager nonetheless was aware of the possibility of an alibi, which the Gardaí were checking out. The Tribunal held that the manager's belief in the guilt of the claimant had not been reasonable and that the investigation did not meet the standard requirements of fullness and fairness.

In *Cooke v Ashmore Hotel Ltd* [1992] ELR 1, the claimant had commenced work as a bar manager in 1988. Problems began to emerge when difficulties concerning stock shortages arose some twelve months later. The plaintiff's status changed to that of barman. Some months later, the proprietor approached him and advised him to take a month off, during which time a stocktake wold be carried out, and that he could return to his job depending on its outcome. Three weeks later, the proprietor indicated to the claimant that he could return but that he would be watched closely all the time.

The Employment Appeals Tribunal held that what had been said to the claimant was tantamount to a dismissal and that he had been entitled to regard it as such. Nevertheless the dismissal had been fair. It was not the Tribunal's function to determine the guilt or innocence of an employee who had been dismissed. Its sole function was to determine the fairness or otherwise of the dismissal. In the circumstances, the respondent had satisfied the Tribunal that its belief that the claimant were responsible for the stock shortages was a reasonable one and that the claimant had been given every opportunity to give his explanation for the shortages. The investigation carried out by the respondent when the claimant was bar manager had been fair and reasonable and the claimant's failure to offer any satisfactory explanation for the shortages had been 'inconsistent with his duties and obligations as bar manager'. The claimant had been given every reasonable opportunity to defend himself in relation to the shortages. These had been brought to his notice on each occasion when a stocktake was done and had been discussed on an ongoing basis with him.

Illegality The question whether an unfair dismissals claim can be maintained in respect of an employment contract tainted by illegality is one raising troublesome issues of justice. Very often, in cases where the employee colludes with a system of tax-fiddling, for example, the employer is acting, not out a sense of generosity to the employee, but rather in a coldly calculating way of reducing his wages bill, since the saving gained from non-deduction of tax often means that the employee will be willing to work for less gross wages than would otherwise have been the market rate.

In *Ebanks v Vinehall Ltd* [1992] ELR 5, the claimant had received overtime payments in cash. His representative told the Tribunal that he had pay slips which recorded overtime payments which were taxed. The company secretary told the Tribunal that the practice of paying cash for overtime had been established before the claimant commenced employment there.

The Tribunal held that it could entertain the proceedings. The parties were not equally at fault. The claimant had come into a situation already in existence and had told the Tribunal that, as far as he was concerned, he had paid his full tax.

In *Tracey v Cheadle Investments Ltd* [1991] ELR 130, the Tribunal held on the evidence that the claimant had at no stage entered into negotiations or an arrangement with the respondent to evade the payment of tax or PRSI and that accordingly the employment contract was not tainted with illegality.

In *Leacy v Harney t/a Harney Stores* [1991] ELR 213, a supermarket proprietor dismissed the claimants, who were sisters, after they had admitted to a garda that they had for some time engaged in a process of discounting goods at well below the retail price. The claimants asserted that the employer was aware that the staff operated a discount system. One of the claimants had been on sick leave and was still under psychiatric treatment—a fact that she deliberately kept from the employer. In evidence she claimed that she admitted a discount of over £1,000 because she had been so distressed she 'just wanted to get out of' the premises. The other sister gave evidence that she had admitted to discount of £1,000 only after constant pressure from the employer and for her sister's sake.

The Tribunal held that the dismissals had not been unfair. It was not for the employer to decide whether the first claimant's statements had been made under personal stress, because information on her condition had been withheld from him. There had been no evidence in her behaviour to indicate a psychiatric problem or a lack of responsibility. Whilst the second claimant's main concern had been to protect her sister by not disclosing her true condition to the employer, '[n]o one could accept that this could be rational or permissible behaviour'. She had breached a relationship of trust and her employer could not have trusted her again.

Incapacity In *Caulfield v Waterford Foundry Ltd* [1991] ELR 137, the Tribunal held that a dismissal for incapacity had not been unfair. The claimant had been injured in 1988 in the course of his employment. He had subsequently taken a case for damages in which it had been contended on his behalf that he would never again be fit for heavy work. Evidence to the Tribunal from the respondent company's doctor supported this view. The advice of a rheumatologist to whom the claimant was referred was similar. Both doctors considered that the claimant would be suitable to do a lighter type of work. The evidence on behalf of the respondent company was that there was no light work which he could do. The jobs that were available required employees to be able to run and bend and to operate below knee level, if required.

The facts and analysis in this case are reminiscent of the Supreme Court decision in *Rafferty v Parsons (CA) of Ireland Ltd* [1987] ILRM 98, analysed by Binchy, '"Light Work": A Dilemma for Employers', 82 Incorp L Soc of Ireland Gazette 47 (1988). If an employer were not entitled to dismiss an employee for incapacity where the employee is capable of doing only light work and only heavy work is available, troublesome issues would arise in a case where the employee was injured from doing the heavy work. The two primary questions would relate to the nature and scope of the duty of care in the circumstances and the possible application of the defence of voluntary assumption of risk. There has yet to be a clear decision in which the individuating characterisation adopted by the Supreme Court in *McComiskey v McDermott* [1974] IR 75 in respect of persons engaged in motor rallying has been applied to the employment context. On this theme, see McMahon & Binchy, *Irish Law of Torts* (2nd ed., 1990), 100-1, 336-8.

Constructive dismissal In *O'Donnell v Browning & Co.* [1991] ELR 210, the Tribunal held that an employee had not been constructively dismissed when she left her employment after a dispute concerning a payment which her employer declined to make in respect of part of the time she had been on sick leave. The Tribunal was satisfied that there had been no pay arrangement for this period. The employer had attempted to facilitate the employer in every possible way. The Tribunal was of the view that the employer had been 'in a highly emotional state following her return to work and not in a position to rationalise her situation'.

Revocation In *Hegarty and Cregan v Easy Sleep Textiles Ltd* [1991] ELR 205, the Tribunal held that the revocation of a decision to dismiss employees, who resisted a request to work overtime on the basis of a prior commitment, could not be unilaterlly revoked by the employer after the employer had tried to withdraw the decision based on certain terms which were not acceptable to the employees. The decision should be regarded as one based on its own facts. There can scarcely be a universal principle that revocation of a decision to dismiss is inevitably defeated by a prior unsuccessful negotiation with the dismissed employee. Such an unqualified principle would defeat rather than facilitate the policies underlying the Unfair Dismissals Act 1977.

Indefinite suspension In *Deegan v Dunnes Stores* [1992] ELR 184, the claimants were suspended indefinitely for refusing to sign an undertaking to participate in all further stocktaking and to adhere in future to all management decisions with regard to day-off arrangements with notice. The Tribunal held that the indefinite suspension was 'a total injustice', since 'an employee is entitled to know the nature and extent of any disciplinary action against him'. The suspension amounted to a dismissal since the refusal to sign the undertaking meant that the claimants could never return to work.

The Tribunal found the dismissal to be unfair because it was too severe a penalty. In considering the question of redress, however, it found that the claimants had contributed to their loss by their lack of co-operation with management, in particular with regard to stocktaking.

PART-TIME WORKERS

The Worker Protection (Regular Part-Time Employees) Act 1991 radically improves the position of part-time workers. For an account of the former law, see Whyte (1989) 11 DULJ 74. The Act seeks to ensure that part-time workers who are normally expected to work for at least eight hours a week for an employer and who have completed thirteen weeks' continuous service with the employer will enjoy the same protection under labour legislation as full-time workers. Whether the Act fully achieves this goal has been questioned by Leo Flynn in an incisive analysis of the Act's provisions in (1991) 13 DULJ 55.

Land Law

CONVEYANCING

Assents In *Mohan v Roche* [1991] 2 IR 560, a widow was personal representative to her late husband's estate. He had died intestate, his house being held under a fee farm grant. By deed of family arrangement two years after his death, their nine children 'granted, released and conveyed' to the widow for natural love and affection any interest they had in the house. The widow died testate. Her personal representative subsequently contracted to sell the house. One of the purchaser's requisitions was that the executor furnish a written assent by the widow, as personal representative of her deceased husband. It transpired that no such assent had ever been executed. The purchaser insisted on the curing of this omission. The vendor resisted on the basis that no such assent was required since the entire beneficial interest in the property had been vested in the widow by the execution of the deed of arrangement; the vendor also contended that, if an assent was required, the deed constituted an implied assent; finally the vendor argued that the widow had acquired a possessory title to the house.

After a close examination of the terms of ss. 52(2), 52(2) and 53(1) of the Succession Act 1965, Keane J concluded that the language used in these provisions indicated clearly that the draftsman had been concerned with the transfer by the personal representative of the relevant estate or interest in the land to other persons who became entitled to that estate or interest by reason of the provisions of a will or the distribution of the estate of the deceased on intestacy. There was no indication that the draftsman had considered it essential that the personal representative should also execute such an assent *where he himself was the person entitled to the property*, either by reason of a bequest or devise in the will or because of the distribution of the estate on intestacy. While it might well be *desirable* that a personal representative should sign an assent in circumstances such as the present case, this was 'far from saying that it is a necessary link in the title'.

Keane J was fortified in reaching this conclusion by the criticism of Pennycuick J's decision in *In re King's Trusts; Assheton v Boyne* [1964] 2 WLR 913 which had been made by Farrand (108 The Solicitor 698) and Garner (28 Conveyancer 298). For further critical analysis of *King's Trusts*, see Paul Coughlan's penetrating comments in (1991) 13 DULJ 155.

Having held in favour of the vendor on the important issue of the necessity for an assent, Keane J went on to express considerable doubt about the strength of the vendor's other arguments. As to the deed of family arrangement, he did not think that it could be read as an assent by the widow to the vesting in herself of the estate to which she was entitled on her late husband's intestacy. Similarly, the exclusive intention of the widow in executing the will had been to vest the interest in the property in those whom she wished to benefit; in no sense could it be read as an express or implied assent by the widow of any interest in the property in herself. Keane J also evinced considerable reluctance to accept the vendor's argument that the purchaser should accept a possessory title. The Supreme Court in *Perry v Woodfarm Homes Ltd* [1975] IR 104 had confirmed the long accepted rule that there is no 'parliamentary conveyance' of the grantee's interest to a squatter at the end of the limitation period; there were clearly serious difficulties in holding that a vendor was entitled to insist on a purchaser's accepting such a title where he had contracted for documentary title.

Easements　In *Drennan v McMahon*, High Court, 30 October 1991, where premises were being conveyed by the defendants to the plaintiffs, a dispute arose about whether there was a way-leave over adjoining premises, with ancillary rights of entry. The defendants contended that there was and served two completion notices on the plaintiffs. The plaintiffs responded with a Vendor and Purchaser Summons. The parties did not seek to make the owners of the adjoining property parties to the proceedings.

The defendants argued that, when the two premises had been in separate ownership, a way-leave had been acquired against the adjoining property which inured to the benefit of the premises that were being sold to the plaintiffs. The defendants had acquired the fee simple in both premises but, during the period it was the fee simple owner, before it had sold the adjoining property, there had been no unity of possession because the premises now being sold to the plaintiffs had been subject to a controlled tenancy. Thus, the defendants argued, the easements that had affected the adjoining property continued to do so undisturbed by the defendants' acquisition of the fee simple interest.

Carroll J was less than fully convinced by this argument: the owners of the adjoining property might well succeed in preventing the enforcement of the way-leave on the basis that it had not been disclosed to them at the time of the sale of the premises to them. But she had a more fundamental reason for rejecting the defendants' argument: it was one that could be made only if the owners of the adjoining property were in court to respond to it. It was not possible for the court to give a judgment binding them if they were not parties. The plaintiffs were totally within their rights in refusing to close because of the non-disclosure to them before the sale of the position regarding the services:

> It is for the defendants as vendors to ascertain the legal position regarding services. . . . It is not for this court to force the purchaser to complete a contract when he does not know if he has an enforceable way-leave with ancillary rights of entry.

Having determined this issue in favour of the plaintiffs, Carroll J considered that it was not necessary for her to decide a separate question that arose regarding enquiries as to whether a road had been taken in charge by the local authority. Whether these enquiries should be made by a purchaser before the contract or whether they constituted a proper requisition on title was left unresolved.

Passing of risk   In its *Report on Land Law and Conveyancing Law: (3) The Passing of Risk from Vendor to Purchaser* (LRC 39-1991), the Law Reform Commission puts forward a compact and sensible series of proposals. The issue is one calling for reform. At present it is the purchaser who from the date of the contract bears the loss of damage caused to the property by fire, flood, storm or other elements. The Law Society's Standard Conditions of Sale go some way towards improving the purchaser's position, but not all sales of land are governed by these conditions. A purchaser who seeks to ensure that the property is insured from the date of the contract can experience practical difficulties, especially in cases where the property is sold by auction.

Several strategies have been suggested or adopted abroad, ranging from granting the purchaser a right to claim on the vendor's insurance policy to treating as a frustrating event the destruction or occurrence of substantial damage to the property between the date of the contract and the completion of purchase.

The Commission proposes that the risk of damage should remain with the vendor until completion unless the purchaser has gone into possession of the property prior to completion.

The Commission recommends that, where substantial damage occurs before the risk has passed to the purchaser, the purchaser shall have the right either to rescind the contract or to require completion of the contract with due abatement of the purchase price. The vendor would have the right to insist on the completion of the contract where the damage is *not* substantial. It goes on to propose that the vendor should be under an obligation to notify the purchaser of the damage; the purchaser would have ten days within which to rescind. Disputes as to whether or not the damage is substantial would be decided by binding arbitration.

The Commission proposes that, where the transaction proceeds to completion, the vendor should as a general rule be entitled on completion to receive interest from the purchaser to cover the period from the completion date fixed by the contract or the date on which the damage has occurred (whichever should be the later) to the date of actual closing, at a rate to be equivalent to the last long-dated Government security. In cases where the purchaser had contended that the damage was substantial and it was later established or conceded that it was not, the rate of interest would be 4% higher than the lower rate.

The Commission goes on to deal with a special case that arises where a purchaser is in delay in completing and the vendor has already served a valid notice requiring the purchaser to complete before the damage occurred. If the damage is *not* substantial, the Commission recommends that the vendor should be entitled to interest on the entire of the purchase money, seven days from a date after the service of the completion notice to the date of completion, the purchaser continuing to be entitled to an abatement of the purchase money in respect of the damage. The Commission makes no special recommendation to cover situations where substantial damage occurs after service of a completion notice since 'the purchaser should still have a right to rescind and completion by the purchaser is likely to be based on terms negotiated between the parties' (para 5.4).

Service of completion notices In its *Report on Land Law and Conveyancing Law: (4) Service of Completion Notices* (LRC 40-1991), the Law Reform Commission recommends the enactment of a statutory provision containing two rules. The *first* is that, once a vendor has served a completion notice on the purchaser, he may be required to complete, giving vacant possession and discharging any encumbrance, within ten days of being requested to do so by the purchaser. The *second* is that the vendor should not be deemed to be other than able, ready and willing to complete at the date of service of a completion notice:

(a) by reason of being unable to deliver vacant possession at that date, or
(b) by reason of not having discharged any mortgage which may affect the property.

The thrust of these proposals is to overrule by statute the unanimous decision of the Supreme Court (Walsh, Griffin and McCarthy JJ) in *Viscount Securities Ltd v Kennedy*, 6 May 1986. There the Court had interpreted clause 28 of the 1978 edition of the Law Society's general Conditions of Sale as requiring the vendor to be in a position to give vacant possession at the time of service of a completion notice. The presence of a large quantity of spoil on the lands, unknown to the vendor's solicitor thus rendered the vendor unable to complete at that time. Clearly this result has not great attraction from the standpoint of common sense and practicality since the lands were being sold for the purposes of development. Nevertheless, once it is accepted that an ability to complete the sale embraces the ability to deliver vacant possession, the Court's conclusion is hard to gainsay. The Commission's examination of English athorities—scarce enough on the precise issue— leads it to support the argument that the absence of vacant possession should be characterised as rendering the vendor unable to complete only where it prevents the vendor from showing a good title. (Perhaps the recommendation would have been improved by the addition of the word 'merely' between 'reason' and 'of' in clause (a): see p. 27 of the Report.)

The strongest argument against a general legal rule (as opposed to contractual provision) requiring the vendor to have vacant possession at the time of service of the completion notice is the practical difficulty that it would create, especially in relation to the sale of residential property. If a family have contracted to sell their home and to buy another, it does not seem very practicable that service by them of a completion notice on a dilatory pur- chaser of their home should require them to put all their possessions into storage.

The Commission notes that, following the *Viscount Securities* decision, 'concern was expressed particularly having regard to the judgment of Griffin J' that a vendor might be required to have discharged any money charges prior to giving a valid completion notice. This would have imposed hardship on the vendor since in many cases it would have required the vendor to raise funds, probably by way of bridging finance, to enable the vendor to discharge the money charge. Accordingly the Commission proposes that any amend- ment of the law in this area should extend to the release of charges as well as to the giving of vacant possession.

JUDGMENT MORTGAGE

In *Allied Irish Banks plc v Griffin* [1992] ILRM 590, Denham J reiterated the strict approach traditionally adopted towards interpreting the formal requirements of the Judgment Mortgage (Ireland) Act 1850. S. 6 requires that the affidavit to register the judgment as a mortgage should state 'the title, trade or profession of . . . the defendant. . . .' Here the affidavit referred to the defendant as a widow; it failed to refer to the fact that she was a farmer. Invoking a number of judicial precedents (especially *Crosbie v Murphy*, 8 ICLR 301 (1858)) and academic authority (J.C. Wylie's *Irish Land Law* (2nd ed.), 709), Denham J held that the word 'widow' connoted marital status rather than a title, trade or profession as required by the Act. If the defendant had *no* clear trade or profession, she could properly have been described as 'gentlewoman' or 'widow', but since she was a farmer, the expression used was a misdescription and thus rendered the affidavit invalid. Accordingly Denham J refused the bank's application for a declaration that the sum of the £165,000 plus interest stood well charged on the defendant's interest in three properties on foot of the judgment mortgage.

LANDLORD AND TENANT

Constitutional aspects In *Shanley v The Commissioner of Public Works in Ireland and the Attorney General,* High Court, 31 October 1991, the plaintiff sought a declaration that s. 4 of the Landlord and Tenant (Amendment) Act 1980 as amended by s. 14 of the Landlord and Tenant (Amendment) Act 1984 was invalid having regard to the provisions of Articles 40.3 and 43 of the Constitution. S. 4(2) provides that (subject to the subsequent subsections of s. 4) the 1980 Act does not bind a State authority in its capacity as lessor or immediate lessor of any premises. The plaintiff's case depended on the application of the Landlord and Tenant Act 1963 to the tenancy that had been granted to him in 1972 giving him rights which were taken away by s. 4(2) of the 1980 Act.

The defendants contended that the Landlord and Tenant Act never applied to State property and that s. 4(2) merely restated what was the law; if that was correct, then the constitutionality of s. 4(2) did not arise. The 1922 Constitution was of crucial relevance. Article 11 set out the different kinds of state property and provided that it should be controlled and administered by the Oireachtas according to such regulations and provisions as should from time to time be approved by legislation. It also provided that State property should not be alienated but might in the public interest be from time to time granted by way of lease or licence to be worked or enjoyed under the authority and subject to the control of the Oireachtas. No such lease or licence could be for a term exceeding ninety-nine years, or be renewable by its terms.

The State Lands Act 1924 incorporated all the major aspects of Article 11. It provided for the granting of leases and licences (excluding mines and minerals) for periods not exceeding ninety-nine years if in the opinion of the Minister for Finance this was in the public interest. The parties might agree upon such covenants, conditions and agreements, other than for renewal, as the Minister for Finance considered proper or desirable in the public interest. Details of all proposed leases and licences had to be laid before each House of the Oireachtas; the Oireachtas had power to modify their terms.

The Landlord and Tenant Act 1931 contained several features that were incompatible with the regime for State property. Its provision that the courts should fix the terms of a new tenancy was inconsistent with control by the Oireachtas. The 1937 Act did not exclude mines and minerals nor did it require that the public interest should be taken into account.

Carroll J was satisfied that as a matter of construction the 1931 Act did not apply to State property. Thus s. 4(2) of the 1980 Act took away no right of the plaintiff, and the question of its constitutionality did not arise. The decision of *Commissioners of Public Works v Kavanagh* [1962] IR 216 did not cast any doubt on this interpretation. It dealt with the position of the State as *lessee* under the Landlord and Tenant Act 1931. Carroll J saw nothing inconsistent in the State's having statutory rights as a lessee under the 1931 Act if it fulfilled the statutory requirements for a lessee. She took no final position on this question, however, since the point did not arise and had not been argued.

Lease or licence?   The courts have faced difficult policy issues when called on to determine whether a particular relationship is one of lease or licence. Formalistic solutions can do a disservice to the complexity of these issues and the formidable difficulty of their resolution. Putting the matter simply, contemporary political mores support the perception of tenants—even of commercial premises—as persons worthy of social protection through law; legislation has sought to encourage security of tenure and proportionality of rent. Faced with this thrust of social policy, lawyers advising lessors have understandably sought ways of mitigating, or sidestepping, its effects. See, e.g., *Bank of Ireland v Fitzmaurice* [1989] ILRM 452, analysed in the 1989 Review, 271-2. One appealing device is that of licence. If would-be tenants can be shepherded into that pen, then the paternalistic legislation applying to leases can effectively be circumvented.

To what extent should the courts intervene to prevent such devices? Is there such an important public policy that courts should characterise as leases contractual arrangements that fulfil the formal criteria of licences? Thus far, the answer from the courts is incoherent. One may reasonably infer from the decisions a desire to favour the characterisation of a licence, but the principles that have emerged fall well short of a frank articulation of the underlying social policies.

In *Texaco (Ireland) Ltd v Murphy t/a Shannonway Service Station*, High Court, 17 July 1991, Barron J had to deal with a long-running dispute. The defendant had operated a filling station owned by the plaintiff since 1969. He had entered into possession on the basis of an oral assurance that he would be a tenant under a lease that was being prepared, though he had signed a licence agreement with the plaintiff company providing only for a three-month licence. Every three months thereafter he had signed a similar agreement. Although it was the plaintiff's policy not to issue leases, the defendant was not told that he would never be given a lease. In 1973 the defendant was required to sell all the stock on the premises to the plaintiffs and to vacate the premises. The purpose of this was apparently to prevent the defendant from obtaining a right to a new tenancy under the provisions of the Landlord and Tenant Acts. He went back into occupation the next day, and a new licence, on terms identical with the previous ones, was given to him three weeks later, though in a corporate capacity. The licence agreements continued over subsequent years with the corporate capacity being dropped in 1976.

In 1981, when a three-month licence had expired, the plaintiff offered the defendant a statutory three year licence, which he refused to accept. In 1985, the plaintiff threatened legal proceedings but the defendant persisted in his stance. Finally in 1988 the plaintiff served a written demand for possession; the defendant refused to give up possession and the plaintiff issued proceedings.

Barron J was impressed by the fact that the defendant had been promised a lease before he had taken up possession in 1969:

> For whatever reason, the plaintiff was anxious to retain the defendant as an operator of the station and notwithstanding all his requests for a lease and objections to the agreements being offered to him, no one came out openly and said, you will never get a lease and it is not company policy to grant leases. I accept that the defendant would not have gone into possession of the station if he had been made aware that he was not a tenant and would never be granted a lease; and that if this had been made clear to him he would not have stayed.

In Barron J's view, the plaintiff had agreed to give the defendant a tenancy of the station. Its terms had been agreed in 1969 before the defendant had taken up the position, at a meeting between the plaintiff's assistant regional manager and the defendant. However, the commencement date for the term had not been agreed. This had prevented an agreement for a lease from coming into being. Once the defendant had been given the licence agreement to sign, it should have been clear to him that this was not the lease he had been promised. The question therefore was whether the observance of the terms of the licence agreement amounted to a concluded agreement between the parties whereby the defendant held the premises as *tenant* from the plaintiff on those terms.

Barron J came to the conclusion that the answer was in the affirmative. The plaintiff's admission to the defendant that he was entering as a tenant under a lease that was being prepared overrode the defendant's admission, in what was acknowledged to be a temporary document, that he was using the premises for three months only as a licensee:

> The normal implication from the granting of exclusive possession would be that a tenancy was being created. It is only where such exclusive possession is given as a personal privilege that no tenancy comes into being. If the grantor seeks to rely upon personal privilege, the onus is on him to establish that. Here, no attempt was made to do so other than in the licence agreement which in [the] circumstances was repudiated by the representation that the lease was being prepared.

No lease had ever been produced. Nor had the tenancy created by the entry into possession by the defendant ever been terminated. It had not been argued that the signing of any of the licence agreements constituted a surrender of the tenancy in favour of a licence. Nor could such contention have succeeded since the defendant had always maintained that he had a tenancy.

Barron J did not consider that the events of 1973 had altered the position. He accepted the defendant's evidence that what had happened had been devised and carried out by the plaintiff and that the defendant had never had any intention of giving up his interest in the premises:

> The plaintiff has never acknowledged this tenancy. For this reason, no step has ever been taken to determine it. It is therefore still subsisting.

The plaintiff had argued, on the basis of *Irish Shell and BP Ltd v John Costello Ltd* [1984] IR 511, that, once the final licence had been terminated, it was entitled to possession following a demand for possession. Barron J distinguished *Irish Shell* on the basis that in that case the licence agreements had been held previously to the tenancy agreements for fixed periods and that the issue accordingly had been the nature of the relationship that had come into existence *on expiry of the tenancy*. In the instant case the tenancy had not been coextensive with the successive periods covered by the licence agreements.

Shopping centre leases   In *Wanze Properties (Ireland) Ltd v Mastertron Ltd, Sui Man Lam and Choi Lin and Lam* [1992] ILRM 746, Murphy J addressed a number of issues of general commercial interest. The case concerned a shopping centre in the Dublin suburb of Hartstown. It consisted of a large supermarket and seven units of about a thousand square feet. The centre depended on a local trade as there were bigger centres with more extensive facilities available to potential customers willing to travel even relatively small distances.

One of the units had been under-leased to a person who used it as a bicycle shop. When this business did not prosper, he surrendered his interest to the immediate lessor, the first plaintiff in the case, who agreed to grant a new underlease to Mr and Mrs Lam. The Lams paid £12,500 to their predecessor to acquire this interest. They obtained planning permission for a change of user to a Chinese take-away. They invested £35,000 in converting the unit to that use.

The head lessors, the defendants in the case, withheld their consent for this change of user. Murphy J was called to decide whether they had acted unreasonably. He derived assistance from the test laid down by Lynch J in *OHS Ltd v Green Property Co. Ltd* [1986] IR 39. This had also involved a shopping centre, though one much larger than in the instant case. The landlord had withheld its consent to a change of user to a building society. Lynch J was reluctant to set a standard that would require the tenant to show that the landlord was acting capriciously or arbitrarily; the court had to take the circumstances of *both* parties into account. He had held that the landlord had not acted unreasonably, since an excessive number of 'dead frontages' which financial institutions involved inhibited the variety of retail outlets on which the success of a shopping centre depended.

In the instant case, since the main part of the business of a Chinese take-away occurs in the evening and the prospects of a significant lunch-time business were not high, the problem of the dead frontage arose, even though the Lams were willing to keep their premises open throughout the day.

The expert evidence in the case was to the effect that a particular range of desirable tenants, such as retailers of fashion goods, electrical goods or jewellery, could not be attracted to a relatively small neighbourhood shopping centre, because people looking for more specialised or expensive goods were more likely to travel the extra distance to a larger shopping centre where all of these facilities would be available. More natural tenants would be newsagents and pharmacies (which were already in the centre) as well, perhaps, as hairdressers, fresh food shops, hardware and dry cleaners. The expert witnesses disagreed on the prospects of actually attracting tenants of the latter category.

Murphy J concluded that the defendants had reasonable grounds for believing that they could succeed in attracting such a tenant, even if it should transpire in the long run that their hopes were not realised. It was true that the relationship between the defendants and the intermediate lessors was that of a 10,000 year lease, at the equivalent of a peppercorn rent; but the whole purpose of creating that structure rather than completing an outright sale was to enable the head lessors to maintain an effective operation of the shopping centre. Thus, Murphy J considered that the reasonableness or unreasonableness of the head lessors' refusal to consent to the change of use had to be evaluated by that consideration and not on the basis of their financial stake or interest in the premises. In the circumstances their refusal was *not* unreasonable.

Murphy J declined to resolve two other arguments made by the plaintiff because they did not fall within the subject-matter of the proceedings, which related to the question of the reasonableness of the defendants' refusal to consent to the change of use. The first of these arguments was that, though the *intermediate lessees* were not entitled to acquire a fee simple interest in the premises, they could create a lease in favour of the Lams which would comply with condition 7(a) of s. 10 of the Landlord and Tenant (Ground Rents) (No. 2) Act 1978, and that this would entitle the Lams to acquire the fee simple interest in the property thus demised to them. The second argument was that the restrictive covenant could be defeated by s. 29 of the Landlord and Tenant (Ground Rents) Act 1967 which provides in effect that an action will not constitute a breach of covenant if the user amounts to a development authorised by planning permission. Neither of these arguments, it was agreed, could prevail if the covenants in the lease protected or enhanced the amenities of any land occupied by the defendants: see s. 28(2)(a) of the 1978 Act.

Murphy J noted that the issue would then reduce itself to the question whether 'amenities' in s. 28 connoted exclusively the *physical* advantages enjoyed in connection with the premises or included the *commercial* advantages that could be derived from control of the use that could be made of different units in a shopping centre.

Sporting leases   In *O'Farrell v Cochrane* [1991] 2 IR 513, Murphy J gave guidance as to how the court should fix the rent for a sporting lease under s. 6 of the Landlord and Tenant (Amendment) Act 1971. The Act gives certain rights of renewal to sporting leases. S. 6(1) provides that, in determining the rent, the court is to fix a fair rent for the grant of a lease of the property for the purpose of carrying on the sport. S. 6(2) provides as follows:

> In fixing the rent the Court shall have regard to the general intention of this Act in relation to sports clubs which is the advancement of outdoor sports, games and recreations and the preservation of open spaces for the common good and, without prejudice to such other considerations as it considers relevant, may take into account the rent or other sum previously paid for the property by the sports club and any covenants and conditions under which it was so paid, to the rent paid by other sports clubs of the same kind in the same or a comparable locality, to the contribution made by the sports club to the enhancement of the property, and to the price paid by any person who is a necessary party to the granting of the lease in the acquisition of his estate or interest.

Murphy J noted that the Oireachtas had not qualified the effect of the several considerations mentioned in s. 6(2). In directing what should be taken into account, however, the Oireachtas had indicated the general approach which the court was to take and the factors which should influence it. Murphy J did not accept that it would be mandatory on the court, having regard to the terms of the section, to follow slavishly each of these considerations. It seemed to him that the court would be bound to have regard to them but might well dismiss them for good and sufficient reasons; even where those factors were properly taken into account there must be considerable difficulty in determining the weight and value to be given to each factor.

The case before Murphy J involved a consideration of s. 6 at one remove. The dispute concerned an arbitration in relation to a lease incorporating in a schedule to it the terms of s. 6. The arbitrator had come to a determination which, on one view, involved the assumption that his only task was to ascertain the full market rental value of the premises and then make a deduction from it based on a calculation of only one factor—the additions made by the club members since the date of the lease and the appropriate element of those improvements which should be attributed to the landlord. Murphy J rejected this interpretation. It seemed inconceivable that the distinguished arbitrator, having had the benefit of the argument of learned leading counsel, should have so misconceived his function as to think that this process would give a fair rent. What the arbitrator was seeking to express was the manner in which one dealt with *the particular issue in relation to which the parties were at odds*. In underscoring this matter, he had not referred in his award to the other factors which manifestly he had considered.

In *Fitzgerald (Trustees of Castleknock Tennis Club) v Corcoran* [1991] ILRM 545, two net points of interpretation arose on a consultative case stated to the Supreme Court by Lardner J. The first was whether the applicant lessee of a sporting lease was entitled to make a claim to a right to enlarge its interest into a fee simple in part only of the demised premises, notwithstanding that the notice it had served under s. 4 of the Landlord and Tenant (Ground Rents) Act 1967 referred to the *entire* of the property and did not by its express terms make any alternative claim to the fee simple in part only of the property. In the light of the decision of the former Supreme Court of *Corr v Ivers* [1949] IR 245 Finlay CJ (Griffin and O'Flaherty JJ concurring) had no difficulty in answering this question in the affirmative.

The second question, premised on the affirmative answer to the first, was whether the lessee was entitled to invoke s. 14 of the 1978 Act to entitle it to acquire the fee simple in the Club House and such ground as was subsidiary and ancillary thereto. S. 14 provides as follows:

(1) Where a person holds land under a lease (in this section referred to

as a partly-built lease) which would entitle him to acquire the fee simple but for the fact that the portion of the land which is not covered by the permanent buildings is not wholly subsidiary and ancillary to those buildings, the following provisions of this section shall have effect.
(2) The partly-built lease shall, for the purpose of this Act, be deemed to compromise two separate leases as follows:

(a) one lease (in this section referred to as the built-on lease) comprising that portion of the land demised by the partly-built lease which is covered by the permanent buildings, together with so much of the land as is subsidiary and ancillary to those buildings, and
(b) the other lease (in this section referred to as the vacant lease) comprising the residue of the said land.

The Chief Justice noted that it was possible to construe the phrase in subs. (1), 'not wholly subsidiary and ancillary to those buildings', as referring either to a situation where the entire of the land was not subsidiary and ancillary, *some portions of it being so and some not,* or to a situation in which it could be said that *the entire of the land was partly, but not wholly, subsidiary and ancillary.* He found the concept of an identifiable piece of land's being *partly* subsidiary and ancillary 'difficult to make logical or sensible'. Subs. (2) referred to 'the residue of the land' in sub-clause (a) and in sub-clause (b) made it abundantly clear that the true meaning of the phrase in subs. (1) must be that it referred to a portion of land held under a lease, some area of which was subsidiary and ancillary and some area of which was not.

Finlay CJ rejected the lessor's argument that the provision regarding the acquisition of a fee simple contained in the 1978 Act should be construed as being inapplicable to sporting leases, in view of the inconsistency between some of the provisions of sporting leases and the provisions of the 1978 Act which the lessor had sought to identify. In the Chief Justice's view, the matter was disposed of by s. 1(2) of the 1978 Act, which provided that the collective citation of the Landlord and Tenant Acts 1931 to 1978 should include the 1978 Act and that those Acts and the 1978 Act should be construed together as one Act. The Landlord and Tenant (Amendment) Act 1971, dealing with 'sporting leases' fell within the scope of this reference.

SUCCESSION

S. 117 applications   In the 1989 Review, 307-10, we analysed the Supreme Court decision of *In the Estate of I.A.C. Deceased; C. and F. v W.C. and T.C.* [1989] ILRM 815, which sought to narrow the range of circumstances in which a s. 117 application should be successful. Finlay CJ (for the Court) emphasised that the section placed 'a relatively high onus of proof' on an applicant for relief. (Parenthetically it may be observed that this is a curious way of articulating the issue: the question is not whether the onus of proof—an exclusively evidential matter—is high; rather is it one of substantive import, relating to the range of factual situations in which it would be appropriate to stigmatise the testator's will as falling short of the discharge of the relevant moral duty. This involves a value judgment, not resort of the law of evidence.) The Chief Justice went on to state that it was not sufficient for the applicant to establish that the provision made for the applicant 'was not as great as it might have been, or that, compared with generous bequests to other children or beneficiaries in the will, it appears ungenerous. . . . A positive failure in moral duty must be established'.

In *In the Estate of J.H. de B. Deceased; J. de B. v H.E. de B. and N. de B. and E.M. de B.* [1991] 2 IR 205, Blayney J applied this test in a case where the deceased's estate had a net value of around £200,000. He had left a widow and seven adult children. In his will he left his farm, worth about £160,000, to his widow for life, remainder to his eldest son H. He gave small legacies to the rest of his children, including a legacy of £5,000 to the plaintiff, a married man aged 49, with three children, whose gross salary was £26,000. The plaintiff's house had been bought twenty years ago with a mortgage of £5,000 which was jointly paid off by the plaintiff and the deceased. Its present value was over £90,000. Two of the older children of the deceased, who had received small legacies, had taken proceedings under s. 117. These had been settled for sums of £44,000 and £20,000 respectively.

Blayney J dismissed the plaintiff's application. He referred to the fact that the deceased had financed six years of higher education for the plaintiff. A more fundamental reason for rejecting his claim was the fact that the only asset out of which the deceased could have made any provision for his children was the remainder interest in the farm which he had bequeathed to his son H. As a result of the other bequests and the settlements in the other s. 117 applications, that interest was charged with nearly £100,000. In Blayney J's opinion, no court would consider it fair to increase the burden to H by adding to that amount an order to make further provision for the plaintiff.

Two aspects of Blayney J's analysis are worthy of comment. First, the manner in which he treated the settlements of the s. 117 claims by two of the testator's children. The plaintiff had not suggested that these had been other than *bona fide* arms' length agreements. Fortified by Barron J's approach in *In the Goods of JH deceased* [1984] IR 599, at 607, Blayney J considered that these settlements came within the category of 'other circumstances which the court may consider of assistance in arriving at a decision': s.

117(2). This is surely a correct interpretation. The second matter is somewhat more debatable. Blayney J noted that, according to the plaintiff's evidence, the farm had always been intended for H. He commented: 'Would it have been fair for the deceased, having encouraged this expectation, to have failed to fulfil it?'. The question of the extent to which a putative claim based on estoppel or representation should be capable of modifying the court's response to a s. 117 application is not easy to resolve. Before holding that an assurance given by the deceased to another party has the effect of reducing the force or scope of a s. 117 application, should the court be satisfied that it generated a *legal* claim on the part of the person to whom the assurance was given? If not, what weight should be given to a moral, as opposed to legally enforceable, representation of this kind?

Desertion In *A.B. v J.B. and M.B.* [1991] 2 IR 501, Blayney J analysed the ingredients of the concept of desertion by a spouse. This analysis arose in the context of s. 120(2) of the Succession Act 1965 which precludes a spouse who has been in desertion for at least two years up to the death of the deceased from taking any share in his or her estate as a legal right or on intestacy. The issue of desertion is, however, a linchpin of family law, in other areas as well, such as in respect of judicial separation, maintenance entitlements and the Family Home Protection Act 1976.

The four ingredients of desertion are (i) the factual separation of the spouses; (ii) the absence of consent to live apart; (iii) the intention to desert; and (iv) the absence of just cause for leaving. In the instant case, the fourth of these elements was in particular focus. The parties had married in 1973. The wife, the applicant in the proceedings, was a widow, then aged thirty eight, with eight children. The husband, who was a bachelor farmer, was then fifty years old. For a few years after the marriage, the husband continued to live with his brothers for part of each week. The spouses then went to live in a house on the husband's farm. The daily pattern was less than pleasant from the wife's standpoint. Her husband would leave early in the morning, usually without having had breakfast, and would spend the day working on the farm. He took all his meals with his brothers and returned home late at night. The only break in this routine was when the spouses went out together to a public house on an odd Sunday night.

In 1978, a year after the spouses had moved into this house, the plaintiff began to spend most of her day in the house where she had lived prior to the marriage. In 1982 she left her husband and went to live permanently in her former home. The husband died five years later, never having visited the wife during this period.

The wife claimed that the reason for her withdrawal was the failure of her husband to maintain her properly. Blayney J rejected this assertion on the evidence. She also claimed that, if her husband had taken all his meals in their home and had spent his evenings there, she would have happily moved back.

Blayney J applied the test for just cause for leaving a spouse which Barrington J had articulated in *P. v P.*, High Court, 12 March 1980. It would be necessary to establish 'some form of serious misconduct' on the part of the spouse who remained. Barrington J had quoted Lord Asquith's observation in *Buchler v Buchler* [1947] 1 All ER 319, at 326, that this misconduct must:

> exceed in gravity such behaviour, vexatious and trying though it may be, as every spouse bargains to endure when accepting the other 'for better or worse'. The ordinary wear and tear of conjugal life does not in itself suffice.

Barrington J had also endorsed William J's statement in *Postlethwaite v Postlethwaite* [1957] 1 All ER 909, at 910, that to constitute just cause there must be 'a grave and weighty matter, i.e., conduct of such kind as, in effect, makes the continuance of married life together impossible'.

Blayney J concluded, apparently with some hesitation, that the wife was in desertion on the basis that she had lacked just cause for leaving. While the deceased's conduct had clearly been a failure on his part to satisfy one of the normal expectations which a wife was entitled to entertain—that she should enjoy her husband's company whenever he was not obliged to absent himself for reasons of work, and making due allowances for his right to use some of his spare time independently of her—this failure could not amount to serious misconduct. Certainly it was not conduct of such a kind as made the continuance of married life together impossible. While it was understandable that the wife should have left, the husband's conduct was not sufficient to constitute just cause. Blayney J noted that in *P. v P.* Barrington J had observed that:

> [w]hen parties marry, they marry for better or worse. This, as I understand it, includes accepting quirks and difficulties in the character of the other marriage partner.

Here, the husband's quirk was his attachment to his home and his brothers—'a not surprising quirk perhaps, in a man who had been a bachelor until the age of fifty; [b]ut obviously one that was hurtful and displeasing to the plaintiff'. It was 'something that she had to accept'.

Blayney J went on to consider the argument that the plaintiff had not been in desertion because the spouses had never established a family home together. On the evidence he rejected this contention, but he was of the view that, even if they had not done so, that was no reason for preventing him from making a finding of desertion. The decision of *Wells v Wells* [1940] NI 88 made this clear.

WILLS

In the 1988 Review, 305-6, we discussed Lardner J's decision in *In re Curtin Deceased; Curtin v O'Mahony* [1991] 2 IR 562. The testator had made a will by whose cumbersome terms he professed to make detailed provision for the disposition of his property in the event of his having sold his dwellinghouse. When he died, the house was still unsold. Lardner J faithfully applied the Supreme Court test of *Rowe v Law* [1978] IR 55, and interpreted the will as meaning that the residue should be distributed in accordance with the statutory rules. The will was not a sensible one; it had been 'badly thought out and ill-constructed', possibly on account of the incompetence of the solicitor who had drafted it; but it was also possible that it did accord with the testator's instructions, however lacking in good sense.

The Supreme Court [1991] 2 IR 562 unanimously reversed Lardner J. O'Flaherty J delivered the leading judgment. He invoked Porter MR's observations in *In re Patterson, deceased; Dunlop v Greer* [1899] 1 IR 324, at 331, to the effect that:

[i]f, having considered the will and the whole will, it is plain that to place a literal meaning upon one clause would defeat the clear intent, it may be necessary to 'do violence' . . . to the language used. The thing to be ascertained is what was the man's *will*.

Porter MR (at 332) had gone on to warn that great care must be taken in applying this doctrine. It had to be clear, not only that words had been omitted, but also what was the substance of the omitted clause; otherwise the court would not be construing, but making, a will.

O'Flaherty J stated:

A judge is to tread cautiously so as not to offend against the judicial inheritance to construe a will but not to make one. However, two injunctions are on a collision course in the case: one is that a court is not entitled to make a will for a testator but on the other hand there is the requirement that effect should be given to the intention of the testator, if at all possible. If the will is given a literal meaning then the intention of the testator is clearly defeated and an absurd result is produced.

It seemed clear to O'Flaherty that the testator had intended that, if he had not sold the house at the date of his death, the person named as the beneficiary of the house should be entitled to it and the rest of the property should go to those identified as being entitled to it in the proportions mentioned in the will as applying if the house *had* been sold. It was reasonably clear that a simple clause would supply a proper sense to the will: the addition of the words 'including the proceeds of the sale of my dwelling-house, if sold, but not otherwise' after the passage in the will which reads '. . . I direct that my estate both real and personal which I die possessed of [and] to which at my death I am be entitled'. With respect, this proposed solution does not quite work. Immediately before the words '. . . I direct that my estate [etc]' there appears in the will the following passage: 'In the event of I (*sic*) selling the dwelling-house . . .'. This phrase clearly incorporates a condition, activated *only* on the sale of the home before the testator's death. Thus it would be impossible for the words 'but not otherwise' ever to attach to any actual situation since, if the home were *not* sold, the condition would not get off the ground. The corrective language necessary to give verbal effect to the testator's probable intent would have to embrace a situation where the house was *not* sold before the testator's death. A clause conditional on such a sale is not an adequate basis on which to rest this quite contradictory scenario. *Pace* Finlay CJ, O'Flaherty J's proposed solution does *not* 'neutralis[e] the conditional consequence of the phrase. . . .'

What is quite striking about the decision is the hostility evident towards *Rowe v Law*. The court went so far as to ask the parties whether they wanted to have this case reconsidered; the parties declined this invitation. Nonetheless, Finlay CJ and O'Flaherty J put it on the record that they reserved for further consideration the question whether the majority judgment in *Rowe v Law* correctly presented the extent of the amendment in the law effected by the enactment of s. 90 of the Succession Act 1965.

Evidential aspects   In *In re the Estate of Myles Deceased* [1993] ILRM 34, Lardner J was left in darkness by the combination of a disastrous home-made will, crowded with deletions, and a paucity of evidence as to when those deletions might have been made. Lardner J proceeded on the basis that there was a rebuttable presumption that an alteration, obliteration or interlineation was made *after* execution (*In the goods of Adamson*, LR 3 PD 253 (1870)) and that this presumption might be rebutted by reasonable evidence including evidence afforded by the will itself (*In re Hindmarsh*, LR 1 PD 307 (1866)).

Lardner J noted that no evidence had been tendered as to the handwriting or the events mentioned in the will which might have thrown some light on when the deletions had occurred. The only useful evidence, by an attesting witness, was not sufficiently helpful to explain which deletion had occurred at any particular time. Lardner J stated that an applicant applying for probate took on the burden of proving on the balance of probabilities what constituted the will at the time of execution. That burden had not been discharged by the evidence that had been advanced. Accordingly he declined to grant liberty to apply for a grant of probate, permitting instead the applicant to apply for administration.

The case is interesting from an evidential standpoint. The rebuttable presumption did not operate in such a way as to sustain a will whose contents were so uncertain. The applicant was not permitted to invoke that presumption to extinguish, albeit artificially, that uncertainty. The poverty of the evidence about the will had the effect of defeating the application without the rebuttable presumption having an opportunity to attach to anything.

Law Reform

The Law Reform Commission was busy in 1991, publishing ten reports and three consultation papers. In the chapter on Conflict of Laws above 92-7, we analyse the Commission's Report on the Hague Convention on Succession to the Estates of Deceased Persons (LRC 36 – 1991). In the chapter on Criminal Law, we consider the Commission's Reports on Confiscation of the Proceeds of Crime (LRC 35 – 1991) (see above 132-4). Indexation of Fines (LRC 37 – 1991) (see above 161-3) and the Crime of Libel (LRC 41 – 1991) (see above 136-41). In the Land Law chapter, we analyse the Commission's Reports on the Passing of Risk from Vendor to Purchaser (LRC 39 – 1991) (above, 279-80) and Service of Completion Notices (LRC 40 – 1991) (above 280-1). In the Torts chapter (below 453-9) we discuss the Commission's Report on the Civil Law of Defamation.

The Commission published a detailed Consultation Paper on Contempt of Court in July 1991. It proposed to publish a Report on the subject in 1992. In view of the developments in the law on so many aspects of contempt in 1992, we defer our consideration of the Commission's approach until it publishes its Report.

Licensing

INTOXICATING LIQUOR

In *Application of Chariot Inns Ltd*, High Court, 12 April 1991 the applicant company sought declarations under ss. 15 and 16 of the Intoxicating Liquor Act 1960 that, having regard to substantial building works in progress and to planning permission received, the premises in its ownership were suitable for the granting of an intoxicating liquor licence and a restaurant certificate. The applicant indicated that it intended to apply for permission to operate the premises, located in Ranelagh in Dublin, as a disco up to 2 a.m. Local residents objected to the application on the basis of, inter alia, the nuisance which would thereby be created. They also objected on the ground that an application under ss. 15 or 16 of the 1960 Act could not be made after building works had commenced. Johnson J granted the declarations sought by the applicant, though not without making some important comments on the unsatisfactory state of the licensing code.

He held that the applications under ss. 15 and 16 could be made at any time before the completion of the building works, and that the extension to the premises clearly made it suitable for an intoxicating liquor licence under s. 15 of the 1960 Act. He then stated that, having regard to the fact that the premises in question were already in possession of a restaurant certificate for accommodation which was far inferior to that planned, and to the fact that planning permission had already been obtained for a restaurant, the applicant had made out a case that the premises were suitable to be certified as a restaurant under s. 16 of the 1960 Act.

While the applicant was thus successful on all counts in the present application, Johnson J pointed out that the declarations granted did not amount to permission for the premsies to be used at any time for any purposes, since these would be dealt with under the relevant legislation and in relevant courts for the determination of such issues. However, he clearly bemoaned this state of affairs and commented that it would be much easier for the Bench and for objectors if cases such as the present were dealt with under a codified system of licensing in which all relevant issues could be considered together, rather than in the piecemeal manner which exists at present. It is to be hoped that this cri de coeur might elicit some much-needed legislative reform in this area. For previous decisions indicating other complexities in the licensing code, see the 1988 Review, 285-90.

PUBLIC MUSIC AND DANCE HALL

In *Sheehan v Reilly*, High Court, 19 April 1991 the respondent Judge of the District Court had granted the applicant a public music licence under s. 51 of the Public Health Acts (Amendment) Act 1890 and a public dance licence under s. 6 of the Public Dance Hall Act 1935. The order of the Court stated that the objectors to the licences were entitled to re-enter the matter at any time during the currency of the licences. On one such re-entry, the objectors stated that the licences were operated in such a manner as to cause a public nuisance and, having heard the evidence, the respondent Judge revoked the applicant's licences. The applicant sought judicial review of the revocation on the ground that the Judge had no jurisdiction to revoke the licence, and that the only basis for revocation under s. 51 of the 1890 Act or s. 6 of the 1935 Act was a conviction for a licensing offence. Barron J quashed the respondent's revocation.

He held that the respondent had no jurisdiction to revoke the licences in the instant case, having regard to the terms of s. 51 of the 1890 Act and s. 6 of the 1935 Act, already referred to. Having granted the licences Barron J concluded that the respondent was functus officio, and he was not entitled to grant, in effect, a reviewable licence. Finally, since this error went to jurisdiction, Barron J concluded that the applicant was not estopped from seeking judicial review by his failure to challenge the re-entry provision in the Order of the respondent.

Limitation of Actions

ACCRUAL OF CAUSE OF ACTION

In the 1987 Review, 253-5, we examined the Law Reform Commission's *Report on the Statute of Limitations: Claims in Respect of Latent Personal Injuries* (LRC 21 – 1987). Since then the meaning of the notion of accrual of a cause of action has been clarified by the Supreme Court in *Hegarty v O'Loughran and Edwards* [1990] ILRM 403; [1990] 1 IR 148. See the 1990 Review, 389-94. The Statute of Limitations (Amendment) Act 1991 gives substantial effect to the Commission's recommendations and, in the confident words of its proposer, Mr Lyons, 'will also remove constitutional doubts' about the position: 126 Seanad Debates, col. 1216 (31 October 1990). It is difficult to see how the Act could quell *all* constitutional uncertainties, since it applies only to personal injuries litigation and not to proceedings where property damage or economic loss is the basis of the claim. For a stimulating discussion of this issue, see Eoin Quill, 'Defective Buildings and the Limitations of Actions' (1992), 10 ILT (ns) 185, 202. For very helpful analyses of the Act see Tony Kerr's Annotation [1991] ICLSA and Dr John White's article (1991) 85 Incorp L Soc of Ireland Gazette 307.

The Act lays down the general rule that an action for personal injuries is not to be taken after the expiration of three years from the date on which the cause of action accrued or the date of knowledge (if later) of the person injured: s. 3(1). S. 2 defines the date of knowledge by setting out what one needs to know in order to be fixed with knowledge for the purposes of the Act and the circumstances in which one may be treated as already having knowledge of a particular fact. That person's date of knowledge is the date on which he first had knowledge of the following facts:

> that the person alleged to have been injured had been injured,
> that the injury in question was significant,
> that the injury was attributable in whole or in part to the act or omission which is alleged to constitute negligence, nuisance or breach of duty,
> the identity of the defendant, and,
> if it is alleged that the act or omission was that of a person other than the defendant, the identity of that person and the additional facts supporting the bringing of an action against the defendant: subs. (1).

Knowledge that any acts or omissions did or did not, *as a matter of law*, involve negligence, nuisance or breach of duty is irrelevant: *id.*

This definition postpones the date of knowledge to the point that the Law Reform Commission recommended, and thus delays accrual considerably longer than under the law formerly. (It wisely eschews any attempt to prescribe the circumstances in which an injury is 'significant'. The attempt to do this in English legislation proved signally unsuccessful.) S. 2(2) enlarges on the circumstances in which knowledge will be attributed to a person. Such knowledge includes knowledge that the person might reasonably have been expected to acquire from facts observable or ascertainable by him or from facts ascertainable by him with the help of medical or other appropriate expert advice that it is reasonable for him to seek. Thus the test is an objective rather than a subjective one.

Cases can arise, however, where a person fails to learn of his medical condition because his medical advisor negligently fails to diagnose it. The Law Reform Commission recommended in its *Report*, p. 46, that in such circumstances the limitation period 'should not run until he ascertains the true position'. (Perhaps the more appropriate test would be based on the date when he *might reasonably have been expected* to have knowledge of that position.)

The Act seeks to give effect to this recommendation in s. 2(3), which provides that, notwithstanding subs. (2),

> a person shall not be fixed under this section with knowledge of a fact ascertainable only with the help of expert advice so long as he has taken all reasonable steps to obtain (and, where appropriate, to act on) that advice. . . .

This draft is modelled on the heads of legislation proposed by the Commission. The sense is clear enough; perhaps it might have been still clearer if the subsection referred, not simply to 'a person', but to 'a person who has not actual knowledge of a particular fact', with consequential modification of the remainder of the provision. Against the need for this clarification, it may be argued that subs. (2), to which subs. (3) is a qualification, refers only to circumstances where a person has *not* knowledge of a particular fact.

Subs. (3), again following the Commission's lead (cf. the *Report*, p. 45), provides that an injured person is not to be fixed with knowledge of a fact relevant to the injury which he or she has failed to acquire as a result of that injury. The Commission considered that, if the effect of the accident is to slow the injured person down so that he is less diligent in finding out about how it was caused than an ordinary healthy person would be, the question of the reasonableness of the discoverability of his injuries should embrace the fact of his debilitated condition. Subs. (3) is drafted somewhat more starkly; it is possible that the degree of indulgence favoured by the Commission might not be fully reflected in a court's analysis of the causal effects of the injury on the plaintiff's attempt to solve the mystery of the provenance of his injured condition.

As well as applying to actions in respect of personal injuries caused by negligence, nuisance or breach of duty, the Act also applies to personal injuries litigation arising under s. 13 of the Sale of Goods and Supply of Services Act 1980 and s. 21 of the Control of Dogs Act 1986. For consideration of s. 21, which prescribes strict liability for attacks by dogs on humans (save for trespassers, who may plead only negligence) and for injuries caused to livestock, see McMahon & Binchy, *Irish Law of Torts* (2nd ed., 1991), 512-16. S. 13 of the 1980 Act establishes an implied condition in certain contracts for the sale of a motor vehicle that it is free from defects that would render it a danger. This condition is not subject to a privity limitation, and amounts in effect to an unusual hybrid between contractual and delictual liability.

Ss. 4 and 6 of the 1991 Act give effect to the Commission's recommendations in respect of survival of causes of action and fatal injuries: see the 1987 Review, 255. S. 5 applies the "date of knowledge" principle to the special provisions in the Statute of Limitations 1957 relating to disability, arising from childhood or mental disability. Under the 1957 Act, in cases where a right of action involving a claim for personal injuries accrued to a person while under a legal disability, the three-year limitation period did not start to run against the person until he ceased to be under a disability. Thus a person injured in childhood might institute proceedings at any time up to three years after reaching the age of majority—which is eighteen or younger if the person marries under eighteen. See McMahon & Binchy, *op. cit.*, 834-8. S. 5 makes it clear that the changes brought about by the 1991 Act do not have the effect of imposing on any child or mentally disabled person the duty of taking proceedings during the period of disability, and that, in a case where a minor or mentally disabled, person has discovered his injury during that period, he should nonetheless have a full three years period, after reaching majority or ceasing to be mentally disabled, within which to take his action.

S. 7 of the Act applies the 'date of knowledge' principle to all causes of action involving personal injuries whether they accrue before or after the enactment of the Act, and also to proceedings pending at that time.

The Act contains no 'long stop' provision akin to Article 11 of the EC Directive on Products Liability. The Commission was against the inclusion of such a provision on the basis that it could frustrate the overriding objective of a discoverability test and that, however long or short it might be, 'it must of its nature be crude and arbitrary and have no regard to the requirements of justice as they arise in individual cases': *Report*, p. 48. The Commission noted the power of the courts to strike out proceedings before the expiration of the limitation period, where there has been 'inordinate or inexcusable delay' in bringing the proceedings and there are no countervailing circumstances. The authority for this was of course *Ó Domhnaill v Merrick* [1984] IR 151. The Commission ventured the view that there was no reason to suppose that this power would be availed of by the courts other than in exceptional circumstances. Subsequent developments, exemplified by *Toal v Duignan (No. 1)* [1991] ILRM 135 and *Toal v Duignan (No. 2)* [1991] ILRM 140, reveal that, while these cases may indeed be exceptional, the Supreme Court has applied what in effect is its own personalised Statute of Limitations, based on somewhat questionable criteria in a manner that is not easy to reconcile with the legislative judgment as to how principles of justice should operate in this area. We need not here rehearse our unhappiness with this development: see the 1990 Review, 394-8.

Finally it should be noted that s. 3(2) of the 1991 Act expressly re-enacts the six year time limit in actions founded on tort other than actions in respect of personal or fatal injuries. In *Tuohy v Courtney*, High Court, 3 September 1992, Lynch J rejected a constitutional challenge to this provision. We shall examine this decision in detail in the 1992 Review.

TRESPASS

McDonald v McBain [1991] ILRM 764; [1991] 1 IR 284 raised important questions of principle relating to limitation of actions in trespass cases, where a plaintiff alleges concealment by fraud on the part of the defendant. The facts were unusual. The defendant had agreed to sell his home to the plaintiff in 1974. He had been so lethargic in doing so that the plaintiff had been obliged to bring specific performance proceedings against him. Before the plaintiff occupied the home, the defendant had gone to the house for a 'farewell party', with cylinders of gas and pieces of carpet underfelt, allegedly saying in effect that he was going 'to put an end to all this'. The house had been burnt to the ground that night. The plaintiff had told the Gardai of the defendant's unusual behaviour. Two years later, two people had apparently reported to the plaintiff that the defendant was the culprit, though they subsequently retracted this allegation when interviewed by the Gardaí.

The plaintiff commenced proceedings in 1985, alleging breach of contract, trespass and negligence. The time limit under the Statute of Limitations 1957 is six years. (This limit was not disturbed by the 1991 legislation, which applies only to cases involving personal injuries.) The plaintiff argued first that her claim was not barred because the defendant had concealed her right to action by fraud. Secondly, she argued that the claim based on trespass could arise only when she had knowledge of the fact that the defendant was the person who had actually set fire to the premises and that she had learnt of this only when in 1983 the defendant had admitted the fact to her.

Morris J rejected both arguments. As to the first the plaintiff had cited in aid Lord Denning MR's judgment in *King v Victor Parsons & Co.* [1973] 1 WLR 29, at 33-4, to the effect that:

> [i]n order to show that a defendant concealed the right of action 'by fraud' it is not necessary to show that he took active steps to conceal his wrongdoing or breach of contract. It is sufficient that he knowingly committed it and did not tell the owner anything about it. He did the wrong or committed the breach secretly. By saying nothing he kept it secret. He conceals the right of action. He conceals it 'by fraud', as those words have been interpreted in the cases. To this word 'knowingly' there must be added 'recklessly'.

Morris J found no difficulty in adopting, 'in the main', this approach. He was of opinion that:

> if the circumstances were such that the plaintiff . . . had her property destroyed by fire deliberately by a third party, either by stealth or silence, succeeded in hiding that fact from the plaintiff, and she was left in complete and total ignorance of the identity of the wrongdoer, then that conduct on the part of the wrongdoer would amount to fraud within the meaning of the Statute of Limitations.

In the present case, however, the circumstances were such that the plaintiff was possessed of sufficient information to enable her to institute the proceedings had she chosen to do so. What had been missing from the case and was supplied in 1983 was an item of proof which could be adduced to strengthen the plaintiff's case if and when it came to hearing:

> Certain proof was already available to the plaintiff upon which she could rely in an attempt to persuade the court that on the balance of probabilities the defendant was responsible for the deliberate burning of the property.
>
> I see a clear distinction between the present case where the plaintiff has evidence which she may adduce to the court to connect the defendant with the deliberate burning and a case where the wrongdoer remains entirely undiscovered. I know of no authority which allows the plaintiff to postpone bringing her case until she has available to her evidence which she believes will copperfasten the matter in her favour.

Accordingly, Morris J was of opinion that s. 71 had no relevance.

In support of her second argument, based on the requirement of knowledge of the defendant's identity as the author of the wrong, the plaintiff invoked a passage from Finlay CJ's judgment in *Hegarty v O'Loughran* [1990] 1 IR 148, at 157 where the Chief Justice had construed s. 11(2)(b) as starting the clock 'when a provable personal injury, capable of attracting compensation, occurred to the plaintiff. . . .' The plaintiff argued that the tort of trespass became 'provable' only at the stage where the defendant acknowledged that he had set fire to the premises.

Morris J did not deal in express terms with this argument, which appears to suffer from the fact that it conflates knowledge of the fact that one has been injured with knowledge of the identity of the author of the injury.

McDonald v McBain raises important questions as to the relationship between the torts of trespass and negligence, so far as limitations of actions is concerned. Thus far, we have no Irish decision holding that the tort of trespass is limited to intentional acts; it is still permissible for a plaintiff to plead trespass and leave it to the defendant to establish the absence of intention or negligence. The trend of thinking in other common law jurisdictions is clearly in the direction of limiting the tort of trespass to intentional acts, leaving negligent trespass to be dealt with under the rubric of negligence. That day has yet to come in Ireland, though the failure of the law to develop on these lines may perhaps be attributed more to the paucity of decisions in which the issue was raised than to any fidelity on the part of Irish judges to the traditional contours of the trespass action.

This matter is important in relation to the question of limitations because there is a clear relationship between fraudulent suppression and intentional conduct. A person who intends to harm another very often will seek to cover his tracks; one who negligently injures another may well attempt to disclaim his guilt but the process is usually less easy and less deserving of the label of fraud. It is far easier to stigmatise as fraudulent the act of one who seeks to cause harm without detection than the act of one who, having negligently injured another, seeks to avoid the consequences. From the standpoint of the plaintiff, there is an argument that the lack of a reasonable opportunity to know that he or she has been the victim of tort should stop the clock until such an opportunity arises. This argument does not depend in any way on the fraudulent conduct of the defendant but rather on the fairness of depriving a person of a remedy before he or she can reasonably be expected to be aware of its existence. When it comes to the question of fraud, there is a strong case in justice for suspending the operation of the Statute of Limitations during the period when a person who intentionally caused another harm succeeded in covering his tracks, by a plan conceived before he set on this course. Here the combination of the intentional wrongdoing and the prior preparation of the plan to avoid the consequences makes the case in favour of stopping the clock a very strong one. It is far different where a person, having negligently caused injury, fails to own up. His cowardice may no doubt be condemned from the moral standpoint but there is no rule of law requiring tortfeasors to confess their wrongdoing. It may be argued that the right approach, so far as trespass actions are concerned, is to suspend the operation of the Statute of Limitations only where the defendant committed the tort intentionally and has done so in circumstances where that intention was accompanied by conduct designed to conceal from the plaintiff either the fact that he or she was the victim of a tort or that the defendant was the author of the tort.

CLAIMS BY PERSONAL REPRESENTATIVES

In *Gleeson v Feehan* [1991] ILRM 783, on a case stated by Barron J, the Supreme Court was called on to determine whether s. 45 of the Statute of Limitations 1957, as amended by s. 126 of the Succession Act 1965, bars claims by, as well as against, personal representatives. S. 45(1), thus amended, provides as follows:

> Subject to s. 71, no action in respect of any claim to the estate of a deceased person or to any share or interest in such estate, whether under a will, on intestacy, or under s. 111 of the Succession Act 1965, shall be brought after the expiration of six years from the date when the right to receive the share or interest accrued.

The Court held that the provision should not be so interpreted. Endorsing McMahon J's approach is *Drohan v Drohan* [1984] IR 311, it considered that s. 13(2) of the 1957 Act governed the position. This prescribed a twelve-year limitation period for actions to recover land brought by persons to whom the right first accrued or those claiming through them. Actions by personal representatives fit 'precisely' into s. 13(2).

Finlay CJ, conscious of the argument that this interpretation involved an anomaly with the next-of-kin, who would be restricted to six years, expressed tentative support for the view that such claims accrued, not on the death of the intestate, but rather when the property in question came into the hands of the personal representative. In an incisive commentary on the decision in [1991] DULJ 164, at 169, Paul Coughlan observes that this gives rise to the 'daunting' prospect of the totality of claims to an intestate's land not being extinguished for eighteen years, thereby frustrating the purpose of s. 45(1).

Characterisation of action In *Sweeney v Duggan* [1991] 2 IR 274, which we examine in greater detail below 386-7, the essence of the plaintiff's case was that the effective owner of the company that employed him owed him a duty to ensure that, if he was injured in the course of his employment, he would be adequately compensated. The plaintiff argued that the defendant should either have ensured that there was a liability insurance policy in place or have warned the plaintiff of its absence.

Barron J held that the claim was statute-barred because it should be characterised as an action where the damages 'consist of or include damages in respect of personal injuries. . . .' (Statute of Limitations 1957, s. 11(2)(b)). He considered taht he could 'not hold . . . that this particular type of claim, where the manager or owner of a business is being sued, differs in substance from a claim against the business itself. Both are equally actions where the damages claimed consist of or include damages in respect of personal injuries'.

There is admittedly a formidable argument against such a characterisation. The entire loss claimed by the plaintiff was of an economic nature. It is true that that economic loss related to personal injuries but those injuries *were at one remove*. In support of Barron J's holding it may be replied that the language of s. 11(2)(b) has sufficient elasticity to encompass a claim of the kind that was made in *Sweeney v Duggan*. The answer to the question should perhaps be sought, not in a neutral passing of the words in the statutory provision, but rather by reference to the policies underlying the reduction from six years of the limitation period for tort actions with a personal injuries ingredient. Whatever those policies may have been—to encourage the early resolution of such claims while the evidence is fresh, for example—they have been turned on their head by the enactment of the Statute of Limitations (Amendment) Act 1991, which *extends* the limitation period for this category of action.

Local Government

BUILDING CONTROL

The Building Control Act 1990 (Commencement) Order 1991 (SI No. 304) brought the following sections of the 1990 Act into effect from 4 December 1991: ss. 1 to 4, 6, 7, 14, 15, 18-21 and 25. All remaining provisions were brought into effect from 1 June 1992. On the Act, see the 1990 Review, 404-6. In conjunction with this Commencement Order, two highly significant Regulations were also made which came into effect on 1 June 1992.

Building Control Regulations The Building Control Regulations 1991 (SI No. 305), made under the 1990 Act, came into effect on 1 June 1992. These require that advance notice be given to a building control authority (in effect, large local authorities) of the commencement of any building works covered by the Act. This includes not merely new buildings but also material alterations to existing buildings (that is, buildings in use before 1 June 1992).

They also require that a fire safety certificate be obtained from a building control authority before building works commence. The form of application for a certificate is included in the First Schedule to the Regulations. Such a fire certificate can only be granted by the authority if the building plans comply with the fire safety requirements of the Building Regulations 1991 (SI No. 306), discussed below. Finally, the building control authority must maintain a register of applications for fire certificates and of decisions on such applications.

Building Regulations The Building Regulations 1991 (SI No. 306), also made under the 1990 Act and also coming into effect on 1 June 1992, are the first statutory code of building standards to be applicable throughout the State. They require compliance with specified building standards in respect of building works commenced on or after 1 June 1992 both in respect of new buildings and also in respect of material alterations to existing buildings. The history of the Draft Building Regulations which preceded them is referred to in the 1990 Review, 404.

One preliminary point is worth mentioning. The text of the 1991 Regulations appears small when compared with that of the Draft Building Regulations. The explanation for this seeming shrinkage is that, whereas the Draft Building Regulations contained detailed descriptions of relevant technical

standards to which buildings should conform, the 1991 Regulations incorporate such standards by reference to what they describe as 'Technical
Guidance Documents.' These are, in effect, the documents which set out the
technical standards, whereas the 1991 Regulations set out the basic framework around which such documents are built. Technical Guidance Documents were published by the Department of the Environment to coincide with
the promulgation of the 1991 Regulations. The advantage of such documents
is that they may be updated as necessary to take account of new standards
without the need to change the structure of the 1991 Regulations.

As mentioned already, the Building Regulations are relatively short,
running to only 13 Regulations in all. However, the First Schedule also
contains the basic headings in relation to which the Technical Guidance
Documents provide information on standards to which building works must
comply. These fall under the following headings:

Part A: Structure
Part B: Fire
Part C: Site Preparation and Resistance to Moisture
Part D: Materials and Workmanship
Part E: Sound
Part F: Ventilation
Part G: Hygiene
Part H: Drainage and Waste Disposal
Part J: Heat Producing Appliances
Part K: Stairways, Ramps and Guards
Part L: Conservation of Fuel and Energy
Part M: Access for Disabled People.

The Technical Guidance Documents published by the Department of the
Environment deals with each of these headings in turn. The Document on
Fire, which is the most lengthy, runs to 129 printed pages.

Like the Building Control Regulations, above, the Building Regulations
apply both to new building works and also to material alterations of existing
buildings. However, Regulation 12 provides that material changes of use to
existing buildings need only comply with Parts A, B, F, G, H, J and L of the
First Schedule.

Finally, it should be mentioned that Regulation 6 provides for a number
of exemptions from the provisions of the Regulations.

CONTROL OF DOGS

The Control of Dogs (Restriction of Certain Dogs) Regulations 1991 (SI No.
123) imposed muzzling requirements on a large range of dogs, in the wake

of highly-publicised cases of children being attacked by dogs, both in Britain and in this State. The Regulations were made under the Control of Dogs Act 1986. The Control of Dogs (Restriction of Certain Dogs) (Amendment) Regulations 1991 (SI No. 146) excluded guide dogs and rescue dogs from the requirements of SI No. 123. These Regulations should now be seen in the context of the Control of Dogs (Amendment) Act 1992, which will be discussed in the 1992 Review.

DERELICT SITES

Derelict sites levy The Derelict Sites (Commencement of Derelict Sites Levy) Regulations 1991 (SI No. 286) designated 1992 as the first year in respect of which a derelict sites levy is payable under the Derelict Sites Act 1990. On the Act see the 1990 Review, 410-11.

Fees The Derelict Sites (Case Stated for the High Court)(Fees) Regulations 1991 (SI No. 148) and the Derelict Sites (Appeal Fees) Regulations 1991 (SI No. 149) are self-explanatory.

ELECTIONS

Part III of the Local Government Act 1991 consolidated, with amendments, the legislation on local elections: see 311, below.

HOUSING

The nature of the legal obligations placed on local authorities by the Housing Act 1988 in relation to the housing of the travelling community was addressed by Barron J in *University of Limerick v Ryan and Ors (Limerick County Council, Third Party)*, High Court, 21 February 1991.

The University applied for an injunction seeking to have the respondents, 50 members of a travelling community family, removed from the University's grounds where they had been parked for some time. The circumstances leading to the family's parking on the University grounds were outlined in detail in the judgment of Barron J. In brief, Limerick County Council had been attempting for some years previously to provide housing and serviced halting sites for the travelling community in its functional area. These had foundered, chiefly because the Council was unable to find a site which was suitable and which did not draw objections from members of the settled community. The result was that many travelling families, including the family involved in the instant proceedings, were unable to stay in any one place for a lengthy period of time and would be required to move on to another place.

Barron J's judgment in the instant case provides a detailed description of the failed efforts of the Council to give effect to its policy to house the travelling community. Significantly, he held that the Council had erred in the interpretation of its duties under ss. 9 to 13 of the Housing Act 1988. The Council had argued that its duties under these sections were fulfilled if it made an assessment of housing needs for travellers and offered accommodation from the Council's existing housing stock to those who were 'in need' within the terms of the 1988 Act. Barron J held that this did not meet the requirements of s. 13 of the 1988 Act in particular. He referred in this context to the judgment of O'Higgins CJ in *McDonald v Dublin Corporation*, Supreme Court, 23 July 1980, where the then Chief Justice interpreted the more limited provisions of ss. 55 and 60 of the Housing Act 1966, which were repealed by the 1988 Act. In *McDonald*, O'Higgins CJ had opined that the duty to prepare a scheme of needs 'would seem to involve a corresponding duty to operate such.' On this basis, Barron J concluded that the specific duty to consider the needs of the travelling community imposed by s. 13 of the 1988 Act required the Council to operate a scheme with the particular housing needs of the travelling community in mind. In this respect, he concluded that the Council had been in breach of its statutory duty to the respondents in the instant case.

In conclusion, Barron J adjourned the application by the University for an injunction for two weeks to enable the Council take steps to reconsider the nature of the duties imposed on it by the 1988 Act in the light of the interpretation which Barron J had placed on these. He made it clear, however, that the University was entitled to obtain the injunction and that the Council's duty was a distinct matter which could not deny the University the equitable relief sought.

LOCAL GOVERNMENT REFORM

The Local Government Act 1991 represents the first legislative response to *Local Government Reorganisation and Reform* (Pl. 7918), the March 1991 Report of the 'Committee of Experts' chaired by Dr Tom Barrington, the eminent public servant who has long called for reform of the local government structure. The Barrington Report made far-reaching recommendations on local government, and a substantial amount of legislation would be required to deal with all matters raised in it, in particular the issue of local government financing. The 1991 Act is a mixture of response to the Report as well as provisions which had been promised for some time.

Commencement orders   The 1991 Act will be implemented in phases, and in 1991 three wide-ranging Commencement Orders were made. The combined effect was to bring into force most of Part I, all of Part II, Part III (except for s. 12), all of Part IV and much of Part VII of the 1991 Act. The timetable was as follows.

The Local Government Act 1991 (Commencement) Order 1991 (SI No. 122) brought the following provisions into effect on 21 May 1991: Part I (except s. 1(9) and s. 4); Part III (except s. 12); Part IV; and the following provisions in Part VII: ss. 47, 52 and 55(1). The Local Government Act 1991 (Commencement) (No. 2) Order 1991 (SI No. 130) brought the following provisions into effect on 7 June 1991: s. 1(9) and some elements of s. 4(1), a repealing provision; and the following from Part VII: ss. 41, 42, 44, 45, 46, 48, 49, 53, 54 (other than 54(a)) and 55(3). Thirdly, the Local Government Act 1991 (Commencement) (No. 3) Order 1991 (SI No. 180) brought the following into effect on 1 August 1991: Part II and ss. 50 and 55(2).

Powers of local authorities   Part II of the Act (ss.5 to 9) deals with the powers of local authorities and represents a direct response to the Barrington Report. S. 6 of the Act considerably relaxes the rigidity of the *ultra vires* rule, which had the effect of limiting local authorities to acts which were authorised directly or indirectly by the legislation creating a particular power. For the effects of the old *ultra vires* rule, see for example *Ballybay Meat Exports Ltd v Monaghan County Council* [1990] ILRM 864 (1990 Review, 406-7) and Hogan and Morgan, *Administrative Law in Ireland*, 2nd ed, pp. 175-8. S. 9 of the 1991 Act also has considerable potential for expansion of local authority competences. It provides for the transfer by Order to local authorities of functions currently carried on by government departments. Although nothing specific is indicated in the 1991 Act in this respect, the Barrington Report indicated a number of areas of activity which could usefully be transferred from central to local control. One such area referred to was enforcement in some sectors of the legislation on safety and health at work. Such transfer might also take place under the terms of the Safety, Health and Welfare at Work Act 1989.

Local elections   Part III of the 1991 Act (ss. 10 to 16) largely provides for the consolidation of existing law on local elections. However, s. 13 also includes a provision by which government Ministers (and Ministers of State) are disqualified from membership of local authorities. While the convention had been that Ministers resigned from local authorities on their appointment, this convention was not always followed, and s. 13 legislates for the convention. The Barrington Report had recommended that members of the Oireachtas and of the European Parliament be prohibited from sitting as members of local authorities. However, this far-reaching recommendation was not accepted by the government or the Oireachtas.

Reorganisation of Dublin County   Part IV of the 1991 Act (ss.17 to 26) provides for a mechanism for the eventual reorganisation of local government in the Dublin County area. It is envisaged that Dublin County Council and Dun Laoghaire Corporation will be dissolved, to be replaced by Fingal (i.e. North Dublin County), South Dublin and Dun Laoghaire-Rathdown. The creation of these three separate local authorities will require, however, further legislation.

Boundary changes   Part V of the 1991 Act (ss. 27 to 35) largely consolidates the law on local authority boundary changes. However, included for the first time is provision for a Boundary Commission to advise the Minister for the Environment prior to any alterations in boundaries. While the recommendations of the Commission will not be binding, the experience with the Dáil Electoral Commission indicates that any recommendations would be ignored at peril. This Part is not yet in force.

Local committees   Part VI of the 1991 Act (ss. 36 to 40) provides for the establishment of committees of local authorities and joint committess (i.e. committees between local authorities) to deal with any matter within the jurisdiction or jurisdictions of the local authorities. This Part is not yet in force.

Planning: section 4 motions   Part VII of the 1991 Act (ss.41 to 55) deals with a number of important miscellaneous matters. The most publicised such matter was the amendment to s. 4 of the City and County Management (Amendment) Act 1955 contained in s. 44 of the 1991 Act. S.4 of the 1955 Act had been used as a procedure for granting planning permission outside the normal planning process, and had become the subject of widespread criticism. The section 4 procedure had also given rise to recent case law, notably *P. & F. Sharpe Ltd v Dublin City and County Manager* [1989] ILRM 565; [1989] IR 701 (see the 1988 Review, 300-1). S. 44 of the 1991 Act requires that, where a section 4 motion concerns a planning application, it must be supported by three quarters of the members for the local authority area in question and also supported by three quarters of the members of the authority itself. The more radical proposal of the Barrington Report that planning matters be excluded from the section 4 procedure was rejected. Nonetheless, s. 44 of the 1991 Act represents a significant limit on section 4 motions.

Tenure of managers   S. 47 of the 1991 Act also provides a mechanism for setting age and tenure limits for city and county managers, giving effect to another recommendation of the Barrington Report. The Local Government

(Tenure of Office) Order 1991 (SI No. 128) provides that the tenure limit will be seven years and the age limit will be 60 years for managers. However, this section does not apply to existing managers and there are transitional arrangements for existing local authority officers aged 50 years or more on 21 May 1991.

Part VII of the 1991 Act also includes provisions concerning allowances for chairpersons of local authorities (s. 42); entertainment expenses of local authorities (s. 46); conferral of civic honours (s. 48); the possible establishment of regional authorities (s. 43, not yet in force); and the twinning of local authority areas (s. 49).

PLANNING

1 Advertisement In *Cunningham v An Bord Pleanála*, High Court, 3 May 1990 (discussed below, 318-9) Lavan J held, applying dicta of Henchy J in *The State (Elm Developments Ltd) v An Bord Pleanála* [1981] ILRM 108, that the advertisement in relation to the planning application involved in the case was not sufficient to comply with the Local Government (Planning and Development) Regulations 1977. However, it should also be noted that he did not grant judicial review to the applicant.

In *O'Donoghue v An Bord Pleanála* [1991] ILRM 750 (discussed below), Murphy J held, applying dicta of Griffin J in *Crodaun Homes Ltd v Kildare County Council* [1983] ILRM 1, that the advertisement in relation to the planning application involved in the case was sufficient to comply with the 1977 Regulations.

2 Advice of inspectors The validity of the planning permission given to the 'Radio Tara' transmission mast was considered in *O'Keeffe v An Bord Pleanála and Anor* [1992] ILRM 237. The case is discussed more fully in the Administrative Law chapter, 16-18, above.

Briefly, the Supreme Court held that in the instant case, the applicant had not discharged the onus placed on him to establish that the respondent Board had acted unreasonably in granting the planning permission for the mast. In particular, even though the Board had before it reports from its own experts which indicated the hazards of granting the permission the Supreme Court held that the Board had been entitled to reach the conclusion it did on a perusal of the entire of the Reports before it, notwithstanding the strength and clarity of the actual recommendations against granting permission made in them.

A similar approach was taken by Murphy J in *O'Donoghue v An Bord Pleanála* [1991] ILRM 750. In this case, the Board also granted planning permission in circumstances in which one of its senior inspectors had reached a conclusion that the development would constitute an overdevelopment of the area in question. Notwithstanding this, Murphy J concluded that the decision could not be quashed on *certiorari*. It is notable that, although Murphy J delivered his judgment after the decision of the Supreme Court in *O'Keeffe*, above, he did not appear to have the benefit of the text of those judgments since he referred only to the 1990 judgment of Costello J in that case. Despite this, his conclusions are entirely in line with that of the Supreme Court.

3 Bord Pleanála: minutes   In the *O'Keeffe* case, above, the Supreme Court also rejected a point on the Board's procedure for keeping minutes. It held that there was no obligation on the Board to keep contemporaneous minutes of its proceedings; and that, in any event, having regard to the failure of the applicant to seek a minute of its proceedings its procedure was not infirm for judicial review purposes. This would appear to limit to some extent the range of the decision of the Supreme Court itself in *P. & F. Sharpe Ltd v Dublin City and County Manager* [1989] ILRM 565; [1989] IR 701 (1988 Review, 296-301).

4 Default permission   The consequencees of granting a default permission in contravention of a Council's development plan were considered by Barron J in *Calor Teo v Sligo County Council* [1991] 2 IR 267. The case arose as follows.

On 12 May 1989, the applicant company sought planning permission for a bulk LPG Depot. The appropriate fee was not paid by the company until 30 June. The company then made enquiries as to the processing of the application. On 31 August 1989, the Council wrote to the company to suggest a meeting concerning the safety aspects of the application. A meeting took place on 6 September 1989, during which the company discovered for the first time that the plans it had submitted with the application omitted details concerning thermal insulation. Details of this were furnished on 8 September 1989. The planning application was refused on 10 November 1989. It was agreed that this decision reached the company within 2 months of the company supplying details of the thermal insulation, but the company sought a declaration that a default permission must be deemed to have been issued on 30 August 1989, 2 months after the appropriate fee was lodged by the company. Barron J held that, although a default permission had been granted, the default permission was invalid as it constituted a material contravention of the Council's development plan.

As to whether any permission had been granted, Barron J held that the company's notice for planning permission complied with Article 15 of the Local Government (Planning and Development) Regulations 1977 since it referred to the physical 'nature and extent' of the development and it was not required to specify the possible or even probable consequences of such development. He distinguished the decision in *Keleghan v Corby* (1977) 111 ILTR 144 on this point. And since the Council had not served any notice on the company under s. 27 of the Local Government (Planning and Development) Act 1963, the time period for a default permission began on 30 June 1989, and thus a default permission was granted on 30 August.

It thus became necessary to examine the nature of a default permission. Barron J referred approvingly to the description given by the Supreme Court *Readymix (Éire) Ltd v Dublin County Council*, Supreme Court, 30 July 1974, namely, that it is permission to carry out the development in accordance with the original plans submitted. Since the company in the instant case had failed to submit thermal insulation plans with its original application and the Council's Fire Officer had indicated that such an application would not conform to the requirements of the Fire Services Act 1981, he concluded that the default permission was not valid because it would constitute a material contravention of the the the Council's development plan, which required compliance with the Fire Services Act 1981.

5 Development plan: interpretation In *Tennyson and Ors v Dun Laoghaire Corporation* [1991] 2 IR 527 Barr J considered the question of the interpretation of a development plan. He applied the tests adumbrated by McCarthy J in *XJS Investments Ltd v Dun Laoghaire Corporation* [1987] ILRM 659; [1986] IR 750 (1987 Review, 101) and in *Attorney General (McGarry) v Sligo County Council* [1989] ILRM 768; [1991] 1 IR 99 (1989 Review, 329-30). Applying that approach, Barr J examined the instant case on the basis of what a lay person, unversed in planning matters, would conclude from an examination of the words used in the development plan. In the instant case, he held that the Corporation had acted in breach of its development plan in granting the planning permission which had been challenged by the applicants. A time limit issue was also considered by Barr J in the case: see 321-2, below.

6 Environmental impact assessment The method of implementation of the Directive on environmental impact assessment (85/337/EEC) by, *inter alia*, the European Communities (Environmental Impact Assessment) Regulations 1989, is criticised in Humphreys (1991) 13 DULJ 135.

7 Extension of permission: 'substantial works' In *Frenchurch Properties Ltd v Wexford County Council* [1991] ILRM 769, the applicant company had purchased land in respect of which planning permission to build two blocks of apartments had been granted in 1985 by Wexford County Council. The purchase took place in December 1989 and the planning permission was due to expire on 8 April 1990. The company began the development of the property with a view to carrying out 'substantial works' before April 1990 in order to qualify for an extension of the planning permission under s. 4 of the Local Government (Planning and Development) Act 1982.

By 8 April 1990, the piling for both apartment blocks had been completed and the pile capping and beaming had been completed for one block. In addition, floor slabs and other steel works, which could not be used for any other purpose, had been manufactured and some had been delivered to the site. The company's application for extension of the planning permission was rejected by Wexford County Council, and this decision was based in particular on the ground that 'substantial works' had not been carried out within the meaning of s. 4 of the 1982 Act. The Council considered that the floor slabs and steel works did not constitute 'works' and these were, therefore, discounted for the purposes of the 1982 Act.

On judicial review, Lynch J granted an order of certiorari quashing the Council's refusal to extend the planning permission period. He was of the view that, since the the floor slabs and steel works wree unique to the development in question and were incapable of being used in any other development, they constituted 'works' within the meaning of s. 4 of the 1982 Act. Since the Council had misinterpreted s. 4 in this context and since it had also failed to give the company an opportunity to deal with the basis on which it had arrived at its conclusion, Lynch J concluded that the rules of fair procedures had been breached and that the refusal would be quashed.

Lynch J noted at the end of his judgment, however, that this did not require that on a renewed applciation the Council was bound to grant an extension. This was because the Council might still conclude that the work to 8 April 1990 still did not meet the 'substantial works' requirement of the 1982 Act. It is noteworthy that, in the course of his judgment, Lynch J held that it was not unreasonable for the Council to have a general poicy that 40% to 50% of work would need to be completed before it would be satisfied that 'substantial works' had taken place. Deferring to the expertise of the Council's advisers in this area, Lynch J had held that such a policy could not be regarded as unreasonable or at variance with common sense, in the sense used by the Supreme Court in *The State (Keegan) v Stardust Victims Compensation Tribunal* [1987] ILRM 202; [1986] IR 642: see the Administrative Law chapter, 16-19, above.

8 Fees The Local Government (Planning and Development) (Fees) (Amendment) Regulations 1991 (SI No. 187) increased the fees concerning planning applications.

9 *Locus standi*   The question of standing was considered by the Supreme Court in *Chambers v An Bord Pleanála and Sandoz (Ringaskiddy) Ltd* [1992] ILRM 296; [1992] 1 IR 134, in a case which attracted considerable publicity: see *Irish Times*, 26 July 1991.

The plaintiffs had instituted proceedings seeking a declaration that the planning permission granted by the defendant planning board to the second defendant was *ultra vires* the Local Government (Planning and Development) Act 1963, as amended. The plaintiffs were residents in the area in which the second defendant proposed to site its pharmaceutical plant in respect of which permission was granted. S. 82(3)(a) of the 1963 Act, as inserted by s. 42 of the Local Government (Planning and Development) Act 1976, provides that proceedings challenging a planning permission must be brought within two months of the grant of permission. The permission in the instant case had been given on 24 July 1990 and the plaintiffs' action was begun on 21 September 1990. The defendants sought to have the action dismissed on the ground that it was frivolous and vexatious or an abuse of the process of the courts. Blayney J dismissed this application.

A preliminary issue was then set down for trial as to whether the plaintiffs had locus standi to bring the proceedings. The defendants argued, *inter alia*, that the plaintiffs had no locus standi since they had not participated at the hearing before the defendant planning board and that since the 1963 Act constituted a comprehensive code the plaintiffs should not be permitted to raise matters in the proceedings which they could have raised, but did not, at the planning hearing. In the High Court, Lavan J held that the plaintiffs had no *locus standi*, but on appeal by the plaintiffs the Supreme Court (Finlay CJ, Hederman, McCarthy, O'Flaherty and Egan JJ) unanimously reversed this decision and held in the plaintiffs' favour.

The defendants had relied on the decision of the Court in *The State (Abenglen Properties Ltd) v Dublin Corporation* [1982] ILRM 590; [1984] IR 381, but this decision was distinguished in the instant case. Applying the test of standing in *The State (Lynch) v Cooney* [1983] ILRM 89; [1982] IR 337, the Court held that since the plaintiffs had instituted the proceedings within the statutory time period specified in the 1963 Act, and since they were also aggrieved persons, in the sense that the permission impacted on them personally, they had *locus standi* to continue the proceedings as part of what McCarthy J (who delivered one of the two reasoned judgments) described as their constitutional right of access to the courts to litigate justiciable issues.

The Court accepted the plaintiffs' explanation that they had not participated in the planning appeal as they were members of the local environmental group which had processed the appeal. In addition, McCarthy J suggested that some of the arguments raised by the defendants might have some relevance to the substantive proceedings, but were not relevant to the issue of standing.

10 Misrepresentation to planning authority In *Cunningham v An Bord Pleanála*, High Court, 3 May 1990 Lavan J considered, *inter alia*, the effect of a misrepresentation in a planning application. Bord Pleanála had granted planning permission in respect of a development which involved the demolition of certain buildings. The developers' advertisement for the application referred to the demolition, but did not indicate whether the buildings involved were fit for human habitation. In their application to an Bord Pleanála, the developers stated that, to the best of their knowledge, the buildings in question were not fit for human habitation.

The applicant initiated judicial review proceedings seeking to quash the planning permission on the grounds, inter alia, that the advertisement was not sufficiently clear to comply with the Local Government (Planning and Development) Regulations 1977 and that the developers had misled An Bord Pleanála on the issue of the habitability of the buildings to be demolished. The applicant initiated the judicial review after a meeting of a group of people, including members of An Taisce and the Irish Georgian Society, who had participated in the planning appeal process.

Lavan J first addressed the question of the adequacy of the advertisement. Applying the well-known *dicta* of Henchy J in *The State (Elm Developments Ltd) v An Bord Pleanála* [1981] ILRM 108, he held that the advertisement was not sufficiently precise to comply with the 1977 Regulations. He concluded that there should have been express reference to the fact that houses which might have been habitable, albeit only with substantial investment, were involved in the planning application. He noted that such a requirement had been imposed in connection with a planning application which post-dated the instant case. Nor did he consider that the matter fell within the *de minimis* rule mentioned by Henchy J in the *Elm Developments* case.

As to whether An Bord Pleanála had been misled, Lavan J accepted that the developers had been less than frank in stating that, to the best of their knowledge, the buildings in question were not fit for habitation. He was prepared to accept that since the developers motivation was one of profit, they might only be interested in complying with the letter of planning requirements. However, he concluded that An Bord Pleanála were fully aware of the condition of the building, and that it was aware that the buildings could only have become habitable with very large investment. In fact, Lavan J stated that An Bord Pleanála were fully supportive of the development involved. In those circumstances, although the Board had erred in omitting to deal expressly with the question of habitability, such error was within jurisdiction, and thus not amenable to judicial review. In this context, he quoted with approval dicta of Henchy J in *The State (Abenglen Properties Ltd) v Dublin Corporation* [1982] ILRM 590; [1984] IR 381.

Finally, it remained for Lavan J to consider whether, in light of the defect in the advertisement, the applicant was entitled to judicial review. He concluded that, in the exercise of his discretion, no relief should be granted. He was particularly influenced in this context by the fact that the applicant appeared to represent a group of people who had been involved in the entire planning process and that the objections raised on judicial review had never been put to An Bord Pleanála. On the basis that these people had, in effect, represented that the developers had defeated all the objections which were likely to be put in their path, Lavan J concluded that it would not be appropriate to grant judicial review. He reiterated the views of Henchy J in the *Abenglen* case that the planning code should be seen largely as a self-contained code with recourse to the courts in exceptional cases only. See also the approach taken by the Supreme Court in *O'Keeffe v An Bord Pleanála* [1992] ILRM 237 in the Administrative Law chapter, 16-18, above.

11 Motorway scheme In *Nolan and Ors v Minister for the Environment and Electricity Supply Board* [1991] ILRM 705; [1991] 2 IR 548, the Supreme Court considered the procedures to be followed in relation to the construction of a motorway.

The respondent Minister had made an order under the Local Government (Roads and Motorways) Act 1974 approving a motorway scheme by Dublin County Council. The motorway path included a number of pylons which the respondent Board sought to remove and relocate. The Board applied to the Minister pursuant to the 1974 Act for his consent to removal and relocation of the pylons. The Minister purported to grant such consent pursuant to s. 10 of the 1974 Act, which authorises that consent may be given by the Minister to a statutory undertaker in relation to excavating any apparatus in the motorway path. The applicants, householders beside which the pylons were to be relocated, sought judicial review of the Minister's consent on the grounds that it was ultra vires: (i) in purporting to permit the respondent Board to perform an illegal act, namely to relocate the pylons without planning permission under the Local Government (Planning and Development) Act 1963 and (ii) in failing to comply with the principles of fair procedures and natural justice.

In the High Court Costello J granted the applicants a declaration that the Minister had acted *ultra vires* the 1974 Act in allowing a development which was not exempted under the 1963 Act: [1989] IR 357 (see the 1989 Review, 332). On appeal by the respondents the Supreme Court (Finlay CJ, Hederman and O'Flaherty JJ) allowed the appeal in part and remitted another aspect of the matter to the High Court, with certain *dicta* indicating that the applicants might, ultimately, be unsuccessful.

On the first issue, whether planning permission was required under the Local Government (Planning and Development) Act 1963, the Supreme Court held by a majority that such was not required. Hederman and O'Flaherty JJ (Finlay CJ dissenting) held that since s. 8 of the 1974 Act prohibited a planning authority from granting permission for any development which is part of a motorway scheme under the 1974 Act, the 1974 Act should be regarded as a self-contained piece of legislation quite separate from the planning code. Thus, it was not appropriate to approach the instant case by considering whether the respondent Board's actions were or were not exempt from the 1963 Act. They concluded that the trial judge had thus erred in finding that the Minister had acted ultra vires. Therefore, the respondents' appeal on this ground was allowed.

On the question of fair procedures, the Court unanimously held that the Minister was required, in the exercise of his powers under s. 10 of the 1974 Act, to consider the views of persons, such as the applicants, who might be directly affected by the proposal which the respondent Board had made to the Minister. This was supported by reference to the Court's decisions in *East Donegal Co-Op Ltd v Attorney General* [1970] IR 317 and *O'Brien v Bord na Mona* [1983] ILRM 314; [1983] IR 255.

However, since the procedures in question had not been considered in the High Court, this aspect of the case was remitted to the High Court. While there is support for the view that matters not considered in the High Court will not be dealt with by the Supreme Court, it must be said that recent case law has appeared to be quite flexible on this: see the cases discussed in the 1988 Review, 125-6, and the 1989 Review, 343. The decision to remit in *Nolan* was further complicated by certain dicta from the Supreme Court judges which appeared to indicate that the applicants would face an uphill struggle in the High Court on remittal. Thus, all three judges felt that the requirements of fair procedures did not require a formal public notice, or an oral hearing for all objections, but would be satisfied if the Minister received and considered the gist of local objections. In addition, O'Flaherty J (with whom Hederman J agreed, the Chief Justice expressing no view on this point) opined that the Minister may have complied with the requirements of fair procedures in the instant case. While O'Flaherty J prefaced this remark by saying that he was not expressing a final view on the point, it might have been better to refrain from expressing any view given that he was consenting to an order remitting this very point to the High Court.

12 Practice: judicial review The Supreme Court in *O'Keeffe v An Bord Pleanála and Anor* [1992] ILRM 237 (see 16-18, above) issued what amounted to a Practice Direction on aspects of appeals in planning cases. Delivering the Court's leading judgment, the Chief Justice made two important points at the end of that judgment. First, an applicant for judicial review must seek to join, and the court should normally join, any party who is likely to be affected by the avoidance of the decision impugned. Second where judicial review is by way of a plenary summons, the action should be presented by way of oral evidence, unless the court by express order directs a hearing on affidavit or accepts from the parties an expressly agreed statement of facts.

13 Section 4 notices The power to grant planning permission pursuant to a motion under s. 4 of the City and County Management (Amendment) Act 1955 was limited by s. 44 of the Local Government Act 1991: see 312, above.

14 Time limits The two month time limit for challenging planning decisions in s. 82(3A) of the Local Government (Planning and Development) Act 1963, as inserted by s. 42 of the Local Government (Planning and Development) Act 1976, arose in two cases in 1991.

In *Colgan v Dublin Corporation*, High Court, 19 March 1991, the applicant instituted proceedings claiming a declaration that he had been granted planning permission by default. The basis of his claim was that he had not received any response to his application within the two month period specified in s. 26(4) of the 1963 Act. The Corporation had actually posted a reply (granting a more limited permission than sought) one day within the two month deadline, but the applicant stated that this had not reached him until after the two month period had elapsed. The case law on the issue is unclear: compare *The State (Murphy) v Dublin County Council* [1970] IR 253 with *Freeney v Bray UDC* [1982] ILRM 29.

In a neat twist of irony, however, the Corporation argued that this issue should not be reached because the applicant had not brought his judicial review proceedings within the two month period specified in s. 82(3A) of the 1963 Act. Costello J agreed. He rejected the applicant's argument that s. 82(3A) did not apply because he had merely sought a declaration. Costello J noted that the instant case manifestly involved a challenge to the validity of the reply from the Corporation: on that basis the two month time limit applied. He therefore dismissed the application on that preliminary ground.

The second case on time limits, *Tennyson v Dun Laoghaire Corporation* [1991] 2 IR 527 involved a different issue arising from s. 82(3A). For other aspects of the case, see 314, above. The applicants had applied for judicial review of a planning permission just one day before the expiry of the two month time limit in s. 82(3A). The application was adjourned by the judge dealing with the matter for over three weeks to seek clarification of certain matters. It was only at the adjourned hearing that leave to seek judicial review was granted. Barr J held that this adjournment had not brought the applicants outside the two month time limit, since it had not been established that the material considered at the adjourned hearing was fundamental to the success of the original application.

15 *Urban renewal: Temple Bar*   The Temple Bar Area Renewal and Development Act 1991 details the special arrangements for the renewal and development of the Temple Bar area in Dublin. The vehicle for this is Temple Bar Renewal Ltd, which is given substantial powers by the Act, including powers of compulsory acquisition. For discussion of the background to the Act see Cooney's Annotation, *Irish Current Law Statutes Annotated.*

SANITARY SERVICES

Dangerous building: support   The extent of a sanitary authority's obligation to support a dangerous building was clarified by the Supreme Court in *Treacy v Dublin Corporation* [1992] ILRM 650. In an earlier decision, *The State (McGuinness) v Maguire* [1967] IR 348, the point had been left in a state under which the Corporation in the instant case believed it had no obligation of support. For discussion of the *McGuinness* case, see Keane, *The Law of Local Government in the Republic of Ireland*, 107-12.

The defendant Corporation, as sanitary authority, declared a building to be dangerous within the meaning of the Local Government (Sanitary Services) Act 1964. Under s. 3 of the 1964 Act, it gave notice in March 1988 to the plaintiff, the occupier of the adjoining building, of its intention to enter and demolish the dangerous building. The plaintiff obtained an interim injunction restraining such demolition unless the defendant provided the plaintiff's building with adequate support and protection against the weather. It was accepted that the plaintiff's premises enjoyed an easement of support from the dangerous building. Costello J granted a permanent injunction in the terms sought. On appeal by the Corporation the Supreme Court (Finlay CJ, Hederman, McCarthy, O'Flaherty and Egan JJ) unanimously affirmed the High Court decision.

The Chief Justice held that where the Corporation exercises its power to demolish a dangerous building under s. 3 of the 1964 Act, this cannot be done unless existing easements of support are protected. Otherwise, he stated, the Corporation would be in breach of its overall obligation under the 1964 Act to prevent the creation or development of dangerous structures. Thus, the Corporation was required to give back support to the plaintiff's premises, distinguishing the instant case from that in *The State (McGuinness) v Maguire* [1967] IR 348, referred to above.

The Court went on to touch on an interesting issue in land law, namely, whether there is a separate easement against 'wind and weather'. In the leading English decision on this point, *Phipps v Pears* [1967] 1 QB 76, the Court of Appeal came down against the existence of such an easement as such. In *Treacy*, although the Supreme Court appeared to favour this view, it also concluded that it would be unrealistic, in the context of terraced buildings, to confine the support requirement to one of buttressing, since in a short time the buttressed wall, having regard to its age, would become unstable and cease to be a support. Thus, the Corporation was required to provide protection against wind and weather, albeit not under the heading of an easement.

On a procedural point, the Court noted that there had been an unexplained delay in processing the appeal from the High Court. The Court noted that, having regard to the dangerous condition of the building, the appeal to the Court should have been expedited and an early hearing would have been granted on application.

Sewer maintenance   The wide reach of a sanitary authority's obligation to maintain sewers was graphically illustrated by the decision of Costello J in *Merriman v Dublin Corporation and Dublin County Council* [1993] ILRM 58; 1992] 1 IR 129.

The plaintiff was injured when he fell into an open gully on the side of a roadway. The gully, road and adjacent housing had been built by Dublin Corporation in Dublin County Council's administrative area, but the roadway had not been taken in charge by the Council at the time of the accident. A grill on the gulley had been removed at some unknown stage prior to the plaintiff's accident. The gully constituted a 'sewer' within the meaning of s. 2 of the Public Health (Irl) Act 1878. Both defendants denied responsibility for the injuries sustained by the plaintiff but, ultimately, Costello J found for the plaintiff against the Council for breach of its statutory duty as a sanitary authority under the 1878 Act.

Costello J first held that the Corporation owed no duty of care at common law to the plaintiff nor was it in breach of statutory duty to the plaintiff either as sanitary authority or as a road authority.

However, as already indicated, he held that although the Council had not taken in charge the road in question, it was in breach of statutory duty since the gully constituted a 'sewer' under s. 2 of the Public Health (Irl) Act 1878 and it was obliged to keep in repair all sewers belonging to it under s. 15 of the 1878 Act. He relied on the decision in *White v Hindley Local Board* (1875) LR 10 QB 219 to support this conclusion.

The Council had argued that, if it was in breach of statutory duty, then it was entitled to an indemnity from the Corporation because the Corporation had agreed with the Council to maintain the road in question until it was taken in charge. However, Costello J held that this did not create any statutory obligations towards third parties and so the defendants were not 'concurrent wrongdoers' under s. 11 of the Civil Liability Act 1961, and the Council was not therefore entitled to an indemnity from the Corporation. This point is further considered in the Torts chapter, 409-10, below.

Finally, on the question of damages, Costello J found that the plaintiff had not been a candid witness in relation to the extent of his injuries; and having regard to the medical evidence he awarded £10,000 in damages.

ULTRA VIRES RULE

The relaxation of the *ultra vires* rule by s. 6 of the Local Government Act 1991 is discussed above, 311.

Practice and Procedure

ABUSE OF PROCESS

The inherent jurisdiction of the courts to dismiss claims as an abuse of process was discussed in *Sun Fat Chan v Osseous Ltd*, Supreme Court, 30 July 1991. Under older forms of procedure, the instant case would have been described as a demurrer action (the most famous of which was *Donoghue v Stevenson* [1932] AC 562), in which the defendant admits facts pleaded by the plaintiff but contends that the pleadings disclose no cause of action.

The plaintiff had instituted proceedings claiming specific performance of a contract with the defendant company for the sale of land. The contract was subject to the plaintiff, as purchaser, obtaining planning permission, within six months, for the erection of a single dwelling on the land. Permission within the stated period was not sought. Some time later the plaintiff successfully obtained, with the encouragement of the defendant, planning permission but this was revoked by An Bord Pleanála on appeal by a third party. The defendant then rescinded the contract of sale. In the High Court, the defendant sought to have the plaintiff's proceedings dismissed on the ground that, on the admitted facts, the plaintiff could not succeed. The plaintiff argued that the right to rescind was vested in the plaintiff only. Blayney J rejected this argument and dismissed the action.

On appeal by the plaintiff to the Supreme Court, the plaintiff did not rely on the ground put forward in the High Court but argued that, since the defendant had encouraged the plaintiff to seek planning permission outside the time limit specified in the contract, the defendant should not be entitled to rely on the right to rescind stated in the contract. The Court (Finlay CJ, Hederman, McCarthy, O'Flaherty and Egan JJ) dismissed the appeal.

The Court noted that since the plaintiff had not questioned the inherent jurisdiction to dismiss a claim at the stage of the delivery of a statement of claim, it would proceed on the basis that such jurisdiction existed. While this approach of the Court may not signal any particular distaste for the jurisdiction to dismiss, there may be some basis in the future for a constitutional challenge to a wide-ranging use of such a power, based on the right of access to the courts protected by Article 40.3 of the Constitution.

Perhaps for this reason, the Court in the instant case was quite cautious in its approach (see also the discussion of *Murphy v Greene* [1991] ILRM 404; [1990] 2 IR 566 in the 1990 Review, 147-50). Referring to the judgment of Costello J in *Barry v Buckley* [1981] IR 306 (in which the jurisdiction was considered at length) the Court stated that in any event the power to dismiss should be exercised with caution. In the particular circumstances of the present case, for example, it was prepared to take into consideration arguments by a plaintiff which were not raised at first instance even if they might have been.

This cautious approach by the Court was to no avail as far as the plaintiff was concerned. The Court noted that the plaintiff's argument on appeal required it to imply a term into the contract between the parties. However, applying the officious bystander test, the Court concluded that since it could not be said that such a term would have been agreed to by the defendant as vendor at the time the contract was made, the court should not imply such a term. The plaintiff's action was therefore dismissed: see the discussion in the Contract chapter, 113-5, above.

A similar cautious approach to striking out proceedings was evident later in 1991 in the judgment of Costello J (who had delivered the judgment in *Barry v Buckley*) in *Olympia Productions Ltd v Mackintosh* [1992] ILRM 204 (see the discussion in the Conflict of Laws chapter, 86-7, above).

ADJOURNMENT

The refusal of a trial judge to adjourn a personal injuries hearing to allow an expert witness to be called was upheld in *Ward v Walsh*, Supreme Court, 31 July 1991. The case is discussed in the context of damages in the Torts chapter, 441-2, below. Briefly, the plaintiff suffered partial paraplegia and other injuries while a passenger in a car which overturned when being driven by a servant or agent of the defendant, the car's owner. The trial judge (Lardner J) concluded that the car was being driven at between 60 and 70 mph at the time of the accident. The driver was wearing a seat belt but the plaintiff was not. The trial judge found the plaintiff to be 20% contributorily negligent for failing to wear his seat belt. The plaintiff appealed against this finding and both parties appealed various headings of the damages awarded. For present purposes, it may be noted that the trial judge had refused to adjourn the trial to enable the plaintiff call an expert to testify on the effect of not wearing a seat belt.

The Supreme Court (Finlay CJ, Hederman and Egan JJ) upheld this aspect of the trial judge's approach. The Court held that the trial judge had correctly exercised his discretion to refuse such an adjournment, having regard in particular to the length of the trial and that the plaintiff had an ample opportunity otherwise to address the court on this point.

APPELLATE COURT FUNCTION

Fresh evidence   The question whether the Supreme Court will allow fresh evidence to be led on appeal from the High Court was again considered in 1991 in *Murphy v Minister for Defence and Ors* [1991] 2 IR 161. For discussion of the case law, see the 1989 Review, 341-3.

The plaintiff had instituted proceedings for damages arising from two separate incidents which occurred while he was a serving member of the Irish Army. In 1983, the plaintiff suffered back injuries while lifting an item under orders from his superiors. In 1986, the plaintiff was required to undergo a fitness test, during which he claimed he aggravated the 1983 back injury. In the High Court, the plaintiff's claim was dismissed. For the High Court hearing, the Army's medical record of the plaintiff was available. On appeal by the plaintiff to the Supreme Court, the plaintiff sought (pursuant to O.58, r.8 of the Rules of the Superior Courts 1986) to introduce additional evidence, namely, an Army Training Circular of 1980 and an Army Medicial Directive of 1979. The Supreme Court (Finlay CJ, Hederman and O'Flaherty JJ) granted the application to adduce the additional evidence.

The question which arose was whether the plaintiff's legal advisers had, in the circumstances, used all reasonable diligence in seeking relevant information for the trial of the action. Delivering the leading judgment, Finlay CJ declined to accept the defendants' submission that the legal advisers could have done more. The Chief Justice accepted that it had not been apparant that, apart from the Army's medical records, there were any other documents relevant to the case. In a concurring judgment O'Flaherty J pointedly noted that the Court should not acquiesce in the suggestion (which, he felt, the defendants' argument amounted to) that there should be a slavish application for discovery in all cases. Of course, discovery will be an important element in many cases but the Court was keen to ensure that the costs of actions would not be increased unnesessarily by, in effect, requiring discovery in all instances. For criticism of the excessive use of discovery and other pre-trial procedures in the United States, see, for example, Armstrong, 'Discovery Abuse and Judicial Management' (1992) 142 *New LJ* 927.

On the contents of the Circular and Directive, the Court noted that they referred to conducting medical examinations in certain circumstances. Clearly such 'best practice' would have had an important bearing on the trial judge's view of the approach taken by the defendants and would also have affected the course of the cross-examination of the plaintiff's superior officers in the trial. Since the defendants had not disputed the credibility of the evidence in question, the Court concluded (applying its decision in *Lynagh v Mackin* [1970] IR 180) that the plaintiff was entitled to the order sought and a re-trial was ordered: [1991] 2 IR at 168.

Review of trial court's findings The well-established limitations on an appeal court's functions of review in an appeal on a point of law were applied by the Supreme Court in *Sinnott v O'Connor*, Supreme Court, 12 February 1991 (see the Torts chapter, 420, below) and in *Browne v Bank of Ireland Finance Ltd* [1991] ILRM 421; [1991] 1 IR 431 (see the Revenue chapter, 360-1, below). Consistent with the general approach, however, the Court has indicated that there are some situations where conclusions of fact by a trial judge will be overturned.

A straightforward illustration of this is the decision of the Court in *In re D.G., an Infant; O.G. v An Bord Uchtála* [1991] ILRM 514; [1991] 1 IR 491. Here, the Supreme Court overturned a High Court decision on the ground that there was no foundation whatever in the evidence for certain findings made by the trial judge: this case is discussed in the 1990 Review, 287-91.

Less easy cases for the Court to deal with were two further decisions in 1991. In *Mullen v Quinnsworth Ltd (No. 2)* [1991] ILRM 439 (discussed in the Torts chapter, 393-5, below), the Court held that where no question arose as to the truthfulness of the witnesses in a case, the Supreme Court was in as good a position as the trial judge to draw its own conclusions or inferences from facts proved or admitted and to decide the case accordingly. A similar statement was made by the Court in its decision just three days later in *Coleman v Clarke* [1991] ILRM 841 (also discussed in the Torts chapter, 404-6, below). In both cases, the Court applied the general principles established in the leading case *Northern Bank Finance Corp Ltd v Charlton* [1979] IR 149.

COSTS

Counsel's fees In *Smith v Ireland and Ors*, High Court, 14 February 1991 and *Smyth and Anor v Tunney and Ors (No. 2)*, High Court, 8 August 1991 the appropriateness of counsel's fees was considered. In *Smith*, Lynch J was required to consider the issue in the unusual circumstances that neither the briefing solicitor or the leading senior counsel in the case was available to give evidence. In *Smyth*, Murphy J concluded that counsel's brief and refresher fees were too high, and the case gives a valuable insight into the level of fees in High Court litigation. For recent discussion of the principles involved, see *The State (Gallagher Shatter & Co.) v de Valera (No. 2)* [1991] 2 IR 198 (1990 Review, 430-1) and *Crotty v An Taoiseach (No. 2)* [1990] ILRM 617 (1989 Review, 346-7).

In *Smith v Ireland and Ors*, High Court, 14 February 1991, the plaintiff had instituted civil proceedings arising from his arrest under s. 30 of the Offences against the State Act 1939, claiming damages for slander, wrongful arrest, false imprisonment, negligence and failure to vindicate his constitutional rights. The trial of the action lasted 5 days. It appeared that the gardaí thought that the plaintiff was another person. The trial judge put two questions to the jury, the first being whether the plaintiff had been arrested as 'Kevin Walsh', to which the jury answered 'Yes', and, secondly, if the first question was answered in the affirmative, to assess damages which the jury assessed at £28,000. On taxation of the costs of the action, the Taxing Master reduced the brief fee allowed to the two senior counsel for the plaintiff. The briefing solicitor for the plaintiff, who had emigrated to the United States, was unavailable to state whether he had exercised an independent judgment on the level of fee to be allowed with the leading senior. The leading senior had since died. The second senior had understood the fee to have been agreed with the leader. The plaintiff had been informed prior to the trial as to the level of the fees. The Taxing Master had also disallowed a pre-trial opinion given by the junior counsel for the plaintiff. On appeal by the plaintiff Lynch J allowed the appeal and remitted the case to the Taxing Master.

As to the exercise of an independent judgment by the solicitor, Lynch J held that the Taxing Master had erred in concluding that the solicitor for the plaintiff had not exercised an independent judgment on the correctness of the fee to senior counsel; and it was to be presumed, in the absence of contrary evidence, that a briefing solicitor would do his duty conscientiously and would consider the appropriate level of fee payable.

Having examined the transcript of the trial of the action, he also held that the Taxing Master had not taken into account the actual complexity of the case even though the questions put to the jury appeared to focus on the issues of false imprisonment.

Then, Lynch J held that the Taxing Master had erred in concluding that the fee agreed with senior counsel was a 'special fee' within the meaning of O.99, r.37(18) of the Rules of the Superior Courts 1986, and he concluded that the briefing solicitor had been correct to inform the plaintiff in advance of the potential fee he might be exposed to if the claim was unsuccessful. Finally, he held that the Taxing Master should have allowed the pre-trial opinion under O.99, r.37(18) bearing in mind again the complexity of the case.

In the second case in this area, *Smyth and Anor v Tunney and Ors (No. 2)*, High Court, 8 August 1991 the parties had been involved in a 17 day civil action in which the plaintiffs contended, inter alia, that the defendants had fraudulently concealed alterations to an agreement between the parties and the defendants argued that the proceedings constituted an abuse of the process of the courts and an attempt to blackmail them: see *Smyth and Anor v Tunney and Ors*, High Court, 6 October 1989 (see the 1989 Review, 127 and 444). Each of the defendants was represented by one senior and one junior counsel. Senior counsel for the first defendant agreed in advance with his instructing solicitor a brief fee of 10,000 guineas, and a refresher fee of 2,000 guineas per day. The instructing solicitor considered these fees reasonable. The Taxing Master allowed a brief fee of £6,875 and a refresher fee of £1,000. The instructing solicitor for the first defendant sought an instruction fee of £90,000, which the Taxing Master reduced to £25,000. Reductions to £12,500 and £8,000 were made in the instructing fees of the two other solicitors for the defendants. On appeal to the High Court, Murphy J upheld some of the alterations which the Taxing Master had made, and reinstated some of the original marked fees.

As to the general practice for marking fees, Murphy J noted that the former practice of a solicitor marking a fee on a brief (referred to in *Robb v Connor* (1875) IR 9 Eq 373, and cited by Murphy J), which had the merit that the solicitor focused on the question of the appropriate fee for counsel, had fallen into disuse and he stated that it was not the court's function to seek to revive the practice.

On the Taxing Master's function, Murphy J applied the leading cases (in particular *Dunne v O'Neill* [1974] IR 180, *Kelly v Breen* [1978] ILRM 63 and *The State (Gallagher Shatter & Co.) v de Valera (No. 2)* [1991] 2 IR 198) in pointing out that it was not the function of the Taxing Master in reviewing counsel's fees to determine whether such fees were correct, but that he did have a discretion to review counsel's fees in that he was required to decide whether a reasonably prudent solicitor acting in a reasonable way would have offered such a fee.

In the instant case, Murphy J held that the Taxing Master had erred in describing the fee charged by counsel as a special fee, since there was no evidence to support this. However, having regard to the fact that a fee of more than 5,000 guineas had rarely been allowed on taxation, and since the instant case did not involve any special scientific evidence but was largely fought on questions of fact, Murphy J concluded that the fee of 10,000 guineas was not one which a reasonable solicitor would have offered; and the appropriate brief fee was 7,500 guineas with a refresher fee of 1,000 guineas.

Turning to the solicitor's instructions fees, he held that the Taxing Master was entitled to determine whether the fee sought was the correct fee, and for this reason the experience of the Taxing Master was especially relied on by the courts. Murphy J stated that an instruction fee could not be used to compensate the solicitor in some way for the low levels of fees allowable under Appendix W of the Rules of the Superior Courts 1986 in respect of other expenses, and in the instant case the solicitors' role had not been dominant but its outcome depended primarily on the forensic skills of counsel. However, he ultimately concluded that in the circumstances the fees allowed by the Taxing Master were too low and instructing fees of £40,000, of £22,500 and of £16,000 should be allowed, bearing in mind that the solicitor for the first defendant had completed much of the paperwork for the case.

Finally, on certain attendance fees, Murphy J held that the Taxing Master had correctly disallowed a fee of £1,500 for senior counsel and of £1,000 for junior counsel for their attendance to take judgment in the case and that the Taxing Master had correctly allowed attendance fees for an estate agent and an architect who, although not called, were correctly regarded as witnesses whose attendance might be crucial. He referred with approval to *Duan v Freshford Co-Op Ltd* (1942) ILTR 220 in this context.

Daily transcript In *Ward v Walsh*, Supreme Court, 31 July 1991 (see the Torts chapter, 441-2, below), the Court held that the unsuccessful defendant should not be required to bear the cost of a daily transcript of the evidence, since there were instructing solicitor and one junior counsel and two senior counsel involved on both sides and there had been no detailed scientific evidence in the case.

Follow the event: limit on rule S. 14 of the Courts Act 1991 introduces certain limits on the general rule that the successful plaintiff is entitled to costs to discourage the bringing of cases in a higher court: see 347, below.

Partnership dissolution In *Baxter v Horgan (No. 2)*, Supreme Court, 7 June 1991 the plaintiff had begun High Court proceedings in 1976 seeking the disso- lution of a partnership between himself and the defendant. The defendant denied a partnership, but the proceedings were compromised in 1977 by a consent order dissolving the partnership. An account by the Examiner of all transactions was ordered, but various disputes arose as to whether certain transactions formed part of the partnership. These disputes led to various High Court hearings, including a judgment of Carroll J that certain invoices produced by the defendant were forgeries (High Court, 21 February 1986). Further disputes between the parties resulted in another reference by the Examiner to the High Court. In relation to some of the items referred, Murphy J found in the defendant's favour, but he awarded the costs of the proceedings to the plaintiff (High Court, 28 May 1990). On appeal by the defendant against the award of costs the Supreme Court (Finlay CJ, McCarthy and Egan JJ) unanimously dismissed the appeal.

The Court noted that while it is usual that in partnership actions the costs of accounts after dissolution are directed to be paid out of partnership assets, the trial judge has a wide discretion in the matter. In the instant case, the

Court agreed that it was appropriate to take into account that the defendant was the partner responsible for keeping proper accounts and that he had failed to do so. Having regard to previous findings that the defendant had produced forgeries, the plaintiff was entitled to put the defendant on proof of each item relevant to the accounts; and while not every issue had been decided in the plaintiff's favour, the Court accepted that the trial judge had strong grounds for awarding the plaintiff the costs of the issues referred from the Examiner.

Professional witnesses: standby fees   In *Aspell v O'Brien* [1992] ILRM 278; [1991] 2 IR 416 Costello J expressed disapproval at the practice of giving 'standby' fees to medical witnesses. The plaintiff's personal injury action against the defendant had been listed for 30 and 31 May 1990. Evidence was heard on 30 May but the action was settled on 31 May. Counsel for the plaintiff had directed the attendance of four doctors, but only one had given evidence when the case was settled. All four doctors had charged standby fees for 30 May, and the plaintiff's solicitor discharged these fees. It was a long standing practice that such standby fees were not allowed on taxation by the Taxing Master, but the Incorporated Law Society of Ireland recommended that such fees be discharged. It was argued that such fees should be allowed on taxation, but the Taxing Master declined to allow them. On appeal, Costello J affirmed the Taxing Master's decision.

While Costello J acknowledged that the listing system for personal injuries actions in the High Court was not very satisfactory, and that this undoubtedly caused inconvenience to all professional witnesses who are not called on the date scheduled for their evidence, he did not accept that it was reasonable, within the meaning of O.99, r.37(8) of the Rules of the Superior Courts 1986, for professional witnesses to charge standby fees. He noted in particular that it had not not been suggested that such professional witnesses necessarily suffer any financial loss for a day on which they have mistakenly made themselves available to appear in court. He considered that any additional inconvenience would be compensated for by the payment of the attendance fee.

In relation to medical witnesses as a particular case, Costello J accepted that they were in a special category, since their inconvenience might be accompanied by hardship to other people, but he noted that the courts took account of this by arranging, for example, to have their evidence heard out of turn or by specially fixing a date for hearing an action.

He went on to hold that the practice of paying such standby fees, albeit recommended by the Law Society, did not mean that such payment was either necessary for the attainment of justice or for enforcing the rights of either party, within O.99, r.37(18) of the 1986 Rules. It had been argued that the principles laid down by Hamilton P in *Kelly v Breen* [1978] ILRM 63 supported the payment of such standby fees in order to protect a party's interests, but Costello J did not accept this and stated firmly that no practice could confer a right to payment outside the terms of O.99.

However, acknowledging the practical difficulties in meeting the needs of justice, Costello J ended his judgment by stating that it would be in the interests of the administration of justice and of the medical profession if agreement could be reached more frequently to accept medical reports as evidence without the necessity to call their authors merely for the purpose of confirming and repeating their contents in court. He stated that consideration should be given to the establishment of pre-trial procedures to permit this to be done formally, as well as the acceptance of reports, maps and photographs from other professional witnesses without the necessity of having to prove them formally. This procedure has, of course, been in place in the United Kingdom for some years and its introduction in the State could make a practical contribution to lowering the overall costs of personal injuries actions as well as encouraging, perhaps, earlier settlements of those cases in which liability is not in issue.

Security for costs   *Fallon v An Bord Pleanála* [1991] ILRM 799 involved an important application of the general principles of security for costs.

The plaintiff, a man in his late 20s, instituted proceedings seeking to have invalidated a decision of the defendant Planning Board granting retention planning permission for certain bungalows which had been built by the second defendant. The plaintiff's claim was dismissed in the High Court. The plaintiff appealed this decision to the Supreme Court. The second defendant then applied, pursuant to O.58, r.17 of the Rules of the Superior Courts 1986, for an order from the Supreme Court requiring the plaintiff to furnish security for costs in respect of the appeal. The Court (Finlay CJ, Griffin and Hederman JJ) unanimously held, in an ex tempore decision, that security should be provided. The Chief Justice stated that the special circumstances required under the 1986 Rules (and the decision of the Court in *Midland Bank Ltd v Crossley-Cooke* [1969] IR 56) which justifed the making of an order requiring security for costs were that: (i) the plaintiff was a young man of modest means; (ii) the appeal would not involve a question of law of public importance; and (iii) there were special circumstances in the case, involving the uncontroverted assertion that the plaintiff had been deliberately chosen as a person of little means to bring the proceedings, which were such that security for costs should be required.

On remittal of the issue to the High Court, the Master fixed security at £2,500, being about one third the defendant's estimated costs in contesting the plaintiff's appeal to the Supreme Court. On appeal to the High Court, Egan J affirmed that sum. On further appeal by the second defendant, who argued that the sum set was, in the circumstances, too low, the Supreme Court by a majority (Hederman and McCarthy JJ; Finlay CJ dissenting) held that the amount set should stand.

The Court accepted the approach taken by the Supreme Court in *Thalle v Soares* [1957] IR 182 that the customary practice of the courts to require one third of the estimated costs of an appeal as security was a good general guide to setting the amount of security. However, this sum was not a fixed amount, and could be departed from in exceptional circumstances, such as where an appeal was bordering on vexatious litigation or devoid of any merit.

Of particular significance in the *Fallon* case, however, was the reference of the majority to the importance of ensuring that the constitutional right of equal access to the courts should not be breached. Thus, Hederman J concluded his judgment by stating:

> The Court should not, in my view, shut out any litigant solely because of poverty. The interest of justice demands that in so far as possible there should be equality before the law.

In the same vein, McCarthy J noted that the decision in *Thalle v Soares* [1957] IR 182 had been made without reference to the constitutional aspect of security. Bearing this new dimension in mind, the majority held that, although the plaintiff was a man of limited means, the interests of justice did not require an increase in the amount of security fixed by the Master, since the defendant would not be in any way prejudiced by the level of security actually set. It was also relevant that the plaintiff's appeal was not devoid of merit as there was an arguable point of law to be made and the plaintiff had also lodged appeal papers and the case was ready for hearing in the Supreme Court.

While the one third rule is likely to continue as the benchmark for most cases of security for costs, the *Fallon* decision indicates that the right of access to the courts may prove important as a factor, at least in relation to the amount of security required.

DIRECTION APPLICATION

The *ex tempore* decision of the Supreme Court in *Hetherington v Ultra Tyre Service Ltd and Ors*, Irish Times LR, 22 July 1991 provided important guidance on the correct approach a judge should take where an application for a direction is made, that is, where the defendant submits that the plaintiff's evidence is not sufficient to establish the case made against the defendant. In the instant case, the trial judge had acceded to an application for a direction by one of the defendants at the end of the plaintiff's evidence.

The Supreme Court (Finlay CJ, McCarthy and O'Flaherty JJ) noted that none of the defendants had actually queried the approach adopted by the trial judge in the instant case, and the substance of the appeal concerned the liabilty of the remaining parties. Nonetheless, the Chief Justice, with whom the other members of the Court agreed, felt that it was appropriate to provide some guidance on the question. He stated that where a defendant in an action being tried by a judge alone applies for a direction at the end of the plaintiff's case, the judge would be entitled to inquire from the defendant applying for the direction as to whether the defendant intends to stand over the application, in other words whether the defendant intends not to call any evidence. If the defendant indicates an intention to call evidence, Finlay CJ indicated held that the trial judge would be entitled to decline to make any decision on the application for a direction and to require that all evidence in the case be heard. Where, as in the instant case, there were a number of defendants, the Chief Justice stated that the possible impact of a non-suit in favour of one defendant should be considered in relation to the other defendants in the case.

DISCOVERY

1 Discovery as substantive action The view that discovery could, in limited circumstances, be sought as a substantive remedy gained support from the decision of the Supreme Court in *Megaleasing UK Ltd and Ors v Barrett and Ors* [1992] 1 IR 219.

The plaintiffs had instituted plenary proceedings against the defendants in which the substantive relief was for orders of discovery concerning certain invoices said to be in their possession. The purpose of such orders was stated by the plaintiffs to be to facilitate them in bringing proceedings against other parties whose tortious acts the plaintiffs claimed had caused them (the plaintiffs) to suffer loss. In the High Court, Costello J granted the plaintiffs the relief sought, and refused to grant a stay of execution upon the order. On appeal by the defendants against the refusal of the stay the Supreme Court (McCarthy, O'Flaherty and Egan JJ) granted the stay.

McCarthy J, in the leading judgment, referred with apparent approval to the decision of the House of Lords in *Norwich Pharmacal Co. v Customs and Excise Commissioners* [1974] AC 133 in which the concept of discovery as a substantive remedy had been accepted. Since the instant case involved an application for a stay on the High Court order, the Supreme Court was not required to express a final view on the matter, but the Court did accept the principle that the courts should aid in obtaining all information relevant and necessary to the true determination of facts. This approach presaged the later approval of the *Norwich Pharmacal* decision by the Court in *Megaleasing*

UK Ltd and Ors v Barrett and Ors (No. 2), Supreme Court, 20 July 1992, although the Court decided that the principle in that case did not apply to the circumstances of the instant case. This second judgment in the case will be discussed in the 1992 Review.

To revert to the Court's decision on the application for the stay, it was noted that the defendants' application involved important constitutional issues concerning the rights of privacy and of communication. Since, if the stay was not granted, an appeal against the order made in the High Court would be rendered moot and a decision in the plaintiff's favour at this stage of the proceedings would determine the action, the Court held that in the circumstances the interests of justice required that a stay be granted. As already noted, the decision of the Supreme Court in 1992 was, ultimately, that the plaintiffs were not entitled to the discovery order sought. None-theless, in appropriate cirumstances, the decisions in the *Megaleasing* case have opened the way for successfully obtaining discovery as a substantive remedy.

2 *Excessive cost*   In *Bula Ltd and Ors v Tara Mines Ltd and Ors (No. 5)*, High Court, 11 January 1991, Murphy J dealt with a further discovery application in this long-running litigation (see the 1990 Review, 433). The plaintiffs sought mining records of the first defendant going back over 15 years. Murphy J was sympathetic to the defendant's argument that this might involve excessive cost, but he ordered discovery of what he considered would be the relevant portions of the company's records. He also stated that, if the cost in fact turned out to be excessive, he would be open to the argument that the plaintiffs provide security for such costs, particularly having regard to a previous order in the litigation that the plaintiffs be given access for exploratory drilling as part of their claim.

3 *Not to be sought automatically*   In *Murphy v Minister for Defence* [1991] 2 IR 161, the notion that discovery should be applied for automatically in personal injuries actions was dismissed by the Supreme Court: see 327, above.

4 *Privilege: European Communities*   In *Duff and Ors v Minister for Agriculture and Food and Ors* [1992] 1 IR 198, Lardner J rejected a claim for privilege against the background of the European Communities Act 1972.

The plaintiffs had instituted proceedings claiming damages against the defendants in respect of farm development plans which they had entered into. In the course of the proceedings, they sought discovery of, *inter alia*, documents which had been prepared by civil servants for the Minister for Agriculture and Food in relation to meetings of the EC Council of Agriculture. The defendants argued that such documents were privileged on the ground that decisions of the Council of Ministers were confidential under the Rules of Procedure of the Council of 24 July 1989. Article 3 of these Rules of Procedure provides that meetings of the Council shall not be in public unless the Council unanimously decides otherwise. Article 18 provides that the deliberations of the Council shall be covered by the obligation of professional secrecy.

Lardner J firstly accepted that the 1979 Rules of Procedure came within the definition of 'acts adopted by the institutions of the Community' within the meaning of s. 2 of the European Communities Act 1972. Thus, these Rules formed part of the domestic law of the State.

However, he did not accept that discovery of the documents would breach the confidentiality provisions of Articles 3 or 18 of the 1979 Rules. After a perusal of the documents in question, he held that they had been prepared solely for the purposes of preparing the Minister for participation in the meetings of the Council of Ministers. They were thus not part of the actual deliberations of the Council and thus their discovery would not breach the 1979 Rules.

5 Privilege: legal professional In *Hurstridge Finance Ltd v Lismore Homes Ltd*, High Court, 15 February 1991 Costello J applied the principles established in *Smurfit Paribas Bank Ltd v AAB Export Finance Ltd* [1990] ILRM 588; [1990] 1 IR 469 (see the 1990 Review, 435-6).

In *Bula Ltd and Ors v Crowley and Ors (No. 3)*, High Court, 8 March 1991 Murphy J upheld a claim to legal professional privilege, holding that none of the documents involved came within the 'dual purpose' rule applied in *Tromso Sparebank v Beirne (No. 2)* [1989] ILRM 257 (1989 Review, 331-4).

In *Breathnach v Ireland (No. 3)* [1992] ILRM 755, Keane J considered legal professional privilege in relation to the Director of Public Prosecutions: 341-3, below.

6 Privilege: public interest The extent of public interest privilege arose for discussion by the Supreme Court in *Ambiorix Ltd and Ors v Minister for the Environment and Ors* [1992] ILRM 209; [1992] 1 IR 277. In the course of the judgments delivered, the Court affirmed the seminal decision in *Murphy v Dublin Corporation* [1972] IR 215. In an earlier decision of the High Court, *Gormley v Ireland*, High Court, 7 March 1991 Murphy J also applied the *Murphy* principles in the context of material connected with internment. A third case, *Bula Ltd and Ors v Tara Mines Ltd and Ors (No. 6)*, High Court, 25 July 1991, considered the manner in which sensitive material could be screened out. Finally, in a fourth case in this area, *Breathnach v Ireland (No.*

3) [1992] ILRM 755, Keane J affirmed the general trend in the context of another sensitive area, police communications.

Because of its pivotal importance, we will discuss *Ambiorix Ltd and Ors v Minister for the Environment and Ors* [1992] ILRM 209; [1992] 1 IR 277 first. The plaintiff companies, all engaged in property development in Dublin, instituted proceedings seeking, inter alia, a declaration that the Minister had acted *ultra vires* the Urban Renewal Act 1986 in determining that a site on George's Quay, Dublin, owned by the fifth defendant Irish Life Assurance plc, was a designated area under the 1986 Act. In connection with the case, the plaintiffs sought discovery of documents from the defendants, including memoranda between civil servants and government Ministers as well as correspondence between Irish Life and the relevant government departments. The Minister resisted the motion for discovery on the grounds that discovery of the departmental memoranda would impair the efficient operation of the civil service and that the correspondence from Irish Life and others, which included financial information, had been treated as confidential. Lardner J ordered discovery, and on appeal by the defendants the Supreme Court (Finlay CJ, Hederman, McCarthy, O'Flaherty and Egan JJ) unanimously upheld this decision.

Delivering the leading judgment, Finlay CJ explained why the Court was not prepared to accept the defendant's submission in favour of privilege and the, mainly, English authority on which it was based:

> It appears to me that the fundamental flaw in the submission . . . is that it ignores the fundamental constitutional origin of the decision of this Court in *Murphy*. . . .

Reiterating the view of Walsh J in *Murphy*, the Chief Justice stated that it was for the judicial power, not the executive, to determine whether certain documents be produced in evidence. Where there is a conflict alleged between the production of documents and the public interest in confidentiality in the exercise of the executive power, the resolution of the conflict was also a matter for the judicial branch. Thus, he concluded, there could not be a general class of documents for which any public interest immunity from production can be claimed; and so any claim to 'class immunity' would involve an interference with the right of access of the citizen to the courts. In this context, Finlay CJ referred with approval to the judgment of McCarthy J in *O'Keeffe v An Bord Pleanála* [1992] ILRM 237 in which the same point had been made (for discussion of the *O'Keeffe* case, see the Administrative Law chapter, 16-18, above). To that extent, therefore, the English case law emanating from *Conway v Rimmer* [1968] AC 910 cannot be considered good law in the light of the *Ambiorix* case.

The Court went on to hold that, in the absence of a claim that production of the documents would affect the safety and security of the State, the trial judge had acted correctly in examining the documents in question. It may be noted in this context that the Chief Justice did not express any view on the question whether State security could be the basis for any future claim to privilege; in *Murphy* Walsh J had suggested that in certain circumstances there might be documents whose very existence could not be acknowledged by the State. As such a case did not arise here, the Court was not required to deal with that any further. However, given the Court's approach to similar problems in recent years, such an exemption seems a possibility at the least: see for example the decision of the Court in *The People v Ryan* [1989] ILRM 333; [1989] IR 399 (1988 Review, 144-7) and the earlier decision of the Chief Justice when President of the High Court in *Savage v Director of Public Prosecutions* [1982] ILRM 385 (criticised by Byrne (1984) 6 DULJ 177).

The extent of disclosure now required by the jurisprudence of the Court gives rise, no doubt, to legitimate concern within the public service as to whether, or when, various sensitive material might be made public in some future litigation. The decision in *Ambiorix* unfortunately does not provide much guidance in this area. However, the three decisions of the High Court in 1991 in this area clearly indicate that the judges are prepared to be highly pragmatic in dealing with this problem. Thus, in *Bula Ltd and Ors v Tara Mines Ltd and Ors (No. 6)*, High Court, 25 July 1991 (340, below), Murphy J ordered a discovery motion, in which memoranda from the Department of Energy were sought, to be heard in camera. And in *Gormley v Ireland and Ors*, High Court, 7 March 1991 (339-40, below) and *Breathnach v Ireland (No. 3)* (341, below), Murphy and Keane JJ, respectively, ordered certain parts of documents to be pasted over to conceal particularly sensitive material.

Reverting to *Ambiorix*, it is notable in the context of the question of sensitivity that the Supreme Court, in addressing the question of confidentiality of financial information supplied to the government departments, held that this could be dealt with either by way of deletion of the information under the direction of the court or through restricting access to the legal advisers for the plaintiffs. In any event, as the Court pointed out, the use of the discovered material for any purpose extraneous to the proceedings would be a contempt of court. See to the same effect the comments of Costello J in *Fitzpatrick v Independent Newspapers plc* [1988] ILRM 707; [1988] IR 132 (see the 1988 Review, 335).

Finally, for completeness, it may be mentioned that the substantive action by the plaintiffs was dismissed in the High Court in a judgment delivered in 1992: this will be discussed in the 1992 Review.

The second case to consider public interest privilege in 1991 was the decision of Murphy J in *Gormley v Ireland and Ors*, High Court, 7 March

1991 which predated the *Ambiorix* decision. Of interest in the context of
Ambiorix was that Murphy J was required to consider documentation which,
it was stated, might affect State security.

The plaintiff, a clerical officer with the Department of Posts and Tele-
graphs, was interned pursuant to the Offences against the State (Amendment)
Act 1940 between July 1957 and November 1958. On release, he was
requested to sign a declaration to respect the Constitution of Ireland and not
to support or assist any unlawful organisation. Between 1958 and 1983, the
plaintiff declined to sign this declaration and he was suspended as a clerical
officer. In 1983, he signed the declaration and he was restored to his position.
He instituted proceedings claiming a salary without regard to the interruption
arising in his suspension from duties. In the course of the action, the
defendants claimed privilege from discovery for certain documents relating
to the plaintiff's internment and also in connection with communications
with the Gardaí. Murphy J ordered discovery of certain documents, but not
others.

He held that while some of the memoranda and letters prepared in
connection with the plaintiff's internment were confidential and sensitive,
they could not be regarded as involving national security, and it was in the
public interest that they be disclosed for the purposes of the proceedings.
Likewise, he ordered that certain documentation concerning the alleged
refusal of the plaintiff to sign the declaration should also be disclosed, except
for some elements which concerned legal advice, and these would be pasted
over.

Finally, he held that certain communications with the gardaí concerning
internment were highly confidential and while they might be of some value
to the plaintiff they were in no sense fundamental to his action and he
concluded that discovery would not be ordered of these documents.

The judgment in *Gormley* indicates a highly pragmatic approach by
Murphy J. Clearly, the defendants in this case did not press their case as far
as the extreme instance mentioned by Walsh J in *Murphy v Dublin Corporation* [1972] IR 215, to which reference has been made in the discussion
of the *Ambiorix* case, above. Nonetheless, the judgment of Murphy J indicates that the judiciary are, in most instances, prepared to engage in a
document by document analysis of material in order to maximise the amount
of material which would be of benefit to a litigant.

The third case on public interest privilege was *Bula Ltd and Ors v Tara
Mines Ltd and Ors (No. 6)*, High Court, 25 July 1991. This was another
discovery motion in this extremely complex litigation. The judgment of
Murphy J in this instance arose out of an affidavit of the Minister for Energy
claiming privilege in respect of certain confidential memoranda generated in
the department concerning some of the parties involved in the litigation.

Murphy J described some of the comments as including a 'frank' analysis of the conduct of certain parties. Indeed, in order to maintain the confidentiality of the documentation, Murphy J had ordered that the discovery motion be heard *in camera*. Having perused the documents, he ordered that some were not discoverable. Even in relation to those in respect of which he ordered discovery, Murphy J stated that certain parts of memoranda would require pasting over or sealing in order to avoid revealing material over which privilege could be claimed.

The fourth case on public interest privilege was *Breathnach v Ireland (No. 3)* [1992] ILRM 755. The plaintiff had instituted proceedings against the defendants arising out of his prosecution, conviction and subsequent acquittal by the Court of Criminal Appeal in respect of a case which became known as the Sallins Mail Train robbery. The civil proceedings largely concerned the circumstanecs in which the plaintiff confessed to involvement in the armed robbery in question. His confession was, ulti- mately, ruled inadmissible by the Court of Criminal Appeal. Previous judgments in the case concerning issue estoppel and *res judicata* have been discussed in the 1989 Review, 358-60. Arising from these previous judgments, the plaintiff was estopped from litigating claims of assault and battery, while the defendants were estopped from denying wrongful arrest and wrongful detention for 48 hours in police custody.

The plaintiff claimed discovery of a large volume of documents, some of them included in the garda file which had been sent to the Director of Public Prosecutions and others which involved legal advice to the Director of Public Prosecutions. The defendants claimed public interest privilege in respect of the documents sought.

In his judgment dealing with the claims for privilege, Keane J called in aid the confirmation in the *Ambiorix* case, above, of the Supreme Court decision in *Murphy v Dublin Corporation* [1972] IR 215. This was important because in Keane J's own judgment in *DPP (Hanley) v Holly* [1984] ILRM 149, he had used the *Murphy* case to conclude that the blanket or 'class' claim to privilege in respect of police communications, asserted in *Attorney General v Simpson* [1959] IR 105, was inconsistent with and had not survived the decision in *Murphy*. He used *Ambiorix* to bolster the conclusion he had arrived at in the *Hanley* case.

Applying this to the instant case, Keane J was aware that particular sensitivities existed in the case of police communication in relation to which the Court was especially alive. He listed three categories of material to which the Court would be particularly sensitive. First, he accepted that material supplied in confidence to the gardaí should not, in general, be disclosed and he referred with approval to the decision of Costello J in *Director of Consumer Affairs v Sugar Distributors Ltd* [1991] ILRM 395 in this respect (see the 1990 Review, 434-5). Second, material on methods of detecting or combatting crime would also, in general, not be disclosed. Third, echoing views expressed by Walsh J in *Murphy v Dublin Corporation*, he stated that the very disclosure of the existence of certain material might be detrimental to the State. In addition, he was prepared to accept that material generated, prior to the initiation of a prosecution, between the gardaí and the Director of Public Prosecutions or between the Director and the legal advisers in the Director's office, could remain privileged even after the criminal proceedings had been completed. Keane J pointed out that a verdict of acquittal in criminal proceedings should not be used as a basis on which the acquitted person could engage in a fishing expedition of garda files for the purposes of bringing civil proceedings.

However, Keane J stated that this approach must be viewed against the general background that the public interest in the investigation of crime was but one matter to be weighed and considered against the countervailing interest in disclosure of relevant evidence for the purposes of court proceedings. Thus, he rejected the defendants' assertion that the public interest in crime detection and prevention could allow for the reintrodcution of a blanket ban on access to files prepared for the Director of Public Prosecutions by the gardaí.

And he also rejected the view, expressed by Wood J in *Evans v Chief Constable of Surrey* [1988] QB 588, that the plaintiff should bear the burden of establishing that disclosure was required. On the contrary, applying the *Murphy* case, Keane J considered that the defendants must bear this burden.

As to the documents which he examined, Keane J held that privilege should be allowed in respect of the documentation which involved legal advice passing between the Director and his legal advisers concerning the plaintiff's prosecution. However, he ordered production of certain material in the garda file prepared for the Director which might be relevant to the approach of the gardaí involved in the plaintiff's interrogation which had led to the confessions on which the prosecution was largely based and which would be relevant to the issues in the civil proceedings instituted by the plaintiff. Finally, it may be noted that while the State originally intended to appeal this decision to the Supreme Court, it was decided ultimately not to proceed with the appeal: see *Irish Times*, 19 February 1992.

7 Pasting over documents   In *Bula Ltd and Ors v Tara Mines Ltd and Ors (No. 6)*, High Court, 25 July 1991, Murphy J sanctioned the pasting over of portions of documents which were being discovered: see 340-1, above. In *Bula Ltd and Ors v Crowley and Ors (No. 3)*, High Court, 8 March 1991, below, he had warned that a party was in error where it pasted over or obliterated parts of documents without the sanction of the court.

8 Shredded documents In *Bula Ltd and Ors v Crowley and Ors (No. 3)*, High Court, 8 March 1991, Murphy J pointed out that an affidavit of discovery should make reference to all documents which were, at some stage, in the possession of the deponent, even where such documents have been shredded by the time the affidavit is filed. And, as already indicated, he also stated that a party was in error where it pasted over or obliterated parts of documents without the sanction of the court.

DISTRICT COURT

Small claims procedure A procedure for processing small claims in the District Court other than through a civil process was introduced by the District Court (Small Claims Procedure) Rules 1991 (SI No. 310). These provide for an initial application to a clerk of the District Court who is empowered to attempt to reach a compromise between the parties in dispute. In the event of continued dispute, the matter can be referred to a judge of the District Court for resolution. The procedure was introduced on a pilot basis in certain areas in early 1992, and it was expected that the procedure might be extended to cover the entire State at some later date. The 1991 Rules provide that certain cases are excluded from the procedure.

EVIDENCE

Formal proof The continuing need to prove by oral testimony the contents of medical reports in personal injuries litigation was decried by Costello J in *Aspell v O'Brien* [1992] ILRM 278; [1991] 2 IR 416. He called for consideration of a pre-trial procedure in which such evidence could be formally proved without the need for oral evidence: see 332-3, above.

Hearsay The general tendency against hearsay was adverted to in *D'Arcy v Roscommon County Council*, Supreme Court, 11 January 1991 and *Johnston v Fitzpatrick* [1992] ILRM 269 (both of which are discussed below, 353-4).

Oaths The decision of the Supreme Court in *Mapp v Gilhooley* [1991] ILRM 695; [1991] 2 IR 253 is discussed below, 348-9.

HIGH COURT

Appeal from Circuit Court The full nature of the re-hearing in the High Court on appeal from the Circuit Court was adverted to by Barron J in *AIF*

Ltd v Hunt, High Court, 21 January 1991 (discussed in the Commercial Law chapter, 27-8, above).

JUDGE AND JURY

Interventions by judge   In *Donnelly v Timber Factors Ltd* [1991] 1 IR 553, the Supreme Court dealt with the thorny issue of judicial interventions in the course of an action.

The background was as follows. The plaintiff had been involved in a collision with a vehicle driven by an employee of the defendant company. Liability was accepted and the trial of the action was confined to an assessment of damages. The plaintiff had had a history of back injury prior to the collision, but her consultant gave evidence that this had cleared up at the time of the collision. He also described the plaintiff as a person who did not exaggerate her condition. The plaintiff stated that she was unable to continue with sporting activities after the collision. The defendant argued that the plaintiff's injuries were not substantial. The defendant's consultant had examined the plaintiff on two occasions. It was accepted on both sides that the first examination had not been satisfactory. The plaintiff described the defendant consultant's attitude as 'hostile' and that he had attempted to minimise her injury. The consultant also had in his possession the plaintiff's medical records.

The trial judge criticised the consultant for his approach to the examination and for his possession of the plaintiff's records. It emerged, however, that the defendant's consultant had been given the medical records by the plaintiff's consultant. The trial judge also intervened on a number of occasions during the examination of the defendant's consultant. The trial judge awarded £35,000 in general damages. The defendant appealed the award, but the Supreme Court (Hederman, McCarthy and O'Flaherty JJ) dismissed the appeal.

The Supreme Court unanimously agreed that the trial judge's criticism of the defendant's consultant was severe, for which there was no support in the transcript. And while the Court accepted that a judge may be required on occasion to intervene to maintain an even balance between the parties, in the instant case the trial judge had, in his criticisms of the defendant's consultant, failed to conduct the trial in a manner which conformed to the division of functions between a trial judge and that of counsel.

However, the Court was divided on the effect of the trial judge's interventions, with McCarthy J being alone in considering that a retrial should have been ordered. Hederman and O'Flaherty JJ were of the view that, while the trial judge had been in error in his criticism, there had not otherwise been an excessive degree of intervention by him in the course of the trial. They concluded that, given the nature of the defence in the instant case where the defendant was attempting to minimise the plaintiff's injuries, it was to be expected that the trial judge would react in a particular way if, as occurred, he accepted that the plaintiff was a very genuine witness.

Taking what O'Flaherty J described as a commonsense view of the gist of the evidence, the majority felt it would be disproportionate to the error made by the trial judge to order a retrial on the assessment of damages. The majority rejected the argument that, in reviewing the trial, they should adopt the view most favourable to the defendant, and in this respect they doubted whether the decision in *Jones v National Coal Board* [1957] 2 QB 55 should be followed in this jurisdiction. See also 447-8, below, in the Torts chapter.

Irrelevant factors considered *Ambrose v O'Regan*, Supreme Court, 20 December 1991 involved a High Court judge taking into account irrelevant factors in reaching his decision. In 1974, the plaintiff was injured while a passenger in the defendant's car which, at the time, was being driven by the defendant's son. The plaintiff issued proceedings against the defendant, but the question of compensation was then discussed in the context of the Agreement operated by the Motor Insurance Bureau of Ireland (MIBI). Not having reached agreement as to whether MIBI was liable under the Agreement, the case ultimately came before the High Court in 1990 on the question as to whether the defendant's son was driving with the defendant's consent within s. 118 of the Road Traffic Act 1961.

In holding that the defendant's son had not been driving with her consent, the trial judge (MacKenzie J) stated that the plaintiff was ultimately entitled to be compensated for his injuries and that the case was an attempt by the MIBI to offload responsibility onto the defendant. On appeal, the Supreme Court (Finlay CJ, McCarthy and O'Flaherty JJ) allowed the appeal and ordered a re-trial.

Delivering the judgment for the Court, McCarthy J pointed out that the reference to the MIBI by the trial judge was an irrelevant consideration to his decision. However, this fact alone would not have automatically required a retrial, since the evidence in the case supported a conclusion one way or the other and this might have been sufficient to warrant the Supreme Court not interfering with the decision reached. However, he concluded that it was appropriate to order a re-trial of the action bearing in mind that the onus to disprove consent under s. 118 of the 1961 Act, in accordance with the decision of the Court in *Buckley v Musgrave Brook Bond Ltd* [1969] IR 440, lay on the defendant: see also the Torts chapter, 435-6, below.

JUDICIAL PENSIONS

The Courts (Supplemental Provisions) (Amendment) Act 1991 extends to the judiciary and other court officers (the Master of the High Court, Taxing Masters and county registrars) certain pension entitlements which were already given to other public servants. The effect is that the persons covered by the Act will be entitled to such pensions for a shorter period of service.

Of some significance is that the 1991 Act has a substantial retrospective content. Thus the provisions on reckoning service are deemed to be effective from 1 August 1978, while those on payment of a death gratuity on the death of a judge or court officer are deemed to be effective from 1 June 1973. This substantial retrospection was explained on the basis that the improved pensions provisions in the 1991 Act had been promised by previous administrations to certain judges on their appointment. This fact gave rise to a certain amount of unusually politicised statements during the passage of the Act, and resulting headlines in the contemporary newspaper coverage. For reaction to the criticism expressed as the Act was being passed, see the comments of the former Chief Justice, Mr Justice O'Higgins, *Irish Times*, 24 April 1991.

The Courts (Preservation of Superannuation) (Judiciary) Regulations 1991 (SI No. 308) provide that pensions may also be reckoned in relation to appointments to the Court of Justice and the Court of First Instance of the European Communities.

JURY DISTRICTS

The Jury Districts Order 1991 (SI No. 337) provides that County Louth is to be a single jury district. The 1991 Order also revokes the Jury Districts Order 1977 (SI No. 59 of 1977) and amends the Jury Districts Order 1976 (SI No. 57 of 1976).

MONETARY LIMITS AND NUMBER OF JUDICIARY

The Courts Act 1991 provided for substantial increases in the monetary jurisditions of the District and Circuit Courts in civil cases, which had been last increased by the Courts Act 1981. It also provided for an increased number of judges and for the new title 'Judge of the District Court' to replace 'Justice of the District Court.' (It may also be noted that the Act provided for the service of summons in summary criminal proceedings by registered post: see the Criminal Law chapter, 149, above.)

The general jurisdiction of the District Court was raised from £2,500 to £5,000, while the jurisdiction of the Circuit Court was raised from £15,000 to £30,000. These changes came into effect on 15 August 1991: see s. 23(4) of the Act. Significantly, s. 16 of the 1991 Act also provides that future changes in the monetary jurisdiction may be done by way of statutory Order, taking account of changes in the value of money.

The 1991 Act should be seen against the general background of a desire to reduce the cost of litigation. The substantial increase in the jurisdiction of the Circuit Court in particular was intended to take many personal injuries actions out of the High Court. One effect of this might be, for example, that only one junior counsel would be briefed to appear, whereas until this change it would be common to brief a junior and senior counsel.

In conjunction with the changes in the monetary limits, s. 14 of the 1991 Act substituted a new s. 17 of the Courts Act 1981 in order to limit the amount of costs which a successful plaintiff can recover in civil proceedings where the amount of the award is less than the jurisdiction of the Court. It also introduces a novel discretion for the trial judge to require such a plaintiff to pay a sum in costs to the unsuccessful defendant. This provision thus introduces a limit on the normal rule that 'costs follow the event.' S. 15 of the 1991 Act provides for the first time that cases may be remitted from the Circuit Court to the District Court. Previously, cases could only be remitted from the High Court to the Circuit Court.

The 1991 Act also provides for an increase in the permanent members of the judiciary in recognition of the changed jurisdictions. S.17 increases the maximum number of ordinary High Court judges (that is, excluding the President of the High Court) from 14 to 16. This is to take account of the increased criminal jurisdiction of the High Court in the Criminal Law (Rape) (Amendment) Act 1990 (see the 1990 Review, 258-62). The maximum number can be 17 where a High Court judge is appointed President of the High Court. S. 18 of the 1991 Act increases the maximum number of permanent ordinary Circuit Court judges (that is, excluding the President of the Circuit Court) from 15 to 17. It should be remembered that temporary Circuit Court judges may also be appointed by the Minister for Justice. Finally, s. 19 of the Act Act increases the maximum number of permanent Judges of the District Court from 39 to 45. Again, it is relevant to bear in mind that temporary Judges of the District Court may also be appointed by the Minister for Justice. In connection wioth nomenclature, s. 21 of the 1991 Act provides that any statutory reference to 'Justice of the District Court' should now read 'Judge of the District Court.' The name change was made in order to acknowledge the status of the District Court Judges as full time members of the judiciary, and came about as a result of representations from the Judges of the District Court. S.21 came into effect on 15 October 1991, so that from that date the name and title 'Justice of the District Court' became obsolete.

OATHS

Less than a year after the Law Reform Commission had published a *Report on Oaths and Affirmations* (LRC 34-1990) which argued for the abolition of oaths (see the 1990 Review, 442-7), the Supreme Court gave its support to the continuance of oaths in *Mapp v Gilhooley* [1991] ILRM 695; [1991] 2 IR 253.

The plaintiff, who was 8 years of age at the date of the trial of his action, instituted proceedings in the High Court claiming damages arising from personal injuries sustained while a pupil in the school managed by the defendant. When he was called to give evidence, he was asked by the trial judge whether he understood the oath, and the plaintiff stated he did not. The trial judge was asked by the plaintiff's counsel to hear his evidence and to judge it as best he could. The trial judge told the plaintiff that it was very important to tell the truth and then proceeded to hear the plaintiff's account of the incident in the school. The trial judge also heard the sworn evidence of teachers who had been supervising the plaintiff, their account of the incident in question being different from the plaintiff. The trial judge concluded that he preferred the plaintiff's account, found that the defendant had been negligent and awarded the plaintiff £8,000 damages (see the 1989 Review, 430-1).

On appeal, the defendant abandoned any argument on the liability issue and instead argued that the procedure adopted by the trial judge in hearing the plaintiff's unsworn evidence amounted to a mistrial. The Supreme Court (Finlay CJ, McCarthy and O'Flaherty JJ) unanimously agreed and ordered a retrial on liability in the Circuit Court.

Delivering the leading judgment, the Chief Justice stated his views in trenchant language:

> It is a fundamental principle of the common law that for the purpose of trial in either criminal or civil cases *viva voce* evidence must be given on oath or affirmation. To this principle there are statutory exceptions contained in the Children Act 1908, as extended by the Criminal Justice Administration Act 1914, which apply to criminal cases only. . . . The broad purpose of the rule is to ensure as far as possible that such *viva voce* evidence shall be true by the provision of a moral or religious and legal sanction against deliberate untruth. Such a rule cannot, therefore, be inconsistent with the Constitution, either on the basis of being

discriminatory or on the basis of being an impermissible restriction on the right of access to the courts.

Finlay CJ also stated that the practice by which documentary evidence can be accepted as proof of matters by agreement of the parties does not constitute an exception to the rule of evidence by oath or affirmation, since such agreement is a method of avoiding the giving of evidence. He concluded that the inevitable consequence of acting on unsworn *viva voce* evidence in a civil case is that a mistrial has occurred.

He went on to state that a party could only be prevented from seeking to argue a mistrial in such a case on the basis of estoppel by acquiescence or on the ground that to allow an appeal would amount to a virtual fraud or an abuse of the process of the courts. In the instant case, while the defendant had appeared to accept the validity of the plaintiff's unsworn account at the trial of the action, the Court ordered a retrial on liability in the Circuit Court having regard to the fundamental nature of the rule that evidence be given on oath. The Court noted that the plaintiff's interests could be preserved by an award of interest under s. 22 of the Courts Act 1981 if he were ultimately to be successful.

On the implementation of the principle established by the Court, the Chief Justice stated that where it appears that a child does not understand the meaning of an oath, the proper course is to adjourn the trial so that the child may be adequately instructed on its meaning.

The effect of the decision is clearly that the Supreme Court supports the continuation of oaths. The reference by the Chief Justice to the religious, moral and legal sanction to prevent deliberate mistruth is in direct conflict with the approach taken by the Law Reform Commission. It will be recalled that the Commission's approach was queried in the 1990 Review, but it is unfortunate that the Supreme Court did not explicitly consider the Commission's Report. In light of the decision in *Mapp*, however, it seems inevitable that the approach in the Report will be regarded as having lost a great deal of authority.

RULES OF COURT

The following Rules of Court were made in 1991.

Companies: examinership The Rules of the Superior Courts (No. 3) 1991 (SI No. 147) concern the provisions of the Companies (Amendment) Act 1990. On the Act, see the 1990 Review, 41-56.

Companies: general The Rules of the Superior Courts (No. 4) 1991 (SI No. 278) update the provisions in the Rules of the Superior Courts 1986 to take account of changes effected in the Companies Acts 1963 to 1990.

Judicial separation The Circuit Court Rules (No. 1) 1991 (SI No. 159) take account of the changes in the Judicial Separation and Family Law Reform Act 1989: see the 1988 Review, 229-42.

Recognition of Diplomas The Rules of the Superior Courts (No. 2) 1991 (SI No. 177) set out the procedures for appeals to the High Court under the European Communities (General System for the Recognition of Higher Education Diplomas) Regulations 1991 (SI No. 1): see the Education chapter, 187, above.

Small claims procedure The District Court (Small Claims Procedure) Rules 1991 (SI No. 310) establishes the procedure by which small claims may be processed by a clerk of the District Court: see 343, above. The District Court (Fees) Order 1991 (SI No. 311) sets out the fees for such applications.

Social welfare appeals The Rules of the Superior Courts (No. 1) 1991 (SI No. 67) amend O.90 of the Rules of the Superior Courts 1986 to take account of Part IV (in particular s. 20) of the Social Welfare Act 1990: see the 1990 Review, 477.

SUPREME COURT

Appellate court Issues concerning the appellate nature of the Supreme Court's jurisdiction are dealt with above, 327-8.

Limit to appellate jurisdiction In *Minister for Justice (Clarke) v Wang Zhu Jie* [1991] ILRM 823, the Supreme Court held it had no jurisdiction to entertain an appeal against a refusal by the High Court for leave to appeal after a consultative case stated from the District Court.

The substantive issue in the case concerned the legality of the defendant's arrest under the Aliens Act 1935. On a consultative case stated from the District Court to the High Court pursuant to s. 52 of the Courts (Supplemental Provisions) Act 1961, Costello J held that the arrest had been lawful: see the 1990 Review, 201. Costello J then declined to grant leave to appeal to the Supreme Court, such leave being required by s. 52 of the 1961 Act. On appeal by the defendant against this refusal, the Supreme Court (Finlay CJ, Hederman, McCarthy, O'Flaherty and Egan JJ) unanimously held that it had no jurisdiction to hear an appeal under s. 52 of the 1961 Act in the absence of leave given by the trial judge.

The case turned on the interpretation of Article 34.4.3 of the Constitution, which provides that the Court has jurisdiction from all decisions of the High Court, except where otherwise provided by law. The decision in *The People v Conmey* [1975] IR 341 is the leading authority in this area, and established that any exceptions to the appellate jurisdiction must be clearly stated.

In the instant case, the Court held that the requirement to seek leave constituted a clear limitation on the power of the Supreme Court to hear appeals from the High Court. Apart from the terms of s. 52 of the 1961 Act, the Court concluded that this interpretation was supported by an application of the mischief rule of statutory construction (though the Court did not use this term). The Court noted that the previous prohibition on appeals to the Supreme Court in cases such as the present under s. 83 of the Courts of Justice Act 1924 had been altered to the qualified right of appeal under the 1961 Act. On this historical view of the 1961 Act, the Court concluded that the Oireachtas had given a clear signal of its intention to limit the Court's appellate jurisdiction.

Stay of execution pending appeal In *Redmond v Ireland* [1992] ILRM 291 the Supreme Court provided important guidelines on the circumstances in which a stay of execution on an award of damages may be granted pending appeal to the Supreme Court. In *Corish v Hogan*, Irish Times LR, 21 May 1990 (see the 1990 Review, 454), the Court had delivered an *ex tempore* judgment on the topic which had led to some difficulties in application at first instance. The *Redmond* case thus offered welcome clarification on the relevant principles.

The plaintiff had been awarded £49,969 damages in the High Court in his action against the defendants in respect of injuries sustained in the course of his employment. The defendants made no application to the trial judge for a stay on the award, but appealed the decision to the Supreme Court on liability and quantum, and then sought a stay on the High Court award. The Court ordered that a payment of £15,000 be made pending determination on the question of a further stay.

By a majority, the Court (McCarthy and Egan JJ; Finlay CJ dissenting) ultimately declined to grant any further stay on the High Court award. The Chief Justice was in the minority in the sense that he would have granted a stay, but he agreed with the statement of the relevant principles set out in the judgment of McCarthy J. Both McCarthy and Egan JJ formed the majority which held that no further stay should be granted, but Egan J expressed no opinion on the statement of principles in McCarthy J's judgment. Since it is clear that McCarthy J's statement of principles commanded at least a majority in the Court, they are likely to be relied on in future cases. It is useful, therefore, to quote in full the relevant passage from McCarthy J's judgment:

> In my view, the matters to be taken into account by this Court in an application for a stay of execution upon the whole or part of an award for damages for personal injury should include the following.

(1) Liability is genuinely in issue.

(2) A heavy responsibility lies upon the legal advisors of those seeking a stay of execution to assist the court on the reality of the appeal on liability.

(3) The court should not be trying the appeal.

(4) The issue is raised upon an argument that findings of fact are unsupported by any credible evidence.

(5) There may be cases in which monies paid on foot of a decree might not be recoverable.

(6) The bringing of an appeal can be, of itself, damaging to an injured person.

(7) Appeals have been brought and may be brought again as a bargaining weapon.

(8) The length of time between accident and trial and and the prospective length of time between trial and the hearing of the appeal.

(9) The absence of any application for a stay at the trial.

Applying these principles to the instant case, McCarthy J noted that since the trial judge had delivered a reasoned decision on liability which was not demonstrably wrong, and since in his view there was no substance in the appeal on quantum, the Court should not grant a stay. As already indicated, Egan J also concurred in refusing a stay. Having reviewed the transcript, but without taking a final view, he felt that it was difficult to conceive that the findings of the trial judge on liability would be set aside and he was of the view that it was 'totally unlikely' that there would be any reduction in damages. Although in dissent, the Chief Justice was clearly reluctant to grant a stay. He appeared to accept that the appeal on liability stood little chance of success, but he considered that there was a better chance on the question of damages. Since he felt that any immediate hardship to the plaintiff had been allieviated by the £15,000 payment out and that the defendants might find it difficult to recover the balance of the £49,969 if their appeal on damages proved successful, he would have granted a stay on that basis.

THIRD PARTY NOTICE

The circumstances in which it is appropriate to join a third party were considered by the Supreme Court in three cases in 1991, *D'Arcy v Roscommon County Council*, Supreme Court, 11 January 1991, *Johnston v Fitzpatrick* [1992] ILRM 269 and *Quirke v O'Shea and CRL Oil Ltd* [1992] ILRM 286. In all three cases, each involving an application to join the parent or parents of an infant plaintiff, the applications were refused. It may also be said that the *Quirke* case involves the most comprehensive examination of the issues to be considered in such cacses. However, we will discuss each case in turn.

In *D'Arcy v Roscommon County Council*, Supreme Court, 11 January 1991 the plaintiff, a minor suing by her mother and next friend, instituted proceedings in negligence against the defendant Council. The Council sought to have the plaintiff's parents joined as third parties in the proceedings. The application was grounded on the affidavit of the solicitor for the Council, who averred that, to his knowledge and belief, the plaintiff's parents had themselves been negligent in relation to the incident the subject matter of the proceedings. In the High Court, MacKenzie J refused the application to join the parents as third parties. On appeal by the Council, the Supreme Court (Hederman, McCarthy and O'Flaherty JJ) unanimously dismissed the appeal, in an *ex tempore* judgment delivered for the Court by Hederman J.

Hederman J held that the allegations against the plaintiffs' parents were inadequate to justify making an order joining them as third parties. He agreed that the trial judge was correct in taking into account two factors: first the lack of clarity in the allegations made, particularly as the power to join under O.16, r.1 of the Rules of the Superior Courts 1986 was discretionary; and, second, the potential intimidating effect that joining the parents might have on their consideration of the running of the case and of any settlement which might be offered.

Hederman J also stated that it was undesirable, in an application to join a third party, that the solicitor for the applicant should swear the grounding affidavit, and it was preferable that it be sworn by the person having first hand knowledge of the events in question. See further 414, below.

The second case on this topic was *Johnston v Fitzpatrick* [1992] ILRM 26. Here the plaintiff was also a minor suing by his mother and next friend. He instituted proceedings in negligence against the defendant. The plaintiff, then 10 years old and in his parents' company, was struck by a car driven by the defendant. The defendant brought a motion to join the plaintiff's parents as third parties. In support of the motion, the defendant's solicitor averred that the plaintiff 'dashed' onto the road in front of the defendant; and that his parents did not, in the circumstances, exercise any reasonable supervision over the plaintiff. In the High Court, MacKenzie J declined to join the parents as third parties. On appeal by the defendant, he was permitted, having regard to the decision in *D'Arcy v Roscommon County Council*, Supreme Court, 11 January 1991, above, to file an affidavit in which he personally deposed to the events of the accident. In this case a five judge Supreme Court (Finlay CJ, Hederman, McCarthy, O'Flaherty and Egan JJ) unanimously declined to join the parents as third parties.

Delivering the leading judgment, Egan J took an approach in line with that of Hederman J in the *D'Arcy* case. He noted that the power of the Court to join a third party under O.16 of the Rules of the Superior Courts 1986 was not mandatory in nature, and the party seeking the order must establish that the proposed third party contributed to the accident. In the instant case, having regard to the child's age, he concluded that the averment in the grounding affidavit did not establish that the parents contributed to the plaintiffs' 'dash' onto the road. He did add, however, that it might be otherwise if there was an allegation that the plaintiff had a disability or that the parents had encouraged him to make a 'dash' across the road.

On the question of affidavits grounding an application to join a third party, Finlay CJ (with whom McCarthy J concurred) was of the view that the *D'Arcy* decision was not authority for requiring a direct affidavit in all applications to join a third party, but he agreed it had been required in the instant case. However, the Chief Justice also added that he was not expressing a final view on this matter. On another point, see 413, below.

The third case in this area was *Quirke v O'Shea and CRL Oil Ltd* [1992] ILRM 286. The plaintiff, an infant, through his mother and next friend, claimed damages for personal injuries arising from an accident involving a lorry which was driven by the first defendant and was the property of the second defendant. The lorry had delivered oil to the house occupied by the plaintiff and his family. The injury occurred as the lorry was driving away from the house. The defendants sought to join the plaintiff's mother as a third party in the proceedings. In an affidavit in support, the first defendant stated that the mother had signed the delivery docket for the oil and was near the plaintiff when he began driving away; that he had assumed that she was in control of the plaintiff but that, in the light of the accident she had not taken reasonable care of the plaintiff. In the High Court, MacKenzie J declined to join the mother as a third party. The Supreme Court (Finlay CJ, Hederman and Egan JJ) upheld this decision on appeal. The judgment delivered in *Quirke* provides more insight into the steps to be considered in such applications.

First, whether a *prima facie* case had been made out. In *Quirke*, the Court accepted that (unlike the *D'Arcy* and *Johnston* cases) the defendant's affidavit had made out a *prima facie* case for joining the mother as a third party. The second factor was whether the application to join the mother amounted to an abuse of the process of the court. The Court held that, although the mother was not a person of great means, this was not in itself sufficient to indicate that the application to join her was an abuse.

The third issue examined was whether a refusal to join would be relevant to the issue of a contribution under s. 27 of the Civil Liability Act 1961. The Court held that if a third party application was refused under O.16 of the Rules of the Superior Courts 1986, this would not be a basis for a court to refuse contribution if the party refused such application instituted separate proceedings against a concurrent wrongdoer. Thus, the Court concluded, the discretion under O.16, r.1 as to whether to join a third party is extremely wide.

Finally, the Court held that it was entitled, in an application under O.16, r.1, to balance the disruption to existing proceedings (where the next friend would have to be substituted if made a third party) against the convenience of trying all the issues in one action. In the instant case, the Court concluded that the disruption involved in granting the application would not be justified, having regard in particular to the limited means of the mother.

Prisons

CONJUGAL RIGHTS

The decision of the Supreme Court in *Murray v Ireland* [1991] ILRM 465, refusing conjugal rights to the plaintiffs (both convicted prisoners) is discussed in the Constitutional Law chapter, 101-4, above.

JUVENILE OFFENDERS

The requirements of rr.223 and 224 of the Rules for the Government of Prisons 1947, requiring the separate accommodation of juvenile offenders, was considered in *G. and McD. v Governor of Mountjoy Prison* [1991] 1 IR 373: see the discussion in the Criminal Law chapter, 184-5, above.

TRANSFER FROM ST PATRICK'S INSTITUTION TO PRISON

S. 7 of the Prisons Act 1970 empowers the authorities in St Patrick's Institution (the detention centre for convicted male juveniles between the ages of 17 and 19, formerly borstal) to transfer any excess population to prison. The Prisons Act 1970 (s. 7) Order 1991 (SI No. 158) continued s. 7 of the 1970 Act in operation for a two year period from 28 June 1991. Previous extensions (see the 1990 Review, 457; the 1989 Review, 364; and the 1988 Review, 353) had allowed s. 7 to continue for, usually, a period of one year only.

Revenue Law

As with previous Reviews, this chapter focuses on case law during 1991. For a detailed analysis of the Finance Act 1991, see Kennedy's Annotation, *Irish Current Law Statutes Annotated*. In addition to changes in personal income tax rates, among the changes were the following.

BES The Act gave effect to significant restrictions in the Business Expansion Scheme (BES), though these were not as extensive as had been originally announced at budget time.

Parent and subsidiary companies S. 36 of the Act implements Directive 90/435/EEC on the Taxation of Parent and Subsidiary Companies.

Acquisition of own shares by companies The Act provides for the taxation of acquisition by a company of its own shares, consequent on the changes effected by the Companies Act 1990, as to which see the 1990 Review, 107-15.

Stamp duty Part IV of the 1991 Act provides for a major overhaul of the Stamp Act 1891. Among the changes were the following. S. 94 of the 1991 Act makes the payment of stamp duty mandatory for the first time by substituting a new s. 1 of the 1891 Act. The previously unclear issue as to who is liable for stamp duty has been clarified by the introduction of the concept of 'accountable persons' by s. 96 of the 1991 Act which introduces a new s. 122 of the 1891 Act.

S. 97 of the 1991 Act introduces a new s. 5 of the 1891 Act, making it incumbent on professional advisers to verify the facts affecting the liability for stamp duty set forth in the instrument in question. S. 98 of the 1991 Act amends s. 12 of the 1891 Act by empowering the Revenue to issue assessments for stamp duty for the first time. S. 100 of the 1991 Act amends s. 15 of the 1891 Act by increasing substantially the penalties for late stamping.

ACCOUNTANT AS TAX AGENT

Quigley v Burke [1991] 2 IR 169 is an important decision on the status of an accountant who acts as tax agent for a taxpayer. In the instant case, the inspector of taxes had assessed the respondent taxpayer, an electrical contractor, to income tax for the year 1986/87 in the sum of £20,000. The taxpayer appealed this to the Circuit Court for a rehearing of the assessment. In the course of the appeal, it was accepted that the taxpayer's accountant, acting as his tax agent, had supplied to the inspector of taxes the trading and profit and loss account, the capital account, the balance sheet and a statement of source and application of funds. The accountant had also compiled a nominal ledger, which comprised information from the books of account which had already been supplied to the inspector, but which also included additional information from the taxpayer. Having compiled this nominal ledger, the accountant concluded that the correct liability to tax was £8,642.

The inspector of taxes sought access to, under s. 174 of the Income Tax Act 1967, the nominal ledger which the accountant had prepared. The accountant submitted that this nominal ledger was not the taxpayer's property, stated that it had been purchased by the accountant and that it therefore constituted part of the working papers which did not come within the terms of s. 174 of the 1967 Act. The Circuit Court judge accepted this submission and substituted the figure of £8,642 for the year in question. However, on a case stated from the Circuit Court, Carroll J reversed this decision.

The taxpayer's accountants had relied on the decision in *Chantrey-Martin v Martin* [1953] 2 QB 286 as supporting the claim that documents 'in their power and possession' could not be produced. However, Carroll J noted that in that case the Court had held that only where accountants are acting as auditors for the taxpayer could production be refused and that where the accountants are acting as the taxpayer's tax agents they could not refuse production since in reality the documents were the client's property. She described as a 'red herring' the point made that the accountants had bought the nominal ledger itself; this was a matter for the accountants to take up with the taxpayer.

Finally, she remitted the case to the Circuit Court on the basis that it had not been possible, without the nominal ledger, for the Circuit Court judge to have arrived at a reasonable conclusion as to the correct liability to tax for the year in question.

The decision of Carroll J is highly significant since it establishes that only where an accountant is acting as auditor can reliance be placed on case law concerning the ownership of documents as between client and professional person. Where the accountant is acting only as tax agent, virtually all documents, even if described as 'working papers' will be deemed to be the taxpayer's property if they include information supplied to the accountant by the taxpayer.

BENEFITS IN KIND: CARS

In *Browne and Ors v Attorney General* [1991] 2 IR 58, Murphy J upheld the constitutional validity of the benefit in kind taxation of cars supplied for use to sales representatives.

The three plaintiffs were all sales representatives. Their respective employers had supplied them with cars for their employment, and they were permitted to use the cars for private purposes. Where such private use occurred, the plaintiffs paid for the petrol involved. One of the plaintiffs did not use the car for any private purpose. Under s. 4 of the Finance Act 1982, the availability of such cars for private use was treated as taxable income. Taking account of various deductions allowed under s. 4, the effect was that the three plaintiffs were taxed for the availability of the cars for private use. They claimed that s. 4 of the 1982 Act constituted an unjust attack on their right to earn a livelihood or alternatively was arbitrary in its effect. Murphy J dismissed their claims.

He dealt first with the presumption of constitutionality. Murphy J quoted with approval the view of O'Hanlon J in *Madigan v Attorney General* [1986] ILRM 136 that, in relation to taxation legislation, the presumption of constitutionality was particularly strong and that the plaintiffs faced an uphill battle to establish their case.

The next issue concerned the nature of the tax imposed under the 1982 Act. The plaintiffs had argued that the 1982 Act taxed the car and its use. Murphy J rejected this argument. Rather, he concluded, it taxed the *availability* of the car for private use.

While he acknowledged that the burden of s. 4 of the 1982 Act fell more heavily on some because of the low level (or nil level in the case of one of the plaintiffs) of private mileage actually used, he was not prepared to accept that this in itself rendered the 1982 Act unconstitutional, because there could be no objection in principle to the imposition of taxation on the availability of an asset any more than on ownership or possession of assets. In any event, he noted, there were alternative arrangements which employers and employees could enter into where the application of s. 4 of the 1982 Act resulted in a heavy burden of taxation on an individual employee.

This led on to the plaintiffs' next argument, based on *Brennan v Attorney General* [1984] ILRM 355, that the 1982 Act operated in an arbitrary manner. Murphy J concluded, however, that the 1982 Act was not arbitrary in its application, but was predicated on the reasonable assumption that a car made available for private use was, in general, likely to be used for that purpose.

Finally, it may be noted that the original benefit in kind tax had been introduced by the Finance Act 1958, where it had been based on an annual income of £15,000. Murphy J noted that the plaintiffs had argued that, bearing this history in mind, the tax was being applied to a far wider number of taxpayers than envisaged by the £15,000 income in 1958. However, he felt that it was not relevant to consider this background since s. 4 of the 1982 Act stood on its own without reference to any earlier statutory provisions on the subject.

CAPITAL GAINS TAX

The Capital Gains Tax (Multipliers) (1991-92) Regulations 1991 (SI No. 139) were the usual Regulations for the tax year 1991-92 by which capital gains were to be calculated to take account of the decrease in the value of money for the purposes of the Capital Gains Tax Act 1975.

COURSE OF TRADE: BANKING

In *Browne v Bank of Ireland Finance Ltd* [1991] ILRM 421; [1991] 1 IR 431 the Supreme Court held that the dividend received by the company from government stocks was income generated in the course of its trade as a licensed bank.

The respondent company was engaged in banking activities, including the provision of credit finance and leasing, but not the operation of current accounts. As part of the conditions of their banking licence under the Central Bank Act 1971, the company was required to hold a specified number of government stocks. The Revenue did not accept that the company's business constituted banking business, and applied to have the dividend from the government stock treated as income from trade under Schedule D, Case 1 of the Income Tax Act 1967. In the Circuit Court (Judge Martin) it was held that the dividend did not arise from the company's trade since it did not deal in investments in the ordinary course of business and the gain did not therefore result from its trade. On a case stated to the High Court, Blayney J declined to interfere with the Circuit Court decision: [1987] IR 346 (1987 Review, 289 and 293). On further appeal by the Revenue the Supreme Court (Griffin, Hederman and McCarthy JJ) allowed the appeal and reversed Blayney J's decision.

Delivering the leading judgment, Griffin J accepted, like Blayney J, that the appropriate test to apply on case stated was set down in *Mara v Hummingbird Ltd* [1982] ILRM 421, namely, that the Court would only set aside primary findings of fact where there was no evidence whatever to support them, and inferences drawn from primary facts would only be set aside where no reasonable court or Appeal Commissioner would have drawn such conclusions. However, Griffin J differed from Blayney J in the application of that test.

Whereas Blayney J regarded the Circuit Court judge's views as supportable, the Supreme Court concluded that the inferences drawn by the Circuit Court judge were not such as could reasonably have been made. The Court held that Judge Martin had erred in concluding that the gains from the government stocks did not form part of the company's trading profits. It held that, since the government stocks had been bought by the company to comply with the conditions attached to its banking licence under the Central Bank Act 1971, it was necessarily done in the course of its normal trading activities and the realised gains made on redemption of such stocks were profits in the nature of trade and were, therefore, chargeable to tax under Schedule D, Case 1 of the Income Tax Act 1967.

On the important fiscal consequences for the State if the Supreme Court had upheld the decision of Blayney J, see *Irish Times*, 9 February 1991.

MANUFACTURING

In *Ó Laochdha v Johnson & Johnson (Irl) Ltd* [1991] 2 IR 287, the High Court again considered the question as to what constitutes 'manufacturing' for tax purposes.

S. 42 of the Finance Act 1980 provides for relief from corporation tax in respect of profits derived from the sale by export of goods manufactured in the State. The respondent company engaged in the production of nappy liners and J Cloths in the State, and these were then exported. They were produced by placing large bales of fabric (1,200 to 3,000 cubic metres) into a machine which, it was agreed, was expensive, sophisticated and required special training for its operatives. In relation to J Cloths, the machine was capable of packaging as well as cutting the cloths. The applicant Inspector of Taxes refused to allow the company relief from corporation tax under s. 42 of the 1980 Act. On appeal the Appeal Commissioner held that the relief should be granted, and this was confirmed on case stated by Carroll J.

She examined the case against the background of the case law in this area, in particular the decisions in *Cronin v Strand Dairy Ltd* (High Court, 18 December 1985) and *Irish Agricultural Machinery Ltd v Ó Cúlachain* [1989] ILRM 478; [1990] 1 IR 535 (see the 1989 Review, 368-9). Applying the principles in these cases, Carroll J concluded that, looking at the end product in the instant case, it was immediately clear that it was commercially different from the bales of fabric, adding more than 70% in value to the J Cloths and 40% to the nappy liners. And the reduction in size involved in the process had utility, quality and worth which were due to the process carried out by the company. Although Carroll J acknowledged that the process did not bring about any change in the raw material itself (just as, she noted, confetti was unchanged from its original state as bulk paper), this did not prevent it from being a manufacturing process. Finally, she concluded that an ordinary person, even if unaware of the actual process, would consider it to be manufacturing.

SCIENTIFIC RESEARCH: EXPLORATION

In *Texaco (Irl) Ltd v Murphy* [1992] ILRM 304; [1991] 2 IR 449, the Supreme Court held that exploration activity conducted by the company qualified for capital relief under the Income Tax Act 1967.

Between 1976 and 1978, the taxpayer company engaged in offshore exploration for petroleum, under licence granted pursuant to the Petroleum and Other Minerals Development Act 1960. The company claimed a capital allowance in respect of the expenditure incurred in the scientific testing involved in the exploration, pursuant to s. 244 of the Income Tax Act 1967, as amended by s. 21 of the Corporation Tax Act 1976. This provides for an allowance in respect of capital expenditure on scientific research which is not related to the trade activities of the company involved. S. 245 of the 1967 Act provides for relief for capital expenditure in relation to certain mining exploration activities, but offshore exploration was excluded from s. 245. The Appeal Commissioners held that the company was not entitled to the allowance under s. 244, pointing in particular to the juxtaposition between s. 244 and s. 245. This view was upheld by Carroll J [1989] IR 496 (1988 Review, 360-1), but on further appeal the Supreme Court (Finlay CJ, Hederman and McCarthy JJ) upheld the company's argument.

McCarthy J delivered the sole judgment for the Court. He concentrated on providing a simple textual interpretation of s. 244 of the Income Tax Act 1967, as amended. He referred to a number of leading authorities on the interpretation of taxing statutes, beginning with the well-known 'no equity about a tax' quotation from the judgment of Rowlatt J in *Cape Brandy Syndicate v IRC* [1921] 1 KB 64. He followed this with a quote from the judgment of Kennedy CJ in *Revenue Commissioners v Doorley* [1933] IR 750, where it was pointed out that the principal canon of interpretation was to have regard to the ordinary meaning of words used by the Oireachtas.

Applying these approaches to the instant case, McCarthy J stated that, while it might be of relevance to look at the overall intention of a statute, this was less the case in a revenue statute. Having regard to the plain meaning of the words in s. 244 of the 1967 Act, he concluded that the company was entitled to the allowance claimed, and that the Commissioners had erred in examining the provisions of s. 245 in this context.

STAMP DUTY

General   As already noted, 357, above, Part IV of the Finance Act 1991 introdcued substantial changes to the stamp duty regime.

Reality of transaction   In *Viek Investments Ltd v Revenue Commissioners* [1992] ILRM 557; [1991] 2 IR 520, Murphy J applied the decision of Carroll J in *Waterford Glass (Group Services) Ltd v Revenue Commissioners* [1990] 1 IR 334 (1989 Review, 371-2) in holding that the transaction in the instant case was, in reality, a 'conveyance' within the meaning of s. 54 of the Stamp Act 1891. Thus, the transaction attracted *ad valorem* duty. He upheld the assessment to duty imposed by the Revenue in this respect. It may also be noted, however, that Murphy J confirmed that, in appropriate circumstances, it was permissible to avoid *ad valorem* duty where a contract for sale was not implemented by a conveyance, approving the decision of Kinsmill Moore J in *McCall v Bradish-Ellames* [1950] Ir Jur Rep 16.

TRAVEL ALLOWANCE

The European Communities (Customs and Excise) Regulations 1991 (SI No. 57) implemented Directive 69/169/EEC by requiring 24 hours travel to qualify for the traveller's allowance. The Regulations were passed to comply with the decision of the Court of Justice in *Commission v Ireland* [1990] 1 ECR 4465. The European Communities (Customs and Excise) (Amendment) Regulations 1991 (SI No. 174) and the European Communities (Customs and Excise) (Amendment) (No. 2) Regulations 1991 (SI No. 368) raised the maximum 24 hour travel allowance.

As a result of the decision of the State not to contest proceedings seeking a refund of duty paid on goods under the previous '48 hour' rule, it appeared that up to 2,500 people on whom duty was imposed would be entitled to refunds: see the report of *Ryan v Minister for Finance, Irish Times*, 22 March 1991. See also Travers (1992) 10 ILT 224, 254, a comprehensive analysis of the new regime.

VALUE ADDED TAX

Cable television   In *Brosnan v Cork Communications Ltd*, High Court, 15 October 1991, Carroll J held that the cable transmission of TV signals did not constitute the supply of electricity within the meaning of the Value Added Tax Act 1972.

The respondent company's business was the relay of cable television and radio signals to domestic householders. The signals were transmitted through cables to each house by means of electric current, at a voltage of about 0.001 of a volt. The evidence indicated that such current is not normally capable of any use except for the relaying of broadcast signals. The supply of electricity is zero rated for the purposes of the 1972 Act. In the Circuit Court, it was held that the respondent was supplying electricity and that the zero VAT rate was applicable. On a case stated, Carroll J reversed the Circuit Court decision.

Applying the leading decision of the Supreme Court in *Mara v Hummingbird Ltd* [1982] ILRM 421, she held that the findings of the Circuit Court judge, whether viewed as a mistaken interpretation of the law or an unreasonable inference from the primary facts, could not be upheld since they were inconsistent with the finding that the company's business was the transmission of TV and radio signals.

As to the substantive question in the case, Carroll J applied the views expressed by Henchy J in *Inspector of Taxes v Kiernan* [1982] ILRM 13; [1981] IR 117 that words in statutes should, in general, be given their ordinary colloquial meaning. In the instant case, she concluded that while the company used electricity to carry the signals, this could not be described as supplying electricity in the ordinary colloquial meaning of those words.

Recording copyright   In *Phonographic Performance (Irl) Ltd v Somers* [1992] ILRM 657, the appellant company had vested in it the recording copyright of the sound recordings of its members, though not the copyright in the products themselves (that is, not the copyright in the songs which had been recorded, for example).

The question was whether the company, in seeking payments from third parties who caused the recordings to be broadcast in public, was supplying a service within the meaning of s. 2 of the Value Added Tax Act 1972. This in turn called for the interpretation of s. 17(4) of the Copyright Act 1963. This provides that the acts restricted by a copyright in sound recording are: (a) making a record or (b) public broadcast without the payment of an equitable remuneration to the copyright owner. The company submitted that it was only entitled, under heading (b), to request an equitable remuneration for public broadcast. It pointed to s. 5 of the 1972 Act, which defines the supplying of a service as including the 'toleration' of any situation. The company submitted that since it could not prevent any public broadcast, but only had a right to receive equitable remuneration for such broadcast (as opposed to the right to forbid a recording under heading (a) in s. 17 of the 1963 Act), its activities in collecting such remuneration did not fall within the 1972 Act.

Murphy J rejected the company's argument, concluding that its interpretation of s. 17 of the 1963 Act was too narrow. He held that, for example, the agreement between the company and RTE amounted, in effect, to an exploitation of the company's copyright, even though the parties had been careful to avoid describing the agreement between the parties as a licensing agreement. Murphy J was prepared to accept that the reality of the agreement was that the company was exploiting its copyright by setting out various terms and condition under which RTE was entitled to transmit the copyright material. In that context, since the company had negotiated particular terms and conditions, it was by implication 'tolerating' a situation within the meaning of s. 5 of the 1972 Act. And even if the company had made no detailed agreement with RTE he held that the company would also be 'tolerating' a situation in which RTE would be, in effect, determining the equitable remuneration for the purposes of s. 17 of the 1963 Act.

Finally, it may be noted that Murphy J adverted in his judgment to the consequence of the decision that RTE would bear between 40% to 50% of the VAT burden to be paid.

Safety and Health

ENVIRONMENTAL SAFETY

Sea pollution The Sea Pollution Act 1991 is an enabling Act which empowers the Minister for the Marine to make Regulations for the purposes of preventing pollution at sea caused by oil, oily mixtures, noxious liquid substances, harmful substance, sewage or garbage. Each of these terms is separately defined in s. 3 of the 1991 Act. The 1991 Act gives legislative effect, *inter alia*, to the MARPOL Convention, that is, the International Convention for the Prevention of Pollution from Ships of 1973 and a 1978 Protocol to that Convention.

The 1991 Act, when brought into effect by Commencement Order, will repeal the Oil Pollution of the Sea Acts 1956 to 1977, though without prejudice to any Regulations made under those Acts.

Finally, it may be noted that the Oil Pollution of the Sea (Civil Liability and Compensation) Act 1988 (1988 Review, 437-9) is not affected by the 1991 Act. However, certain consequential and clarifying amendments were effected by s. 37 of the 1991 Act.

FIRE SAFETY

Calor Teo v Sligo County Council [1991] 2 IR 267 dealt with the planning implications of non-compliance with the requirements of the Fire Services Act 1981: see the discussion in the Local Government chapter, 315, above.

FOOD SAFETY

Contact with foodstuffs The European Communities (Materials and Articles Intended to Come into Contact with Foodstuffs) Regulations 1991 (SI No. 307) introduce further measures to ensure that the materials in which foodstuffs are sold do not transfer their constituents to the food. The 1991 Regulations revoke SI No. 60 of 1988 of the same title.

Food imitations The European Communities (Food Imitations) (Safety) Regulations 1991 (SI No. 265) implement Directive 87/357/EEC. They revoke the Industrial Research and Standards (Section 44) (Resemblance to Food of Non-Food Products Used by Children) Order 1983.

Inspection The Health (Official Control of Food) Regulations 1991 (SI No. 332) implement Directive 89/397/EEC and prescribe certain matters to be subject to inspection. The Health (Sampling of Foods) Regulations 1970 have been revoked. The European Communities (Health Act 1947, Amendment of Sections 54 and 61) Regulations 1991 (SI No. 333) make the necessary consequential amendments to ss. 54 and 61 of the Health Act 1947 in order to comply fully with Directive 89/397/EEC. The Health (Official Control of Food) Approved Laboratories Order 1991 (SI No. 335) sets out the approved laboratories for the purposes of SI No. 332, above.

Jams etc The European Communities (Fruit Jams, Jellies and Marmalade and Chestnut Puree) (Amendment) Regulations 1991 (SI No. 319) implement Directive 88/593/EEC and amend the 1982 Regulations of the same title.

Marketing of foodstuffs The European Communities (Labelling, Presentation and Advertising of Foodstuffs) (Amendment) Regulations 1991 (SI No. 228) implement further Directives on the marketing of foodstuffs.

Nutritional claims The Health (Food for Particular Nutritional Uses) Regulations 1991 (SI No. 331) further restrict the claims which are made for particular foods. They also revoke the 1982 Regulations of the same title.

Solvents in food The European Communities (Extraction of Solvents in Foodstuffs) Regulations 1991 (SI No. 334) implement Directive 88/344/EEC.

LABORATORIES

General The European Communities (Good Laboratory Practice) Regulations 1991 (SI No. 4) implement Directives 87/18/EEC, 88/320/EEC and 90/18/EEC. They establish the Irish Laboratory Accreditation Board as the Competent Authority for approval purposes. They also provide that laboratory tests done under Directive 67/548/EEC (on the Classification, Packaging and Labelling of Dangerous Substances) or any other similar EC requirement must comply with the provisions of the Regulations.

Food tests The Health (Official Control of Food) Approved Laboratories Order 1991 (SI No. 335) sets out the approved laboratories for the purposes of the Health (Official Control of Food) Regulations 1991 (SI No. 332 of 1991): see above.

MANUFACTURING STANDARDS IN THE EC

As part of the drive for an Internal Market, the European Communities has adopted a series of Directives on general industrial products, which are now being transposed into Irish law at an increasing rate to comply with the 1992 Programme. Following the overall approach indicated in the European Commission's 1985 White Paper on the Single Market, the Directives (generally described as 'New Approach' or 'Approximation' Directives) establish minimum safety and health criteria for the products covered. Manufacturers are required to ensure that products covered by any such Directive comply with the criteria. The manufacturer may affix to the product the 'CE' mark to indicate that it so complies. In essence, the system is a self-certifying procedure, though the manufacturer also has the option of having the product tested by a national certifying body. In Ireland, the certifying body for many such products is Eolas. In addition to self-certification, the Directives also permit the State authorities to conduct independent examination in certain cases.

It may also be noted that these Standards Directives also incorporate by reference detailed technical standards, or European Norms (EN), developed by the European Standards bodies such as CEN and CENELEC, in accordance with the general terms of Directive 83/189/EEC, as amended (see the reference to this Directive in *United States Tobacco (Irl) Ltd v Ireland*, High Court, 19 February 1991, below, 377). Although CEN and CENELEC are not, as such, EC institutions the standards they set amount to EC standards. Once an EN standard is agreed and published in the Official Journal of the European Communities, it then is deemed to override any domestic standard in that area. Eventually, it is hoped that EN standards will replace all domestic standards, such as IS or BS standards, thus removing further technical barriers to trade in the EC.

From the point of view of liability, it is significant that the Regulations which transpose the Directives into domestic law require manufacturers to comply with the criteria set out in the Directives. Where any injury occurs arising from non-compliance with these criteria, a strong case for breach of statutory duty would seem to arise.

Relevant Regulations in this area in 1991 were as follows.

Electrical equipment: explosive atmospheres   The European Communities (Electrical Equipment for Use in Potentially Explosive Atmospheres) (Amendment) Regulations 1991 (SI No. 289) implemented Directives 88/571/EEC and 90/487/EEC and further amend the 1981 and 1986 Regulations of the same title. As required by the Directives themselves, the implementing Regulations state that compliance with the safety and health criteria set out in the Directives is deemed to be compliance with the relevant provisions of domestic electrical safety legislation, such as the Factories (Electricity) Regulations 1972 and Regulations made under the Dangerous Substances Act 1972 in relation to work with petroleum.

Industrial trucks   The European Communities (Self- Propelled Industrial Trucks) Regulations 1991 (SI No. 12) implemented Directives 86/663/EEC and 89/240/EEC.

Lifting equipment   The European Communities (Electrically, Hydraulically, or Oil-Electrically Operated Lifts) Regulations 1991 (SI No. 41) implemented Directive 90/486/EEC. They amended the European Communities (Electrically Operated Lifts) Regulations 1989, which had implemented the Principal Directive 84/529/EEC.

Pressure vessels   The European Communities (Simple Pressure Vessels) Regulations 1991 (SI No. 115) gave effect to Directive 87/404/EEC, as amended by Directive 90/488/EEC.

OCCUPATIONAL SAFETY (GENERAL)

Dangerous preparations   The European Communities (Paints etc.) (Classificationn, Packaging and Labelling) (Amendment) Regulations 1991 (SI No. 152) implement Directive 89/451/EEC. This requires that the labels of packages of paints and varnishes must contain a warning that the paint or varnish contains lead where the level of lead exceeds 0.15%. Previous Regulations of 1987 had required such a warning where the level of lead exceeded 0.25%.

Laboratory tests   See the European Communities (Good Laboratory Practice) Regulations 1991 (SI No. 4), above 367.

Manual lifting   *Dunleavy v Glen Abbey Ltd* [1992] ILRM 1 is a very important decision on the interpretation of the Factories Act 1955 (Manual Labour) (Maximum Weights and Transport) Regulations 1972: see the discussion in the Torts chapter, 406-9, below.

Mines: women   The Employment Equality Act 1977 (Employment of Females on Underground Work in Mines) Order 1989 (SI No. 153 of 1991) finally removes the restriction on women working underground contained in the Mines and Quarries Act 1965. Prior to this Order it was not permissible, for example, for a women geologist to conduct underground surveys. Under the Order, all restrictions have been removed.

Mines and quarries: duty of quarry manager   *Sweeney v Duggan* [1991]
2 IR 274 is discussed in the Torts chapter, 386, below.

Offshore safety   We discuss the Regulations made in 1991 under the
Safety, Health and Welfare (Offshore Installations) Act 1987 below, 371-2.

The Continental Shelf (Protection of Installations) (Ballycotton Field)
Order 1991 (SI No. 226) may also be noted in the present context: see the
Electricity and Energy chapter, 189, above.

Radiation   We discuss the Radiological Protection Act 1991, which repealed the Nuclear Energy Act 1971, under the Radiological Pro- tection
heading, 372-5, below. We also discuss there the European Com- munities
(Ionising Radiation) Regulations 1991 (SI No. 43), which revoked the
Factories Ionising Radiations (Sealed Sources) Regulations 1972 and the
Factories Ionising Radiations (Unsealed Radioactive Substances) Regulations 1972.

Substances banned   The Safety Health and Welfare at Work Act 1989
(Control of Specific Substances and Activities) Regulations 1991 (SI No.
285) had the effect of banning, subject to limited research exceptions, the
use at all places of work of four dangerous substances specified in the
Schedule to the Regulations. The substances are: 2-naphtylamine and its
salts; 4-aminobiphenyl and its salts; benzidine and its salts; and 4-nitro-
diphenyl. These substances are regarded as being potentially carcinogenic.

The 1991 Regulations give effect to Council Directive 88/364/EEC, the
fourth in a series of Directives (based on a 1980 'Framework' Directive
80/1107/EEC: see the 1989 Review, 378) aimed to protect workers from
exposure to chemical, physical and biological agents. The 1991 Regulations,
which came into force on 1 December 1991, also revoke the Factories
(Carcinogenic Substances) (Processes) Regulations 1972.

It is notable that the 1991 Regulations implement an EC Directive under
the power given to the Minister for Labour by s. 28 of the Safety Health and
Welfare at Work Act 1989 (as to which see the 1989 Review, 379-393). Prior
to this, the implementation of Directives had been through regulations made
under s. 3 of the European Communities Act 1972. A criticism of Regulations
made under the 1972 Act is that they create summary offences only, thus
limiting the penalties which may be imposed where prosecutions for breach
are taken. On the other hand, with Regulations made under the 1989 Act
prosecutions on indictment may be taken where there is no monetary limit
to the fine which may be imposed. The change in policy indicated by the
1991 Regulations is a welcome indication that EC safety and health requirements are being placed on a par with domestically inspired legislation.

OFFSHORE INSTALLATIONS

In 1991, four Regulations (SI Nos. 13 to 16) were made under the Safety, Health and Welfare (Offshore Installations) Act 1987 (see the 1987 Review, 299). Most of the Regulations took effect in May 1991. The 1987 Act came into force in November 1990 (see the 1990 Review, 475-6).

The Safety, Health and Welfare (Offshore Installations) (Installation Managers) Regulations 1991 (SI No. 13) set out the form of the notification to the Health and Safety Authority of the appointment, and where relevant the termination of appointment, of an installation manager, as required by s. 11 of the 1987 Act.

The Safety, Health and Welfare (Offshore Installations) (Emergency Procedures) Regulations 1991 (SI No. 14) require the maintenance of an Emergency Procedures Manual specifying the action to be taken in the event of an emergency on the installation. The Regulations also require that drills and musters be carried at at specified intervals. They also require that a stand-by vessel be on hand at all times in the neighbourhood of the installation (unless climatic conditions do not allow). The stand-by vessel must have two rescue craft. Detailed requirements as to the nature of the stand-by vessel are also specified. All provisions of these Regulations came into effect on 1 May 1991, except the requirement that the stand-by vessel 'be highly manoeuvrable and able to maintain its position', which came into effect on 1 May 1992. This was to enable the offshore industry to investigate the suitability of craft to comply with this particular provision.

The Safety, Health and Welfare (Offshore Installations) (Life-Saving Appliances) Regulations 1991 (SI No. 15) specify the life-saving appliances which must be provided on offshore installations, including survival craft, life rafts and survival suits, life buoys, life jackets and other personal emergency equipment. They also require the provision and maintenance of an emergency position-indicating radio beacon.

The Safety, Health and Welfare (Offshore Installations) (Operations) Regulations 1991 (SI No. 16) are the most lengthy of the four 1991 Regulations under discussion. They contain detailed requirements concerning what might be described as day-to-day activities on offshore installations. Among the requirements of these Regulations are the following. Regulation 5 specifies a written 'work permit' procedure for potentially dangerous work, including welding, flame cutting or any other 'hot work'. Regulation 7 requires the preparation of a plan for the regular maintenance, examination and testing of the installation and its plant. Regulation 14 requires protection of workers from any noise level likely to cause harm. In particular, persons on an installation must not be exposed to noise levels over 85dBA unless the intensity or duration is sufficiently abated to protect them or ear protection is provided. These requirements are expressly stated to be in addition to the requirements of the European Communities (Protection of Workers) (Exposure to Noise) Regulations 1990 (SI No. 157 of 1990) (see the 1990 Review, 474-5). Regulation 19 requires that every dangerous part of machinery be 'securely fenced', unless it is, by reason of its position or of such construction as to be as safe to every person on the installation as if securely fenced. This provision is modelled on s. 23 of the Factories Act 1955. Regulation 23 requires the provision and maintenance safe means of access to and egress from places of work. All floors etc. must have a non-slip surface. Regulation 25, and the Sixth Schedule, lay down specific requirements relating to drilling and production procedures. Regulation 26 specifies the personal protective equipment required on offshore installations. Regulation 27 requires the provision and maintenance of suitable signalling equipment approved by the Department of Tourism, Transport and Communications, and that it be installed in a Radio Room. Regulation 31 deals with the radio or other communications required before a helicopter may depart for or return from an installation. Regulation 33 states that the master, captain or person in charge of any vessel, helicopter, hovercraft, jetfoil or any other type of vessel must obtain the permission of the Installation Manager to come alongside or land on an installation. Regulation 34 provides that no person can be permitted manually to lift, carry, move or manipulate any load in excess of that person's personal capacity. Regulation 35 requires the notification of certain accidents and other dangerous occurrences to the Health and Safety Authority. Under s. 27 of the 1987 Act, fatal accidents must be notified. Regulation 35 adds accidents involving bodily injury which disables a person from performing normal duties for more than three consecutive days. Regulation 38 requires the provision and maintenance of a Sick Bay.

RADIOLOGICAL PROTECTION

General The Radiological Protection Act 1991 is an important development in Irish legislation concerning nuclear safety. There are two essential elements of the Act, which reflect the domestic and the international genesis of the Act.

First, s. 6 of the Act provided for the establishment of the Radiological Protection Institute of Ireland, which replaced and took over the powers and functions of the Nuclear Energy Board. The Institute was established on 1 April 1992, pursuant to the Radiological Protection Act 1991 (Establishment Day) Order 1992 (SI No. 48 of 1992). The effect of that Order was that the Nuclear Energy Board stood dissolved on 1 April 1992, and the Nuclear Energy Act 1971 was also repealed and replaced by the 1991 Act. In recent years in Ireland, public disquiet about environmental protection generally has reached a high level. The Environmental Protection Agency Act 1992 (which will be discussed in the 1992 Review) reflects the general upgrading of legislation in this area. In relation to nuclear safety, perceived dangers associated with the Sellafield nuclear plant in Cumbria have been the focus of much public attention. It may be said that the passage of the Radiological Protection Act 1991 represents the upgrading of the legislative response to the dangers of nuclear energy.

The second major impetus for the 1991 Act was the Chernobyl nuclear disaster. In the wake of that disaster, two International Conventions were adopted at a conference held under the auspices of the International Atomic Energy Agency in September 1986. These are known as the Assistance and the Notification Conventions. An earlier Protection Convention had been adopted at a 1979 Conference under the Agency's auspices. The opportunity was taken in the 1991 Act to incorporate these three Conventions into Irish law, and the text of each is included in Schedules to the Act. A very useful summary of the effects of the three Conventions was included in the Explanatory Memorandum to the 1990 Bill which became the 1991 Act; and this summary is also included in the General Note to the Act in *Irish Current Law Statutes Annotated*. Briefly, the Assistance Convention allows a party State to call for assistance from another party State in the event of a nuclear accident; the Notification Convention requires a party State to notify other affected States in the event of a nuclear accident; and the Protection Convention requires States to take appropriate preventive measures in relation to the international transport of nuclear material.

As to the detail of the Act, Part II (ss. 5 to 26) deals with the establishment of the Radiological Protection Institute of Ireland, its general functions and staffing and the transfer of the powers and functions of the Nuclear Energy Board to the Institute. S. 7 of the Act confers monitoring and advisory functions on the Institute in connection with ionising radiation, whether affecting environmental or human (and other animal) life. S. 8 of the Act empowers the Institute to co-operate with other States in the implementation of the Conventions referred to above.

Under s. 8(n) of the Act, the Institute also has the important function of carrying out, pursuant to an Order under s. 30 of the Act:

> a licensing system relating to the custody, use, manufacture, importation, distribution, transportation, exportation or other disposal of radioactive substances, nuclear devices or irradiating apparatus.

This comprehensive licensing provision provides for continuity between the Nuclear Energy Board and the Institute. The Board was responsible for the licensing system contained in the Nuclear Energy (General Control of Fissile Fuels, Radioactive Substances and Irradiating Apparatus) Order 1977, which was made under the 1971 Act, and which has been continued in force by s. 44 of the 1991 Act as if it were an order made under s. 30 of the 1991 Act. The Institute is now responsible for licensing under the 1977 Order. Of course, the 1977 Order may in the future be expanded under the terms of the 1991 Act. In addition to the 1977 Order, the Institute takes over the functions given to the Board under the European Communities (Ionising Radiation) Regulations 1991 (SI No. 43), which we consider below. Additional monitoring powers may be conferred on the Institute under s. 9 of the 1991 Act.

Part III of the Act (ss. 27 to 34) sets out the detailed provisions concerning the control of radioactive substances, nuclear devices or irradiating apparatus.

These include the appointment of inspectors (s. 28) and the extensive powers of such inspectors (s. 29), provisions which reflect the entry and inspection powers given to inspectors of the Health and Safety Authority under s. 34 of the Safety, Health and Welfare at Work Act 1989 (see the 1989 Review, 391). S. 30 of the Act empowers the Minsiter for Energy to made orders controlling the use of radioactive substances, nuclear devices or irradiating apparatus. The 1977 Order already mentioned comes under this heading.

S. 31 of the Act also allows the Minister to establish by Regulation maximum levels of radioactive contamination—referred to in the Act as 'prescribed levels'—for food and for water supplies. Where these prescribed levels are breached, any food or water will be deemed unsuitable for human consumption. S. 32 of the Act permits other relevant Ministers to make Regulations in connection with their respective functions, setting out what the Act describes as 'specified levels' of radioactive activity which would require remedial action. As a follow on, for example, s. 33 of the Act permits the slaugther of animals, destruction of crops and the disposal of eggs which exceed any 'specified levels' contained in Regulations made under s. 32.

S. 34 of the Act is an important provision on notification. It requires that, where there has been a theft of (or the threat of a theft of), or an accident or loss involving any radioactive substance, nuclear device or irradiating apparatus, the holder of a licence under the Act must notify the Institute that any such act has occurred.

Part IV of the 1991 Act (ss. 35 to 47) sets out, inter alia, the various offences and penalties under the Act. The Radiological Protection Institute is empowered to prosecute offences under any Order made pursuant to s. 30 of the 1991 Act, including the 1977 Order carried forward by the 1991 Act. All other offences under the Act, including for example failure to the notify the Institute under s. 34, would appear to be matters for the Garda Síochána (and the Director of Public Prosecutions, in respect of prosecutions on indictment) or the relevant Ministers referred to in s. 41 of the Act.

S. 35 of the Act provides that the Minister for Foreign Affairs may by Order designate the countries which are party to the 1980 Protection Convention referred to above. The Radiological Protection Act 1991 (Designation of Convention Countries) Order 1991 (SI No. 373) was made under s. 35.

Finally, under s. 42 of the Act, the Minsiter for Energy may make appropriate arrangements for the compensation of persons who suffer injury arising from co-operation given to another State under the 1986 Assistance Convention. The Minister is also empowered to lodge claims for reimbursement from the State which requests assistance under the Convention.

Regulations on ionising radiation The European Communities (Ionising Radiation) Regulations 1991 (SI No. 43) implement Directive 80/836/ Euratom, as amended by Directive 84/467/Euratom. They came into force on 5 April 1991, that is, before the Radiological Protection Act 1991 was passed, and so before the establishment of the Radiological Protection Institute: see above.

The Regulations apply to any work activity that involves the production, processing, handling, use, holding, storage, transport and disposal of natural and artificial radioactive substances and any other activity which involves a hazard arising from ionising radiation (Regulation 3). This means the Regulations apply to virtually all places of work, not just factories as with previous Regulations. The person responsible for any activity covered by the Regulations must ensure that exposure is within the prescribed limits. There are also requirements on disposal of radioactive material. Notification of activity covered by the Regulations must be given to the Radiological Protection Institute (because the Regulations were made before the Institute was established, they refer to the Nuclear Energy Board, but this should be adapted to refer to the Institute).

One regrettable and unusual lacuna in the Regulations may be noted. Although Regulation 28 creates criminal offences for non-compliance with the terms of the 1991 Regulations, there is no indication as to who is empowered to prosecute the 'person responsible' in the event of such non-compliance. In this unusual situation, the Garda Síochána are the enforcement authority, though one would have thought that the Institute or the Health and Safety Authority would have been designated as the appropriate authority. The Institute is not empowered to prosecute for non-compliance with the 1991 Regulations under the Radiological Protection Act 1991 since prosecutions may only be brought in respect of non-compliance with Orders made under the Act: the 1991 Regulations do not come within that category. No doubt, the Health and Safety Authority would be empowered to prosecute in appropriate cases under the Safety, Health and Welfare at Work Act 1989 (see the 1989 Review, 379-93), though again this is only a second best.

It is also of interest to note that Regulation 29 of the 1991 Regulations revoked the Factories Ionising Radiations (Sealed Sources) Regulations 1972 and the Factories Ionising Radiations (Unsealed Radioactive Substances) Regulations 1972. Under the 1972 Regulations, the prosecuting authority was the Health and Safety Authority, as successor to the Minister for Labour.

Perhaps the issue of prosecuting authority will be addressed when regulations to implement another Directive, already agreed at EC level in this area, is implemented in Irish law.

TOBACCO

Advertising and Promotion The Tobacco Products (Control of Advertising, Sponsorship and Sales Promotion) Regulations 1991 (SI No. 326), which came into effect on 31 December 1991, update the regime concerning the limits on advertising and promotion of tobacco products which have been in place for a number of years. The 1991 Regulations replace the Tobacco Products (Control of Advertising, Sponsorship and Sales Promotion) (No. 2) Regulations 1986.

Ban on oral tobacco The ban on the importation of oral smokeless tobacco in s. 6 of the Tobacco (Health Promotion and Protection) Act 1988 was unsuccessfully challenged in *United States Tobacco (Irl) Ltd v Ireland*, High Court, 19 February 1991. For an earlier successful challenge to a previous ban, see *United States Tobacco International Inc v Minister for Health* [1990] 1 IR 394 (1989 Review, 377-8). In both cases, the challenge was brought by companies which intended to import into the State an oral smokeless tobacco product called 'Skoal Bandits.'

The principal argument made in the instant case was that s. 6 of the 1988 Act was an impermissible quantitative restriction within the meaning of Article 30 of the Treaty of Rome, and that it was not saved by the 'protection of human health' exception in Article 36 of the Treaty. A second argument made was that s.6 amounted to a technical specification within the meaning of Directive 83/189/EEC, as amended by 89/622/EEC, and should therefore have been notified to the European Commission by the Goverment. In his judgment, Blayney J rejected both claims.

As to Article 30 of the Treaty of Rome, Blayney J noted that the defendants accepted that the ban fell foul of Article 30 of the Treaty of Rome, citing the leading decision of the Court of Justice in *R. v Henn and Darby* [1979] ECR 3795 in this context.

The main focus in the case was, however, on Article 36, and Blayney J accepted the defendants' submission that the ban was a permissible quantitative restriction under the 'protection of human health' exception. In coming to this conclusion, the Court was required to examine detailed expert evidence on the possible carcinogenic effects of oral smokeless tobacco products. Blayney J's conclusion was that, although the plaintiffs' witnesses doubted the connection between oral tobacco and cancer, the vast majority of the published scientific material, as well as the defendants' witnesses, supported the view that there was such a connection. In this light, Blayney J held that the State had a duty to act as it did, though perhaps such a strong comment might be viewed as *obiter*. The *ratio* of the case was, no doubt, that the ban in s. 6 of the 1988 Act was supportable by reference to the scientific information available. Nor did he consider that the objective of protecting human health could have been achieved by the type of warnings which apply to other tobacco products such as cigarettes. Therefore, Blayney J concluded that the ban did not offend against the principle of proportionality. Blayney J's judgment contains a useful analysis of the relevant jurisprudence of the Court of Justice in this area. This includes the decisions of the Court on the general principles, beginning with *Simmenthal SpA v Ministero della Finanze* [1976] ECR 1871, as well as the decisions on proportionality such as *Officier van Justitie v de Peijper* [1976] ECR 613.

The other argument addressed to the Court was that s. 6 amounted to a technical specification within the meaning of Directive 83/189/EEC, as amended by 89/622/EEC, and should therefore have been notified to the European Commission by the Goverment. Blayney J rejected this submission, noting that although the 1988 Act defined 'smokeless tobacco' for the purposes of the Act this definition did not include matters which the 1983 Directive indicated would amount to a 'specification', such as requirements as to quality, dimensions or any particular characteristics. He therefore concluded that there was an important difference between a definition and a specification for the purposes of the 1983 Directive. Thus, the State was not obliged to notify the Commission of the contents of s. 6 of the 1988 Act. Finally, it may be noted that Blayney J was not required to address the question whether failure to notify under the 1983 Directive would affect the validity of the ban contained in s. 6 of the 1988 Act.

Tar yield The European Communities (Tar Yield of Cigarettes) Regulations 1991 (SI No. 327) implement Directive 90/239/EEC concerning maximum tar yields.

Social Welfare

For a detailed analysis of the Social Welfare Act 1991, see Clark, Annotation, *Irish Current Law Statutes Annotated*. As well as giving effect to the changes in benefits announced in the 1991 Budget, the 1991 Act introduced a number of important substantive changes. Among these were the inclusion of part-time workers, changes to the Family Income Supplement (FIS), anti-fraud provisions and changes to the Pensions Act 1990. S. 43 of the 1991 Act is also intended to reverse the effect of the decision of Lavan J in *McHugh v AB (Deciding Officer)*, High Court, 23 November 1990 (see the 1990 Review, 478), a decision which was appealed to the Supreme Court.

REGULATIONS

The following Regulations were made in 1991 in relation to social welfare.

Social Welfare Act 1991 (Section 17) (Commencement) Order 1991 (SI No. 207).

Social Welfare Act 1991 (Section 26) (Commencement) Order 1991 (SI No. 312).

Social Welfare Act 1991 (Section 27(1)(b)) (Commencement) Order 1991 (SI No. 313).

Social Welfare Act 1991 (Section 43) (Commencement) Order 1991 (SI No. 280).

Social Welfare (Agreement with Canada on Social Security) Order 1991 (SI No. 317).

Social Welfare (Amendment of Miscellaneous Social Insurance Provisions) Regulations 1991 (SI No. 206).

Social Welfare (Contributions) (Amendment) Regulations 1991 (SI No. 370).

Social Welfare (Employment of Inconsiderable Extent) Regulations 1991 (SI No. 28).

Social Welfare (Employment of Inconsiderable Extent) (Revocation) Regulations 1991 (SI No. 71) (revoked SI No. 28 of 1991).

Social Welfare (Employment of Inconsiderable Extent) (No. 2) Regulations 1991 (SI No. 72).

Social Welfare (Family Income Supplement) Regulations 1991 (SI No. 279).

Social Welfare (Full-Time Education) Regulations 1991 (SI No. 261).

Social Welfare (Lone Parent's Allowance and Other Analogous Payments) (Amendment) Regulations 1991 (SI No. 170).

Social Welfare (Lone Parent's Allowance and Other Analogous Payments) (Amendment) (No. 2) Regulations 1991 (SI No. 262).

Social Welfare (Miscellaneous Control Provisions) Regulations 1991 (SI No. 196).

Social Welfare (Miscellaneous Provisions for Self-Employed Contributors) (Amendment) Regulations 1991 (SI No. 121).

Social Welfare (Modification of Insurance) Regulations 1991 (SI No. 94).

Social Welfare (Modification of Insurance)(Amendment) Regulations 1991 (SI No. 369).

Social Welfare (Old Age and Blind Pensions) Regulations 1991 (SI No. 263).

Social Welfare (Old Age (Contributory) Pension and Retirement Pension) Regulations 1991 (SI No. 314).

Social Welfare (Overlapping Benefits) Regulations 1991 (SI No. 281).

Social Welfare (Overlapping Benefits) (Amendment) Regulations 1991 (SI No. 374).

Social Welfare (Pay-Related Benefit) Regulations 1991 (SI No. 253).

Social Welfare (Pre-Retirement Allowance) (Amendment) Regulations 1991 (SI No. 93)

Social Welfare (Preservation of Rights) (Amendment) Regulations 1991 (SI No. 39).

Social Welfare (Rent Allowance) Regulations 1991 (SI No. 208).

Social Welfare (Subsidiary Employments) Regulations 1991 (SI No. 73).

Social Welfare (Temporary Provisions) Regulations 1991 (SI No. 291).

UNEMPLOYMENT ASSISTANCE

In *Corcoran v Minister for Social Welfare* [1992] ILRM 133; [1991] 2 IR 175 the applicant received unemployment assistance after his redundancy. A social welfare Deciding Officer investigated whether he was entitled to continue to receive the assistance. He concluded that the applicant was not entitled to a qualification certificate pursuant to s. 138 of the Social Welfare (Consolidation) Act 1981, having regard in particular to the applicant's purchase of a Nissan van in a trade-in of an older van which the applicant had bought while he was employed. The applicant had retained a firm of solicitors to deal with his claim to assistance, and they wrote to the Department asking to be represented at any appeal hearing. The Department had arranged an appeal for the day after this letter was sent and the firm was not aware of the hearing, although the applicant had been informed of the hearing a week earlier. At the appeal hearing, the Appeals Officer upheld the decision not to grant the applicant social assistance. A further appeal, at which the applicant was represented by his solicitor, also declined to grant the applicant the unemployment assistance. On judicial review by the applicant, Murphy J dismissed the application.

He held that the Deciding Officer was entitled to take account of the applicant's personal circumstances, particularly his continued ownership of the van bearing in mind the obvious demands on his limited resources; and the inference that he had a more substantial income or an undisclosed income in excess of the statutory maximum permitted under s. 138 of the 1981 Act could not be described as unreasonable, in the sense used in *The State (Keegan) v Stardust Victims Compensation Tribunal* [1987] ILRM 202; [1986] IR 642. He concluded that similar reasoning applied to the decision of the Appeals Officer.

Murphy J noted that the Social Welfare (Assistance Decisions and Appeals) Regulations 1953 did not provide for a right to legal representation at an appeals hearing, and the appeals notice in the instant case had conformed to the requirements of those Regulations; and, in any event, the applicant had not been prejudiced by the absence of his solicitor from the first appeals hearing.

The applicant had relied on *dicta* of Barron J in *Flanagan v University College Dublin* [1989] ILRM 469 (1989 Review, 14-5) to support a claim of a right to be legally represented at the appeals hearings. However, Murphy J did not accept that these dicta supported any general proposition that the applicant was entitled to be represented by legal advisers at an appeal hearing, even where such legal advisers notified the Department of their intention to appear. Nor did he consider that there was any basis for the suggestion that such representation should be at the expense of the State, bearing in mind that a refusal of assistance was not final and could be reviewed in the light of new evidence as to means. The refusal to acknowledge a right to legal assistance outside the criminal context is consistent with existing case law: see the 1990 Review, 144-7. However, Murphy J did comment that although the solicitors had no right to appear, it would have been churlish if they had been refused permission to appear. Of course, in the instant case such permission had been granted.

Solicitors

APPRENTICESHIP

The Solicitors Acts 1954 and 1960 (Apprenticeship and Education) Regulations 1991 (SI No. 9), which came into effect on 18 January 1991, prescribe the arrangements for obtaining apprenticeships as well as the requirements concerning the Law Society's School in Blackhall Place, Dublin. They revoked all previous Regulations.

EUROPEAN COMMUNITIES

The Solicitors Acts 1954 and 1960 (European Community Lawyers) (Fees) Regulations 1991 (SI No. 84) set out the fees required for sitting examinations for European Community lawyers. The Solicitors Acts 1954 and 1960 (European Communities) Regulations 1991 (SI No. 85) specify the basis on which lawyers qualify for recognition in accordance with the European Communities (General System for the Recognition of Higher Education Diplomas) Regulations 1991 (SI No. 1).

NEGLIGENCE

Cases involving solicitors' liability in negligence are discussed in the Torts chapter, 387-90, below.

Statutory Interpretation

Breach of statutory duty   In *Dunleavy v Glen Abbey Ltd* [1992] ILRM 1, the causative connection between breach of a statutory duty and liability for an accident at work was considered: see the Torts chapter, 406-9, below.

Ordinary or plain meaning   In *Texaco (Irl) Ltd v Murphy* [1992] ILRM 304; [1991] 2 IR 449, the Supreme Court applied the ordinary meaning rule in the context of taxation legislation: see the Revenue chapter, 362, above. A similar approach was used by Carroll J in *Brosnan v Cork Communications Ltd*, High Court, 15 October 1991: see also the Revenue Law chapter, 363-4, above.

See also the decision of the Supreme Court in *In re Atlantic Magnetics Ltd*, Supreme Court, 5 December 1991: see the Company Law chapter, 33-5, above.

Repeal by substitution   In *The People v Gilligan (No. 2)* [1992] ILRM 769, the Court accepted that a statutory provision which substituted a section in an existing Act with a new section effected a 'repeal' of the existing statutory provision within the meaning of s.21 of the Interpretation Act 1937: see the Criminal Law chapter, 163-4, above.

Strict construction   In *D.P.P.(Jennings) v Go-Travel Ltd* [1991] ILRM 577, the Supreme Court applied the strict construction test to road transport legislation which created criminal offences: see the Transport chapter, 464-5, below.

Subsequent legislation   In *D.P.P.(Jennings) v Go-Travel Ltd* [1991] ILRM 577, the Supreme Court considered the relevancy (or otherwise) of legislation enacted after the statutory provision under consideration: see the Transport chapter, 464-5, below.

Telecommunications

BROADCASTING

European programmes   The European Communities (Television Broadcasting) Regulations 1991 (SI No. 251) require certain programmes on RTE to be European-based.

Restrictions on broadcasting   Under the Broadcasting Authority Act 1960 (Section 31) Order 1991 (SI No. 6), effective until 19 January 1992, spokespersons for certain named and proscribed organisations are prohibited from broadcasting any material on Radio Telefís Éireann, including party political broadcasts. For discussion of Orders under s.31, see *The State (Lynch) v Cooney* [1983] ILRM 89; [1982] IR 337.

Retransmission and Relay   The Wireless Telegraphy (Television Programme Retransmission and Relay) Regulations 1991 (SI No.252) prohibit the use of certain unauthorised retransmission and relay equipment, commonly known as deflectors.

VIDEO RECORDINGS

Licensing of outlets   The Video Recordings Act 1989 (Commencement) Order 1991 (SI No. 32) brought ss. 1, 18, 21, 23, and 31 to 35 of the Video Recordings Act 1989 (see the 1989 Review, 408-9) into effect from 20 February 1991. These provisions relate primarily to licensing of video outlets as well as the power to make Regulations under the Act. The Video Recordings Act 1989 (Licences) Regulations 1991 (SI No. 33) provide for the registration of licence holders with the Official Censor of Films. The Video Recordings Act 1989 (Fees) Regulations 1991 (SI No. 38) set out the different fees for wholesale and retail outlets.

Unauthorised supply   The Video Recordings Act 1989 (Commencement) (No. 2) Order 1991 (SI No. 104) brought ss. 2, 19, 20, 22, 24, 25, and 26 to 28 of the 1989 Act into effect from 1 May 1991. These provisions provide for offences in relation to the sale or supply of videos from unlicensed outlets.

Certification and prohibition   The Video Recordings Act 1989 (Commencement) (No. 3) Order 1991 (SI No. 216) brought into effect from 26 July 1991 the following provisions of the 1989 Act: s. 7 (except for subs.(3)), ss. 8 and 9, s. 10 (except for subs. (4)(a)), s. 11 (except for subs. (1)(a)) and ss. 15 to 17. These sections relate to the power of the Official Censor of Films to classify certain videos on the basis of age suitability as well as the power to prohibit videos entirely. The sections also provide for appeals to the Censorship of Films Appeal Board. The subsections which were not brought into force by the Order relate primarily to revocation of a prohibition order. The Video Recordings Act 1989 (Register of Prohibited Video Works) Regulations 1991 (SI No. 217) specify the form of the register to be maintained by the Censor. The Video Recordings Act 1989 (Appeals) Regulations 1991 (SI No.218) prescribe the procedure for appeals to the Appeal Board under the Act. Finally, the Video Recordings Act 1989 (Fees) (No. 2) Regulations 1991 (SI No. 221) set out the different fees payable for certification under the Act.

One of the effects of the implementation of the 1989 Act is that, because notice of a prohibition order must be published in *Iris Oifigiúil*, the contents of that heretofore austere Official Gazette have, since July 1991, made for somewhat distracting reading for those searching, for example, for notice of the publication of the latest Acts or Statutory Instruments.

Torts

THE STANDARD OF CARE

It is a truism that, in determining the standard of care in negligence actions, the courts are to be governed neither by how people normally behave nor by the norms that particular groups may establish as controlling their behaviour. Even in the case of professional negligence, where enhanced deference is given to customary norms and practices, the test is one over which the courts retain ultimate control. Against this background, what relevance should be ascribed to safety standards set by a particular body or institution to govern the behaviour of those working for it?

The question arose in *Murphy v Minister for Defence* [1991] 2 IR 161. The case concerned an application for liberty to adduce further evidence, under Order 58, rule 8 of the Rules of the Superior Courts 1986, in a pending appeal brought by a soldier against Costello J's dismissal of his action for damages for personal injuries arising from the army's alleged negligence in requiring him to undergo a fitness test without a prior medical examination. The further evidence consisted of training and medical circulars issued by the army authorities which required that such an examination be carried out. Under *Lynagh v Mackin* [1970] IR 180, the further evidence must be such that, if given, would probably have an important influence on the result of the case.

The Supreme Court was satisfied that the circular passed this test. Finlay CJ considered that knowledge of their existence 'would be likely to have an important effect on the view of a trial judge' as to whether the defendants had discharged their duty of care: see also 327, above.

Why should such knowledge have been likely to change Costello J's mind? Not because the army sets its own standard of care in negligence. If that were so, the *absence* of such circulars would have been equally crucial. A more plausible rationale is perhaps that the existence of such circulars enhanced the credibility of the plaintiff's claim that reasonableness demanded a prior medical examination. It would seem essential that courts should not place too much emphasis on the safety regime actually in operation. Otherwise those who take extra precautions would be punished, rather than rewarded, for their concern for their employees.

THE DUTY OF CARE

Over the past decade, courts in Britain have been greatly exercised by the issue of liability in negligence for causing pure economic loss. The radicalism of *Junior Books* [1983] 1 AC 520 has given way to a strong opposition to any general principle of liability for this category of loss. In Ireland, no such development can be clearly discerned, though this may be simply because the issue has yet to present itself in stark form at appellate level.

The decision of *Sweeney v Duggan* [1991] 2 IR 274 involved a consideration of the subject; Barron J's observations are of much interest. The plaintiff, a drilling machine operator employed by a company at a quarry, was injured in an accident at work when the drill he was operating fell on him. His claim against his employer, was, ultimately, not defended, and this resulted in judgment in his favour, but the company had be this stage gone into liquidation and the plaintiff was entitled to recover only 15% of his damages, as a preferential creditor.

The plaintiff sued the defendant, who was effectively the owner of the company (his wife having a one-pound share in it) as well as being its quarry manager. The essence of the plaintiff's case was that the defendant, in his capacity as quarry manager under s. 23 of the Mines and Quarries Act 1965, owed a special duty of care to the plaintiff and that, as controller and effective owner of the company, aware of its financial position, he had a duty of care to employees engaged in a dangerous occupation to ensure that the business would be capable of paying com- pensation to them for injuries arising out of their work, by securing an appropriate policy of insurance.

Barron J dismissed the claim. He approached the matter as follows. Applying the principles enunciated by the Supreme Court in *Ward v McMaster* [1989] ILRM 400; [1988] IR 337, it was necessary to consider three elements: *proximity, foreseeability* and *public policy*. The nature of the loss was 'not material'. Liability in negligence extended to both personal injury and economic loss suffered by reason of the defendant's wrong. Foreseeability was not in question; the real issue related to the other two elements.

Barron J had several reasons for rejecting the plaintiff's case. Perhaps the most formidable was that an employer's duty to ensure the safety of employees did not extend to a duty to have regard to their economic well-being. If a duty to provide employers' liability insurance should be imposed, this was a matter solely for the Oireachtas. Moreover, while quarrying was obviously a dangerous employment, the evidence as to its dangerous nature had not been 'very compelling'. At the time of the accident, the company had been in good financial shape; its business had failed because of outside circumstances which arose subsequently.

The other main reason for dismissing the claim was that to allow it 'would in effect be depriving the defendant of his protection under company law and to nullify all the essential principles of that law'. There are, of course, circumstances in which those in charge of companies may be reached civilly: see, e.g. the Companies Act 1990, ss. 38, 39, 109, 133, 142 and 163. Moreover s. 52 of the 1990 Act requires directors, in the performance of their functions, to have regard to the interests of the company's employees in general: see the 1990 Review, 74-5. S. 52 would not avail the plaintiff, however, since the duty it prescribes is owed to the company.

Barron J's reluctance to extend the duty of care into such a contentious area of pure economic loss is understandable. *Ward v McMaster* was admittedly a case where liability was imposed for a loss of this type, but the element of reliance was there a good deal stronger and the paternalistic policy underlying the legislation was easy to discern. The absence of legislation mirroring a common law duty of care in *Sweeney* suggested that none should be imposed gratuitously by the courts.

Later in the chapter, under the heading 'Tort Law and the Constitution', we examine another unsuccessful line of argument pursued by the plaintiff in *Sweeney v Duggan*.

PROFESSIONAL NEGLIGENCE

Solicitors In *Kehoe v C.J. Louth & Son* [1992] ILRM 282, the Supreme Court addressed one straightforward issue of liability and a somewhat more complex secondary issue relating to damages. The plaintiffs had bought a licensed premises in a country village. The property was held on a yearly tenancy. At the time of the signing the contract, the managing clerk of the defendant solicitor's firm advised the plaintiffs, who were the firm's clients, that the tenancy was 'as good as freehold', since they had the legal right to acquire the freehold. An offer by the plaintiffs shortly afterwards to buy the freehold for £500 was rejected by the agents of the owners of the freehold. Later, when the business did not prosper, the plaintiffs sought to sell the premises but found that this was virtually impossible as they did not in fact have the right to buy out the freehold. Under s. 15(1)(d) of the Landlord and Tenant (Ground Rents) (No. 2) Act 1978 (as subsequently amended by s. 9 of the Landlord and Tenant (Amendment) Act 1984) the right to acquire the freehold was conditional on the yearly rent's being less than the rateable valuation. Here the yearly rent was £9.67 and the valuation £9.

One solution to the difficulty would be to have the Commissioner of Valuation revalue the premises; the drawback to this course was that the liability for rates would be likely to increase greatly. The Supreme Court, overruling Lardner J on this issue, held that the failure by the managing clerk to advise the plaintiffs of these implications was negligent.

The measure of damages under this heading was the capital value of the annual increase in rates discounted by the consideration that the existing valuation might not, in any event, have remained permanently at this low figure. Egan J (McCarthy and O'Flaherty JJ concurring) acknowledged the difficulty of this calculation. The speculative element is surely high.

A second heading of damage related to the price of buying out the freehold, which was in the region of £3,500. Lardner J had rejected evidence from one of the plaintiffs that the managing clerk had said that the freehold could be purchased at a 'nominal price'. This finding was not disturbed on appeal. Moreover, Egan J considered it clear on the evidence that the plaintiffs knew that they would have to buy the ground rent if they wanted a freehold interest. Nonetheless the Supreme Court held the defendant should compensate the plaintiffs to the tune of £3,000 under this heading. Egan J observed that:

> [a]lthough they were not promised that the rent could be bought out for a nominal sum, it is reasonable to assume that they could not have known that it would cost as much as £3,500 (or something in this region) to buy out an annual rent of a mere £9.67. A layman would probably think that the actual offer of £500 would be sufficient. . . .

This finding seems harsh. It should be noted that this second 'heading' of damages in fact involves an entirely *different basis of liability in negligence* from the first. It would apply even if the managing clerk had given the plaintiffs full information of the implications of an increase in the rateable valuation. One wonders whether solicitors have a customary practice of answering unasked financial questions that might be relevant to the exercise of commercial judgment by clients contemplating the acquisition of commercial premises. The purchase price of the premises was £43,000. An extra expense of less than 10% in converting a yearly tenancy in a freehold does not seem inordinately large. Certainly, if the customary practice does not involve disclosure of the detailed information considered proper by the Supreme Court, it would be hard to stigmatise it as involving an inherent defect such as would fail the test laid down by the Court in *O'Donovan v Cork County Council* [1967] IR 173, and reiterated *Roche v Peilow* [1985] IR 232.

The decision of *McCabe v Dolan Cosgrove & Co.*, High Court, 14 October 1991 might at one level seem to be of no consequence in the development of the law of negligence. At another level, the legal issue raised was one of considerable interest. Lynch J confessed that its facts appeared to be 'very confusing and difficult to follow'. It involved a negligence action brought by the plaintiff, a lay litigant, against a firm of solicitors with regard to the advice they were giving to the executor of a purported will. The plaintiff claimed that, in giving this advice, the defendant firm was doing wrong to her and her family. The defendant successfully applied under Order 19, rule 28 of the Rules of the Superior Courts 1986 to have the claim struck out.

Lynch J was anxious not to take any concluded position as to the merits of the facts of the case, though his comments seem designed to encourage the plaintiff to investigate the matter further before starting costly litigation. His remarks on the legal reason why he was striking out the case are worth quoting in full:

> Every citizen is entitled to consult a qualified lawyer for advice as to his or her legal rights on the facts as the citizen sees them; and lawyers are entitled to advise their clients on those facts as stated to them. If the advices are wrong, which most often is because the instructions as to the facts turn out to be wrong, the client may be sued by the opposing party, but not the lawyer for advising the client. Lawyers do no wrong in advising clients on the facts as put before them by their clients. If the advices are wrong, not because the instructions are wrong but because of negligence, then of course the client could sue the lawyer. But the opposing party has a remedy as against the client, not against the lawyer.

At first sight, this analysis would seem difficult to reconcile with the fact that our courts have for long recognised that lawyers can be liable to persons who are not their clients on the basis of the *Hedley Byrne* principle: see, e.g., *Wall v Hegarty* [1980] ILRM 124. This basis of liability can extend to the broader 'neighbour' principle of *Donoghue v Stevenson* where the relationship is of sufficient proximity and no countervailing policies exist: see *Wall v Hegarty*, above and *Ross v Caunters* [1980] Ch. 297. The answer to this apparent inconsistency is revealed by consideration of the fact that there must be limits to the scope of a solicitor's liability to third parties. In *Ross v Caunters* (at p. 322), Megarry VC observed that:

> [i]n broad terms, a solicitor's duty to his client is to do for him all that he properly can, with, of course, proper care and attention. . . . The solicitor owes no such duty to those who are not his clients. He is no guardian of their interests. What he does for his client may be hostile and injurious to their interests; and sometimes the greater the injuries the better he will have served his client. The duty owed by a solicitor to a third party is entirely different. There is no trace of a wide and general duty to do all that properly can be done for him. Instead, in a case such as the present, there is merely a duty, owed to him as well as the client, to use proper care in carrying out the client's instructions for conferring the benefit on the third party.

This approach found support in *Business Computers International Ltd v Registrar of Companies* [1987] 3 All ER 465 and in the English Court of Appeal decision of *Al-Kandari v JR Brown & Co.* [1988] 1 All ER 833. In *Al-Kandari* (at 838-9), Bingham LJ observed that:

> [i]n the ordinary course of adversarial litigation a solicitor does not owe a duty of care to his client's adversary. The theory underlying such litigation is that justice is best done if each party, separately and independently advised, attempts within the limits of the law and propriety and good practice to achieve the best result for himself that he reasonably can without regard to the interests of the other party. The duty of the solicitor, within the same limits, is to assist his client in that endeavour, although the wise solicitor may often advise that the best result will involve an element of compromise or give and take or horse trading. Ordinarily, however, in contested civil litigation a solicitor's proper concern is to do what is best for his client without regard to the interests of his opponent.

Lord Donaldson MR invoked *Rondel v Worsley* [1969] 1 AC 191—the advocates' immunity case—in support of the proposition (at 836) that, in the context of 'hostile' litigation, 'public policy will usually require that a solicitor be protected from a claim in negligence by his client's opponent, since such claims could be used as a basis for endless re-litigation of disputes'.

The Court of Appeal was, however, willing to impose liability on a solicitor, even in the course of contested litigation, who for a limited purpose steps outside his or her role as agent of one party and assumes a different role, either independent of both parties or as agent of both.

Doctors   In *Maguire v Randles, Jordan and the North Eastern Health Board*, High Court, 21 June 1991, Lynch J dismissed the plaintiff's claim for negligence relating to the insertion in her womb of the intra-uterine contraceptive device known as the coil when she was pregnant. The plaintiff alleged that she had suffered a miscarriage three weeks later. After a review of the evidence, Lynch J concluded that there had been no negligence. At the time the coil was inserted, the plaintiff was already at the early stage of a miscarriage. It would not have been possible to have distinguished this condition from menstruation, which would have been the appropriate time for the insertion of the coil.

In the section of this chapter, dealing with the doctrine of *res ipsa loquitur*, below, 415-7, we examine Morris J's decision in *Lindsay v Mid-Western Health Board*, High Court, 30 May 1991.

Architects The question of the duty of care of those engaged to inspect properties prior to purchase has generated much litigation in Ireland and in other common law jurisdictions. See R. Jackson & J. Powell, *Professional Negligence*, ch. 2, McMahon & Binchy, *op. cit.*, 256-7. In *Sunderland v McGreavey* [1987] IR 372, at 385, Lardner J defined the duty of an architect in a case where a 'walk through' visual inspection was envisaged as being:

> to inspect the building with the eye of a competent architect and to draw the inferences which such an architect would draw from what he sees. If there are physical signs which would alert him to the existence or possible existence of some problem or danger he would be obliged to warn or recommend that they be investigated further. . . .

This test was endorsed by Barr J in *Bedford v Lane, practising as P.D. Lane Associates*, High Court, 22 November 1991, where the defendant architect had failed to observe what were referred to in evidence as 'alarm signals' indicative of possible structural problems. Barr J considered that, if there were defects or signs in a building which a competent surveyor ought to observe and which should suggest to him the possibility of structural instability, he had a clear duty to advise his principal that a more detailed inspection should be made to ascertain whether the building was structurally sound.

Engineers In *Moran v Duleek Developments Ltd and Hanley*, High Court, 7 June 1991, the plaintiff bought a house from the first defendant which turned out to be susceptible to flooding. The second defendant was an engineer working in the public service, who had been engaged by the builder to prepare appropriate layout plans for the estate to enable planning permission to be obtained. He did not in any sense supervise the construction of the buildings but he did provide certain important levels in connection with the development of the estate, and also provided certificates as to the compliance with the conditions contained in the planning permission that was ultimately granted.

Planning permission was subject to a condition that all houses should be erected above maximum flood level, which should be agreed with the Council's engineer before development commenced. In fact no such level was agreed with the Council's engineer, though the level which the second defendant provided was a perfectly satisfactory one. After the plaintiff's house had been built and sold to him, he was provided with a certificate by the second defendant to the effect that, to the best of his knowledge and belief, all conditions in the planning permission relating to that site had been complied with. When the flooding occurred it transpired that the house had been constructed at a level lower than what had been prescribed as the minimum by the second defendant.

The second defendant argued that he had not been guilty of negligence since he had enquired of a third party in the litigation whether the plaintiff's house had been constructed in accordance with the minimum ground level which he had directed and this third party had negligently confirmed that it had been. The third party, a director of the company, was a young man; according to the evidence, he was either still at university, where he was a student of commerce, or else was a recent graduate. His function was to assist in a very minor way by holding the pole when the second defendant was taking measurements. Murphy J considered it highly improbable that the second defendant should have sought the third party's confirmation as to the level at which the house had been constructed; if such a question had been posed, it 'must have been of a most casual nature'. Murphy J did not believe that its significance would have been understood by the third party, nor could he accept that a qualified engineer would place any reliance on the answer to a casual question asked of a young inexperienced employee, albeit a director of the company, who was not a builder by profession.

Murphy J had great sympathy for the second defendant, who had not been in the position of an architect or engineer exercising a constant supervision after the development and thus having a full body of knowledge not merely of what had been planned but what had been achieved. In the nature of the information available to him, it was probably true that he would have to make further measurements himself before the certificate could be given. Perhaps it would not be necessary to make additional measurements for *every* house and certificate, but it seemed clear to Murphy J that the second defendant 'had to satisfy himself in an appropriate professional manner that the crucial measurements had been observed'.

The second defendant's professional expertise with regard to the maximum water levels had been vindicated; at the very least he had been let down by the workmanship of the company and the persons taking control of it.

In holding the second defendant liable in negligence for providing a certificate that proved to be erroneous and in an area falling particularly within the expertise of an engineer, Murphy J made the following important observation:

> Whilst evidence was given by engineers as to what they believed was the appropriate standard of care which should be exercised by engineers or architects I believe that this is essentially a matter for the court. The nature of the duty can be better seen from the point of view of the purchaser who is invited to rely on the express written certificate of the engineer which is addressed to the particular circumstances of his case

and without which it is clear that the transaction would not have proceeded.

Clearly what Murphy J was seeking to stress here was the element of reliance placed on certificates. Professional people are concerned with the norms of their profession; naturally they will have regard to the reliance dimension but it will not always be as central to their considerations as to what constitutes neglectful conduct as it will be to a court. Once reliance enters the picture, the traditional judicial indulgence to customary professional practice is displaced by a more stringent generic test of negligence. (The implications of this development in the context of informed consent to medical treatment are, incidentally, intruiging.)

OCCUPIERS' LIABILITY

Supermarkets In the 1990 Review, 515-21, we discussed the Supreme Court decision in *Mullen v Quinnsworth t/a Crazy Prices* [1990] 1 IR 59. It will be recalled that the plaintiff, a woman aged seventy four, had slipped and fallen on some cooking oil when shopping in the defendants' supermarket. There was at the time a big end display of cooking oil in one of the aisles nearby. Barrington J had withdrawn the case from the jury; the Supreme Court reversed and directed a new trial. It held that the case was one to which the *res ipsa loquitur* doctrine applied.

The retrial was heard by Lynch J, who dismissed the action. During the hearing he had permitted evidence to be given by the defendants' assistant manager that, only moments before the plaintiff slipped, he had been told by a customer that there was oil spilled on the floor. Lynch J had himself later asked the assistant manager what exactly the customer had said, and the assistant manager replied that she had said 'I have just dropped a bottle of oil'.

On appeal, [1991] ILRM 439, the Supreme Court reversed Lynch J. Griffin J (Hederman J concurring) laid much emphasis on the (essentially uncontradicted) evidence of the plaintiff's expert witness that the plastic bottles of oil were easily breakable, that the manner in which they were stacked as a pyramid was unstable and that the employment of only one 'floater' to traverse a distance of 500 yards in ten or fifteen minutes was wholly inadequate.

Griffin J rejected as 'clearly inadmissible in evidence' the assistant manager's statement that the customer had told him that oil had been spilt and that she had spilt it. With respect, whereas the second of these statements may perhaps have offended the rule against hearsay, the first did not, if it had been admitted in evidence merely to establish that the assistant manager had become alert to the danger only moments before the plaintiff fell. In 'slip and fall' cases, the crucial issue usually concerns the length of time between the commencement of the danger and the moment the store's employees learnt, or could reasonably have learnt, of it. The assistant manager was *rightly* permitted to give evidence of what he had been told by the customer, so far as it impinged on the issue of *alacrity of response*. The *existence* of oil on the floor moments before the accident was not in issue between the parties. The second statement is a certainly good deal more problematical; it should have been excluded under the hearsay rule so far as its adduction sought to address the question of *how long the oil had been on the floor before the assistant manager was told of its existence there.*

It will be recalled that, in the first appeal, McCarthy J mentioned that it remained for another day to consider whether or not, by way of application of the rule in *Rylands v Fletcher* or otherwise, balancing the rights of people and the rights of property, 'a principle of absolute liability' might be appropriate to claims arising out of 'certain forms of accidents occurring in large supermarkets'. Prior to the retrial, the plaintiff had given notice of a particular of breach of duty expressed in terms of 'escape' of the cooking oil from a place under the defendants' control onto a 'public aisle' in the supermarket. It seems that this intriguing attempt to echo the traditional concepts of the rule in *Rylands v Fletcher* was not strongly pursued in the hearing. On appeal, at the Supreme Court's invitation, the argument excluded this issue. Thus, as McCarthy J repeated, that question 'must therefore remain for another day'.

In the 1990 Review, 518-21, we discussed McCarthy J's approach. We need say no more here than that the principle of 'absolute liability' that he postulated could not easily have been based on the rule in *Rylands v Fletcher* and was in truth a *modernistic* strategy relating to a form of enterprise liability. It is interesting to see how the plaintiff's lawyers had sought to mould that principle into a more traditional framework; such an approach might have been considered more likely to appeal to the other members of the Court had the outcome of the case depended on it.

Nevertheless, the argument in favour of strict (if not absolute) liability in relation to 'slip and fall' injuries has some attraction. The reality of how supermarkets conduct their lucrative business is that there is a certain measurable level of attrition in terms of customers who fall on products dislodged by the inevitable process of throngs of customers passing down aisles containing thousands of relatively fragile products. The design and operation of supermarkets throw up a predictable incidence of casualties, who will be customers or employees of the enterprise. It would of course be possible to apply the traditional negligence test stringently (cf., e.g.,

McGovern v Clones UDC [1944] IR 282), but it is not, perhaps, illegitimate to contemplate a strict liability regime on the basis that, if not an inherently dangerous activity, the enterprise has an unavoidable risk of injury, the price for which should be paid by the enterprisers rather than their customers.

Dance floors   The *Mullen v Quinnsworth* litigation may be contrasted with an issue raised, but ultimately not requiring resolution, in *McSweeney v Garda Síochána Boat Club*, High Court, 5 June 1991. The plaintiff had fallen on the dance floor at a disco run by the defendants. She claimed that she had slipped on 'drink of some description' which had been spilt on the floor. O'Flaherty J held that the plaintiff was mistaken in her recollection, which would have been affected by the shock of the fall, and he upheld Judge Martin's dismissal of the case. Of more general interest are O'Flaherty J's comments on what would have been the position had there been a spillage. The defendants had conceded that, since patrons were allowed to bring glasses of drink into the area where dancing took place, inevitably from time to time drink would get spilt. They claimed that they had in operation a system of control whereby those supervising the disco would watch for spillages and try to have them mopped up as promptly as possible.

O'Flaherty J, impressed by the evidence on the issue, would have been disposed to hold that the system operated by the defendants was a reasonable one; if that were so, 'the likelihood is that it would have been explained that [the spillage] could have been there only for a very short length of time and it would be a counsel of perfection to expect the spillage to be cleared up immediately'.

It is interesting to contrast this somewhat gentle approach to liability for spillage with that adopted in *Mullen v Quinnsworth*. The defendants were a club, rather than a supermarket; the profit motive and the capacity to pay would differ greatly as between the two. Nevertheless, the risk of spillages was surely not insignificant in the instant case, yet, in contrast to the supermarket regime, the judgment does not suggest that anyone had been given the *exclusive* function of removing dangers resulting from spillages. The actual *discharge* of this function would also be likely to be a good deal more difficult in relation to a disco floor, with its mixture of darkness and multicolored lighting.

Is there not in O'Flaherty J's approach some tacit endorsement of the traditional judicial approach to leisure activities with a risk factor? The operation and management of these activities are given a fairly wide margin of appreciation, the courts recognising that very often, if they are to be permitted to take place at all, some risk of injury is inevitable. The conceptual categorisation variously adopted to articulate this policy shows a bewildering inconsistency. Some judges have argued (quite unconvincingly) that the risk is unforeseeable; others (more credibly) that the cost of preventing the risk would be too onerous; still others have addressed the issue in terms of the absence of a duty of care or the existence of a modified, individuated, duty of care; finally, that old reliable, voluntary assumption of risk can always be invoked when all else fails. Irish decisions in which these several approaches have been adopted—sometimes within the same judgment—include *Callaghan v Killarney Race Co. Ltd* [1958] IR 366, *Coleman v Kelly*, 85 ILTR 48 (1951), *Donaldson v Irish Motor Racing Club*, Supreme Court, 1 February 1957 (extracted in McMahon & Binchy's *Casebook on the Irish Law of Torts* (1st ed., 1983) 220, and *McComiskey v McDermott* [1974] IR 75.

National monuments   In the 1987 Review, 334-5, we discussed Barr J's judgment in *Clancy v Commissioners of Public Works in Ireland* [1988] ILRM 268, so far as it impinged on the issue of contributory negligence. In an appeal by both parties [1991] ILRM 567, the Supreme Court upheld Barr J's finding of liability, and allowed the plaintiff's cross-appeal on the issue of contributory negligence.

It will be recalled that the plaintiff, a 13 year old boy, was injured when he fell through a large unprotected ope on the first floor of Donegal Castle, an ancient, partly ruined building. The defendants were the guardians of the building under the National Monuments Act 1930. S. 16 of that Act provides as follows:

> (1) Where the Commissioners or a local authority are the owners or the guardians of a national monument, the Commissioners or such local authority (as the case may be) shall, subject to the provisions of this section, admit the pubic to enter on and view such monument upon payment of such (if any) charge for admission and subject to such conditions and limitations as the Commissioners or such local authority shall prescribe.
>
> (2) Where the Commissioners or a local authority are the guardians of a national monument by virtue of a deed made under an Act repealed by this Act, the public shall not be admitted to such monument under this section without or otherwise than in accordance with the consent of the owner of such monument given by such deed or otherwise.

Finlay CJ (Hederman J concurring) construed this section as imposing an *obligation* on the defendants to admit the public to enter on and view the castle, subject to such conditions and limitations as they should prescribe. They were accordingly entitled to confine the public, if they saw fit, to viewing the castle only from outside its actual buildings or to permit access to the first floor only. The Chief Justice was satisfied that these conditions and limitations had to be carried out 'reasonably and with care, so as to avoid danger or injury to persons who it could reasonably be foreseen would be affected by the discharge of that duty'. He rejected the argument that the conditions and limitations could relate only to *preservation of the fabric of the monument*; such an interpretation would lead to the 'extraordinarily anomalous position' that, if part of the monument fell, by reason of decay, on a member of the public, the defendants would be liable but if a member of the public fell through a hole in the monument which was not attributable to non-repair, he or she would have no claim.

The Chief Justice was satisfied that, in carrying out their statutory duty under s. 16, 'the Commissioners were obliged to take such reasonable steps as were necessary to avoid foreseeable risk to persons likely to be affected by the discharge of that duty, that is to say, to persons who might gain access to the national monument by virtue of the admission of the public to enter upon and view it'. He accepted that in general the Commissioners, in admitting members of the public to enter upon and view national monuments, 'should not be equated, in regard to standards of care, with the obligation which may be imposed on persons such as hotel owners or shop owners in relation to the care which would be taken of members of the public having access to buildings in use for purposes connected with commerce or trade'. Anyone entering upon and viewing a partly ruined building expected to find opes which were unprotected and staircases which did not contain a bannister or side rail. It was a matter for determination in each individual case whether protection should be provided or whether, in the alternative, where this was not reasonably possible, the public should be prevented from having access to some particular part of the building.

In the present case, the ope was large—seven feet by three feet; it was in a dark coloured stone floor sixteen feet above ground level and was apparently straddling the path from the top of the stairs to the most obvious viewing point, the bay window. Such a situation, in Finlay CJ's view, created 'a very real and present risk of injury' to persons gaining access to the castle. This fact imposed on the Commissioners an obligation either to close the aperture by a grill (as they had subsequently done) or to prevent access to the first floor. The defendants had failed in this obligation and accordingly Barr J had been correct in holding them guilty of negligence and breach of duty.

This analysis is probably best understood as involving a process of statutory interpretation rather than as impacting on the common law rules relating to occupiers' liability. The Supreme Court's reluctance to work out the implications of *McNamara v ESB* [1975] IR 1 for 'lawful' entrants has frequently inspired comment: see, e.g., Eoin O'Dell, 'Reform of Occupiers' Liability?' (1992) 86 Incorp L Soc of Ireland Gazette 303, 359, McMahon

& Binchy, *op. cit.*, 225-31 and the 1987 Review, 331-2. Nothing in Finlay CJ's comments suggests that he was seeking to take a definitive stand on a matter on which, as recently as in *Rooney v Connolly* [1986] IR 572; [1987] ILRM 768, the Court (by a majority) had taken no view in default of argument by the plaintiff raising this issue. *Clancy* can therefore be treated simply as a case limited to its distinctive statutory context.

EMPLOYERS' LIABILITY

In *Heeney v Dublin Corporation*, High Court, 16 May 1991, a fatal injuries action brought under Part IV of the Civil Liability Act 1961, the deceased had been employed as station officer with a fire brigade. He died after inhaling gasses while fighting a fire in a building without breathing apparatus. His death took place in October 1985. The evidence established that the fire authority in 1977 had started to provide their crews with breathing apparatus and to organise courses for the training of firemen. By 1984, all the *permanent* fire brigades in the country had been issued with breathing apparatus, but certain *retained* brigades, including the one employing the deceased, had not yet received any training nor had been issued with the apparatus.

The deceased had enquired when these matters would be remedied and had been informed that breathing apparatus training would be provided for retained firemen when the training programme had been finalised. An order for the purchase of breathing apparatus for the deceased's appliance had been made in 1983 but it was not issued until 1988 because personnel were not trained in its use until then.

In imposing liability, Barron J had no doubt that the fire authority ought to have provided breathing apparatus for its retained crews before it had done and that the brigade where the deceased was employed should not have been allowed to go into buildings without breathing apparatus in cases where the station officer would have authorised the use of breathing apparatus, had it been available. The absence of any instruction to the station officer or his men not to enter the building without breathing apparatus had been wrong. Barron J rejected the argument that the deceased should have waited at the fire for the arrival of a brigade with breathing apparatus before going into the building. The deceased 'was in control of the fire and had to act as he saw fit when he arrived at that fire. . . .'

A second basis for imposing liability was that the fire authority ought to have carried out a medical examination of the deceased, who was aged over fifty five years at the time of his death and who suffered from coronary artery disease. The question of retirement at fifty five and of annual medical examinations for employees had been the subject of proceedings before the Labour Court. That Court's recommendation for changes seven months before the death of the deceased had been resisted by the union, which had sought to reach agreement first as to what was to happen to firemen who would be compelled to give up their employment. The employers felt unable to concede the union's demands and as a result the changes had not been implemented. Barron J commented that, '[r]egrettably, financial considerations on both sides were allowed to take priority over safety, which does not redound to the credit of either side in the dispute'. He considered that the existence of the dispute and the failure to implement safety rules which both parties had recognised as being necessary could not be ignored in the context of what the defendants could or could not reasonably have foreseen. The defendants had been under a duty to consider the interim period until the Labour Court recommendations could be introduced. There was no evidence that they had done so. There was no prohibition on medical examinations and the union could not have objected to a decision to impose a medical examination on any particular officer. Had they examined the deceased, they would have discovered the fact that he suffered from hypertension. Coupled with his age, this would have put the fire authority on notice to take the matter of his health further. If they had done so, it was reasonable to suppose that his coronary artery disease would have been discovered.

Barron J's approach is consistent with the generally high standard of care that the Irish courts have imposed on employers. Whether such jealous concern will always lead to improved employment practices is, however, less than certain. The policy issues in relation to the employment of physically fragile employees are more subtle than may at first appear. See, e.g., *Rafferty v Parsons (CA) of Ireland* [1987] ILRM 98, analysed by Binchy, *'Light Work': A Dilemma for Employers*, 82 Incorp L Soc of Ireland Gazette 47 (1988). See also Wriggleworth, *Legislation and Injury Control*, 18 Med Sci & L 191, at 193 (1978), discussing the practical effects of the House of Lords' decision in *Paris v Stepney Borough Council* [1951] AC 367. See also 275, above.

NERVOUS SHOCK

The subject of liability for negligently caused 'nervous shock' is one on which Irish courts led the way at the end of the last century. In two decisions, *Byrne v Southern & Western Ry Co.*, unreported, CA, February, 1884, and *Bell v Great Northern Ry Co.*, 26 LR (Ir) 428 (Ex Div, 1890), the Irish judges showed themselves disposed to grant compensation for foreseeable psychology injury consequent on fright. The timidity of the Privy Council is *Victoria Ry Commissioners v Coultas* 13 App Cas 222 (1888) held no appeal for the Exchequer Division in *Bell;* Palles CB and Murphy J emphasised the physical basis underlying mental disturbance.

In both *Byrne* and *Bell*, the plaintiff's fright was caused by a sudden emergency in which his or her life appeared to be in danger. The facts were thus similar to those of the English decision of *Dulieu v White & Sons* [1901] 2KB 669. It was not clear whether the strong concentration in the Irish decisions on the foreseeability of the plaintiff's shock would lead to the imposition of liability outside the context of fear for one's own physical safety. The slow progress of British decisions over the past twenty years has been towards a gradual extension of the range of recovery but it still can not be said that the mere foreseeability of shock guarantees compensation for the plaintiff. The classic situation in which the issue can arise is where the plaintiff suffers shock having come upon the aftermath of an accident involving a loved one.

In *Mc Loughlin v O'Brian* [1983] 1 AC 410, there was a clear division of opinion among the judges. Lords Wilberforce (supported by Lord Edmund-Davies) considered that a threshold policy-based limitation on foreseeability should be made. First, only those with a very close relationship to the person injured in the accident could sue. This class would certainly include parents, children, husbands and wives, but beyond them he took no final position, save to note that '[t]he closer the tie (not merely in relationship, but in care) the greater the claim for consideration'. As regards proximity to the accident, he regarded it as 'obvious that this must be close in both time and space'. A strict test of proximity by sight or hearing should be applied, save for those who came on the scene very soon after the accident or those 'of whom it could be said that one could expect nothing else than that [they] would come immediately to the scene—normally a parent or spouse.' As regards communication, Lord Wilberforce ruled out cases where a person suffers nervous shock on being *informed* of an accident affecting a loved one: the shock would have to come either through sight or hearing of the event or its immediate aftermath, or possibly through some equivalent of sight and hearing, such as simultaneous television.

In contrast to this approach, Lords Bridge Scarman and Russell favoured an unqualified foreseeability test. When examined closely, however, it seems that this 'foreseeability' test is not uninfluenced by the policy considerations spelt out by Lord Wilberforce. The same approach was adopted by Tobriner J in the California Supreme Court decision of *Dillon v Legg*, 68 Cal 2d 728, at 740-1 (1968). That 'foreseeability' here translates in practice into a policy-based limitation is evident from *Thing v L. Chusa*, 48 Cal 3d 644 (1989), where the California Supreme Court made it clear that 'a bright line in this area of law is essential'. See Vande Weghe, 24 Loyola of LA L Rev 89 (1990) and Bartolini & Calibrey, 64 Conn Bar J 275 (1990).

Recently the House of Lords returned to the subject. In *Alcock v Chief Constable of the South Yorkshire Police* [1991] 4 All ER 907, the question arose at to whether relatives of victims of the Hillsborough Stadium disaster, who witnessed events on live television and subsequently suffered shock, should be entitled to compensation. In rejecting the claims, the judges of the House of Lords substantially endorsed Lord Wilberforce's approach in *McLoughlin v O'Brian*, interpreting the first of his policy considerations somewhat more broadly than his words would suggest. Thus, the relationships warranting compensation should be determined on the basis of a foreseeability test. This meant that even a bystander might, exceptionally, be permitted to recover damages in very shocking circumstances, such as where a petrol tanker careered out of control into a school in session and burst into flames. But normally the relationship of brother or brother-in-law of the direct victim would not render the shock foreseeable. As regards communication by means of simultaneous television, the judges considered that shock would not normally be foreseeable as broadcasting guidelines prohibited the transmission of shocking pictures of persons suffering and dying. For analysis of *Alcock*, see Davie, 43 NILQ 237 (1992) and Lynch, 108 LQR 367 (1992).

In 1991 an Irish court addressed the issue for the first time in many years. In *Mullally v Bus Éireann* [1992] ILRM 722, the plaintiff's husband and children were involved in a serious bus accident caused by the negligence of the defendants' employee. The plaintiff learned of the accident when on a visit to another town with her brother and mother. Her brother received a telephone message from his sister in law as well as a visit from the Gardaí. The plaintiff, aware that something was wrong, telephoned one hospital and was told that one of her sons, Francis, was 'very bad'; she telephoned another hospital and was told that her husband was dying and that a second son, Tom, was also there. She could not at this time establish where her third son, Paul, had been taken.

The plaintiff was first driven to her home, when she was told that Paul was in the same hospital as Francis. She went to that hospital where she discovered a scene similar to a field hospital. Denham J stated that '[t]here were bodies' everywhere, people moaning and groaning and many distressed relatives around. Her son Paul presented a most distressing sight, with blood oozing from his wounds and with tubes attached to his arms and nose and in his mouth. The plaintiff became very aggressive and angry with the medical personnel. She later came upon Francis, who was 'beyond recognition', with serious injuries to his face, nose, teeth and head.

The plaintiff then went to the other hospital. The scene there was not as bad because the passage of time since the accident had enabled matters to be more under control. Her husband nonetheless presented a very distressing sight. He was obviously very ill and fighting for his life. The plaintiff then went to see Tom, who was having his ear stitched. He was crying and upset but in a much better condition than his father. At this time the plaintiff was walking and talking mechanically but when she went home she became hysterical and rejected attempts by others to comfort her.

In the months afterwards, the condition of plaintiff's husband and of Francis and Tom gradually improved. The outcome for Paul was tragic. After nine months' of disability, accompanied at times by great suffering, and after several operations, he died.

The plaintiff's psychological state had changed radically from what it had been before the accident. Denham J noted that:

> [s]he put down the shutters. She became very reserved. A new person emerged. She put all emotion aside. . . . Her personality changed. She appeared frozen. . . .

Denham J found that the plaintiff had the symptoms consistent with post-traumatic stress disorder. She accepted the DSM III-R criteria for this condition, as set out in Brian McGuire's article in the Irish Journal of Psychology 1990, at p. 4. These are:

> 1. Exposure to a recognisable stress or trauma outside the range of usual human experience, which would evoke significant symptoms of distress in almost anyone.
> 2. Re- experiencing the trauma through intrusive memories, nightmares or flashbacks or intensification of symptoms through exposure to situations resembling or symbolising the event.
> 3. Avoidance of stimuli related to the trauma or numbing of general responsiveness indicated by avoidance of thoughts or feelings, or of situations associated with the trauma, amnesia for important aspects of the trauma, diminished interest in activities, feelings of estrangement from others, constricted affect, sense of foreshortened future.
> 4. Increased arousal indicated by sleep disturbance, anger outbursts, difficulty concentrating, higher vigilance, exaggerated startle response, psychologically reactivity to situations resembling or symbolising the trauma.
> 5. Duration of disturbance at least one month.

Denham J, for the purposes of the judgment, found that post-traumatic stress disorder 'is a very psychiatric disease'. The plaintiff's condition had been caused by the accident and its aftermath, not her grief: cf. *Heeney v Dublin Corporation*, High Court, 16 May 1991, discussed above, 398-9. Applying 'the ordinary criteria of reasonable foreseeability' to the facts, and in view of the 'ever-advancing awareness of medical knowledge of mental illness', Denham J considered that it was readily foreseeable that a mother exposed to the experience that the plaintiff had gone through would break down and suffer illness. She considered that there was 'no policy in Irish law opposed to a finding of nervous shock, an old term covering post-traumatic stress disorder. Indeed the Irish courts were one of the first to find that such an illness existed and was compensatable. . . .'

Denham J here quoted passages from *Byrne v Southern & Western Railway Co.* and *Bell v Great Northern Railway Co.* In a crucial passage, she stated:

Thus the law is that a person who suffers nervous shock which results in psychiatric illness may succeed against the person who caused the nervous shock. The question then is whether the causation nexus exists between the defendants' negligence and the plaintiff's illness as the plaintiff was not at the scene of the accident.

It appears to me that the causal link is there; that the illness was reasonably foreseeable. The facts of this case clearly establish an horrific situation for the plaintiff from the time of learning of the accident, through her journey to the hospital, to the appalling sights at the hospital, the terrifying sights of her sons Paul and Francis, and the fact of her apparently dying husband. All these events were caused by the accident caused by the defendants. It would be unjust, and contrary to the fundamental doctrine of negligence, not to find that there is a legal nexus between the actions of the defendants causing the accident, and the resultant aftermath in the scenes in the hospitals . . . and the injuries of the plaintiff's three sons and husband. There was no . . . cause of the scenes in the hospital or the injuries to the children and the husband other than the defendant's negligence. The shock of the plaintiff was foreseeable. The duty of care of the defendants extends as to injuries which are reasonably foreseeable. Thus the defendants had a duty of care to the plaintiff. I consider that there is no bar in law, or under the Constitution, to this determination. If it causes commercial concern then that is a matter for another place, where a policy can be established in the law. It appears to me to come under the fundamental principles of the law of negligence to hold the defendants liable for reasonably foreseeable psychiatric illness caused by [their] negligence'.

Denham J went on to observe that she had been assisted by the House of

Lords decision in *McLoughlin v O'Brian*. She added that, while the instant
case appeared to fall within the parameters set by Lord Wilberforce, she was
'guided more by Lord Bridge'.

It should be noted that at the time when Denham J delivered her judgment
in *Mulally*, the House of Lords had not yet handed down judgment in *Alcock*.
There is a striking contrast between Denham J's approach and that favoured
by the Lord Wilberforce in *McLoughlin* which was substantially endorsed in
Alcock. For Denham J, the policy question as to compensation for nervous
shock was a *threshold* one, which should be resolved in favour of permitting
compensation for this category of injury. Denham J evinces no interest in
prescribing the three limitations favoured by Lord Wilberforce. Does this
mean, therefore, that *Mulally* is a clear precedent for a victory for plaintiffs
in a factual situation similar to *Alcock?* Specifically, should brothers and
brothers-in-law be entitled to recover, and should the fact that they witness
the shocking event on television be no barrier to their claims? The general
tenor of Denham J's judgment would suggest that these plaintiffs would
succeed, but it is wise to sound two notes of caution. First, she expressed no
dissent from Lord Wilberforce's approach and went so far as to note that the
facts of *Mulally* appeared to fall within the parameters that Lord Wilberforce
had set. Secondly, Lord Bridge's favoured approach of foreseeability, as we
have seen, contains a strong element of underlying policy. This suggests that,
even applying a foreseeability test, an Irish court could well hold against
some plaintiffs who suffer nervous shock. There are precedents in other
jurisdictions that show that such an outcome could well occur: see, e.g., *King
v Phillips* [1953] 1QB 429, critically analysed by Goodhart, 69 LQ Rev 347
(1953) and *Brown v Hubar,* 3 Or (2d) 448 (1974), criticised by Binchy, 9
Ottawa L Rev, at 350-2 (1977). But see *Bechard v Halibruton Estate*, 10
CCLT (2d) 156 (Ont CA, 1991).

NEGLIGENCE ON OR NEAR THE HIGHWAY

A duty to veer? What should a driver proceeding at 30 mph along a
suburban road do when confronted by a vehicle coming in the opposite
direction which drifts into his direct path? Brake severely and sound his horn,
might seem to be the obvious answer. This the defendant did in *Coleman v
Clarke* [1991] ILRM 841. It proved to be ineffective in preventing a fatal
accident. MacKenzie J held that the defendant had been negligent in failing
to veer to the left and even go so far as to mount the pavement. He reduced
the plaintiff's damages by 60% on account of her contributory negligence.
The Supreme Court, but only by a majority, reversed.

Griffin J (Finlay CJ concurring) considered that, having regard to the
suddenness of the emergency, which was not of his making, the defendant

should not be blamed 'for omitting to take, in the heat of the moment, an additional step which would not, in the event, have avoided the collision' unless the defendant mounted the pavement. In Griffin J's view, it would be wholly unreasonable to expect the defendant to have risked the danger of a collision with a solid stone wall close to the pavement and to make that positive decision in the short time available.

O'Flaherty J , dissenting, was of the view that the MacKenzie J's holding that the defendant should have done more did not impose an extravagant or artificial duty of care. He noted that, in the course of argument, he had asked whether, before the Civil Liability Act 1961, the defendant might have been held wholly responsible for the accident if a question in relation to the 'last opportunity' rule were to be answered in favour of the plaintiff. He observed that:

> [t]he injustice that the Civil Liability Act cured was that prior to it any contributory negligence on the part of a plaintiff disentitled him to recover but, of course, if he could prove that, despite his negligence, the defendant had the 'last opportunity' to avoid the accident then the defendant was saddled with the full burden of blame. Instead of purpose of the Civil Liability Act was to enable the court to apportion blame between the parties.

These remarks are of course unexceptionable so far as they contain propositions of law, but they are *nihil ad rem*, so far as the threshold question of the defendant's liability is concerned. The possibility of apportionment of damages has not rendered tortious any conduct that was not previously so. If the defendant's driving should not have been characterised as negligent before 1961, the statutory changes in relation to the last opportunity rule and contributory negligence could have no effect on that question. The last opportunity doctrine did not render any defendant liable who was not guilty of negligence.

One finds in *Coleman v Clarke* an interesting contrast with the approach favoured by O'Flaherty J in *Moore v Fullerton* [1991] ILRM 29, discussed in the 1990 Review, 526-7. In *Moore*, O'Flaherty J, dissenting, would have reversed the trial judge and held it negligent for a lorry driver to proceed at 14 miles per hour down a village street when a mart was being held in the vicinity. In *Coleman*, he stressed that the remit of the Supreme Court's function did not extend to dissecting the minutiae of the evidence and of the trial judge's findings:

> It must look at the broad sweep of the evidence that was available to the trial judge. If the evidence is clear so as not to justify a finding of

negligence then, of course, this Court must say it on appeal. But this is surely a case where there was a ground on which the defendant could have been faulted.

Contrast this with Griffin J's invocation of the old reliables of *SS Gairloch* [1899] 2 IR 1, at 18 and *Northern Bank Finance Corporation v Charlton* [1979] IR 149, at 177-180 (*per* O'Higgins CJ) and at 189-92 (*per* Henchy J) in support of an interventionist appellate strategy with respect to 'conclusions or inferences from the primary facts found'.

What is at stake here, of course, as we indicated in the 1990 Review, 527, is the extent to which the Supreme Court should engage in the process of characterising as rules of law detailed propositions of negligence in particular factual circumstances. With the demise of juries in personal injuries litigation and the growth of written judgments by High Court judges, the point is one of very considerable relevance. The proper approach would be one giving a fairly considerable margin of appreciation to the trial judge but, frankly, in the case of *Coleman v Clarke*, it was the duty of the Supreme Court to intervene to preserve the integrity of the fault principle at the heart of the law of negligence.

Condition of footpath In *Condon v Cork Corporation and an Bord Telecom*, High Court, 1 February 1991, Barr J imposed liability on the first defendant for resurfacing a footpath without providing expansion joints every thirty to forty feet to enable the concrete, which is an elastic substance, to expand and contract in appropriate weather conditions. This had caused the surface concrete to become cracked and broken in parts over the years. The elderly plaintiff had tripped on a broken part. For consideration of Barr J's disposition of the issue of contributory negligence, see below, 439.

BREACH OF STATUTORY DUTY

Employment relationship *Dunleavy v Glen Abbey Ltd* [1992] ILRM 1 is a decision that should cause understandable alarm among employers who perceive the law as one involving effectively strict liability for accidents involving their employees. The plaintiff, whose duties included moving heavy loads, was injured when carrying a very heavy package. The background to the accident was that he would have used a fork lift truck but this was inoperative because its battery was dead; so he had asked another person to assist him. The employee had let go of the package when it was near to the ground. The result was that the plaintiff was jerked by the weight of the load and suffered an injury to his back.

Barron J's judgment is confined to the issue of breach of statutory duty. Since he held that liability arose on this basis he did not address possible common law grounds for liability, such as the employer's failure to take reasonable care to provide proper equipment, competent co-employees or a safe system of work. The crucial issue related to the Factories Act 1955 (Manual Labour) (Maximum Weights and Transport) Regulations 1972, made under s. 67 of the 1966 Act. Regulation 6 provided as follows:

(1) Every person shall, prior to being assigned to—(a) a process to which these regulations relate . . . , receive adequate training or instruction in working techniques relating to the process for the purposes of safe-guarding health and preventing accidents.
(2) The training or instruction mentioned in paragraph (1) of this regulation shall include methods of lifting, carrying, putting down, unloading and stacking different types of loads, and shall be given by a suitably qualified person.
(3) Whenever a person receives training or instruction required by this regulation, such training or instruction shall, whenever practicable, be followed by adequate supervision to ensure that the correct methods are used by the person while engaged in the process to which the training or instruction relates.
(4) In case a person is required by this regulation to receive training or instruction it shall be the duty of the person by whom such person is employed to provide or arrange for the provision of such training or instruction.

Also of crucial relevance was regulation 7, which provided that,

[i]n order to avoid the necessity for the manual transport of loads, suitable mechanical devices shall be used, so far as is reasonably practicable, in . . . every factory or premises mentioned in regulation 3(1). . . .

The regulations applied to the plaintiff, who had received no training such as the regulations envisaged. There was no dispute on the evidence that the plaintiff was aware that the fork lift truck was inoperative from time to time and that he had complained about this. In these circumstances, Barron J concluded that the defendant was in breach of its statutory duties both as to training and as to the provision of suitable mechanical devices.

Breach of statutory duty is not tortious unless there is a sufficient causative link between the defendant's breach and the plaintiff's injury: cf. *Martin v Millar & Co. Ltd*, Supreme Court, 12 May 1972, *CIE v Carroll* [1986] ILRM

312. The defendant urged that this causal link was missing. Even if the plaintiff had been property trained in accordance with the regulations, he would still have carried out his work in the way that he had done. The plaintiff had used the proper posture for lifting and putting down loads. Barron J rejected this argument, on the basis that, if the employer had carried out its statutory obligations, the plaintiff would have learned more than the correct posture:

> He would have learned that in some circumstances it is safer to take the whole weight himself rather than to share it with another. He would have learned that in appropriate circumstances of which this was one it is advisable to break up the load. Had he been given such advice, it is clear that he would not have set about his particular task in the way he did. It is reasonable to suppose that because of this he would not have met with the accident.

As regards the fork-lift truck, Barron J was satisfied that, if the truck had been available, the plaintiff would have used it and thus not met with the accident. He did not accept that regulation 7 applied only to *repetitive* actions. In his view the failure to have the fork-lift truck adequately maintained when the employer was aware that it was breaking down from time to time was itself a breach of the regulations.

Having regard to the view that he had taken of the case, it did not seem to Barron J that any question of contributory negligence could arise:

> The plaintiff had been carrying out the job with the proper posture in the belief that he was doing all that he could to minunise the problem which arose by reason of the failure of the fork-life truck to start.

It may be worth reflecting in this context on the relationship between the operation of the defence of contributory negligence in common law actions for employers' liability and in actions for breach of statutory duty. The courts have evinced an intuitive understanding that the defence of contributory negligence should not be given a wide range of operation in cases where the statutory duty involves safety in the employment environment. The true reason why this is so is that the defence would subvert the important protective and paternalistic policies underlying the imposition of civil liability for breach of statutory duty in this context. The articulated reasons do not give proper credit to these policies. Instead, they seek, disingenuously, to draw distinctions based on the degree of inadvertence of the employee. see *Stewart v Killeen Paper Mills Ltd* [1959] IR 436, *Kennedy v East Cork Foods Ltd* [1973] IR 244, *Higgins v South of Ireland Asphalt Co. Ltd*, 101

ILTR 168 (1961). Just as the defence of voluntary assumption of risk is carefully constricted by the courts in this context, so also is the defence of contributory negligence. The reason is not that the basis of liability is statute rather than common law but rather that the strength of the policy considerations relating to protection of employees from injury is more patent in the former case. See further our discussion of this issue in relation to the same Judge's decision in *Dunne v Honeywell Control Systems Ltd and Virginia Milk Products Ltd* [1991] ILRM 595, in the 1990 Review, 504-5.

Relationship with common law negligence and contribution In *Merriman v Dublin Corporation and Dublin County Council* [1993] ILRM 58; [1992] 1 IR 129, Costello J confronted a conundrum as to the relationship between breach of statutory duty, the common law duty of care in negligence and actions for contribution. The plaintiff had fallen on an open gully at the side of a road. At the time of the accident, the road had not yet been taken in charge by Dublin County Council. Dublin Corporation had erected the gully, with the County Council's agreement, in accordance with plans submitted for the Council's approval under the Planning Acts. The gully had included a grille when it was installed but this 'had been removed sometime before the accident'.

Costello J imposed liability on the County Council for breach of statutory duty since the drain constituted a 'sewer' under s. 2 of the Public Health (Ireland) Act 1878 and had not been kept in repair, as s. 17 of that Act required of the body in which the sewer vested under s. 15. He relieved the Corporation from liability for breach of statutory duty either as a sanitary authority or as a road authority. No legislation had imposed on it any obligation to maintain the road in question. Nor was the Corporation liable in negligence to the plaintiff since, in the circumstances of the case, it owed him no duty of care at common law. Costello J noted that the case had not been made that it owed such a duty. No question of contribution or indemnity from the Corporation arose. The Corporation was under a liability to the Council to maintain the road until it had been taken in charge by the Council; the source of this liability was a condition imposed in the permission to develop granted to the Corporation by the Council. But this condition did not confer any statutory obligations towards *third parties* such as would entitle a claim for damages for personal injuries to be brought in the event of non-fulfilment of the obligation.

Costello J's analysis is entirely conventional if one accepts the premise that the Corporation had no duty of care at common law to the plaintiff. This is not perhaps self-evident. The judgment throws no light on the circumstances in which the grille was removed. No doubt complex questions of liability could arise as to the *discharge* of a duty of care in respect of the supply and ongoing supervision of a product capable of being interfered with by others, but the threshold question concerns the imposition or non-imposition of such a duty in the first place. Why should the Corporation have been exempt from such an imposition? Suppliers of products, capable of causing personal injury to third parties, fall well within the scope of the duty imposed under *Donoghue v Stevenson*. That case was of course famous for its rejection of the 'privity of contract fallacy' at the root of such Irish decisions as *Corry v Lucas*, IR 3 CL 208 (1868). For further discussion, see McMahon & Binchy, *op. cit.*, 170-4.

Another occupiers' liability case dealing with the relationship between breach of statutory duty and common law negligence is *Clancy v Commissioners of Public Works in Ireland* [1988] ILRM 268; [1991] ILRM 567. We examine it, above, 396-8, in the section dealing with Occupiers' Liability.

REMOTENESS OF DAMAGE

Inability to borrow   In *Latham v Hibernian Insurance Co. Ltd and Peter J Sheridan & Co. Ltd*, High Court, 4 December 1991, some interesting questions of remoteness of damage fell for consideration. The plaintiff had sought to have his premises insured. He retained the second defendant, an insurance broker, to insure the premises with the first defendant. Some time after this had been done the plaintiff was arrested and charged with receiving stolen goods. The second defendant, who learned of this, failed to advise the plaintiff that he ought to disclose this fact when the policy was being renewed. By reason of non-disclosure, the first named defendant lawfully repudiated the policy when the premises were subsequently destroyed by fire.

In an earlier judgment, on 22 March 1991, Blayney J had found the second defendant liable for negligence and breach of contract: see 30-2, above. He now addressed the issue of damages. The first question that Blayney J faced was to determine the position if the second defendant had *not* been negligent. It emerged that, had the fact of the arrest and charge been disclosed to the first defendant or, indeed, *any* insurance company in Ireland, it would have refused to accept the risk. The question thus arose as to what the plaintiff would have done in the event of that refusal. On relatively slight evidence, not rebutted by the second defendant, Blayney J concluded that the plaintiff would have been able to obtain cover in England for a substantially increased premium.

Another question of general interest related to the plaintiff's claim to be compensated for loss of profits from his business from the date of the fire up to the date of the judgment. The plaintiff argued that the second defendant ought to have foreseen that the plaintiff would be left with a burnt out building which he would not have the funds to repair until he received compensation.

Blayney J accepted that the second defendant should have foreseen this problem but he did not agree that he could reasonably have anticipated that the plaintiff *would not be able to borrow what was required.* Had the plaintiff borrowed these funds, he would have been entitled to recover the interest he paid on the loan, on the authority of the Supreme Court decision of *Murphy v McGrath* [1981] ILRM 364.

The question of the extent to which the impecunious plaintiff should be treated in the same way as the 'egg-shell skull' plaintiff is one to which there is no easy answer. The gradual movement of the judicial decisions has been away from the strictness of the House of Lords decision in *Liesbosch Dredger v Edison SS* [1933] AC 448 towards recognising that many businesses (cf. *Riordans Travel Ltd v Acres & Co. Ltd (No. 2)* [1979] ILRM 7) and private individuals (*Murphy v McGrath*, above) cannot be expected always to have sufficient assets to prevent the need for them to borrow. To a large extent this development may perhaps not reflect a greater sensitivity to *subjective* elements, on a par with the 'egg-shell skull' rule, but rather merely the application of an *objective* test of foreseeability as to the general likelihood of credit playing a vastly more central role in business and personal finance than it did six decades ago.

If this is so, then Blayney J's approach can be regarded as orthodox. One aspect of the case is nonetheless worth considering. If, in the particular circumstances, the plaintiff's inability to borrow could have been foreseen by the second defendant then, in spite of the fact that no such likelihood would apply to plaintiffs in general, it would have justified the enhancement of the damages awarded. For an excellent analysis of the issues, see Kerr, 'The End of the 'Edison'?, (1980) 74 Incorp L Soc of Ireland Gazette 51.

In *Amethyst Ltd (in liquidation) v Galway Insurance Brokers Ltd*, High Court, 16 May 1991, Barron J gave a detailed analysis of how damages should be computed where, because of the admitted negligence of the defendant, polices for fire insurance were not in place when the plaintiff's premises were destroyed by fire. The decision is essentially one of fact, but is worth noting so far as it addresses the question of the projected expansion of a business.

Novus actus interveniens In the High Court decision of *Cowan v Freaghaile* [1991] 1 IR 389, the plaintiff was injured by a wall which collapsed on him while he was attending the All Ireland Hurling Final at Croke Park in September 1985. The wall lacked strengthening bars or dowel rods, contrary to what was already good building practice at the time of its construction.

O'Flaherty J concluded on the evidence that these elements had been specified in the construction contract but, through the negligence of the builders, had not been included.

In May 1985, tragedies had occurred at two football stadiums when spectators had died in a fire in Bradford and had been crushed to death following a riot at Heysel. Counsel for the plaintiff argued that the owners of Croke Park ought to have carried out an examination of all facilities in their stadium, in the knowledge of these disasters. O'Flaherty J accepted this contention. He found as a fact, in conjunction with his own 'knowledge of sporting occasions and not just at this particular venue', that, almost invariably there was a certain amount of pushing and jostling around entrances to toilets, which was likely to create pressure on the screen walls. In the light of the recent tragedies, the authorities 'were required to be extra vigilant in making sure *all* structures and installations which were subject to crowd pressure were given the benefit of a full expert examination in advance of any big sporting occasion'. The owners were thus liable in negligence, since such an examination would have disclosed a hairline crack in another wall, which would have alerted the expert to carry out a better examination, using ultrasonic equipment, which in turn would have revealed the faulty nature of the wall which fell on the plaintiff.

O'Flaherty J rejected the argument of counsel for the builders that the *novus actus interveniens* principle should cocoon them from liability. The Supreme Court decisions of *Conole v Redbank Oyster Co.* [1976] IR 191 and *Crowley v Allied Irish Banks Ltd* [1987] IR 282 had established that one who ignores a patent defect negligently caused by another should be held to relieve that other from liability to a person injured subsequently by that defect. O'Flaherty J commented:

> Those cases clearly deal with a patent defect which is known, or (at most) ought to have been known, to the intermediate wrong-doer. However, the principles embodied in those cases would require a considerable extension to be applicable to the facts of this case. Here, there was no patent defect which was known or ought reasonably to have been known to the owners. The most that can be said against them was that they neglected to have an examination carried out which would, probably, have revealed the need to carry out further examinations and tests which, in turn, would no doubt have shown up the defective structure. As I say, that would require a considerable extension to the existing law and I am not disposed to say that the law should be extended this far. Such an extension of the law would not be consistent with the concept of concurrent wrong-doers in my judgment. . . .

Accordingly O'Flaherty J held that the builders and the owners were concurrent wrongdoers. He apportioned 80% of the fault to the builders, and 20% to the owners.

The resolution of the issue of *novus actus interveniens* in convincing. The doctrine should not be used as a way for an 'original' defendant to unload his responsibility merely because his negligence was supplemented by negligence of another party before the plaintiff sustained injuries. It is only in cases where the intermediate party has engaged in a deliberate or reckless act or omission that he should relieve the original actor from liability.

RES IPSA LOQUITUR

Parental control of Children In *Johnston v Fitzpatrick* [1992] ILRM 269, the question of when a third party notice should be permitted to be issued was examined somewhat inconclusively: see The Practice and Procedure chapter, above, 353-4. Of present relevance is the doctrine of *res ipsa loquitur*, never mentioned by the court but surely worthy of attention.

The plaintiff, a boy aged ten, had been struck by the defendant's car when crossing a road. In seeking to join the boy's parents as third parties, the defendant contended that the boy had been accompanied by them and some others who were apparently intending to cross the road, and that the plaintiff suddenly dashed out onto the road and ran into the side of the defendant's car. The defendant alleged that in the circumstances the parents had not exercised reasonable supervision of their son nor had taken sufficient care to ensure his safety.

Egan J's disposition of the issue, which received the express endorsement of the Chief Justice, should be noted:

> The plaintiff in this case was aged ten and this fact *per se* would not, in my opinion, support an allegation that his parents or either of them contributed to his alleged 'dash' onto the road. It would probably be otherwise if there was an allegation that he was retarded or if there was an allegation that he had been encouraged by them or either of them to make a 'dash' across the road.

With respect, this analysis may be questioned. How can it be that the defendant failed to establish 'a stateable or *prima facie* ground' for issuing third party proceedings on the basis of this allegation? The alleged facts appear to embrace all the necessary ingredients of a statable case based on the *res ipsa loquitur* doctrine: the child was under the control of his parents, and children do not usually dash under cars if their parents are exercising due care. This is not, of course, to suggest that the allegation, if established by the evidence, would necessarily have resulted in imposition of liability, in part or in whole, on the parents, and of course the allegation might well have proved incorrect, but the idea that the alleged facts fell short of a *prima facie* allegation of actionable negligence seems to be at variance with established jurisprudence.

One has only to recall the Supreme Court decision of *Curley v Mannion* [1965] IR 543, where it was held that a parent could be found liable in negligence for failing to prevent his twelve-year-old daughter, who was a passenger in his car, from opening a door in the path of a cyclist. The later Supreme Court decision of *Moynihan v Moynihan* [1975] IR 192 was scarcely stinting in the breadth that was willing to ascribe to the notion of 'control'. As to the doctrine of *res ipsa loquitur*, it may be remembered that as recently as 1988, in *Hanrahan v Merck, Sharp & Dohme (Ireland) Ltd* [1988] ILRM 629 the Supreme Court held that the doctrine applied even in a case where it had not been established by express evidence that the thing that caused the damage was under the defendant's control. Perhaps the crucial difference between children and barrels (cf. *Byrne v Boadle*, 2 H & C 722; 159 ER 299 (1863)—the progenitor of the *res ipsa loquitur* doctrine) is that children have the power of self-propulsion, but it is the existence of that capacity which creates the special duty of control imposed on those charged with the care of children.

If one wants to understand why in *Johnston v Fitzpatrick* the same court was so unmoved by the allegation of negligence, the key is provided by *Darcy v Roscommon County Council*, decided six months previously, on 11 January 1991: see the Practice and Procedure Chapter, above, 353. There the defendant had also sought to join a plaintiff child's parents as third parties. Hederman J stressed the discretionary and equitable nature of the third party order:

> To grant such a discretionary order, which necessarily is intimidatory on the parents and in particular on the parent who is at present the next friend, might well affect their ability to exercise their parental independence in considering the running of the case and any settlement which might be offered.

Now of course, the court should zealously protect litigants against intimidation, by exercising its discretion so as to prevent it. (It should not be forgotten that the tort of malicious institution of civil proceedings or abuse of the process of the court would be available as a remedy in some cases: cf. the 1990 Review, 444-5, *Smyth v Tunney*, High Court, 6 October 1989). It is one thing to deal with actual or threatened instances of intimidation; it is quite another to decline to grant a third party order against parents of an infant plaintiff because to do so would 'necessarily [be] intimidatory on the parents'. The use of the word 'intimidatory' here suggests a judicial perception that the very granting of a third party order where such a relationship exists has, of itself, a frightening effect on parents, which is not necessarily attributable to any wrongful intent on the part of the defendant.

For the court to refuse a third party order because of its concern that the parents might be encouraged to settle the case on terms not in their child's best interests seems to involve a radical departure from sound principle. If we assume a case where the parents were mainly, or even entirely, responsible for their child's injury, it is surely unjust to the defendant that he should be prevented from joining the parents as parties and should have to pay compensation for which he may not be responsible. This seems to involve a resort to crude pragmatism.

If such pragmatism were to be applied consistently, should it not prevent the taking of appeals by defendants against child plaintiffs whose parents would often be 'intimidated' by the prospects of losing the action on appeal? And what about the situation where a defendant chooses *not* to seek to have a child parents joined as third parties, so as to encourage them to settle the case at an undervalue as the tacit prize of being excused from having their liability identified?

Medical negligence In *Lindsay v Mid-Western Health Board*, High Court, 30 May 1991, extracted in McMahon & Binchy's *Casebook on the Irish Law of Torts* (2nd ed., 1991), p. 91, the plaintiff, aged eight years, underwent an appendectomy at a hospital in 1982. After the operation, she failed to regain consciousness. The medical evidence was to the effect that she never would do so in the future and that her probable life expectancy was only fifteen years.

The plaintiff's proceedings for negligence and breach of duty included a plea of *res ipsa loquitur*. As to the express allegation of negligence, the plaintiff's expert witness said that there were three possible causes for the plaintiff's condition: (1) sub-arachnoid haemorrhage; (2) hypoxic insult and (3) miscellaneous possibilities, such as cardiac arrest, a sudden drop in blood pressure and a serious drug reaction. He excluded the first and third of these and favoured the second explanation.

After a detailed review of the evidence from all experts called by both parties, Morris J was not satisfied that the plaintiff had discharged the onus of proof that her condition had resulted from the second possible cause. Morris J then turned to consider the *res ipsa loquitur* claim. The defendants were admittedly in control of the event. All who were working in the hospital were persons for whose negligence the defendants would be vicariously liable. Moreover, the accident was of such nature as in ordinary circumstances did not happen if those having control of the procedures used proper care. At no stage had the defendants sought to argue that the appendectomy operation was other than routine or that the procedure could give rise to any hidden or unusual problems or risks.

One commentator has taken issue with this part of Morris J's analysis. Citing the death statistics resulting from anaesthesia (Buck, Devlin & Lynn, *The Report of the Confidential Enquiry into Preoperative Deaths* The Nuffield Provincial Hospitals Trust, 1987), pp. *vii*, 71, 76)), Dr Clive Symmons (*Professional Negligence* 17, at 18 (1992)) observes that:

> *both* the type of operation and the administration of anaesthetics (in *any* operation) involve some small statistical risk. And it is this aspect that may cause alarm bells to ring now in Irish medical circles as it amounts to a step towards stricter medical liability, particularly as the application here seems to by-pass possible problems of causation.

Echoing Henchy J's rationale for the doctrine in *Hanrahan v Merck Sharp & Dohme (Ireland) Ltd* [1988] ILRM 629, at 634-5, Morris J was satisfied that in a case such as the one before him it would be palpably unjust to require that plaintiff to prove something that was beyond her reach and was peculiarly within the range of the defendants' capacity of proof.

Having held that the *res ipsa loquitur* doctrine applied, Morris J addressed the troublesome question of its procedural effect. He was of opinion that there was 'an onus cast upon the defendants to provide an explanation for the injuries sustained by [the plaintiff] which was not due to their negligence'. He sought to reconcile the Irish decisions on this issue with the Privy Council decision of *Ng Chun Pui v Lee Chuen Tat* [1988] RTR 88. Whether *Ng Chun Pui* imposes quite as heavy a burden as the Irish cases, or the formula supported by Morris J, may be debated. That decision may more easily be interpreted as requiring the defendant to adduce evidence that he was not negligent, but not going so far as to require him to prove on the balance of probability that he was not negligent.

Morris J examined in detail the evidence of the defendants' experts which supported the theory of viral encephalitis as an explanation for the plaintiff's condition. He concluded that it amounted to speculation rather than a reasonable explanation for what had occurred. Accordingly the defendants had failed to discharge the onus cast on them and the plaintiff succeeded in her claim.

The finding in favour of the plaintiff may perhaps be debated, so far as it depends on the application of the *res ipsa loquitur* doctrine. If a fact situation is such that the only ways by which a defendant could have been negligent are identified and the evidence establishes that the defendant was not negligent in any of these ways, then there is no residual area of operation for the doctrine. It would be different if the situation were such that a defendant might have been negligent in a wide variety of ways and the plaintiff sought, unsuccessfully, to show that the defendant was negligent in one or more of a limited number of such ways. The plaintiff's failure to do so would still leave unanswered the residual ways in which the defendant might have been negligent. While Morris J's approach finds echoes in some recent American decisions, concern has been expressed there (65 Tulane L Rev, at 1289 (1991)) as to whether this development could stifle the availability and quality of health care.

DEFENCE OF PROPERTY

In the Circuit Court decision of *MacKnight v Xtravision*, 5 July 1991 (extracted in McMahon & Binchy's *Casebook on the Irish Law of Torts* (2nd ed., 1991), 407-10), Judge Carroll addressed the limits of the defence, in proceedings for trespass to the person, of defence of property.

The defendants were tenants of a lockup shop in a shopping centre in Palmerstown, County Dublin. In the course of a dispute with their landlord, the owner of the centre, the defendants withheld payment of service charges to the landlord. One morning the defendants' staff arrived to find that they were unable to enter the shop because a chain and lock had been placed on the floor by the landlord. The plaintiff, 'a security man about the place', was aware of the fact that the landlord had done this because of the defendants' non-payment of the service charges. In taking this step, the landlord was, in Judge Carroll's view, a trespasser.

Some time later the defendants' marketing manager and the head of their security department arrived, as did the Gardaí. The plaintiff was in the vicinity of the shop, allegedly telling passers-by that the rent was unpaid. He told the Gardaí that this was a civil matter and that they had no jurisdiction. The Gardaí, 'perhaps unwisely', accepted what the plaintiff said and departed.

The defendants consulted their solicitor at some stage and were advised that they might use force to remove the lock and chain. The exact terms of this advice were not given clearly in evidence.

The Xtravision party went to Donnybrook where they purchased bolt clippers and collected 'another very hefty member' of the security department; asked, when giving evidence, whether he was a heavyweight boxer, he explained he was a light-middle weight.

On their return the Xtravision party found that the plaintiff had anchored himself to the handles of the double doors of the shop, facing the doors, an arm through each handle. In acting this way he was a trespasser, in the judge's view.

An altercation then ensued in which, it appears, the plaintiff's arms were restrained and he was punched by the marketing manager and the boxer. His arm and upper chest were bruised and his back and abdomen were very painful.

Judge Carroll was satisfied that the 'roughing up' administered to the plaintiff would certainly support a charge of assault causing actual bodily harm against the defendants. The question was whether it could be justified on the ground that it was the consequence of using no more force than was reasonably necessary to remove from the shop doors a man who was undoubtedly a trespasser.

Judge Carroll's forceful, yet highly thoughtful, discussion of the issue is worth recording here:

> What is reasonable force? Is it merely the amount of energy which is required to move a man out of a room [or] a house or, as here, to loosen his grip on a door and move him away from it, no matter what may be the other consequences? I think not. It is necessary to take into account the occasion upon which the force is used. It is here essential to point out that the present case bears only . . . remote resemblance to that of a householder who is disturbed by an intruder who invades his or her house or flat, the shopkeeper or tradesman who finds a person forcing his way into his shop or premises where business is being carried out so as to threaten or discommode his customers or staff or one who refuses to go when asked; even less does it resemble the case of any such person who has to deal with a criminal who forces or tries to force an entry with threat to life or limb or property.
>
> The danger of causing confusion in the minds of such persons is one of the features of the case which has troubled me. The degree of force used here would be perfectly justifiable in such types of case and much more if necessary to defend a man's home. Nothing which I am about to say should in any way render such citizens hesitant or fearful about defending their persons or property.
>
> In this case, up to the arrival of [the Xtravision party], no one had been in any way threatened or put in fear: it was a simple case of the defendants, being prevented from entering a lock-up shop and, no doubt, some threat to commercial interests.
>
> The Xtravision party were undoubtedly entitled to lay hands lightly on the plaintiff to move him aside. But when that failed, in the circumstances of the case, they should have desisted. They were not upon such cause entitled to assault him so as to inflict the type of injuries [he sustained].

On their way to Donnybrook to buy the bolt clippers and pick up the

> light-middleweight . . . they must have passed the open doors of these courts where, their solicitors might have advised them, they could have had an injunction against [the plaintiff] and his employers for the asking. It may be objected that this would have involved a delay which would have been damaging to their commercial interests. But it is of the essence of a civilised state regulated by law that its citizens in very many—indeed in all but a very small minority of—cases, forego the right to redress their grievances by private violence and instead look to the courts for their remedy. If parties were to resort to private violence in cases such as this, there would be an end to all law or order.

While imposing liability, Judge Carroll reduced the plaintiff's damages by a half on account of his contributory negligence.

Judge Carroll's analysis is of particular interest because it represents a novel articulation of traditional principles in terms of contemporary social mores. The right of an occupier to expel a trespasser has been established for centuries (cf, eg, *Green v Goddard*, 2 Salk 641, 91 ER 540 (1798)). The old plea in defence was that the defendant *molliter manus imposuit* (gently laid hands) upon the trespasser. What Judge Carroll requires it that, in some circumstances, even such gentle imposition must be abandoned in the interest of the public peace.

The circumstance envisaged by Judge Carroll are far removed from the context of violation of the home which, as well as being a tort, can amount to a breach of constitutional rights (cf. *DPP v Gaffney* [1986] ILRM 657; [1988] ILRM 39, discussed in the 1987 Review, 85-6). What Judge Carroll has in mind are cases of trespass on *commercial* premises. The idea of resorting to private violence to accomplish what is a purely commercial goal is understandably abhorrent to many people. Nevertheless, one may wonder whether there should, in effect, be an absolute veto on acts of defence of commercial property. If, for example, a performance of an artistic work were taking place in a theatre or concert hall and an interruption took place which could be dealt with fairly easily by the organisers with no risk of injury unless those interrupting resorted to violence, should be proper legal advice invariable be to seek an injunction instead? In the *Xtravision* case, there were no similar circumstances of urgency; all that was at stake was a day's business to which a value could relatively easily be ascribed when calculating damages. An interruption of an event scheduled to last only a couple of hours raises different considerations, for which the injunctive remedy may not always be sufficient.

FRAUDULENT MISREPRESENTATION

In *Sinnott v O'Connor* Supreme Court, 12 February 1991, there was an unsuccessful appeal against Murphy J's dismissal on 20 July 1989 of a claim for fraud, misrepresentation and breach of contract arising out of an agreement designed to settle differences between owners of a company. Hederman J (Finlay CJ and O'Flaherty J concurring) entertained 'no doubt whatever' that not only had Murphy J been entitled to come to the findings that he had done but that he 'could not reasonably have come to any other findings'.

PRODUCTS LIABILITY

1 Defective products The Liability for Defective Products Act 1991 belatedly gives legislative effect to the EEC Directive on Products Liability. The Directive supplements, rather than replaces, the existing remedies in tort and contract. In conjunction with the Jurisdiction of Courts and Enforcement of Judgments (European Communities) Act 1988, the Directive has the effect of broadening the options available to injured parties, as regards the type of liability, the range of potential defendants, the choice of jurisdiction, and the modes of enforcement of judgments. For analysis of the Act, see Alex Schuster, ed., *The New Product Liability Regime* (Irish Centre for European Law, 1992).

Article 19 of the Directive requires Member States to bring into force, not later than three years from the date of notification of the Directive—30 July 1985—the laws, regulations and administrative provisions necessary to comply with the Directive. In fact, the 1991 Act came into operation on 16 December 1991 (SI.No. 316 of 1991), thus raising the spectre of State liability under European law.

The main features of the Directive The essence of the Directive is contained in Article 1, which is drafted with commendable simplicity:

> The producer shall be liable for damage caused by a defect in his product.

There are, of course, some important qualifications to this statement of general principle, but the main notion is clear: liability is based, not on *wrongful conduct* by the producer, which (in theory at least) is the hallmark of negligence, but merely on proof of a *fact*, that a defect in the product caused the plaintiff damage. But inevitably normative considerations enter into the picture when deciding what constitutes 'defectiveness' in this context. As we shall see, the range of liability under the Directive is not radically different from that arising under common law principles. S. 2(1) of the Act makes it clear that the liability prescribed by the Directive falls within the characterisation of tort under Irish law.

1. The meaning of 'product' A 'product' is defined in Article 2 as including all movables *except* 'primary agricultural products' and game, even where the movables are incorporated into other movables or into immovables. 'Primary agricultural products' are defined by the same Article as meaning 'the products of the soil, of stock-farming and of fisheries, excluding products which have undergone initial processing'. Electricity is deemed a 'product' for the purpose of the Directive.

This exception relating to 'primary agricultural products' is an important one for this country, but the dividing line between products that have undergone 'initial processing' and those that have not may sometimes be difficult to draw. As the English and Scottish Law Commissions have observed (Eng Law Com No. 82 & Scot Law Com No. 45, para 85):

> even fresh vegetables, which at first sight would seem to be a good example of unprocessed natural products, may have been sprayed by chemicals and the land in which they grew artificially fertilised.

It is doubtful whether the concept of 'initial processing' ranges quite so far, but the point worth noting here is that the exception relating to primary agricultural products is a good deal narrower than might at first appear. Any Member State may, by way of derogation form Article 2, provide in its legislation that 'products' are to include primary agricultural products and game. Ireland did not avail itself of this opportunity: see s. 1(1) of the Act. 'Initial processing' is defined in s. 1(1) as processing 'of an industrial nature . . . which could cause a defect' in the agricultural product. Of course the defect of which the plaintiff complains need not necessarily have resulted from the initial processing.

The general exclusion of immovables should be noted. In the law of negligence, immoveables (or, in ordinary tort parlance, land) tended to remain outside the scope of a full duty of care. It is only in recent years that the exemptions from liability for owners and builders have gradually been swept away. (See *Ward v McMaster* [1988] IR 337; cf. *Curling v Walsh*, High Court, 23 October 1987, discussed in the 1987 Review, 333.) The Directive does not apply, for example, to a defective house which collapses, save to the extent that any movable 'incorporated into' the house is defective. Thus, if a girder installed in a home is defective and this brings about the collapse, the Directive may apply. Since most immovables are composed of movables which are 'incorporated into' the whole, this potential range of application should not be ignored. But in such a case it would be necessary to show that the particular movable (or movables) was itself (or were themselves) defective; in other words, *a defective combination* into an immovable of movables which themselves are not defective would not appear to fall within the scope of the Directive.

Finally, it should be noted that Article 17 provides that the Directive is not to apply to products (as defined by Article 2) put into circulation before the date on which the legislative and administrative provisions necessary to comply with the Directive enter into force. S. 13 of the 1991 Act restricts the retrospective operation of the Act even further, so as not to apply to products put into circulation before the commencement of the Act. Since the Directive should have been implemented by 30 July 1988, s. 13 is not in harmony with Article 17.

2. *Who is a 'producer'*   Article 3.1 provides that a 'producer' is one who is:

(a) the manufacturer of a finished product;
(b) the producer of any raw material;
(c) the manufacturer of a component part; or
(d) any person who, by putting his name, trade mark or other distinguishing feature on the product, presents himself as its producer.

Moreover, a person who imports into the Community a product for sale, hire, leasing or any form of distribution in the course of his business is deemed to be a producer within the meaning of the Directive and is responsible as a producer (*id*, para 2).

Finally, where the producer of the product cannot be identified, each supplier of the product is treated as its producer unless he informs the injured person 'within a reasonable time' of the identity of the producer or of the person who supplied him with the product (*id*, para 3). The same rule applies, in the case of an imported product, if this product does not indicate the identity of the importer, even if the name of the producer is indicated (*id*).

It is scarcely surprising that manufacturers of finished products, producers of raw materials and manufacturers of component parts should be treated as 'producers' for the purposes of the Directive. Nor, on reflection, should it be a matter of serious debate that those who present themselves as producers by putting their name, trade mark or other distinguishing feature on a product should also be treated as 'producers'. This practice is 'particularly common amongst large retail organisations' (Eng Law Com No. 82 & Scot Law Com No. 45 para 99) and has been part of Irish mercantile life for several years. It would be curious if, having presented products as their own to the public, retail organisations should later be allowed to disclaim strict liability on the basis that the articles were not really 'their' products.

So far as imported products are concerned, it should be noted that only the person who imports the product 'for sale, hire, leasing or any form of distribution in the course of his business' is deemed a 'producer': Article 3 para 2. Thus, for example, there is no question that the Directive affects the non-commercial importation of food or gadgets purchased abroad by holiday-makers—a fear that troubled the English and Scottish Law Commissions (*op. cit.*, para 103). The argument in favour of imposing strict liability on the commercial importer is that this business involves exposing consumers within the Community to the risk of being injured by the imported products. Realistically, consumers will be grateful for being presented with a relatively easy target within the Community rather than having to face the prospect of expensive and uncertain litigation in some foreign jurisdictions outside the Community.

Where the producer cannot be identified, there is much to be said for effectively treating the supplier as the producer, unless he discloses the identity of the actual producer. As the English and Scottish Law Commissions observed (*op. cit.*, para 101):

> First, it assists the injured person in tracing the 'anonymous' producer in circumstances where assistance is needed; second, it encourages retailers and other suppliers to keep records from which it may be possible to establish the identity of the supplier (or producer) of the product in question; third, by making it harder for the producer to remain anonymous, it encourages him to reveal his identity by labelling his products where practicable.

3. When is a product defective? Article 6 is concerned with the circumstances in which a product is defective. Under Irish law, a person may, in some circumstances, be liable in negligence for producing a defective, non-dangerous product: see McMahon & Binchy, *op. cit.*, 180-6, *Ward v McMaster* [1988] IR 337. But under Article 6 'defectiveness' does not have this wider meaning. Products that are safe but shoddy do not fall within its scope.

The key word in this Article is *safety:* a product is defective when *it does not provide the safety which a person is entitled to expect*, taking all the circumstances into account. Article 6, paragraph 1 mentions three specific circumstances, giving them no particular weight relative to each other or relative to other, unspecified, circumstances. What weight each should have must depend on the facts of the particular case. The first of these circumstances is 'the presentation of the product'. If, for example, a product is represented in the advertising literature or in the detailed descriptive literature accompanying its sale as being of a particular quality, then a consumer who is injured or suffers damage as a result of the product's dangerousness in lacking this quality may have a right to action. So, where a hot water bottle is represented as being capable of taking boiling water, and it is not, an injured user who relies on this representation may well succeed, on this account, in showing that the hot water bottle did not provide the safety which he or she was entitled to expect. It would appear that the 'presentation' of the product includes an *omission* to provide information which ought to have been given, to protect the user from harm. Thus, the failure by a producer to refer to an allergic reaction which was known to the producer to affect the product could in some instances be relied on by an injured consumer. Similarly the failure to warn of a product's latent dangerous condition, such as inflammability, would be taken into consideration under this heading of Article 6, as it is at common law: see *O'Byrne v Gloucester*, Supreme Court, 3 November 1988, and the 1988 Review 433-4.

The second circumstance specified in Article 6 is 'the use to which it could reasonably be expected that the product would be put'. Clearly there are limits to what reasonably may be expected: it is unreasonable, for example, to expect that a hammer should be capable of being used successfully as a car jack. Moreover, a competent adult who deviates widely from the specified instructions as to the use of a product may have no right to complain about injuries resulting from his or her failure to comply with the directions.

The third circumstance specified by Article 6 is 'the time when the product was put into circulation'. This factor may operate in one or two ways. First, the passage of time may be relevant as throwing light on what a person is 'entitled to expect'. To take an obvious case, one would not be entitled to expect that a chocolate cake would be edible after a year. Indeed, one should surely expect that any consumer product, after sufficient wear and tear, will eventually become likely to be unsafe.

The second way the time factor specified by Article 6 operates is somewhat different. It relates to the fact that safety standards may change over a period of time. This change may be as a result of a development in the state of scientific and technical knowledge: such a case is also covered by Article 7, clause (e) and will be considered below. But safety standards may also change without direct reference to such scientific and technical developments. What may have been an acceptable risk from a product twenty years ago may simply cease to be acceptable to the community over this period. For example, there is a greater sensitivity to questions of hygiene and road safety today than there was some time ago. The thrust of Article 6 is to seek to ensure that producers will not suffer unduly from these changes in attitude. The Article does not give the producer an absolute defence to show that the product complied with the standards of the time when the product was put into circulation; but this will be a factor to be considered, as one of a number of circumstances, in determining whether the product was defective.

The passage of time since the product was put onto the market may also be relevant to the question of proof, which is addressed by Article 4. As *Prosser & Keeton on Torts*, 696 (5th ed., 1985) note, '[t]he older the product, the less likely it is that evidence of malfunctioning will suffice as an inference of a construction flaw, although some courts would permit [the] plaintiff to negative misuse and overuse in such a case'.

Finally in this context it should be noted that Article 6, paragraph 2 states that a product is not to be considered defective 'for the sole reason that a better product is subsequently put into circulation'. This recognises the fact that production processes are inevitably subject to constant technological change: to stigmatise a product as 'defective' merely because a better one has later been produced would be unfair and impractical. But in some cases the later circulation of a better product may be potent evidence that greater safety could earlier have been achieved. Article 6, paragraph 2 does not prevent this inference from being made.

4 The scope of 'damage'   'Damage', for the purposes of Article 1, is defined by Article 9 as meaning:

> (a) damage caused by death or by personal injuries;
> (b) damage to, or destruction of, any item of property other than the defective product itself, with a lower threshold of 500 ECU, provided that the item of property:
>
>> (i) is of a type ordinarily intended for private use or consumption, and
>> (ii) was used by the injured person mainly for his own private use or consumption.

Article 9 is specified as being without prejudice to national provisions relating to non-material damage.

It is perhaps significant that the ninth recital to the Directive, having referred to the fact that the protection of the consumer requires compensation for death and personal injury as well as damage to property, goes on to state that the Directive 'should not prejudice compensation for pain and suffering and other non-material damages payable, where appropriate, under the law applicable to the case'. This could be interpreted in three ways. First, that, in conjunction with Article 9, it excludes any recovery of damages for pain and suffering under the Directive, leaving claimants to look only to such other remedies as may be available to them under the national law. The effect of this interpretation would be to deny claimants recovery of damages for pain and suffering save to the extent that they *already* have this entitlement. This would represent no improvement of claimants' rights so far as pain and suffering are concerned. A second interpretation would permit recovery for pain and suffering in cases of death and personal injury but not for mental suffering resulting from property damage. Whether this was the intention of the framers of the Directive may, however, be doubted. Finally, the ninth recital and Article 9 could be interpreted as entitling States, at their option, when implementing the Directive, to provide for the entitlement to recover damages for pain and suffering *under the strict liability regime prescribed by the Directive*. Against this interpretation, it might be considered curious that the option should not have been expressly identified and highlighted, as are other options under the Directive. Whether this is a serious objection may, however, be doubted, since this interpretation appears the most convincing of the three in terms of both the language of the ninth directive and Article 9 and the policy implications.

The 1991 Act does not resolve the question definitively. Its definition in s. 1(1) of 'personal injury' as including 'any disease and impairment of a person's physical or mental condition' has been interpreted by Alex Schuster, *op. cit.*, at 13-14, as supporting the inclusion of damages for pain and suffering. Professor McMahon, *id*, at 25, has no doubt that this is so. The characterisation of the liability by s. 2(1) as resting on tort supports this view.

So far as property damage is concerned, Article 9 requires, first, that the damage be to any item of property *other than the defective product itself*. Thus, if an electric kettle self-destructs and burns to a cinder, but causes no damage to other property, no liability accrues under the Directive.

Article 9 requires, secondly, that the items of property damaged by the defective product be of a type 'ordinarily intended for private use or his own private use or consumption'. Clearly what the Directive is seeking to exclude is damage to property used in the course of a trade, business or profession: the draft Directive makes this clear.

The language used in the Directive is perhaps unfortunate. It would seem, in its express terms, to exclude property damage sustained by an innocent third party as a result of an accident brought about through the innocent use of an unsafe product by its owner. For example, if A buys a car with defective brakes and smashes through B's front window, leaving A physically un-scathed, B is surely morally entitled to compensation for the property damage, but it cannot be said that the car was '*used by the injured person* [B] mainly for his own private use or consumption'. B never 'used' the car: he first became acquainted with it in his living room after the damage was done.

S. 3 of the Act gives effect to Article 9 in a controversial manner, by requiring the deduction of £350 (equivalent to 500 ECU) from all awards of that figure or more. The purpose of Article 9 is to exclude trivial claims for property damage, rather than to reduce the defendant's liability. There is, however, support for the approach taken in s. 3 of the French text of the Directive, as Alex Schuster, *op. cit.*, at 80, points out.

It should be noted finally that, by virtue of Article 14, the Directive does not apply to injury or damage 'arising from nuclear accidents and covered by international conventions ratified by the Member States'. On this area, see 372-5, above.

Questions of proof and causation   Article 4 provides tersely that:

> [t]he injured person shall be required to prove the damage, the defect and the causal relationship between the defect and damage.

The onus of proof is thus clearly on the injured person, but what must be proved is, of course, less conceptually encumbered than what is necessary to establish in a negligence action. There is no need to establish any breach of a duty of care on the part of the defendant: all that need be shown is that the product was defective, that the plaintiff suffered damage and that 'the causal relationship between the defect and damage' existed.

Two questions arise about this approach. To what extent, if at all, may the *res ipsa loquitur* doctrine, or some analogue, apply? This is a formidable issue since, under present law, it is less than fully clear what precisely the doctrine means and what are its effects on the onus of proof: see our discussion above, 415-7, of Morris J's decision in *Lindsay v Mid-Western Health Board*, High Court, 31 May 1991. If the classic rationale for *res ipsa loquitur* applies, it can surely have no relevance to Article 4, since liability under the 1991 Act is not premised on proof of *negligence*. If, however, the true rationale for the doctrine is the defendant's superior access to the true explanation for the injury, then the doctrine, or some analogue, may indeed apply.

Secondly, what is meant by 'the causal relationship between the defect and damage'? Obviously, if there is *no* causal relationship, the plaintiff cannot succeed, but the converse is not necessarily the case, as the doctrine of 'proximate cause' or remoteness of damage, makes clear. In tort law not every case involving a causal relationship will be sufficient to impose liability on the defendant see, e.g., *Latham v Hibernian Insurance Co. Ltd and Peter J Sheridan & Co. Ltd*, High Court, 4 December 1991 and *Cowan v Freaghaile* [1991] 1 IR 389, discussed above, 410-13, and this limitation applies even in cases of strict liability. Article 4 specifies no similar limitations. Perhaps it should be interpreted as implicitly imposing liability, however indirect and distant the causal relationship may be. Alternatively, it could be read subject to implicit limitations to be filled in by judicial exegesis. Of course, the language of the Directive and of the Act narrows the potential scope of causal attribution. Liability arises only where a defect in the product wholly or partly caused the damage of which the plaintiff complains. A product is defective when it 'fails to provide the safety which a person is entitled to expect. . . .' This emphasis on reasonable expectation as to safety will exclude liability for many freak accidents, without even reaching the question of causation.

Defences   The Directive, in Article 7, provides five defences to the strict liability principle. A producer will not be liable if he proves:

> (a) that he did not put the product into circulation; or
> (b) that, having regard to the circumstances, it is probable that the defect which caused the damage did not exist at the time when the product was put into circulation by him or that this defect came into being afterwards; or
> (c) that the product was neither manufactured by him for sale or any form of distribution for economic purpose, nor manufactured or distributed by him in the course of his business; or
> (d) that the defect is due to compliance of the product with mandatory regulations issued by the public authorities; or
> (e) that the state of scientific and technical knowledge at the time when he put the product into circulation was not such as to enable the existence of the defect to be discovered; or
> (f) in the case of a manufacturer of a component, that the defect is attributable to the design of the product in which the component had been fitted or to the instructions given by the manufacturer of the product.

Regarding the first defence, that the producer did not 'put the product into circulation', the Commission was of the view that it was not necessary to define this term further since it was 'self-explanatory in the ordinary meaning of the words'. The Commission considered that '[n]ormally, an article has been put into circulation when it has been started off on the chain of distribution'. Thus, if a product is released onto the market as a result of a third party's act, the producer could in some circumstances be liable in negligence but strict liability would not attach.

The defence contained in ground (b) in Article 7 is designed to protect the producer from liability for defects coming into being some time after the product was put into circulation by him. As the Commission noted, '[o]ne of the conditions for the liability of the producer is that the defect in the article should arise in the producer's production process. . . . Liability is therefore excluded where the defect arose only after th[e] time [it was put into circulation]. . . .' But, although the difference may be easy enough to state in the abstract, it does raise some troublesome conceptual—indeed philosophical—issues. If a defect appears in a product two years after the product was put into circulation, by what criteria can it be judged to have 'come into being' at any particular time? And when should that time be? Are we not here attempting to resolve the problem of 'actualisation of potential', which has troubled philosophers since the time of Aristotle? If a car develops a weakness in its brakes after two years, and the technical evidence is to the effect that a car is so manufactured that the brakes generally start weakening dangerously at this time, is that a defect 'coming into being' at the time of manufacture or two years later? Would the answer be the same if the relevant period were two weeks? Or twenty years? One is here reminded of the notion, canvassed in *Pirelli General Cable Works Ltd v Oscar Faber & Partners* [1983] 2 AC 1, at 16, of a product being 'doomed from the start'.

The defence contained in ground (c) of Article 7 protects the non-commercial producer. Ground (d) ensures that a commercial producer will not be faced with the dilemma of having to comply either with mandatory regulations issued by the public authorities or with the terms of the Directive: if such a potential clash arises, the producer will have a good defence under the Directive where he complies with the mandatory regulations.

Ground (e) of Article 7 contains an important modification to the strict liability principle. A producer will be relieved of liability that would otherwise attach if he can prove that the state of scientific and technical knowledge at the time when he put the product into circulation was not such as to enable the existence of the defect to be discovered. In other words, if the product was as safe as the 'state of the art' would allow at the time of production, subsequent improvements in safety in the production process with respect to this product may not be relied on by an injured plaintiff as setting the standard of safety. To some degree this specific defence is contained, in general terms, in Article 6: for why should a person be 'entitled to expect' standard of safety which, *ex hypothesi*, was *impossible* to attain at the time the product was put into circulation? Moreover, Article 6, as we have seen, specifies 'the time when the product was put into circulation' as a circumstance to be taken into account in determining whether a product is defective. This would appear to give some scope to the 'state of the art' defence to operate, even without the express ground to this effect contained in Article 7.

It is perhaps worth raising the question whether the 'state of the art' defence contained in Article 7 of the Directive would be more effective in exempting a producer from strict liability under the Directive than from liability in negligence at common law. Mere proof that the state of scientific and technical knowledge at the time the product was put into circulation 'was not such as to enable the existence of the defect to be discovered' will relieve the producer of strict liability; but in a negligence action the matter would not be so easily decided in his favour. A separate question could arise in some cases as to whether, in view of the limited level of scientific knowledge and relatively undeveloped 'state of the art', it was negligent to have put the product into circulation at all. The risk to the consumer could well outweigh the benefits, especially where the desire to make profits encouraged a premature release of a product onto the market. Cf. *Best v Wellcome Foundation Ltd* [1992] ILRM 609, reversing High Court, 11 January 1991.

It should be noted that any member State may, by way of derogation from Article 7(e), provide that the producer is to be liable even where he proves that the state of scientific knowledge at the time when he put the product into circulation was not such as to enable the existence of a defect to be discovered. Ireland did not avail itself of this possibility

Ground (f) of Article 7 allows the manufacturer of a component to escape liability under the Directive where, in effect, the responsibility lies with the manufacturer of the product in which the component is fitted. That responsibility can arise where the defect is attributable (i) to the *design* of the product in which the component is fitted, or (ii) to the *instructions* given by the manufacturer of the product. It is possible to imagine cases where the defect is attributable to a *combination* of causes, including the act of the manufacturer of the component and the instructions given by the manufacturer of the product. In such instances joint and several liability under Article 5, rather than liability imposed solely on the manufacturer of the product, would appear appropriate. In other words it seems that, 'attributable' in ground (f) should be interpreted as meaning 'attributable exclusively' to the matters specified in the ground. In view especially of the terms of Article 8.1, it might indeed have been better if ground (f) had determined this issue more clearly.

Limitation period and extinction of liability   The idea of a limitation period is based on two policies: first, that a defendant should be protected from stale, possibly fraudulent, claims, where accessibility to evidence has been diminished; and secondly, that a plaintiff who sleeps on his rights is not entitled to an indefinite period within which to take the action.

The thrust of the Directive seems, on balance, to favour the first school of thought. Though Article 10 is framed in terms generous to plaintiffs, the benefit of this is largely, if somewhat arbitrarily, subverted by Article 11.

Article 10 requires Member States to provide in their legislation that a limitation period of three years is to apply to proceedings for the recovery of damages as provided for in the Directive. The limitation period begins to run from the day on which the plaintiff became aware, or should reasonably have become aware, of the damage, the defect and the identity of the producer. However, the laws of Member States regulating suspension or interruption of the limitation period are not affected by the Directive.

Article 11 requires Member States to provide in their legislation that the rights conferred on the injured person pursuant to the Directive are to be extinguished on the expiry of a period of ten years from the date on which the producer put into circulation the actual product which caused the damage, unless the injured person has in the meantime instituted proceedings against the producer.

Some points about these two Articles should be noted. First, as mentioned in relation to Article 10, time begins to run from the time the plaintiff was, or ought to have become, aware of the damage, the defect and the identity of the producer. Under the Statute of Limitations (Amendment) Act 1991, which we analyse in the Limitation of Actions chapter, 299-301, above, this is the test favoured in relation to tort law in general, where the gravamen of the case involves personal injuries.

It should also be noted that the effect of Article 11 in extinguishing the injured person's rights after the expiry of ten years from the date the producer put the product into circulation, is to render inoperative the law of Member States regulating suspension or interruption of the limitation period on the basis of minority or mental incapacity, for example. True, Article 10 provides that these laws 'shall not be affected by this Directive'; but Article 11 is concerned, not with a limitation period within which an action must be taken, but the extinction of rights.

The merits and disadvantages of Article 11 have been widely debated. In favour of the absolute cut-off point, it has observed that:

> [i]t is in the producer's interests that he should be able to close his books on a product after it has been in circulation for a fixed period. It assists him in assessing the risk and it facilitates insurance and amortisation, thus keeping the insurance premium down. There is thus some saving, albeit marginal, which redounds to the general benefit of the public. More important, perhaps, it sets a date after which the producer no longer has the burden of proving that a product which has caused an accident was not defective when he put it into circulation. This burden is increasingly difficult for him to discharge as the years pass and it seems only fair that there should come a point when it is entirely removed. (Eng Law Com No. 82 and Scot Law Com No. 45, para 152.)

As against this, several objections may be made to the ten-year cut-off point. First, it is crude and arbitrary. Some products—various types of machinery or aircraft, for example—may well be expected to last for more than ten years, so that it could properly be said of them, say, twelve years after they were put into circulation, that, in spite of their age, they were 'defective'. For other products—a loaf of bread, for example—ten years is an entirely inappropriate figure. The Council of Europe, which favoured the same approach as was ultimately adopted by the EEC Directive, was conscious of the problem but none the less considered ten years 'an acceptable period in view of the need to fix some limit (ten years being a fair average) and the desirability of affording producers some security': *Explanatory Report to the Strasbourg Convention on Products Liability in Regard to Personal Injury and Death*, para. 68.

Similarly, the framers of the draft Directive considered that ten years 'appeared appropriate as an average period'. This notion of an 'average period' may be challenged; the vast range of products, each with their appropriate life-span of use, makes it quite inapt to select *any* particular period as a cut-off point, since that period will be quite unsuitable for many of these products.

The ten-year cut-off period has not been met with universal support by producers, some of whom

> argue that the period is too long, that for them to maintain records to establish that goods were not defective when originally sold will be an expensive exercise, and the longer the period for which records must be kept the greater the expense. As the consumer must bear this cost in the price of the goods is it to his advantage to pay for record keeping which can be of benefit on only the most rare occasion? (Marriott, 3 J of Products Ly 15, at 16 (1979)).

One of the grounds on which the Scottish Law Commission objected to the ten-year cut-off point was that it would be unfair to an injured person, who normally would not know on what date the product had been put into circulation. Different cut-off periods would apply in respect of each component:

> an injured person wishing to sue a component maker would have at the very least a complicated task in ascertaining whether his action was likely to be time-barred, and evidence to this effect might not emerge until after the injured person had incurred considerable expense in pursuing his claim. (*Op. cit.*, para. 158.)

S. 7 of the Act implements Articles 10 and 11, incorporating them into the Statutes of Limitations 1957 and 1991.

Contributory negligence   Contributory negligence comes into play under
the Directive. Article 8.2 provides that:

> [t]he liability of the producer may be reduced or disallowed when,
> having regard to all the circumstances, the damage is caused both by a
> defect in the product and by the fault of the injured person or any person
> for whom the injured person is responsible.

Thus, contributory negligence is permitted to have much the same role as
it does at present in a negligence action. Even the notion of imputed
contributory negligence is allowed to operate: cf. McMahon & Binchy, *op
cit*, 365-7.

Relevant to Article 8.2 is the present uncertainty under Irish law as to how
a case should be resolved where the plaintiff is guilty of contributory
negligence and the defendant is strictly liable (for breach of statutory duty,
for example) without any 'fault', as that notion is understood under the Civil
Liability Act 1961. In the Supreme Court decision of *O'Sullivan v Dwyer*
[1971] IR 275, Walsh J interpreted s. 43 of the 1961 Act as disentitling the
plaintiff to any compensation in such circumstances. However, in *Daly v
Avonmore Creameries* [1984] IR 131, McCarthy J raised a question as to
whether s. 43 was mandatory or discretionary. It is perhaps worth noting that
in several jurisdictions in the United States it is possible to operate contributory negligence rules of apportionment in products liability cases where
the defendant is strictly liable and the plaintiff is guilty of contributory
negligence.

Article 8.2 seems clearly in accord with this approach. Unlike s. 34(1) of
the 1961 Act, it does not require the Court to compare the respective degrees
of fault of the plaintiff and defendant. On the contrary, it envisages reduction
or disallowance of the claim by virtue of a consideration of 'all the circumstances' where the damage is caused by a defect in the product and the fault
of the plaintiff or his proxy. The drafting strategy adopted by s. 9(2) of the
Act, whereby the defect is treated as though it were due to the fault of the
defendant, amounts to a formalistic resolution of the issue raised in
O'Sullivan v Dwyer.

Prohibition on 'contracting out'   Article 12 of the Directive prohibits 'contracting out'. It provides that the liability of the producer arising from the
Directive may not, in relation to the injured person, be limited or excluded
by a provision limiting his liability or exempting him from liability. In its
original draft, the relevant provision limited contracting out, without
reference to any 'provision' to this effect. The original draft, therefore,
overrode not merely contractual exclusions of liability but also any assertion

by the producer that the consumer, by using the product, had voluntarily assumed the risks that might arise from the defectiveness of the product. The inclusion in the final text of the reference to a 'provision' limiting the injured person's liability appears to restrict the scope of the Article. The precise extent of the change is a matter for debate: there may, of course, be a 'provision' in a contract, but it would also seem possible for there to be a 'provision' in a non-contractual agreement, or even (perhaps) in a unilateral notice, involving some degree of communication between the parties. The parallel with the construction of the *volenti* defence as a result of s. 34(1)(b) of the Civil Liability Act 1961 is worth considering.

Concurrent wrongdoers The net of liability among several defendants is cast widely by the Directive. In view of the broad range of liability under Part III of our Civil Liability Act 1961 and our liberal third-party procedure, this approach is generally in harmony with the present law. Article 5 provides that:

> [w]here, as a result of the provisions of this Directive, two or more persons are liable for the same damage, they shall be liable jointly and severally without prejudice to the provisions of national law concerning the rights of contribution or recourse.

And Article 8.1 provides that:

> [w]ithout prejudice to the provisions of national law concerning the right of contribution or recourse, the liability of the producer shall not be reduced when the damage is caused both by a defect in [the] product and by the act or omission of a third party.

Ss. 8 and 9 of the 1991 Act give practical effect to these two provisions.

2. Negligence In *Best v Wellcome Foundation Ltd*, High Court, 11 June 1991, Hamilton P held that the defendant had been negligent in releasing a particular batch of a whooping cough vaccine, but that this had not caused the plaintiff's injuries. The Supreme Court on 3 June 1992 reversed the finding as to causation: [1992] ILRM 609. We shall examine this case in detail in the 1992 Review.

VICARIOUS LIABILITY

Traffic accidents The doctrine of vicarious liability in tort law has caused understandable controversy since it represents an uneasy conjunction between the principles of fault-based and absolute liability. By and large, tort law still looks for fault before it imposes liability. The idea that a person innocent of any carelessness should be made liable, on a vicarious basis, strikes a note of dissonance with the search for fault at a personal level. Nevertheless, the courts have not shrunk from casting a wide-ranging net of vicarious liability in relation to tort. The Supreme Court decision in *Moynihan v Moynihan* [1975] IR 192 is perhaps the most notorious example of this tendency.

Traffic accidents have tempted courts throughout the common law world to engage in dubious ascriptions of the elements of the vicarious liability doctrine in order to bring about, *sub rosa*, a liberal regime of compensation for those injured on the road: see Lattin, 'Vicarious Liability and the Family Automobile', 26 Mich L Rev 846 (1928). In Ireland legislative initiative nearly sixty years ago (the Road Traffic Act 1933, s. 172) dispensed with the need (or temptation) to engage in undue extension of the doctrine. S. 172 of the 1933 Act became s. 118 of the Road Traffic Act 1961, which provides as follows:

> Where a person (in this section referred to as the user) uses a mechanically propelled vehicle with the consent of the owner of the vehicle, the user shall, for the purposes of determining the liability or non-liability of the owner for injury caused by the negligent use of the vehicle by the user, and for the purposes of determining the liability or non-liability of any other person for injury to the vehicle or persons or property therein caused by negligence occurring while the vehicle is being used by the user, be deemed to use the vehicle as the servant of the owner, but only in so far as the user acts in accordance with the terms of such consent.

In *Ambrose v O'Regan*, Supreme Court, 20 December 1991, reversing High Court, 14 November 1990, MacKenzie J had held that the driver of a car involved in an accident had been driving without the consent of his mother, the owner, and that accordingly proceedings against the owner under s. 118 should be dismissed. In his judgment he had observed that the case concerned a question:

> as to . . . the night of the accident where poor Mr Ambrose . . . sustained most serious injuries for which he has not yet been compensated and which he will be compensated for. That is really an attempt by the Motor Insurers' Bureau who are primarily responsible for paying the damages which Mr Ambrose sustained to offload their obligations onto Mrs O'Regan, either personally or through her insurance company as to what is determined under the agreement with the Minister and the insurer

concerned. What I am asked to say is that Mr O'Regan, on the night of the accident, was driving the motor car with the consent of his mother, either expressly or implied.

These observations echoed comments made during the hearing of the evidence.

The Supreme Court upheld the appeal and directed a new trial on the issue of liability. McCarthy J (Finlay CJ and O'Flaherty J concurring) considered that MacKenzie J's comments reflected an incorrect approach. If he had been influenced by a consideration that the plaintiff would recover damages irrespective of the outcome of the issue, he was wrong. The evidence in the case would support a conclusion either way on the issue of the owner's consent. The conclusion, 'based as it clearly was, in part upon irrelevant considerations', could not be allowed to stand.

The Supreme Court decision is welcome, but it raises a broader question of principle. MacKenzie J's approach was easy to strike down because it frankly expressed inappropriate judicial concerns: but what should be the situation where an appeal comes to the Supreme Court in circumstances indicating that the trial judge may well have delivered a verdict for the plaintiff in the knowledge (but without overt reference to the fact) that the defendant's insurance company would foot the bill? If the Supreme Court gets a whiff of such a sentiment, is it to order a re-trial, or is it confined to cases where the trial judge leaves a paper trail? The fixation of courts in the last century with establishing 'error on the record' strikes us today as bizarre. Should there not be a way for the Supreme Court, in civil appeals, to break through the form of judgments to examine their substance?

In *Kenny v Motor Insurers' Bureau of Ireland and the Minister for the Environment* [1991] 2 IR 441, the plaintiff, aged 12 years at the time of the accident, was injured when, having been thrown off a truck because of the dangerous way it was being driven, he was crushed by its back wheel. The plaintiff had been on the truck in somewhat unusual circumstances. The vehicle was a small one with a flat open body. It was usually parked outside its owner's house and there 'constituted an irresistible invitation to children in the neighbourhood to play on it'. The owner was aware of this and was not averse to giving them rides for some distance towards the entrance of the housing estate where they lived.

On the fateful day, the plaintiff and four or five other children were on the back of the truck when the defendant came out of his house. The plaintiff asked the defendant if he was going out in the truck, as he did not want to take a ride if the vehicle was being moved. The defendant did not answer him but, knowing that he and his friends were on the back of the truck, got into it and drove off. The plaintiff tried to get down, but could not because of the press of children around him. The defendant drove the truck some considerable distance and at some considerable speed. The plaintiff got on the floor of the truck and then stood up holding onto an iron bar behind the cab. It was from this position that he was thrown off the vehicle.

The plaintiff's action against the defendant yielded a judgment in his favour but the defendant was uninsured. The plaintiff thus looked to the Motor Insurers' Bureau of Ireland for compensation.

Paragraph 2 of the MIB agreement with the Minister for Local Government requires the MIB to satisfy any unpaid judgment obtained 'in respect of any liability for injury to persons or which is required to be covered by an approved policy of insurance under s. 56'. S. 56 of the Road Traffic Act 1961 requires all users of mechanically propelled vehicles in public places to insure against claims of injury caused by negligent use to any person other than 'excepted persons'. An excepted person is defined by s. 65 of the 1961 Act, as amended by the Road Traffic Act 1968. It includes anyone claiming in respect of personal injures sustained 'while he was in or on' the vehicle, other than when in or on a vehicle which has been specified by the Minister. (No such specification applied in the case). S. 65(2) provides that references to injury sustained while in or on a vehicle include injury sustained while entering, getting onto, being put into or on, alighting from, or being taken out of or off, the vehicle, and injury caused by being thrown out of or off the vehicle.

Costello J concluded that the plaintiff could not circumvent the breadth of s. 65. The plaintiff had argued that he had not sustained his injury by being 'thrown off' the vehicle, but rather had done so, *after* he had been thrown off, when the wheel of the truck went over him. Costello J rejected this argument because the causal and temporal connection between the act of being thrown off and having the wheel go over him was a very close one.

Costello J also rejected the plaintiff's contention that he had not been voluntarily on the truck at the time of the accident and that the Act had to be construed as only exempting vehicle owners from liability to insure persons who are *voluntary* passengers on vehicles. Costello J accepted that the plaintiff had not been voluntarily on the truck but he could not construe the section as applying only to voluntary passengers:

> Subject to a Ministerial Order, the effect of s. 65 is that owners of vehicles are not required to insure against claims arising from injury to passengers in their vehicles. I cannot construe it as imposing a liability to insure passengers who are not on the vehicle with their consent. Firstly, the section does not say so—it refers to 'any person' claiming in respect of any injury sustained while in or on the vehicle. Secondly, interpreting the section by reference to the Act as a whole I can find no

reason why it should be construed as urged on the plaintiff's behalf—on the contrary, such an artificial construction would be a most implausible one.

The plaintiff thus being an excepted person, his claim against the Motor Insurers' Bureau failed.

One may perhaps debate the merits of the outcome. Legislation relating to the obligation to insure and to the implications for plaintiffs of defendants' failure to insure has a clear social purpose. No one could argue that the court should take a liberal interpretation of statutory provisions simply to carry the paternalistic and social goals of the legislation some distance further than the legislators wished; to do so would constitute unwarranted and indefensible judicial legislation. It is an entirely different matter, however, to examine the language of s. 65(2), not by strictly applying the literal rule but by adopting the 'mischief' approach. What was the legislature seeking to achieve in making a distinction between injuries on and off vehicles? Surely it must have been based on the crucial difference that those who share a vehicle *share a common purpose*, whether it be a journey that is paid for or a pleasure trip together. The relationship between the driver of a vehicle and a person who is not in or on the vehicle with him is a remote one. In the normal case no prior relationship or common purpose between the parties can be presumed. In the case of an individual involuntarily on a vehicle, the relationship between him or her and the driver lacks the element of common purpose which is the prime justification for categorising a person as an 'excepted person'.

Having said this, it must also be stressed that a ruthless application of a test of involuntariness in this context could lead to conclusions that clearly could not be justified; there would, for example, be no sound basis for holding an infant of six months not to be an 'excepted person'. The law already makes accommodation for cases such as this in other areas; cf. *Murray v Harringay Arena Ltd* [1951] 2 KB 529.

Medical Negligence   In *Lindsay v Midwestern Health Board*, High Court, 30 May 1991, which we discuss above, 415-7, in the section dealing with the doctrine of *res ipsa loquitur*, Morris J held that all who were working in the defendants' hospital were persons for whose negligence the defendants would be vicariously liable. We thus have to wait and see whether an Irish court will be disposed to adopt the robust approach favoured by the Supreme Court of California in *Ybarra v Spangard*, 25 Cal 2d 486, 154 P2d 687 (1944), which imposes a duty to give an explanation on all those involved in the treatment of unconscious patients, even when they are not bound together by the ties of vicarious liability.

CONTRIBUTORY NEGLIGENCE

Elderly persons The extent to which the objective test of the reasonable person, in determining negligence and contributory negligence, should be modified by individual factors is one that raises issues far more subtle than might at first appear: see Seavey, *Negligence-Subjective or Objective?*, 41 Harv L Rev 1 (1927). There is no problem where physical disabilities are concerned: the courts have qualified the test so as to set the standard as that of *the reasonable person affected by the particular disability in question.* Similarly, children are not judged by an entirely objective test: the degree of subjectivity which the courts apply to them is even more extensive than in relation to the physically disabled, since they take into account the *age, mental development* and *experience* of the particular child: *Fleming v Kerry County Council,* [1955-1956] Ir Jur Rep 71, *Brennan v Savage Smyth & Co.* [1982] ILRM 223.

The elderly are treated with a good deal less indulgence. There is no inevitable legal deference to seniority: courts do not generally speak of 'the reasonable sixty-six year old', for example. Nevertheless, some recognition of the realities of old age can at times be gleaned from the decisions. One such case in *Condon v Cork Corporation and An Bord Telecom*, High Court, 1 February 1991, where a sixty-six year old woman fell on a pavement with broken concrete. Barr J imposed liability in negligence on the first defendant for the manner in which it had resurfaced the pavement: we consider that issue, above, 406. Barr J also acquitted the plaintiff of contributory negligence. The question he considered appropriate concerned the degree of care for his or her own safety that ought reasonably to be expected of an adult pedestrian in the situation in which the plaintiff was at the time of the accident. Pedestrians were not obliged to watch where they placed each step. They should avoid *significant obstructions or defects* in a footpath or roadways, but were not obliged to look out for and avoid every minor defect:

> If the law so required, then, bearing in mind the state of numerous footpaths in the older parts of our cities and towns, pedestrians not infrequently would find themselves involved in something broadly action to hop-scotch which, for elderly people in particular, might well be more dangerous than the minor hazards sought to be avoided.

The small hole that caused the plaintiff to fall was not a significant defect which she ought to have observed and avoided.

There is in this decision a recognition that physical agility decreases with age and that older people cannot reasonably be expected to engage in physical exertion more demanding than their condition allows.

Pedestrians The question of the contributory negligence of pedestrians has generated several appellate decision over the years. This was especially so when juries determined liability issues in the High Court frequently had to determine whether to characterise the plaintiff's carelessness as contributory negligence as a matter of law: see, e.g., *Connolly v Murphy*, Supreme Court, 11 October 1971, *O'Connell v Shield Insurance Co. Ltd*, [1965] IR 700. When it comes to apportion responsibility between the pedestrian and car driver, there is an understandable tendency to be unduly lenient towards the pedestrian. This cannot be reconciled with sound prin- ciple. In *Harrison v Ennis* [1967] IR 286, at 294, Walsh J sounded the following caution:

> While I would agree . . . that the position in the case of a collision between a motor car and a pedestrian is not the same as for two motor vehicles, it does not follow that in every collision between a pedestrian and a motor vehicle, in which both parties are negligent, a greater degree of fault must always be apportioned to the driver of the motor car and the circumstances attendant upon the accident must be taken into account including [such questions as whether] the accident occurred at night and in circumstances in which the [pedestrian] had a better opportunity of seeing the [driver] than the [driver] had of seeing the [pedestrian].

In *Shields v Boyle*, High Court, 6 November 1991, O'Hanlon J addressed the question of the contributory negligence of a pedestrian injured when crossing a street in a country town after dark. There was two hundred yards' clear visibility up the street and the lighting in the area was good. The road was about thirty two feet wide. The plaintiff, emerging from between parked cars, had formed the view that the vehicle that struck her was sufficiently far away to make it safe for her to cross in its path. O'Hanlon J held that the driver of that vehicle had been negligent in driving at an unsafe speed and in failing to keep a careful look out. He held that the plaintiff was guilty of contributory negligence in clearly having failed to ensure that it was safe for her to cross and in having failed to keep the car in view as she crossed the road. O'Hanlon J reduced the plaintiff's damages by 33⅓% when appor- tioning fault between the parties. If it had been a simple matter of appor- tioning *causation*, he would have tended towards a decision in equal shares, but since fault was the test, a 33⅓% reduction was more correct on the basis that the negligent driving of the defendant's car was a source of real danger to all other users of the road in that vicinity, whereas the plaintiff's negligence was merely a careless failure to take care for her own safety.

It is fortunate that Irish law, is contrast to English law, apportions liability on the basis of the respective degrees of fault of the parties (Civil Liability

Act 1961, s. 34(1)) rather than 'the potency of the causative factors moving from each side': *Kelly v Jameson*, Supreme Court, 1 March 1972, *per* Walsh J. The language of causative ascription too often involves tacit value judgments as to how people should act. In some contexts—such as that relating to the failure to use a seat-belt, which we consider below—it does make sense to engage in a process of severing the respective causal contributions of the parties, but these are the exception rather than the rule.

The seat-belt defence In contrast to their counterparts in the United States of America, Irish judges have taken a fairly robust attitude to the seat-belt defence. Generally they are content to reduce the damages by relatively small amounts ranging from ten to twenty per cent without examining the causal question in any nuanced fashion. Thus in the Supreme Court decision of *Hamill v Oliver* [1977] IR 73, at 76, Griffin J could assure prospective defendants that 'in most cases' no special evidence was required to prove that the wearing of the seat belt would have prevented or reduced the injuries. Indeed, there is even a willingness to infer from circumstantial evidence that the plaintiff must not have been wearing a seat belt and that this failure contributed to the gravity of the plaintiff's injuries: see *Conley v Strain*, High Court, 5 August, 1988, analysed in the 1988 Review, 453.

Ward v Walsh, Supreme Court, 31 July 1991 is of interest in that it indicates a willingness to move away from the simplistic formulae favoured by the English Court of Appeal in *Froom v Butcher* [1976] QB 286; the criteria it propounds are controversial but are nonetheless worthy of serious consideration, leading to a refinement of the Court's earlier approach.

The plaintiff passenger had been severely injured in an accident caused by the defendant driver's negligence. The defendant had been travelling in excess of 60 mph (and possibly at 70 mph) on a wet road 'through typical Connemara countryside'. The car had gone out of control and overturned. The plaintiff had been thrown out and had come into contact with stones and rocks. He had suffered an incomplete paraplegia.

Lardner J, applying *Carroll v Clare County Council* [1975] IR 221, had reduced the plaintiff's damages by 20%. He was satisfied that, if the plaintiff had worn his seat belt, he would probably not have sustained any paraplegia. The Supreme Court affirmed. The evidence disclosed that the plaintiff had not worn his seat belt because he had 'decided firmly' not to do so, since he had a fear of being trapped in a car; 'probably' he had been advised by the defendant, with whom he was friendly and with whom he had often travelled as a passenger, to wear a seat belt on other occasions. The defendant's driving was of 'a high degree of recklessness'. Finlay CJ considered that the plaintiff's refusal to wear a seat belt had been 'a definite and conscious decision', and that the plaintiff had 'continued in that decision notwithstanding the extremely high speed at which the car was being driven in these bad road conditions'.

Ward v Walsh is significant because it reminds us that, in all cases where contributory negligence is alleged against the plaintiff, the court must engage in a *serious* exercise of investigating the respective degrees of fault of the parties in the light of the particular circumstances. Here we had a defendant travelling at a high speed—though it must be admitted that sixty to seventy miles an hour, even on a Connemara road, scarcely strikes one as shocking— and a plaintiff who resolutely refused to buckle up. The difficulty with the case is that the plaintiff's failure to wear a seat belt was attributable to his 'definite and conscious decision'. Normally recklessness (in the sense of *advertent* negligence) and, *a fortiori*, intention are punished more seriously than inadvertent carelessness, but the facts of the instant case should give pause for thought. The plaintiff had acted on the basis of fear of being trapped in the car. The nature of this fear is not examined; unfortunately, since the resolution of this question would seem to impinge on the quantum of contributory negligence. It is possible that the plaintiff acted on the *mistaken view* that the balance of caution lay against using a seat belt, on account of the dangers that attached to cases where a passenger was trapped in a car. If the plaintiff acted on this basis, his failure to wear a seat belt, though deliberate, was scarcely to be penalised heavily since his 'fault', judged by the *Carroll* test, was simply one of mistaken assessment of empirical data impinging on risk. If, on the other hand, the plaintiff's fear was attributable to some phobia on his part, the question should surely have arisen as to whether a phobia constitutes 'fault'. The former Supreme Court paid scant attention to this distinction in *Kelly v McElligott*, 85 ILTR 4 (1949) but, four decades later, sensitivities should have improved.

At the heart of the matter is the question of the extent to which judicial deference should properly be afforded to the psychological profile of plaintiffs in negligence litigation. Sadly, little or no attention is paid to the psychological profile of *defendants*: cf. the Law Reform Commission's *Report on the Liability in Tort of the Mentally Disabled* (LRC 18-1985). Whatever the tacit policy considerations in favour of imposing liability on mentally disabled defendants—and we hasten to assert our scepticism as to their merits—there are no obvious equivalent policies in favour of reducing the amount of compensation to *plaintiffs*.

Where compensation of plaintiffs injured by mentally disabled defendants is concerned, the policy in favour of ensuring that the plaintiff is not left without any compensation has encouraged courts to ignore the defendant's lack of mental capacity. It is quite different to suggest that a plaintiff who suffers from a mental disability should be fully compensated regardless of his or her condition. To ignore the condition may result in obliging the defendant to pay for what is essentially attributable to the plaintiff's condition.

Trespass to the person In the Circuit Court decision of *MacKnight v Xtravision*, 5 July 1991 (extracted in McMahon & Binchy's *Casebook on the Irish Law of Torts* (2nd ed., 1991), 407-10), Judge Carroll reduced the plaintiff's damages by 50% where he had sued for trespass to the person. We examine the case above, 417-9, in the section dealing with defence of property. Here we need only note that Judge Carroll had no hesitation in applying the defence of contributory negligence in proceedings for battery— a matter on which courts in other jurisdictions have displayed a bewildering inconsistency.

DAMAGES

Provision of domestic care In *Ward v Walsh*, 31 July 1991, the Supreme Court had to deal with the issue of how damages should be assessed in respect of the necessary provision of domestic care. Lardner J had applied the conventional actuarial multiplier of 4%. The plaintiff argued that the (larger) multiplier of 2% interest was appropriate on the basis that the gross cost of providing wages for services, historically and probably into the future, would be significantly greater than the net increase of such wages and therefore would be significantly more than the rate of inflation.

The Supreme Court rejected this contention, on the basis that Lardner J, in calculating these figures, had been 'assessing a calculation for services of this nature in a rural area, and not in a form of employment or service which has been structured and organised on a regular basis of regular wages increases' (*per* Finlay CJ, for the Court).

Collateral damages In *Ward v Walsh*, 31 July 1991, the Supreme Court confronted the question of collateral benefits: see McMahon & Binchy, *Irish Law of Torts* (2nd ed., 1990) 794-7. The plaintiff had been severely injured in a traffic accident caused by the defendant's negligence. He had suffered an incomplete paraplegia. In regard to the in-hospital treatment which the plaintiff would require, the court had to determine the extent to which compensation should be awarded on the basis that the plaintiff 'genuinely and reasonably' required that treatment to be given to him *as a private patient*.

Much of the treatment that was appropriate to the plaintiff was best supplied at the Cedars Rehabilitation Hospital, where the plaintiff would not be charged. But there were other forms of treatment which either could be provided in other hospitals or required to be given in these hospitals. Finlay CJ, in awarding compensation on the basis that treatment would be provided in these hospitals, stated:

> It seems to me reasonable that the plaintiff, who established his genuine desire about this matter by indicating that he and his family had arranged, prior to any accident, for Voluntary Health Insurance, enabling them to have private hospital treatment, that that is a reasonable desire and that it should have been allowed to him [by the trial judge].

One may wonder whether this is quite the way to formulate the question. Whether compensation in respect of fee-charging hospitals is appropriate should not depend on the contingent decisions made by plaintiffs *before* they sustained the injuries for which they sue. The real issue was whether or not it was appropriate for the plaintiff to seek care in a fee-charging hospital. If it was, then the issue of whether he had not protected himself by a form of insurance against the payments arising from such care was entirely irrelevant on the basis of the collateral benefits principle.

Personal injuries   In *McKenna v Murphy*, High Court, 29 July 1991, Hamilton P assessed the quantum of damages for knee injuries. The plaintiff was aged twenty-two years at the time of the accident in 1988, in which he suffered (*inter alia*) injuries to both his knees and his spine. The knee injuries included an inter-articular vertical fracture of the right knee, and a detachment of the medial collateral ligament from the lateral epicardial of the left knee, which caused laxity in that knee. He was on crutches for three months. When he went back to work he suffered pain and stillness in his right knee and occasionally in his left knee. When medically examined, his right knee showed quite marked patella femoral crepitus indicating disturbance of the patella femoral joint. The medical expert was of opinion that any significant problem from arthritic change in his right knee would be delayed for about fifteen years. The laxity in the plaintiff's left knee was very much at risk of developing degenerative changes. The plaintiff's employment as a motor mechanic involved bending, lifting, and working in a confined space.

In awarding damages, Hamilton P had regard to the probability that the plaintiff might not be able to continue his employment if the arthritis ultimately developed as predicted. He awarded £25,000 for pain and suffering to date, £75,000 for future pain and suffering, and over £28,000 for out-of-pocket expenses. The economic loss that the plaintiff suffered in terms of the future risk to his employment was thus, unusually, computed under the heads of pain and suffering. This made no difference in the instance case, since the plaintiff would receive the same amount regardless of the heads under which it was computed. Had the plaintiff died before the action, however, the point would cease to be academic, since damages for pain and suffering do not 'survive' so as to pass to a deceased's estate: see the Civil Liability Act 1961, s. 7(2), McMahon & Binchy, *op. cit.*, 730.

Death of parent

Fatal accidents In the 1990 Review, 568-74, we discussed two High Court decisions dealing with the troublesome question of computation of damages for the death of a parent. To give an appropriate answer, the court must engage in a complex reconciliation between prediction about likely future occurrences and value judgments about sex roles in contemporary society.

In *McDonagh v McDonagh* [1992] ILRM 841; [1992] 1 IR 119, these difficulties were present, supplemented by the complication that the defendant whose negligent driving had brought about the death of the mother of two young children was the mother's husband and father of the children. A further element in the case was that, since the husband had only fitful employment, the mother had been the main breadwinner for the family.

Costello J went to considerable lengths to isolate from the general contribution the mother had made to the family finances the element that was specifically attributable to the children's benefit. This was no easy task since family life generally runs on informal lines, with parents regarding themselves as having a considerable degree of discretion as to how money will be spent on their children's behalf. Nonetheless, Costello J was surely fully justified in engaging on this enquiry, since otherwise there would be a prospect of indirectly compensating the defendant for some of *his* loss resulting from his wife's death. It is in situations such as this that the artificiality of tort litigation is manifested. The truth of the situation is that it is the defendant's insurance company that may be presumed to have paid the bill. The fact that the part of the economic loss resulting from the death of the defendant's wife was suffered by the defendant rather than some other person would not have played a significant part in the calculation of the premium.

Costello J then turned to the domestic services which the mother had rendered to her two children. He described these as gratuitous. On the evidence, he rejected the suggestion that these services would be replaced by a live-in nanny/housekeeper. On the balance of probabilities, he did not think that this would occur. It had not been shown that such a person was available for this type of employment in the Sligo area, where the family lived. (This seems a debatable conclusion; a sufficiently attractive salary might well have attracted applicants from Sligo or from further afield). Moreover, Costello J thought it probable that the defendant would continue to avail himself of the help that his sister had most generously given since his wife's death. The sister would be entitled to be remunerated on a daily basis. In assessing these damages, Costello J thought that the amount should be reduced gradually over the years. The young children-both girls-would not require someone to take them to school when they were older; nor, when they were teenagers, would they require someone to be in attendance every afternoon when they returned from school and every morning during the school holidays. This approach is similar to that adopted in some recent English decisions: see Denyer, 'What's A Carer Worth?', 22 Family L 119 (1992).

Costello J referred only briefly to the possibility that the defendant, aged twenty-eight, might remarry. He took this into account as a discount which, in conjunction with others, would reduce by one half the compensation for the domestic services that his wife had rendered to the children. He did not discuss the broader question of whether it is reasonable for a court in the 1990s to proceed on the basis that a woman who marries a widower may be expected to perform domestic services for the children of the deceased wife. As we have mentioned, we sought to analyse this issue in the 1990 Review: see especially pp. 572-4.

Mental distress In *McDonagh v McDonagh*, above, Costello J, when awarding damages for mental distress, concluded that a girl whose mother died in a traffic accident when the girl was one and a half, was too young to have suffered distress, 'whatever about emotional deprivation', by her mother's death. He considered that her sister, aged four at the time of the fatal accident, must have suffered greatly, and he divided the sum of £7,500 between the sister and the parents of the deceased woman. No claim had been made by the woman's husband as it had been his negligent driving that had resulted in his wife's death; the principle that a wrongdoer should not benefit from his wrongdoing applied.

In *Heeney v Dublin Corporation* High Court, 16 May 1991, the liability issues of which we discussed above, 398-9, the dependants of a deceased fireman—his widow and son—took proceedings under Part IV of the Civil Liability Act 1961. The deceased had died after inhaling gases when fighting a fire. Barron J stated:

> The circumstances of the deceased's death were traumatic and I am satisfied that the full figure of £7,500 should be awarded to the plaintiff for mental suffering.

This passage calls for some comment. The statutory provision is designed to compensate dependants for mental distress rather than nervous shock: see *Mulally v Bus Éireann* [1992] ILRM 722, which we analyse in the section of this chapter dealing with nervous shock, above, 401-4. The maximum figure of £7,500 constitutes an artificial limitation which has no parallel in a common law claim for compensation for nervous shock. Of course the two psychological states can intermingle, and it seems reasonable to envisage cases in which the traumatic circumstances of the death might enhance the dependants' mental distress; but, if the essence of the claim is psychological disturbance or trauma rather than grief, it should be pleaded and compensated separately from the statutory claim.

Denigration of expert witness by trial judge In *Donnelly v Timber Factors Ltd* [1991] 1 IR 553, a troublesome issue arose as to how the Court should exercise its appellate function where the trial judge had made a damaging and professionally offensive criticism of an expert medical witness for the defence. This witness had examined the plaintiff in relation to her back injuries sustained in a crash caused by the admitted negligence of the defendant.

The members of the Supreme Court were agreed that the trial judge's intervention had been improper: see the Practice and Procedure Chapter, above, 344-5. But should such impropriety *require* a re-trial? This issue divided the Court. McCarthy J thought that it should, primarily because the trial judge's approach to the question of which witness he should accept must clearly have been coloured by his mistaken belief that this expert witness had acted improperly. He noted that it had been suggested in argument (in support of upholding the award) that really there was little difference in the opinion of the expert medical witnesses for both parties. He doubted that this was so. He added that:

> it may well be that the damages awarded are not in any sense out of proportion to the injuries sustained. But that is not the point. Damages range between certain extremes having regard to the evidence accepted by the arbiter of damages. Where the manner of acceptance is flawed, in my view the award of damages cannot stand.

In contrast, O'Flaherty J (with whom Hederman J concurred) was willing to leave the award of damages undisturbed. The crucial evidence on the issue had been that of the plaintiff. Once it was believed, corroborated as it was by the unchallenged evidence of her general practitioner, the award was proper. O'Flaherty J did not follow the course that the court was generally required to adopt in cases such as this, namely to take the view of the evidence most favourable from a respondent's point of view. He preferred to 'take a commonsense view of the gist of the evidence'. To order a retrial in the circumstances would be to adopt a remedy disproportionate to the mistake that had been made in the case.

This divergence of judicial opinion provokes reflection. As a threshold issue, it must surely be the case that the mere fact of improper treatment of a witness by a trial judge should not, *of itself*, warrant a retrial. It would seem essential to show that this improper treatment either *revealed* that the judge had a mistaken or biased understanding of that witness which in turn affected his disposition of a crucial issue or issues in the case or that the treatment had an *effect* (on the witness or otherwise) which may have altered the subsequent conduct of the trial in some potentially crucial way. McCarthy J's view of the case clearly falls within the first of these categories; O'Flaherty J also proceeds on the basis of the correctness of this approach but comes to a different conclusion relative to its application to the facts.

McCarthy J's view that, where the manner of acceptance of evidence is flawed, the award of damages 'cannot stand' might be criticised on the basis that it ought to be subject to the possibility of qualification. Clearly there will be cases where the manner of the acceptance of evidence was quite flawed but the award of damages was nonetheless of a quantum which was entirely justifiable, judged by the correct criteria. The context in which McCarthy J's observation is made suggests that perhaps it was intended to be read as being subject to an implicit qualification on these lines.

Exemplary damages   In the 1988 Review, 460-1, we analysed Barron J's decision in *Conway v Ireland* [1991] 2 IR 305. The Supreme Court dismissed the appeal (*sub nom Conway v Irish National Teachers Organisation*) [1991] ILRM 497; [1991] 2 IR 305.) It will be recalled that the case involved an action for damages for conspiracy to interfere with the constitutional right to primary education of several school pupils whose education was disrupted by the Drimoleague National School dispute. The issue of *liability* had been determined by the High Court in *Crowley v Ireland* [1980] IR 102. The instant proceedings were accordingly heard as an assessment of damages only. Barron J had awarded the plaintiff £10,000 for general loss and the loss of career prospects; to this he added the sum of £1,500 for exemplary damages.

Finlay CJ set out the following analysis of the relevant principles:

> In respect of damages for tort or for breach of constitutional right, three headings of damage in Irish law are, in my view, potentially relevant to any particular case. They are:
>
> (1) Ordinary compensatory damages being sums calculated to recompense a wronged plaintiff for physical injury, mental distress, anxiety, deprivation of convenience, or other harmful effects of a wrongful act and/or for monies lost or to be lost and/or expenses

incurred or to be incurred by reason of the commission of the wrongful act.

(2) Aggravated damages, being compensatory damages increased by reason of:

> (a) the manner in which the wrong was committed, involving such elements as oppressiveness, arrogance or outrage, or
> (b) the conduct of the wrongdoer after the commission of the wrong, such as a refusal to apologise or to ameliorate the harm done or the making of threats to repeat the wrong, or
> (c) conduct of the wrong-doer and/or his representative in the defence of the claim of the wronged plaintiff, up to and including the trial of the action.

Such a list of the circumstances which may aggravate compensatory damages until they can properly be classified as aggravated damages is not intended to be in any way finite or complete. Furthermore, the circumstances which may properly form an aggravating feature in the measurement of compensatory damages must, in many instances, be in part a recognition of the added hurt or insult to a plaintiff who has been wronged, and in part also a recognition of the cavalier or outrageous conduct of the defendant.

(3) Punitive or exemplary damages arising from the nature of the wrong which has been committed and/or the manner of its commission which are intended to mark the court's particular disapproval of the defendant's conduct in all the circumstances of the case and its decision that it should publicly be seen to have punished the defendant for such conduct by awarding such damages, quite apart from its obligation, where it may exist in the same case, to compensate the plaintiff for the damage which he or she has suffered.

The Chief Justice, after a discussion of the exact interrelationship between the terms 'exemplary' and 'punitive' damages—which we examine in detail below—went on to address the question whether it is open to a judge in assessing damages for a wrong consisting of a deprivation of a constitutional right, such as the right to free primary education, to assess exemplary damages. For an answer to this question he thought it only necessary to refer to the famous passage from Ó Dálaigh CJ's judgment in *The State (Quinn) v Ryan* [1965] IR 70, at 122, where he stated:

> It was not the intention of the Constitution in guaranteeing the fundamental rights of the citizen that these rights should be set at nought or

circumvented. The intention was that rights of substance were being assured to the individual and that the Courts were the custodians of these rights. As a necessary corollary it follows that no one can with impunity set these rights at nought or circumvent them, and that the Courts' powers in this regard are as ample as the defence of the Constitution requires.

It seemed clear to Finlay CJ that the court could not be availing itself of powers as ample as the defence of the Constitution and of constitutional rights required unless, in the case of breach of those rights, it held itself entitled to avail itself of one of the most effective deterrent powers that a civil court had: the awarding of exemplary or punitive damages. In an important passage, the Chief Justice added:

> This does not mean that every wrong which constitutes the breach of a constitutional right in any sense automatically attracts exemplary damages. It does not, in my view, even mean that in every such case, irrespective of the facts or circumstances surrounding it, the court should specifically concern itself with the question of exemplary damages. Many torts, such as assault and defamation, constitute of necessity a breach of constitutional rights, but there are many types of assault and many types of defamation as well in which no conceivable question of awarding . . . exemplary damages could arise.

In the particular case the intended consequence of the defendants' acts had been the direct deprivation of the plaintiff of her constitutional right to free primary education, coupled with the special relationship which the defendants bore to the general rights of children to free primary education. These circumstances clearly made it a case in which the question necessarily arose whether exemplary damages should be awarded. The Chief Justice was satisfied that this was an appropriate case in which the court should feel obliged to mark its disapproval of the defendants' conduct to the extent of awarding exemplary damages, for four reasons:

> (a) The right which was breached on this occasion was one expressly vested in a *child* by the Constitution;
> (b) The right which was breached was one which, having regard to the education and training of a child, was of supreme and fundamental importance;
> (c) It must be presumed that the defendants were aware of that importance;
> (d) The breach of the constitutional right involved was an intended, as distinct from inadvertent, consequence of the defendants' conduct.

Finlay CJ found it impossible to ignore the fact that the defendants were persons who, in the form of a trade union, constituted an organisation dealing with all the primary teachers in Ireland. It seemed particularly important that, if such a body acted as it had done, the courts 'should, with particular severity, mark their disapproval'. Barron J's assessment of exemplary damages had not been excessive.

Griffin J, concurring, observed that exemplary damages might be awarded where there had been on the part of the defendant wilful and conscious wrongdoing in contumelious disregard of another rights:

> The object of awarding exemplary damages is to punish the wrong-doer for his outrageous conduct, to deter him and others from any such conduct in the future, and to mark the court's (or the jury's . . .) detestation and disapproval of that conduct. Such damages are to be awarded even though the plaintiff who recovers them obtains the benefit of what has been described in the case law as a fortunate windfall.

What may be noticed about this analysis is that it makes no attempt to distinguish between torts and infringements of constitutional rights. The restraint against awarding exemplary damages for such infringements, which Ó Dálaigh CJ's statement in *The State (Quinn) v Ryan* represents, is not evident in Griffin J's criteria. Nowhere does he state expressly that an award of exemplary damages for such infringements is permissible only where the defence of the Constitution and of constitutional rights *requires* the court to take such a step.

Griffin J went on to reject in the clearest of terms the limitation of the award of exemplary damages to cases involving 'oppressive, arbitrary or unconstitutional action by the servants of Government', the *first* category which Lord Devlin prescribed in *Rookes v Barnard* [1964] AC 1129, at 1226-7. Griffin J could see 'no valid reason, in logic or common sense' for this restriction. He thought it unnecessary to discuss the other categories.

Finally Griffin J endorsed the approach that O'Flaherty J had taken in *McIntyre v Lewis* [1991] 1 IR 121, in adopting the three considerations which Lord Devlin in *Rookes v Barnard* had said should always be borne in mind when considering awards of exemplary damages. These are, *first*, that the plaintiff may not recover exemplary damages unless he is a victim of the punishable behaviour; *secondly*, that restraint should be exercised; and, *thirdly*, that the means of both parties should be taken into account. One may perhaps wonder about what possible rationale could justify the third consideration in cases involving infringements of constitutional rights. Why should it make any difference to the *exemplary* element of an award for damages for interference with the right to a free primary education that a

particular child came from a well-off family? If a servant of the State violates
the bodily integrity of a citizen, why should the means of the citizen play any
part in determining the quantum of exemplary damages?

McCarthy J, also concurring, drew inspiration from the analogy with the
exclusion of evidence generated by a breach of the constitutional rights of
the citizen: *The People v Lynch* [1981] ILRM 389; [1982] IR 64, *The People
v Kenny* [1990] ILRM 569; [1990] 2 IR 90, analysed in the 1990 Review,
202-5. He quoted from Warren CJ's proclamation in *Terry v Ohio* 392 US
1, at 13 (1968) (which had received O'Higgins CJ's benediction in *Lynch*):

> Courts which sit under our Constitution cannot and will not be made
> party to lawful invasions of the constitutional rights of citizens by
> permitting unhindered governmental use of the fruits of such invasions.

McCarthy J's derivation of a common denominator between constitutional aspects of the rules of evidence and the courts' power to award
exemplary damages for infringement of constitutional rights merits quotation
in full:

> The stringency of the rule is apparent; it is in force regardless of the
> immediate consequences. In that instance, it was a case of governmental
> or State wrongdoing; in such case, if in any case, it must be open to
> award exemplary damages. Where the wrongdoer is not a governmental
> or State agency, the relevant consideration is in amount rather than
> liability. The purpose of awarding such damages is truly to make an
> example of the wrongdoer so as to show others that such wrongdoing
> will not be tolerated and, more to the point, will not be relieved on
> payment of merely compensatory damages. It does provide a windfall
> for the successful plaintiff; the application of the evidentary rule to
> which I have referred may well provide the most handsome windfall—
> that of freedom—to the person charged with a criminal offence.
>
> The Constitution in guaranteeing rights imposes corresponding
> duties. In the instant case, the defendants in deliberately interfering with
> the plaintiff's rights have failed in their own duties. Every member of
> the judiciary has made a public declaration to uphold the Constitution;
> it would be a singular failure to do so if the courts did not, in appropriate
> cases such as this, award such damages as to make an example of those
> who set at naught constitutional rights of others. As the Chief Justice
> has said, that is not to say that in every case, such as defamation or
> assault, where there is also, by definition, a breach of a constitutional
> right, there should be an award of exemplary damages. In my judgment,
> there was here a compelling case for the award of such damages.

It may perhaps be debated whether the analogy with the exclusionary rule in evidence holds up. Only at the most general level would there seem to be a conjunction between this rule and the power of the courts to award exemplary damages for infringement of constitutional rights. When one moves from the general to the specific, it may be argued that the exclusionary rule in evidence operates quite differently from the power of the courts to award exemplary damages. The exclusionary rule applies regardless of its consequences; it is justified not on the basis of the circumstances of the individual case but for reasons having no necessary significance in the particular instance. The power to award exemplary damages is quite different: it depends entirely on the requirements of the particular case.

DEFAMATION

The Law Reform Commission's *Report on the Civil Law of Defamation* (LRC 38-1991), together with the Commission's earlier *Consultation Paper*, published in March 1991, present a comprehensive analysis of the subject. See Eoin O'Dell's incisive comments on the *Consultation Paper* (1991) 9 ILT 181, 214. Many of the Commission's recommendations for reform of the law will be widely welcomed; others are more controversial and unlikely to form part of the legislation that may emerge in due course.

Uncontentious proposals Of the sixty or so recommendations put forward, the uncontroversial include such proposals as that the distinction between libel and slander should be abolished (para 3.3), that the defendant be able to make payment into court without admission of liability (para 3.20) and, that an apology should not be construed as an admission of liability (para 3.21).

Tying the hands of the jury Let us now turn to consider the more controversial proposals. Perhaps the clearest instance is the proposal (para 10.6) that, in High Court proceedings for defamation, the jury should assess issues of fact *other than damages*, save to the extent that they should be entitled to include in their verdict a finding that the plaintiff is entitled to nominal damages only. This approach modifies that favoured by the Commission in the Consultation Paper, which would have given the jury the function of determining the *category* of damages that should apply (compensatory, exemplary or nominal), with the judge determining the appropriate amount of compensation in the light of this categorisation.

There are some difficulties with this approach. First, and fundamentally, no coherent empirical evidence is put forward in either the *Consultation Paper* or the *Report* which supports the contention, made by the media and accepted without dissent by the Commission, that juries have a tendency to award disproportionately high damages. Of course there has been the odd case where the jury awarded too much but the Supreme Court is well capable of dealing with such excesses (cf, e.g., *Barrett v Independent Newspapers Ltd* [1986] IR 13, analysed by McGonagle, (1987) 9 DULJ 3155). In fact, very few appeals are taken by media or other defendants. On the contrary there have been several instances where the media either settle without fight or let the case run for a couple of days in the High Court before throwing in the towel. When it is borne in mind that the media have financial resources well in excess of most (though not all) defamation plaintiffs, the failure of the media even to appeal jury awards on any widespread scale weakens their argument that juries should lose their entitlement to make awards.

There is something curious about the willingness to remove from the juries the function of assessing damages, while leaving them determine lability issues. Defamation law is notoriously complex, yet juries' capacity to understand and apply principles of liability are nowhere called in question in the Report.

A major difficulty with the recommendation that juries should determine liability but not damages is that this leaves the trial judge in an invidious position. He or she may have come to the conclusion that the plaintiff should lose either on the facts (because, for example, the witnesses on the plaintiff's side were lying) or on the law. Faced with a jury finding of liability, and without any guidance as to the seriousness with which the jury viewed the case, how much should the judge award? This division of functions involves blindfolding the judge and frustrating the jury. The proposal in the *Consultation Paper* that the jury should prescribe the *category* of damages is an indication of some appreciation by the Commission that the judge should not be left completely in the dark as to the jury's perception of the seriousness of the injury. That proposal had its own difficulties and was rightly abandoned by the Commission but its replacement in the Report enhances the problem for the trial judge.

The Commission's proposals regarding the role of juries, in chapter 10 of the Report, are not easy to reconcile with its recommendations, in chapter 8, relating to exemplary damages. There the Commission proposes (para 8.16) that exemplary damages for defamation should be awarded only where:

> (i) the defendant intended to publish matter to a person other than the plaintiff, knowing that such matter would be understood to refer to the plaintiff, that it would tend to injure the plaintiff's reputation and with knowledge, or in reckless disregard, of its falsity; and
> (ii) the conduct of the defendant has been highhanded, insolent or vindictive or has exhibited a disregard for the plaintiff's rights so gross

as clearly to warrant punishment over and above that which has been inflicted upon him by an award of compensatory damages.

Nowhere does the Report clarify whether the function of awarding exemplary damages should be that of the trial judge or of the jury. It would seem from chapter 10 that the judge is intended to have this function; yet the first of the criteria for an award of exemplary damages seems to involve exclusively a *finding of fact*, concerning the defendant's intent and knowledge. If the trial judge is of the view that the plaintiff's witnesses were liars and that the defendant thus did not say the words attributed to him, yet the jury bring in a verdict of liability, and the alleged defamation is of the most serious and scurrilous type, what is the judge to do? Apply his or her view of the evidence onto the exemplary damages issue and deny the plaintiff damages that would flow inevitably from the jury's finding of fact or defer to the jury's findings and make an award of exemplary damages based on a 'finding of fact' which is not truly that of the judge?

Falsity of allegations and the burden of proof Under present law, the onus rests on the defendant to proved the truth of a defamatory allegation. The Commission by a majority of three (Keane J, Mr Buckley and Ms Gaffney) to two (Professor Duncan and Mr O'Leary) recommends that the onus should be shifted onto the plaintiff to establish the falsity of the defamatory allegations.

The minority present a potent argument (para 7.35) against this change:

Reversal of the onus of proof would result, in effect, in a presumption that anything said of the plaintiff, no matter how damaging, is true. Any plaintiff who wished to vindicate his or her own name through defamation proceedings would so in the teeth of an assumed defect in his or her reputation. A situation in which the plaintiff would be required in effect to prove his or her innocence is, in our view, inconsistent with the sprit of the constitutional requirement that the State vindicate the good name of every citizen in the case of injustice done.

It is not always easy to prove a negative—for example, that the plaintiff was not at a particular place at a time when a crime was committed. In some cases the plaintiff will be able to do little more than deny the truth of what has been alleged against him or her, without being able to offer supporting evidence. It is then a matter for the court to decide whom it believes. If there is substantial uncertainty on this issue, under the majority's proposal the plaintiff will fail because he or she will not have discharged the onus of proving the falsity of the allegations against him or her on the balance of probabilities. The court will decide against the plaintiff, not because it is satisfied that the allegation made against him or her is true, but because in a case of doubt, its truth is assumed.

The majority's central rationale for its proposal (para 7.31) is as follows:

> The claim that an alteration in the present law may create difficulties for some plaintiffs is an argument based on pragmatic considerations rather than principle. The principled objection to the proposal that it is unjust, and arguably unconstitutional, to presume that the defendant's assertion is true is based, in our view, on a misconception. The proposal we favour would not involve, as in sometimes mistakenly suggested, the reversal of the existing presumption. It would simply mean that there were no presumptions of any sort in this area. The law would, in the result, adopt a neutral position: there would be no presumption that the defendant had wronged the plaintiff by the publication of an untrue defamatory statement and, equally, no presumption that what the defendant said about the plaintiff was true. The plaintiff would thus be required to prove the commission of the alleged wrong by the defendant, in accordance with the general principles of the civil law.

There is a real risk here of confusing the relevant evidential principles. To impose an onus of proof on one or other party in civil proceedings does not involve the establishment of any *presumption* against that party. The failure to appreciate that the 'presumption of innocence' in a criminal trial in fact connotes no true presumption can lead a court into error, as the notorious decision of the United States Supreme Court in *Coffin v The United States* (1895) 156 US 432 makes plain. Nor is it true that, if the onus of proof were reversed so that proof of the falsity of the allegation rested on the plaintiff, the law would 'adopt a neutral position'. On the contrary, in the absence of discharging this onus successfully on the balance of probabilities, *the plaintiff would inevitably lose the case*, as the minority point out.

There is surely merit in the minority's suggestion that, to prevent the plaintiff from benefiting by not giving evidence, there should be an explicit statutory rule to the effect that 'when, without reasonable explanation or excuse, a plaintiff refuses to deny in evidence the truth of any statement complained of, the court may, having regard to all the circumstances, draw what inference it thinks proper from such refusal, including the inference that the statement was in fact true'. (From a drafting standpoint it might be advisable to modify this proposal by replacing the reference to refusal by a reference to the plaintiff's *failure* to deny the truth of the statement. Otherwise a plaintiff who failed to give evidence would not come within the scope of this rule).

The defence of reasonable care The Commission proposes that the defence of reasonable care should be available to defendants, save to the extent that the plaintiff has suffered financial loss. The defence would consist of the exercise of reasonable care prior to publication in attempting to ascertain the truth of the allegation. It may be worth reflecting on the implications of this proposal in conjunction with the majority's proposal to place the burden of proof as to the falsity of the allegation on the plaintiff. If a person fails to answer questions posed by a newspaper, for example, the newspaper might well be considered to be acting with reasonable care if it makes an allegation based on this failure of response.

The proposed distinction between financial and non-financial loss is difficult to defend. The law of defamation seeks to protect a person's right to his or her good name. Some of the nastiest calumnies, such as an allegation that an elderly person is guilty of sexual abuse, may devastate that person's interpersonal relationships but yet cause no financial loss. No coherent argument emerges in favour of the distinction; all that is proposed for a plaintiff whose life has thus been ruined is the doubtful benefit of a declaratory order or a correction order stating the matter to be false and defamatory: cf. para 9.15. The Commission itself admits that, 'in certain cases, a correction order may not be appropriate, because the defendant is not a person or media organ' (para 9.14). A declaratory order would scarcely be any more efficacious to remedy the non-financial loss caused by a non-media defendant.

Privilege The Commission makes some radical proposals in relation to the defence of privilege. Regarding *absolute* privilege, it recommends that 'any rule of law whereby communications between members of the executive are absolutely privileged should be abrogated' (para 4.15). In support of this recommendation, it argues that there is no public interest in this context equivalent to that relating to statements made in the Oireachtas or in judicial or quasi-judicial proceedings; it was 'not . . . able to identify any principled reason' for maintaining absolute privilege in respect of communications between members of the Executive.

The Commission recommends that communications between solicitor and client should attract only qualified privilege. Its rationale is brief (para 4.16):

> [A]bsolute privilege represents a substantial intrusion on the right to a good name. Although we have recommended its retention, we have done so on the basis that it should be retained only in areas relating to State business. Communications between solicitor and client, or counsel and client, are not of this type and we see no reason why qualified privilege should not be an adequate protection.

The Commission recommends (para 4.23) that communications between spouses should not be immune from liability for defamation and the general principles of qualified privilege should afford the only protection. The judicial authority for this immunity is slight enough: the only reported decision, *Wennhak v Morgan*, 20 QBD 635 (Div Court, 1888) was based on the legal unity of the spouses—a notion already obsolescent at the time—and Manisty J's concern lest removal of the immunity might lead to results 'disastrous to social life'. The Commission considers that the question of *justice to plaintiffs* is largely overlooked in this analysis:

> A person who loses his life, his family, his job or simply his reputation as a result of a defamatory communication between spouses is no less a victim that one who similarly suffers from a defamatory communication between parent and child or between close friends.

In the area of *qualified* privilege, the Commission recommends that the rule somewhat reluctantly endorsed in *Hynes-O'Sullivan v O'Driscoll* [1988] IR 349 should be abrogated, so that the defence would not fail by reason only of the fact that the recipient had no actual interest or duty to receive the communication if a reasonable person would have believed the recipient to have such an interest or duty (para 4.27). This proposal would clearly conflict in no way with the approach favoured by Henchy J in *Hynes-O'Sullivan*, since he there expressed the view that 'the suggested radical change in the hitherto accepted law should more properly be effected by statute. The public policy which a new formulation of the law would represent should more properly be found by the Law Reform Commission or by those others who are in a position to take a broad perspective as distinct from what is discernible in the tunnelled vision imposed by the facts of a single case'. What is not so clear is whether the Commission's recommendation harmonises with McCarthy J's analysis, which invoked the Constitution in support of the rule that a reasonable, mistaken belief that the recipient had an interest or duty to receive the communication should afford no defence. In the 1988 Review, 444, we questioned whether McCarthy J's rationale was fully convincing. Certainly there is no majority support in *Hynes-O'Sullivan* for the view that the Commission's proposal would offend any provision of the Constitution.

TORT LAW AND THE CONSTITUTION

In the 1988 Review, 462-6, we examined the troublesome question of the relationship between tort law and compensation for infringements of constitutional rights under the principles stated in *Meskell v C.I.E.* [1973] IR 121. It will be recalled that in the Supreme Court decision of *Hanrahan v Merck Sharp & Dohme (Ireland) Ltd* [1988] ILRM 629, at 636, Henchy J (for the Court) regarded tort law as substantially encompassing the damages remedy for infringements of constitutional rights:

> A person may of course in the absence of a common law or statutory cause of action sue directly for breach of a constitutional right . . . ; but when he founds his action on an existing tort he is normally confined to the limitations of that tort. It might be different if it could be shown that the tort in quesiton is basically ineffective to protect his constitutional right.

Henchy J went on to note that the guarantee to respect and defend personal rights given in Article 40.3.1^o applied 'as far as practicable' and that the guarantee to vindicate rights given by Article 40.3.2^o referred only to cases of 'injustice done'.

In *Sweeney v Duggan* [1991] 2 IR 274, which we examine in greater detail above, 386-7, the plaintiff, an employee whose successful action against his employer, a company, was largely unenforceable because the company had gone into liquidation, sought to establish a duty on the part of the effective owner of the company, under the Constitution, to safeguard his bodily integrity 'in and about his employment' and to ensure that any bodily injuries he suffered in the course of his employment would be duly compensated. He relied in particular on the undertaking by the State in Article 40.3.2°, to protect by its laws 'as best it may from unjust attack and, in the case of injustice done, [to] vindicate the life, person, good name and property rights of every citizen'.

Barron J disposed of this argument in two sentences:

> In my view there is nothing in that provision to assist him. It gives him no more than a guarantee of a just law of negligence, which in the circumstances exists.

This summary dismissal of the constitutional dimension can perhaps be justified on the basis that Barron J had already engaged in a detailed investigation of whether the law of negligence should be extended to embrace the circumstances arising in the case. The flexibility and potential for growth in the principles of negligence law should, however, be contrasted with some other torts, notably trespass, whose parameters have long ago been settled: see our comments in the 1988 Review, 465. While Barron J's observations may seem to evince no sympathy with the argument, it would be unwise to ignore the words 'in the circumstances'. Barron J appears to accept that a court would be wrong to proceed on the *a priori* basis that the present scope of the law of negligence *necessarily* affords full protection to constitution-ally-protected rights. For further consideration on the subject, see Binchy, 'Constitutional Remedies and the Law of Torts', in J. O'Reilly, ed., *Human Rights and Constitutional Law* (1992), 201.

Transport

AIR TRANSPORT

The European Communities (Sharing of Passenger Capacity and Access to Scheduled Air Service Routes) Regulations 1991 (SI No. 53) gave effect to Council Regulation 2343/90. The European Communities (Scheduled Air Fares) Regulations 1991 (SI No. 54) gave effect to Council Regulation 2342/90.

INTERNATIONAL CARRIAGE OF GOODS BY ROAD

The International Carriage of Goods by Road Act 1990 (Commencement) Order 1991 (SI No. 22) brought the 1990 Act into effect on 1 May 1991. The effect is that the CMR Convention came into effect on that date for all international travel, except for travel to Great Britain and Northern Ireland. On the licensing of UK drivers in Ireland, see the 1990 Review, 585. On the 1990 Act in general, see the 1990 Review, 129-39.

The International Carriage of Goods by Road Act 1990 (CMR Contracting Parties) Order 1991 (SI No. 160) specifies the current list of CMR Contracting Parties.

INTERNATIONAL CARRIAGE OF PERISHABLE FOODSTUFFS

The International Carriage of Perishable Foodstuffs (Amendment) Regulations 1991 (SI No. 266) amend the 1989 Regulations of the same title (see the 1989 Review, 446-7).

MERCHANT SHIPPING

Access to report to Minister In *Haussman v Minister for the Marine* [1991] ILRM 382, Blayney J refused access to the plaintiff to a copy of a report prepared under s. 728 of the Merchant Shipping Act 1894.

The defendant Minister had ordered a report to be furnished to him under s. 728 of the 1894 Act in respect of the sinking of a fishery patrol vessel near Ballycotton wich occurred on 7 July 1990. The plaintiff was the widow of one of the persons who died in the sinking. Subsequent to the s. 728 report, the Minister ordered a formal inquiry into the sinking under s. 466 of the 1894 Act, to be conducted by a Judge of the District Court. The plaintiff, who was legally represented at the inquiry, sought a copy of all documentation in the hands of the Minister relevant to the inquiry. The Minister agreed, after the institution of the proceedings, to give the plaintiff copies of the documents on which the s. 728 report had been based, but declined to give her a copy of the report itself. As already indicated, Blayney J declined to order access to the report.

The decision of Blayney J was not based on the secrecy of such reports, but rather on whether access would assist the plaintiff. He held that non-production of the report would not prejudice her right to have a full and thorough inquiry conducted by the formal inquiry under the 1894 Act. Nor did he consider that the s. 728 report amounted to necessary evidence for the purposes of the formal inquiry since it constituted third party findings based on evidence which would be available to the inquiry itself. Finally, he considered that the plaintiff would not be prevented from availing adequately of the inquiry since she did have access to all the documentation on which the s. 728 report was based.

Blayney J distinguished *The State (Shannon Atlantic Fisheries Ltd) v McPolin* [1976] IR 93 on the basis that that case had concerned an application to quash a report (made under a different provision of the merchant shipping legislation). He also distinguished *Holloway v Belenos Publications Ltd (No. 2)* [1988] ILRM 85; [1988] IR 494 (1988 Review, 328-9) on the basis that that case concerned the inherent jurisdiction of the courts to order discovery.

It is of interest to note that, while the policy of the Department of Marine had, up to and including the Ballycotton tragedy, been to decline to publish reports under the Merchant Shipping Act 1894, it was announced that this policy has since been changed: see *Irish Times*, 14 April 1992. It seems unlikely, therefore, that a case similar to *Haussman* will arise in the future.

Ballycotton Inquiry   The Inquiry which led to the *Haussman* case, above, was chaired by Judge Michael Reilly, Judge of the District Court. The Inquiry's report was published in July 1991: *Report of the Formal Investigation into the Shipping Casualty Off Ballycotton, Co Cork on 7 July 1990*. The Report included a number of recommendations on the design of fishery patrol vessels.

ROAD TRAFFIC

Bye-Laws   The Road Traffic General Bye-Laws (Amendment) Regulations 1991 (SI No. 204) amend the 1964 Bye-Laws in relation to railway crossings.

Construction standards The European Communities (Road Traffic) (Vehicles Type Approval) Regulations 1991 (SI No. 34) provide that vehicles complying with EC Approval (or Technical Standards) Directives are deemed to comply with the Irish Construction, Equipment and Use of Vehicles Regulations. For further amendments of the EC standards see the European Communities (Motor Vehicles Type Approval) Regulations 1991 (SI No. 186) and the European Communities (Motor Vehicles Type Approval) (No. 2) Regulations 1991 (SI No. 367), which amend the Principal Regulations of 1978.

In view of SI No. 34 of 1991, above, see also the Road Traffic (Construction, Equipment and Use of Vehicles) (Amendment) Regulations 1991 (SI No. 273), the Road Traffic (Construction, Equipment and Use of Vehicles) (Amendment) (No. 2) Regulations 1991 (SI No. 358) (introducing the 1.6 mm thread depth requirement for tyres, based on Directive 89/459/ EEC) and the Road Traffic (Construction, Equipment and Use of Vehicles) (Amendment) (No. 3) Regulations 1991 (SI No. 359) (introducing the requirement for rear seat anchorages and child restraints, based on Directive 91/671/EEC).

Construction warranty The Road Traffic (Control of Supply of Vehicles) Regulations 1991 (SI No. 35) have the important effect of implementing s. 8 of the Road Traffic Act 1968, with effect from 1 March 1991. The result is that, from that date, vehicles sold in the State now carry a warranty that they comply with the numerous Construction, Equipment and Use of Vehicles Regulations: see above.

Lighting The Road Traffic (Lighting of Vehicles) (Amendment) Regulations 1991 (SI No. 182) give effect to EC requirements.

Railway crossings The Road Traffic (Signals) (Amendment) Regulations 1991 (SI No. 205) provide for the yellow box system at railway crossings. See also the Road Traffic General Bye-Laws (Amendment) Regulations 1991 (SI No. 204) which amend the 1964 Bye-Laws in relation to railway crossings.

Registration and licensing The Road Vehicles (Registration and Licensing) (Amendment) Regulations 1991 (SI No. 30) and the Road Vehicles (Registration and Licensing) (Amendment) (No. 2) Regulations 1991 (SI No. 357) amend the 1982 Regulations of the same title, further updating licence display plate provisions.

Removal of vehicles The Road Traffic (Removal, Storage and Disposal of Vehicles) (Amendment) Regulations 1991 (SI No. 185) further amend the 1983 Regulations.

Speed meter detectors The Road Traffic (Speed Meter Detectors) Regulations 1991 (SI No. 50) prohibit the importation, supply, fitting and use of speed meter detectors.

Testing The European Communities (Vehicle Testing) Regulations 1991 (SI No. 356) implements the requirements of Directive 88/449/EEC on MOT testing for light vehicles.

ROAD TRANSPORT LICENCE

Licence under old regime In *D.P.P.(Jennings) v Go-Travel Ltd* [1991] ILRM 577, the Supreme Court dealt with the licensing requirements of the Road Transport Act 1932.

The defendant company hired a coach from another company, Greenline Coaches Ltd, to carry passengers from Dublin to Macroom. Each passenger paid the defendant £11 as a contribution towards the hiring of the coach. The coach was driven by an agent of Greenline Coaches. No passenger licence was obtained for the journey, and the defendant was charged under s. 7 of the Road Transport Act 1932 with carrying on a passenger road service without a licence contrary to s. 2 of the 1932 Act. The defendant argued that, since it merely hired a vehicle for a specific journey it was not engaged in the carrying on of a road passenger service. The defendant was convicted, but on case stated to the High Court, Lardner J held that no offence had been committed. On further appeal by the Director of Public Prosecutions the Supreme Court (Hederman, McCarthy and O'Flaherty JJ) agreed with the conclusion reached by Lardner J.

Delivering the leading judgment, McCarthy J pointed out that since s. 7 of the 1932 Act created a criminal offence it was, as part of penal statute, to be strictly construed. Since the provisions of ss. 2 and 7 of the Act were only applicable to cases in which the defendant both receives the charges for each passenger and also owns or otherwise controls the vehicle, and since the defendant company in this instance did not own or control the vehicle in question, he concluded that the defendant could not be convicted under the 1932 Act. In this respect, he distinguished this case from the circumstances in *Attorney General v Pratt* [1942] IR 478, in which the defendant had owned the vehicle in question and had made a separate charge of each passenger.

McCarthy J also noted that, while it was not an appropriate canon of construction to look at subsequent legislation, it was perhaps indicative of current legislative thinking that the European Communities (Road Passenger Transport) Regulations 1977 excluded from the definition of road passenger transport business the situation in the instant case. Pointing to the wider debate on the possible liberalisation of the road passenger market, he opined that in the future legislation might require the organisers of coach trips to hold licences, but that this was a matter for the legislature.

It is of interest that, shortly after the Supreme Court decision, a new licensing regime was introduced in this area through three sets of Regulations.

The 1977 Regulations referred to in *Go-Travel* were revoked and replaced by the European Communities (Road Passenger Transport) Regulations 1991 (SI No. 59), which introduced a new licence, the Road Passenger Transport Operators' Licence. The 1991 Regulations give effect to Directive 89/438/EEC.

The European Communities (Merchandise Road Transport) Regulations 1991 (SI No. 60) revoke 1988 Regulations of the same title (1988 Review, 209) and prescribe requirements for obtaining a merchandise road transport licence, as well as providing for the recognition of diplomas and other qualifications. These Regulations implement Directive 89/438/EEC.

The Road Transport (Road Freight Carrier's Licence Application Form) Regulations 1991 (SI No. 61) are self-explanatory. They revoke 1988 Regulations of the same title.

Index